Human Rights at the UN

This book is a publication of

Indiana University Press
601 North Morton Street
Bloomington, IN 47404-3797 USA

http://iupress.indiana.edu

Telephone orders   800-842-6796
Fax orders   812-855-7931
Orders by e-mail   iuporder@indiana.edu

The paper used in this publication meets the minimum requirements of American National
Standard for Information Sciences—Permanence of Paper for Printed Library Materials,
ANSI Z39.48-1984.

Manufactured in the United States of America

Library of Congress Cataloging-in-Publication Data

Normand, Roger, date
  Human rights at the UN : the political history of universal justice / Roger Normand and
Sarah Zaidi.
      p. cm. — (United Nations intellectual history project)
  Includes bibliographical references and index.
  ISBN-13: 978-0-253-34935-4 (cloth : alk. paper)
  ISBN-13: 978-0-253-21934-3 (pbk. : alk. paper) 1. United Nations—History. 2. Human
rights—History—20th century. I. Zaidi, Sarah. II. Title.
  JZ4984.5.N67 2008
  341.4'8—dc22
                              2007029689

1 2 3 4 5   13 12 11 10 09 08

Dedication

To William Clay Normand (1922–2006) and Taqia Sajida (1926–2006):

Your hopes continue in us.

Contents

Series Editors' Foreword

It is surprising that there is no comprehensive history of the United Nations family of organizations. True, in the last few years, histories of the UN Development Programme[1] and the World Food Programme[2] have been completed, to add to the two histories of UNICEF, the UN Children's Fund, produced in the 1980s and 1990s.[3] And the UN Educational, Scientific and Cultural Organization; the World Health Organization; and the UN Conference on Trade and Development have been preparing volumes bringing together different perspectives of the evolution of their own organizations. But sixty years after the founding of the UN, these are still patchy and incomplete. More serious and complete accounts of UN activities and contributions must be expected of all public organizations, especially internationally accountable ones, along with enhanced efforts to organize their archives so that independent researchers can also document and analyze dispassionately their efforts, achievements, and shortcomings. All this is an essential part of the record of global governance during the last half century.

Faced with this major omission—which has substantial implications for the academic and policy literatures—we decided to undertake the task of writing an *intellectual* history—that is, a history of the ideas launched or nurtured by the United Nations. Observers should not be put off by what may strike them as a puffed-up billing. The working assumption behind our undertaking is straightforward: ideas and concepts are a main driving force in human progress, and they arguably have been one of the most important contributions of the world organization. And as the various volumes of our project have been completed, our early assumptions about the importance of ideas among the UN's various contributions, and for its wider influence, have been confirmed by the record.

The United Nations Intellectual History Project (UNIHP) was launched in 1999 as an independent research effort based at the Ralph Bunche Institute for International Studies at The Graduate Center of The City University of New York, with a liaison office in Geneva. We are grateful for the enthusiastic backing from former Secretary-General Kofi Annan and other staff, as well as from scholars and analysts and governments. We are also extremely appreciative for the generosity of the governments of the Netherlands, the United Kingdom, Sweden, Canada, Norway, Switzerland, Finland, and the Republic and Canton of Geneva; of the Ford, Rockefeller, and MacArthur Foundations, the Carnegie Corporation of New York, and the Dag Hammarskjöld and UN Foundations; and an individual contribution of Ms. Alice Lobel of Paris. This support ensures total intellectual and financial independence. Details of this and other aspects of the project can be found on our web site: www.UNhistory.org.

The work of the UN can be divided into two broad categories: economic and social development, on the one hand, and peace and security, on the other. The UNIHP is committed to producing fifteen volumes on major themes, mainly in the first arena but penetrating also the second. These volumes are all being published in a series by Indiana University Press. Oxford University Press is publishing a related volume titled *The Oxford Handbook on the United Nations.*[4]

In addition, the UNIHP has completed an oral history collection of some seventy-nine lengthy interviews of persons who have played major roles in launching and nurturing UN ideas—and sometimes in hindering them! Extracts from these interviews were published in 2005 as *UN Voices: The Struggle for Development and Social Justice,* and authors of the project's various volumes, including this one, have drawn on these interviews to highlight substantive points made in their texts. Full transcripts of the oral histories were made available in electronic form in early 2007 to facilitate work by researchers and other interested persons worldwide.

There is no single way to organize research, and certainly not for such an ambitious project as this one. This UN history has been structured by topics—ranging from trade and finance to human rights, from transnational corporations to development assistance, from regional perspectives to sustainability. We have selected world-class experts for each topic, and the argument in all of the volumes is the responsibility of the authors whose names appear on the covers. All have been given freedom and responsibility to organize their own digging, analysis, and presentation. Guidance from ourselves as the project directors as well as from peer review groups has been provided to ensure accuracy and fairness in depicting where the ideas came from, how they were developed and disseminated within the UN system, and what happened afterward. We are hoping that future analyses will build upon our series and go beyond. Our intellectual history project is the first, not last, installment in depicting the history of the UN's contributions to ideas.

Human Rights at the UN: The Political History of Universal Justice is the ninth volume in the series—and in some respects the most challenging and outspoken. Roger Normand and Sarah Zaidi bring to bear an enormous range of professional expertise, country experience, and personal commitment as human rights scholars and activists, including recent first-hand involvement in the traumas of Iraq and Afghanistan. They have traced the developments and advances in the main areas of human rights within the UN, from the Charter and the Universal Declaration in the 1940s through the tortuous debate and negotiation of the two conventions on economic, social, and cultural as well as civil and political rights in the 1950s and 1960s and the later developments in the rights of special groups and the right to development in the 1980s to the World Conference on Human Rights in Vienna and the establishment of the Office of the High Commissioner in the 1990s. They deal with the most recent restructuring of the Human Rights Council, whose first session took place in June 2006.

At every stage, the authors bring out the different forces and interests behind governments in this story, the vision and roles of some of the key professionals within the UN secretariat, and the important roles played by what we have called the "third UN"—the experts and committed activists in nongovernment positions and organizations that lobby publicly and privately and often contribute expertise to achieve what they think will be a better outcome. Indeed, in the area of human rights, the role of the third UN may have been more significant and strategic in explaining advances than that of either the first or second UN, the names we have given in this project to the member governments and secretariat staff successively.

For all their recognition of the positive elements represented by these advances, Normand and Zaidi underline a darker and more hypocritical side of government policy at each stage, namely that with few exceptions, each negotiation has continued and reinforced the position set out by the major powers from the beginning, to the effect that human rights in their international manifestation are not to be subject to any legal international enforcement mechanism. Normand and Zaidi argue that more often than not, when international action has been taken in the name of human rights, it has been driven by big-power politics rather than by law or principle.

The concluding message in the final chapter is an even more sobering one, based on their analysis of the long historical record of human rights but sharpened by their recent first-hand involvements. This message is that the present international system of human rights, for all its strengths and weaknesses, is under serious worldwide threat from two more current challenges: the war against terror and the steady advance of globalization. The war against terror has sacrificed human rights in many countries all over the world, including in those that most loudly proclaim their allegiance to them. In parallel, globalization is giving sway to the economic priorities of the market over human rights (and other considerations such as the environment). This, Normand and Zaidi argue, not only reflects the power of economic interests but the principles on which international institutions such as the World Trade Organization have been constructed. Principles in this case *are* backed by legal enforcement mechanisms of the sort that were set aside, consciously and consistently, in the construction of declarations and conventions for human rights.

These are tough messages, and the authors back them up with a wealth of analysis and evidence. As with other volumes in this series, we do not agree with every detail but are proud to have commissioned this well-documented volume. All who care about human rights need to carefully ponder the challenge that the authors present.

We are convinced that the UN story in general deserves to be better documented if it is to be better understood and appreciated. *Human Rights at the UN: The Political History of Universal Justice* makes a significant contribution. Secretary-General Kofi Annan wrote in the foreword to *Ahead of the Curve? UN Ideas and Global Challenges*: "With the publication of this first volume in the United Nations Intellectual History Project, a significant lacuna in twentieth-century scholarship and international relations begins to be filled."[5] This present volume is yet another step in closing the gap in the historical record.

We hope that readers will feel engaged, confronted, and perhaps provoked by this account, at once a journey through time and ideas and a challenge for all who are committed to the extension of human rights. Normand and Zaidi's analysis raises questions about the unfinished revolution, not the least whether the world, as too often before, may be entering a phase of reversal in what was a major area of human advance, a revolution "finished off" rather than "left unfinished." We hope that the authors' premonitions of the demise of human rights as a central concern and activity of the United Nations are exaggerated. But this volume's lesson is that if human rights are to be guarded from further setbacks and the human rights revolution is to be continued and not abandoned, critical actions and inputs must come from committed citizens within individual countries and from nongovernmental organizations (NGOs) acting on a global scale—a call to arms by the third UN.

There are glimmers of hope. Over the last ten years, a momentum has been built up by the adoption of rights-based approaches to development among many international and national NGOs. There has been a sea change toward rights-based approaches to development in Latin America, just as there is new energy in the fight for access to treatment for HIV/AIDS from groups in South Africa. In a different way, many long-term supporters of civil liberties in the United States and other developed countries are being energized by their dismay over the retreats from human rights commitments by the major powers.

These efforts are evidence of important advances and continued strong support for human rights in civil society which will not easily be reversed by the war on terror. Normand and Zaidi are right to direct attention to the challenges presented by recent worldwide setbacks to human rights. But the battle is not over—and the outcome, as so often before, will depend on the pressures brought to bear by civil society and, within and around the UN, by the third UN. This volume will, we hope, serve as a stimulus to these efforts.

As always, we welcome comments from our readers.

Louis Emmerij
Richard Jolly
Thomas G. Weiss
New York
August 2007

Foreword

Among the most improbable developments of the previous hundred years or so is the spectacular rise of human rights to a position of prominence in world politics. This rise cuts against the grain of both the structure of world order and the "realist" outlook of most political leaders acting on behalf of sovereign states. We live in a globalizing world that is still largely dominated by states whose governments jealously guard their sovereign rights. Those who exert influence within these governments overwhelmingly shape policy by relying upon perspectives that tend to marginalize matters of law and morality. Given these background conditions, it is rather remarkable that human rights has received any serious attention within the United Nations, which is above all an organization of, by, and for sovereign states. The whole field of international human rights is haunted by the question "Why would states voluntarily subvert their own sovereign authority?"

And yet, despite impediments, the issue of human rights has steadily moved from the marginal domains of public piety and nationalistic propaganda toward consistent policy relevance and frequent societal preoccupation. An array of ex post facto explanations exists for the unlikely emergence of international human rights. To begin with, there has been a widespread recognition among the citizenry of democratic states since World War I that upholding human rights is connected with international stability—in effect, that an improvement in the life circumstances of domestic society will over time contribute to the avoidance and mitigation of armed conflict. This conviction, anticipating "democratic peace" thinking, was reinforced by the aggressive behavior of the fascist countries and imperial Japan.

Further, in wartime, political leaders solemnly promised their citizens a new dawn of enhanced global justice once victory was achieved. This sense of moral purpose as a goal of war was given an initial push by the establishment of the League of Nations after World War I, which, despite failing miserably to fulfill its role of preventing war, represented an altogether novel institutional commitment to placing the interests of humanity above and beyond the interests of states. Without doubt the strongest of all antecedent developments to the rise of human rights was the psycho-political impact of the Holocaust and the sense of guilt felt within the liberal democracies about how little had been done to block Adolf Hitler's genocidal path of action. The core conviction that such governmental abuse should not be shielded in the future by the protective claims of national sovereignty was the foundation of the post-1945 movement to embed fundamental human rights in international law. The UN was established to carry this momentum forward, but in fact the world body was largely stymied by the intrusion of power realities and colonialist sensitivities.

Over the decades, the UN has often disappointed human rights supporters, yet it has also provided several impressive success stories. The disappointments have generally involved rude awakenings to the continuing potency of power politics and state sovereignty that seemed always, in the crunch, to trump urgent human rights challenges. It has become normal not to expect too much of a response from the UN even in the face of impending humanitarian catastrophes unless there happens to be a compelling geopolitical motive for taking strong protective action. Here again, the terrain is slippery. If the geopolitical stakes are high, suspicions will abound that human rights considerations are being invoked as a pretext for recourse to aggressive war. The ongoing Iraq war is the textbook case of this pattern, which casts a dark shadow of hypocrisy across the whole spectrum of what is presented as humanitarian diplomacy.

As of 2007, Iraq is slipping deeper into violent chaos because the geopolitical stakes are seen as high. Yet the killing in Darfur is getting comparatively little attention since such stakes are treated as trivial. Furthermore, despite the existence of a framework of international law mandating the protection of human rights, it remains difficult for the United Nations or outside forces to act without the backing of major powers and the consent of the territorial government. It is obvious that countries such as Russia and China are too strong to challenge, however reprehensible their behavior with respect to human rights. Nothing effective can be done to uphold the rights of the people of Chechnya, Tibet, and Xinjiang except to subject the situations in those parts of the world to periodic media scrutiny. Even less formidable countries such as Sudan have demonstrated that it is not currently feasible to protect victims of abuse when the territorial government or de facto leaders are sufficiently opposed to "humanitarian intervention."

Yet major human rights successes exist and sustain hope for the future. Largely under UN auspices, governments have constructed over the years an authoritative architecture of human rights norms and practices through

the negotiation of widely ratified international treaties. The Universal Declaration of Human Rights, the International Covenant on Civil and Political
Rights, and the International Covenant on Economic, Social and Cultural
Rights together form what is known as the international bill of rights. In
1993, the United Nations held a world conference in Vienna on human
rights and development that brought together governments and civil society
forces to debate and discuss human rights. Besides strengthening transnational networks of human rights activists and organizations, the conference
resulted in an upgrading of human rights within the UN system. A high
commissioner for human rights was created to give greater influence to the
human rights agenda within the UN. Unfortunately, subsequent experience
has been mixed as political pressures have seriously eroded the credibility
of the world body's work in the area of human rights; the United States
has mounted attacks because of its inability to focus attention more or less
exclusively on its adversaries, as have countries of the global South that are
frustrated by the unwillingness of the UN to take steps to implement what
has been agreed upon.

More notable, perhaps, than these organizational achievements, was the
backing the UN gave, especially the General Assembly, to political movements seeking to overcome oppressive conditions. Despite some political
friction, the UN eventually lent its support to anticolonial struggles and
through an endorsement of the right of self-determination turned its back on
exploitative forms of imperial rule. Even more vigorously, the UN created an
important aura of legitimacy for the anti-apartheid campaign that included
lending its moral authority to the sanctions imposed on the government of
South Africa.

The UN cannot escape this contradictory profile of achievement and
frustration. A mixed message is written into its Charter, which affirms the
equality of states and the norm of nonintervention yet confers on five states
permanent membership in the Security Council coupled with a right of veto.
This Westphalian tension between a world of equally sovereign states and
a formal acceptance of the privileged role of dominant states is responsible
for an unending sense of uncertainty as to what to expect from the United
Nations—nowhere more so than in relation to the international protection
of human rights.

It is against such a background that Roger Normand and Sarah Zaidi have
written their extraordinary historical account of the complex evolution of a
human rights dimension in the theory and practice of the United Nations.
Their book illuminates the extent to which human rights has so often taken
a back seat to geopolitics over the years, but they go further, arguing that the

only true test of achievement is the behavioral impact of human rights on the lives of women and men. Normand and Zaidi find a disturbing gap between the proliferation of norms and the absence of implementing mechanisms, leaving poor and oppressed peoples without much discernible relief that can be traced to the incorporation of human rights into international law. They explain this gap as not only a reflection of a statecentric world order but as also significantly connected with the workings of neoliberal globalization that they believe has intensified disparities between rich and poor within and among countries without appreciably diminishing the magnitude of poverty and other forms of avoidable human suffering. Normand and Zaidi adopt a comprehensive view of human rights that gives equivalent weight to economic and social rights and are sharply critical of capital-driven policies pursued by international financial institutions and market forces.

Because of their well-evidenced and well-reasoned skeptical assessments, their affirmations of the human rights movement have great weight. *Human Rights at the UN* affirms the potential and reality of this human rights tradition even as it has operated within the constraints of the United Nations. The book argues convincingly that despite repeated failures of implementation, the authority and acceptance of human rights has contributed an invaluable language to the pursuit of universal justice that has encouraged debate and communication within and outside the UN and crosses civilizational and religious lines of difference. These consensus-forming activities at the UN have also helped to identify agreed limits on permissible behavior. The human rights perspective has often highlighted illegitimate government practices in ways that can (under certain conditions) mobilize political opposition and produce desirable changes in behavior. In this regard, the UN must be credited with hastening the collapse of both colonialism and apartheid.

Normand and Zaidi provide readers with a fascinating narrative of the role of human rights discourse prior to the existence of the United Nations that makes two elements of the story much more clear than ever before: first, the links between support for human rights, major wartime conditions, and postwar global reform; and second, the crucial role both charismatic political leaders and popular agitation played in bringing human rights in from the cold. Their telling of these stories also helps us understand why both hope and disillusionment surround the experience of human rights as it has developed within the United Nations.

The book is particularly informative about how such wartime leaders as Woodrow Wilson and Franklin Delano Roosevelt presented hopeful images of their postwar visions of humane societies *during* a war only to have those visions shattered by entrenched political elites at home and abroad as soon as the war was over. It was one thing to talk about racial equality and freedom for all peoples in the midst of a war, when the mobilization of support was crucial to the war effort, and quite another to confront reactionary forces in control of allied governments that were committed to racism and colonialism once the war ended. Normand and Zaidi's provocative yet persuasive thesis is that these reactionary forces generally prevailed both before and after the establishment of the United Nations. This assessment leaves readers somewhat uncertain as to whether they think the idealistic efforts of global reformers fell short because of naiveté or the constraints of power or, more likely, some combination.

What is certain, however, is that *Human Rights at the UN* is a great book, filled with insight, empathy, and understanding. It encourages what all genuine supporters of human rights and of the United Nations should welcome—an authoritative text that approaches this delicate subject matter with eyes wide open. Above all, it helps us grasp the complex double truth that the emergence of human rights as a major concern at the UN is both a political miracle and a large contributor to disillusionment about the real impact of UN activities on the human condition.

Richard A. Falk
Princeton University
August 2007

Preface

We do not believe that history is objectively knowable, only a snapshot of the almost infinite voices, personalities, and events that comprise a given moment in time can ever be captured through words on a page. The issue is not only whose stories get told but also who tells the stories. In writing this book, we have made an effort to canvass a range of primary and secondary materials and draw from them reasonable inferences and make fair conclusions, but we cannot pretend that our own viewpoints are irrelevant. Before presenting the substantive themes and ideas of the book, therefore, we will try to situate our own voices through a brief sketch of our shared journey in human rights.

We come to this topic from the perspective of having spent most of our careers as "professional" human rights activists. This has given us opportunities to travel the world, work with talented and committed people, investigate the causes as well as effects of various violations, and, above all, experience the resilience of the human spirit in the face of countless oppressions. However, through these experiences, we have also come to question many of the pat assumptions we once held about the inherent value of human rights, concerning not only means and methods but also concepts and ideology. Today we consider ourselves to be human rights believers and human rights skeptics at the same time.

In 1993, we established an international human rights organization to fight for economic, social, and cultural rights, rights central to the lives of the most exploited and dispossessed people on earth.[1] We worked together until 2005 on a series of research, education, and advocacy projects in some of the world's most intractable conflict zones. When we first started, it seemed that the end of the Cold War had opened an important new frontier to work for peace, human rights, and development, and we wanted to do our part. A few years earlier, our group would have been hard pressed to win political, let alone financial, support to challenge economic oppression on human rights grounds. But the new political climate was conducive to new ways of thinking.

Our methodology incorporated a multidisciplinary approach—human rights lawyers, social scientists, and community groups working together to document violations, educate the public, and advocate for social change. Our principle was solidarity; we felt fortunate to work with inspiring and dedicated activists and organizations in so many different countries, and we came to understand the genuine universality of people's hopes and struggles.

At the same time, we constantly ran up against the political limitations of human rights advocacy. Despite entering the field with a measure of worldly realism, the intransigence of power was nonetheless a disillusioning experience. The lessons we learned contributed to our interest in examining the historical foundations of the human rights idea, if only to better understand how a potentially revolutionary ideology with popular appeal could be so ineffective at improving people's lives on the ground—in our view, the single most important litmus test for judging the worth of the human rights system.

Our own personal decision to collaborate in the first place illustrates the power and promise of human rights as an overarching justice framework capable of uniting diverse people with diverse interests. Identity politics essentializes cultural and other differences; human rights reveal the common ground of being. By all appearances, we two came from different backgrounds and were destined to head in different directions—a Pakistani Muslim female social scientist trained in international public health and development and a Jewish male lawyer from the United States trained in international law and theology. Political interests brought us together, and human rights defined our career paths.

Human rights made sense to us as a natural, almost self-evident choice for carrying forward our shared commitment to social justice. No other ideological framework offered a set of principles that we both could accept wholeheartedly. Equally important, no other framework seemed to offer comparable practical avenues for contributing to social change—the entire community of nations, so called, had recognized human rights as the moral and legal foundation for international justice. The widespread acceptance by states of a common set of legal norms provided the theoretical basis for accountability. On the other hand, we knew full well that these commitments made little difference to people without a strategic capability to win them on the ground. The task, as we saw it, lay in closing the gap between rhetoric and reality.

We would like to offer uplifting testimonies of great victories won in partnership with dedicated local groups and fearless activists. There are such stories, though the triumphs are often small and personal, reflected more in the process of struggle than in any outcome that might be recognized as a triumph by history. Instead, we will recount, in highly abridged form, the results of campaigns we undertook in Iraq and Afghanistan, both of which illustrate the challenges inherent in using human rights as a tool for social change. To what extent the obstacles we encountered are built into the human rights model itself is one of the subjects of this book.

Iraq presents one of the most shameful failures of the international community this century. Few serious observers doubt that the Baath Party under Saddam Hussein committed gross human rights violations. The height of these violations occurred in the 1980s, when Iraq was receiving financial and operational support from the United States and other western powers in its war against Iran. Due to political pressure, the United Nations maintained silence in the face of documented abuses against political dissidents and, more broadly, the Kurdish and Shi'a populations. It was only when Iraq upset the geopolitical balance by invading and occupying Kuwait in 1990 that the Security Council, again directed by the United States and western powers, authorized war and sanctions against Iraq. Between 1991 and 2003, when a U.S.-led coalition invaded Iraq for a second time, this time toppling the regime, the Iraqi population suffered a precipitous and unprecedented decline in living standards under policies approved and executed by the United Nations, an organization meant to secure peace, development, and human rights.[2] The entire nation was impoverished, and more than a million civilians died as a result, the majority of them children.

Our human rights group was one among the first and most persistent critics of this international policy, sending four assessment missions—comprised of lawyers, medical experts, economists, engineers, and other social scientists—to Iraq during the 1990s, the first only three weeks after the end of the 1991 war.[3] We also participated in several other UN assessment missions.[4] The findings from these investigations were dramatic and incontrovertible. War had systematically destroyed Iraq's modern infrastructure, while sanctions prevented its reconstruction and caused the collapse of Iraq's import-dependent economy. The poorest and most vulnerable sectors of society, those without the means to fight for scarce resources, were the most adversely affected. Perversely, sanctions also obliterated the private sector and the middle class while strengthening the regime's grip on power by increasing its leverage over remaining resources and making the population dependent for survival on a government rationing system. A cycle of malnutrition, disease, and death took hold; our epidemiological surveys documented a sharp rise in infant and child mortality. By the late 1990s,

UN studies corroborated the finding that more than 500,000 children under the age of five had died as a result of sanctions-related conditions.[5] These results were not unexpected, given that sanctions were deliberately designed to cripple Iraq's economy and force the government to redraw its borders, eliminate weapons programs, and make other concessions demanded by the United States. It is within this calculus that U.S. secretary of state Madeline Albright termed the suffering of civilians an "acceptable price to pay" for keeping the pressure on Saddam Hussein.[6]

Our findings contrasted with U.S. claims of a "clean" war and a humane sanctions policy aimed at isolating the regime rather than harming the population as a whole. Other groups issued similar reports, the media covered the growing humanitarian crisis in Iraq, and a global movement arose to demand an end to sanctions. Yet the U.S.-led Security Council remained unmoved, modifying sanctions to allow a limited "oil-for-food" program but otherwise assigning all responsibility for the suffering of Iraqis to the demonized figure of Saddam Hussein. In effect, the people of Iraq were caught in a double oppression, punished by their own authoritarian government in its desperation for power and by the international community for the sin of living under the formerly western-backed Hussein regime without managing to overthrow it.

Our human rights position was simple and, on its face, difficult to refute—namely, that it was a breach of the fundamental premise of human rights to hold the lives of innocent citizens hostage to the behavior of their leaders.[7] If human rights are the birthright of every individual, they are not forfeited en masse because the dictator of a particular country refuses to bow to the will of a particular superpower. A reasonable reading of human rights, in our view, indicated that sanctions which have the foreseeable and documented effect of killing civilians on a large scale are illegal, illegitimate, and immoral—especially when they have a relatively minor impact on the offending government and an enormously harmful impact on children and other vulnerable groups. But arguments on paper do not change policy, and there was no international legal authority capable of challenging the Security Council to which one could appeal. Without the possibility of judgment or enforcement, the only option was public pressure. Within the human rights community, southern groups and activists were united in opposition to sanctions against Iraq, but influential northern-based organizations with global reach, like Amnesty International and Human Rights Watch, were unwilling even to address the issue until the late 1990s, when they belatedly and timidly began to criticize U.S. and UN policies.[8] Their reticence was partly due to fears of being labeled sympathetic to Saddam Hussein, an indication of the limits of impartiality when operating in overtly political contexts.

By the time human rights concerns began to influence the sanctions debate, the attacks of 9/11 came, and U.S policy on Iraq shifted from regime containment to regime change. When the Security Council refused to authorize the use of force, a U.S.-led "coalition of the willing" ignored the UN Charter, invaded Iraq in March 2003, and toppled the government. The occupying powers promised to deliver democracy and reconstruction, but instead the country has been consumed by military resistance to occupation, sectarian violence, a generalized breakdown of law and order, and an increasing spiral of poverty and economic hardship. Saddam Hussein was captured, tried, convicted, and hanged after a legal process that was condemned as farcical by international human rights observers. As this book goes to press, the crisis in Iraq has deteriorated into an escalating conflict that threatens regional and perhaps global stability.[9]

Afghanistan presents a different script with the same message: the irrelevance of human rights concerns in the face of great-power politics and the UN's structural weakness. Afghanistan has long suffered under the "great game" of geopolitics, condemned by its location as a strategic crossroads between competing empires. After the Soviet invasion in 1979, it became the last Cold War battlefield as the United States poured billions of dollars in weapons and training to a fractious alliance of local and foreign mujahideen, from which Al Qaeda would eventually emerge. Upon the triumph of the mujahideen in 1992, the United States and its allies lost interest. The country descended into violent chaos as the victorious warlords turned against each other and established competing fiefdoms. The chaos lasted until the Taliban reunified the country in 1996, backed by Pakistan, Saudi Arabia, and, covertly, the United States.[10] After the attacks of 9/11, a U.S.-led military coalition toppled the Taliban and returned the warlords to power.

In December 2001, shortly after the war in Afghanistan, we sent a team to investigate human rights conditions, under contract with the local UN human rights office. At the time there was intense global interest in rebuilding the country. The media was full of stories about the unfolding humanitarian disaster due to war, displacement, poverty, and drought. Western political leaders made solemn commitments never again to turn their backs on the Afghan people, and international donors pledged billions of dollars to a World Bank–sponsored, UN-coordinated reconstruction effort. Upon arrival, however, we found an enormous contingent of UN staff and consultants holed up in Kabul, restricted from traveling the country due to security concerns, and therefore unable to involve the people of Afghanistan in the planned rebuilding of their own country. Yet they were under tremendous pressure to draft detailed funding proposals with ten-year horizons and multimillion dollar budgets for reconstruction, replete with buzzwords about Afghan participation, democratic capacity-building, and human rights.

Working with local organizations, we traveled throughout the country to undertake a survey of human rights attitudes. We found a surprising level of awareness and support for human rights among ordinary Afghans. They had two general priorities. First was an end to the violence and insecurity that accompanied the return of the warlords. While western media broadcasted images of Afghan women in Kabul removing their burqas, most rural women we interviewed experienced increased fear and insecurity. The survey showed that Afghans uniformly favored immediate disarmament of the most brutal militias, some mechanism for human rights accountability, and the extension of international peacekeepers outside Kabul. As one high school principal said, "For many years you have contributed to war and bloodshed, it is your turn now to help us with peace and security."[11] Their second priority was to guarantee rights to food, water, health, and other economic rights in the midst of severe drought and hardship. Contrary to conventional perceptions, most Afghans were eager to educate their girls, but due to high levels of poverty, they required some form of subsidy to offset lost income. They also considered international aid to be a matter of rights and duties, not charity, as expressed by one tribal elder:

> Before talking about reconstruction, the Americans should first stop the destruction. Then they should rebuild what they have destroyed: our homes, our roads, our farms. The same goes for Russia, Pakistan, and all the other countries that talk about helping us. Rebuilding what you have destroyed is not something you do for us. That is your duty as a human being.[12]

Returning to Kabul, we met with the international teams planning Afghan reconstruction and shared the results of our surveys. In essence, our report called for the UN to embrace its own much-publicized commitments to mainstream human rights in operational programs and implement guidelines for rights-based development. UN staff members, especially those with country experience, were enthusiastic about focusing on human rights and Afghan participation but at the same time were deeply frustrated by the politicization of their own work. They had low expectations that Afghan priorities would be taken account at UN headquarters in New York, particularly since they conflicted with U.S. imperatives to support friendly warlords and World Bank imperatives to establish market-friendly policies. Among the more egregious examples, the reconstruction plan called for cutting school subsidies and even imposing user fees for education. The priorities of the U.S.-led coalition of donors and the Afghan people were at loggerheads, and it was crystal clear which side would come out ahead.

From these and similar experiences, we derived several broad lessons. They may strike the reader as self-evident, but they are nonetheless important to spell out for their larger implications about the human rights system as it has developed through the UN. First, we found that the human rights paradigm resonated with ordinary people, and civil society groups in particular, even those concerned not specifically with rights but with broader issues of social justice. In every country we worked in, including Afghanistan, Iraq, Haiti, and Ecuador, human rights could provide a unifying banner to link diverse individuals and organizations engaged in common struggles for justice. It sounds like a cliché, indeed it is a cliché, but people everywhere shared common dreams for a better life free from various oppressions and indignities and could find their hopes reflected in the civil, political, social, economic, or cultural rights recognized in the human rights regime. Who does not want food on the table, a place of one's own, a good education, work at a living wage, an opportunity to express one's views and conscience, a chance to develop and thrive?

People we met were rarely, if ever, concerned with metaphysical debates about the origins of human rights or historical controversies over Eurocentrism. Their calculations were based on the more immediate and practical desire to improve their welfare and uplift their communities; they understood human rights as a vocabulary of justice ostensibly endorsed by the key power brokers and decision makers at the international level. Especially in regions scarred by war and conflict, they saw human rights as a peaceful means to pursue their goals.

The second contrasting lesson was of the impotence of the existing human rights model as a tool of leverage when it is isolated from other social and political factors; this has resulted in the UN's inability to vindicate its own human rights principles. It is one thing to understand intellectually that human rights are a tough sell in the "real" world of realpolitik; it is another to confront those limits in the process of struggling for change. In the absence of effective mechanisms to enforce human rights at either the international or national levels, we found that the machinery of government was not easily moved by appeals to higher principles and supposedly legally binding norms. Even public indignation generated by media exposés and the support of well-organized NGO communities working across local and international lines were insufficient to force policy change.

It is here that the failure of human rights to engage and mobilize larger popular constituencies became most apparent. The human rights system has neither mechanisms for passing and enforcing legal judgments nor mass support for compelling change through political pressure. Without the support, or at least acquiescence, of the more powerful states, the prospects for justice are extremely limited. This was especially evident in Iraq, where the United States and its allies co-opted the world organization into serving as a proxy for their geopolitical interests. But even in Afghanistan, where the UN had more political space to implement its own human rights mandate and guidelines, bureaucratic inertia, limited resources, and the low priority given to human rights combined to undercut the prospects for a meaningful and effective program on the ground.

It is instructive to compare the enforcement failures of human rights over the past sixty years with the powerful legal tools available to effectuate the purposes of international economic law.[13] Although the World Trade Organization was established only in 1994, it came equipped with judicial bodies empowered to pass judgment against sovereign states and impose considerable financial penalties—powers that human rights advocates have long dreamed of in vain. The United Nations has in principle enthroned human rights law at the apex of the global moral order, recognizing the universal and inalienable rights of individual dignity. But the truth of the matter is that human rights have been granted the fewest means of practical implementation of any comparable system of international law. This conclusion comes as no surprise to observers of global affairs. But important questions still remain unanswered: How and why did member states of the United Nations design the human rights system to privilege principles over practice, in stark contrast to the hopes and expectations of the peoples of the United Nations?

Acknowledgments

This book emerged out of our long collaboration in human rights, starting with a humanitarian mission to postwar Iraq in March 1991. Since then we have had the good fortune to work with many courageous activists and organizations in many parts of the world. It is not possible to thank everyone who, by sharing their ideas and experiences and inspiring us with their examples, helped shape our understanding of human rights. But without them, this book would not have been written.

We learned about human rights in "the field"—that place where human beings live and struggle and suffer for justice—through work associated with the Center for Economic and Social Rights (CESR), a nonprofit organization we established together with Christopher Bertil Jonas af Jochnick. We are indebted to Chris for the long and intense hours of discussion and debate during which our ideas about human rights were formed and reformed. While failing to change the world, perhaps we managed to change ourselves.

We also want to express our appreciation and gratitude to all those who provided us with expert guidance and meaningful support, especially in the early years when our enthusiasm overmatched our experience. Deserving of special mention are Philip Alston, Elisabeth Benjamin, Clarence Dias, Richard Falk, Scott Leckie, Henry Steiner, Sarah Leah Whitson, and Alicia Yamin. We also thank Phyllis Bennis, Lincoln Chen, Larry Cox, Paul Epstein, Leilani Farha, Paulina Garzon, Nadia Hijab, Stephen Marks, Makau Mutua, Bruce Porter, Mike Posner, Ken Roth, Eric Stover, Jack Tobin, and Mona Younis.

Our projects and travels provided the opportunity to work with a wide range of dedicated individuals such as Ghassan Abu Sitta, Shahbano Aliani, Chris Caruso, Anna Cody, Brenda Coughlin, Mary C. Smith Fawzie, Saad Hamid, Nasser Kafarneh, Nick Lundgren, Lucy Mair, Abdullah Mutawi, and Jacob Park. The influence of these and many other unnamed friends and colleagues is invisibly marked in these pages.

We want to say that this book was a labor of love; it may be more accurate to simply call it a labor. For keeping us on track and stubbornly believing that we would one day complete the manuscript, we extend thanks to Tom Weiss, Richard Jolly, and Louis Emmerij, the series editors of the United Nations Intellectual History Project. Other UNIHP staff provided invaluable and much-needed assistance, including Kate Babbitt, Tatiana Carayannis, Danielle Zach Kalbacher, Nancy Okada, Sophie Theven de Gueleran, and Zeynep Turan. We also are grateful to the participants at UNIHP seminars and review sessions for offering helpful feedback and suggestions.

The book covers a lot of historical ground, and we are very thankful for the able and timely research support of Jean Carmalt, Benjamin Cohen, Ahsan Kamal, Sara Qutub, Gilbert Sembrano, and Sara Van Der Pas. Special appreciation goes to Naila Baig Ansari, whose help always went far beyond the call of duty.

Last but far from least, we were sustained by the unstinting love of our families, who have not just tolerated but encouraged our various wanderings and causes and crusades during these years. With so much support and advice from colleagues, friends, and family, any errors and shortcomings in the manuscript are ours alone.

Abbreviations

AJC	American Jewish Committee
BSSR	Byelorussian Soviet Socialist Republic
CEDAW	Convention on the Elimination of All Forms of Discrimination against Women
CHR	Commission on Human Rights
CRC	Convention on the Rights of the Child
CSW	Commission on the Status of Women
ECOSOC	Economic and Social Council
EU	European Union
FAO	Food and Agriculture Organization
HDR	Human Development Report
ICC	International Criminal Court
ICERD	International Convention on the Elimination of All Forms of Racial Discrimination
ICJ	International Court of Justice
ICRC	International Committee of the Red Cross
ILO	International Labour Organization
IMF	International Monetary Fund
MDG	Millennium Development Goal
NAACP	National Association for the Advancement of Colored People
NAM	Non-Aligned Movement
NGO	Nongovernmental Organization
NIEO	New International Economic Order
NNC	National Negro Congress
UNCTAD	United Nations Conference on Trade and Development
UNDP	United Nations Development Programme
UDHR	Universal Declaration of Human Rights
UNESCO	United Nations Economic, Social and Cultural Organization

UNICEF	United Nations Children's Fund
UNRRA	United Nations Relief and Rehabilitation Administration
WTO	World Trade Organization

Human Rights at the UN

Introduction

- Human Rights and Justice
- Human Rights as Universal Ideology
- Historical Origins of Human Rights
- The Modern Conception of Human Rights
- Historical Methods and Limitations
- Themes and Structure of the Book

Human Rights and Justice

In what was billed as an historic reform, the United Nations voted on 15 March 2006 to abolish the Commission on Human Rights (CHR) and replace it with a new Human Rights Council.[1] Politically charged questions about the nature of human rights and the proper means of enforcing them dominated the highly contentious debates preceding the UN's decision. These debates pitted a group of largely western states against a larger group of developing countries.

The former pushed for sweeping changes to exclude states with dubious human rights records, primarily in the area of civil and political rights, and to make it easier to condemn and punish human rights violations. They argued that non-democratic states such as China, Cuba, and Sudan had taken over the commission and politicized its agenda to shield themselves from scrutiny rather than uphold the impartial banner of human rights. On the other side, a group of "like-minded" countries in the Non-Aligned Movement (NAM)[2] argued that powerful countries such as the United States and Britain were exploiting human rights to advance their geopolitical interests, sitting in judgment of poor nations and ignoring their own policies of economic and military imperialism.

In a sense, this debate reflects the extraordinary success of human rights. In little more than half a century, the issue of human rights has become the preeminent signifier of international morality and legitimacy. Notwithstanding the lack of enforcement mechanisms, the "soft power" of human rights to define acceptable behavior in international affairs and, crucially, to determine who is the accuser and who stands accused has become an increasingly important feature of the global landscape.[3] It is also increasingly contested, as non-European states have challenged the traditionally dominant interpretation of the United States and its allies. For example, China, which has routinely been subject to scathing criticism in the U.S. State Department's annual human rights report, turned the tables in a thoroughly documented 2006 report detailing U.S. abuses at the domestic and international levels.[4] While China was elected to the first Human Rights Council by secret ballot on 9 May 2006, the United States chose for the first time not to seek a seat on the world's preeminent human rights body.[5]

This squabble between the world's sole superpower and its fast-emerging rival illustrates the paradoxical role of human rights as both a source of universal values and an arena of ideological warfare. The paradox is greater still insofar as states themselves have, through the UN, purported to limit their own sovereignty by establishing and codifying the universal values that are being politically contested. The stakes in this battle are significant: states defined as violators become susceptible to various forms of public condemnation and pressure. In extreme cases, depending on their status in the global hierarchy and the extent of alleged violations, they could face the prospect of unilateral or international military intervention.[6]

The debate also highlights fundamental fissures in the universal project of human rights. Human rights, in theory and principle, are meant to occupy a nonpartisan space by virtue of their accepted status in public morality and international law. Basic to human rights is the equal dignity of every individual, abstracted from his or her personal conditions. Yet this concept is not empirically realistic; human beings come into the world decidedly unequal. For hundreds of millions of children born into abject poverty, the prospects for achieving their "inherent" dignity are not high. The proclamation of universal human rights cannot erase, in one fell swoop, the hierarchies and divisions of power reflected in nation, class, race, and all other categories that separate humanity. Given the inevitable (mis)use of human rights to advance particular agendas, the question becomes whether human rights mechanisms reconcile or aggravate such divisions. Do they reflect the interests of the dominant categories (whether state, class, or race) or of the international community as a whole? Are they a bridge between civilizations or a locus for the clash of civilizations?

It is not only states that figure in the human rights drama; equally important is the role of civil society organizations and ordinary citizens. It is undeniable that the primary engine driving human rights forward, both during the establishment of the framework after World War II and its subsequent expansion, has been the passion and energy of people fighting for their rights. The relationship has been mutually reinforcing: UN recognition of human rights principles has encouraged, and to an extent channeled, the struggles of oppressed groups, which have in turn added flesh and blood to the principles on paper.

However, the quest for justice predates and prefigures the modern human rights paradigm. People have always struggled to improve their lives and claim their just portion. The persistence—some would argue increase—of persecution, exploitation, and inequality since the triumphant arrival of the Universal Declaration of Human Rights (UDHR) in 1948 raises serious questions about the value added to this ongoing struggle for justice: Does the human rights paradigm provide an effective outlet for popular energies? To what extent does the UN system, in addition to representing state interests, accommodate and reflect values common to the masses of human beings alive today? Do people's deeper beliefs about human rights find expression in the set of international laws and institutions that have developed over the past sixty years?

These questions require us to closely examine the historical development of human rights. From the establishment of the United Nations, the Commission on Human Rights played a central role in shaping the international human rights framework. It was the only human rights body established through a specific provision of the UN Charter.[7] In its early years, the CHR had the monumental task of creating an international bill of rights—in effect, defining and elaborating the practical meaning of human dignity in the new system of nation-states that arose from the wreckage of World War II.

The questions it faced did not lend themselves to easy answers. What were the sources and contents of human rights? What were to be recognized as the "right" relationships among and between individual human beings, the communities with which they associated, the states in which they lived, and international society as a whole? Were human rights standards to be expressed as moral imperatives or legal mandates? How were human rights to be monitored and enforced, if at all, in an international system of states divided by myriad practices, beliefs, and traditions? In short, how could a new standard of universal ethics be established and made meaningful for the diverse peoples and nations of the world?

These dilemmas were shaped by the context of the times. World War II was an unprecedented global catastrophe; people everywhere wanted an end to wars and massacres and oppressions. The intense and understandable yearning for a better world expressed itself in widespread public support for a universal system of justice that linked practices at the domestic level with global standards of rights. The call was for a human rights system that worked; citizens pushed their governments to accept and develop such a system.

The CHR was tasked with designing the new human rights paradigm. State representatives on the commission negotiated and formulated the Universal Declaration and the two international covenants that followed. While the image persists of an international consensus behind human rights, in fact the divisions—between the United States and Soviet Union, between great powers and weaker nations, between states and public opinion—were manifold and ever-shifting depending on the issues involved. Most states, while accepting the idea of human rights in principle, were unwilling to tolerate international interference in their domestic affairs, putting them at loggerheads with public demands for a meaningful legal framework. As colonies of Europe, the majority of nations now recognized as independent had no say in the affairs of the emerging United Nations. Meanwhile, the great powers—the United States and Soviet Union in particular—insisted on maintaining hegemony in the global organization and rejected restrictions on their sovereign powers and prerogatives. The shield of domestic sovereignty was successfully raised against proposals to establish even a weak international monitoring and supervisory capacity in human rights.

As a result of these pressures, the human rights system established at the UN emphasized a particular set of values as moral norms only rather than enforceable rights. That legacy continues to influence human rights discourse and practice, even if current debates appear oblivious to the fact that "politicization" was always part and parcel of the human rights regime. Human rights are, in our view, rightly acclaimed as the first relatively broad-based effort to establish a global ethics. It is not possible, however, to assess their present role and potential relevance without understanding the historical circumstances of their origins. The political and ideological tensions, impositions, and compromises that characterized the earliest debates and decisions have come to define and delimit the parameters of the modern human rights framework we have inherited today.

Consider, for example, the controversy over the new Human Rights Council, which has been portrayed as a governmental dispute along North-South lines. The role of public opinion does not appear as a factor in this equation, outside of targeted advocacy interventions by the larger, well-established international nongovernmental organizations (NGOs).[8] Yet it is not difficult to imagine that many, if not most, ordinary citizens of the world hope and expect that effective reform of an admittedly flawed human rights system should seek to protect the rights of all people. A properly constituted impartial human rights body should condemn, when they are investigated and proven, human rights violations associated with weak states as well as strong—China's political persecution and U.S. military adventurism, for example—not to mention violations by nonstate actors ranging from Al Qaeda to the International Monetary Fund (IMF).

Of course a genuine program of universal enforcement of human rights against all abusers is hardly feasible under present political conditions. But even keeping in mind the distinction between what is and what should be, the issue becomes whether the UN human rights system is capable, over time, of effectuating its lofty principles. Is it moving in the right direction, does it reflect the highest consensual values of states and the peoples they claim to represent, or is it fatally compromised by a deliberately designed gulf between accepted moral principles and negligible means of legal and political enforcement?

These profound questions and dilemmas have lain submerged beneath the relatively calm surface of universal human rights acceptance for much of the past sixty years. Their emergence today results from multiple factors, in particular the heightened rhetorical use of human rights by diverse political actors in the divisive context of a purported clash of civilizations, the sudden and dramatic escalation in human rights violations associated with the war on terror, and growing gap between rich and poor linked to globalization. It is difficult to predict how these forces will play out in the coming years. However, it seems evident to us that human rights structures—and indeed the UN system as a whole—faces a significant challenge to its basic relevance, a challenge that can be effectively confronted only through an honest accounting of the past. How and why did human rights develop as they did? What are the implications and limitations for our present and our future?

The human rights movement tends to ignore such issues—an unusual omission given the liberal intellectual roots of many advocates, academics, diplomats, and informed citizens who count themselves part of this movement.[9] Instead, universal human rights are often simply asserted as a matter of positive law and self-evident truth. The intention may be to safeguard the legitimacy and power of human rights in international discourse, but in our view the impact is quite the opposite. The debate over human rights becomes reduced to a matter of competing faiths and dogmas, thereby intensifying rather than reducing the politicization of the concept.

Our purpose in writing this book is to shed light on the political history of human rights. Greater awareness of the achievements and disappointments, conflicts and compromises, and bargains and betrayals that marked

the establishment and development of human rights is, in our view, a precondition for realizing their potential to improve people's lives. We address
not the philosophical basis of human rights but rather their emergence
in the twentieth century through the crucible of the United Nations—the
public hopes and expectations, concrete power struggles, national rivalries,
and bureaucratic infighting that molded the international system of human
rights law. We emphasize the period before and after the creation of the
UN, when human rights ideas and proposals, generated largely by nongovernmental actors, were shaped and transformed by the hard-edged realities
of power politics and bureaucratic imperatives. We look also at the more
recent expansion of the human rights framework in response to demands
for equitable development after decolonization and organized efforts by
women, minorities, and other disadvantaged groups to secure international
recognition of their rights.

It has been a sobering experience to study the extent of governmental
hypocrisy regarding human rights throughout the conflict-ridden twentieth
century. Then again, power is always reluctant to stay its bloody hand on
moral appeal alone. Whether one sees progress or loss in the overall human
rights balance sheet is a matter of perspective, bearing in mind that the story
is still unfolding. For our part, despite skepticism concerning the structural
weakness of human rights in a global system dominated by nation-states
and unaccountable financial powers, we remain partisans of the universal
struggle for justice that underlies the human rights idea.

Human Rights as Universal Ideology

The human rights paradigm is resilient; one of its more remarkable characteristics is the capacity to mean different things to different people while retaining overall ideological coherence. Consider these contradictory propositions:
human rights are as old as the first societies; human rights are a moral and
legal innovation born half a century ago through the United Nations. Human
rights are rooted in religious and ethical traditions; human rights overturn
the old collective duty of obedience to higher law, recognizing instead the
inalienable rights of every single person. Human rights are universal, applicable to all people in all cultures, transcending time and place; human rights
derive from western, primarily Anglo-American history and philosophy and
are fully open to critical scrutiny. Human rights uphold individual dignity
against state abuse, posing a revolutionary challenge to the prerogatives of
sovereignty; human rights were established, shaped, and ratified by sovereign
states, comprising just another ideological weapon in the arsenal of power

politics. Human rights are impartial and nonpartisan; human rights challenge the prevailing political orders in virtually every nation—if ever truly implemented they would overturn these orders.

As Walt Whitman might have said, human rights contain multitudes; there may be as many human rights ideas as there are human beings.[10] Yet in spite of, or perhaps because of, these contradictions, the concept of human rights enjoys broad acceptance among people of every background. Despite being highly contested, human rights are still widely considered to be the best, if not the only possible, universal global ethic.

The success of human rights in becoming the accepted standard of international morality is one of the more improbable stories of the twentieth century. It stands out as an anomaly in the bloodiest and most destructive period in human history, an age marked by world wars and myriad lesser conflicts, genocides, holocausts, massacres, and all manners of abuse. While the impulse to mass violence is not a modern invention, the scale and intensity has been something new, a phenomenon historically associated not only with our exponentially expanding technological powers but also the establishment and consolidation of the current international system of territorially defined nation-states.

The question therefore arises: Why in the midst of so much state-initiated violence should a universal ethic arise based largely on protecting the sanctity of the human individual from state abuse? Are human rights a form of wishful thinking—false consciousness for mass consumption—or an expression of the irrepressible human spirit? How did human rights come to occupy a privileged moral position above rival ideologies? How were they shaped and defined, and what are their origins and impacts?

Human rights are concerned, first and foremost, with questions of justice. The struggle for justice is a mysterious and enduring aspect of human existence. Of the characteristics that distinguish our species from all others, the idea of justice stands apart, especially in its universalist dimensions. Justice cannot be readily reduced to the simple conditioned instinct for survival and adaptation that at a basic level drives the biological and evolutionary imperatives of life. The greatest thinkers of every age have struggled to understand the origins and contents of justice, the moral sense of right and wrong, the link between finite, personal truths and immutable, universal Truth. From one perspective, their answers are as varied as the cultures that produced them. From another, they all appear as shadows cast from a common source of light—the hero with a thousand faces, as Joseph Campbell has written to explain how one core mythology seems to permeate all human societies.[11]

In our modern age, the idea of human rights is, for better or worse, the predominant incarnation of this universal yearning for justice. Yet the source of human rights remains undefined by design. All references to an ultimate source were deleted from draft versions of the 1948 Universal Declaration of Human Rights. The group of states that the UN recognized as independent (excluding the vanquished powers of World War II and colonized peoples) could not reach consensus on whether God, nature, positive law, self-evident reason, human reciprocity, social construction, class struggle, or some combination thereof should be credited with the creation of human rights. So they agreed to disagree, leaving the source blank and negotiating a set of moral principles that were nevertheless declared to be inherent and inalienable, presumably valid from all possible origins. This fundamental claim to universal justice has proven remarkably durable despite lacking an accepted foundation.

The speed with which human rights has penetrated every corner of the globe is astounding. Compared to human rights, no other system of universal values has spread so far so fast. A few decades ago, the concept of human rights was hardly discussed outside a small circle of mostly western intellectuals. In what amounts to an historical blink of the eye, the idea of human rights has become the lingua franca of international morality. In the words of Louis Henkin, we live in "the age of rights."[12] Other universal ideologies—Christianity, Islam, capitalism, and communism, for example—have conquered large parts of the world at various times but have also provoked intense, militant opposition. Devotion to human rights may be less deep and committed than devotion to these worldviews, but it is also less contentious and divisive. In part this can be attributed to the ostensibly legal and nonpolitical nature of human rights. Virtually the entire community of nations, representing every culture, religion, and ethnicity, has in principle assented to human rights, marking a universal acceptance of positive law. In theory, if less often in reality, human rights provide a common ground for the Christian and the Muslim, the communist and the capitalist. A U.S. writer sums up the phenomenon: "Who can bad-mouth human rights? It is beyond partisanship and beyond attack."[13]

Of course, human rights are criticized all the time; there is no shortage of individuals and even governments opposed to human rights. But the dissenter is immediately thrown on the defensive and assumed to be an apologist for atrocities. Most people feel little compunction in rejecting the universal claims of religions to which they do not adhere. But those who deny the universality of human rights are placed in a different category altogether. In this sense, human rights, as conventionally understood, comprise a hegemonic moral discourse. Dissent is tolerated; indeed, free speech is a core value of human rights. But the dissenter is nevertheless assumed to have dubious ethical values. To question human rights is not merely in bad taste, it is immoral. The foundation of human rights rests on the claim of moral consensus; the center does not hold if it becomes acceptable for you to reject while I believe.

That is why disbelievers are generally placed beyond the pale of accepted international ethics. Critics of human rights run a very real risk of moral isolation, with attendant political consequences. Cultural practices that transgress conventional notions of human rights may invite humanitarian intervention; states that deny the universal validity of human rights may become international pariahs subject to regime change. The "may" is important, because it is common knowledge that not all abuses and abusers are equal in practice. The theory of impartiality is belied by the absence of consistently applied legal mechanisms interpreted and enforced by objective decision makers. Instead, human rights rely for their impact on media attention, public outrage, and, especially, the sponsorship of powerful states. The latter have always deployed human rights in a selective, self-serving manner, underscoring the geopolitical nature of an ideology premised on universalism.

Apart from inconsistent application, it is often said that the Achilles heel of human rights lies in the persistence of gross abuses of human dignity throughout the world. It is doubtful whether a single state can claim to be in compliance with the full range of human rights—the gap between pious international commitments and brutal domestic and global practices is stark indeed. The proliferation of human rights ideas and norms at the UN has clearly not solved the problems of injustice. In fact, the rapid ideological rise of human rights since the 1960s, and especially the 1990s, has coincided with the greatest expansion of social and economic inequality the world has ever seen.[14] On the other hand, many point to human rights successes—the fall of dictatorships in the Soviet bloc and Latin America and the extraordinary growth of NGOs and civil society movements in virtually every country—to argue that the world would be worse off but for the imperfect protection offered by human rights.

Either way, the undeniable chasm between rhetoric and reality appears to pose a fundamental challenge to human rights. It is hard to escape the conclusion that the idea of human rights has gained surface acceptance across the globe without sufficiently influencing the practice of states and other powerful actors. Yet despite all these conceptual and practical problems, human rights remain a powerful expression of people's hopes and demands for a better world. States are widely blamed for violating human rights, but the system that they themselves created to prevent such violations has escaped systematic critique. Human rights continue to claim the allegiance of people of different nationalities and backgrounds, religious and secular, liberal and socialist, rich and poor alike.

Our postmodern intellectual age, with its skeptical disciplines of anthropology, sociology, and other comparative social sciences, has little tolerance for the so-called universality of dogmatic belief and unquestioned truth. Even sacred scriptures have been subject to exhaustive historical and literary analysis. But not human rights. No one believes that human rights were handed down on stone tablets; we know that they were formed in the minds and made through the efforts of human beings, often representing nation-states. We know that universality is a rhetorical device that not only masks specific power relations but also papers over a wide range of differences within the human rights concept itself.

Why then do human rights appear relatively immune not only to ideological critique but even probing intellectual scrutiny? Mark Mazower, a historian who has turned his attention to human rights, states:

> We will look in vain to scholarship to shed much light on this question. Lawyers . . . shy away from any hint that the origins of legal regimes lie in a set of cultural, political, and ideological struggles. . . . Historians [have] turned the history of law into a ghetto in historical studies while the history of how law has been deployed in international politics remains a ghetto within a ghetto.[15]

Historical Origins of Human Rights

One problem of history is where to begin. We have chosen to focus on the establishment of human rights in modern international law, starting with the codification of humanitarian principles in the late nineteenth century and emphasizing the incorporation of human rights into the UN Charter and subsequent treaties. While the book does not address the history of the idea of human rights in any depth, we feel it is nonetheless important to sketch briefly the philosophical and historical antecedents of human rights in order to contextualize the perspectives of supporters and detractors alike.

These antecedents are anything but immediately apparent or conveniently traceable. Some proponents claim that human rights emerged in ancient history from myriad philosophical, ethical/moral, and religious sources: "The idea of the inalienable rights of the human being was often articulated by poets, philosophers, and politicians in antiquity."[16] Yet this dubious assertion seems based more on ideological than historical considerations; one of the ways that the human rights idea maintains and extends its powerful position as the most widely accepted benchmark of international morality is by encompassing other ethical systems under the broadest possible umbrella. By this method divine law and religious edicts, ancient philosophies, natural law, and legal positivism are all claimed as the common ancestors of the human rights idea.

Such a broad-brush approach, while defensible at the most generic level, fails in our view to account for the particular characteristics integral to the human rights idea. Human rights should not be conflated with any and every ethical system of justice, ideas which have indeed been around since the dawn of recorded history. In contrast to this view, we argue that the concept of human rights emerged specifically from Anglo-American and French natural rights traditions in the seventeenth and eighteenth centuries. It arose not as a set of disembodied ideas but was linked to a series of revolutions—scientific, industrial, and ultimately military. Just as these revolutions overthrew the old feudal order in favor of a capitalist society based on negotiable contractual and property relations, the ideological revolution of individual rights overthrew the feudal conception of divine rights and natural hierarchies. And just as the old order grounded its legitimacy in an unchanging eternal law, the victorious concepts of natural law and human rights proclaimed their own universal validity, applicable to all humanity for all time—despite arising out of specific historical circumstances and despite privileging the rights of wealthy white men in law and in fact.[17]

The claim of modern human rights to represent a secular version of religious traditions likewise does not bear scrutiny.[18] It is true that all religions uphold universal values and delineate duties that people owe both to each other and to the transcendent force of creation. It is also true that religious texts speak of the worth, dignity, and integrity of every person without distinction. Hinduism considers "all human life to be sacred . . . the first and foremost ethical principle is non-injury to others." Judaism "urged people to extend beyond themselves and take action on behalf of others in this world." Confucian thought advised all people to honor their duty and responsibility toward others and recognize that "within the four seas, we are all brothers."[19] Similar sentiments can be found in all religious traditions.

Yet religion offers an entirely different conception of dignity than does human rights. The source of human value in religious thought is established and decreed by a divine order, whereas under the human rights idea, people recognize their own worth and on that basis enter into an understanding to respect one another's integrity as a fundamental, inviolable right. This definitional difference between human rights and religious duties can be seen in the example of Judaism, although the same point can be made in reference to other traditions: "Judaism never accepted natural law, only one law was recognized and that was divine law. . . . Judaism knows not rights but duties, and at bottom, all duties are to God."[20]

As far as secular antecedents are concerned, the earliest conceptualization of rights is attributed to ancient civilizations such as the Greeks, Persians, and Romans. Aristotle argued that universal natural law based on equality of rights of citizenship could not be abridged by government. Roman jurists extended natural law into jus gentium, the law of nations, establishing the theoretical basis for universal rights in the world community. Hammurabi famously decreed, "Let the oppressed man come into the presence of my statue for equal protection under the law."[21]

However, these various ideas of equal justice are belied by their intended and actual application. Hammurabi's code, for example, offered a limited set of legal protections to aristocrats only, thereby preserving the accepted hierarchies between social classes. Greco-Roman philosophy reflected an idealized version of what the law ought to be rather than an accurate portrayal of actual laws that legitimized the rights of autocratic leaders to rule at home and plunder abroad. As one historian notes:

> In Rome, as in the ancient Near East, the emperor ruled as the son of gods; against his will there was no recourse. Only Roman citizens, a small percentage of the population, had specific rights, and these were minimal indeed: if condemned to death, the citizen had the privilege of being beheaded rather than tortured to death in the public arena, as noncitizens were.[22]

The idea that all individuals had universal claims of right against their governments was present in these societies, but only at the margins of thought and the very outer margins of power. The overriding legal ethic condoned the subordination of individuals to society as a whole and the ruling class in particular on the grounds that "society confers upon its members whatever rights, privileges, or exemptions they enjoy. According to this pattern, ultimate value derives from the social order," not the rights-bearing individual.[23]

The classical period did, however, exert a profound influence on the Enlightenment philosophers whose ideas would help spark revolutions in all spheres of European life. In their battle with the "dead hand" of absolute church power and the divine right of feudal monarchies, these thinkers hearkened back to a classical golden age of personal freedom and natural rights. The scientific and industrial revolutions, which challenged state and religious authorities, found their ideological counterpart in a political philosophy that challenged ruling ideas of law and governance. These philosophers represented the intellectual vanguard of historical struggles centered in Britain and its American colonies, led by the rising power of merchants and bourgeoisies seeking to wrest political control from feudal structures and reduce their arbitrary authority over property and trade.

Key events in England included the rise of the Levelers movement against the monarchy in the seventeenth century, based on a platform promoting the natural rights of all people to life, property, election of representatives, freedom of religion, and freedom from conscription; the enactment of the Petition of Right in 1628, asserting the right to be free from arbitrary arrest and punishment; the Habeas Corpus Act of 1679; and the adoption of the 1689 Bill of Rights, a landmark in the history of civil and political rights establishing a limited monarchy, security of law and property, representative government, freedom of speech, trial by jury, and prohibitions against cruel and unusual punishment.[24]

These struggles for redistribution of political and economic power were based on an understanding of rights emanating from natural law doctrine. The most influential proponent of these theories was John Locke, who argued famously that "every individual possessed certain 'natural rights' in the state of nature prior to the existence of organized societies."[25] A crucial element of Lockean theory is that people formed societies and set up governments to preserve those natural rights, meaning that governments are a product of man and not the other way around and are authorized to rule only with the consent of the governed under a social contract.[26] Thomas Paine also argued that natural rights are the original source for subsequent civil rights of man in society, although unlike Locke, he linked natural rights to divine principles.[27] In his famous pamphlet *Rights of Man*, he asserted that man "enters" into society with natural rights and, together with other citizens, grants society power to safeguard some of these as civil rights, particularly rights to security and protection.[28] Since rights are not granted by society but inherent in individuals, the constitution, as an expression of natural rights, is antecedent and superior to the government that must adhere to it.[29] Other prominent members of the group known as the philosophes included Jean-Jacques Rousseau, Montesquieu, Voltaire, and David Hume. Their work shared common themes opposing clerical, feudal, and monarchical power and advocating individual liberty and freedom of choice based on inviolable fundamental rights arising out of human nature and reason.[30]

These thinkers played a crucial role in providing ideological justification for the American and French revolutions and the general triumph of capitalist modes of economic and political relations over the old feudal order. The enumeration of "self-evident" and inalienable natural rights in the American

Declaration of Independence and the French Declaration of the Rights and Duties of Man elevated these concrete historical struggles into the realm of universal justice, proclaiming principles applicable to all men—and perhaps a few women—everywhere. Not only political freedom but also notions of property and free trade were grounded in natural rights theories, legitimizing the shift of control from the landed aristocracy to the mercantile bourgeoisie as a natural progression rather than a bloody struggle for power.

The idea of a mythical state of nature is now understood to be a fiction contradicted by evolutionary science, sociology, anthropology, and common sense. But at the time, liberal individual rights as universal natural rights served as a ringing ideological battle cry to defeat the ancien régimes of Europe. Of course, not all philosophers agreed with such ideas. The hypocrisies were self-evident to many critics, who pointed out that these universal principles were belied by slavery, suppression of women, expanding imperialism, and fundamental inequalities between people at all levels. Moreover, liberal governments tended to enforce property rights far more vigorously than other ostensibly universal human rights.

Edmund Burke denounced revolutionary thinkers' rejection of tradition for encouraging chaos and raising false expectations among the masses, who were, in his view, inherently weak and irrational. "Metaphysical declarations that produced the monstrous fiction of human equality" were not grounded in the reality of human nature or experience; according to Burke, progress was best achieved through tradition and stability.[31] Jeremy Bentham argued that pious proclamations of universal natural rights only masked the realities of inequality under the domination of the propertied classes, just as the divine right of kings masked feudal oppressions. Famously declaring that "natural rights is simple nonsense: natural and imprescriptible rights, rhetorical nonsense, nonsense upon stilts," he argued that real rights derive from positive law and specific legislation, which should be aimed at maximizing the public good rather than enshrining false ideas about individual rights.[32] Thomas Hobbes critiqued liberal rights for disregarding the ceaseless human grasping for power, the natural state of "war of every man against every other man," which necessitated the establishment of a strong government, the Leviathan. In his view, the power of the state, holding all rights to itself, was the only reliable guarantor of security and stability.[33]

These philosophies of state power, the common good, and conservative tradition gradually overtook theories of individual liberal rights, which increasingly fell into disfavor after their heyday in the late eighteenth century. The Napoleonic era ended France's flirtation with individual rights and ushered in a period of nationalization in Europe, in which the consolidation of state power took precedence over theories of the individual. A series of increasingly bloody wars placed the needs of the nation and the community above the individual and directed people to serve the state rather than assert rights against it. Socialism, which arose in reaction to the economic brutalities and excesses of capitalist development, also stressed the interests of collectivities—the working class in theory, the party in practice. Marx himself argued that individual rights served only to separate and isolate every person from the other, elevating the interests of egoistic, selfish man and leaving the poor masses vulnerable to capitalist exploitation.[34]

This broad overview takes us to the end of the nineteenth century, the first efforts to codify public international law, and the point at which our historical inquiry into the development of the modern human rights framework begins. By this time, human rights as individual rights were a spent political force and barely retained intellectual currency. Spurred by nationalism and socialism, the main thrust of international law development focused on group rights, in particular the rights of workers, women, minorities, and nations seeking self-determination. Individual rights would wait until the establishment of the United Nations to make their dramatic comeback. The advent of human rights at the UN was to an extraordinary extent a U.S. initiative, as we will discuss. But it was also supported by many other states, including non-European states, not to mention global public opinion. Throughout the book, we will consider this interplay between universal acceptance of human rights and the particular historical circumstances of their birth.

The Modern Conception of Human Rights

Human rights assert the radical idea that everyone everywhere shares an equal birthright of dignity that should be recognized in law and politics as matters of principle and practice. Modern human rights therefore presuppose the possibility of international law and international organization based on global agreement and consensus. In addition, they recognize the human person as a key subject of law and uphold the sanctity of individual conscience. Many other systems of justice have proclaimed universal values while in fact limiting membership to a chosen group based on belief, nationality, wealth, or other restrictive criteria. Still others understand universality as the hegemony of one culture, or one nation uber alles, and demand universal submission to the laws of a particular empire along the lines of the Pax Romana. While critics note that human rights have also been used to advance narrow political interests hypocritically, it is important to point out that this is not done openly. Such motives must always be disguised, as they contradict the primary values of the human rights idea.

In asserting that universality is the core ideological principle of human rights, we do not argue that human rights are "truly" universal; such metaphysical inquiries are beyond the scope of this book. Nor do we dismiss the oft-leveled charge of Eurocentrism. On the contrary, a recurrent theme of the book is the extent to which not only European but specifically U.S. values shaped the human rights project. Based on the historical record, it would be difficult to overstate the level of U.S. control over every aspect of the early human rights system. Such hegemony in the construction of international human rights norms does not, however, prove that the norms were simply an imposition of U.S. values on the world. The widespread resonance of human rights ideas, then and now, suggests a real measure of global support.

The same point can be made in relation to the global ideologies of liberalism, communism, and fascism, which originated in Europe yet have influenced virtually every nation owing to Europe's predominant place in the world over the past few centuries. But Europe does not as a result hold a monopoly on ideas concerning individual rights, class struggle, or ethnocentrism. Similar ideas and philosophies have been expressed by other cultures throughout the world. The fact that the specific form of an idea can be traced to European rather than African lineage does not automatically disqualify its claim to universality. At minimum, however, the proponent of human rights must be willing to engage in a dialogue with other cultures and ideas to assess the genuine basis for the claim of universality; yet for years, appeals by non-European activists for cross-cultural approaches have fallen on deaf ears and failed to penetrate the human rights establishment.[35]

A distinguishing feature of human rights, even from other ethical systems within the western tradition, is their specific assertion of the theoretical primacy of the individual in the face of organized powers such as state and church. While human rights also recognize group and national rights, arguably even global solidarity rights, they do so at the margins of the discourse: the fundamental basis remains the individual. The highest value of human rights is humanity itself, conceived as a collection of self-contained, sovereign individuals. As a result, human rights are, in theory, subversive of established centers of organized power—even the powers that established the human rights system, to the extent that such powers transgress the limits imposed by the inalienable principles of individual human dignity. To avoid this potential subversion, states supported human rights as rhetorical ideals without accompanying means of enforcement. The much-denounced split between principles and practice is not an accident of history; it lies at the very heart of the UN human rights system as designed by state powers.

The main characteristics we attribute to human rights—recognition in law and politics, radical universality, primacy of the individual—are those that were expressly asserted during the establishment of human rights at the United Nations. Alternative conceptions of human rights that stressed, for example, groups more than individuals, duties more than rights, the state as fulfillment of rather than limitation on rights did not survive the UN process of creation. There were winners and losers in these original interstate debates and negotiations; some ideas were discarded while others triumphed and were incorporated into the declarations, treaties, and norms of the modern human rights system.

It is also important to bear in mind that there is no one monolithic entity called the United Nations responsible for shaping human rights ideas. The UN has at least three distinct and interrelated components: the first UN of member states, which sets the policies, debates the positions, and funds the activities; the second UN of the Secretariat and specialized agencies, the international civil service responsible for running the organization and carrying out functional programs; and the third UN of NGOs, independent experts, and think tanks, which contributes to UN thinking through consultation and advocacy.[36] There are hierarchies within these categories as well, for example, between the permanent members of the Security Council and relatively powerless members of the General Assembly.

This book focuses largely on the decision-making and law-making aspects of the first UN, although there is also some emphasis on civil society interventions. While the second and third UNs have undoubtedly played an influential role in expanding the reach of human rights, it is the member states that have negotiated the instruments and set UN policy on issues of global importance. The UN is not a democracy; the examples of Afghanistan and Iraq discussed in the preface illustrate how a handful of the most powerful states are able to override the concerns of most individuals and institutions associated with the second and third UNs.

Historical Methods and Limitations

Writing history used to be the job of official scribes hired by the rulers of a given society. It was considered self-evident that most people had no place in their own histories. The explicit task of history-making was to serve power and legitimize the policies of decision makers as natural, justified, and even universal. In every society, shaping how people viewed the past has been a primary goal of rulers seeking to maintain power. This concept was expressed succinctly in George Orwell's famous phrase: "He who controls the present controls the past, he who controls the past controls the future."[37] Today the battle to shape how people understand past, present, and future events is called "information war."[38]

If modern historians believe that all people are created with an equal right to be present and heard in their own histories, the vast range of people's different voices must somehow be captured and recorded. But how can one sketch an accurate picture of history when it is comprised of so many different actors and points of view? What does it mean to provide an objective accounting of past ideas and past events? Whose ideas and whose histories count? These concerns are only heightened in writing a history of human rights, an ideology meant to reflect universal values existing above and independent of individual ideas and historical circumstances. In this context, the question becomes, whose rights count?

While such questions preoccupied us in writing this book, we did not attempt to provide an exhaustive account of all the protagonists, events, and ideas that shaped the journey of human rights in the twentieth century. Our goals were more modest—to present a balanced picture of these forces in the context of their times, focusing on struggles and challenges that do not generally appear in more triumphalist versions of human rights history. The book begins with the first efforts to internationalize rights in the framework of peace and security through the Hague Peace Conference and the League of Nations and then turns to the process whereby the original unity of human rights ideas became eviscerated at the United Nations. Several broad themes run throughout: the power of human rights ideas as a unifying expression of popular desires for peace and justice; the use and abuse of these ideas by governments, great powers in particular, to advance military, political, and economic interests; the interplay between public pressure and state sovereignty in the creation of human rights norms; the politicization and fragmentation of human rights within the UN system; and the struggles of postcolonial states and civil society groups to close the gap between strong "promotion" and weak "protection" of rights.

In preparing this book we relied on various sources for research and ideas. Of great value were the proceedings of the conferences and meetings at which state representatives shaped various ideas and proposals into the declarations, treaties, and instruments that constitute the human rights system. These materials give a flavor of the power dynamics and shifting interests involved in the process of creating the human rights system. For example, UN records of negotiations and discussions between member states regarding the establishment of human rights institutions and the drafting of treaties reveal the intensely political character of debates, the closely contested nature of votes, and the historical contingency of decisions that we now take for granted and view as inevitable. The official reports, resolutions, and other communications of UN human rights bodies were also useful to show the public face of human rights after the dust of backroom negotiations had settled.

On the other hand, government representatives at these conclaves tend to deliver high-minded speeches that hide as much as they reveal about state policies and positions. It is a well-known but underanalyzed fact of geopolitics that diplomatic pronouncements prepared for public consumption rarely correspond with the actual considerations that drive government policy. Wherever possible, therefore, we have relied on internal government communications, as reported in secondary sources, to assess underlying political motivations. Such records were more readily available in the case of the United States (and the United Kingdom) than other countries, but we feel the resulting focus on U.S. policy is justified. The United States wielded overwhelming influence over not just the human rights agenda but all aspects of the UN as part of a larger project to restructure the world's economic, social, and political landscape in line with U.S. hegemony in these fields. As international correspondent James Reston noted at the time:

> The United States has changed overnight from the role of observer at international conferences to the role of leader. . . . We ran the Food and Agriculture Conference at Hot Springs, the first session of UNRRA Council at Atlantic City, the Monetary and Financial Conference at Bretton Woods, the Civil Aviation Conference at Chicago, the preparatory security conference at Dumbarton Oaks, and the United Nations Security Conference at San Francisco. . . . We have established our league of nations.[39]

There is also an enormous volume of legal and academic literature on the development of human rights, which we found useful to review, despite its tendency to ignore sociopolitical context and focus on positive law issues. More helpful in this regard were historical sources that delved into the political and strategic considerations driving the human rights policy of key states and UN bodies. Another extremely useful source was biographies, and even more the personal and public writings, of such key founding figures and NGO leaders as Eleanor Roosevelt, John Humphrey, René Cassin, Hersch Lauterpacht, Joseph Proskauer, James Shotwell, Roger Baldwin Nash, and many others. These sources give important insight into the hopes and frustrations of those most directly involved in establishing the new human rights regime.

This book addresses the pivotal role of the United Nations in shaping the human rights system, providing a broad political history of how and why the key features of this system came into being. It is impossible to understand the sudden emergence of human rights on the world scene without an appreciation of the decisive role played by the world body. In essence, the United Nations gave birth to the modern human rights regime. It was through the UN that the idea of individual rights based on inherent human dignity was recognized and enshrined in international law and institutions. The tripartite international bill of rights—comprised of the Universal Declaration of Human Rights and the two international covenants on civil and political rights and economic, social, and cultural rights—as well as a multitude of subsequent treaties, declarations, and instruments were negotiated at the UN, ratified by its member states, and then interpreted and monitored by an array of human rights institutions, agencies, and bodies.

The most critical period was the 1940s, before the start of the Cold War, when global attention centered on the effort to establish a new international morality with human rights as the cornerstone. It was a time of great hope and creativity, with ideas and proposals proliferating among a broad range of engaged civil society groups and public intellectual circles, although ultimately state representatives would have the final say. Their rejection of the more-far-reaching and innovative ideas, not to mention the core concepts of enforcement and protection, would set the track along which human rights developed as a fragmented and weakened set of norms and institutions. The bulk of the book therefore recounts the story of how human rights ideas were incubated in the early twentieth century, burst into prominence during and after World War II, were routinized and bureaucratized at the UN, and were shaped by major geopolitical factors such as the Cold War and decolonization.

Focusing on the trajectory of human rights through the UN system rather than, for example, popular struggles for human rights by civil society and oppressed communities inevitably emphasizes the tarnishing of the dream once it became embedded in the rough-and-tumble of great-power politics, intergovernmental negotiations, and institutional forms of expression. The dilution of human rights ideas has been so pronounced that it is easy to overlook the achievements of countless groups and activists who have fought to make something real of the rights on paper. This important topic has been addressed elsewhere, although a "peoples' history" of human rights remains to be written.[40]

There are many other issues that we do not cover or mention only in passing. We do not address the complex bureaucracy established to oversee the UN's human rights machinery. This proliferating network of human rights institutions might appear to indicate the priority of human rights within the world organization; however, the ad hoc way in which their different mandates have developed, with overlapping and often-competing responsibilities, has resulted in turf wars, duplication of some activities, and neglect of others. As one expert laments, the human rights system

> has grown "like Topsy" and the boundaries between the different organs are poorly delineated. . . . Its expansion has depended upon the effective exploitation of the opportunities which have arisen in any given situation from the prevailing mix of public pressures, the cohesiveness or disarray of the key geopolitical blocks, the power and number of the offending state(s) and the international standing of their current governments, and a variety of other, often rather specific and ephemeral, factors.[41]

Regional systems to promote and protect human rights are likewise not discussed. Focusing on the development of legal procedures and precedents in the European system, for example, would have painted a more positive picture of the prospects for judicial enforcement and domestic incorporation of human right principles by like-minded states within a more cohesive regional grouping than the "international community" of the United Nations. Nor do we cover the evolution of specific rights, such as freedom from torture, and beyond the international bill of rights, we discuss the major human rights treaties only briefly.

Themes and Structure of the Book

We do not accept that human rights constitute a new theology, a self-evident set of objective principles, an unchanging verity from a mythical state of nature, or an unassailable body of positive law legitimized by state consensus. To take for granted the universality of human rights based on God, reason, nature, or positive law serves only to obscure the historical factors behind the emergence of this ideologically powerful yet increasingly vulnerable modern concept.

This book is premised on a more mundane set of explanations—that human rights derive in the first instance from ideas of justice expressed in the organized struggles of people seeking a better world; that western liberal states initially proclaimed allegiance to human rights in order to mobilize popular support for world wars; that postwar public pressure to fulfill such promises compelled states to negotiate the adoption of international laws recognizing human rights; that the resulting human rights framework inevitably reflected sovereign state interests more than public expectations; that the victorious powers, the United States in particular, played a "more equal than others" role in channeling human rights toward rhetorical promotion and away from practical protection; that the human rights idea in the UN was further split into numerous treaties and quasi-legal instruments, with oversight responsibility divided among a host of overlapping bodies with competing bureaucratic interests; that the weak set of existing enforcement measures, such as they are, came about primarily through civil society activism and the increased international power of southern states after decolonization; and that, broadly speaking, the fragmented and relatively toothless international human rights system we have today is a consequence of this overall political history.

In addition to this introduction, the book has nine chapters grouped in three roughly chronological parts and a tenth concluding chapter. Each part begins with a summary of chapters and themes. To avoid repetition, the following overview presents only a brief exposition of the main ideas developed in each part.

Part I begins with the effort to develop the laws of war at the Hague Peace Conference of 1899, examines the rise and fall of the group-rights system established by the League of Nations after World War I, and discusses how, on the eve of World War II, the ideologies of fascism and communism seemed to be on the verge of eclipsing the brief rule of liberal international rights epitomized by the League. It was during this period that the idea of protecting humanity from state power through international law first entered world politics, although the legal regimes that arose conceived of rights in collective terms as belonging to nations, minorities, workers, and noncombatants. The idea of human rights as individual rights was not yet in vogue, hardly even discussed outside of a small circle of international jurists and theorists.

The increasingly brutal European wars of the nineteenth century, in which advancing technology brought more and more people under the shadow of military violence, gave rise to citizens' movements for peace and justice, the first seeds of what would become a far more powerful lobby during the creation of the United Nations. In an age marked by the consolidation of increasingly powerful nation-states, the emergence of public opinion and organized popular movements forced governments to confront the issue of international rules limiting their freedom of action in such crucial areas as the waging of war and treatment of minorities. The ideology of rights came into full prominence during World War I, when U.S. president Woodrow Wilson's call for a new world order based on self-determination and equality of nations galvanized worldwide sentiment and created enormous expectations at the Paris Peace Conference of 1919; hopes were dashed when the victorious nations carved up the spoils of war according to great-power interests. The asserted universality of rights stood in flat contradiction to the realities of the world system: most nations were under foreign domination; minorities in the advanced western democracies suffered various forms of segregation and oppression; and racism against non-Europeans was the norm. In the interwar years, fascist movements successfully attacked the hypocrisies of liberal international rights to undermine and eventually dismantle the League of Nations, proposing instead a world openly dominated by the strongest races and nations.

Human rights ideas regained prominence in the context of another world war. President Roosevelt's call for Four Freedoms set the stage for an Anglo-American ideological offensive against fascism that stressed human rights and freedom from tyranny. Almost overnight, the idea of human rights was transformed from a dead letter into a vigorous global discussion, especially in the United States and Europe. However, when the three victorious powers—the United States, the United Kingdom, and the Union of Soviet Socialist Republics—met in secret to chart a new international organization, human rights were dropped from the blueprint; their respective policies of Jim Crow, colonialism, and the gulag were hardly conducive to a human rights approach. After concerted lobbying by civil society groups and smaller nations, especially the Latin Americans, human rights were reinstated at the United Nations Conference on International Organization held in San Francisco that established the UN, albeit in vague and general terms only.

Part II describes how the idea of human rights was transformed through the UN into the foundations of the modern human rights framework. The victorious powers were most influential in shaping the human rights agenda, but it was the United States above all that controlled and dictated the proceedings, determined to establish a system of universal values reflecting the globalization of U.S. principles rather than a set enforceable legal standards. The Soviet Union was equally insistent that human rights should be recognized as moral principles without any mechanisms for international enforcement; real power was to reside with the permanent veto-wielding members of the Security Council exercising a monopoly over global security enforcement and controlling the right of intervention in the affairs of sovereign nations. This superpower axis against genuine human rights protection would prove a significant roadblock to popular hopes for an effective system.

The Commission on Human Rights, chaired by Eleanor Roosevelt, became the primary vehicle for negotiating and creating the human rights system at the UN. The group of eighteen government representatives made important decisions that would shape the human rights system we have inherited today—which ideas to accept, which rights to recognize, and which instruments to draft. The most fateful decision in this regard, made by joint U.S.-Soviet diktat over the objections of the rest of the commission, was to split the bill of rights into three distinct parts—a declaration of principles, which became the Universal Declaration of Human Rights; a binding convention, which was delayed eighteen years and split again into two separate treaties for civil and political rights and economic, social, and cultural rights; and measures of implementation, which were never actually implemented. Even more than the distorting impact of the Cold War, this fragmentation of the UN human rights system prevented it from fulfilling its revolutionary potential.

Part III looks at changes in the human rights field due to the increased activism of civil society groups and the process of decolonization, which shifted the dynamics in the UN by giving greater voice to the concerns of developing countries. These developments are examined through the lens of two major trends: the establishment of treaties protecting the rights of specific groups and the emergence of the right to development.

The liberal bias of the human rights system made it hostile to claims that people had rights as members of collectivities rather than as individuals. However, growing civil society movements for racial justice, women's rights, and child rights were able to leverage the support of constituencies through-out the world as well as sympathetic states and agencies within the UN to negotiate and establish new human rights treaties. These treaties generally viewed group rights through the lens of discrimination, promoted formal rather than substantive equality, and had limited means of implementation based largely on voluntary state reporting. At the same time, they broke new ground in overcoming the artificial divide between civil and political rights and economic, social, and cultural rights and provided a platform to link local activism with international principles and movements. Minorities and indigenous peoples, on the other hand, did not fare as well in their quest for recognition at the UN. Their call for national expression and self-determi-nation threatened the territorial power base of the state system and faced particular hostility from developing countries, both postcolonial states and established multiethnic states in Latin America and Asia. As a result, the various UN reports, recommendations, and draft declarations recognizing indigenous and minority rights have never received official state sanction, and these groups have continued to suffer oppression and abuse with virtu-ally no protection under international law.

The right to development also has a mixed record. After decolonization, the new states of Africa and Asia joined with those of Latin America to call for a New International Economic Order (NIEO) to redress the inequities of colonialism. When northern countries resisted direct transfers of wealth and technology, these states turned to the right to development as a means to close the gap between rich and poor. However, it took a working group ten years to resolve bitter disputes between states over the scope and meaning of the right—northern states insisted that the right be confined to individuals rather than states or groups and entail no obligatory transfers from rich to poor countries. By the end of the negotiations, the right to development had been so watered down that it merely recognized the centrality of respecting existing human rights in the development process and urging international cooperation to resolve the crisis of global poverty but with few practical means to address the growing divide between the haves and have-nots.

The concluding chapter focuses on human rights developments since the 1990s. The end of the Cold War raised hopes of overcoming the ideological divisions that have split the human rights idea; the UN proclaimed that the time had come to mainstream human rights in development activities and reintegrate civil, political, economic, social, and cultural rights. Despite this auspicious context, human rights today are under attack as never before; the very framework is increasingly subject to question. This is partly due to the failure to address, let alone correct, the contradictions and imbalances described throughout this book—between public expectations of justice and the determination of states to protect their sovereignty, between powerful states seeking geopolitical hegemony and others seeking the protection of international law, and between rhetorical promotion and lack of protection. Added to these long-standing concerns are two critical new developments: economic globalization and the war on terror.

Unlike the weak implementation mechanisms of human rights, the economic rules of neoliberal globalization are strictly imposed both by the Bretton Woods institutions through structural adjustment programs and the World Trade Organization (WTO) through enforcement of a series of free trade agreements. As a result, states have lost significant autonomy over social and economic policy, and citizens have no democratic means to influence, let alone hold accountable, these distant global lending and trade institutions. Despite a growing gap between rich and poor at all levels of the world, the human rights framework is less equipped to redress socioeconomic injustice than ever before.

While states have lost power over social and economic decisions, they have increased repression of civil and political rights under the rubric of the war on terror. The United States is openly questioning the relevance of human rights and humanitarian law to the new global war. States throughout the world have followed the superpower's lead, resulting in a marked increase in violations of such previously sacrosanct rights as freedom of speech, freedom from torture and basic due process, and peaceful assembly. People therefore face heightened abuse under the looming threat of war.

Given its subservience to state interests, the United Nations has been unable to develop an effective response to the threats posed by both globalization and the war on terror. Instead, the debate around reforming the UN human rights system has focused on relatively marginal changes to the Commission on Human Rights. Unless these central challenges are faced head on, the idea of human rights will continue to lose relevance among masses of people until its original promise of justice becomes an historical memory or is replaced by something new.

Part 1. Human Rights Foundations in the First Half of the Twentieth Century

In the following four chapters, we review the main trends in the first half of the twentieth century that eventually culminated in the emergence of human rights at the United Nations. Our emphasis is not on philosophical debates about the nature of rights but rather on the concrete historical events and political forces that shaped human rights discourse and led to human rights ideas being incorporated into international laws and organizations. In covering such a broad sweep of history in a few pages, we briefly sketch major issues to set the context in which human rights ideas would develop.

It is important to note that human rights per se were not a common topic of international conversation until the 1940s. Before that time, human rights ideas were promoted and kept alive through the committed efforts of a handful of individuals and nongovernmental groups at the margins of international politics and diplomacy.[1] It was only with the onset of World War II and in response to the ideological challenge of fascism that human rights took shape as a distinct and coherent set of ideas and eventually found expression within the legal and institutional framework of the United Nations.

We are not suggesting that human rights suddenly materialized in world politics without antecedents; the introduction traced the historical, philosophical, and legal roots of human rights in previous centuries.[2] These chapters demonstrate that core human rights principles, such as freedom, equality and nondiscrimination, the rights of individuals and groups, and lawful limits on state sovereignty, did not arise de novo through the United Nations but rather developed gradually in international law throughout the first half of the twentieth century. These principles appeared as interrelated aspects of common popular struggles for justice, yet they were not incorporated within a broad overarching framework. Eventually they would coalesce into the modern human rights regime, based largely on the concept of protecting individual rights from state transgression and abuse.

At the most general level, however, and at the risk of oversimplification, it can be said that human rights grew out of the triumph of liberalism over its two main rivals—communism and fascism—a victory assured more through military confrontation than ideological battle. Had the pivotal and closely contested political and military conflicts of this era ended differently, the human rights idea would certainly never have assumed its present form and reach.[3]

History, including the history of ideas, is written by the winners. Until very recently, the triumph of liberal rights over its main ideological rivals seemed self-evident: a straight path of victory through two world wars and the Cold War. After the fall of the Soviet Union, western commentators spoke triumphantly of the "end of history," based on the assumption that the unchallenged hegemony of formal democracy was inevitable and irreversible.[4] But history did not end, and soon some of the same commentators were postulating an inevitable "clash of civilizations,"[5] with U.S. political and military leaders predicting a "global war" that will endure for decades.[6] Similar twists and turns characterized the unsteady and uncertain journey of liberal rights during the early part of the twentieth century.[7] The eventual enshrinement of human rights in the international order came only after many reversals and seeming dead ends, as we shall see.

Another theme that emerges from this period is the contradiction at the heart of liberalism itself, the extraordinary gulf between liberal theories of universal rights and the behaviors of states espousing them. It is no secret that the major powers that promoted these rights and eventually established the UN system, the United States and the British empire in particular, did so from within the framework of an explicitly imperialist and racist world order of which they were leaders and beneficiaries. To protect their hegemony while still leading the ideological crusade for universal principles, the great powers drew a clear distinction between the rhetorical promotion of rights for strategic purposes, especially during wars, and the concrete enforcement of these rights, particularly when their perceived political interests were at stake. How these powers managed to separate the promotion of human rights principles from their ineffectual and selective enforcement without discrediting the universal basis of the entire human rights project is one of the subjects of these chapters and the book as a whole.

We do not mean to imply that any state had a monolithic policy on issues of human rights or that the development of human rights resulted solely from cynical manipulation by governments. On the contrary, the divide between high-minded human rights principles and abusive human rights practices created dynamic spaces in governments and civil societies. Within these spaces, competing interests and factions fought for and against the realization of rights.

On the one hand, governments were often divided between and within themselves regarding human rights. Small states tended to favor strengthening international law to protect their interests against large states. Within strong states, bureaucratic battles were fought over whether, and how much, to concede elements of sovereignty to some form of international authority. On the other hand, governments had to answer to their citizens and popular constituencies. The unprecedented degree of public awareness of and involvement in international issues at the turn of the twentieth century, spurred by growing literate classes, the spread of media, and the beginnings of global information exchange, posed a new constraint on the customary state practice of secrecy and deception in diplomatic affairs.

These tensions spurred the development of human rights in part through the law of unintended consequences. States often found that rhetorical declarations and toothless international agreements pertaining to human rights, when taken seriously by the public, had an unwelcome tendency to develop a life of their own. In the context of popular desires for justice, such human rights rhetoric heightened general expectations and civic mobilization, which in turn increased pressure on governments to fulfill their vague promises, even at the cost of limiting sovereignty. A classic example is the boost to nationalist and anti-imperialist demands after World War I given by President Woodrow Wilson's repeated pronouncements in favor of the right to self-determination, pronouncements that came to be invested with far greater global significance than Wilson, and certainly his foreign policy advisors in the State Department, ever intended.[8] In this way, the very idea of human rights shaped people's consciousness, generated expectations, and translated into concrete pressures, with ripple effects felt across the globe.[9]

Notwithstanding such advances, it is unwarranted to exaggerate the role of public demands, which managed significant yet, in the final analysis, limited inroads into the traditional and long-standing sovereign prerogative to abuse and mistreat people within state borders. An examination of the diplomatic maneuverings behind the establishment of human rights and their antecedents in international law—particularly the laws of war established at the Hague Peace Conference and the group-rights regime established at the Paris Peace Conference—reveals the boundaries of realpolitik beyond which powerful states would brook no interference. Throughout this book we discuss the role of such boundaries in the development and institutionalization of human rights at the United Nations.

The supremacy of state sovereignty points to an inherent structural weakness of the human rights system—the need for individual states to voluntarily accept lawful limits on their freedom of action. Conceiving their interests narrowly, states, especially great powers, have generally proven unwilling to accept enforceable legal restrictions on their authority to control and coerce their own populations, or other populations for that matter. Human rights have always been, and remain, caught within this dilemma: what makes sense for the people of the world, individually and collectively, appears different when viewed through the prisms of governmental interests that purport to represent those same people. This political tension has been a fundamental obstacle in the creation, and even more in the enforcement, of international human rights. As a result, the rule of the lowest common denominator has often held true in the development of human rights norms.

These four chapters review the major trends in international law aimed at promoting individual and group rights during the first half of the twentieth century. Such trends include the protection of civilians in war, principles of self-determination and racial equality, and the rights of minorities, workers, and women—all of which foreshadowed the development of human rights as a coherent politico-legal framework. These separate struggles for justice derived from, and helped advance, the cardinal notion that all human beings possess an inherent dignity that ought to be protected at all times, irrespective of race, religion, nationality, gender, and other characteristics.

From the turn of the century until the dawn of World War II, human rights were conceived largely in collective terms as rights of nations and minority groups as well as workers and women. It was only after the failure of the group-rights paradigm established through the League of Nations and the growing ideological threat the rise of communism and fascism posed to liberalism that individual human rights became a serious topic of international discussion. Individual jurists and activists promoting human rights were lone voices in the interwar period with no backing from governments and little support even from liberal intellectuals. It was the Anglo-American appeal for human rights as an ideological weapon in the crusade against Nazi tyranny that energized the human rights idea, attracted the attention of civil society organizations, and culminated in the establishment of human rights at the UN.

Chapter 1, "First Expressions of International Human Rights Ideas," is divided into two sections. Section one focuses on the birth of international humanitarian law, the precursor of human rights, at the Hague Peace Conference of 1899. Coming after a century of intensifying war in Europe, the Hague conference marked the first time that the world's leading states, responding to popular demands for peace and disarmament, agreed to negotiate international law limits to war. Despite high public expectations, the effort to develop meaningful protections for civilians in war and uphold principles of humanity against military necessity largely failed. The resulting treaty, which was weak and unenforceable, did nothing to prevent the rapid advancement of military technology that would culminate in World War I. Nevertheless, the Hague conference was a novelty in international affairs, and the unprecedented mobilization of public opinion across the globe in response to the possibility, albeit illusory, of disarmament, laid the groundwork for the emergence of civil society activism and the subsequent development of human rights.

The second section of the chapter examines the global effort to construct a new world order after the unbridled ferocity of World War I, which redrew the map of Europe and its colonial possessions. The Paris Peace Conference of 1919 raised enormous, and unrealistic, hopes for a post-imperialist international system founded on rights to self-determination and equality between nations and races. President Wilson's Fourteen Points symbolized the temporary ascendancy of liberal ideology based on the formal recognition of international rights. But once the war was over, these ostensibly universal principles were applied selectively by the great powers at the Paris Peace Conference as they got down to the business of carving up old empires, creating new states, and consolidating control over global resources.

Chapter 2, "The Decline of Human Rights between World Wars," discusses the period between the two world wars, which began with the triumph of Anglo-American liberal principles after the Paris conference and ended with fascism on the verge of establishing European, and seemingly global, dominance. The League of Nations was crippled at the outset by the withdrawal and isolation of the United States and the inability of European victors to establish a common security policy. The League's failure to vindicate its system of international rights—especially self-determination rights for colonized peoples and just treatment of German and other minorities in the states of Central and Eastern Europe—opened the door to the rise of totalitarian ideologies of the right and left. Human rights also failed to take root at the domestic level; a wave of constitutional democracies guaranteeing individual rights produced, instead, political instability, economic paralysis, and xenophobic nationalisms throughout Europe. In contrast to the widely perceived hypocrisies of liberal rights, whose universal principles were belied by selective practices, communism championed radical equality for oppressed peoples, while fascism openly celebrated inequalities between races and nations as the natural order of a conflict-ridden world. Defense of universal rights was left to a handful of international jurists and public intellectuals. These thinkers waged a lonely struggle to keep human rights ideas alive during this period, drafting the first examples of international bills of human rights and preparing the way for a burst of renewed interest during World War II.

Chapter 3, "The Human Rights Crusade in World War II," examines the revival of human rights ideas during World War II, leading to their eventual establishment through the United Nations. After years of being urged by human rights advocates to formulate a positive vision of "what we are fighting for," the United States and Britain belatedly took up the cause as part of an ideological crusade against Germany and Japan, which had already conquered continental Europe and East Asia, respectively. President Roosevelt's declaration of the Four Freedoms, widely considered to be the cornerstone of the UN human rights project, was aimed at asserting American leadership in defining the war's aims and shaping the postwar order. Alone among the great powers, the U.S. government drafted detailed blueprints for the new global organization even before entering the war, including a limited, largely declaratory, role for international human rights. Anglo-American support for human rights in the Atlantic Charter and the United Nations Declaration, even though clearly subordinate to the goal of securing total victory over the Axis powers, succeeded in galvanizing an outpouring of public enthusiasm—dozens of versions of international bills of human rights were drafted, discussed, and promoted by a diverse array of legal, diplomatic, and religious organizations, primarily in the United States and Latin America. These private initiatives, some in open collaboration with the U.S. State Department, emphasized the need to combine civil and political rights with economic, social, and cultural rights and to establish clear means of international enforcement so as to avoid states using domestic jurisdiction as a shield for abuses.

Chapter 4, "Human Rights Politics in the United Nations Charter," describes how the great powers managed to control public enthusiasm for human rights. The Three Policemen, the United States, Britain, and the Soviet Union, were eager to mobilize popular support for the war but had no interest in sacrificing their sovereign power on "the altar of human rights."[10] This tension would bedevil, and ultimately undermine, the development of an international human rights system capable of offering practical protections to people who most need them. At a series of secret meetings, the great powers negotiated the blueprint for a new world order. The centerpiece was a security council in which the powers would dominate the rest of the world and maintain exclusive responsibility for peace and collective security. The issue of human rights was dropped altogether from their calculations; at

Dumbarton Oaks, the major preparatory meeting for the United Nations, human rights merited a mere eight words at the very back of the proposal.

The San Francisco conference of 1945 was an American show from start to finish. Not only was the entire event organized by the U.S. government, but American spy agencies monitored all aspects of the event, supplying the U.S. delegation with daily briefings on the positions of other countries. Human rights were a major topic of discussion; smaller states and NGOs made it the centerpiece of their advocacy after the disappointment of Dumbarton Oaks. The United States was happy to play along, intending to capitalize on American ideological leadership and years of State Department planning by elevating human rights to the moral apex of the United Nations, with the caveat that they should have no means of enforcement. A consultative group of NGOs accompanying the official U.S. delegation were effectively co-opted into supporting the separation of human rights principles from their practice, a split that would undermine any hopes for a meaningful legal system to take shape. Thus human rights were recognized several times in the Charter, including among the purposes and principles of the organization, but were not given any means of implementation. The crucial task of drafting an international bill of rights was given to the newly established Commission on Human Rights.

1

First Expressions of Human Rights Ideas

- Humanitarian Law at The Hague
- Human Rights at the Paris Conference

Humanitarian Law at The Hague

The seeds of what would become the international human rights system were planted at the Hague Peace Conference of 1899. There the modern law of war, or international humanitarian law, was born through international agreement among the world's leading nation-states. Humanitarian law, in theory, seeks to strike a balance between principles of humanity and military necessity and to protect the lives and property of individuals rather than states. These concerns appear as the first international legal expression of similar doctrines that eventually coalesced into the human rights framework.[1] Humanitarian law and human rights law are today considered separate yet overlapping fields of international law; however, before human rights took shape as a distinct set of ideas and norms, the basic mechanism of protecting human beings through international agreement between states was first discussed at the Hague conference in the context of peace and disarmament. As noted legal scholar Josef L. Kunz emphasizes, "The whole law of war, including the norms regulating its conduct, is humanitarian in character; it is in the truest sense a part of the law for the protection of human rights."[2]

At the Hague conference, powerful and weaker states alike met to consider accepting limitations on their most jealously guarded sovereign prerogative, the waging of war. The idea of protecting individuals from state abuse at the international level, thereby separating the interests of citizens from those of their governments, was novel in its own right and marked the emergence of human rights as distinct from state rights. Weighing in on the side of restricting national sovereignty through law, popular opinion made its first meaningful intervention in international diplomacy, an area that hitherto had been characterized more by government intrigue and secret agreements than by negotiations open to public scrutiny.

The manner in which negotiations took place at the Hague conference foreshadowed the complex set of meetings and agreements that led to the establishment of human rights at the United Nations fifty years later. The conflicts that eventually determined the nature of human rights were already present, in incipient form, at the Hague conference—conflicts between unlimited rights of sovereign states and lawful restrictions on that sovereignty, between strong states eager to preserve their dominance and weak states seeking the protection of international law, between governments intent on maximizing their powers of action and popular demands for universal principles of justice.

The Hague conference failed, and failed miserably, to limit military technology or protect civilians in conflict. This failure contributed to the imminent and ultimately catastrophic world war. Yet the Hague conference can be seen as the first halting step on a long journey marked by ever-stronger popular efforts to develop universal standards of justice that culminated in the establishment of the human rights regime after World War II.

The nineteenth century had seen a series of successively more brutal conflicts. As Jean Pictet, a leading advocate of humanitarian law, observed, the French Revolution and the Napoleonic wars heralded the dawn of "an epoch of unbridled ferocity," in which the state mobilized all its forces and resources, including its citizenry, to wage war.[3] Over the next hundred years, the great powers fought each other on the European mainland and throughout their far-flung empires, and independence movements in the colonies were put down with genocidal violence. Civilian casualties mounted as military technology advanced and modern forms of warfare increasingly brought the battle into the heart of densely populated areas. Wars were no longer fought solely by professional armies, with limited impact on and investment by the country as a whole. War became a truly national effort, a matter of survival not just for the government but for the entire people, affecting all levels of society.[4]

By the end of the nineteenth century, the world was poised at the brink of a major new conflict. The rising power of Germany, recently established through the consolidation of princely fiefdoms first into a unified state and then an empire, threatened to overturn the balance between Europe's imperialist powers. The fight over prized colonial possessions grew fiercer. These tensions upset the fragile system of collective security that had been in place since the Peace of Westphalia of 1648, whereby European states had accepted each other's sovereign independence, recognized religious freedom and tolerance (although only within the Christian world), and focused military expansion overseas, conquering the Americas, Africa, and Asia.[5]

The threat of war produced an unprecedented public reaction and mobilization; citizens began to express opposition to the frequency and ease with which their leaders resorted to war as an instrument to further state interests. Cognizant of the unprecedented destructive potential of a future conflict, public sentiment against war grew stronger and became organized around protecting the rights of individuals and groups rather than promoting purely state interests. The emergence of popular activism was partly a testament to the power of print media, exemplified, for instance, by the proliferation of newspapers that served ever-growing literate classes. Nongovernmental associations were established to promote peace and protect the rights of civilians in war. The first international NGO, the International Committee of the Red Cross (ICRC), was founded after a public outcry in response to Swiss journalist Henri Dunant's moving eyewitness account of carnage at the battle of Solferino in 1859.[6]

Today we take public involvement in international affairs for granted. A century ago it was a new phenomenon that ran counter to the long-standing sovereign prerogative to conduct diplomacy without popular participation. As we shall see, the biggest surprise of the Hague Peace Conference was that it happened at all. States that otherwise would never have agreed to negotiate limitations on war were forced by public opinion to do exactly that. For this reason, the Hague conference marked an important moment in relations between citizens and their governments. From that point on, civil society grew increasingly active in global affairs, pushing states to develop new forms of international law and organization.

The Russian Disarmament Offensive

It was in this context of public war-weariness that Russian czar Nicholas II dropped a diplomatic bomb.[7] On 4 August 1898, he circulated a letter calling for an international conference to examine "the most effectual means of insuring to all peoples the benefits of a real and durable peace, and, above all, of putting an end to the progressive development of all armaments . . . as a happy presage to the century which is about to open."[8]

It is not clear whether the czar understood the extent of worldwide enthusiasm his letter would unleash, as there were few precedents for mobilizing popular opinion on a global scale. His unexpected proposal provoked a storm of public approval. Peace movements throughout Europe, led by prominent activists such as W. T. Stead in England and Frederic Passy in France, made use of their extensive publishing networks to mobilize support, hailing the czar as a humanitarian visionary.[9] U.S. peace groups such as the Quakers, the Universal Peace Union, and the American Peace Society urged their members to lobby U.S. officials in support of the Russian proposal.[10] Religious associations were particularly active in promoting the peace agenda. A lively debate ensued in newspapers and parliaments throughout the world.[11] In all these efforts, the central idea was that governments had a duty to put the interests of humanity above sovereign self-interests, premised on the understanding that the state was serving its people and not the other way around.

Caught off guard by what they regarded as a Russian propaganda ploy, governments were forced to welcome the proposal of an international conference. But privately they reacted with skepticism and outright hostility, suspecting a trick, aware that Russia's shattered economy could not support the expense of purchasing the new rapid-fire field gun that was already standard issue in the German, French, and Austrian armies.[12] One damning assessment by a historian probably captures the mood of European governments at the time: "The offer to the nations of the world to meet for the purpose of limiting armaments was in truth a sort of masterpiece of diplomatic finesse, worthy of study by aspiring statesmen of the future. . . . The truth was that the peace rescript had been conceived in fear, brought forth in deceit, and swaddled in humanitarian ideals."[13]

The Russian appeal for public support was seen by competing states as an admission of weakness that would only encourage rather than prevent war. French diplomat Paul Cambon remarked, "This proposal for disarmament will have the result of convincing everyone that war is imminent."[14] German Kaiser Wilhelm II speculated that the conference would "add not a little to the prospects for war."[15] The Japanese prime minister maintained that the czar's effort would not only fail but would lead instead to war with Japan—as did happen six years later.[16]

Despite suspicion that the letter was motivated in greater part by military vulnerability than humanitarian vision, Russia's rivals preferred to graciously accept the invitation rather than risk losing public approval. As a result, twenty-eight states, including the world's leading powers, agreed to meet for the ostensible purpose of restricting their sovereign right to war through the acceptance of a binding international agreement.[17] Government spokespersons effusively praised the czar's proposal, even appropriating the language of peace activists.[18] This had the effect of raising popular expectations even more and energizing the newly formed civil society groups to redouble their lobbying efforts. Their goal—though not formulated in human rights language—was to pressure states to negotiate and agree to new international laws.

In his opening address to the conference, Baron de Staal of Russia played to public expectations, urging "a tangible result which the whole world awaits with confidence."[19] But privately, other delegates did not share his enthusiasm. Count Munster, head of the German delegation, told his U.S. counterpart, Ambassador Andrew White, that the conference was "a political trick—the most detestable ever practiced"[20] yet at the same time admitted that "we can, in regard to Russia, not allow the conference to end with an entire fiasco and must try to cover it with a peaceful-looking cloak."[21] Hearing similar concerns from other delegates, Ambassador White concluded, "Since the world began, never has so large a body come together in a spirit of more hopeless skepticism as to any good result."[22] White's assessment was firmly grounded in his own diplomatic brief; it has since come to light that the U.S. and British delegations had been secretly instructed in advance by their respective governments to reject any restrictions on the development and production of any weapons.[23]

Given the atmosphere of cynicism and political intransigence at the conference, which was unknown to the public at the time, it was inevitable that grandiose hopes would be dashed. Expecting powerful states to abandon or even meaningfully limit their traditional reliance on war as a means to further political ambitions and resolve disputes was unrealistic. After all, the idea that principles of humanity should trump state sovereignty arose not from the efforts of an ideologically motivated political movement but rather from a deep-seated popular yearning for a safer and better world that gained sudden and unexpected international expression in response to a diplomatic gesture by a declining European power.

Government delegations at The Hague were conscious of the need to safeguard their nations' military interests while at the same time projecting a cooperative public image to the throngs of newspaper reporters from all over the world. Such scrutiny forced diplomats into an unwelcome balancing act in which they appeared to address popular concerns about peace and disarmament without compromising sovereign prerogatives. This balancing act led state representatives to make declarations and even sign vague agreements appearing to favor disarmament while in the end ensuring that no binding enforceable restrictions to warfare would be placed on state powers.

Once the conference got under way, delegates made the right noises, further encouraging the mood of popular optimism, but behind closed doors, the negotiations were quickly deadlocked by familiar rivalries and divisions.[24] States proposed only such limitations on armaments that would run contrary to the interest of rival states. Disarmament proposals by Russia and weaker powers went nowhere; Germany, with its growing army, rejected French and Russian proposals to limit land forces; sea powers such as Britain and the United States rejected German proposals to limit naval forces.[25] Most states hid their bare-knuckled negotiating tactics behind a public façade of accommodation, although the German delegation was more forthright in declaring that Germany's "patriotic" population would not tolerate any reduction in military spending.[26]

With strong states intent on retaining their military advantages, there was no possibility of reaching meaningful agreement that might slow either the development of new weapons systems or the forward march to war. At the end of the day, only two weapons were banned, asphyxiating gases and dum-dum bullets, both of which were generally considered to have limited or no practical military value.[27] The United States and Britain cast the sole dissenting votes, the U.S. military delegate arguing that the prohibition on poison gas would be disregarded once an effective delivery system could be developed[28] and the British delegate insisting that the disfiguring dum-dum bullets, manufactured in India for use in colonial Africa, were useful and indeed necessary for killing savages who were otherwise impervious to standard projectiles.[29]

Words without Substance; Agreements without Teeth

The consensus document that came out of this debacle was the Hague Regulations on Land and Naval Warfare of 1899, signed by all twenty-eight nations present. The text of the treaty did mark a breakthrough of sorts; it spoke of "rights" of civilians, of wounded, and of prisoners.[30] However, provisions touching on military limitations were left deliberately vague, ill defined, and unenforceable, serving mostly as a formal mask behind which to hide the failure of states to accept practical humanitarian limitations on warfare. For example, Article 22 declared that "the right of belligerents to adopt means of injuring the enemy is not unlimited"[31] without specifying any particular limits; similarly, Article 23 prohibited, without definition, the infliction of "superfluous injury."[32] The treaty's most famous and stirring turns of phrase, drafted by prominent Russian jurist Frederic de Martens, were found in the nonbinding preamble. The oft-cited language, which has since become known as the de Martens clause, placed war victims "under the protection . . . [of]

the laws of humanity, and the requirements of public conscience . . . until a more complete code of the laws of war is issued."[33]

Such language sounded impressive but provided little in the way of concrete protections for civilians in war. International jurists, who thereafter began to produce a flood of legal commentary debating the interpretation and application of the Hague laws, seemed to be the only constituency that found something to discuss and even cheer about.[34] The entire exercise can be seen as setting a disturbing precedent—states' strategy of signing unenforceable international agreements to mollify popular pressure in place of having to accept genuine limits on sovereign freedom of action.

As we shall see, this strategy would resurface, again and again, during negotiations to incorporate human rights into international law, at both the League of Nations and the United Nations. The same balancing act between state interests and popular expectations would be a recurring theme in international negotiations over the development of human rights law. States have always found it easier to agree on seemingly empty rhetoric; the battle lines are drawn when it comes to practical enforcement with real-world consequences. However, the public would also play a role in pressing governments to bridge the gulf between words on paper and actions in the world.

With such meager returns on the investment of hope and energy, the mood among those who followed the ups and mostly downs of the Hague conference was severely deflated. Upon returning to America amid a flood of negative press coverage, Ambassador White lamented that "the evil I dreaded, as regards the formation of public opinion in relation to the work of our conference, is becoming realized."[35] Diplomats did their duty and put a positive spin on the outcome; peace activists were critical but still tried to rally the troops; and press reaction was muted at best, otherwise caustic. The *Times*, the most influential paper in Britain, summed up the public mood in a devastating assessment: "The Conference was a sham and has brought forth a progeny of shams, because it was founded on a sham. We do not believe that any progress whatever in the cause of peace, or in the mitigation of the evils of war, can be accomplished by a repetition of the strange and humiliating performance which has just ended."[36]

By the time the Second Peace Conference at The Hague was convened in 1907, popular expectations had been considerably scaled down. In light of the Russo-Japanese War, the Italian invasion of Turkey, and growing tensions between the European powers, the public mood was one of cynicism and indifference.[37] Needing to rebuild his defeated army, the czar dispatched de Martens, famed drafter of the first Hague treaty's humanitarian language, on a European tour to argue against disarmament in advance of the Second

Peace Conference.[38] The provisions of the second Hague treaty, therefore, did not challenge the existing balance of power: principles of humanity remained subordinate to military necessity, the march toward more destructive weaponry continued to accelerate, and civilians were left more vulnerable than ever to the scourge of war, as would soon be amply demonstrated in World War I. One historian drew the following conclusions: "The two great peace conferences of modern times, along with their lesser predecessors, did not succeed in reducing armaments, or in restricting the development and improvement of weapons.... [They] demonstrate rather that a weapon will be restricted in inverse proportion, more or less, to its effectiveness."[39]

In the stark light of history, the Hague conferences appear to be an unmitigated defeat for humanitarian principles.[40] The mood of public optimism was based, to a large extent, on organized political deception by powerful states intent on covering ongoing military planning and preparations with a "peaceful-looking cloak." People would not be protected by the new international laws, nor would the scourge of war be diminished. Just over the horizon was the most destructive military conflict the world had yet seen—until the next, even more horrific conflict.

But the real contribution of the Hague conferences was in terms of ideas not laws—the idea that human beings and not just states mattered, the idea that people had universal rights to be protected from abuse by states. Never before had these ideas been expressed with so much public enthusiasm in a setting where the world's governments had agreed, even if under duress, to take them seriously as the basis for creating international law. Hearing only the public praise, and not the private damnation, of diplomats and politicians, it was only natural that the popular imagination was seized by the prospect of establishing humanitarian principles to limit war. It is a fact of history that ordinary citizens have always fought harder for genuine peace and justice than their leaders. Powerful states in all ages have tended to seek the Pax Romana, the peace of empire and domination. At The Hague, the peace of peoples made a brief, albeit unsuccessful, appearance on the world stage.

In effect, the Hague conferences marked the birth of global efforts to inscribe the rights and interests of human beings into international law. The birth was premature but not stillborn; the public energies unleashed in this period would continue to grow, opening space for the universal project that would become human rights. Many of the activists and organizations that emerged at the Hague conferences would continue to advance human rights principles in the coming years. In this way, misplaced expectations that principles of humanity might be elevated over state reliance on war gave rise to the beginnings of a global movement, which over time developed the confidence and experience to demand a place at the table that had long been dominated by governments and their professional diplomatic corps.

Human Rights at the Paris Conference

Efforts to protect humanitarian principles in war and limit civilian damage were swept away by the violent convulsions that shook Europe and the rest of the world in World War I. Advances in military technology transformed the battlefield, and the immense human suffering that resulted raised anew the question of establishing enforceable rights at the international level. As old empires were carved up and new states assumed their place, human rights emerged as an issue of global concern. The primary emphasis was on the national right to self-determination and group issues such as minority rights and labor rights, as opposed to the focus on individual rights that eventually predominated in the modern human rights framework.

The unprecedented conflict transformed the global map, not only in terms of new borders but in terms of new ideas as well. During the war itself, the victorious powers had gained allies and mobilized popular opinion on the basis of promises to extend universal rights to oppressed and subordinated peoples. The military victory laid the ground for the ideological victory of liberalism, with Anglo-American principles ascendant on the world stage. Full of hope and excitement, representatives of various nations and minority groups gathered at the Paris Peace Conference to press their claims for recognition in the new international order that was to be built on the ruins of war.

U.S. president Woodrow Wilson, the leading proponent of liberal international rights, proclaimed a new era of democracy and self-determination through his Fourteen Points. In Paris and throughout much of the world, he was viewed as a conquering hero, a visionary who would do away with the hypocrisies and double standards that had previously characterized great-power politics.

The victorious powers shouldered an enormous responsibility as they sought to balance their own hegemonic interests with the demands of new and aspiring states, especially oppressed colonies in Asia and Africa. Not surprisingly, the demands of sovereign self-interest took priority over the promises of liberal rights. Secret agreements concluded during the war and the realpolitik of dividing the spoils effectively undermined Wilsonian principles of self-determination and equal rights. The League of Nations reflected these contradictions: on the one hand, it established a hierarchy of nations, with great powers maintaining colonial possessions in the mandates despite the fiction of autonomy rights, and on the other hand, it protected a range of human rights in the minority rights treaties and the International Labour Organization (ILO).

It is easy to criticize the failures of the Paris Peace Conference and the League of Nations in light of the tragic consequences only twenty years later. But the task of establishing the first truly global organization, the League of Nations, based on international law and treaties, was an enormous undertaking, especially given the historical absence of anything resembling an international community of nations.[41] The liberal principles introduced by the League, even if abrogated by their own superpower sponsors, would be enshrined in the new constitutions of European and Latin American nations. Sustained by the global diffusion of popular belief in equality, freedom, and self-determination, the human rights idea would not be buried in the rubble of the League of Nations but rather would resurface even stronger after World War II.

The Advent of Total War

Within a few years of the Hague peace conferences, the world was embroiled in conflict. There are different theories about what sparked the conflagration, but regardless it is clear that Europe was primed for war. For centuries a rough balance of power, volatile yet ultimately contained, had enabled European states to build empires by projecting military power outward to the Americas, Asia, and Africa rather than concentrating the destruction at home. With Germany rising, British power waning, the Ottoman empire on the verge of collapse, new nationalisms being asserted, and states everywhere engaged in a rapid buildup of military forces and capabilities while paying lip service to peace and disarmament, it was perhaps inevitable that the old order would be remade through war.[42]

Public hopes to protect individual rights in war and separate civilians from combatants, which lay at the heart of unsuccessful efforts to develop humanitarian law at The Hague, were overwhelmed by the historical forces sweeping across Europe and the world. The twin trends toward industrialization and militarization changed the face of modern societies, culminating in the organized violence of World War I.[43] The development of heavy industry through the introduction of methods of mass production powered the rapid advance of military technology and the growing interdependence of the military and civilian sectors.[44] The development of aerial bombardment and long-range artillery deprived civilians, especially urban populations, of the relative immunity they had once enjoyed when war was a contest between professional armies.[45] Air power began to be used openly as a weapon of terror to attack civilians directly as a means of breaking the national morale and will to fight on the theory that "the man in the street, the voter, not the soldier or sailor, is the master, the principal, the person to be impressed and won over."[46] As one historian noted, these trends marked the advent of total war "fought by entire nations wherein all are considered 'combatants' without any limitation on the means of injuring the enemy in order that he may be so utterly defeated that his entire system of life may be subordinated to the will and the system of the victor."[47]

World War I mobilized 65 million men, of whom more than 8 million were killed and 30 million wounded.[48] From the heart of Europe, the conflict spread outward to European colonies and possessions in the Middle East, Asia, and Africa and to the Ottoman empire, Japan, China, Australia, and the Pacific. Once unleashed, the violence seemed to take on a life of its own. Any country with a territorial score to settle took advantage of the generalized atmosphere of militarism to launch its own aggression. Of the major regions, only the Americas remained untouched by the scourge of war.

World War I redrew the map of the world, eliminating four empires—the German-Hohenzollern, the Austro-Hungarian, the Russian, and the Ottoman. In continental Europe, three former sovereigns were carved into thirteen new republics.[49] Never before had a single conflict so dramatically reshaped global politics and territorial borders in so short a time.

National and Group Rights and Racial Equality

The breakup of traditional power structures liberated long-suppressed struggles for self-determination and justice at both the domestic and international levels. Human rights per se were not yet on the global agenda, but within many states, the military conflict and accompanying industrialization sparked rapid advances in the areas of labor rights and women's rights. Historian Eric Hobsbawm observed that "even in industrial societies so great a manpower mobilization puts enormous strains on the labour force, which is why modern mass wars both strengthened the powers of organized labour and produced a revolution in the employment of women outside the household; temporarily in the First World War, permanently in the Second World War."[50]

Mass production enhanced the economic position and bargaining power of industrial workers and sharpened class divisions as unions leveraged their crucial military contributions into growing social and political power. Union membership grew dramatically, and workers became more organized and politicized. Communist parties also increased their ranks and vied for power through both revolutionary movements and mainstream politics.[51] In Russia, the Bolsheviks launched their globe-shaking revolution, forcing European governments to pay greater attention to the demands of their workers, if only to forestall more radical developments. The mass entry of women into the workforce at all levels during the war, including manufacturing, challenged traditional gender roles and marked a decisive shift toward economic independence.[52] Although most male war veterans would return to claim their former jobs, millions of women were introduced to wage-earning for the first time, changing their consciousness as well as their socioeconomic status. Empowered by their wartime experiences, women in the United States and Europe fought for and won the right to vote and participate in politics, changing the face of their societies.[53]

The banner of international rights was raised high during the war as a means of mobilizing support against Germany. The Entente powers had rallied international allies by framing the war as a broad-based crusade for liberal rights and national freedoms. This rhetoric was exemplified in President Woodrow Wilson's memorable appeal for allies in a global war "to make the world safe for democracy."[54] The deployment of rhetorical appeals to universal rights encouraged oppressed peoples around the world to step up their struggles for national rights and self-determination. In the heart of Europe, suppressed nationalisms arose with a vengeance. Communities long defined as minorities within larger states—Czechs, Slovaks, Estonians, Poles, and Romanians—demanded states of their own and formed political and military organizations to fight for them.[55] For the victorious powers, such unfulfilled promises loomed as a considerable postwar challenge as they sought to remake the world order and manage the competing claims of various parties clamoring for rights and recognition.

The worldwide emergence of strong nationalist movements also called into question the stability of the imperialist order outside Europe. Throughout their colonies and empires, European states had recruited millions of soldiers, organized as segregated military units, to fight, kill, and die in the Great War. Asked to sacrifice their lives for European interests, these soldiers came face to face with ultimate double standards—racism and second-class citizenship. But having gained valuable combat experience, fighting with and against white Europeans, and coming to question the natural superiority of the imperialist nations, battle-hardened veterans like Ho Chi Minh and Zhou Enlai returned to their occupied homelands to lead independence movements against their former masters.[56] Everywhere the demand was for freedom and change: the Congress Party in India began its campaign for home rule; Irish nationalists launched the Easter Rebellion against British domination.

The drive for national liberation at the global level had its domestic counterpart in movements for racial equality and minority rights. Groups whose collective interests and identities had been suppressed sought redress through an explicit demand for rights. Throughout Europe, religious, civic, and rights-based groups organized to promote issues of racial equality and justice. U.S. blacks, who provided almost one-third of their nation's armed forces only to return home to segregation and legal apartheid, joined the struggle for civil rights in increasing numbers. During the war, W. E. B. Du Bois and the National Association for the Advancement of Colored People (NAACP) had broken with the antiwar left and urged members to "close ranks shoulder to shoulder with our white citizens and allied nations that are fighting for democracy."[57] Determined to win democratic rights at home after the war, they would be disappointed and angered by the continued power of white supremacy in the legal, political, social, and economic systems of the United States.[58]

Non-European states were also strong supporters of the principle of racial equality. In Japan, which had played a significant role in defeating German forces in the Asia-Pacific region, state-owned and private media consistently reported on the humiliating forms of legal discrimination Japanese business-men faced in the United States, Britain, and elsewhere in Europe.[59] Although European states had formally renounced extraterritorial rights in Japan by this time, Japanese continued to be subjected to racist laws and treatment when they visited Europe and the United States.[60] The Japanese public was outraged, especially given Japan's emerging military and economic parity with European states, and demanded that its government fight for postwar recognition of equality between races and nations as an essential condition of the upcoming peace conference at Paris. At the same time, disdain for western racist policies did not prevent Japan from practicing similar double standards in dealings with minorities within its borders, as well as with China and other Asian nations.[61]

It is noteworthy that during this period the broad spectrum of public and private initiatives to advance freedom and equality shared a common emphasis on national and group rights rather than individual rights. The concept of the individual as a holder of rights in international law would not emerge meaningfully until World War II and the development of the modern human rights system at the UN. At the Paris Peace Conference of 1919, however, individual rights did not even appear on the agenda; self-determination, racial equality, minority rights, and labor rights were the main issues of the day. The failure of the League of Nations and its framework of group rights was one of the main factors that led to a changing conception of human rights in international law.

The Paris Conference and the Triumph of U.S. Liberalism

The atmosphere at the Paris Peace Conference could not have been more different than the mood of official cynicism at the Hague conferences. Established powers and aspiring nations alike sent their highest political representatives to Paris, eager to participate in the creation of an international regime to replace the old order. As W. E. B. Du Bois remarked, the heads of "thirty-two nations, peoples, and races" gathered to raise their voices and press their claims, creating a colorful atmosphere "unique in the annals of global diplomacy"[62]; another participant observed that "Chinamen, Japanese, Koreans, Hindus, Khirgizes, Lesghiens, Circassians, Mingrelians, Buryats, Malays, and Negroes and Negroids from Africa and America were among the tribes and tongues forgathered in Paris to watch the rebuilding of the world political system and to see where they 'came in.'"[63]

Everyone present in Paris knew that the stakes had never been higher. Throughout the world, all eyes were on the peace negotiations. Expectations for positive change were enormous. With perhaps a little hyperbole, a British diplomat captured the mood: "We were journeying to Paris not merely to liquidate the war, but to found a new order. . . . We were preparing not Peace only, but Eternal Peace."[64] Paris also marked the entrance of the United States onto the center stage of world affairs, a spectacular triumph for President Wilson and his principles of liberal democracy. Despite America's comparatively minor contribution to the military victory, Wilson was seen to embody the hope for a more effective system of international security than the old imperialist order presided over by the fratricidal European powers. Having boldly announced early in the war that his country "puts human rights above all other rights" and that "her flag is the flag not only of America, but of humanity," Wilson continued to step up the oratory.[65] From his pulpit as chairman of the Commission on the League of Nations, Wilson pressed his famous Fourteen Points and stressed that self-determination is "not a mere phrase. It is an imperative principle of action, which statesmen will henceforth ignore at their own peril."[66] His own secretary of state, Robert Lansing, privately regretted these rhetorical flourishes, wondering how Wilson planned to fulfill such promises given the unrealistic expectations for national independence they inevitably engendered.[67]

It is important to recall that Wilson's vision of liberal rights, while dominant at the time, was not the only ideology vying for public support in the aftermath of the war. To the East, Soviet leader Vladimir Lenin also proclaimed a new era of rights. But for the Bolshevists, these rights were the property of workers and the oppressed proletariat, not isolated individuals or insular groups. They were achievable through revolutionary communism, not capitalist democracy, and aimed for full economic and social emancipation, not superficial political freedom.[68] Lenin also promoted rights for women and minorities and argued that self-determination was a universal right to be immediately realized not only by Europeans but by all colonized peoples of Asia and Africa.[69]

The Bolsheviks initially made good on these promises in Russia itself, extending rights without discrimination to women and minorities and abolishing privileges based on class and status.[70] In so doing they "won over the new non-Russian nationalities by offering them real political power through participation in government, economic power by enjoying the benefits of social revolution, in which previously dominant ethnic groups from among the urban bourgeoisie and the landowning classes found themselves dispossessed, and peasants took over the cities; and cultural power through new educational rights with the spread of mass literacy and compulsory schooling."[71] In the postwar climate of economic hardship and political uncertainty, these developments had wide appeal, and the Soviet model won significant support in Europe and its colonies.

The period after World War I marks a watershed in human affairs. It is hard for us to recapture the ferment, the sense of both possibility and dread that must have gripped people at that time. Principles of freedom and equality were proclaimed not only by activists and intellectuals but by governments of the world's leading powers. Both Wilson's liberal universalism and Lenin's revolutionary communism promised to emancipate people from political and economic servitude. Wilson's memorable phrase "a war to end all wars" may sound hopelessly naive from our perspective in history, but at the time his words were broadcast by media throughout the world and discussed by intellectuals in Parisian cafés and students in Chinese universities. To masses of people struggling for self-expression after years of foreign domination, such rhetoric resonated and appeared as a light at the end of a dark tunnel.

The Return of Power Politics and Double Standards

It was not long before Wilson's idealistic declarations ran headlong into the reality of power politics. The Europeans were perfectly happy to let the U.S.

president take center stage provided he did not take too seriously those high-minded pronouncements. While the principle of self-determination posed the most obvious contradiction for those powers intent on retaining, if not expanding, their colonial possessions, all of Wilson's proclaimed principles were problematic. Take, for example, the first of the Fourteen Points: "Open covenants of peace, openly arrived at, after which there shall be no private international understandings of any kind but diplomacy shall proceed always frankly and in the public view."[72] Abiding by this one sentence would have overturned centuries of statecraft and rewritten the ethics of traditional diplomacy, whereby deception, intrigue, and secret agreements were not only the common currency of international practice but also the preferred strategy of leading political theorists across cultures.[73]

The issue was of practical, not merely theoretical, significance. To mobilize support during the war, European powers had already concluded a whole host of secret agreements. These understandings had been crucial to winning the war and were now expected to serve as the basis for dividing the spoils and shaping the postwar order; they could not simply be disregarded by Wilson's liberal triumphalism. Among other things, these agreements allocated territories to new states, granted Japan concessions in China and the Pacific, and, in the infamous Sykes-Picot Agreement, divided the Middle East between Britain and France even though Britain had promised independence to Arab nationalist leaders in return for their military efforts against German forces. Arab interests would be dealt a further blow at the Paris Peace Conference when the Zionist movement, with British assistance, gained the support of the United States and the League of Nations to establish a Jewish national home in Arab Palestine, as the British had previously promised the Zionist movement in the Balfour Declaration.[74]

With large chunks of the world already spoken for, European diplomats resisted what they saw as Wilson's attempt to open a Pandora's box of vague, unworkable notions of liberal rights. Instead, they continued to conduct secret negotiations and got on with the business of dividing the spoils of war, paying lip service to universal rights only so far as necessary to mollify popular expectations.

In this context, there was bound to be a clash between public hopes and practical outcomes. Inspired by the promise of self-determination, representatives of established and aspiring nations flooded Paris to press their territorial claims and political ambitions and argue for redress of past grievances. Responsibility for adjudicating these claims and disputes rested almost entirely with the war's victorious powers, the so-called Council of Four: Britain, France, the United States, and Italy. There were frequent and sharp disagreements between these four powers. Eventually four would be reduced to three when President Wilson, with French and British support, refused Italy's territorial demand for the port city of Fiume on the Dalmatian coast and the Italian delegation, supported by an outraged and nationalistic public back home, walked out of the Paris conference.[75] Noting the double standards involved in striking a balance between imperial interests and self-determination, an Italian diplomat remarked, "Now President Wilson, after ignoring and violating his own Fourteen Points, wants to restore their virginity by applying them vigorously where they refer to Italy."[76]

Britain, France, and the United States faced enormous and contradictory responsibilities at the Paris Peace Conference. While committed to extending their own spheres of influence, they also had to negotiate a durable peace, approve the creation of new states, develop a system of treaties, and establish a global organization to maintain collective security—all without alienating either international or domestic support. And they had to accomplish this within the contradiction of a liberal rights framework whose rhetoric of freedom and equality resonated across the globe but whose actual implementation, if taken seriously, would have undermined their own strategic interests in geopolitical hegemony.

The nineteenth century may have seen an unending succession of wars, but the resulting political changes were incremental and piecemeal; in Paris the whole world suddenly seemed up for grabs. The result was a frenzied mix of, on the one hand, official negotiations to develop a principled, rights-based international organization, the League of Nations, and on the other, Machiavellian horse-trading conducted at breakneck speed, old-style power politics carving up the pie behind a façade of liberal rights.

The hypocrisy of Paris was exemplified by the drama surrounding Japan's attempt to include an article on racial equality in the charter of the League of Nations. Japan attached great importance to the conference and sent an experienced delegation familiar with European diplomatic traditions headed by Prince Saionji, a distinguished member of the royal family who had been educated partly in France.[77] The Japanese delegation in Paris was not eager to push the issue of racial equality, correctly anticipating its unfavorable reception with the great powers. However, public opinion at home was inflamed by the persistence of open European racism despite Japan's status as an emerging world power. A joint statement of thirty-seven Japanese NGOs declared that without racial equality, "all the alliances and treaties will only be castles in the sand, and the general peace of the world will not be secured."[78]

Meeting with their U.S. and British counterparts, Japanese delegates expressed a willingness to accept watered-down language so long as there

would be something at the end of the day to show their public. The delegation of the British empire, which included Australia, South Africa, and other
colonial territories, was adamantly opposed. Australian prime minister Billy
Hughes saw an insidious threat to "White Australia" and argued, "either the
Japanese proposal means something or it means nothing: if the former, out
with it; if the latter—why have it?"[79] Wilson was more sympathetic but equally
intransigent, believing that racial equality was a nonstarter in the Jim Crow
south and would jeopardize Senate approval of the peace treaty.

Nevertheless, after an assiduous and highly effective lobbying campaign,
Japan gained the support of several European and all non-European delegations at Paris, assuring majority support for the racial equality clause.
Ironically, the issue was brought to a vote before the League commission on
the very day that it had agreed to accept the U.S. right of unilateral military
intervention throughout Latin America under the Monroe Doctrine.[80]

The watered-down clause Japan proposed did not specifically mention
legal equality; instead, it spoke of "the principle of equality of nations and just
treatment of their nationals." Despite strenuous objections from the United
States and the United Kingdom, the Japanese motion easily passed, by a vote
of 11 to 6.[81] In a dictatorial maneuver in clear breach of legal procedure, Wilson used his authority as chairman of the League commission to quash the
proposal without further deliberation, on the grounds that there were "too
serious objections on the part of some of us."[82] Even delegates accustomed
to the arrogance of power were shocked by Wilson's blatant manipulation
and disregard of the majority vote.

The news traveled fast. The media trumpeted the rejection as a betrayal
and humiliation of Wilson's own high-minded declarations; the contradiction
was captured in headlines such as "Peace Delegates Beat Japan's Proposal for
Racial Equality."[83] People around the globe reacted with anger to the open
and cynical disregard of the supposed principles for which the war had been
fought. Cities in Asia, Africa, and even the United States saw violent street
demonstrations, with one commentator likening the scene to a "race war."[84]
Wilson was condemned as a hypocrite and his public image as a visionary
peacemaker suffered a heavy blow.

This seemingly resounding defeat for human rights needs to be placed
in historical context. Racism, as it is commonly understood today, was the
rule, not the exception, throughout the United States and Europe. The great
powers openly practiced racism, especially in their colonies and dependent
nations. In addition to the discriminatory laws that offended Japanese and
Asian citizens, the United States imposed a form of legal apartheid on its
own black citizens, and British and French imperialism was grounded on
the distinction between superior white Europeans and inferior natives, a

distinction often accepted and internalized by the colonized as well.[85] Such practices and attitudes reflected not only the political and cultural zeitgeist of the times but also the latest eugenic theories ostensibly derived from Darwinian evolution.[86] The national and racial bigotries that would manifest so violently only a few years later in World War II did not arise out of thin air but had historical antecedents in centuries of slavery, imperialism, and colonialism. As one historian has noted: "In an age of empire and social Darwinism, notions of racial hierarchy were ubiquitous, and few Europeans of Left or Right did not believe in ideas of racial superiority in one form or another, or accept their relevance to colonial policy."[87]

Just as the authors of the American Declaration of Independence saw little contradiction between the peculiar institution of slavery and the self-evident philosophy that all men are created equal, western politicians at Paris could comfortably proclaim universal rights to self-determination and equality within a common understanding of white superiority. Their public and private pronouncements at Paris are littered with references to backward races and nations being unable to govern themselves without the help of white European civilization.[88] For them, the real issue raised by the Japanese proposal was not whether nations and races were truly equal—of course they were not—but whether the interest of the great powers in maintaining global dominance and colonial possessions were truly threatened by a vague and unenforceable clause in the League of Nations charter that enshrined some form of equality between races. The French thought that they were not and accordingly voted with the majority in favor of the Japanese proposal; the United Kingdom and United States disagreed.

In Japan, the debacle of the racial equality clause strengthened the hand of nationalists who had long warned that western powers would never accept Japan as an equal. This encouraged the country to turn inward, undertake an aggressive program of military industrialization, and seek to dominate the Asia-Pacific region as a counterweight to U.S. and European hegemony.

Paradoxically, the more immediate consequence at the Paris conference was a stiffening of Japan's demand for concessions in the Chinese province of Shandong, revered as the birthplace of Confucius. Japan had seized the strategic peninsula from Germany, who in turn had occupied it as a seaport and railway transportation hub. Japan's claim, ostensibly based on a wartime agreement with China but clearly understood as an imperialist land grab, was backed by the threat to abandon the League if the great powers returned Shandong to China. Wellington Koo, a U.S.-educated scholar who would later successively serve as China's ambassador to the United States, the United Kingdom, and France, made an impassioned plea for territorial integrity, citing established international law and the nascent principles of the League of Nations, in what was widely considered one of the most impressive presentations before the League commission.[89] Wilson, with British and French backing, nevertheless supported Japan's claim to Chinese land. Wilson complained about losing sleep over the decision—he also lost several staff members, who quit in protest—but in the end decided that Japanese participation in the League was too important to risk over a small piece of land in Asia.

As with so many decisions taken at Paris, the unintended effects would reverberate across the globe in the coming decades. Chinese nationalists were outraged, organizing petition drives against both western governments and their own leaders. The recollection of a Chinese student captures the mood of anger among intellectuals:

> When the news of the Paris Peace Conference finally reached us we were greatly shocked. We at once awoke to the fact that foreign nations were still selfish and militaristic and that they were all great liars. A group of my friends and I talked almost the whole night. We came to the conclusion that a greater war would be coming sooner or later, and that this great war would be fought in the East. We had nothing to do with our Government, that we knew very well, and at the same time we could no longer depend upon the principles of any so-called great leader like Woodrow Wilson, for example. Looking at our people and at the pitiful ignorant masses, we couldn't help but feel that we must struggle.[90]

Students organized protests throughout the country. A large demonstration at Tiananmen Square against Japan turned violent; student leaders were arrested and the movement grew more radicalized. Many of the leading activists, including Mao Zedong and Zhou Enlai, went on to establish the Communist Party the following year.[91] This series of events provides another example of the historical consequences western powers unleashed at Paris in first raising and then shattering public expectations for a new era of liberal international rights.

The League's Hierarchy of Nations

Another clear illustration of power trumping principle at Paris can be seen in the organization of the League itself and the ranking of its members. Nations were grouped into different classes through an explicit hierarchy of rights. The victors of World War I ensured that there would be one set of rules for themselves, another for the vanquished European powers, and yet another for non-European races whom they considered inferior in all respects.[92] At the top of the heap sat the Council of Four, who not only assumed responsibility for policing the world but also increased their dominions by seizing new lands in the former Ottoman and German empires.[93] At the bottom were the colonies and possessions in Africa, Asia, and the Middle East, now renamed mandates. These were invested with the appearance of autonomy through the legal sanction of the League of Nations and a complicated set of treaty rights for the three separate tiers of mandates, ranked by how capable the natives were of self-government.[94] But in reality, all the mandates were subject to the continued domination of their European masters; independence would eventually be won through political confrontation and military force after World War II rather than through legal petition on the basis of universal rights.

A notch below the victors, but well above the mandates, were the new European states carved out of former empires—Poland, Czechoslovakia, Yugoslavia, Romania, Greece, Austria, Bulgaria, Hungary. These enjoyed sovereignty but were forced, despite bitter protests, to accept a series of agreements called the minorities treaties, which recognized a wide range of civil, political, and religious rights of minorities within their borders and placed their protection under League guarantee should the new states fail in their responsibilities.[95]

Nevertheless, the very establishment of an international organization comprised of the globe's recognized states (excluding, of course, colonized and dependent peoples) marked an unprecedented achievement in international law and organization. The innovative structures of the League—a deliberative assembly of all "reorganized" nations, a governing council of the great powers, a professional secretariat to administer the organization, an international court, and a legal charter and accompanying set of treaty-based rights—was resurrected as the institutional foundation for the next postwar effort at global security, the United Nations.

Selective Imposition of Minorities Rights

Minority rights enjoyed broad public support, especially after the well-publicized Turkish assault on its Armenian population in 1915, the first genocide of the twentieth century.[96] Jewish groups, who were already cognizant of the dangers of resurgent European nationalisms and constituted a highly effective lobby in Paris, pushed hard for legal protections for minorities. After the embarrassing episode of the racial equality clause, the United States threw its weight behind minority rights as one area in which Wilson's liberal vision could bear fruit. The British understood minority rights to be necessary to curb the power of the chauvinistic majorities in the "new and immature states of Eastern Europe or Western Asia" while at the same time safeguarding the newly drawn borders by reducing the chances of interstate conflict and refugee flows.[97] The dismemberment of the German empire had resulted in large German populations being incorporated into the new Eastern European states. The British were concerned, rightly so, as it turned out, that mistreatment of these minorities could give rise to territorial claims and eventually threaten the balance of power in Europe as a whole.

The new states resisted the imposition of the minority treaties in the absence of a similar commitment from established states. They argued that it was unfair and hypocritical to expect them to protect minority rights when the victorious powers refused to accept the same obligations regarding treatment of minorities in their own territories, let alone in the mandates, which also fell under their jurisdiction and responsibility. They therefore proposed a general clause to protect minority rights that would be applicable to all members of the League. This position had a sound basis in law and logic but was not grounded in the political realities of the time. The United States and Great Britain were in no position to apply minority rights domestically without upsetting the basis of white superiority on which their societies still depended, politically, economically, and legally. As one British diplomat observed, universal enforcement of minority rights would have "involved the right to interfere in the internal constitution of every country in the world. . . . Even if the denial of such right elsewhere might lead to injustice and oppression, that was better than to allow anything which would mean the negation of the sovereignty of every state of the world."[98] In the end, the proposal to extend universal protections to minorities in every country through treaty rights was dismissed without serious discussion.

This debate highlighted, again, that the great powers built double standards into the very notion of human rights. At issue was not the existence of minority rights and the right to self-determination per se but the universality of these rights. The principle was recognized but the scope was applied selectively, as a matter of law as well as practice. Rights were to be a critical element of the new order for European citizens but not their colonized subjects. Limitations on sovereignty were required for "immature" European states but not for great powers, which could dictate international laws without having to abide by them. This was the established hierarchy of nations, the calculations of power behind the formal equality of liberal rights.

The Surprising Success of Labor Rights

The establishment of the International Labour Organization at Paris appears to be the most unambiguous victory for human rights advocates.[99] Labor had emerged from World War I in a strengthened position; the role of workers in the military effort was crucial and undeniable. During the war, the major trade unions in industrialized countries had agreed to boost working hours and production in return for promises of improved social and economic conditions.[100] After the war they expected a return on their investment and sacrifice and began to agitate for sweeping changes to advance workers' interests. As part of this movement, unions and labor leaders called for the establishment of a global charter, applicable to workers worldwide, to guarantee a basic set of rights in the areas of working conditions, social welfare, and economic benefits.[101] The internationalization of the struggle for labor rights was no doubt influenced by the growing power of communist parties and the successful revolution in Russia. Before President Wilson left for Paris, U.S. labor leaders urged him to prioritize the rights of workers, warning that "organized labor must have this recognition."[102]

A labor commission was established at the Paris conference to study these issues and draft recommendations.[103] This would prove to be the most exciting and dynamic initiative in Paris. The commission met thirty-five times, inviting a broad range of labor groups, human rights advocates, suffragists, and other activists to present a range of proposals linking peace, labor rights, and social justice. The commission ended up drafting two documents: a proposal for the establishment of a permanent international labor organization based on a tripartite system of representation consisting of government, business, and labor; and a charter of general legal principles, including rights of association and collective bargaining, equal rights for women, abolition of child labor, and limits on working hours.

It came as somewhat of a surprise when the great powers approved both proposals and incorporated them into the peace treaties with little amendment or discussion. Thus was the International Labour Organization born, first as a partner of the League of Nations and eventually as an independent organization.[104] It has been speculated that the establishment of the ILO was part of a deliberate strategy to co-opt organized labor and forestall a more radical global movement influenced by the Bolshevik call for worker uprisings.[105] This may well be the case, but it is also clear that governments and industry needed the cooperation of labor to rebuild their war-ravaged economies. Whatever the reason, in one fell swoop, labor gained an international institution with a broad mandate to promote social justice and workers' rights that was separate from the League and thereby insulated from its political weakness and constraints. While the League was destined to disintegrate within a few years, the ILO would survive World War II, develop an associated but independent relationship with the United Nations, and promulgate a wide array of treaties and norms promoting labor rights worldwide.[106]

Sowing the Seeds of the Next War

Time has been a harsh judge of the Paris Peace Conference and its failure
to establish a system of collective security capable of resolving conflicts and
promoting peace and justice. Knowing the horrors just around the bend of
history, it is easy to condemn Paris and its liberal principles as a sham. The
punitive treatment of Germany and the scattering of its population as vulnerable minorities in hostile new European states would provide the perfect foil
for Adolf Hitler's irredentist claims. John Maynard Keynes predicted that the
economic subjugation of Germany would prove to be ruinous for Europe as
a whole.[107] The haphazard and arbitrary manner in which states were established and territories allocated further aggravated nationalist tensions. The
disrespectful and openly racist treatment of Japan and China drove those
countries away from a course of cooperation with the West. The continued
subjugation of peoples in Africa, Asia, and Latin America undermined faith
in western values (or revealed them in true light, as the case may be) and set
the stage for future independence struggles.

It may have been premature to establish a world organization that required the voluntary support of independent states, most of which were
newly created and lacked coherent internal governance systems, let alone a
consistent approach to international affairs. Yet public expectations had been
deliberately raised by the European powers as part of the war effort and then
intensified by Wilson's human rights rhetoric. The results of Paris proved
that the peace was harder to win than the war; the language of freedom was
more effective at rallying the troops than at providing the basis for a new
global security arrangement.

Countless millions, especially outside Europe, who had placed hopes in
the stirring vision of a new age of equal rights and self-determination were
bound to be disappointed by the revelations of business as usual once the
results of the Paris conference were known. Throughout the territories designated as mandates, masses of people demonstrated against the betrayal of
their hopes and new organizations formed to fight for national independence.
Meanwhile, Wilson's star had fallen low since those heady first days in Paris;
he would return to the United States weakened, exhausted, and incapable
of pushing the Versailles Treaty through a recalcitrant Senate, a telling early
blow to the prospects of the League of Nations.

Human rights ideas are intangible, their influence on people and events
the subject of constant debate between idealist and materialist views of history. But whatever the interplay between cause and effect, it appears that

Wilson's role in raising unrealistic popular expectations in favor of universal rights nevertheless energized the spread of his liberal vision. New civic associations and networks were organized to promote principles of freedom, self-determination, and racial equality. The power and prerogatives of state sovereignty were increasingly subject to the spotlight of public scrutiny and challenge. More important, the idea of universal justice established through international law and organization had been introduced to every corner of the world. Although destined to wither during the interwar years, human rights concepts enjoyed a dramatic revival during and after World War II.

In a sense, Paris marked the launch of a global discussion on rights and justice. And while that discussion ended in disappointment, people's anger was largely directed not against the idea of human rights but against the hypocrisy of power reserving rights for the privileged few.

2

The Decline of Human Rights between World Wars

- Early Challenges for the League of Nations
- The Failure of Liberal International Rights
- Constitutional Rights and Subsequent Challenges
- Keeping Human Rights Alive
- Losing the Battle of Ideas
- Waiting for World War

This chapter discusses the period between the two world wars, when the hope for a new global regime based on liberal international and domestic rights proved to be a short-lived illusion.[1] The effectiveness of the League of Nations was crippled by the early defection of the United States; the inability of European rivals, particularly Britain and France, to develop common positions in defense of the rights proclaimed at Paris; and the League's overall failure to deliver on promises of minority rights and equality of nations and races. The weakness of the League's enforcement mechanism allowed for the suppression of minorities and the rise of chauvinistic nationalism throughout Europe. Continued imperialist competition negated the promise of self-determination for colonized peoples worldwide. These trends and the poor political and economic performance of Europe's liberal governments paved the way for fascist regimes to win over the masses, ascend to power through largely democratic means, pursue aggressive and racist policies at home and abroad, and bring total war to the heart of Europe and eventually the world.

While the new constitutional democracies in Europe represented a temporary triumph for Anglo-American principles of universal rights, their inability to deliver effective governance or economic benefits to their populations and their ruthless suppression of communist parties paved the way for the rapid rise of fascism. As an ideological program, the concept of liberal rights suffered a steep decline in public enthusiasm because of paralysis at the constitutional level and at the League of Nations. Human rights ideas were kept alive during this period through the efforts of NGOs and individual jurists and activists, but they could not compete with the mass appeal of racist nationalism. As a result, the human rights idea entered a period of retreat during the 1920s and 1930s. On the eve of World War II, the military and ideological strength of totalitarian regimes seemed poised to overwhelm the fragile framework of liberal rights before it had taken root in the international system.

Early Challenges for the League of Nations

Despite public disappointment with power politics at Paris, the League of Nations still marked a spectacular triumph for the ideology of liberal international rights. The map of the world had been redrawn along lines developed primarily by Britain and the United States. Anglo-American power and principles were predominant. The British empire had actually expanded its territory, while the United States emerged not only as an ideological beacon for the world but a leading economic power as well. The demands of decolonization had been forestalled and managed within the system of mandates that preserved imperialist privileges while holding out the illusory promise of self-government and autonomy. Germany had been neutralized, its empire dismantled, and much of its population scattered between various new nation-states. The vexing problem of European nationalism had been resolved, albeit temporarily, through the establishment of new states with supposedly international safeguards for their minority populations to prevent the tyranny of the democratic majority. These states owed their existence to the system set up through the League, despite misgivings about their inferior status within the international hierarchy. In the face of many challenges, a new order had emerged from the ashes of war, seemingly able to provide a measure of stability and a global framework for resolving nationalist tensions without resorting to war. The ideological framework and justification for this new system was the idea of liberal rights.

Making Rights Meaningful

The main issue for the League was how to make these rights meaningful within a system of privileges for and ongoing conflicts between the great powers. This was a difficult task in the context of the times. After centuries of intensifying imperialist rivalries, it was unrealistic to expect the leading

European states suddenly to set aside their differences and throw their collective weight behind a set of principles to which they had only a half-hearted commitment, especially given the limitations on sovereign power that these rights implied. At the domestic level, it was challenge enough to institute a political system of governance based on the equal rights of citizens under a constitutional system. At the international level, sovereign equality and the rule of law flew in the face of existing geopolitical power relations between states and colonies with vastly unequal abilities to promote and enforce their national interests.

The primary architects of the League of Nations never intended it to "correct" these imbalances but rather to ensure a measure of international stability within great-power hegemony based, in principle at least, on a liberal rights framework. Yet if this first experiment in international organization and collective security was to succeed, it needed workable mechanisms to resolve conflict and move the world system toward greater recognition and respect for principles of self-determination, minority rights, and peaceful resolution of disputes. The ultimate failure of the League lay in its manifest weakness to effectuate these principles. This failure undermined the credibility and effectiveness of the underlying ideology of liberal rights and in so doing cleared the way for alternative ideologies, first communism and then fascism, to develop broad popular appeal in the years leading up to World War II.

Structural Weakness of the League

The first blow to the League of Nations was the failure of the United States to join the new organization. Had the United States been actively involved in European affairs during the interwar period, history might look very different.[2] At minimum there would have been a stronger ideological counterweight to the rise of fascism. But Wilson proved unable to sell his vision of global leadership to the public and the political establishment of the United States. Wilson had long been criticized as arrogant and inflexible even by his allies in Congress. Exhausted and ill after six months of difficult negotiations in Paris, he was simply not up to the arm-twisting and compromise necessary to sway a majority of senators to his cause.[3] On the left, especially among sectors of civil society that had previously supported Wilson's liberal internationalism, there was disappointment that old-style great-power politics prevailed at the Paris Peace Conference. But the major opposition came from isolationists in the Senate, who appealed to chauvinistic myths of purity and individualism, portraying Europe as mired in unending conflict that would only sap America's moral and economic strength and the League itself as a motley collection of nations unfit for cohabitation with America.[4] Typical of the overt racism prevalent at the time, a senator from Missouri asked his colleagues to imagine "submitting questions involving the very life of the United States to a tribunal on which a nigger from Liberia, a nigger from Honduras, and a nigger from India . . . each have [sic] votes equal to that of the great United States."[5]

Wilson's increasingly desperate efforts to win ratification contributed to nervous exhaustion and a debilitating stroke, ending his presidency and his life. The United States subsequently turned inward, ushering in a period of unbridled consumerism and capitalist excess that came crashing down ten years later with the Great Depression.

The defection of the United States might not have proven fatal had there been a basis for unity and collective action among the European powers sitting on the League's Council, although, as one historian notes, "a peace settlement based on Britain and France alone—for Italy also remained dissatisfied—could not last. Sooner or later, Germany, Russia, or both, would inevitably reappear as major players."[6]

The differences between Britain and France were especially pronounced concerning Germany's role in Europe. France naturally wanted to dominate the continent by suppressing Germany and strengthening its buffer in Eastern Europe. The rights of German minorities in the new European states were therefore of little interest. The British, on the other hand, favored a balance of power on the continent, preferring to rehabilitate Germany as a counterweight to both France and the emerging Soviet Union. This stalemate over Germany and indifference toward the League's role in dispute resolution prevented the two foremost European powers from working together to provide stability for the new postwar global arrangements.[7] There was, of course, broad agreement about the need to maintain hegemony over the mandates regardless of promises of local self-government. But the insurmountable political obstacle was a lack of consensus necessary to enforce other treaty rights and obligations, ensure balance of power between states, and deter political repression within states.

The Failure of Liberal International Rights

The League's inability and unwillingness to enforce the rights framework it had established contributed to a loss of political and popular support for the larger ideological system of liberal democracy. The consequence of abandoning these rights was a return to explicit power politics and eventually to global conflict. This can be seen in the neglect and demise of three of the intended pillars of the postwar order—international restraints on war, self-determination and the rights of colonized peoples, and rights of minorities.

Ongoing international negotiations to safeguard humanity from war met with complete failure. Efforts organized by jurists, diplomats, and activists simply did not enjoy the political backing of states or the mass public support to overcome this weakness. In 1923, a commission of distinguished international jurists convened, at the request of their respective governments, to draft a new treaty protecting civilians from the growing threat of aerial bombardment.[8] One historian described the resulting Hague Air Laws, which essentially banned the use of air power in urban areas at the same time that states were investing massively in offensive air power, as "the high water mark in legal fantasy."[9] As the jurists had neither formal governmental authority nor a popular mandate to put political weight behind their proposals, not a single country signed the treaty.[10] In another act of legal utopianism, the French and British foreign ministers met in 1928 to ban war altogether, following the theory that "it is by the development of a law of peace, rather than by renewing the attempts to codify the law of war, that a stable international system can be built up by the League of Nations."[11] The Kellogg-Briand Pact was the type of unenforceable legal diplomacy that played well to public sentiment but only papered over the great-power rifts that would soon erupt in global conflict.

Similarly, the right to self-determination was ignored once the ink had dried on the Treaty of Versailles. Throughout the mandates, the European powers failed to allow meaningful progress toward independent political parties or self-government, let alone genuine self-determination. None of the mandates gained sovereign independence during the interwar period. Instead, nationalist leaders were suppressed, jailed, and killed, and the mass movements they led were put down with brutal violence.[12] All this was done without triggering condemnation of the mandatory powers for violating their legal duty under the League of Nations "to secure just treatment of the native inhabitants of territories under their control."[13] It is perhaps not surprising that the League's powerful members refused to condemn their own actions; nevertheless, national and minority groups that petitioned for redress were bitterly disappointed by the lack of response.[14] It soon was understood that the League had neither the means nor the authority to entertain the rights of colonized and oppressed peoples, especially against the great powers that dominated the global organization.

This policy toward colonized peoples weakened the League's standing in international opinion and left it powerless to prevent new military aggressions, first in non-European territories and then in the heartland itself. By the 1930s, the League had lost all deterrent powers and become, in effect, a "useless debating society."[15] Japan's invasion of Manchuria, Germany and Italy's intervention in the Spanish civil war, and Italy's invasion of Ethiopia merely confirmed the League's incapacity to maintain peace, the end game of its failure to enforce liberal rights.[16] In 1935, having deployed saturation bombing, poison gas, and the full force of its modern army to massacre untold thousands of civilians, Italy appeared before the moribund global organization to declare "the honor of informing the League of the progress achieved in its work of civilizing Ethiopia."[17]

The League's inability to uphold the minority rights treaties was an even greater factor in the rise of fascism and the advent of World War II. France had never been interested in enforcing the rights of German minorities or any other vulnerable groups, in Eastern Europe or elsewhere. Even the British, who at Paris had advocated minority rights as a guarantor of European stability, took a laissez-faire attitude toward the plight of minorities in hostile majority states. As one British diplomat remarked, "More harm would be done by unnecessary interference than, even at the risk of a little local suffering, allowing these minorities to settle down before their present masters. So long as these people imagine that their grievances can be aired before the League of Nations, they will refuse to settle down and the present effervescence will continue indefinitely."[18]

Given the League's indifference, the new European states, which had bitterly resisted the minority rights treaties in the first place, felt free to adopt increasingly xenophobic policies. The general rule for minorities became forced assimilation and second-class citizenship: members of minority groups were stripped of rights, and their language schools and cultural institutions were shut down.[19] Abuse of German minorities, for example, was widespread in Eastern Europe and eventually became a major factor that fueled Hitler's rise to power. The inability of the League and the liberal European powers to take on the Nazi challenge stemmed in part from their legacy of failure to respect self-proclaimed moral and legal principles; in other words, it was the product of ideological as much as military weakness. The end result was that throughout Europe, virulent strains of racism and nationalism spread unchecked, provoking counternationalisms and providing justification for the fascist worldview of warring races and nations.[20]

The consequences of inaction were fatal not just to victims of rights abuses but to the entire rights framework underpinning the League of Nations. As it became clear that the League's international principles were inoperative in practice, sovereign power exercised its traditional prerogatives without fear of accountability. In the absence of even the threat of enforcing the League system of rights, it was impossible to deter or resolve breaches to the peace and achieve a measure of security. When totalitarian governments came to power in Europe, they justified aggressive policies by pointing to the blatant hypocrisy and double standards pervasive in the rights-based ideology of the liberal European powers.

Constitutional Rights and Subsequent Challenges

After the Paris Peace Conference, liberal rights did enjoy one significant success, in the area of democratic governance and formal constitutionalism. The new European states organized governments exclusively along parliamentary lines, reflecting the most tangible triumph of postwar liberalism.[21] As governments came into power, there was a veritable wave of new constitutions promoting the latest legal theories of individual rights. For example, just before adopting a constitution for a democratic republic, Czech nationalist leaders proclaimed: "We accept the American principles as laid down by President Wilson: the principles of liberated mankind—of the actual equality of nations—and of governments deriving their just power from the consent of the governed."[22] Similarly, article one of Germany's new constitution affirmed, "The Reich is a republic. All political authority is derived from the people."[23]

In addition to the standard list of civil and political rights derived from Anglo-American and French legal traditions, these constitutions included a more limited set of social and economic rights. Whether motivated by the popular appeal of communist principles, the influence of leftists within governing alliances, or the desire to contain Soviet influence and weaken more radical alternatives, the new constitutions enshrined as basic rights such socioeconomic concerns as health care, land reform, and social security. Hugo Preuss, the eminent jurist who drafted the Weimar constitution, declared: "Either Wilson or Lenin."[24] However, formal recognition of these rights did not translate into changed economic relations within societies, let alone a systematic policy to redistribute wealth or property. Even in governments that favored legal enforcement of social justice goals, "constitutional commitments to socio-economic rights were undermined by the depression and mass unemployment."[25] But for most liberal nations, economic policy still operated very much along laissez-faire capitalist lines. This was the age when industrial capitalist empires were built on the strength of new forms of mass production and mechanization.

In contrast, the adoption of civil and political rights within democratic governance had a significant impact on the political culture of these states, for better and for worse. Throughout Europe there was a proliferation of political parties of all stripes, competing in open elections for the allegiance of masses of voters newly mobilized by the prospect of national self-expression after a long period of subordination within larger empires. Democratic elections were the rage as people lined up to celebrate independence and exercise their rights. This marked the heyday of legal positivism, the theory that formal recognition of rights by government could establish the foundation for a culture of rule of law. Such an optimistic thesis would suffer precipitous decline once political and economic conditions in Europe no longer favored the rule of liberal rights.

The honeymoon of constitutional rights was short lived; facism lurked around the corner. The problem was that liberal democracy did not seem to work well in practical politics at either the international or national levels, except in the United States and Britain, where it was rooted in long-standing tradition. Rights had been recognized on paper, proclaimed in law, even enshrined in national constitutions, but with neither the political machinery to support them nor a popular culture that understood them.[26] In a sense, liberalism was victimized by its own success after World War I. Just as Wilsonian principles of self-determination and equality were undermined by the extraordinary expectations they engendered, the enthusiasm for liberal rights resulted in the hasty and haphazard implantation of constitutional democracies in diverse countries burdened by uncertain identities and beset by profound socioeconomic crises. As one historian remarks: "Democracy's shallow roots in Europe's political tradition helped explain why anti-liberal regimes were established with such ease and so little protest."[27]

Challenge from the Left

The spread of a rights-based culture through domestic law and politics was undermined by widespread poverty in the aftermath of the war and challenged by the growing influence of communist parties and their supporters. The war had devastated the global economy, especially in continental Europe, where much of the physical infrastructure lay in ruins. Misery and hardship affected all classes of society. Hunger was so widespread that massive aid and charity programs were launched, the first time that systematic humanitarian efforts extended beyond national borders.[28] It was in this context that communists made a strong appeal for fundamental change. The call was not just for social and economic justice but for a radical restructuring of social and economic relations through violent revolution to displace bourgeois capitalist elites with worker-based associations. Communist parties were influential throughout Europe, especially in Eastern Europe, Italy, and Germany. But their biggest strength was the model of Soviet Russia.

Having destroyed the power base of old ruling elites, the Bolsheviks were carrying out a radical and, by all appearances, successful program of land reform and industrial revolution. They made remarkable progress in transforming, seemingly overnight, a backward peasant society into a modern state, especially compared to the economic stagnation in Europe at the time.[29] While Europe was riddled by competing nationalisms coexisting uneasily within artificial boundaries, Russia was extending its empire by granting minorities real economic and political power within a federal system of quasi-independent nations called the Union of Soviet Socialist Republics.[30] Even if still dominated by Russia, neighboring countries willingly abandoned sovereign statehood in return for the benefits of rapid industrialization, mass literacy and education campaigns, and the suppression of former parasitic elites.[31]

Thus, in the immediate postwar period, an ideological battle raged throughout Europe and the rest of the world. Two rival systems vied for power: Anglo-American liberal democracy globalized as the League of Nations and Soviet communism embodied in the Communist International. Both offered a vision of human freedom but through vastly different means, with liberalism promoting incremental, politico-legal reform while communism advocated revolutionary change. At the time, the outcome of this battle was in doubt: "Soviet communism claimed to be an alternative and superior system to capitalism, and one destined by history to triumph over it. For much of this period, even those who rejected its claims to superiority were far from convinced that it might not triumph."[32]

These political battles cannot be compared to the tame, almost ritualized skirmishes between right and left parties in the modern era, especially since the disintegration of the Soviet system.[33] This was politics as war, a fight for control of government by capturing the allegiance of the masses that had newly entered the political arena. World War I had effected an unprecedented mobilization as millions were conscripted into armies and channeled into economic production. The 1920s continued this popular upheaval; millions of citizens gained literacy and education for the first time, millions of workers were inducted into the ranks of industry and organized into labor associations, and millions of women earned the vote. Political parties battled for the support of these constituencies through grand ideological programs that promised change on a global scale.

While the liberal European states had the lion's share of political, economic, and military power, communism held wide appeal during this period of socioeconomic dislocation. The postwar popularity of communist ideology was so threatening to liberal European governments that they ruthlessly suppressed local leftist parties. In established and new states alike, communist parties were outlawed or suppressed; their leaders were harassed, jailed, and assassinated; their funding sources were cut off; and their organizations were penetrated by agents and provocateurs.[34] When communists briefly took power in Hungary and Bavaria in 1919, the rest of Europe united to topple them through a combination of diplomatic pressure and direct military intervention.[35] This systematic crackdown was largely successful in reversing the growing strength of communist parties in Europe and breaking their ability to win political power. But it had an unintended consequence: the rise of fascism, which moved into the political vacuum with a rapidity that stunned its ideological rivals.

Rise of Fascism

Several liberal governments, German, Italy, and Spain in particular, sealed their own fates by making anticommunist alliances with the very fascist parties that eventually dethroned them. Fascist parties won support from the mass base that had once gravitated toward the left, often using similar rhetoric, describing the struggle for political power as a fight for national survival that would culminate in a victory of historic proportions.[36] The ascendance of the totalitarian right was so rapid and unforeseen that within a decade it was threatening to eclipse both liberal democracy and revolutionary communism.

Fascism was the most Eurocentric of the grand ideologies, simultaneously deriding U.S. consumer capitalism and Russian communism. With remarkable success, fascists espoused a specifically European superiority regarding race, history, and destiny. As one historian comments: "National Socialism, in particular, fits into the mainstream not only of German but also of European history far more comfortably than most people like to admit. . . . Its revolutionary rhetoric masked greater continuities of ideas and institutions with the past."[37]

Belief in European superiority and privilege was not peculiar to fascism but was shared by leading liberal thinkers as well. As a useful comparison to Nazi rhetoric, consider the following private communication from Winston Churchill to his foreign secretary on 21 October 1942, just as the Soviet Red Army was turning the tide against the German invasion after suffering horrific losses. With Allied victory seemingly secure if still far off, Churchill expressed hope for "the revival of the glory of Europe, the parent continent of the modern nations and of civilization. It would be a measureless disaster if Russian barbarism overlaid the culture and independence of the ancient states of Europe."[38]

The rise of fascism was facilitated not only by the suppression of the left but also by the dramatic failures of liberalism and its philosophy of individual rights. During the 1920s and 1930s, a string of ineffectual democracies across Europe were paralyzed by petty political infighting and appeared incapable of delivering political stability or economic prosperity to their populations. Parliaments were plagued by factionalism and dominated by splinter parties, which proliferated under systems of proportional representation. In 1930, sixteen parties secured seats in the Reichstag, and nineteen were successful in the 1929 Czech elections.[39] Because of political infighting, governments rose and fell with astonishing regularity while the business of government remained undone. During the 1920s, the pinnacle of the era of parliamentary democracy, most European cabinets lasted less than a year before being replaced by equally short-lived successors. In Germany, Austria, and France, the average cabinet lasted for eight months, in Italy five, and in Spain four.[40] Naturally this political instability impeded the effective working of governments and undermined public confidence in democratic politics. Hans Kelsen, the eminent Austrian jurist whose philosophy of legal positivism provided the theoretical underpinnings for constitutional democracy, spoke gravely at the time of "the crisis of the parliamentary system."[41]

The most common response of liberal parties to the threat of fascism was to adopt the authoritarian tactics of the right while retaining the façade of constitutional legitimacy. In Germany, Austria, and other formal democracies, governments preferred to rule unilaterally through the executive branch by invoking extraordinary constitutional powers rather than working through fractious parliaments to pass necessary legislation. It became increasingly common throughout Europe to circumvent parliament altogether and rule by executive decree, thereby implicitly rejecting liberal rights as the basis for governance. In the German Weimar Republic of 1932, for example, just before the Nazi Party won a plurality of the popular vote, the government issued fifty-nine emergency decrees while passing just five laws by parliamentary means.[42] The authoritarian mode of politics was thus already well entrenched in liberal Germany even before Hitler assumed power.

Especially after the 1929 global Depression, fascist parties appealed to masses of Europeans who were discouraged by declining socioeconomic conditions and the inability of their democratic parliaments to alleviate social conditions. One historian summarizes this sweeping trend to the political right:

> A world economic crisis of unprecedented depth brought even the strongest capitalist economies to their knees and seemed to reverse the creation of a single world economy, which had been so remarkable an achievement of nineteenth century liberal capitalism. Even the U.S.A., safe from war and revolution, seemed close to collapse. While the economy tottered, the institutions of liberal democracy virtually disappeared between 1917 and 1942 from all but a fringe of Europe and parts of North America and Australasia, as fascism and its satellite authoritarian movements and regimes advanced.[43]

Still more fearful of the waning threat of communism than the rising power of the right, weakened liberal and centrist parties were willing to shore up their support by joining ranks with increasingly popular fascist parties.[44] These coalition governments moved steadily toward totalitarianism without a forceful public reaction. The first fascist European government, headed by Benito Mussolini in 1923, was possible only in coalition with the main liberal party in Italy. As with Hitler, Mussolini rode into power by democratic means, until the laws could be changed and the system rigged to further strengthen the executive at the expense of parliament.[45] The constitutional system in Italy, as in many other countries, was rife with corruption and incompetence, leading many citizens to favor the discipline of the totalitarian state, which looked with disdain at individual rights. In 1933, Mussolini wrote: "One should not exaggerate the importance of Liberalism in the last century and make of it a religion for all present and future times when in reality it was one of the many doctrines of that century. . . . The present century is a century of authority, a century of the right, a Fascist century."[46]

On the eve of World War II, fascism had already begun to eclipse Europe's weakened parliamentary democracies. Germany, with Austrian and Italian support, dominated Europe politically and economically, as Japan did the Asia-Pacific region. Their authority was based not on a few fanatical individuals adept at manipulating the levers of power but on an enormous base of mobilized popular support that swept into power well-organized political machines. The masses exulted in an unabashed celebration of collective destiny that promised glory to the strong nations and races.

Fascist politics and ideology were by no means confined to these few powers; the idea of the totalitarian state was gaining popularity throughout Europe and its colonies, even in Britain and the United States, where a "realist" U.S. diplomat like George Kennan could see "greater possibilities for good in benevolent despotism" and suggested that the United States travel "along the road which leads through constitutional changes to the authoritarian state."[47] Fascism was not an abrogation of European ideals but an intensification of genuinely populist strands of racism and communalism, promising a form of egalitarian social justice to those inside the system while delivering conquest and subjugation for those outside. It was the popularity of these ideas as much as Germany's growing military power that threatened the whole of Europe:

> Its construction of a racial-nationalist welfare system simply pushed to extremes tendencies visible in European thought more generally and it held power in Europe's most technologically advanced economy. This is why it is the Third Reich [not the Soviet Union] which posed the most serious challenge to liberal democracy this century, and why an analysis of the changing content of European democratic thought and practice means acknowledging the very real possibility that emerged in the late 1930s of a continent organized along Nazi lines.[48]

Fascism challenged liberal principles of self-determination and sovereign equality, arguing, with obvious justification, that these formal legal concepts masked the realities of repression and inequality. In response to this critique, human rights advocates acknowledged liberal hypocrisies of the interwar years yet argued that the answer was more freedom, not less; they insisted that the League of Nations failed because it paid lip service to rights instead of seeking to implement them. A true human rights regime, in their view, required political support and legal authority, especially practical enforcement of core principles such as freedom and equality.

In contrast, Nazis celebrated inequality as an illustration of the Darwinian struggle of competing races to dominate the riches of the earth.[49] They argued that the double standards of the international rights framework were part and parcel of the natural order and unabashedly dismissed the bourgeois idea of individual rights in favor of the communal duty of service to blood, race, and nation. Jews were an ideal scapegoat in this ideological system, blamed by the Nazis for the betrayal of World War I and the rise of both international capitalism and international Bolshevism.[50] Hence Jews were portrayed as racially and ideologically alien to the German nation, a treacherous threat to the purity of the *Volk.*

It should not be forgotten that fascism was primarily a positive ideology that appealed to a shared sense of strength, ethics, and honor based upon service to the community. Under fascism, individual members of a community were mobilized through an idealized version of one destiny by one will under one leader, as opposed to the egoistic self-interest of bourgeois liberalism that set each man against his compatriots: "Against liberalism's glorification of the selfish individual they [fascists] proposed the spirit of self-sacrifice, obedience and communal duty."[51]

If many outside Germany were seduced by this vision, it is attributable equally to the failure of liberal democracy to deliver economic benefits or political leadership and the success of fascism in achieving both. It is undeniable that during the interwar period, the most enviable records of growth and stability belonged to authoritarian regimes. The Soviet Union was widely viewed as an economic success compared to moribund Europe, transforming Russia and surrounding countries from peasant societies to an industrial powerhouse. Japan also built power based on chauvinistic authoritarian nationalism and had a militarized economy to rival any in Europe.[52] And with Britain's waning power and weakening grip over its far-flung empire, Germany and Italy were seen as Europe's most successful and dynamic states.

Their political and economic weakness rendered it more difficult for liberal European states to mount an ideological counterattack against Nazism, even though international morality appeared to be the weak point in the totalitarian armor, given the explicit threat to subjugate most of the world's population under the rule of a handful of powerful nations. However, the only clear-cut liberal success story in political and economic terms, the United States, was widely disdained across Europe for its unbridled individualism and crass commercialism. For their part, U.S. residents remained indifferent to the looming war; Congress passed the Neutrality Laws of 1935–1937 to insulate the United States from direct involvement in Europe's internecine conflicts.[53]

Keeping Human Rights Alive

The idea of human rights did not fade away completely, even during the interwar decades when governments undermined public faith in the efficacy of liberal rights and ceded ideological ground to fascism. But given the failures of the system of group rights established at the League of Nations and the subsequent ideological weakness of liberal states, it fell to prominent jurists, public intellectuals, and legal associations to preserve and further develop the idea of international human rights. An impressive array of these thinkers, many of them veterans of peace conferences at The Hague and Paris, continued to advance the cause of universal rights for all people as the only hope for saving humanity from the scourge of war and the threat of totalitarian ideologies.[54] The connections and cross-fertilization of ideas that had taken place at these conferences coalesced around a shared vision of codifying human rights as enforceable international law.

The main human rights ideas discussed and accepted at Paris had focused on the rights of groups rather than individuals. In the context of national struggles for sovereign independence and the burning issue of equality between races and nations, it is understandable that human rights ideas came to be seen as synonymous with self-determination, minority rights, and racial equality.[55] The rights of workers and women were also conceived of largely in collective terms, deriving momentum from the labor and suffragist movements that championed them at the political level. Moreover, both communism and fascism exalted the concept of duty to class and nation above that of individual rights. To the extent that individual rights were held to have universal validity in the reigning liberal paradigm, they were understood as domestic rights—civil-political liberties and, occasionally, socioeconomic guarantees to be effectuated through constitutions within the framework of democratic governance.

During this period, the idea that later became central in the human rights regime established by the United Nations—that all individuals, regardless of status and place of birth, had inherent rights that must be recognized and protected at the international level—was put forward by scholars and activists largely outside mainstream political discourse. One of the first and most prominent of these pioneers was Chilean diplomat and intellectual leader Alejandro Alvarez. Influenced by juridical Pan-Americanism, Alvarez participated in the Paris conference, was a co-founder and secretary-general of the American Institute of International Law, was nominated for the 1932 Nobel Peace Prize, and eventually served ten years as a judge at the International Court of Justice upon its founding in 1946.[56] In 1917 he wrote a draft declaration on principles of international law for the American Law Institute that included a section titled "International Rights of the Individual," a detailed listing of universal human rights enjoyed by all people and applicable to all states.[57] The rights enumerated covered traditional civil and political rights to life, speech, religion, and political participation.

Human Rights Pioneers

Perhaps the most prolific and active proponent of human rights during these years was Andre Mandelstam, an international lawyer who once headed the legal office of the Russian Foreign Ministry before fleeing to Paris in exile after the Bolshevik revolution.[58] His passion for human rights derived not only from opposition to communist repression in Russia but also from outrage over the Armenian genocide, which he witnessed first hand as a diplomat posted to Turkey in 1915.[59] In 1921, he proposed a set of legal mechanisms for the protection of minorities in particular and human rights in general as rapporteur of a commission established by the International Law Institute in 1921. In Paris, he acted as a magnet for like-minded international lawyers, who gathered there and wrote articles and established organizations to promote human rights. One protégé, a Russian émigré law professor named Boris Mirkine-Guetzevitch, published a survey of human rights provisions in various constitutions and wrote in favor of international human rights treaties.[60] Another, Antoine Frangulis, Greek representative to the League of Nations until fleeing his country after the military takeover in 1922, teamed up with other prominent jurists, including Alvarez and Colonel House, former adviser to President Wilson at Paris, to establish the International Diplomatic Academy in 1926.[61]

This academy, along with the International Law Institute and a host of other legal associations, adopted resolutions and declarations aimed at establishing binding human rights at the international level. Mandelstam himself drafted the most prominent of these efforts after consulting "the teachings of the most qualified publicists."[62] The "Declaration of the International Rights of Man" included a preamble and six articles enumerating the right to life; liberty; property; education; nondiscrimination on the basis of nationality, race, gender, religion, language, and economic activities; and the freedom to practice the religion and use the language one chose.[63] It also posed a direct challenge to the state monopoly on determining just treatment of citizens by emphasizing the need to establish binding and enforceable limitations on sovereignty for the purpose of protecting individual rights.

Mandelstam energetically publicized the declaration and gained the support of prominent legal associations such as the Institut de Droit International, the International Law Institute, the International Diplomatic Academy, and the Carnegie Endowment for International Peace as well as noted individual diplomats and jurists including, among others, James T. Shotwell, U.S. delegate to the Paris conference and later the San Francisco conference; prominent French jurists George Scelle and René Brunet; and Belgian Henri Rolin, future president of the European Court of Human Rights.[64] The declaration was adopted by the Fédération Internationale des Droits de l'Homme, a French human rights federation founded at a 1922 meeting of fourteen human rights advocates from across Europe, Latin America, and China. A modified version of the declaration, with fourteen articles emphasizing social and economic rights as well as civil and political rights, was put forward in July 1936 by another French-based human rights organization, the Ligue pour la Défense des Droits de l'Homme, whose leader after World War II, René Cassin, played an important role in drafting the Universal Declaration of Human Rights.[65] Once again, the drafters declared that state immunity for human rights abuses was no longer acceptable: "The international protection of human rights must be universally organized and guaranteed in such a manner that no state can deny the exercise of these rights to any human being living on its territory."[66]

The Global Crusade of H. G. Wells

The honor of launching the most remarkable, quixotic, and influential of the prewar campaigns to revive the human rights idea belongs to Herbert George Wells, the famous British author. At the age of seventy-three, H. G. Wells took it upon himself not only to draft a bill of human rights but also to enlist some of the world's most notable intellectuals to review and contribute to the text. Wells had the bill of rights translated into more than thirty languages (literally all European languages as well as Chinese, Japanese, Arabic, Urdu, Hindi, Bengali, Gujarati, Hausa, Swahili, Yoruba, and Esperanto) and solicited reactions from the world's leading political figures, a list of presidents and prime ministers that included many of those who would have a formative influence on the Universal Declaration of Human Rights—Franklin Delano Roosevelt, Jan Christiaan Smuts of South Africa, Jan Masaryk and Eduard Benes of Czechoslovakia, Mohandas Gandhi and Jawaharlal Nehru of India, and Chaim Weizman of Israel, among others.[67]

Wells had grown increasingly discouraged by the lack of effective response to the forward march of fascism throughout the 1930s. At frequent public lectures, he urged audiences to become "enlightened Nazis" by matching the ardor, willpower, and sacrifice of their political foes.[68] Recognizing the gravity of the ideological battle for hearts and minds, Wells, a committed social democrat, insisted that "the necessity for restating the democratic ideal is the most fundamental question for us all just now." His most bitter attacks were reserved for British prime minister Neville Chamberlain and his coterie of liberals, whom he accused of "a string of incredible blunders" based on their fervent desire to ignore the German threat in order to "go back to their golf links or the fishing stream and doze by the fire after dinner."[69]

Once the war actually started, Wells began to feverishly promote the idea of an enforceable universal code of rights to serve as the basis of postwar security. To ensure support for this enormous undertaking, Wells formed a blue-ribbon drafting committee that included Lord Ritchie Calder, later director of Plans of Political Warfare in the Foreign Office; Lord Lytton, former viceroy of India and leader of the Conservative Party; Viscount Sankey, former lord chancellor of the House of Lords and a member of Frangulis's International Diplomatic Academy; Margaret Bondfield, a prominent Labour Party politician; John Orr, future director-general of the Food and Agriculture Organization (FAO); Norman Angell, recipient of the 1933 Nobel Peace Prize; and a number of eminent professionals.[70]

Wells published an initial draft of "The Declaration of Rights" in the *Times* of London on 23 October 1939.[71] The declaration consisted of a short preamble and ten articles covering a comprehensive list of social, economic, civil, and political rights: the right to food and medical care; the right to education and access to information; the right to work; the right to free discussion, association, worship, and movement; and the right to protection from violence and intimidation. In an accompanying letter to the *Times*, he recalled the British tradition of overcoming political crises by defending and expanding human rights:

> At various crises in the history of our communities, beginning with the Magna Carta and going through various Bills of Rights, Declarations of the Rights of Man and so forth, it has been our custom to produce a specific declaration of the broad principles on which our public and social life is based. . . . The present time seems peculiarly suitable for such a statement of the spirit with which we face life in general and the present combat in particular. . . . I think this statement may serve to put the War Aims discussion upon a new and more hopeful footing.[72]

The draft declaration was continuously revised as comments poured in from the famous and ordinary alike. During February 1940, the *Daily Herald* of London published sections of the final draft daily in serialized form, with comments from distinguished public figures worldwide. Large public meetings were held in Britain to promote the declaration; tens of thousands of copies were distributed internationally. According to Lord Ritchie Calder, who served as secretary of the drafting group, discussion of Wells's proposal took place in twenty-nine countries; it was attacked on the front page of Mussolini's daily paper and derided for an entire week in the radio addresses of Joseph Goebbels, Hitler's propaganda minister.[73] After Wells caused a political controversy by publicly attacking Prime Minister Chamberlain and Foreign Minister Lord Halifax, leading to the resignation of several members of the drafting committee, formal chairmanship of the committee was handed over to Lord Sankey and the document became known as the "Sankey Declaration."[74] However, once Germany opened its military offensive on the western front in May 1940, British public interest in the declaration subsided, though it continued to be discussed and debated in intellectual and legal circles outside Britain.

Losing the Battle of Ideas

The committed advocacy efforts of Wells, Mandelstam, and other intellectuals and jurists eventually helped lay the groundwork for the establishment of international human rights. However, in their own time, they remained on the margins of political discourse, dismissed by intellectual circles and ignored by the leading liberal states despite the mortal threat—ideological as well as military—fascism posed. Only when human rights were taken up during the war as part of an ideological offensive by the Allied coalition, in particular the United States under Roosevelt's leadership, did the issue begin to be taken seriously as a basis for planning the postwar order.

That human rights advocates in the prewar period were essentially acting as voices in the wilderness is illustrated by the dearth of references to human rights even in the works of forward-thinking intellectuals. A 1940 edited volume of essays on freedom by Europe's leading intellectuals, including Benedetto Croce, Jacques Maritain, Albert Einstein, and Harold Laski, did not even mention the term "human rights"; in contrast, a similar exercise commissioned by the United Nations Economic, Social and Cultural Organization (UNESCO) in 1947, with many of the same contributors, focused exclusively on human rights.[75] Reviewing the intellectual and diplomatic output in Europe during the 1930s, one legal historian was surprised to discover the negligible role human rights played: "I found that the wish to set positive concepts against right wing and left wing totalitarian ideologies was a characteristic trend indeed of the intellectual climate of that period, but this trend was expressed mostly in terms of freedom and democracy and almost never in a reassertion of the human rights idea itself."[76]

Even the role of democracy and its organic link to formal constitutional rights was subject to question. The interwar experiment in democratic rights had been such a failure and the attack from fascism so withering and relentless that few were willing to defend the old ways. As leader of the Free French, General Charles de Gaulle recognized that "the mass of the French people confuse the word democracy with the parliamentary regime as it operated in France before the war. . . . That regime has been condemned by events and by public opinion."[77] Former French premier Leon Blum concurred: "A weak and perverted bourgeois democracy has collapsed and must be replaced with an energetic and competent democracy, popular instead of capitalist, strong instead of weak."[78]

By the late 1930s, when military conflict seemed inevitable and principles of liberal democracy and universal political rights were on the brink of defeat, many intellectuals despaired of the ideological weakness of the liberal order. To these intellectuals, the refusal to engage with Nazi propaganda meant that "there is no recognition of the war of ideas or of the social revolution through which we are living."[79] Democracy was "effete and worn-out," as even a champion of the stature of British economist John Maynard Keynes acknowledged: "The positive argument for being a Liberal was very weak."[80]

Waiting for World War

Unable to stem the rising tide of racism and military aggression, the League of Nations could only watch as the borders of its liberal world order began to crumble. By 1932, even a committed internationalist like U.S. president Franklin D. Roosevelt, once a supporter of the League, would dismiss the organization as "a mere meeting place for the political discussion of strictly European political national difficulties."[81] Mistreatment of German minorities in Eastern Europe was the cutting edge used to dismember the fragile international system. Germany insisted on redrawing national boundaries to incorporate its disenfranchised minorities and gain "breathing space" for the Aryan nation.[82] James G. McDonald, League of Nations High Commissioner for Refugees, who was responsible for resettling German Jews in Palestine, quit when the organization refused to challenge Nazi racial policy.[83] With no effective international organization or collective security system to defend Europe's borders and check German ambitions, it was only a matter of time before the League's house of cards came tumbling down.

The onset of World War II marked the definitive demise of the League of Nations and the brief ascendancy of liberal rights in the interwar years. Its vision of collective security, ostensibly based on constitutional protections for individual rights and international protection of national and group rights, had been flawed from inception, dependent on double standards that would increasingly be exposed as the fascists rose to power. Had the League been able to fulfill some level of commitment to protect minority rights in the new states and increase self-determination through the mandates, its authority might have developed over time. The umbrella of its rights might have expanded toward universal application, much as the coverage of the U.S. Constitution grew over time to encompass previously excluded groups without changing its underlying legal and political principles.

But with the early defection of the United States from the League, the indifference and disunity of the European powers, the parliamentary crises across continental Europe, and the growing power of a resentful Germany—not to mention the disappointment of Japan and China, the competing power of the Soviet Union, and the growing revolt in Europe's colonies—the League was never able to establish the authority and will to enforce its vision of liberal international rights. Lacking a system of collective security to check the rising ambitions of ideologically fueled nationalisms, the world would soon be thrown back into the cauldron of war.

3

The Human Rights Crusade in World War II

- The Catastrophe of War
- Planning an American Peace
- The Declaration of the United Nations
- The Proliferation of U.S. Human Rights Initiatives
- European Visions of Social Rights
- The State Department Bill of International Rights
- State Sovereignty or Human Rights?
- Conclusions

International rights in general and human rights in particular appeared to be dead letters on the eve of World War II. The failure of the interwar democratic regimes was so profound that democracy had become a pejorative term, a synonym for inefficiency in governance and lack of conviction in personality. There were no popular liberal alternatives to the discredited system of international rights established by the failed League of Nations. The countries of Europe were consumed in various stages of chauvinistic nationalism and were preparing for the ruthless mechanized war that Hitler was about to unleash on the continent. Non-European nations were preoccupied with maintaining their independence or winning it in war against the imperialist powers; Asian nationalist movements initially welcomed the Japanese blitzkrieg against their European masters. Only in the United States and Latin America, with their relative isolation from the conflicts raging across the Atlantic and Pacific oceans, did human rights ideas continue to be discussed and promoted as a positive program to replace the excesses of unlimited sovereignty in the nation-state system.

As so often before in human history, ideas of peace and justice were born out of war and destruction. U.S. president Roosevelt in particular played a critical role in rallying public opinion, at home and abroad. His speech to Congress setting forth the Four Freedoms—freedom of thought, freedom of worship, freedom from want, and freedom from fear—was a direct ideological response to Nazi tyranny and a bid for his version of U.S. values to shape the postwar order. Even before the United States joined the war, Roosevelt had instructed the State Department to develop the blueprint for the future United Nations. The Four Freedoms appealed to intellectuals and mass movements across the globe as a middle ground between the selfish individualism of prewar laissez-faire capitalism and the brutal collectivism of both communist and fascist mass mobilization. Once human rights rhetoric was introduced into international discourse—albeit as a propaganda weapon against the Axis powers—it quickly developed into a powerful ideological current in the Americas, across Europe, and throughout the colonies in Asia and Africa. As was the case after World War I, the ultimate content of the human rights framework was shaped by the conflict between public demands for genuine legal protections and state reluctance to extend human rights beyond wartime rhetoric.

The Catastrophe of War

World War II was the most cataclysmic conflict in history. The sheer magnitude of destruction was previously unimaginable, even compared to the horrors of World War I. Rapid advances in modern mechanized military technology had transformed war, erasing the distinction between civilian and soldier through the widespread use, for the first time, of aerial bombardment and long-range artillery. While the belligerents promised to restrict bombing of civilian areas, terror bombing designed to break the popular will to fight and maximize civilian casualties soon became the order of the day, practiced by all sides with increasing ferocity.[1] The failure of states to set any lawful humanitarian limits on war and weapons at the Hague conferences and subsequent international gatherings had come back to haunt governments and especially their populations. Vast armies marched across Europe, Asia, and Africa; ancient cities were bombed and blitzed; countries were occupied, their governments toppled and replaced. Hundreds of millions of workers and soldiers were mobilized. Though impossible to calculate with any certainty, it is commonly estimated that up to 50 million people—a majority of them civilians, up to half of them from the Soviet Union alone—were killed in the slaughterhouse of global war.[2]

Today we take for granted the total victory of the Allied powers, but at the time the future of democratic government had never been dimmer. It was clear that a new international order would again be constructed from the ruins and ashes of world war, but it was less clear who would be the victors and therefore which ideology would be ascendant. As Germany swept across

Europe and Japan swept across the Pacific, it must have seemed to many that the ideological, political, and economic triumphs of totalitarianism would soon be followed by its military triumph.

The position of Britain as a hegemonic power was precarious. Developments in aerial warfare and naval invasion had undercut the protective geographic barrier of the English Channel. The island homeland itself was vulnerable to attack, let alone the farther reaches of the British empire. Once it became evident that the states of continental Europe would be unable to withstand the German blitzkrieg, Britain's position as the sole Allied power left standing became untenable. This was especially true in the period before Germany broke the nonaggression pact with the Soviet Union and launched its ill-fated invasion to the East in June 1941, and before Roosevelt was able to maneuver the United States into war in response to the Japanese bombing of Pearl Harbor in December 1941.

While the British policy of appeasement has been derided for failing to understand and take seriously the nature of German military intentions, it was equally responsible for ceding the moral high ground to fascist ideology by abdicating the fight in the war of ideas. For years, British intellectuals and public figures had urged the government to take a more proactive ideological position by making a positive case for "what we are fighting for." This failure seemed especially unforgivable given the natural repugnance many millions of people around the world felt for the fascist ideology of racial superiority and master-slave relations. It was well understood that under a totalitarian order, popular yearnings for freedom, in terms of both national self-determination and human rights, would be brutally suppressed.

Launching an effective ideological counterattack aimed at gaining global backing for the war against fascism was therefore a matter of national survival for Britain. One of the chosen vehicles for this attack was human rights. While the call for human rights had originated with prominent jurists and intellectuals, the Allies eventually, and belatedly, took it up in recognition of its ideological power to mobilize support for the war effort. Rather than simply expressing an antifascist position, human rights offered a positive vision to those who deplored race-based nationalism and militarism but were also dissatisfied with the weakness and hypocrisy of the interwar liberal order. For states fighting Germany, human rights became a cornerstone of their appeal for allies and military support.

Prime Minister Churchill had already made freedom the buzzword for opposition to the Nazi Thousand Year Reich. To this foundation he added human rights. In 1939, Churchill proclaimed that the war was being fought "to establish, on impregnable rocks, the rights of the individual."[3] But it was

President Roosevelt who laid the ideological groundwork for the human rights regime. When the Allied counterattack in the war of ideas finally began to pick up steam, it was the United States that took the lead. And later, when it came time to establish the basis for the postwar world order, it was again the United States that set the agenda and determined the (limited) extent to which human rights would serve as its moral and legal foundation.

Planning an American Peace

The United States began planning for what would become the United Nations in 1939, well before entering, let alone helping the Allies win, the world war. The extraordinary influence of the United States in shaping nearly every aspect of the UN can be attributed to these preparations as well as to the dominant military and economic position the United States enjoyed after World War II. Initial planning focused on economic and security relations with Europe on the assumption that there would be a negotiated peace between Britain and Germany that would leave Hitler in control of much of Europe; only after the United States entered the war did total victory and unconditional surrender become the twin goals of U.S. war policy.[4] Roosevelt kept most of this preparatory work for the United Nations under cover and instructed his staff to withhold information even from key allies such as Britain.[5]

The U.S. near-monopoly on postwar planning was due to its own vast resources and to its distance from the ravages of war. While the U.S. government was able to operate in relative isolation from the battlefield, the other two ultimately victorious powers, the Soviet Union and Britain, were from the very onset of war involved in titanic struggles for national survival that consumed nearly all their human and economic resources. They were simply unable to devote the time, energy, and manpower required to match the U.S. effort in the field of postwar planning. One historian noted that the British official in charge of the postwar reconstruction office "ploughed at first a somewhat lonely furrow . . . since many Foreign Office officials thought that the immediate priority was to win the war, not dream dreams of the peace."[6]

It has long been part of historical myth that the United Nations was a truly global undertaking, developed through discussions and consultations not only between the great powers but all the Allied nations fighting World War II. Recent scholarship has demonstrated that, on the contrary, the global organization was to a remarkable degree planned, designed, and brought to life through the efforts of the United States, acting almost alone.[7] In fact, two U.S. diplomats, whose names remain little known outside of specialized circles, share responsibility for drafting most of the provisions of the Dumbarton Oaks proposals and the United Nations Charter itself.

Sumner Welles: Forgotten Architect of the UN

In late 1939, Roosevelt instructed Under-Secretary of State Sumner Welles, a close personal friend since childhood, to establish the Division of Social Research, a postwar planning department. Welles had a reputation as a progressive internationalist and frequently clashed with conservative isolationists in the foreign policy establishment. Among the Washington press corps, he was considered aloof and arrogant and was given the nickname "Mr. Icicle."[8] His reputation as Roosevelt's handpicked advisor also earned him the unofficial title of "chief administrative officer of U.S. foreign policy"—much to the displeasure of U.S. secretary of state Cordell Hull.[9] At the same time, Welles was hard-nosed about protecting U.S. interests. As assistant secretary of state for Latin America in 1933, he visited Cuba to fulfill Roosevelt's directive to crush a popular revolution and install the Fulgencio Batista dictatorship.[10] C. D. O'Sullivan, one of Welles's biographers, has noted, "Despite his oratory about freedom and individual rights, he supported and worked closely with authoritarian regimes throughout his career, readily accepting them so long as they did not interfere with American interests."[11]

In the lead-up to war and during the war itself, Welles acted as Roosevelt's public voice, urging the spread of U.S. values to the larger world. As O'Sullivan observed, "To many it seemed that Roosevelt had given Welles the task of defining why Americans fought and of preparing the country for its preeminent role in the peace."[12] In public addresses throughout the country, Welles stressed the themes of human rights, economic opportunity, and anticolonialism:

> Of two things I am unalterably convinced: First, that the abolition of offensive armaments and the limitation and reduction of defensive armaments and of the tools which make the construction of such armament possible can only be undertaken through some rigid form of international supervision and control. . . . Second, that no peace which may be made in the future would be valid or lasting unless it established fully and adequately the natural rights of all peoples to equal economic enjoyment. So long as any one people or any one government possesses a monopoly over natural resources or raw materials which are needed by all peoples, there can be no basis for a world order based on justice and peace.[13]

Through these speeches, Welles became as popular with media and civil society groups as he was unpopular with bureaucratic rivals fighting for the president's ear.[14] Hull and other foreign policy conservatives were suspicious of such rhetoric and misunderstood its underlying motivation and rationale. Welles, who was more realpolitik than utopian, recognized earlier than most of his fellow diplomats how U.S. military power could clear the way for global economic dominance based on an ideology of freedom, not just for individuals and nations but also in commercial relations.[15] His vision of a new world order, based upon free markets and republican institutions under a U.S. security umbrella, was rooted in moral persuasion rather than military coercion.[16] O'Sullivan notes, "Prior to the attack on Pearl Harbor, he publicly called for the United States to lead the way toward an internationalist future where world markets would be free, trade barriers nonexistent, and colonialism and economic nationalism unnecessary."[17] With Roosevelt's full support, Welles couched U.S. interests in the language of universal values in order to enhance their appeal both inside and outside U.S. borders:

> He had calculated that the war effort would be better sustained by moral arguments than appeals to self-interest. While he understood that his vision of the postwar order would allow American commerce to flourish alongside universal ideals and values, he used idealistic rhetoric because he assumed the American people would be more willing to sacrifice for ideals that they believed were consistent with their deepest moral, religious and political convictions. . . . The quasi-religious over-tones of Welles's wartime utterances made many of his public addresses sound like sermons, casting an aura of spiritual and moral zeal around what otherwise might have sounded like nothing more than a call to American nationalism.[18]

Hull did not appreciate being displaced by his ostensible subordinate in the foreign policy hierarchy, and as a counterweight to Welles appointed his longtime advisor Leo Pasvolsky to direct research for the State Department's postwar planning division. A Russian-born economist with a deep skepticism of "soft" international law concepts such as human rights, Pasvolsky was a tenacious bureaucratic infighter with an encyclopedic retention of detail. Referred to as "the brain that walked like a man," he was loyal to Hull and could be counted on to keep an eye on Welles, whose direct access to Roosevelt Hull bitterly resented.[19] As one historian notes, "Pasvolsky was the perfect public servant for Hull, endowed with a sharp analytical talent, a non-confrontational but principled personality, a library-like mind on global issues, a faith in free trade, and a passion to remain invisible."[20]

Hull also established a bipartisan blue-ribbon advisory panel to consult with the postwar planning division. The panel consisted of top government officials, such as Dean Acheson, who was later secretary of state under President Dwight D. Eisenhower; and Republican senator Arthur Vandenberg, later a key member of the U.S. delegation in San Francisco; as well as editors of leading opinion-making publications such as the *New York Times* and *Foreign Affairs*.[21] While the panel only met four times before disbanding, it nevertheless served the function of bringing key political and media elites into the secret circle of postwar planning. This was consistent with Roosevelt's strategy for avoiding a repeat of the debacle following World War I, when the United States rejected the League of Nations and withdrew from global leadership.

Hull was too preoccupied with wartime diplomacy and his own failing health to play a significant part in the postwar planning division. While Pasvolsky ran the day-to-day operations, Welles was its driving intellectual force. However, his centrality as the architect of a new world order came to a sudden and abrupt end in August 1943, when Hull engineered his resignation by threatening to go public with unsavory details of Welles's alleged homosexual acts.[22] His political career was over, and his contribution to the UN soon forgotten.[23] However, Welles accomplished a great deal during his brief tenure at the planning division. He commissioned a wealth of reports on the main issues facing the new organization, from membership to structure to security enforcement. He also prepared the first draft of the UN Charter largely on his own, based upon the old League of Nations structure of council, assembly, secretariat, and court. He discussed the draft with Roosevelt and British foreign minister Anthony Eden, winning their approval of key points.[24] Many of his ideas and even phrases would be retained in the final UN Charter approved at San Francisco.

Edward Stettinius, who replaced Welles as under-secretary, essentially turned the entire postwar planning operation over to Pasvolsky, who established and staffed a number of expert committees to draft preparatory materials for the new organization. Pasvolsky also set to work amending those sections of Welles's draft Charter that Hull found objectionable. While retaining most of the substantive and procedural details and the overall structure of the organization, Pasvolsky made several changes that Roosevelt later approved. First, he did away with the "regional principle." Welles had favored the establishment of regional representation on the council as well as recognition of separate councils in Europe, Asia, and the Americas, partly in deference to Churchill and Stalin, who both wanted explicit approval for their regional spheres of influence. Hull and Pasvolsky felt that a universal and centralized organization would best suit U.S. designs to establish global hegemony. Second, he stripped the assembly of any role in security matters, a holdover from the League of Nations structure that allowed for some areas of joint security responsibility between the council and assembly. Third, he expanded the council from four to eleven members while retaining the veto of the great powers, thereby reducing the appearance of a "dictatorship of four." Senator Tom Connally, chair of the Senate Foreign Relations Committee, wrote of Pasvolsky's efforts: "Certainly he had more to do with writing the framework of the charter than anyone else."[25]

FDR and the Four Freedoms

While secret postwar planning gathered momentum in the State Department, it remained confined behind closed doors. Roosevelt recognized the need to engage in the public debate over war and peace and shape the global agenda along U.S. lines. His bold foray into the war of ideas is considered one of the strategic masterpieces of his presidency.

In the annual address to Congress on 6 January 1941, almost a year before declaring war on Japan, Roosevelt announced his vision of security based on four freedoms—freedom of speech and expression, freedom of worship, freedom from want, and freedom from fear.[26] This far-ranging and ambitious speech accomplished many things at once. It was both a specific defense of his New Deal policies and a broad vision of universal justice; it was an attack on fascism and an argument for war; it promoted a liberal ideology based on an expanded notion of freedom that explicitly incorporated economic rights; and it laid the ground for both the U.S. welfare state and the international human rights regime.[27] In effect, the Four Freedoms speech represented Roosevelt's intellectual defense of his presidential legacy and a powerful argument for U.S. leadership not only during the war itself but also in the shaping of the postwar international order.

The New Deal had fundamentally altered the state's role in relation to the well-being of its citizens by establishing a system of public responsibility to provide individuals with entitlements to unemployment compensation, social security, and other matters of general welfare. As a result of the Great Depression, these radical reforms had broad popular support, reflected in Roosevelt's electoral success, yet they still faced significant obstacles from the business and legal elite. The Supreme Court had frequently overturned New Deal legislation as unconstitutional based on a very narrow interpretation of negative liberty embodied in the doctrine of "freedom of contract," which precluded an active government role in providing for the common welfare.[28]

Having succeeded in overcoming domestic political and legal objections, Roosevelt declared the Four Freedoms in order to entrench his vision of economic justice in U.S. society.[29] At the same time, he aimed the message at the international community from which the United States had been largely disengaged since the debacle of the League of Nations. Roosevelt had already decided to enter the war and harbored ambitions for America's role in shaping and controlling a new global organization. But "any grand design for US global dominance had to address one fundamental problem: how to structure American domestic politics for such an external role."[30] The answer was to globalize the New Deal and establish the United States as a superpower on ideological grounds even before its economic and military might became fully apparent to its own population and the world at large.

The idea of four freedoms marked an innovation in U.S. political and legal discourse. The first two freedoms were central to the constitutional tradition of negative freedom, based on the right of the individual to self-expression without restriction by state power. Freedom from want and fear, on the other hand, represented a new vision of positive freedom, a departure from the U.S. ethic of rugged individualism and unrestrained capitalism—although still a far cry from socialist state planning.[31] Roosevelt declared that freedom from want was meant to "secure to every nation a healthy peacetime life for its inhabitants" and freedom from fear "a world-wide reduction of armaments to such a point and in such a thorough fashion that no nation will be in a position to commit an act of physical aggression against a neighbor."[32] The principles Roosevelt declared were a forceful summation of the ideological arguments against fascism and communism, linking individual political rights and broader social rights together within a common framework and tying the survival of independent nations to the development of a shared system of collective security based on a larger vision of human freedom.

Roosevelt emphasized that the supreme objective of security could not be gained by military power alone but only through the political, economic, and social development of free citizens. Freedom from fear therefore required a commitment to public welfare as well as international peace. In this vision, human rights and security were not merely interdependent but identical—alternative ways of describing the aspirations and interrelationships of all people. Raising high hopes among civil society and human rights advocates, Roosevelt stated, "Freedom means the supremacy of human rights everywhere. Our support goes to those who struggle to gain those rights or keep them."[33] By situating the war in Europe as a clash between rights and repression, freedom and tyranny, Roosevelt found his essential justification, indeed his imperative for taking sides in the great conflict raging across the Atlantic. In this way, human rights were made the centerpiece of the U.S. argument for both war and peace.

While the United States was officially neutral, Roosevelt had already been laying the ground for America to enter the war by becoming the "arsenal" for the British and Russian militaries. Desperate to pull the United States out of isolationism, he had already adopted a policy of open support for the British, working closely with Churchill to present a united front against Germany. It would be another year before the United States declared war on Japan and Germany, and then only after the devastating Japanese attack on Pearl Harbor. But in the meantime, Roosevelt kept himself busy by building the case for America to enter yet another war to make the world safe for democracy.

The Four Freedoms speech has become famous as a cornerstone of the human rights project at the United Nations, but it is important to recall that Roosevelt was advocating justice through war. To overcome widespread domestic resistance, Roosevelt mustered his impressive powers of persuasion to paint the dangers of totalitarianism and offer a positive vision of universal rights. By raising public hopes for human rights as the basis of the postwar order, Roosevelt seemed to be threatening the sacred cow of state sovereignty and engaging in the same overstatement that thirty years earlier had complicated Wilson's vision of the League of Nations.[34] Unlike Wilson, however, Roosevelt took care to initiate planning for the postwar order well before the end was in sight, working both unilaterally and with close allies to flesh out the contours of a new global organization dominated by the great powers, the United States above all.

Human Rights in the Atlantic Charter

Britain responded positively to the U.S. human rights initiative, albeit cautiously given her intention to maintain a postwar colonial empire. Foreign Secretary Anthony Eden publicly associated the Churchill government with Roosevelt's Four Freedoms, stating, "We have found in President Roosevelt's message to Congress in January 1941 the keynote of our own purpose."[35] Former foreign secretary Halifax, by then ambassador to the United States, fleshed out the British position in a white paper submitted to the War Aims Committee, in which he explicitly defined and endorsed human rights:

> For all men the right to speak, write and think freely within the law and to have access to the thoughts of others; the right of free association, both national and international, with their fellow men; the right to live without fear of aggression, injustice or want; the right to believe and worship as conscience may dictate. It is the vindication of these rights that all men passionately desire . . . the principal war aim of my people and of those who are fighting with us is to win this life and death struggle for the cause of human freedom.[36]

It was against this backdrop that Roosevelt and Churchill met on August 1941 in Argentia Bay, Newfoundland, shuttling between the British battleship *Prince of Wales* and the U.S. cruiser *Augusta*.[37] Their purpose was to exert Anglo-American leadership in both developing a united front against the Axis powers and plotting a blueprint for the postwar order. The document they proposed, known as the Atlantic Charter, constituted an eight-point declaration of war strategies and peace goals. Originally an understanding between two countries, it was deliberately drafted as a declaration rather than a treaty to encourage other governments to sign on without the additional burden of involving national parliaments and acceding to international law.

The Charter underwent numerous revisions during negotiations between Roosevelt and Churchill and their two principal deputies, Welles and Alexander Cadogan, permanent under-secretary at the Foreign Office. The main bones of contention were, first, U.S. insistence on declaring the Charter to be in favor of free trade, which Churchill rejected as an impingement on the system of trade preferences within the British empire, and, second, British interest in declaring the eventual establishment of a new organization to replace the League, which Roosevelt rejected as premature (while continuing with the secret postwar planning at the State Department).[38]

It should be noted that during these and other wartime negotiations, Britain and the United States clashed over U.S. proposals for the self-determination of colonized peoples and for international free trade, which the British suspected, quite rightly, were covers for the U.S. agenda of dismantling the remains of European empires and establishing in their place a collection of nominally independent states subservient to U.S. economic and military power.[39] Churchill once remarked "I am not going to accept less favorable terms . . . than I could get from Hitler"; while the British secretary of state for India expressed a preference for Hitler's "New Order" rather than Hull's "Free Trade."[40] Welles himself was very clear that anticolonialism was a fundamental question of U.S. commercial interests:

> Welles resolved to stretch the meaning of the Atlantic Charter to ensure that the imperial powers would not seek a return to the status quo at the end of the war. . . . He also assumed that the United States stood to gain from any weakening of the colonial economic systems because it would enable the U.S. to obtain valuable raw materials as well as offering new potential markets and opportunities to extend its free trade regime.[41]

In the end, Roosevelt and Churchill agreed on vague but stirring language focused primarily on the battle for democracy and freedom and the need for total victory against the forces of tyranny. The British Foreign Office was unimpressed with the results, describing the Atlantic Charter as "a terrible woolly document full of all the old clichés of the League of Nations period. . . . However I think it will go down well in America where they like resounding phrases and also in Liberal and Labour circles here."[42]

The final document made no mention of individual rights or human rights per se, a surprising omission in light of its reputation as a founding document of the coming human rights system. The Charter referenced only "freedom from fear" in the sixth clause and "the rights of all peoples" to choose their governments and "sovereign rights" in the third clause. This latter reference became subject to disputing interpretations by the United States, which saw in it a general right to self-determination in line with an anticolonial position, whereas Britain insisted that it referred only to self-determination for nations under Nazi tyranny, and certainly not to its own dominions.

A number of the other nations that were invited to sign the Atlantic Charter criticized the lack of any positive mention of human rights, especially given public pronouncements in favor of such rights from both Roosevelt and Churchill. Representing the Free French, René Cassin objected to the failure to reference human rights, stating: "The French also consider it as necessary to the establishment of a real peace the practical ratification of the essential liberties of man."[43] Roosevelt fudged the issue, at one point falsely claiming that "the declaration of principles includes of necessity the world need for freedom of religion and freedom of information."[44]

The Declaration of the United Nations

After the United States entered the war in December 1941, Roosevelt sought to restate the Allied war aims by means of a new global declaration. Before sending the declaration to other nations for approval, Roosevelt proposed a change that would alter the ideological terms of the debate. To widen the appeal beyond the two original powers and their close military allies, he substituted the term "United Nations" for that of "Associated Powers." Churchill appreciated the rhetorical power of this semantic change, invoking Byron's Childe Harold: "Here, where the sword united nations drew / Our countrymen were warring on that day! / And this is much—and all—which will not pass away."[45]

The United Nations Declaration of 1 January 1942 was even more explicit than the Atlantic Charter in seeking to rally international support against the Axis powers. It was essentially a call for allies to join the fight. Human rights were mentioned directly for the first time, though only once, in the preamble, and even there in the context of the larger goal of military victory:

> Being convinced that complete victory over their enemies is essential to decent life, liberty, independence and religious freedoms, and to *preserve human rights and justice in their own lands as well as in other lands,* and that they are now engaged in a common struggle against savage and brutal forces seeking to subjugate the world. (emphasis added)[46]

The declaration was an extraordinarily successful appeal at the diplomatic level, the first step in assembling a grand coalition that would form the basis for the postwar international organization. Twenty-six nations signed the declaration, including the governments-in-exile of Nazi-occupied Europe, pledging to fight together against "tyranny, cruelty, and serfdom." This marked the first time the countries that would eventually constitute the United Nations took any form of collective action. By signing the declaration, they agreed to commit their full resources to the crusade against the Axis powers and refrain from signing a separate peace until total victory was achieved. Roosevelt, who rejected any idea that states were equal, insisted that the Big Four sign before other nations, in presumed order of importance—the United States, the United Kingdom, the Soviet Union, and China.[47]

The declaration's focus on human rights was clearly subordinate to its purpose of establishing a united war front; human rights were mentioned in the conservative sense of a cause to be preserved rather than rights to be extended to new areas. This phrase could hardly have inspired those whose basic complaint was the lack of human rights protection throughout the world, including within the Allied states. Two of the Four Freedoms, freedom from want and fear, were reaffirmed in clause six as an essential foundation for domestic peace and international security without mention of any mechanism to achieve these goals. The declaration also recognized the need to uphold "sovereign rights and self-government."[48] However, this phrase fell short of declaring the principle of self-determination for all peoples and furthermore left open the interpretation of whether sovereign rights of imperialist nations would continue to trump non-European aspirations for independence.

Anglo-American Double Standards

For both the U.S. and British governments, the contradictions between principled rhetoric and practical policies were quite stark. On the one hand, they were responsible for introducing human rights into the center of international discourse, even if primarily as a propaganda weapon. As one historian notes, leaders from both countries continually "emphasized the need for exorcising the Fascist and Nazi tyranny and safeguarding human rights in the peace settlement."[49] In his annual message to Congress the year after his Four Freedoms speech, Roosevelt stated that in the battle between good and evil, "only total victory can reward the champions of tolerance and decency, and freedom, and faith."[50]

On the other hand, neither power showed any willingness to alter its own policies to fulfill human rights principles. The British had no intention of dismantling their colonial empire. Churchill told Parliament that the self-determination clause did not apply to India, Burma, or to any other country within the British empire, only to European nations occupied by the Nazis.[51] India was allowed to sign the declaration as a nation but not as an independent state. In the United States, where blacks lived under racist laws and oppressive practices, government propaganda and popular media quickly termed the war in the Pacific "the Yellow Race against the White Race." Soon after the United Nations Declaration was announced to the world, Roosevelt signed an executive order forcibly removing U.S. citizens of Japanese descent from their homes to mass detention camps, a policy upheld by the Supreme Court in its infamous decision, *Korematsu v. United States*.[52]

Double standards notwithstanding, the Atlantic Charter and its follow-up United Nations Declaration marked the official entry of human rights per se into the international discourse of states. Specific aspects of what would become the human rights framework had already been the subject of negotiations and treaties, notably humanitarian law principles at The Hague and labor and minority rights at the League of Nations. Nevertheless, it was an innovation for states to expressly recognize the larger idea of human rights, especially the need to protect human dignity from state abuse and the centrality of the individual as the bearer of international rights. Perhaps no one in the U.S. or UK governments seriously thought that one innocuous phrase in a nonbinding preamble to a war declaration would provide the impetus for the complex and far-reaching human rights system eventually established through the United Nations.

One historian of human rights argues, on the basis of an exacting reading of diplomatic history, that civil society subsequently exaggerated the role of human rights in great-power calculations, in effect "rewriting history" to reflect a liberal, rights-based ideology.

> The Charter contains not the least hint of any commitment to the international protection of human rights. U.S. thinking, developed out of the Charter, placed primary emphasis on securing freedom of want by establishing a better economic system. The Charter acquired its significance in the history of human rights retrospectively by the rewriting of history.[53]

This complaint is technically accurate but nonetheless misses the mark. History is not comprised solely of government instructions, diplomatic cables, and international texts. Popular expectations and actions also make history, in dynamic interaction with state politics. In this instance, the rhetorical sponsorship of human rights by powerful states, however half-hearted or even duplicitous, gave new impetus to civil society efforts, just as these efforts had pushed states to adopt human rights ideas in the first place. The mutual cycle of alternating reinforcement and suspicion between governments and civil society actors would continue to play a major role in shaping the human rights regime over the years.

The Proliferation of U.S. Human Rights Initiatives

Given that Anglo-American governmental support for human rights was largely an outgrowth of realpolitik and great-power interests, it was inevitable that the Atlantic Charter and the United Nations Declaration would be viewed with disappointment by progressive civil society forces.[54] The mere acknowledgement of human rights as a legitimate concern by the presumed architects of the postwar order galvanized nascent discussions among legal, religious, and social justice circles. This resulted in a veritable explosion of private efforts to draft bills of human rights, especially in the United States, encouraged by the inclusion of prominent NGOs and activists in State Department deliberations on human rights.

This chain of cause and effect provides another illustration of the law of unintended consequences. Popular enthusiasm for human rights was so deep that the mere acknowledgement of the concept by the great powers was sufficient to unleash a wave of private human rights initiatives. While the U.S. and UK governments certainly intended to mobilize popular support for their war and peace aims, they did not intend to be bound and constrained by such hopes and expectations. But they had raised high the banner of human rights, and it would now be difficult to put it down without a public backlash. At the same time, the sudden enthusiasm for human rights confirmed the ideological power of the leading states to shape global political discourse. Just as government neglect of human rights during the interwar years had consigned private initiatives to the margins of international politics, notwithstanding the tireless work of a handful of individuals, so too government promotion of human rights during the war catalyzed activists and scholars to put their ideas forward in an organized fashion and provided an outlet for their hopes of a better future than a world at war.

Jewish groups played a prominent role in these private efforts, spurred not only by a legacy of grievance against state abuse but also by a dawning awareness of the extent of Nazi atrocities. These efforts focused, in addition to promoting Zionism, on securing traditional liberties such as equality before the law, freedom of religion and expression, and guarantees for minority rights. The American Jewish Committee (AJC), founded in 1906 "to prevent the infraction of the civil and religious rights of Jews, in any part of the world," produced a report recommending, above all other concerns, effective enforcement of human rights against the demands of state sovereignty, pointing to the failures of implementation that had doomed the minority rights system after World War I.[55] Two prominent members of the AJC, former appellate judge Joseph M. Proskauer and philanthropist Jacob Blaustein, later played important roles as NGO delegates at the San Francisco conference. The U.S. chapter of the World Jewish Congress adopted by resolution an international bill of rights that included sections on the protection of life and liberty and equality before the law for all religions, ethnic and cultural groups, and citizens of every country.[56] In January 1943, soon after official confirmation of Nazi Germany's genocidal policy toward the Jews of Europe, a new organization of the AJC was established as an umbrella group for existing Jewish organizations. At its first meeting, the group expressed "hope that a world order based on the Four Freedoms and the Atlantic Charter will also find its expression in an International Bill of Rights" that would provide real protection from violations for all individuals.[57]

Established international law and policy organizations were also very active in promoting the human rights idea. The Commission to Study the Organization of Peace and the American Law Institute played leading roles, no doubt in part because they both participated in the State Department's legal subcommittee responsible for drafting a bill of human rights for the United Nations. Under the leadership of James T. Shotwell and the sponsorship of the Carnegie Endowment, the organization commissioned a number of papers and reports that examined issues of international governance, state sovereignty, and human rights.[58] In 1943, the commission released a report on "Human Rights and the World Order," authored by political scientist Quincy Wright. Wright argued that the sacred cow of nationalism was ruining civilization and that human rights needed to be protected across borders irrespective of state sovereignty.[59] He also recommended establishing a world court with jurisdiction over national governments to enforce a bill of rights, an idea that had been proposed in 1920 by Austrian jurist Hans Kelsen.[60]

The American Law Institute prepared an influential private draft of an international bill of rights. William Draper Lewis, the institute's director since its creation in 1923, established a panel of twenty-four prominent legal advisors, representing thirteen cultures; its goals were "to ascertain to what extent the liberal elements of the major cultures have similar ideas of human rights; and to ascertain how these rights on which all can unite can be expressed in a manner acceptable to their different traditions and cultures."[61] It was soon discovered that the cultures, or rather the individuals involved, could not unite and instead split into two camps. One, led by Ricardo J. Alfaro, former president of Panama, put forth a minimalist conception of traditional liberal rights; the other insisted on a broad new charter of social justice.[62] The dispute was resolved through a compromise in which both conceptions of rights were incorporated into a single document. The first ten articles focused on traditional freedoms and the last five on the rights to education, work, food, housing, and social security.[63] The drafting process for the Universal Declaration of Human Rights would later engender similar disputes and result in a similar outcome—incorporating all rights into one document while the drafters agreed to disagree.

These were among the most prominent of a diverse array of U.S.-based initiatives to discuss, formulate, and promote international bills of human rights. The Christian ecumenical movement also mobilized its members to participate in building a new international order with human rights as its moral foundation. John Foster Dulles, later President Eisenhower's secretary of state, and O. Frederick Nolde of the Federal Council of Churches were both significant forces in educating U.S. residents to support the United Nations and its human rights system.[64] Academics were also active, presenting a consensus international bill of rights from forty-six faculty groups after a series of independent discussion panels in colleges and universities throughout the country.[65] Under the leadership of Manley O. Hudson, a consultation of 196 U.S. and Canadian lawyers, academics, and officials—including John Foster Dulles; John P. Humphrey, future head of the UN's Human Rights Division; Hans Kelsen; Robert H. Jackson, Supreme Court Justice and later chief prosecutor at the Nuremberg Trials; Roscoe Pound, dean of Harvard Law School; and a host of other familiar figures on the human rights circuit such as Draper Lewis, Ricardo Alfaro, and Quincy Wright—published proposals for international law and an "organization of the Community of States" that gave a general assembly legislative power in international law and an executive council "general power to deal with any matter of concern," although state sovereignty was also to be respected.[66]

All of these efforts grappled with the vexing problem of defining the substantive content of human rights by attempting to reconcile the competing claims of various cultures and the different legal traditions of liberal and social rights—within the predominant tradition of the United States. But despite disagreement over the specific provisions that might be included in a bill of human rights, there was widespread consensus that human rights should form the moral and legal foundation of the new international order and, more important, that the traditional prerogatives of state sovereignty must give way to the demands of human rights enforcement and protection. The carnage of World War II drove home the point that there had to be a universal law above the brute force of national authority. Perhaps the most remarkable aspect of this human rights consensus is that it developed so rapidly over a period of several years after decades of neglect and inaction.

European Visions of Social Rights

Europeans did not experience a similar outpouring of enthusiasm for discussing and drafting international charters of human rights—probably because they were too preoccupied with fighting and surviving the world war. Instead they focused on developing a new, empowered vision of democracy and rights as both a war strategy and a solution to the postwar order. In part this was in response to the success of fascism and communism in mobilizing the masses on socioeconomic issues and the corresponding failure of liberal ideas to do so. Democratic rights on paper were clearly seen as insufficient without a popular national will to give them practical effect. Alva Myrdal of Sweden wrote, "Political freedom and formal equality will not be enough; real democracy, social and economic democracy, will be expected."[67] In a similar vein, British historian E. H. Carr decried the empty form of democracy that recognizes "the right to vote but forgets the right to work and the right to live."[68] Some, like French philosopher Jacques Maritain, argued that social responsibility was an individual duty as well as a right; he published the first book-length treatment of human rights, though it was concerned more with Catholic moral philosophy and social theory than with the legalisms that characterized the debate in the United States.[69]

The most thorough treatment of human rights was that offered by Hersch Lauterpacht, Whewell Professor of International Law at Cambridge University and one of the most distinguished international lawyers at the time.[70] Lauterpacht's interest in human rights was given added urgency after the Nazis killed his entire family, save one niece. He first proposed an International Bill of the Rights of Man in a 1943 article for the Grotius Society, taking his cue from Churchill's declaration that "the enthronement of the rights of man is one of the major purposes of the war."[71] He expanded this treatment into a full-length book divided into two parts: the first contained an exhaustive review of the historical and philosophical development of the idea of inalienable natural rights, the second a bill of rights with detailed commentary on each of its twenty articles.[72] These articles covered three main subjects: traditional civil and political liberties; state duties to provide, within their means, the right to work, health care, education, and social security; and, crucially, measures of implementation and enforcement. Lauterpacht wanted to create a legal instrument with definite and enforceable rights and duties apportioned clearly between states and citizens. Rather than proposing an international court with universal jurisdiction, he preferred these rights to be incorporated directly into the law and constitution of every nation, with an international monitoring body to review state practice.[73] In addition to his writings, Lauterpacht participated in several conferences and meetings in the United States where he criticized human rights initiatives that failed to propose a binding system of legal guarantees and internationally supervised domestic protections.

Economic Planning and Human Rights

The acceptance of social and economic rights by a prominent liberal jurist such as Lauterpacht demonstrated the changed mood throughout Europe. State planning, once considered the domain of Soviet bureaucrats and Nazi ideologues, became a standard part of Allied social and economic policies during the war. State intervention was critical in channeling the economy toward the war effort. German and Japanese success in economic planning had inclined many in liberal Europe toward a similar model. Britain, the bellwether of prewar laissez-faire, provides a telling example of this sudden turnabout. Starting with the crucial and life-saving public intervention of the government rationing system, staunchly capitalist Britain inevitably turned to state-controlled economic planning during the war, much to the delight of Keynes and his fellow welfare economists.

When asked by the British war office in 1940 to rebut Nazi propaganda broadcasts on the success of their economic model, Keynes had flatly refused, arguing that "in my opinion, three quarters of the passages quoted from the German broadcasts would be quite excellent if the name Great Britain were substituted for Germany. . . . It is just what we ourselves ought to be thinking of doing."[74] He did agree, however, to develop research and policy briefs on Britain's economic future, producing memos that advocated full-employment policies and constructing the first official national income statistics. This work led to government white papers on full employment and a national health service and laid the groundwork for the transformation of British socioeconomic policy after the war from laissez-faire toward a welfare state. Keynes was also responsible for a 1941 proposal to set up an international clearing union that induced the British government to enter into the Bretton Woods negotiations of 1944, out of which arose an agreement to establish the International Monetary Fund and the International Bank for Reconstruction and Development, the World Bank.[75]

Another key convert to social democracy was William Beveridge, formerly a loud critic of welfare capitalism. Asked by the government to undertake a technical assessment of social insurance, he came away from studying the Soviet war economy convinced that Britain needed to undertake similar measures: "I would very much like to see communism tried under democratic conditions."[76] Beveridge became an energetic champion of social security and employment policies within the finance and economic divisions of the British government. These moves toward Keynesian economics heralded the development of a new postwar economic consensus in Europe: "Post-war capitalism . . . was a sort of marriage between economic liberalism and social democracy (or, in U.S. terms, Rooseveltian New Deal policy), with substantial borrowings from the U.S.S.R, which had pioneered the idea of economic planning."[77] While postwar European economies were not modeled along the lines of the Soviet Gosplan, there were increasing similarities between the two models.

The convergence of legal theory and economic policy toward a welfare model of social democracy demonstrated a remarkable consensus after decades of bitter ideological struggle—almost as remarkable as the bizarre and short-lived political and military alliance of western democracy and Soviet communism.[78] One historian has argued that human rights and welfare economics represented conflicting tendencies of individualism and collectivism during these years:

> If one tendency in wartime thought was to stress the evils of pre-war economic individualism and laissez-faire and the need for greater state intervention in the interests of social harmony, another was to argue that the struggle against Hitler had revealed the importance of human and civil rights. In the legal and political sphere, in other words, the trend was to reassert the primacy of the individual vis-à-vis the state. The wartime rehabilitation and redefinition of democracy moved between these poles.[79]

However, it seems evident that at this particular moment, individual rights and social welfare were seen throughout the world as complementary rather than competitive values, such that everyone could be guaranteed a certain level of well-being as a right. Certainly this is the direction toward which human rights advocates were moving, even in the more traditional Anglo-American jurisdictions. The tensions between individual and group conceptions of rights or between political and social conceptions that would come to bedevil the human rights project during the Cold War and escalate into full-blown ideological confrontation were not yet apparent. Instead, there was a remarkable consensus on a holistic vision interlinking individual human rights with generalized socioeconomic welfare.

The State Department Bill of International Rights

Roosevelt was a hard-nosed pragmatist who believed that the victorious great powers were entitled to dominate the new organization, with the United States playing the leading role.[80] In planning for the United Nations, he instructed the State Department to develop human rights ideas as part of the blueprint for the new international organization but to support rather than challenge his intended global hierarchy.[81] He was also a former navy man and an enthusiastic proponent of exercising military power to enhance America's global economic position. As assistant secretary of the navy in 1914, Roosevelt had declared himself in favor of military expansionism: "Our national defense must extend all over the western hemisphere, must embrace the Philippines and over the seas wherever our commerce may be."[82] He viewed human rights as supporting his vision of free trade in a liberalized global economy, in part as a means to enable the United States to break the British and European monopoly of protectionist trade with dependent territories. This explains the enthusiastic support of the U.S. business community for Roosevelt's global aspirations, despite sharp previous differences with him over domestic New Deal policies. As Peter Gowan has noted, "What this bipartisan coalition of big capital wanted from Roosevelt was an assurance that international expansion would be in safe hands from the point of view of American business."[83]

A legal subcommittee within the postwar planning division was given responsibility for developing the human rights framework for the new organization. The State Department's best legal minds were seconded to serve on the subcommittee, including Green Hackworth, legal advisor to the State Department; Benjamin Cohen, Roosevelt's personal legal advisor; Durward Sandifer, later legal advisor to Eleanor Roosevelt during her tenure as chair of the Commission on Human Rights; Harley Notter, later legal advisor on UN affairs at the State Department; and Alice McDiarmid, who would play an important role at the 1945 San Francisco conference. The legal subcommittee also included James Shotwell, the veteran diplomat from the Paris Peace Conference now affiliated with the Carnegie Endowment for International Peace, and representatives from two NGOs, the Commission to Study the Organization of Peace and the American Law Institute, both of which were actively promoting versions of an international bill of rights in civil society circles.[84] This overlap between the State Department and NGOs was part of a deliberate and extremely successful strategy to bring civil society on board at the outset in support of the postwar arrangements.

Sumner Welles and the legal subcommittee had to reconcile a number of contradictions inherent in the task of drafting an international bill of rights. First was the need to project universal values in a global organization explicitly dominated by great-power politics. Second was the need to emphasize individual liberty and freedom of trade within a global drift toward social democracy and equality. And third was the need to safeguard state sovereignty within the context of powerful public pressures, especially in the United States, for meaningful enforcement of human rights.

As a result of these tensions, the State Department effort barely mentioned economic and social rights, despite Roosevelt's much-publicized call for freedom from want. It drew entirely on sources from U.S. and western legal traditions: the U.S. Bill of Rights, the English Bill of Rights, the French Declaration of the Rights of Man and the Citizen, and various constitutional protections.[85] In addition, Welles and his team referred to the declaration developed by the Institute of International Law—originally drafted by Mandelstam—which included some social rights alongside traditional political liberties and judicial guarantees; for example, the guarantee of equality before the law with respect to employment, education, and social security. The State Department's 1942 declaration ultimately included sixteen articles that were weighted heavily in favor of due process and judicial rights, though mention was also made of rights to minimum standards of social welfare.[86]

Once the declaration was finalized, there was debate within the legal subcommittee on the issue of enforcement. The essential clash was between Welles, who favored some weak form of implementation measures in the United Nations to ensure U.S. moral leadership and provide a tool for intervention in other states, and Hull, who opposed any mention of enforcement on grounds of state sovereignty and was not prepared to undermine U.S. power in the name of soft principles of human rights.

State Sovereignty or Human Rights?

Human rights scholars and activists had long warned that without the imposition of concrete obligations on states, declarations and agreements would remain mere words on paper. Yet just as nongovernmental actors insisted, almost with one voice, that sovereign limitations were indispensable to the effective enforcement of human rights worldwide, governmental representatives, especially those from great powers, were loath to permit any encroachment on sovereign prerogatives. The attitude taken by the United States, the primary architect of the postwar global regime, was no exception and would prove decisive for the emerging human rights system.

The issue of state sovereignty posed a direct challenge and dilemma for the State Department legal subcommittee tasked with addressing human rights issues in postwar planning. While members had been able to reach agreement on the content of rights in drafting the 1942 declaration, they differed significantly about the proper means of enforcement, if any.[87] Secretary of State Hull and several key advisors, especially Pasvolsky, had great difficulty reconciling a legal instrument on human rights with the imperatives of state sovereignty and domestic jurisdiction.[88] This was, of course, a valid concern; binding international law is meant to limit sovereign freedom of action.

The legal subcommittee discussed and debated the question of how to assign responsibility for violations of human rights under several practical scenarios.[89] Since much of the U.S. and British wartime rhetoric about preventing human rights abuses concerned the need to deter tyranny and avoid war, the international body responsible for collective security needed the coercive power to prevent human rights violations in the first place. On the other hand, for violations of a socioeconomic nature, such as extreme poverty, the key responsibility for the international organization would be to bring about humanitarian cooperation rather than forcefully impose solutions. Finally, for addressing individual grievances against the state, there needed to be a system for reviewing petitions and adjudicating claims. Yet any mechanism for enforcement, even one limited to mandating economic cooperation, would inevitably infringe upon a state's domestic jurisdiction—a point the various private initiatives concerned with human rights protection emphasized repeatedly.

The subcommittee was split between those who favored some means of enforcement, albeit limited, and those who rejected the concept out of hand. The first camp recommended that measures of implementation should be either included within the declaration itself or appended to it as an integral annex, with some even suggesting that entrance into the new organization of states be conditioned on signing an international bill of rights.[90] On the other side of the debate, it was argued that human rights should under no circumstances be given express means of legal enforcement at the international level but rather should be issued in the form of a declaration of nonbinding principles to guide and inspire nations to voluntarily incorporate such principles in their domestic legal frameworks. The debate was summarized in a confidential State Department memo:

> The arguments in favor of an international bill of rights are that (1) it would promise individuals security and freedom, which are basic human desires of direct concern to everyone; (2) it would constitute a barrier to doctrines of state supremacy and racial superiority which are inimical to individual rights; (3) by establishing a universal standard it might prevent complaints by one state against another or dissatisfaction by nationals who felt that citizens of other states fared better; (4) it might help create conditions of tranquility and well-being which are basic to international peace; (5) it would eliminate any necessity for protecting special groups, especially minorities.
>
> The arguments against a bill of rights are that (1) it would lack the juridical basis on which national bills of rights are founded, for there is no international sovereignty or true international government to grant or enforce individual rights; (2) it would mark the extension of international influence into a field which has traditionally been regarded as domestic; (3) it might make the protection of individual rights paramount to the safety of the state; (4) it would be very difficult to enforce.[91]

Closing the Door on Enforcement

The possibility that the United States, under the influence of public opinion and in response to the horrors of the world war, might seek to impose meaningful human rights limitations on states was of great concern to the British Foreign Office, especially where the colonies were concerned. One official warned:

> It seems evident that ideas connected with a "Bill of Rights" for individuals and groups occupy a prominent place at the moment in American liberal thinking.... Echoes of them appear to haunt the pronouncements of Mr. Hull and Mr. Welles on colonial and minority problems. There are only faint signs that the real difficulties in these proposals have been understood, viz. that they involve . . . a degree of interference with municipal law that no State, and certainly no Great Power, is likely to tolerate. It is hard to imagine the US "recognizing the rights of individuals" e.g. Negroes in the South "to petition the United Nations Commission on Human Rights" to obtain redress.[92]

As it happens, British fears that the State Department was not cognizant of the dangers human rights enforcement posed to U.S. interests were entirely unfounded. Durward Sandifer, a legal specialist who would later advise Mrs. Roosevelt, recommended a way out of the sovereignty dilemma: agree (with great fanfare) to human rights principles without accepting coercive enforcement measures, judicial review of any kind, or even specific language that might eventually give rise to concrete obligations. By this method, strong states could still promote human rights in foreign policy, pressuring other states to respect the same, without themselves being bound to take any action against interests. In a classified document, he wrote: "It is a device used many times in the past. States agree on the adoption of new rules of law or formulation of existing rules and proclaim them to the world in a formal international agreement. Reliance is placed primarily upon the good faith of the contracting parties."[93]

While there is no record that this was the approach formally adopted by the State Department and the U.S. government, the circumstantial evidence is rather strong. In the first place, the idea of a bill of rights appended to the UN Charter was dropped from U.S. proposals at both Dumbarton Oaks and San Francisco. Moreover, Sandifer himself acted as primary advisor to Mrs. Roosevelt, who, as chair of the Commission on Human Rights, would play a critical role in stripping the Universal Declaration of Human Rights of any implementation measures and limiting its scope to hortatory principles. Finally, Sandifer's suggestion had the bureaucratic virtue of corresponding to the views of his boss, Cordell Hull. Referring in unmistakable terms to the minor role being contemplated for human rights at the United Nations, the secretary of state warned that "no nation should interfere in the domestic affairs of another, that the colonial powers should not be forced to dismantle their empires too precipitously, that the proposed United Nations organization should not be given too much power, and that the doctrine of national sovereignty should not be sacrificed on any altar of human rights."[94]

Conclusions

Once again, history seemed to be repeating itself in equal parts tragedy and farce. With the existence of liberal democracy under mortal threat, the Allied powers had called for an ideological crusade to defeat the evil enemy, based on widespread popular convictions of human dignity and equality embodied in human rights ideas. Their appeal was successful, and nations and individuals joined the fight with great enthusiasm, expecting that through their sacrifices a better world would rise from the unprecedented carnage of modern technological war. Twenty-six countries signed the United Nations Declaration, and people around the world placed their hopes in human rights as a unifying legal and moral framework for the postwar international order.

As in World War I, the success of human rights principles in mobilizing mass support for military victory strengthened their appeal with public constituencies. Civil society actors and small states were more willing and better prepared to fight for human rights than ever before. Especially in the United States, diplomatic, legal, and religious groups engaged in intense public discussions about the best means to effectuate genuine human rights protections across national and cultural boundaries. Reflecting both the bitter experience of the ineffectual League of Nations and the new middle ground created by the grand alliance of western capitalism and Soviet communism, the various efforts came together on two key issues: the need for enforceable legal limitations on state sovereignty and the interdependence of civil-political liberty and socioeconomic security.

Such public discussions and initiatives did not, however, guarantee sufficient political pressure on the great powers to ensure that human rights would be incorporated in a meaningful way into the emerging new world order. The three victorious powers, the United States, Britain, and the Soviet Union, intended to establish a postwar order aligned with their ambitions and interests; enforceable human rights were not on the agenda. The United States, which invested significant resources to plan a United Nations it could dominate and control, envisioned a declaratory role for human rights as the ideological framework for international free trade and democracy but without enforcement mechanisms that might interfere with domestic sovereignty. Britain was willing to go along so long as its colonial interests were not threatened. The Soviet Union was focused on establishing its sphere of influence in Europe and Asia; human rights were of little concern.

Thus, on the eve of the critical negotiations that would establish the shape of the new international order, it was by no means clear whether human rights would have any role to play or whether that role would be substantive or merely rhetorical.

4

Human Rights Politics in the United Nations Charter

- Betrayal at Dumbarton Oaks
- The United Nations and Its Charter
- Conclusions: The American Dream

Betrayal at Dumbarton Oaks

Human rights had served its purpose well, mobilizing public and state support in the war against the Axis powers. The great powers had recognized the ideological value of human rights principles and sparked both public expectations that human rights would be the legal and moral foundation of the postwar order and private initiatives recommending practical measures for achieving this goal. At the same time, the powers had not committed to any specific forms of human rights recognition, protection, or enforcement beyond making stirring rhetorical pronouncements. When it came time for the Big Three—the United States, the United Kingdom, and the Soviet Union—to negotiate concrete postwar arrangements, human rights were summarily dropped from the list of core concerns. At Dumbarton Oaks, during a series of preparatory negotiations for the United Nations between the Big Three, human rights were inserted at the last minute in a single vague reference at the end of the document. Their ultimate resurrection at the United Nations, albeit in a declaratory and nonbinding form, would depend upon an unlikely alliance of western civil society groups, small states, and, crucially, the U.S. government.

A Dictatorship of Great Powers

By the end of 1943, with the tide of war clearly in the Allies' favor, planning for the United Nations between the Big Three began in earnest. Having learned the lessons of World War I, where the victorious powers had failed to reach prior agreements and were often at loggerheads during the Paris Peace Conference, Roosevelt was determined to leave nothing to chance. The United States served as the main organizer for a series of meetings in late 1943 to hammer out the contours of the new world order. These meetings addressed and resolved a number of critical security issues facing the proposed organization; none of them addressed the issue of human rights. Significantly, no states beyond the Big Three were granted access to these negotiations, although the fate of the world, so to speak, was being determined. Never before had so few decided so many fundamental global issues. The result, as one historian of world affairs has remarked, was a global organization completely dominated by the Big Three, centered on "a breathtaking dictatorship by a handful of great powers."[1]

In August 1943, Hull had Pasvolsky draft what became known as the Four Powers Agreement, a set of principles that bound the Big Four, which included China, to work together to establish "a system of general security."[2] These principles, which did not mention human rights, were based on the draft charter prepared by Welles, revised by Pasvolsky, and approved by Roosevelt but not shared with the other powers. On 17 August 1943, Churchill and Roosevelt met in Quebec and agreed to a declaration favoring "establishing at the earliest practical date a general international organization, based on the principle of the sovereignty of all nations."[3] Human rights were not mentioned in the declaration. At Moscow in October 1943, the foreign ministers of Russia, the United States, and Britain and the Chinese ambassador signed a declaration reiterating the need to establish a global organization based not on human rights but on "the principle of sovereign equality of all peace-loving nations."[4] Roosevelt, Stalin, and Churchill met in Teheran on 1 December 1943 to discuss postwar security arrangements; the resulting declaration did not mention human rights.[5]

These critical meetings divided the spoils of victory and forged a peace of great-power hegemony. All other states and civil society groups were excluded from deliberating on the main issues of the day—global security and policing, establishment of national borders and regional spheres of influence, respect for sovereignty and domestic jurisdiction, treatment of defeated nations, disposition of colonies and dependent territories. With no democratic distractions, the Big Three were able to reach agreement on the basic content of the new organization. The Four Policemen—China was added at Roosevelt's insistence—would have sole authority over peace and security as permanent veto-bearing members of a small executive council whose other members would serve brief rotating terms. This made intervention in the domestic affairs of other states subject to the agreement of all great powers on the council. The global organization would be structured along universal centralized lines, although regional groupings were allowed as parallel but not competing formations. Smaller states would play no role in the urgent affairs of the "international community" beyond promoting economic and social cooperation and talking to each other in a general assembly. Human rights, the supposed linchpin of the global crusade against tyranny, were so irrelevant to these great-power negotiations that they simply dropped from the radar screen.

Even after these meetings, a number of issues divided the Big Three that had to be worked out before other countries could be invited to ratify the new world order. The British were resisting U.S. proposals for a trusteeship council, which was intended to have more intrusive supervisory mechanisms than the former system of mandates, to facilitate the eventual independence of colonial territories. The Soviet Union, correctly anticipating that it would be outvoted by the much larger U.S. and European blocs, held firm to an absolute veto over all UN affairs, whereas the United States pushed for a veto on substantive security issues but not on procedural matters. There was also the issue of whether defeated and even neutral nations would be allowed to join the organization. To iron out these remaining details and resolve outstanding conflicts, Roosevelt authorized Hull to make final changes to the draft charter and plan for a major preparatory summit of the Big Three to be held six months later in the United States. In preparation, Pasvolsky, who had been elevated to executive director of the Committee on Postwar Programs, convened seventy meetings of various planning committees to draft the necessary documents and background analyses.[6]

Negotiations between the great powers culminated in a series of meetings between 21 August and 7 October 1944 at Dumbarton Oaks, a former plantation outside Washington, D.C., owned by Harvard University. The talks were conducted at the technical level with foreign affairs experts negotiating the basic agreements, which were to be signed later by their respective foreign ministers. Edward Stettinius, who would soon replace the ailing Hull as secretary of state; Sir Alexander Cadogan, British under-secretary for foreign affairs; and Soviet ambassador to the United States Andrei Gromyko headed the delegations.[7]

The delegations exchanged position papers, but only the United States arrived with detailed policies prepared on every aspect of the organization.[8] The foremost historian of the Dumbarton Oaks meetings has written that Pasvolsky's proposal, "which was by far the most complete and detailed of the three, became—albeit unofficially—the basic frame of reference for building a plan of world organization."[9] At the conclusion of the conference, Hull exulted that "all the essential points in the tentative [U.S.] draft were incorporated in the draft now accepted by the conference."[10]

The negotiations focused on establishing and finalizing details of the principles, procedures, and powers of the organization and its various bodies. Given the scope and complexity of the negotiations, there were remarkably few major disputes, no doubt because many issues had already been agreed in principle and, more fundamentally, because the power structure of the organization was so heavily weighted in favor of the Big Three. The Security Council was given authority over security matters with veto rights for the victorious powers. There was some debate over how these powers would relate to the principle of noninterference in domestic affairs, which was accepted by all present as the basic right of states. The General Assembly, on the other hand, was accorded minimal authority to discuss and debate various social and economic issues. Roosevelt reportedly envisioned this body as meeting once a year for a limited time "to allow all the small nations to blow off steam."[11] Churchill echoed this sentiment later at Yalta,[12] explaining that "The eagle should permit the small birds to sing and care not wherefore they sang."[13]

China joined the talks on 21 September, after most of the important negotiations concerning the structure of the organization had been concluded. The Chinese delegation was represented by Wellington Koo, ambassador to the United Kingdom, who had also participated in the Paris Peace Conference. Throughout the entire series of great-power negotiations, Churchill had bitterly resisted the inclusion of China, recognizing that it would line up with the United States on almost all issues, especially the colonial question. He disparaged China as a lesser power whose participation represented a "faggot vote on the side of the United States in any attempt to liquidate the British overseas Empire," but Roosevelt would not be swayed, insisting on the need to strengthen the government of Chiang Kai-shek against the communist forces of Mao Zedong.[14] Churchill eventually retaliated by insisting that France be given a permanent veto on the Security Council, hoping to encourage the rebuilding of French imperialism and check U.S. designs on Indochina and North Africa.[15]

In any case, the Chinese spent much of the negotiations waiting in their hotel rooms while the Big Three hammered out the various agreements.[16] However, China did offer a proposal "that the principle of equality of all states and races be upheld," partly in response to racist immigration policies in Australia, New Zealand, and the United States.[17] This presented a potentially difficult situation, as the Allied wartime rhetoric on equality, freedom, and human rights would have made rejection of such a clause highly embarrassing. It appears that the Soviets supported the proposal, and even Britain was willing to vote for inclusion.[18] However, the United States, fearing a repeat of the racial equality debacle with Japan at the Paris Peace Conference yet unwilling to risk political opposition in the Senate, persuaded China to drop the proposal before it saw the light of day.[19]

Another potentially troublesome issue was the fate of the colonies. The U.S. position envisioned transferring the mandates to a trusteeship system with stronger international legal protections to ensure self-government and eventual independence. This, of course, did not sit well with the British delegation. A dispute was temporarily avoided only after the United States withdrew the proposal because of concerns the army chiefs of staff expressed that implementation of the principle of self-determination under a trusteeship system might jeopardize plans to establish an extensive network of U.S. bases on annexed and occupied islands in the Pacific.[20]

The two major issues that remained unresolved throughout the Dumbarton Oaks discussions concerned the extent of the veto and individual membership for the Soviet republics. Pasvolsky was dead set against an absolute veto, fearing that the other powers could thereby paralyze the new organization on even minor issues. He first convinced Hull and Roosevelt that a limited veto was in the interest of the United States, given its clear global advantages in economic, political, and moral leadership as compared to Britain or the Soviet Union. Then he convinced his counterparts, Gladwyn Jebb and Arkadei Sobolev, to accept a compromise whereby the veto could only be used on "substantive" issues related to enforcement rather than "procedural" issues of peaceful settlement or general discussion.[21] However, both Stalin and Churchill rejected the limited veto, postponing resolution of the issue until the San Francisco conference. Stalin also insisted that all sixteen Soviet republics be given UN membership to balance the otherwise overwhelming majority of European and U.S. states: "Stalin could see the reality: the membership of the new organization would have a stack of states from the Western hemisphere brigaded under American control and another stack from the British empire, under UK control. So the USSR could easily be isolated on all the bodies and committees of the new organization."[22] Recognizing that this idea could scupper the entire project in the Senate, Roosevelt instructed Stettinius to convey that the Soviet proposal would be seriously considered; meanwhile he would find a way to derail it before it became public.[23] At Yalta he convinced Stalin to accept just two extra General Assembly seats for Ukraine and Byelorussia.

In the end, the basic structure of the United Nations conformed to the

U.S. planning documents. While it was similar to the League of Nations, an even greater share of power was invested in a Security Council of the "Four Policemen" (France was added on 7 May 1945 as a fifth veto-wielding power), with additional members rotating on to provide the appearance of global inclusion. A General Assembly of lesser nations was set up as a talking shop on social and economic cooperation and a number of subagencies to address specialized issues such as food and health, a professional secretariat to manage the organization, and an international court with jurisdiction to handle a limited set of legal disputes were also to be established.[24]

Human Rights as an Afterthought

None of the proposals submitted at Dumbarton Oaks by any of the three powers mentioned the concept of human rights; the work of the State Department's legal subcommittee in preparing a draft bill of rights was not included among the preparatory materials. Once the major issues had been settled, Roosevelt instructed the U.S. delegation to secure recognition for human rights.[25] Benjamin Cohen, Roosevelt's personal advisor and an active member of the State Department's legal subcommittee, was tasked with preparing a draft human rights clause. He was particularly concerned that the absence of human rights would cause a scandal in U.S. civil society in light of Roosevelt's own championing of the concept, not to mention public outrage in response to the Holocaust and other wartime atrocities.[26]

Stettinius dutifully informed Cadogan that "the president attaches the greatest importance to the inclusion in the document of some reference to human rights"—perhaps an exaggeration, given the absence of human rights in previous great-power negotiations.[27] But Cadogan, worried about the impact on British dominions, was unwilling to agree without a corresponding reference to the principle of nonintervention in domestic affairs.[28] Cohen incorporated British concerns, which in any case were shared by Washington and Moscow, into the first draft:

> The International Organization should refrain from intervention in the internal affairs of any state, it being the responsibility of each state to see that conditions prevailing within its jurisdiction do not endanger international peace and security and, to this end, respect the human rights and fundamental freedoms of all its people and to govern in accordance with principles of humanity and justice.[29]

Pasvolsky sought to minimize its significance, explaining that in the absence of any mechanism for international monitoring or supervision, sole responsibility for respecting human rights would fall on each member state as an internal domestic matter. However, Cadogan pointed out that the second phrase on human rights contradicted the first on nonintervention and expressed concern that in the absence of universal agreement on the content and meaning of human rights, criticism might at some point be leveled at any member state; for example, the British empire. Gromyko, the Soviet delegate, opined that "the reference to human rights and basic freedom was not germane to the main task of an international organization."[30] The Soviet government instructed Gromyko to accept the human rights clause but only if fascist states were excluded from membership in the organization, a condition the U.S. and British delegations rejected.[31]

After lengthy negotiations and deliberations, the Soviets relented, but only if the human rights idea was buried out of sight "at the end of the first section of Chapter IX Section A para 1." Chapter IX dealt with "Arrangements for Economic and Social Cooperation," perhaps the fuzziest and least enforceable concept in the entire document. The final agreed-upon text read:

> With a view to the creation of conditions of stability and well-being, which are necessary for peaceful and friendly relations among nations, the Organization should facilitate solutions of international economic, social and other humanitarian problems and *promote respect for human rights and fundamental freedoms.* (emphasis added)[32]

Despite misgivings, Britain also accepted this language. Cadogan explained to his superiors in London: "The Americans pressed very hard for the inclusion of . . . some reference to 'human rights and fundamental freedoms' since otherwise they would be subject to great criticism in the United States." As another British delegate, Gladwyn Jebb, explained to his U.S. counterpart, Alger Hiss, "It would be farcical to give the public the impression that the delegates could not agree to the need to safeguard human rights."[33] From the public point of view, it would indeed have been farcical, yet it also would have been an accurate reflection of the negotiations, which concluded with a pledge to merely "promote" human rights instead of safeguarding them. In the legal lexicon of international agreements, "to promote" is a far weaker term than, for example, to safeguard, to protect, to guarantee, to fulfill, to mandate, or to enforce. Promotion implies little in the way of concrete obligations.

A British historian offers a cynical, albeit realistic, interpretation of the belated insertion of human rights in the Dumbarton Oaks Charter:

> So it was that Roosevelt's wish that the proposals should say something about human rights, combined with the difficulty of finding a form of words which would not encourage trouble-making intervention . . . produced this vague reference to the

subject. It is difficult to believe that Stettinius or Gromyko imagined it was going to make any difference in life. Indeed the aim was to ensure that it did not.[34]

On the other hand, it is also possible to imagine that Roosevelt and some of his savvy advisors in the State Department had a more strategic goal in mind than simply throwing a sop to civil society actors to win their support for U.S. global dominance and leadership in the new organization. Human rights eventually proved to be a much used and, some would argue, highly effective ideological weapon in the U.S. arsenal. Especially once the Cold War heated up, human rights became one of the primary means by which the United States distinguished its morally superior values and leadership from the tyranny of the Soviet "evil empire." More broadly, in its role as a hegemonic power, the United States successfully deployed human rights as a form of "soft power" to reward friends and punish enemies without incurring the costs, risks, and exposure of more coercive forms of intervention and significantly, without facing a meaningful backlash for some of its own less savory human rights practices at home or abroad. To what extent such strategic and selective use of human rights was anticipated at Dumbarton Oaks is a matter for speculation, but there is no question that over the years U.S. governments have derived significant geopolitical benefits from invoking human rights in support of various policies and practices. As one human rights author notes:

> Western governments have consistently reaped rewards for the [human rights] cause and have returned to it again and again. In forties America, President Roosevelt showed that it could be invoked to win domestic support for new politics and institutions, and to silence critics at home. In the seventies, President Carter used it as a national pick-me-up at a time of disillusionment and decay. And as Presidents Bush Sr. and Clinton have more recently demonstrated, it can provide a sugar coating for potentially unpalatable interventions. As these examples show, human rights campaigns are almost always triggered by domestic impulses within the most powerful nations.[35]

Nevertheless, an overall reading of the Dumbarton Oaks Charter would not have inspired human rights proponents at the time. The three great powers seemed intent on securing the fruits of their victory in a bloody world war by maintaining a firm and controlling grip on the United Nations. If the fundamental realpolitik principle of the new organization was great-power interests, its fundamental legal principle was state sovereignty and noninterference in domestic affairs. All the stirring and forceful Anglo-American rhetoric about a war fought to enthrone the rights of man, all the declarations aimed at rallying other nations and peoples to fight for freedom found expression at the very last moment in eight words relegated to the back of the bus: "promote respect for human rights and fundamental freedoms."

Philanthropy of the Masters

Civil society groups and individuals in the United States that had been agitating for human rights and limitations on state sovereignty initially viewed the Dumbarton Oaks proposals as a fiasco and a great betrayal. Many of the same private initiatives that had promoted international bills of rights, on their own and in cooperation with the State Department, began to mobilize against the plan for the new international organization and expressed their opposition in meetings, conferences, and media appeals and through direct lobbying with the government.[36] There was much cause for concern: human rights had been abandoned and state sovereignty reinforced, there was no pretense of equality between races and nations, and only states could bring complaints to the Security Council or appeals to the International Court of Justice. Instead of a forward-looking blueprint for peace and justice, they saw "the crass self-interests and old politics of the Great Powers alone."[37] W. E. B. Du Bois described the results as "intolerable, dangerous" and irreconcilable "with any philosophy of democracy." Expressing the disgust of many critics, he summed up the message that Dumbarton Oaks sent to oppressed nations, races, and minorities: "The only way to human equality is through the philanthropy of masters."[38]

The State Department moved quickly and effectively to quiet the rising chorus of opposition on the home front. On the recommendation of the Office of Public Affairs, a confidential decision was taken to launch a massive campaign to shape favorable public opinion toward Dumbarton Oaks and the upcoming San Francisco conference. The public relations campaign was directed by Archibald MacLeish, whom Roosevelt persuaded to leave his position of librarian of Congress, and assisted by Adlai Stevenson.[39] Over the next few months, teams of speakers organized by the State Department gave over 500 off-the-record briefings to professional and civic associations throughout the country. The State Department mailed out 1.25 million copies of the Dumbarton Oaks proposals, placing it on the best-sellers list. Prominent figures in the peace movement, such as Clark Eichelberger and James Shotwell, gave public lectures to promote U.S. participation in the United Nations, and mass-based groups including the Congress of Industrial Organizations, the League of Women Voters, and the Woodrow Wilson

Foundation mobilized their members to support the State Department's campaign.[40]

Relying on an extensive network of contacts within the NGO community that had developed through previous human rights planning work, the State Department arranged conferences with leading organizations, promising to develop joint strategies to better incorporate human rights into the emerging organization of the United Nations. The potential access to power and influence proved irresistible to civil society groups despite the human rights debacle at Dumbarton Oaks. In September 1944, fifty groups met at a New York conference, and on 16 October, Stettinius held off-the-record discussions with representatives from ninety-five of the largest and most powerful organizations—including the American Society of International Law, the American Bar Association, and the American Jewish Committee—under the chairmanship of Judge Proskauer.[41] Most of the organizations agreed to use their considerable public voice and influence to support U.S. global leadership, on the condition that human rights were reintroduced as a central feature in the new organization. Soon these NGOs were engaged in a well-organized campaign to promote the Dumbarton Oaks proposals and rally public support in advance of the San Francisco conference.[42] The joint government–civil society public relations campaign was an unqualified success. By April 1945, 80 percent of the U.S. public had a positive view of the U.S. role in the United Nations. Dissenting civil society voices concerned about the seeming betrayal of human rights principles at Dumbarton Oaks were drowned out in the massive wave of government-orchestrated public enthusiasm.

The State Department's collaboration with civil society received another boost when the U.S. delegation to San Francisco agreed to issue an open invitation for NGOs to attend the conference as observers, hoping thereby to ensure public support for the results of the conference. Roosevelt supported the idea, but in addition he proposed that selected groups be invited and given semi-official status as consultants to the delegation. Stettinius chose forty-two groups to participate in the U.S. delegation. The invitations were made in such as way as to mislead the NGOs into believing that their own persistent pressure had won them inclusion in the U.S. delegation. James T. Shotwell, who eventually chaired the group of 102 civil society consultants, claimed that Stettinius was initially reluctant to accept the NGO arrangement until Proskauer pointed out that the organizations involved represented 4 million votes and considerable public clout, after which time "we had no further trouble with the State Department."[43] Shotwell was not aware that a decision had been taken at the highest levels of the U.S. government not only to cultivate NGO participation as a means to shape public opinion but also to encourage an exaggerated sense of NGO independence from and influence over U.S. human rights policy.[44]

Opposition from Small States

While U.S. public opinion and most civil society groups were swayed to support the emerging shape of the United Nations, there was significant opposition in other countries throughout the world. Many had sacrificed lives and resources to the war effort. They were shocked by the results of the secret Dumbarton Oaks meetings and dismayed that the Big Three had not offered even a small gesture of consultation or respect for other views. Based on the Anglo-American ideological offensive, states had high expectations for a new world order based on democracy, freedom, and human rights.[45] Instead, the realization of great-power manipulation and abandonment of wartime principles prompted them to openly denounce the proposal for international organization. India and non-European countries protested the complete omission of references to self-determination or racial equality. Stung by their exclusion from the negotiations, New Zealand and Australia met in Wellington and issued a joint declaration pledging to fight for more powers for the General Assembly and the inclusion of explicit human rights provisions, especially relating to socioeconomic welfare.[46] Criticizing the Dumbarton Oaks charter, New Zealand's ambassador to the United States commented: "Too much emphasis on Great Powers, too little on Assembly, not much real machinery for joint action. . . . No adequate opportunity for small countries like New Zealand to exercise influence or express views. . . . No adequate machinery for securing peaceful change and economic justice—only words."[47]

Latin American countries in particular felt snubbed and humiliated. Having dutifully signed the Atlantic Charter and United Nations Declaration and generally done whatever the United States asked of them, they were taken aback by the total neglect of small and medium countries, the overwhelming dominance of great powers, and the absence of any principles of human rights and equality in the plans for the new organization. Leading Latin American statesmen and diplomats had participated in various U.S. human rights initiatives, only to see their efforts ignored. Many countries voiced official complaints that the Dumbarton Oaks proposals trampled on their aspirations; Mexico even circulated a reform proposal that highlighted the human rights contributions of various NGOs and individuals, including Mandelstam and Alvarez, and listed the specific Anglo-American appeals for human rights and wartime solidarity.[48]

CHAPULTEPEC: REBELLION OR REACTION?

The dissatisfaction of Latin American governments found expression in an extraordinary meeting in February 1945 at the Chapultepec Castle in Mexico City, where twenty Latin American countries and a large delegation from the United States participated in the Inter-American Conference on Problems of War and Peace. They reviewed the Dumbarton Oaks proposals in details and introduced 150 draft resolutions urging substantial reforms, many addressing human rights.[49] The Mexican Ministry of Foreign Affairs advanced a program of "Protection of the International Rights of Man," referencing the historical development of human rights principles and insisting that they be incorporated in the postwar order. Bolivia urged that the rights and responsibilities of individuals and nations be precisely defined and made part of the new international organization. Cuba submitted two detailed proposals for consideration, a "Draft Declaration of the International Rights and Duties of the Individual" and a "Draft Declaration on the Rights and Duties of Nations."[50]

These proposals were reintroduced in San Francisco and during the drafting of the Universal Declaration of Human Rights. Latin America's significant intellectual production supporting human rights is a major reason the region has been called "the forgotten crucible" of universal human rights.[51] Latin American jurisprudence was particularly well suited to bridging cultural divides in human rights by linking civil and political rights with economic and social rights. This derived from its historical intermarriage of traditional Anglo-American natural rights theories with Catholic and Thomist moral philosophy linked to the injustices of the Spanish conquest.[52] With their dominant voting bloc, the Latin American countries would play a significant role in advancing human rights throughout the UN process.

However, there was another side to the Chapultepec meeting, one rarely commented on by historians of human rights. Although the mid-1940s in Latin America were "a moment of idealistic optimism and democratic euphoria" characterized by progressive governments in states such as Mexico, Cuba, and Panama, idealism and democracy are relative terms.[53] The majority of Latin American governments were still repressive and right wing, hardly paragons of human rights virtues. There was significant support for the Axis powers throughout Latin America, with Argentina pursuing openly fascist policies. Seven governments refused to break relations with Nazi Germany until the last months of the war, when Stalin laid down an ultimatum at Yalta that if they did not do so, they would be ineligible for membership in the United Nations. These and other Latin American states were more concerned with countering Soviet influence and repressing domestic opposition than with any serious implementation of human rights.

Moreover, Nelson Rockefeller, assistant secretary of state for Latin American affairs, organized the Chapultepec conference for the primary purpose of establishing a regional security system under U.S. protection and hegemony. While human rights concerns were expressed in nonbinding resolutions, the military alliance was formalized in the Chapultepec Pact, in principle committing the United States to Monroe Doctrine–style defense against external aggression. But in practice, the U.S. goal was "to protect pro-American regimes from internal subversion, in exchange for US access to whatever resources it wanted in the various states involved."[54] For each country in the region, Rockefeller had established advisory committees comprised of conservative business interests such as United Fruit, Standard Oil, and General Electric to, in his own words, "lessen the dependence of Latin America on Europe as a market for raw materials and a source of manufactured articles."[55] Less diplomatically, it was understood in the State Department that there were "good properties in the British portfolio" and that "we might as well pick them up now."[56] Rockefeller's support for the right-wing political and business elite angered colleagues like Nicolo Tucci, head of the State Department's Bureau of Latin American Research, who resigned in protest: "My bureau was supposed to undo the Nazi and fascist propaganda in South America but Rockefeller is inviting the worst fascists and Nazis to Washington."[57]

The Chapultepec Pact caused considerable concern throughout the State Department about establishing a regional security organization at the very time that Roosevelt was trying to dissuade similar British and Soviet moves in their spheres of influence. Stettinius recognized that this would complicate U.S. proposals to establish the United Nations along universal rather than regional lines. Moreover, the delegates at Chapultepec resolved to establish a regional pact with strong protections for human rights and to that end requested the Inter-American Juridical Committee to prepare a draft Declaration of the International Rights and Duties of Man for the Americas.[58] This marked the beginning of regional human rights systems parallel to and distinct from the emerging global system. The first crack in the edifice of universal human rights had appeared even before the United Nations was a reality.

Conclusions

The roller-coaster ride of human rights was on a precipitous downswing in the months leading up to the San Francisco conference and the founding of the United Nations. Human rights burst onto the international scene through a combination of Anglo-American wartime rhetoric and popular hopes for universal justice. These hopes found legal expression through an explosion of public discourse about human rights and private initiatives, most of which were based in the United States, to draft an international bill of rights.

When the danger of war subsided, however, and the planning for peace accelerated, the victorious powers lost their fervor for human rights. Absorbed by momentous decisions about the postwar division of power and the structure of the new international organization, they showed little interest in, and even significant hostility to, the idea of incorporating human rights into international agreement. It took U.S. pressure to overcome British and Soviet objections to the concept of human rights in international agreements and to win agreement on a vague and unenforceable phrase belatedly inserted at the back of the Dumbarton Oaks proposals.

However, just as had happened in World War I, political proclamations of grandiose peace goals raised public demands for action in the postwar order, demands that would crystallize into specific proposals and interventions that helped alter the terms of the human rights debate. The persistent complaints of smaller states, especially from Latin America, made it impossible for the war's victors to completely disregard popular calls for human rights. In the end, the world would have its say in San Francisco. But the words would be carefully shaped, and stripped of enforceability, by the great powers—especially the United States, which exerted control over nearly every aspect of the proceedings. The dream of realizable human rights would, for the time being, remain an unrealized dream.

The United Nations and Its Charter

President Roosevelt, the man who did more than anyone else to bring the United Nations into being, died on 12 April 1945, thirteen days before the start of the San Francisco conference. In the last few months of his life he had become almost obsessed with ensuring the success of the global conclave, driving himself to exhaustion in an effort to overcome last-minute objections by Stalin and Churchill and reach agreement on the final details. Some of his close advisors believed that Roosevelt was done in by "the hard, perhaps fatal, trip to Yalta" that was undertaken to reassure Stalin of his commitment to the great-power alliance.[59]

But for Roosevelt, the trip was a necessity, meant to establish the basis for lasting peace according to U.S. power and U.S. ideals. He had even confided to members of his inner circle that once the war was ended, he planned to leave the presidency to become the first secretary-general of the United Nations.[60] In his final interview, Roosevelt explained to his closest confidante in the media that the UN was to be his historical legacy:

> He was looking to the inauguration of the San Francisco conference as the crowning act of his career. This was his project. He prepared it, set the time and place of the meeting, speeded up the preparations in the belief that it was supremely urgent. He dreamed of going down in history as the president who succeeded where Wilson had failed in making the United States the great bastion of an armed security system while the forge of war was still hot enough to fuse nations together.[61]

While Roosevelt did not live to see the birth of the United Nations, his basic vision remained as both the animating ethic and the pragmatic operating principle for the new organization. As with his call for Four Freedoms, which galvanized U.S. and global public opinion to wage a ruthless war to the finish based on the highest ideals of humanity, in his plans for the United Nations, Roosevelt showed an uncanny ability to accomplish two seemingly contradictory goals at the same time. His vision combined an appeal to universal principles of peace, freedom, and human rights with an organizational structure carefully planned and designed to expand U.S. political and economic dominance of world affairs. This remarkably effective "two-faced" policy is described in a recent analysis of Roosevelt's strategic vision for the UN:

> In resolving its task, the Roosevelt Administration hit upon a fundamental insight: that international institutions could be constructed to face simultaneously in two radically different directions. One face would be turned in the direction of mass popular politics, both within the US and internationally. This would be the inspiring ethical face, offering promise of a better world. But simultaneously, the internal face of the organization could be shaped in an entirely different and indeed opposite way, as a framework for the power politics of the hegemon. . . . Far from being an attempt to escape from the realities of great-power politics, Roosevelt's scheme for the UN was his way of confronting and pursuing them.[62]

One of Harry Truman's first acts upon assuming the presidency was to assure Eleanor Roosevelt of his commitment to seeing the president's global vision through to the end. He reaffirmed this commitment to top administration officials and refused to postpone the conference. Despite his low opinion of Stettinius, whom he later termed "dumb as they come . . . never an idea new or old,"[63] Truman kept him as head of the U.S. delegation to San Francisco for the sake of continuity. He also kept in place the entire U.S. team, whose members Roosevelt had shrewdly handpicked to ensure the broadest bipartisan support for the new organization.

The seven-member delegation included three influential Republicans: Arthur Vandenberg, a senior senator and former isolationist with deep ties to the Republican establishment; John Foster Dulles, foreign policy advisor to failed presidential candidate Thomas Dewey; and Harold Stassen, a naval reserve office and former governor of Minnesota.[64] Democrat Tom Connally, chair of the Senate Foreign Relations Committee, was chosen to smooth passage in the Senate, and Virginia Gildersleeve, dean of Barnard College, to act as main liaison to NGO consultants and civil society observers.[65] This team would prove effective not only in negotiating the final details of the UN in San Francisco but, more importantly, in ensuring widespread political and public support for the UN upon conclusion of the conference, thereby preventing a repeat of the League of Nations debacle.

The American World Charter

High-level delegations from forty-six nations, headed by prime ministers and foreign ministers, gathered in the city of San Francisco to discuss, modify, and ratify the Dumbarton Oaks proposals for the creation of the United Nations.[66] For nine weeks, beginning on 25 April 1945, the delegates debated changes to the blueprint of a new international organization. It was an extraordinary gathering, promising a chance to remake the world—an illusory promise given that the Big Three had already constructed the global architecture. Over 5,000 people attended the conference: 850 delegates, 2,600 media, 1,000 U.S. residents working at the secretariat, 300 security officers, and 120 translators working in five languages. Upon reaching San Francisco, Virginia Gildersleeve wrote of "the exaltation as every heart and mind turned hopefully towards the City of the Golden Gate."[67]

The San Francisco conference was, by one standard, an unprecedented global event, truly the first of its kind. Intensifying the trend established at the Hague Peace Conference fifty years ago, the international public witnessed as never before the daily welter of political negotiations and disputes between government representatives. The media was by far the largest contingent in San Francisco; its constant reports blanketed the globe. People followed the twists and turns of the conference through front-page headlines and analysis of every relevant detail of the talks, and delegates were praised or damned for their performances in upholding national interests and pride.

At the same time, from the perspective of history, there was an unreal element to this global media frenzy. Almost all major issues, including the fundamental structures and powers of the new organization, had already been resolved between the great powers in a series of open as well as secret agreements. All that remained was for the rest of the world to ratify the package after tinkering at the margins in a public show of due diligence and careful deliberation. In this way, the angst and drama of San Francisco was much ado over nothing, sound and fury signifying very little substance.

It was impossible at the time to know the extent to which the great powers had already sealed various deals. On the contrary, there was an understandable belief that the Dumbarton Oaks proposals could be significantly modified to reflect the views of additional actors on the world stage beyond the big players once they had a forum to air their concerns and lobby for their interests. Despite disappointment with Dumbarton Oaks, there was hope among smaller nations and civil society groups that with enough public pressure and international solidarity, the postwar peace could still be constructed on the basis of equality and respect for human rights.[68] In some ways this belief was borne out by subsequent developments in San Francisco, at least in the area of human rights, which did in fact undergo significant change and revision from the Dumbarton Oaks version. But the core structure of the organization and the great-power interests it reflected were to remain unchanged.

Preparing the Stage for U.S. Hegemony

It is impossible to exaggerate the extent to which San Francisco was a U.S. show—in the literal sense of the word. The United States funded and organized every detail of the conference, including where the various delegations slept at night. The conference took place at the San Francisco Opera House, which had been remodeled by Broadway stage designers just for the occasion.[69] In the central auditorium, four golden pillars tied together with olive branches were built to symbolize Roosevelt's four freedoms. The flags of participating nations were raised on a semicircle of pikestaffs illuminated by 24-hour spotlights with blue filters for cosmetic effect. The stage was garlanded with flowers, and specially designed maps, posters, and UN organizational charts adorned the walls.[70]

The key honorary and bureaucratic positions were also arranged to maximize U.S. influence on the proceedings. Stettinius was named president of the conference, over the objection of Soviet foreign minister Vyacheslav Molotov, who favored a rotating presidency between the Big Four. Molotov's objection was easily overridden when Latin America voted as a bloc with the United States, setting a precedent that would hold for the rest of the conference. Alger Hiss was named acting secretary-general of the UN, overseeing the schedules and devising the rules of procedure for the multitude of committees and plenary sessions. U.S. delegates dominated the proceedings, setting agendas, distributing relevant discussion documents, and acting as conveners and moderators throughout the conference.

The mood of elegance and solemnity at the Opera House and the grind of constant plenaries, meetings, and caucuses were offset by a carefully planned strategy of wining and dining. Stettinius's penthouse suite at the nearby Fairmont Hotel was the scene of both crucial secret meetings of the great powers and frequent social events where the delegates had a chance to mix and unwind. Throughout the nine-week affair, the U.S. delegation threw a series of lavish parties and receptions throughout the city, with dancing girls, musical bands, and special consignments of top-quality liquor and cigarettes made available through a relaxation of the rationing rules then in place.[71] Hollywood movies were shown daily at a special screening room. Stettinius even took the British and Soviet negotiators on a secret trip to visit "the fleshpots of Manhattan . . . and the stately homes of Virginia."[72] All of these perks made an enormous impression on delegates from countries that had suffered years of devastation and shortages. One British participant recalled the scene: "I had flown straight from blacked-out London into a fantastic world of glitter and light and extravagant parties and food and drink and constantly spiraling talk."[73]

Even the train ride that transported delegates from the East Coast to San Francisco carried a propaganda message, reinforced by U.S. escorts. One of them, Claiborne Pell, later a senator from Rhode Island, recalled that his charges "were given a powerful picture of the United States. They could not miss the contrast with their ravaged countries, as they saw miles and miles of our extraordinarily productive pastures and our seemingly endless fields, punctuated by mighty industrial cities and prosperous towns."[74]

Some of the underlying realities of U.S. society, however, could not be so easily covered up. Underneath the gilded façade of equality, racism was deeply entrenched. On the train to San Francisco, black waiters refused to serve Indian delegates until whites had finished their meals. At San Francisco itself, a vibrant symbol of U.S. progressive internationalism, the State Department had difficulty finding hotels to accommodate nonwhite delegations; in one publicized incident, seven waitresses walked out of a local hotel rather than serve a group of African delegates.[75]

As regards civil society participation, the United States dominated the conference from start to finish. NGO representatives and individual activists constituted the second-largest contingent after journalists; some 1,500 of them outnumbered the assembled delegates two to one.[76] Virtually all were from the United States; the dominance of U.S. NGOs in their sphere of influence mirrored the dominance of the U.S. government. Several charismatic individual voices from Asian and African colonies called for the elimination of imperialism and colonialism, but they were few and far between.[77] In part, this dominance reflected logistical realities, in particular the extraordinary difficulties of travel from war-ravaged parts of the world: "British and continental European organizations played virtually no part in the San Francisco Conference; indeed at this time foreign travel was almost impossible for private individuals, and in continental Europe the business of living occupied more attention than missionary activity."[78]

But the disproportionate representation of U.S. civil society also reflected the remarkable hold on human rights discourse exerted by U.S. groups since Roosevelt's call for the Four Freedoms. Simply put, U.S. initiatives, often incorporating input from Latin American jurists, had monopolized intellectual and legal production concerning human rights in recent years. After surveying U.S. civil society initiatives, one British historian commented: "American enthusiasm did not appear to be driven by concern over internal arrangements in the USA or embarrassment over the Southern States, but rather by religiosity and a desire to exercise moral leadership in the world."[79] The result was an outward-looking morality that sought to reform an evil and degenerate world while paying lip service to removing the evils closer to home. Of the forty-two influential civil society groups invited to provide consultants by the State Department, only one, the NAACP, emphasized racial inequality within the United States. The vast majority focused on peace, justice, and human rights issues outside U.S. borders.

A Massive Spying Operation

While the delegates and observers were focused on the daily business at hand and the evenings of entertainment, the United States was engaged in a range of covert activities designed to enhance the already-considerable advantages of being the host nation. The extent of the spying operation has only recently been revealed, based on a wealth of documents declassified after almost fifty years in government archives, many of them still heavily redacted.[80] The overall picture is one in which the U.S. government left no stone unturned in its effort to shape a global organization to suit its interests.

From an army base at the Presidio nearby the Opera House, military intelligence ran an enormous and elaborate eavesdropping and code-breaking operation, intercepting the communications and cable traffic of every participating delegation in attendance, including U.S. allies. A summary of these decoded messages landed on Stettinius's breakfast table every morning, giving the U.S. delegation a huge advantage in ongoing negotiations. After the conference ended, the officer in charge of the spying operation wrote of his unit's achievements: "Pressure of work has at last abated and the 24-hour day has shortened. The feeling in the Branch is that the success of the Conference may owe a great deal to its contribution."[81]

Even the artistic and logistical sides of the event were staged by U.S. intelligence. The Office of Strategic Services (OSS), precursor to the Central Intelligence Agency, sent a huge team of artists, designers, and technicians to create the proper ambience from both the aesthetic and information-gathering points of view. OSS teams created the familiar UN "brand," a world map, with the United States in the center, set against a sky-blue background. OSS decorators designed conference credentials, badges, lapel pins, flags, and assorted paraphernalia, all stamped with the UN logo. OSS operatives ran the photocopying facilities that churned out 500,000 pages a day, a recording studio to memorialize the proceedings, and a team of photographers who snapped 3,000 pictures daily and distributed them to the assembled press. This comprehensive surveillance network captured, digested, analyzed, and spoon-fed any information of strategic value to the U.S. delegation, helping to ensure that the conference went according to the U.S. plan.[82]

The FBI also played a surveillance role in San Francisco, keeping close tabs on potential subversive elements among the 1,500 representatives of NGOs and peace groups who attended parts of the conference. Of particular interest were a handful of "Negro communists," men like W. E. B. Du Bois of the NAACP, Max Yergan of the Council on African Affairs, and Ben Davis, a New York City councilman.[83] The FBI was particularly anxious about their plans to meet with delegates from Africa and Asia and "influence them considerably" toward decolonization—even though this was ostensibly one of the policy goals of the U.S. delegation itself. As a result of these concerns, the FBI tapped phones, used informants to gather information, and assigned agents to tail these delegates.[84]

While it is difficult to pinpoint the concrete impact of the U.S. spying operation, one small example illustrates the advantages of tapping into other countries' confidential internal communications. The overriding concern of the United States was to safeguard the veto from expected challenges by most of the world's nations. Intercepted cable traffic indicated that a growing coalition of smaller powers, including several Latin American countries, planned to oppose the veto as a violation of "sovereign equality" that would place "permanent members of the council above the law."[85] France, angered at being shut out of Yalta, was refusing to accept the Anglo-American offer of a permanent veto and instead was leading the emerging coalition of recalcitrant states against great-power domination. Armed with decoded messages, Stettinius intensified his diplomatic overtures, exploiting differences within the French government, and eventually won France's acceptance as a member of the permanent five on the Security Council, after which the campaign against the veto abruptly collapsed.[86]

The Fight for Human Rights

From the outset of the conference, the lack of human rights in the draft charter was a contentious public issue. The energy and activism that had gathered steam among U.S. organizations over the previous several years focused on San Francisco as a do-or-die moment.[87] From civil society, the fight for human rights was spearheaded by the core group of U.S. NGO consultants, in particular five notable Washington insiders who had been involved in planning the new organization from the beginning: James T. Shotwell, veteran diplomat and distinguished professor of history at Columbia University, who strongly believed that the UN Charter should include provisions for consultations between the international organization and NGOs;[88] Dr. O. Fredrick Nolde of the Federal Council of Churches, a committed advocate on behalf of a human rights commission;[89] Clark Eichelberger, who headed the principal citizens' lobbying group of the American Association for the United Nations and worked closely with the State Department's public relations campaign on behalf of the UN;[90] and two prominent members of the American Jewish Committee, Judge Joseph Proskauer and Jacob Blaustein. Blaustein had met with President Roosevelt in March 1945 and had been told: "Go to San Francisco. Work to get those human rights provisions into the Charter so that unspeakable crimes like those by the Nazis will never again be countenanced by world society."[91]

Among participating NGOs, Jewish and Christian groups were the most organized, the best funded, and most vocal, especially given the outraged public reaction to revelations of the Holocaust and other Nazi atrocities against civilians. Their focus was on promoting human and religious rights as well as equality and nondiscrimination. A number of proposals were put forward to both the assembled delegations and the plentiful media in attendance. The most common demands were for a commission on human rights to promote worldwide recognition and for an enforceable bill of human rights to guarantee concrete protections.

The Joint Committee of the World Jewish Congress, which represented forty countries; the American Jewish Conference; and the Board of Deputies of British Jews submitted a memorandum calling for an enforceable bill of human rights that would trigger concrete state obligations on the grounds that "only detailed and clearly defined obligations can either be guaranteed or violated. . . . A clearly stated catalogue of human rights and fundamental freedoms can guarantee their international observance, as only their enumeration in a domestic act makes them effective on the national scene."[92] They purchased advertisements in newspapers throughout the country with a ten-point human rights statement that began with an international bill of rights and went on to propose rights for Jews, including the reconstitution of Palestine as a "free and democratic Jewish commonwealth."[93] An interfaith group of religious forces, led by the Federal Council of Churches, the Synagogue Council of America, and National Catholic Welfare Council, also issued a ten-point pronouncement of moral principles for a just world order.[94] Point nine proposed an international bill of rights and an international commission to advance human rights and liberties. In another well-publicized initiative, a group of 150 prominent U.S. academics and public intellectuals, many of them veterans of previous human rights initiatives such as Quincy Wright and William Draper, signed a report calling for the UN to establish a commission on human rights to develop legal standards and monitor state compliance with them.[95]

These civil society proposals for human rights found strong support among non-European states, especially in Latin America.[96] Many of these states had recently written human rights into their own constitutions, and their delegations included prominent jurists whose primary focus was to advance human rights. Peace and security, they argued, could be based only on the protection of human rights, not just traditional civil and political rights but also economic and social rights. Chile, Cuba, and Panama resubmitted the proposal for a binding international bill of rights from the Chapultepec conference.

One perspective within the Big Three saw the Latin Americans' human rights initiatives as hypocritical public grandstanding, given the spotty human rights record of their own governments. A British delegate observed: "The Latin American jurists are, I understand, raring to 'get a move on' with a string of pious [human rights] platitudes which seem to place them in the vanguard of progress yet involve no enforcement of inconvenient standards in their home towns!"[97] At the same time, the great powers could not afford to ignore the combined pressure from NGOs and Latin American countries, especially when magnified by considerable press coverage. After championing human rights during the war, it was one thing to ignore them in secret closed-door meetings but another thing to do so before the eyes of the world. As one historian who observed the proceedings noted: "Though at San Francisco the fervor of the speeches concerning justice, human rights and fundamental freedoms, sometimes seemed in inverse ratio to the practice of those making them, they represented forces which none of the statesmen present could ignore, since in the long run, power is a moral as well as physical entity."[98]

U.S. NGOs: Triumphant or Manipulated?

It had been Roosevelt's brainchild to invite forty-two NGOs to serve as semi-official consultants to the U.S. delegation with the expectation that they would take the lead in lobbying Congress and persuading civil society and the general public to support ratification of the United Nations Charter.[99] Once in San Francisco, these consultants played a pivotal role, liaising between hundreds of other civil society groups, representatives from smaller nations, and the U.S. delegation. During the first week of the conference, they organized petitions and interventions on human rights issues and succeeded in focusing media and public attention on the abysmal failure of the Dumbarton Oaks proposals with respect to human rights. However, at first their efforts did not pay off with the powerful states. On the contrary, the main objective of civil society groups and smaller states—an international bill of rights with enforceable standards incorporated into the Charter—appeared to be a dead letter with the Big Three. As a result, there was a growing sense of frustration among the NGOs about the prospects for making human rights the moral and legal foundation of the new international organization.

It was in this context that a fateful meeting took place on the evening of 2 May between Stettinius and the NGO consultants. The standard history of the meeting portrays a great victory for the NGOs in shifting the position of the U.S. delegation toward greater recognition of human rights.[100] According to subsequent accounts and memoirs written by some of the consultants, their spirited intervention changed the course of human rights at the United Nations.[101] State Department officials attached to the U.S. delegation, probably Alice McDiarmid and Walter Kotschnig, had apparently warned the consultants that human rights were in danger of being lost. Virginia Gildersleeve met with several of them on the morning of 2 May and urged them to force the issue and take a stand with Stettinius.[102] According to Frederick Nolde, "confidential remarks by delegates" convinced the consultants that "prompt and virtually drastic action was needed."[103]

Stettinius opened the session by explaining that he had pushed hard for human rights in Dumbarton Oaks and did not think that the United States could be any more successful in San Francisco.[104] On behalf of the NGOs, Nolde introduced the principal shared demands of civil society: (1) human rights must be identified as a fundamental purpose of the organization; (2) member states must assume obligations of guaranteeing human rights; and (3) a human rights commission must be stipulated by name in the Charter. Judge Proskauer then rose and forcefully urged the U.S. delegation into action: "If you make a fight for these human rights proposals and win, there will be glory for all. If you make a fight for it and lose, we will back you up to the limit. If you fail to make a fight for it, you will have lost the support of American opinion—and justly lost it. In the event you will never get the Charter ratified."[105]

Upon hearing this "eloquent appeal," Stettinius "rose to his feet impulsively" and declared that he would ask the entire U.S. delegation to fight for these ideals. Walter Kotschnig later praised the consultants and credited them with changing the nature of the debate: "I have never seen democracy in action demonstrated so forcefully. . . . It is the participation we had in this room when Mr. Nolde first introduced the matter, which really changed history at this point."[106] McDiarmid concurred, lauding the intervention of the NGO coalition and singling out Nolde and Proskauer as particularly effective advocates.[107] Most subsequent histories of the San Francisco conference repeat this version of events.[108]

But there are a number of problems with this story. In the first place, a recent history of human rights concludes that examination of "the verbatim records of the meeting . . . [show] that things did not unfold in the way that was later recounted [by the consultants]." In particular, the consultants' speeches were somewhat less eloquent, and Stettinius's reaction somewhat less dramatic.[109] Moreover, the United States had already transmitted a set of amendments on that same day to Britain, the Soviet Union, and China proposing to add human rights language in the Charter, including in the purposes of the organization.[110] The subsequent meeting with NGOs therefore could not have prompted these changes. Most important, it is not plausible that a U.S. diplomatic strategy carefully crafted over months and years would simply be tossed aside after one meeting, regardless of the persuasive power of the NGO leaders.

In fact, prior to the San Francisco conference, McDiarmid had drafted and Kotschnig had reviewed a secret State Department memo recommending change in the Dumbarton Oaks human rights provisions. The memo proposed recognizing human rights as one of the purposes of the UN and ensuring that a commission on human rights was established in the Charter.

These changes, according to the memo, would advance U.S. interests without infringing on the principle of state sovereignty, so long as the Commission on Human Rights was prohibited from serving "as a court of appeal from national courts or a means of super-national government."[111] The fact that the NGO proposals so closely tracked those already approved by the State Department, with the notable exception of state obligations to guarantee human rights, indicates that the consultants "had been advised by State Department officials, or consultants closely involved with the State Department's postwar planning, about what would be acceptable."[112] Indeed, several NGO consultants, including Shotwell, had served on the same State Department prewar planning legal committee as McDiarmid had. What Kotschnig referred to as an "NGO coup" appears instead to have been NGO co-optation:

> Government officials thus found themselves in the agreeable position of being exhorted by their guests to do the very thing that they wanted to do anyway. At the same time, the consultants were flattered into feeling personally responsible for the initiative. With both parties benefiting from this conceit, there was no reason to challenge it, and it duly became accepted as truth . . . immortalized in human rights histories.[113]

The outcome of the meeting served U.S. interests, transforming civil society skeptics into enthusiastic backers of U.S. human rights proposals without changing the substance of U.S. policy. It also forestalled demands for enforceable human rights provisions, the top human rights priority of most NGOs prior to San Francisco. Finally, it gave the U.S delegation leverage to overcome resistance by Britain and the Soviet Union to inserting additional human rights language into the Charter. Gladwynn Jebb, a British diplomat involved in the great-power negotiations to establish the UN, referred derisively to the naiveté of the U.S. NGOs: "We had quite underestimated the apparent power of the U.S. administration to delude these simple folk and to make them think that their objectives were achieved in the present Charter. I very much doubt whether 42 British groups of the same character would have come to the same conclusion."[114]

In retrospect, however, it is by no means clear that the NGO coalition served merely to advance State Department policy.[115] The inclusion of any human rights language seemed like a victory after the concept had been buried during great-power negotiations over the previous year. And regardless of what really happened at the 2 May meeting, there is no question that the public pressure mobilized by NGOs helped ensure that human rights could not be ignored in San Francisco as they had been at Dumbarton Oaks.

Nonbinding Human Rights Language in the Charter

Throughout the conference, the great powers held a series of secret and informal meetings, generally in Stettinius's penthouse suite at the Fairmont, to develop consensus positions before presenting them in a unified front to the assembled nations. This strategy was designed to maximize great-power control during the debates and minimize the chance that differences between them could be exploited by smaller countries to create public controversies and derail progress toward a final agreement. Once it became apparent that human rights was a potential wedge issue and that a conference-wide consensus had developed in support of human rights, Britain and the Soviet Union softened their previous resistance to adding human rights language to the draft charter. U.S. proposals therefore elicited few challenges as long as the language stayed within the bounds of nonenforceable and vaguely defined hortatory standards. Thus, the standards enshrined in the Charter stressed recognition and promotion of human rights without empowering an international supervisory mechanism to interfere in domestic sovereignty and jurisdiction.

The main challenge to the Big Three's human rights strategy came from the insistence of Latin American countries, supported by civil society groups, on proposing a binding international bill of rights. With support from Cuba, Chile, and Mexico, Panamanian foreign minister Ricardo Alfaro put forward the American Law Institute's draft bill of rights, to which he had contributed along with a range of other distinguished jurists. To nip this controversy in the bud, Stettinius announced at a press conference on 15 May, apparently without prior consultation, that while the idea was not feasible at the moment, a commission on human rights could take it up later:

> I believe that when the Organization is established the Economic and Social Council, through the Commission on human rights, should promptly undertake to prepare an International Bill of Rights which can be accepted by all the member states as an integral part of their own system of law, just as our Bill of Rights has been an integral part of our system of law.[116]

The British were initially dismayed by his statement and suspected that it was a sop to the Latin Americans to appease their anger at the U.S. failure to support recognition of the regional security arrangement established at Chapultepec.[117] After discussions among the Big Three, however, it was clarified that the United States would support not binding measures to be enforced at the international level but rather a statement of principles that member states could incorporate into domestic law at their own discretion. Eleanor Roosevelt as chair of the commission would successfully push such an approach on human rights during the drafting of the Universal Declaration of Human Rights. The Soviet and British delegations found the U.S. position acceptable,[118] and the British Foreign Office recorded its guarded approval: "Our own attitude was to welcome the idea but caution against guarantees by the United Nations of all individual rights and liberties within each country—as opposed to undertakings by countries to observe these rights and liberties."[119]

Once the issue of the bill of rights was resolved, U.S. proposals for incorporating human rights into various sections of the Charter, particularly the Preamble and Article 1 on fundamental principles and purposes of the organization, were accepted with little debate, first by the great powers and then by the entire conference.[120] While virtually every human rights proposal was forwarded by the U.S. delegation, the Soviet Union did try to advance its own conception of human rights, stressing social and economic issues. The Soviets proposed that the statement of purpose in Article 1 should recognize "the promotion and encouragement of respect for human rights *in particular the right to work and the right to education* and also for fundamental freedoms for all without distinction as to race, language, religion, or sex" (emphasis added).[121] However, at a meeting of the four powers it was agreed that all the Charter articles mentioning human rights would remain general and undefined without reference to specific rights. Article 1 on the purposes of the UN therefore dropped the right to work and to education while retaining the general language; the Preamble to the Charter requested all members to "reaffirm faith in fundamental human rights, in the dignity and worth of the human person."

Including the Preamble and Article 1, human rights were mentioned seven times in the United Nations Charter. Article 13(1)(b) empowered the General Assembly to promote cooperation in the realization of human rights and to initiate studies and make recommendations "assisting in the realization of human rights and fundamental freedoms for all, without distinction as to race, sex, language or religion." Article 55 provided that all member states of the United Nations should "promote universal respect for, and observations of, human rights and fundamental freedoms for all." Article 62(2) empowered the Economic and Social Council "to make recommendations for the purpose of promoting respect for, and observance of, human rights and fundamental freedoms for all"; Article 68 mandated it to establish a commission to promote human rights; and Article 71 instructed it make suitable arrangements for consultation with NGOs.

Colonialism and Self-Determination

Beyond these specific articles, the main human rights issue confronting the delegates at San Francisco concerned the equality of races and the interlinked colonial question. China picked up where it had left off at Dumbarton Oaks, this time buoyed by strong support from small states and civil society groups, partly in return for the backing it had given on human rights issues.[122] What changed the equation was the unequivocal support announced by the Soviets, who no doubt hoped to win accolades in a setting in which they were often isolated and outvoted.

The British fought hard against any mention of the right to self-determination and any establishment of supervisory mechanisms to monitor developments in the colonies.[123] Colonial powers—Britain, France, Australia, Belgium, the Netherlands, New Zealand, Portugal, South Africa, and the United States (in relation to military bases on Pacific islands)—did not want an international organization to oversee independence for former colonies and were determined to sidestep the issue of self-determination and racial equality. U.S. NGOs such as the NAACP urged the U.S. delegation to support independence for all colonized peoples; Stettinius replied that the idea was legitimate only for peoples he considered capable of exercising it.[124]

In the end, the U.S. brokered a compromise: the Charter would recognize "the principle" of equal rights and self-determination, but mechanisms for giving effect to this principle would be referred to a Trusteeship Council that was chaired by Peter Fraser of New Zealand and under the effective domination of Britain and the United States.[125]

The Trusteeship Council drafted several position papers in which the rights of colonized people were left vague and subject to the control of the colonizers. For example, the colonial powers "accepted the general principle that it is a sacred trust of civilization to promote to the utmost the well-being of the inhabitants of these territories . . . [and] to develop self government in forms appropriate to the varying circumstances of each territory."[126] These positions were incorporated into Chapter XI of the Charter, the Declaration Regarding Non Self-Governing Territories, which recognized neither human rights, rights of equality, nor the right to self-determination. As one historian notes, the declaration was "expressed as a voluntary statement by the colonial powers, imposing no obligations on them, and conferring no rights on the organs of the United Nations."[127] Even in territories placed under trusteeship, an exception was made under Articles 82 and 83 for designated "strategic areas" to be supervised by the Security Council directly; thus the

U.S. Army Chiefs of Staff were able to develop their Pacific island bases as fortress colonies without having to either annex them or open their governance to external scrutiny.[128]

The Domestic Jurisdiction Clause

The most important human rights development in the Charter had nothing to do with rights themselves but rather with the protection afforded to states by Article 2(7): "Nothing in the present Charter shall authorize the United Nations to intervene in matters which are essentially within the domestic jurisdiction of any state." This simple phrase, which provoked the most bitter and protracted negotiations of the entire conference, did more to limit the scope and application of human rights than any other.[129] The limited application of nonbinding human rights language in the Charter was reinforced by this legitimization of the principles of sovereignty and nonintervention in the domestic affairs of sovereign states.[130] As one analyst noted, "What the sponsoring states sought was to retain the emphasis on human rights demanded by public opinion while ensuring that the new principles of universal human rights did not interfere with a return to normal international politics."[131]

International jurists such as Hans Kelsen and D. J. Llewelyn Davies observed that the domestic jurisdiction clause essentially limited international law even more stringently than the article included in the Covenant of the League of Nations.[132] Moreover, its prominent placement in Chapter I made it clear that it applied to all provisions within the Charter. Kelsen noted that it would be impossible to fulfill the functions of Articles 55 and 56 (on human rights and economic and social cooperation) without intervening in domestic matters.[133] In fact, the principle of noninterference in domestic affairs was hardly compatible with many of the proposed functions of the United Nations.

Despite the controversial nature of the domestic jurisdiction clause, most delegations ended up supporting it. One historian notes, "One way or another, the major powers and many of the lesser powers were united in wishing to have a Charter that clipped the wings of the new organization."[134] China and France led a coalition of states that preferred to empower the UN to intervene in support of human rights, but they could not command a majority. Most small states, championed by Australia, insisted on a restrictive clause to limit the possibility of great powers meddling in their affairs.[135] Even Latin American states supported this interpretation, notwithstanding their vocal support for human rights. The big powers likewise agreed with the policy of maintaining control over internal affairs without the possibility of international scrutiny and intervention. In "an unholy example of Soviet-American solidarity," John Foster Dulles was chosen to present the position of the Big Three.[136] After listening to a number of countries criticize the domestic jurisdiction clause, he made it clear that the clause was America's price for participating in the cooperative elements of the UN that required resources and financial contributions: "If it is rejected, we shall be forced to reexamine our attitude toward increases in the economic and social activities of this organization."[137]

By confining the potential of human rights to the straitjacket of domestic jurisdiction, the United States planted a contradiction deep in the purpose and functioning of the new organization. As a historian of U.S. human rights policy has observed, "The United States thus contributed substantially to the creation of basic inconsistency between the ambitious goals of the UN and its capacity to give effect to them, a source of much unjustified subsequent criticism of the UN for 'failure to act' in a wide range of issues."[138] As W. E. B. Du Bois pointed out, the priority placed on protecting national sovereignty and the corresponding lack of human rights enforcement meant that the United Nations could not prevent another Holocaust, even though, in the public imagination, that was one of its primary reasons for being.[139]

Conclusions: The American Dream

At first glance, the UN Charter marked a dramatic improvement over the Dumbarton Oaks proposal. The great powers had been able to ignore public pressure for human rights enforcement during their secret negotiations to shape the postwar order. The situation changed under the media glare at the founding conference of the United Nations, especially given the new organization's ostensible mandate to pursue peace and justice. Persistent advocacy efforts by small states and civil society groups succeeded in focusing global attention on the need to incorporate human rights into the new world order. Human rights were recognized multiple times in the text, and a commission was established to draft an international bill of rights. The United States, as the driving force behind the entire conference, played a crucial role in winning British and Soviet approval of these changes while at the same time forestalling more radical demands for enforceable rights.[140] The words of Archibald MacLeish, well-known poet and State Department front man for the publicity campaign to support the UN, appeared to be prophetic: "There are some who will say that the liberation of humanity, the freedom of man and mind, is nothing but a dream. They are right. It is. It's the American dream."[141]

A few activists, in particular those whose agenda focused on racial equality and decolonization, were dismayed by the results of San Francisco. The NAACP and allied groups, which had invested significant time, resources, and hopes in using the global forum to highlight the evils of entrenched racism inside the United States and internationally, were bitterly disappointed at the outcome.[142] To no avail, they criticized the failure to dent the vastly unequal power relations operating both between states and within their borders. Rayford Logan, civil rights activist and chair of the history department at Howard University, characterized the human rights articles in the Charter as a "tragic joke."[143]

But these were minority voices. Just as Roosevelt anticipated, the NGO consultants were thrilled with the role they had played in establishing the organization and fanned out across the country to spread the good news. They generally found enthusiastic and receptive audiences. However, some observers noticed the gap between rhetoric and hopes for a new human rights regime; after a rousing performance by Proskauer before a civil society gathering in New York, one critic observed that "Judge Proskauer glossed over the fact that most of the Human Rights provisions of the Charter are in fact, permissive, not mandatory."[144] This crucial problem also troubled Frederick Nolde, who, even though he strongly supported the Charter, worried that its human rights language "leaves unanswered two very crucial questions: It does not say what human rights shall be sought; nor does it say how they shall be promoted."[145]

These were glaring omissions in what was considered to be the ideological foundation of the new world. The failure to define the content or meaning of human rights raised a number of questions and uncertainties. Were human rights actual rights or mere aspirations? Were they rights of individuals or groups or both? Did they imply any concrete duties or obligations or confer any specific advantages to the intended holder of the rights? Were they to be realized at the domestic or international level? Did they include economic, social, and cultural rights? And what limits, if any, did recognition of human rights in the UN Charter impose on state sovereignty and jurisdiction?

On the crucial issues of structure and power, the final shape of the UN—with its dominant Security Council overshadowing the General Assembly and Secretariat—closely resembled the Dumbarton Oaks proposals forged by the Big Three according to Roosevelt's vision of a U.S.-dominated global system.[146] Led by the great powers, the consensus of nations at San

Francisco insisted on retaining a shield of sovereignty against intervention in domestic affairs and rejected a human rights system in which they might be held accountable to the demands of their peoples or subject to international supervision. As a result, the domestic jurisdiction clause, Article 2(7), was enshrined in the UN Charter as the underlying legal principle of the postwar order, thereby undercutting the primary purpose of human rights efforts. This prompted one author to bluntly dismiss the "delusions" of the NGO cheerleaders for the United Nations:

> Because they wanted to believe that San Francisco heralded a brave new world of human rights, they shut their eyes to the realities of power politics. Instead of seeing the United Nations for what it was—a security organization run for and by the world's most powerful states—they saw it for what they wanted it to be: a vehicle for the advancement of the rights of the disenfranchised and dispossessed.[147]

Part 2. Establishing the UN Human Rights Framework

This section examines the building of the human rights foundation at the United Nations. The critical story is how it came to pass that the primary task of the Commission on Human Rights—the drafting of a single, enforceable bill of human rights—turned into a twenty-year project that produced three separate documents: the Universal Declaration of Human Rights, the Covenant on Civil and Political Rights, and the Covenant on Economic, Social and Cultural Rights. The fragmentation of the bill of rights and the separation of the powers of promotion and protection at the UN set the stage for human rights to develop as a universally recognized set of international law principles but without the enforceable duties that are central to an effective legal system.

Chapter 5 focuses on the formation of the Commission on Human Rights, the great-power rivalries that defined its proceedings, and its fateful decisions not to accept individual petitions and not to draft a single bill of rights. The CHR began its work in a glare of publicity and high expectations; the world placed immense hopes in the formation of an effective human rights regime to prevent a recurrence of the recent horrors of war. However, one of the first decisions of the Economic and Social Council (ECOSOC), which oversaw the CHR, was that its members should be government representatives rather than independent experts, thereby ensuring a high degree of politicization at the outset of the human rights project. The eighteen members included a number of extremely prominent personalities, foremost among them Eleanor Roosevelt, widow of the American president, who was elected first chair of the commission and exerted significant influence over its proceedings. In general, the United States played a predominant role due to its geopolitical power as well as the priority the State Department gave to shaping the human rights agenda. In contrast, the United Kingdom's representatives were lackluster and ineffective, and the Soviet role was largely obstructionist once it became clear that the American vision of individual rights would win the day.

The first key decision of the CHR was to declare its lack of power to receive and review any of the thousands of petitions alleging human rights abuses that flooded into the UN from individuals and groups around the world. Many members wanted to take action in response to the enormous public expectations surrounding human rights, and international jurists also urged concrete implementation measures. But the United States and Soviet Union joined forces to reject such pressures, leading the CHR to adopt the "no power doctrine." As a result, the United States was able to quash a public effort by leading NGOs to raise the mistreatment of American blacks as a human rights issue before the commission.

The United States and Soviet Union were at ideological loggerheads on most human rights issues. However, they combined forces to ensure that there would be no implementation measures of any kind at the international level and that efforts to establish enforcement would either be rejected outright or postponed for future consideration. Superpower opposition was crucial in overcoming a strong consensus, in both the CHR and the public at large, for adopting a single binding bill of rights. Instead, the bill was fragmented between a declaration of moral principles, a binding legal treaty, and measures of implementation. Working groups of the CHR were established to develop each of these three areas. However, the working group on implementation disbanded after several years of proposing various measures, including a human rights court and a human rights attorney general, without getting them past the full commission.

Chapter 6 reviews the politics of drafting the Universal Declaration of Human Rights. It is an irony of history that the UDHR has gained the reputation of expressing the unanimous consensus of the international community concerning fundamental moral principles, for its drafting history was fraught with ideological rivalries, practical disagreements, power politics, and numerous compromises. Yet given the differences between states, it was no mean feat to reach agreement in just two years. The source materials for the early drafts of the Universal Declaration were exclusively western, and the overall paradigm was based on the western model of individual rights. Soviet efforts to emphasize the role of the state as guarantor and provider of rights were rejected, although the Soviet bloc and Latin American countries did join forces to ensure that economic and social rights also had a place in the document.

The great powers defeated a number of rights promoted by the majority. For example, the United States and Britain worked together to undermine the right to rebellion, even though it was recognized in previous human rights statements as a fundamental safeguard against tyranny. Similarly, Anglo-American opposition prevented acceptance of minority rights and the right to self-determination; colonized nations were not members of the UN and therefore had no say on these matters. Economic and social rights were recognized, but after a bitter debate they were placed in a subordinate position within the UDHR. While the reputation of universality is belied by this historical record, the General Assembly resolution passed without a negative vote, testifying to the ideological power of the human rights concept and its mass public appeal. Eight countries, including the Soviet representatives, voted to abstain despite being openly hostile to the human rights philosophy expressed in the UDHR. Today these critics of the Universal Declaration are submerged within its image of unanimous support.

In Chapter 7, we describe the continuing withdrawal from universality through attempted limitations based on federalism, colonialism, and the procedure of reservations. This trend culminated in the fragmentation of the human rights regime into separate covenants with weak reporting and monitoring mechanisms. By the 1950s, the Cold War had heated up; the Soviet Union was increasingly hostile to human rights initiatives, and the United States had abandoned its previous commitment to human rights, in part because the McCarthyite right wing viewed the idea of international treaties with suspicion. As a result, progress in developing the human rights regime ground to a halt, regaining momentum only in the 1960s and 1970s with the increased UN membership due to decolonization.

The United States and several other federal states, notably Canada and Australia, sought to introduce a clause denying the application of human rights treaties to constituent states within a federal system unless they too ratified the treaty. This was strongly opposed by the majority of UN members on the grounds that it was a legally fallacious argument that would undermine the universal foundation of human rights. A similar argument put forward by the United Kingdom and France sought to limit the applicability of human rights in their colonies. Both the federal and colonial clauses were eventually defeated after years of protracted debates.

The biggest debate centered on whether there should be one or two covenants. While the UDHR included both civil and political rights and economic, social, and cultural rights, the United States and its western allies were unwilling to accept the latter rights in a binding treaty, arguing that they were not immediately realizable rights susceptible to judicial enforcement. The Soviet Union and most developing countries were unwilling to separate the two. In the end, it proved impossible to impose a single covenant over such powerful opposition; the two were separated despite common language about to the "indivisibility and interdependence" of all rights. Economic and social rights were not given any mechanisms of enforcement. The committee that was established to review state reports on civil and political rights had only minor powers, mostly to engage in dialogue with state parties. Thus, the fragmentation of the human rights idea was accompanied by a complete neglect of implementation. There would be no meaningful impact on people's lives until a human rights movement based on civil society activism arose in the 1970s and 1980s to challenge gross abuses of human dignity.

5

Laying the Human Rights Foundation

- Human Rights: An Unparalleled Undertaking
- America Takes the Lead
- Petitions: The Case for Individual Complaints
- Interlude: The African American Petition
- The Call for a Single Bill of Rights
- The Fragmentation of the Bill of Rights

Today we are accustomed to the idea that human rights serve as an ideological battleground highlighting differences as much as commonalities between individuals, nations, and cultures. But in the unique atmosphere after World War II, it appeared not just desirable but feasible to push for a global order based on universal human rights. People expected and demanded change. With the unconditional surrender of the Axis powers, the victorious governments seemed willing and able to overcome ideological differences and establish a new international order. The Cold War was still a few years away. The general policies of the western democracies and the Soviet Union, even on matters of state intervention in social and economic affairs, were not incompatible. The United States and the United Kingdom had moved significantly toward welfare economics and recognition of social and economic rights. The Soviets had abandoned calls for global revolution in favor of a focus on rebuilding their war-torn economy and establishing a security zone in Eastern Europe—with tacit acceptance by the western democracies. From any perspective, conditions for states to establish human rights protections had never been more favorable. This is why the story of the Commission on Human Rights and its drafting of the Universal Declaration is as much about opportunities missed and hopes betrayed as about the triumphant emergence of the modern human rights regime.

The Commission on Human Rights has faced a drumbeat of criticism in recent years as being too large, too unwieldy, and too politicized to take meaningful action in support of its ostensible mandate. On 15 March

2006, the General Assembly voted overwhelmingly to replace it with a new, streamlined Human Rights Council. At the time of its creation, however, the CHR was a model of bureaucratic efficiency and played an indispensable role in creating the basic instruments of the modern human rights system. All important decisions—what rights to recognize, how to prioritize rights, whether to establish enforcement mechanisms—fell within the commission's purview. While in principle its decisions were subject to review and approval by ECOSOC[1] and the General Assembly as a whole, in practice the CHR had tremendous discretion to shape the form and content of human rights.[2] The initial decisions taken by its eighteen members would create the framework, set the tone, and circumscribe the discourse within which the idea of human rights would develop over the next half-century.[3] In this context, what was not done often had greater consequences than what was done. For example, U.S.-Soviet agreement to reject human rights enforcement measures and the U.S-British agreement to omit the right to self-determination and the right to rebellion had a decisive influence on the shape of the human rights system. Such decisions about which human rights ideas to recognize and pursue and which to drop or postpone, though often taken quickly at the behest of the CHR's most powerful members, would assume far greater historical significance than the intense and lengthy negotiations over the text of particular articles.

Given the intense global interest in human rights, numerous outside interests sought to influence the workings of the commission. Civil society organizations, private initiatives, and individuals turned their attention to the UN as the hope for establishing a new system of international morality.[4] The energy and enthusiasm during the war years to establish the concept of human rights now turned to more practical questions of implementation: How were human rights to be incorporated as meaningful standards into the new international organization, and what could be done to remedy past and ongoing violations? The idea of an international bill of human rights received particular attention. The UN Secretariat staff noted that as of 1946, it had received twelve different draft bills of rights, all from western representatives.[5] These included drafts submitted by the delegations of Panama, Chile, and Cuba and the American Federation of Labor as well as private drafts from Hersch Lauterpacht of Cambridge University, Alejandro Alvarez of the American Institute of International Law, Rev. Wilfrid Parsons of the Catholic Association for International Peace, Prof. Frank McNitt of the faculty of Southwestern University, and H. G. Wells.[6]

In addition, even before the first official meeting of the CHR, the Secretariat had received thousands of individual petitions from around the world alleging violations of various kinds and pleading for redress.[7] The common assumption behind these external interventions was that the CHR would be empowered, or rather would empower itself, to address the most pressing human rights issues of the day. This assumption turned out to be mistaken. The CHR avoided, or more accurately postponed, the urgent question of how to put the human rights idea into operation. And as often happens when a specialized committee is entrusted with important matters, public interest and involvement faded over time, especially once the bureaucratic routines and formal political channels of the commission's daily workings became established. In the end, the most important issues of universal human rights were decided by a handful of governments and their appointed representatives. The public had no opportunity for input.

Conventional history lauds the commission's crowning glory, the Universal Declaration of Human Rights, as a milestone of global cooperation and achievement.[8] But this account masks a more telling failure. Under the dynamic leadership of Eleanor Roosevelt, the CHR took a series of actions that resulted in the progressive fragmentation and weakening of the human rights idea. Very early on, the commission declared that it had no power to receive and act on individual petitions until an effective mechanism could be agreed upon and established.[9] Such a mechanism would not be established for twenty-two years, and then in a weak form.[10] More important, the CHR made the fateful decision not to adopt a single legally binding bill of rights in the form of a multilateral treaty with state obligations—an approach favored by virtually every significant human rights proposal on record. Instead, the bill of rights was divided into three separate components, each proclaimed to be an integral pillar of the larger human rights edifice: a broad declaration setting out principles acceptable to most governments, a legally binding convention with specific state obligations, and, finally, a separate instrument spelling out means of implementation.[11]

The separation of principles, rights, and remedies cast a long shadow over the human rights project and undermined its legal character and capacity. Indeed, it proved disastrous to public hopes for an effective human rights system capable of providing redress at least for the worst violations. While the first component, the UDHR, was completed within two years, the accompanying human rights convention took twenty-eight more years to come into force, during which time it was further fragmented into two treaties—civil and political rights, championed by western states, and economic, social, and cultural rights, supported, albeit less forcefully, by Third World states and the communist bloc and therefore given an inferior legal and political status in the UN system.[12] The third component of the bill of rights, measures of implementation, proved to be weaker still, as the United States and Soviet Union joined forces to block enforcement. As a consequence, the international law of human rights has from its inception focused more on rhetoric promoting a common standard of achievement than on meaningful legal protection for people facing violations of their human dignity.

Human Rights: An Unparalleled Undertaking

Before the CHR could take ownership of the human rights idea, Latin American states made one last attempt to attach a bill of rights to the UN Charter itself. At the first session of the General Assembly, held in London in January 1946, Dr. Richard J. Alfaro of Panama reintroduced the proposal for immediate adoption of a bill of rights in both the First Committee (political) and Third Committee (social, humanitarian, and cultural).[13] The idea enjoyed significant support among member states, but the U.S. delegation, led by Eleanor Roosevelt, and the British delegation forcefully argued for the issue to be sent directly to the Commission on Human Rights.[14] The Soviet Union similarly opposed the immediate enactment of a bill of rights. The Latin American maneuver received good publicity but had no chance of winning the day. As expected, the General Assembly decided not to review the substance of the human rights proposal, instead relying on procedural grounds to avoid a vote and refer the matter to ECOSOC, requesting that it be sent to the CHR for further consideration and deliberation.[15]

Membership in the commission itself was another critical preliminary issue whose outcome would help to determine the shape of human rights at the UN. The preparatory committee established by ECOSOC, which included such prominent future members as Eleanor Roosevelt and René Cassin, had recommended that the CHR be composed of independent experts unattached to their respective governments.[16] This reflected the influence of civil society pressure; the goal was to shield the bill of rights from undue state interference. While independent experts would have been subject to political pressure, they would not have answered directly to their respective foreign offices. At the first meeting of ECOSOC, the great powers rejected this recommendation and decided instead to appoint government representatives from the five permanent members of the Security Council as well as thirteen additional members from different regions of the world.[17] John P. Humphrey, the influential first director of the Human Rights Division of the UN Secretariat, felt that this decision made political sense, on the grounds that "there would be no point in preparing texts which would not be accepted by governments."[18] However, this simple procedural change provided a high degree of government control over the daily workings of the CHR and ensured that state concerns would predominate as the basic contours of the human rights system were established. It also marginalized the role of civil society groups and individuals, as predicted by a prominent jurist at the time:

> If the United Nations is to draft a charter of human rights that drafting in its final stages must be an act of government. But the very nature of rights is that they are claims on the part of individuals that they should have liberty not only from other individuals but also from the state to act in the manner indicated by any particular right. That the Economic and Social Council should so arrange its constitutional procedure that the individual as distinct from the state should take no part, or only a minor part in it, should have no constitutional opportunity of asserting his rights against encroachment by governments, would seem to be a most unfortunate break in historic tradition. . . . The problem of individual rights has thus been prejudiced from the outset.[19]

The first session of the commission was held in an abandoned gyroscope factory at Lake Success, New York, between 27 January and 10 February 1947. Humphrey described the mood of excitement at the opening session:

> All the visitors' seats in the Council chamber were occupied when the session opened. The importance which governments attached to the commission was manifested by the quality of their representatives, many of whom were also playing or would later play important roles in the General Assembly and the Security Council. Two of them, Charles Malik and Carlos Rómulo, later became presidents of the General Assembly.[20]

At the same time, the CHR meetings were anticlimactic in comparison to the gathering in San Francisco. Gone were the large crowds, the klieg lights, and the constant stream of journalists and publicity. While human rights still attracted media interest, most of the CHR's work took place behind closed doors through mundane meetings of various subcommittees and working groups and endless revisions of text. The task of drafting an international bill of rights was nonetheless a staggering responsibility for all involved. The weight of public expectations coupled with the constant political scrutiny of member states, in particular the great powers, weighed heavily on commission members. Humphrey emphasized the enormity of the task: "What the United Nations is trying to do . . . has no parallel in history. We are attempting nothing else than to define and regulate the relationship between the individual and Society, a problem that has puzzled mankind since Old Testament times and before."[21] In a similar vein, Assistant Secretary-General Henri Laugier, the most senior UN official to have oversight responsibility for the CHR, expressed the following sentiments as he convened the first meeting: "No one part of the action undertaken by the United Nations to make peace more secure had more power or a wider scope than this. The task of the Human Rights Commission amounted to following up in the field of peace the fight which free humanity had waged in the fields of war."[22]

America Takes the Lead

Of the eighteen states represented on the CHR, some were more equal than others. Just as the great powers had created the United Nations as a "breathtaking dictatorship" that enshrined their status as global enforcers, they also used their influence to dominate from the outset the proceedings of the CHR and how it would define human rights. But whereas the great powers had agreed on the basic structures and authorities of the UN, they had major differences over the scope and purpose of human rights.

The fact that almost all these disagreements were resolved in favor of the U.S. position cannot be explained on the basis of geopolitical power alone. America emerged from World War II as the dominant global power, due both to its geographic distance from the devastation in Europe and its enormous economic capacity, but its power was balanced by the British and Soviet empires.[23] Britain still maintained extensive colonial holdings and influence over the independent Commonwealth countries and enjoyed the residual prestige of having been the strongest empire over the past several centuries. The Soviet Union possessed formidable military power and held sway over half of Europe. That the influence of the United States on the human rights project far overshadowed that of Britain and the Soviet Union can also be attributed to the priority the State Department placed on planning and working toward a successful outcome and on the personal strengths of the U.S. representative.

In essence, the United States hit the jackpot with Eleanor Roosevelt. She was the widow of an American hero who had steered the country through the Great Depression, united the population behind the war effort, and spearheaded the establishment of the United Nations. Yet she was impressive in her own right—an elegant figure of world renown and an articulate advocate of human rights whose regular newspaper columns reached millions weekly.[24] She was popular with other members of the commission and was duly elected as chair for the first six sessions, from 1947 to 1951, the period when the Universal Declaration was drafted and the most important decisions about the shape of the human rights system were taken.[25]

As chair she could guide the discussion by recognizing or not recognizing particular speakers at critical moments—an advantage she exploited to its maximum, leading a British official to deplore her penchant for using "her position of chairman to try to force through American ideas with the result that we have to be constantly on guard."[26] Despite her political bias, criticism of Mrs. Roosevelt was rarely heard at the CHR, outside of the communist delegates, with whom she was consistently at loggerheads. Charles Malik, the commission's rapporteur, expressed a common feeling of gratitude for her leadership, maintaining that he "didn't see how they could have accomplished what they did without her."[27]

Mrs. Roosevelt cultivated the support and friendship of other members through personal invitations and used these connections to advance the human rights agenda of the United States. Her charisma was such that the State Department came to count on her behind-the-scenes persuasion to line up votes. Durward Sandifer, her main State Department liaison throughout her tenure with the commission from 1947 to 1952,[28] advised his colleagues:

> Always remember that there are some votes which can be secured only if Mrs. Roosevelt speaks to the delegates herself. As you know, Mrs. Roosevelt makes it a practice of entertaining all the delegates on the Third Committee during the course of the session. This is done by small luncheons and by evening sessions. . . . In each case the group invited must be carefully picked out so as to secure maximum efficiency in lining up votes.[29]

For all her personal charms, it is important to keep in mind that she acted at all times as a representative of the U.S. government, not as an independent champion of human rights.[30] Her involvement in shaping the UDHR was political, not idealistic; her success owed more to the extensive behind-the-scenes preparatory work of her government advisors than to her famous skills of persuasion. She was especially close to Sandifer, who later said: "She adopted me as her confidential and personal adviser, and cultivated her relations with me herself during the course of the Assembly."[31] Alger Hiss, another State Department official, remarked that "it was a case with Sandy and Mrs. Roosevelt of love at first sight."

Throughout her work as commission chair, Mrs. Roosevelt was in constant communication with advisors from an interagency committee comprised of representatives from the departments of state, commerce, labor, and interior and the Federal Security Agency.[32] Every major position she took was laid out in advance and memorialized in position papers and memoranda. At every session of the CHR, she was accompanied by one or more advisors who provided recommendations on all aspects of negotiations, passing notes such as: "If there is a subcommittee of three, suggest—Malik, Dukes, Mora" and

"Our position paper finds 'serious difficulties' with the right to work. On the other hand, you can't very well argue against the President's speech."[33]

That she performed valuable service for the U.S. government is beyond question; reports of her work are uniformly glowing. There is no indication that she ever strayed from her role in faithfully carrying out U.S. policy, although there are reports that she tried to persuade the State Department to drop its rejection of implementation.[34] The decision by the CHR to reject implementation in favor of rhetorical principles—far and away the most damaging decision for the long-term viability of the human rights system—was accomplished through her lobbying skills, in accordance with specific instructions that "discussion of implementation was to be avoided, but if this could not be done, discussion was to be on only a tentative level and should not involve any commitments by this Government."[35] She was also the driving force behind denying the right of petition, and she personally intervened to bury a detailed complaint documenting horrific race crimes in the United States that was submitted by the NAACP, on whose board she served at the time.[36]

Mrs. Roosevelt's status as a revered and respected public advocate of human rights was sufficient to mask her contradictory behind-the-scenes role as a representative of U.S. power politics, even though she frequently engaged in ideological debate with representatives of communist bloc countries at the behest of the State Department. Admiring her skills in demolishing the position of a Soviet delegate, one observer noted, "Never before have I seen naiveté and cunning so gracefully blended."[37] In his private diary, John Humphrey lamented this dual role following one of her speeches in 1948:

> The crowd had come to hear the Chairman of the Human Rights Commission and the widow of a very great man. It heard a speech that had obviously been written by the State Department and ninety percent of which was devoted to an attack against the U.S.S.R. I do not blame the Americans for talking back; but I do regret that they are using Mrs. R. as their spokesman in these polemics.[38]

Britain Punches Below Its Weight

Compared to the United States, British influence at the CHR was negligible. This was not due to lack of interest; the Foreign Office recognized the importance of the commission, correctly predicting that human rights would become the locus of "big battles in the United Nations on the fundamental ideological issue of Western democracy as opposed to Soviet totalitarianism."[39] Moreover, the British considered themselves natural leaders on human rights, given their heritage as founders of liberal individualism in both political philosophy and domestic law. The main obstacle, of course, was the colonial question, but once the issue of human rights in the colonies had been shunted off to the unthreatening Trusteeship Council, the Foreign Office expected to play a lead role in promoting the idea of enforceable human rights through domestic incorporation of international standards.

None of this came to pass, partly because the Foreign Office devoted a fraction of the resources the U.S. State Department expended and partly because the British representatives lacked the knowledge, qualifications, and charisma to establish a leading presence on the commission. While the government was undoubtedly preoccupied with rebuilding the nation and stabilizing its far-flung empire, it missed an opportunity for global influence by neglecting human rights. In contrast to the United States, Britain favored a bill of rights with measures of implementation and therefore was in a position to act as a champion for smaller nations as well as civil society at large.[40] Such a role would have magnified British influence not only in the human rights debate but in the larger ideological discourse of international affairs.

The first British nominee, former trade union leader Charles Duke, was unenthusiastic about assuming the position and had little substantive knowledge of human rights.[41] As the Foreign Office soon discovered, he was unreliable and failed to follow instructions.[42] He did not vigorously oppose the establishment of a subcommission on minority rights, despite the opposition from the Foreign Office, and initially supported the right to petition when the British government had no such policy.[43] In addition, he was elderly and sick and died shortly after assuming his position, before the third session of the CHR. He was replaced first by Marguerite Bowie, who also served on the Commission on the Status of Women (CSW), and then by Geoffrey Wilson, who was similarly inexperienced in matters of human rights.[44] Wilson was well connected in Britain and had accompanied Churchill to the meeting in Crimea with Roosevelt and Stalin but nevertheless lacked international reputation and influence. In the end, even the support of qualified advisors from the Foreign Office was not enough for the British delegates to make a mark on the proceedings of the CHR.

The most obvious candidate to represent the United Kingdom, international jurist Hersch Lauterpacht, had a global reputation. He had written the seminal book on human rights, engaged in numerous academic and private human rights initiatives across the world, and was a respected advocate of a legally binding bill of rights.[45] Nevertheless, he was passed over by the foreign policy establishment. Top legal advisor Eric Beckett felt that Lauterpacht would make a "disastrous" representative:

Professor Lauterpacht, although a distinguished and industrious international lawyer, is, when all is said and done, a Jew fairly recently come from Vienna. Emphatically, I think that the representative of HMG [Her Majesty's Government] on human rights must be a very English Englishman imbued throughout his life and hereditary to the real meaning of human rights as we understand them in this country.[46]

Such reasoning while Europe was still in the shadow of the Holocaust illustrates the difficulties inherent in the effort to implant respect for human rights in a world that was riven by racism and inequality and whose great powers were still wedded to the ideology of superiority and domination.

The Soviet Union: Isolated and Outvoted

The stance of the Soviet delegation, which had one slot each for Russia, Ukraine, and Byelorussia, was half-hearted, ambiguous, and contradictory toward the work of the CHR. Stalin had long since dismissed the importance of the United Nations itself. He accorded "far more importance to his control of Eastern Europe than to the structure of the new global institution, and to gain the acceptance he wanted for the one, yielded any significant say over the other."[47] He consistently underestimated the "soft power" of ideological warfare and misunderstood the role of human rights in mobilizing public opinion on the fundamental moral questions of legitimacy and governance. Moreover, communist theory was genuinely ambivalent, if not hostile, to liberal individual rights, which Karl Marx himself had viewed as a bourgeois form of alienation separating each person from all others and establishing individual interests in opposition to the state that was meant to represent them.[48]

As a more practical matter, the Soviet Union felt that the UN was stacked against its interests in terms of numerical votes and generally adopted a defensive and ultimately obstructionist approach to human rights issues. The grand alliance of Roosevelt, Stalin, and Churchill was fraying, and along with it the balance-of-power compromises reached in the aftermath of war. While in practice Stalin had accepted a modus vivendi with the western powers, he delivered an infamous speech in 1946 declaring that peaceful coexistence between communism and capitalism was impossible.[49] Churchill followed with his famous "Iron Curtain" speech warning of the dangers of Soviet hegemony, while U.S. diplomat George Kennan sent his influential telegram from Moscow arguing that the Soviet regime would respond only to strength, not appeals to humanity—the first step in the U.S. Cold War policy of containment and confrontation.[50]

These tensions spilled over into the CHR, as Soviet delegates attacked the United States for race-based discrimination, lynching, and other forms of violence and were attacked in turn for lack of civil and political freedoms.[51] Moreover, Soviet delegates challenged the individualist framework of human rights as biased toward western liberalism but rarely offered a positive alternative vision of socialist or group rights. Advocating an alternative perspective on human rights could have given them more bargaining power to influence the proceedings and more legitimacy when they ultimately decided to abstain in the General Assembly vote on the Universal Declaration. But apart from Vladimir Koretsky, a prominent Russian professor of international law, Moscow sent unimpressive and unimaginative delegates to the commission and kept them on a tight leash.[52] This meant that Soviet delegates were constantly fighting defensive rearguard actions. Even those rights they supported in theory, for example the abolition of the death penalty, the right to work, and economic and social rights in general, were framed at the CHR not as socialist rights guaranteed by the state but as individual rights within western-style judicial arrangements. The Soviets therefore adopted an inflexible stance that opposed all forms of international implementation of human rights on the grounds of national sovereignty while at the same time advocating, without success, state obligations to provide economic and social rights. In the end, the Soviet stance toward human rights came to be viewed in the UN and the broader public as hypocritical and obstructionist, and the U.S. role as proactive and pragmatic—even though, on crucial issues such as human rights enforcement and the right of petition, both superpowers were equally rejectionist.[53]

In the available literature on human rights, there are few mentions of positive contributions by Soviet delegates. At the first meeting of the CHR, James Hendrick, one of Mrs. Roosevelt's State Department advisors, dismissed the Soviet representative with the following comment: "Mr. Borisov, U.S.S.R., arriving at the last moment, was a completely inflexible exponent of the messages he had received from Moscow"—momentarily forgetting his own government's role in predefinining the policies Mrs. Roosevelt advocated.[54] The most forceful of the communist delegates was Mr. Ribnikar, representing Yugoslavia. His family owned the major Belgrade newspaper *Politka*, and he was trained in political theory as well. While friendly toward western countries, he was a committed Marxist and had cast his lot with Tito.[55] Throughout the CHR's proceedings, Ribnikar attacked liberal individual rights, emphasizing the collective spirit of humanity, "a consciousness of solidarity and personal freedom" that could in his opinion "only be attained through perfect harmony between the individual and the community."[56] Such philosophical musings provoked sharp replies from western-inclined intellectuals such as Charles Malik, P. C. Chang, and René Cassin. But however rhetorically vigorous these disputes and arguments, they were one-sided in outcome, as the communist countries found themselves outvoted and outmaneuvered on almost every significant point of dispute.

Other Leading Members of the Commission

Although the United States exercised predominant power over the workings of the CHR, other members made important contributions to shaping the early human rights system within the given parameters. Many of the state representatives were respected personalities with internationally recognized human rights expertise. One of the senior statesmen was the Australian delegate, Colonel Hodgson.[57] A passionate advocate of internationalism, he was nearing the end of a long and distinguished military and diplomatic career. He had been wounded in Gallipoli and represented Australia at the Paris Peace Conference of 1919. While siding with the United States and Britain on most issues and relishing intellectual combat with his communist counterparts, Hodgson also held some iconoclastic views. In particular, he was a strong proponent of enforceable human rights and favored the establishment of an international court of human rights that could adjudicate individual claims against the state.

The only other woman besides Mrs. Roosevelt was Hansa Mehta, representing India.[58] An intellectual and activist, she came from a privileged background as a Brahmin, an upper-caste Hindu. Mehta had been deeply involved in the battle for self-determination and sovereignty. During the independence struggle, she had been imprisoned several times by the British. Her background in national politics gave her confidence to push for human rights as an effective means to combat oppression. She was also a determined advocate of women's rights and championed a human rights bill with effective enforcement measures to address the discrimination suffered by Indians who had been forcibly transplanted to other countries, such as South Africa.

Several other non-European delegates played leading roles in the commission. Charles Malik of Lebanon presented an interesting mix.[59] A Harvard-educated scholar, he was also an avowed Christian believer, Thomist philosopher, and advocate of natural individual rights. Though representing a predominantly Muslim country marked by communal political alliances, he was a traditionally trained intellectual who had little time or patience for practical politics and, for example, had been dismayed by the intrigues and backroom negotiations at the San Francisco conference. His primary concern at the commission was to work on a tangible set of rights. In recognition of his diligence, experience, and legal background, he was elected as rapporteur.[60] Malik would go on to serve as the president of the General Assembly.

Another prominent western-educated scholar was Peng Cheng Chang, who has been hailed as a Renaissance man of Chiang Kai-shek's China.[61] Chang identified himself as a pluralist in his approach to human rights; he sought to bridge East and West, individual and collective approaches to human rights.[62] By many accounts, he had an agreeable personality and was a master of the art of compromise. Humphrey termed him a conciliatory presence who often would provide a Confucian quote to enable the commission to escape from a deadlock or impasse.[63] He was elected vice-chair of the CHR and generally ran meetings in Roosevelt's absence.

The three leaders of the commission, Roosevelt, Chang, and Malik, enjoyed a close working relationship that proved crucial to the success of the overall endeavor; together they were instrumental in moving the drafting forward, resolving disputes, and promoting a fundamentally shared vision of the human rights idea despite their divergent backgrounds: "This triumvirate, symbolically representing East, West, and in the case of Malik, a crossroads of many cultures, constituted the leadership of the Human Rights Commission throughout the entire period of the preparation of the document that became the Universal Declaration of Human Rights."[64] Such camaraderie did not sit well with all the members. The Soviet delegate, Valentin Tepliakov, sent a pessimistic early report to Moscow on the prospects for influencing the CHR: "We weren't able to make the changes that we wanted to make, such as to bring the representative of the Soviet Union or Yugoslavia into the leadership of the Commission. . . . The Chinese representative as well as the Lebanese representative are partisans of the position of the representative of the United States."[65]

There were other prominent personalities on the CHR. General Carlos Rómulo, professional newspaperman and owner of a chain of papers in the Philippines, had also been present in San Francisco and at the United Nations Monetary and Financial Conference at Bretton Woods.[66] He was an outspoken advocate of economic and social rights, self-determination, and the rights of smaller nations and openly criticized the dominance of the United States and its western allies in establishing the political and economic structures of the postwar world. One of the more flamboyant characters at the United Nations, he went on to serve as the president of the General Assembly. The Chilean representative, Hernán Santa Cruz, was a leading voice in the Latin American human rights movement and a resolute champion of economic and social rights and economic self-determination. He was later appointed UN special rapporteur on issues of racial discrimination and wrote one of the first studies on discrimination in economic and social rights.[67]

It is noteworthy that almost all representatives of what would soon be called the Third World enjoyed close working relations with Mrs. Roosevelt and the U.S. delegation, despite differences on such critical issues as human rights implementation, the right to self-determination, and economic and social rights. The representatives of the United States and the United Kingdom considered Malik a star for his "fervent individualism" and the lead role he played in challenging the Soviets on their materialist philosophy.[68] Notwithstanding her status as an anticolonialist champion, Mehta was a British favorite and gave them "constant and powerful support."[69] The United States similarly counted on tacit alliances with Chang, Rómulo, and even Santa Cruz, despite significant differences over economic and social rights.[70] That such prominent and experienced representatives did not object more effectively to the marginalization of their political views probably reflects their limited room for maneuver under the U.S. umbrella.

From the Anglo-American perspective, French representative René Cassin presented the biggest challenge. Cassin was the foremost legal intellectual on the CHR, the only member with an international stature rivaling that of Mrs. Roosevelt.[71] Although he was a secular Jew, he professed great respect for religion and Christian thought. He had served on the League of Nations, was legal advisor and close friend to President Charles de Gaulle, and later served as the president of the European Court of Human Rights. Cassin enjoyed prestige not only as a prominent jurist but also as representative of a powerful European country, a colonial empire, and a member of the permanent five, yet with some distance from the power politics that produced the UN's antidemocratic political structures. The British Foreign Office decried his stubborn independence, branding him the most "difficult Commission member to work with as he can rarely be persuaded to compromise on his favorite principles."[72] The United States found objectionable his firm commitment to enforceable human rights and his eloquent defense of economic and social rights, even though he considered them to be of lesser legal stature than civil and political rights. The U.S. ambassador to France went so far as to accuse Cassin of "manifesting fellow traveler tendencies" for his "crypto-communist habit of directing criticism against the United States while maintaining silence on the worst features of Soviet regime."[73] Nevertheless, Cassin played a significant part in drafting the UDHR and was called by biographers the "father of the Universal Declaration," based on a misunderstanding that he had contributed the first draft of the document.[74]

One of the key figures behind the UDHR and other UN human rights initiatives was not even a member of the CHR. John Humphrey, director of the Human Rights Division in the Secretariat's Department of Social Affairs, was responsible for supporting the CHR's work, and he did so with great enthusiasm, diligence, and expertise. An international lawyer from Canada, he possessed extensive knowledge of international law and was an ardent supporter of universal human rights protection. It was Humphrey, not Cassin, who produced the first draft of the UDHR, working mainly from a wealth of materials supplied by the United States. He was also an invaluable mediator between different philosophical factions and a central actor in the history of human rights at the United Nations.[75] He remained with the Secretariat until 1966, guiding work on human rights issues as smoothly as possible through the intricate and elaborate machinery of the UN. His memoirs provide valuable insight on the inner workings of the human rights project.[76]

We now turn to one of the first key decisions facing the members of the CHR—what action to take with respect to the great number of petitions flooding the UN from peoples and organizations alleging that their human rights had been violated.

Petitions: The Case for Individual Complaints

The individual right of petition was a recent innovation in international law. Under the League of Nations treaties, individuals had for the first time become subjects of international laws safeguarding the welfare of religious, ethnic, national, and racial minorities. Members of an aggrieved minority were given the right to petition the League directly.[77] Prominent international legal minds at the time, such as Hans Kelsen, Hersch Lauterpacht, and U.S. political scientist Quincy Wright, supported this mechanism as crucial to protect minority groups from nationalistic majorities in the newly created states of Europe.[78]

In the beginning, several hundred petitions were sent to the League, but their numbers gradually dropped as the League took little or no action; only a handful were submitted after 1935. There were several reasons for the League's inaction: members were reluctant to get involved in internal disputes between states and their citizens, there was no remedy for violations, and protection of minorities was not incorporated into domestic law.[79] More broadly, the effectiveness of the whole system had come into question with the unchecked rise of Nazism and fascism in Europe and the League's inability to protect Jewish minorities.[80]

The Jewish lobby groups that had supported League of Nations framework for minority rights quickly adopted the UN's individual human rights framework as better suited to their cause. The acting director of the American Jewish Committee's Institute for Peace and Postwar Problems noted: "The protection of Jewish rights is a part of the general protection of human rights. If the fundamental human liberties are sufficiently secure, there is no need for a special status for the Jews."[81] Great hope, therefore, was placed on the CHR and the international bill of rights to check human rights violations through an effective petition mechanism, despite the domestic jurisdiction clause in the Charter.[82]

The UN Charter laid down the fundamental principle of nondiscrimination on the basis of race, sex, language, or religion. However, it did not provide any machinery for implementation other than observance and respect for human rights. And the domestic jurisdiction clause limited interference in domestic affairs unless the violation constituted a threat to peace. Many international jurists, including Lauterpacht, had interpreted the UN Charter to include, at minimum, a right to petition as a means of safeguarding human rights.[83] In Lauterpacht's view, human rights was not within the purview of the domestic jurisdiction clause. He argued that because human rights had been "included among the principal purposes of the United Nations and [had] become a persistent theme of the Charter, that question has become one which, far from being essentially within the domestic jurisdiction of States, is essentially of international concern."[84] He noted that the provisions of the Charter with respect to human rights were obligatory on member states and obligations were not decisively affected by the limiting clause of Article 2(7). The Charter recognized "the individual as subject of international law. Such recognition may be legitimately expected to enhance the international procedural capacity of the individual for the purposes of the effective petition to the organs of the United Nations in vindication of his human rights and fundamental freedoms thus recognized."[85] Gross forms of discrimination and persecution were violations under the legal obligations of the Charter, thus, a "detailed definition of human rights was neither essential nor desirable."[86]

Another prominent international lawyer, Herbert Briggs, observed that the domestic jurisdiction clause became inapplicable when states themselves created law, constituting obligations of international concern.[87] Wright remarked that the provisions of the Charter were ambiguous and could be interpreted "to bar consideration of almost all questions by the United Nations organs. On the other hand, it might be held that matters cease to be domestic when placed within the competence of United Nations agencies."[88] He listed those matters as including "all matters threatening or disturbing international peace and security; all matters concerning the promotion of higher standards of living, full employment, conditions of economic and social progress and development; the solution of international economic, social, health, and related problems; international cultural and educational cooperation, as well as promotion of universal respect for and observance of, human rights and fundamental freedoms."[89]

In keeping with expert opinion, the nine-member preparatory committee to establish the CHR initially foresaw a role for itself in addressing human rights issues, especially grave violations that might lead to war and undermine the purposes of the United Nations. At its first meeting in spring 1946, the preparatory committee proposed to ECOSOC that "pending the eventual establishment of an agency of implementation the Commission on Human Rights might be recognized as qualified to aid the appropriate organ of the United Nations . . . by pointing to cases where violation of human rights committed in one country may, by its gravity, its frequency, or its systematic nature constitute a threat to peace."[90] However, once the CHR was constituted as an official body of government representatives, subject to state influence and prerogatives, its position on the question of petitions and other forms of implementation changed dramatically.

The Commission's Self-Denial of Power

Despite public opinion and legal arguments in favor of the right of petition, Assistant Secretary-General Henri Laugier, in his opening speech to the members of the CHR, expressed doubts as to whether they had the authority to investigate individual complaints. Nonetheless, he noted that "these appeals established a direct link between the United Nations and men in quest of justice" and a reply was necessary, as tens of millions had died to preserve human rights. He stated: "The problem for the Commission lay in discovering and defining its competence, its procedure, its means of action and its peaceful weapons for the defense of justice."[91]

To most members of the CHR, the large number of appeals that had arrived at their doorstep indicated a need to develop implementation machinery to redress human rights violations. Implementation mechanisms created separately from the international bill of rights had the advantage of coming into force sooner than those connected with the bill of rights. Cassin, Hodgson, and Mehta were of the opinion that the CHR needed to establish a mechanism to respond to petitions regarding urgent crises.[92] Mehta pointed out that India

faced a problem of exceptional magnitude for reasons beyond its control: during the past one hundred years, four million Indians [have] been transplanted to various parts of the world under the aegis of the colonial governments concerned, and

[are] now residing abroad in special communities, created at the request of those governments. As a result of this transplantation, numerous cases of denials of rights in law and equally complicated questions of nationality and citizenship [have] arisen due to certain administrative practices on the part of the governments concerned. Such problems [must] be solved within the meaning of the terms of reference of the Commission on Human Rights and the principles of the Charter. [An] effort should be made to define in precise legal terminology the terms "discrimination" and "minority." It [is] also necessary to define what specific safeguards should be incorporated in the proposed bill of rights against the dangers of assimilation. [The] proposed bill of human rights [will] be meaningless unless an unequivocal definition [is] given of the relationship between the individual, the community, the state, and the international organization.[93]

Mrs. Roosevelt had taken a position in favor of linking the development of implementation measures with the international bill of rights.[94] At the opening of the first session, she declared that the key task before the CHR was how to enforce the international bill of rights the commission was going to write.[95] She had received explicit instructions from the State Department to avoid any direct measures of implementation relating to the petition mechanism. In a private memorandum, Sandifer, her legal advisor, noted that any suggestion of a special organ to supervise and enforce basic rights or receive petitions was a radical and dangerous concept and that Article 2(7) of the Charter specifically denied authority to the UN to intervene in any matters that are essentially of a domestic nature. He therefore noted that "the view of the United States [is] that the establishment of machinery for international supervision of human rights . . . cannot be an immediate objective of the Commission on Human Rights."[96] The American Bar Association and its president, Frank Holman, charged that the UN human rights program and any measures of enforcement that it would propose were an invasion of the domestic jurisdiction of the United States and other states and that it had nothing to do with maintenance of peace.[97]

Given the sharp exchanges between delegates on the issue of petitions in this first session, it was apparent that any decision was going to be very difficult. The British delegate remarked, "greater progress could be made in subsequent discussion if the Commission defined the meaning of individual rights, before proceeding to deal with the other subjects."[98] Philippines' General Rómulo proposed that a subcommittee be set up to review the petitions and determine their merit. The three-person subcommittee met on 1 February 1947 with Charles Duke, the British representative, as the chair, joined by the representatives of Lebanon and Uruguay. It recommended that in the future the Secretariat prepare a confidential list of communications and then grant members access to the original complaint even though Rómulo and Duke felt that sharing these communications with members of the CHR might lead to state reprisals against the petitioners.[99]

The United States, however, maintained that the CHR had been instructed to draft an international bill of rights and that any discussions on measures of implementation were premature.[100] Other states shared U.S. apprehensions about creating enforcement measures under the prerogative of a supranational structure that might be turned against their own governments at some point. In several comments made during the first session, Tepliakov noted that neither the CHR nor anybody considering the bill of rights had any authority to consider implementation, as that would be a violation of the domestic jurisdiction clause of the Charter.[101] Colonel Hodgson, despite his broad personal views supporting immediate enforcement, expressed the official Australian view that considering petitions at this time was a hasty measure. Chang also objected but on procedural grounds. In his view, the CHR, given its current composition with only three legal experts, was not a qualified body to receive such complaints and should refrain from raising false hopes.[102]

Before the end of the first session of the CHR, Mrs. Roosevelt expressed the view that the CHR had no power to take any action on alleged violations of human rights and that the matter should be left for consideration under the international bill of rights. She concluded, "The United Nations is not yet in a position to take effective and comprehensive action upon petitions. . . . The U.S. believes that complaints should for the time being be handled under the Convention."[103] Writing in *Foreign Affairs* magazine, Mrs. Roosevelt reiterated that the CHR was not a court and could not take any action on petitions.[104] Upset by the defeatist attitude of his colleagues, Cassin insisted that ECOSOC be informed of the serious gap resulting from the CHR's refusal to address communications of alleged human rights violations, but Mrs. Roosevelt convinced him that an oral explanation was sufficient.

The CHR's repudiation of its power to make recommendations regarding human rights violations set the stage for ECOSOC to adopt Resolution 75(V) confirming the no-power doctrine. Adopted on 5 August 1947, the resolution stated that "neither the Commission on Human Rights nor the Commission on Women had any power to take any action in regard to any complaints concerning human rights or the status of women."[105] Egypt, India, and the Philippines attempted to reverse the decision, but ECOSOC instead worked in changes such that members of the CHR could not even review the original text of the complaint.[106] The Secretariat was supposed to receive and record communications, compile a list, send summaries of the communications to the governments of concern (deleting the names of complainants), and prepare a confidential list for members of the CHR, who were to review them in a closed meeting. The petitioner was to be informed that the complaint had been noted and referred to the CHR, which had had no power to act in response to the complaint. According to Humphrey, "It was probably the most elaborate wastepaper basket ever invented. At every session the commission went through the farce of clearing the conference room for a secret meeting which lasted only a few minutes, time enough for the commission to adopt a resolution taking note of the list."[107]

Interlude: The African American Petition

The no-power doctrine the CHR adopted frustrated the efforts of anti-racism groups such as the NAACP to raise the problem of racial injustice in the United States as a human rights issue. Stymied by government indifference and encouraged by changes in world politics as a result of World War II, the African American leadership made a strategic decision to shift its focus from civil rights to human rights as the best means to end the segregationist Jim Crow laws of the south.[108] This change was induced by Roosevelt's promise of justice for all peoples based on the Four Freedoms, the recognition of human rights in the UN Charter, and the moral shock of the Holocaust. The move seemed particularly appropriate given that the United States was the leading architect of the emerging human rights framework.

W. E. B. Du Bois, activist, educator, and co-founder of the NAACP, rejoined the organization to champion the cause of black equality through human rights at the United Nations. He began with a critique of the Dumbarton Oaks proposal, focusing on the issue of colonialism and the disfranchisement of 750 million people of color and the failure to develop an international mechanism to address complaints of human rights violations. He attended the San Francisco conference on behalf of the NAACP as one of the forty-two NGO consultants and lobbied hard for an end to racial discrimination and colonialism, only to end up disappointed by the Charter's emphasis on protecting domestic jurisdiction—the same argument used to perpetuate Jim Crow laws.

In 1946, a wave of violence that included murder and lynching erupted against returning black veterans who dared to challenge the Jim Crow laws of the south.[109] Efforts to bring the perpetrators to justice failed; instead, tight-lipped southern society and a racist judiciary protected the lynchers. Georgia governor Eugene Talmadge openly preached violence against blacks and warned them against entering the voting booths, while Senator

Theodore Bilbo, a Democrat from Mississippi, championed the deportation of blacks to Liberia. Despite appeals, the federal government refused to get involved, citing jurisdictional issues. The contrast to the U.S. government's vigorous pursuit of Nazi and Japanese war criminals confirmed the hypocrisy and double standards: the United States flexed its moral muscle in the international arena while maintaining an appalling human rights record on the domestic front.[110]

The UN itself was forced to confront U.S. racism at a very practical level. When the Secretary-General's office tried to reserve accommodations for UN delegations in New York, the Waldorf-Astoria hotel refused rooms to representatives from Ethiopia, Liberia, and Haiti. The Secretary-General intervened personally, meeting with the chair of the hotel's board, who agreed to accept the African delegates but not the Haitians. The State Department had to intervene to find enough hotel rooms and keep the scandal out of the papers.[111] Later that same year, 200 UN employees of color signed a petition in protest against racial discrimination in housing.[112]

In response, the NAACP decided to seek international justice for the black minority in the United States, hoping to link up with antiracist and anticolonialist movements in Asia and Africa. The initial idea of a human rights petition came from an organization Ralph Bunche had co-founded, the National Negro Congress (NNC), which submitted an eight-page report to the UN in 1946 outlining government oppression against blacks.[113] The Secretariat responded that the evidence provided was insufficient to prove that the rights of American blacks were being violated and that in any case the Charter did not allow intervention into the domestic affairs of states. The NNC was unable to advance the petition after black churches and unions withdrew support following an FBI campaign that branded the organization as communist and un-American. Leadership of the petition passed to Du Bois and the NAACP.

Du Bois decided that a scholarly treatise documenting both human rights abuses against blacks and UN obligations to intervene was necessary to spur action against the United States. The purpose was to unequivocally document structurally entrenched racial discrimination in the United States, as reported in an academic study by Swedish economist Gunnar Myrdal, *An American Dilemma*,[114] which examined the social, economic, and political conditions of African Americans and revealed an ever-widening gap between the U.S. principle of equality and the reality of African American lives. Written in three months, Du Bois's 155-page petition titled "An Appeal for Redress" included six chapters detailing the history of legal obstacles to black equality in the United States, setting forth the human rights framework, and presenting a pattern of systemic discrimination using sociological data on employment, wage differentials, illiteracy, housing, infant mortality, low life expectancy, and inadequate health care.[115] The petition documented that even wealthy well-educated blacks faced discrimination purely based on skin color, "and it is this that we denounce as not only indefensible but barbaric," asserted Du Bois.[116] However, at every turn, one question plagued the petitioners: how to overcome the domestic jurisdiction clause.

Before the NAACP had a chance to make its case, the UN found itself embroiled in a high-profile test case of its powers to intervene in domestic affairs concerning state abuse of a racial minority. The Indian government charged South Africa with human rights violations for disregarding treaties meant to grant Indian workers full benefits and rights of citizenship and instead passing a series of discriminatory laws, including the Asiatic Land Tenure and Indian Representation Act, which prohibited Indians from buying land in the whites-only areas.[117] Turning to the United States for support, South Africa contended that the issue was an internal matter and in any case that no such internationally recognized rights existed. The ability of South Africa's Indian population to bypass their own government and complain directly to the UN raised U.S. concerns that its own minorities might do the same. To forestall this, the United States tried to limit the dispute before the General Assembly to violations of treaties between India and South Africa. But this strategy failed once the Soviet Union and developing countries insisted that the UN confront the underlying issue of racial discrimination. As a result, the General Assembly issued a landmark resolution in 1946 condemning the racist character of South African policies as human rights violations contrary to the spirit of the Charter.[118]

The stage was now set for the African American petition; Du Bois was eager to take up the challenge. Earlier John Humphrey had warned him that only member states could place a petition before the UN and that the United States was firmly opposed on the grounds that "no good" would come of it.[119] Mrs. Roosevelt, who sat on the board of the NAACP, had also discouraged Du Bois, advising that it would be in the best interest of African Americans to work within the domestic context instead of exposing the United States to distorted accusations from hostile countries at the UN. Nevertheless, the activist scholar, indefatigable at almost eighty years of age, contacted every UN delegation as well as the Secretary-General, requesting that the petition be given a full hearing before the General Assembly session in November 1947. In an attempt to get the UN to act, Du Bois had the NAACP leak the petition to the press. The story was covered on the front page of the Sunday *New York Times*, which quoted Du Bois's argument that racist elements in the U.S. south posed a greater threat than the Soviets: "When will nations learn that their enemies are quite as often within their own country as without?"[120] Humphrey capitulated and received the petition on 23 October 1947 but under conditions that minimized its impact. He rejected the NAACP's request to present the petition publicly to the UN, transferred it to the Sub-Commission on Prevention of Discrimination and Protection of Minorities—the lowest tier in the UN human rights hierarchy—and insisted that the petition be treated as confidential in accordance with the no-power doctrine under ECOSOC resolution 75(V).[121]

To counter the NAACP petition, the U.S. government embarked on a public-relations campaign to control the damage. The President's Committee on Civil Rights issued its own official report, "To Secure These Rights," spelling out U.S. commitments and activities at the highest levels to improve the conditions of U.S. blacks, thereby countering the argument of government neglect and inaction. Simultaneously, the State Department issued a study of discriminatory practices by other UN member states, singling out human rights problems in the Soviet Union. These reports served as ammunition during debates over the NAACP petition at the UN subcommission, where the Soviet Union took up the cause of African Americans with gusto, exposing U.S. hypocrisy at every opportunity. The United States countered by dismissing the petition as Soviet propaganda and a double standard; Mrs. Roosevelt noted that the Soviet Union had opposed any international implementation of human rights and failed even to provide basic free speech rights to its citizens.[122] Concerning the substance of the petition, Mrs. Roosevelt admitted to "remaining imperfections in the practice of democracy" but insisted that the allegation of government-based discrimination against "Negroes was baseless."[123] After a series of rancorous exchanges, the subcommission rejected the Soviet resolution to investigate racism in America by a vote of 4 to 1 with seven abstentions. The *New York Times* noted that the striking feature of the vote was that delegates uniformly cited procedural rather than substantive reasons for rejecting or abstaining on the resolution, namely that it made no sense to single out one petition for action when the CHR had not taken decisions on the larger issue of enforcement measures.[124]

The failure of the NAACP petition had important human rights consequences in both the UN and the United States. It marked the first time, and for many years the last time, that human rights would be used in the UN as a weapon against U.S. policy. In subsequent decades, the ideological power of human rights would be turned almost exclusively against the Soviet bloc. That an empirically documented and legally powerful complaint submitted by a well-organized minority in the world's most powerful state could be dismissed on technical grounds revealed the fundamental weakness of the UN human rights system: it was simply not designed or equipped to address violations of rights. The millions of people suffering violations of their human rights, including African Americans, who had looked to the UN with such hopes and expectations and would not find comfort or assistance in the new world organization. The failure was so disillusioning to the NAACP and its allies that they abandoned the brief experiment with international justice and refocused the struggle at the domestic front, eventually culminating in *Brown v. Board of Education,* the landmark 1954 Supreme Court decision to desegregate public schools, and the successful civil rights movement in the 1960s. Du Bois did not mince words in noting the rigged foundation of the new world order:

> If the United Nations today face contradiction and frustration in their great effort to build the international community, no small cause of this is that democracy on earth is too often falsifying its own foundation, principles, and for that reason cannot honestly build or cooperate in a just world.[125]

The Call for a Single Bill of Rights

At the end of the first session, the CHR had agreed to convene a smaller drafting group to meet over the summer to prepare an international bill of rights for the second session of the CHR. On 9 June 1947, this group, consisting of Roosevelt, Chang, Malik, Santa Cruz, Cassin, Wilson (replacing Dukes, who was ill), and Vladimir Koretsky (replacing the relatively junior Tepliakov), met at the UN headquarters at Lake Success. The task at hand was to produce a preliminary document of suggestions concerning the international bill of rights. The drafting committee initially discussed two basic options for the bill of rights: a declaration in the form of a General Assembly resolution, and thus primarily a moral statement, or a convention to be adopted by the General Assembly and ratified by governments, and thus legally binding upon states parties.[126] They also received a set of documents prepared by Humphrey on a draft bill of rights.[127]

At the outset, there were sharp differences over what was meant by an international bill of rights, especially between the United States and the United Kingdom.[128] Mrs. Roosevelt, supported only by Koretsky and the Soviet bloc, recommended that a declaration or manifesto with moral standing but no legal compulsion be presented to member states. The other view, expressed most strongly by Wilson and Cassin, favored drafting a legally binding convention applicable only to the signatories. Unable to reach consensus, the group agreed to work on both types of documents at the same time.

The drafting committee, while recognizing that the decision on the form of the bill was a matter for the full commission, decided to prepare two working papers: a preliminary draft of a declaration setting forth general principles and the outline of a draft convention of binding obligations.[129] The drafting committee also found it necessary to take into account possible methods of enforcement. This report was submitted to the full commission at its second session, held at Geneva from 2 to 17 December 1947.[130]

The pace of work in Geneva was grueling, as Mrs. Roosevelt was determined to get a draft bill of rights, or declaration, finished before the end of the session.[131] There was a new Soviet delegate on board, Alexander Bogomolov, who according to Humphrey was the most cooperative of the communist representatives.[132] The session opened with the documents prepared over the summer. Lord Dukeston immediately laid out the British view opposing a declaration, which was recorded in the summary records of the commission:

> A declaration can hardly deal with anything but very general principles, already embodied in the Charter. If the Commission confines itself to producing such a declaration without any means of enforcement it will produce a text too vague to be of real value. . . . It should proceed immediately to drafting a Convention binding the signatory Governments so that it will be possible to set up machinery for appeal. . . . His delegation is prepared to accept a Draft Declaration if that were to precede a Convention, but if the Draft Declaration were to take place of the Draft Convention his Delegation will be unable to support it.[133]

The British derided a declaration of such vague goals as "nothing more than a document of propaganda."[134] Instead, they submitted a draft treaty focused entirely on civil rights derived from British domestic legal traditions that included detailed and precise obligations.[135] The CHR subsequently referred to the British submission as a covenant to indicate "the solemn and inviolable nature of the obligations which states would accept by adhering to it."[136] According to the British, particular violations of human rights, unless they were a threat to peace, were matters essentially within domestic jurisdiction, but once a state became party to a convention or covenant on human rights it waived the protection given to it by Article 2(7) of the UN Charter. Belgian representative Ferdinand Dehousse, whose prestige as an international lawyer was second only to that of Cassin, commented on the shortcomings of the British draft convention; it excluded certain political freedoms, the economic and social rights of workers, and any implementation machinery.[137] Dehousse suggested that three working groups be set up—one on the general declaration, a second on the question of convention, and a third on the machinery for implementation.[138]

Before the CHR could turn to the text of the documents that had been prepared, Hodgson and Mehta began to push the members of the CHR for some form of enforcement mechanism to address pressing global issues requiring international attention, such as the vast number of people that had been made stateless by World War II. Hodgson proposed a General Assembly resolution that could be ratified by states and thereby assume binding force under both municipal and international law.[139] He also advocated establishing an international court of human rights to resolve interstate controversies and adjudicate individual petitions, noting that "similar principles were incorporated in the Peace Treaties following the 1914–1918 war."[140]

Mehta insisted on a legally binding convention and summarized the consensus view of commission members: "The bill should be a simple and forthright document which can be easily understood, with the assurance that there will be adequate machinery for its enforcement whenever human rights are violated."[141] Her view was echoed at the highest levels of the UN Secretariat, which gave strong support to the idea that the CHR should develop human rights enforcement mechanisms. Support for an enforceable bill of human rights was universally shared by human rights advocates of all perspectives. A number of civil society reports and proposals to that end were distributed in the commission by NGO consultants, including reports by the World Jewish Congress and Roger Baldwin Nash, founder and director of the American Civil Liberties Union.[142]

The global consensus for implementation was based on the simple understanding that human rights were above all a matter of practice, not theory, and that it made little sense to proclaim recognition of human rights in grandiose terms if neither the political will nor the practical machinery existed to bring the concept down to earth. Without enforcement, rights would remain abstract and out of reach. By the same token, enforcement would be meaningless without a definition of what human rights actually were in substance. The two sides of the coin—theory and application, principle and practice, content and enforcement—could not be separated without doing injustice to the fundamental idea of human rights. The dilemma was aptly summarized by Lauterpacht in a report prepared for the commission while it was deliberating these issues:

> The two main problems connected with an International Bill of Human Rights are those of its contents and its enforcement. Both these problems are intimately connected one with the other. For the machinery of implementation and the willingness of States to agree to a system of implementation must depend upon the substantive provisions of the Bill. Governments may agree to a measure of enforcement if the

substantive obligations of the Bill are few in number, limited in their scope, and in keeping with their national requirements and policies.[143]

The U.S.-Soviet Anti-Enforcement Pact

Only two voices spoke out clearly and consistently against adopting a binding treaty or any measures of implementation, and they belonged to the two most powerful states in the world. Bogomolov repeatedly asserted that any treaty with supranational adjudication was unacceptable, since implementation was a matter of national sovereignty as expressly stated under the domestic jurisdiction clause of the Charter.[144] In their written comments, the Soviets opposed any form of implementation at the international as opposed to the state level, arguing against "a system of international pressures to be exercised through special organs established for this purpose (e.g. an international court, international committee or United Nations public prosecutor, etc.) and intended to force individual states to take particular steps connected with the execution of the Convention on Human Rights."[145]

The Soviets went on to note that if adopted, such measures would transform disputes between private individuals and their governments into international disputes, which could potentially aggravate international relations and undermine the foundations of peace. They also noted that it would upset the balance of power so carefully crafted under the provisions of the Charter. Throughout the drafting process of the international bill of rights, the communist countries never wavered from this position. Humphrey remarked that the Soviet stance had at least the virtue of frankness, unlike the United States, which often disguised its opposition to implementation on procedural and technical grounds.

Mrs. Roosevelt made a similar point, though in a more diplomatic and less categorical manner. She stated that the United States favored the preparation of a declaration of principles and claimed that the time was not yet right for a convention: "The position of the United States has been that it would be impossible in these initial meetings to do more than write a Declaration."[146] The State Department had prepared a paper for Mrs. Roosevelt setting out U.S. terms that were acceptable for the project, which stated that "there is a need of cataloguing human rights in an international instrument, but that the establishment of machinery for their international supervision and enforcement is not an immediate, practicable objective."[147] Mrs. Roosevelt's statements to the CHR revealed more troubling undercurrents in the U.S. position:

> Her delegation thinks that priority should be given to the draft Declaration, and
> the latter should not be drawn up in such a way as to give the impression that
> Governments will have contractual obligations to guarantee human rights. As
> regards the draft Convention or Conventions, the United States considers that the
> Commission should not proceed to draw them up until . . . it can be accepted and
> applied in all good faith by the participating states.[148]

Mrs. Roosevelt was not freelancing in her refusal to consider measures of
implementation, any more than the Soviet delegates were. There are reports
that she tried to persuade the State Department and key senators to drop
their blanket opposition to enforcement measures, but having failed, she did
not stray from instructions.[149] Her advisors were so insistent on this point
that it became a mantra of U.S. human rights policy. Every position paper
and memo on the topic takes an adamant and inflexible line on the need to
eradicate even the suggestion of implementation. Responding to one proposal
for a legal convention, Hendrick warned:

> The proposal goes beyond what has been outlined in the United States agenda for
> the Commission and is bound to be highly controversial. Its strongest proponent
> on the Commission is Professor Cassin who . . . feels that had the world been able
> to stop the monstrous acts of Germany towards the Jews after Hitler's accession to
> power, war might have been avoided. There is no question but that the Commission's
> work will be of little use without implementation. The difficulty is that effective
> implementation cannot be achieved unless the Commission interferes with the
> internal problems of nations.[150]

In other words, the United States clearly understood that the UN human rights system would have little practical value without some means of
realizing high-minded principles in the concrete practice of states. But the
purpose of human rights, in the U.S. conception, was not to provide accessible remedies to citizens of various nations, especially U.S. citizens, but to
export U.S. principles of justice across the globe at the rhetorical level, thereby
providing a means of ideological intervention in the affairs of other states
without risking outside scrutiny of domestic practices. Moreover, the legacy
of Woodrow Wilson's failure to convince the Senate to ratify the Covenant
of the League of Nations meant that the U.S. government was especially
wary of promoting a bill of rights that might be opposed by Congress. Given
the controversy human rights enforcement had sparked on the home front
through the NAACP's petition for the rights of African Americans, the U.S.
government was particularly apprehensive about supporting an intrusive
enforceable covenant.[151]

U.S. aversion to any form of human rights enforcement at the international level was so extreme that near the end of the drafting process, when almost all provisions of the UDHR had already met with U.S. approval, Sandifer found it necessary to caution his colleagues against allowing any last-minute changes that might reintroduce the bugbear of implementation:

> If changes must be made in the Declaration, I believe the one tendency which must be fought more strongly than any other is the tendency to put measures of implementation in the Declaration. This is a matter you will have to watch like a hawk because once any member has succeeded in putting in only one sentence indicating implementation the precedent will have been established and you will be lost. You remember the fight we had to take out of the Declaration the statement that "the Government shall conform to the will of the people." . . . Had it not been deleted we would have been completely lost when it came to social and economic rights.[152]

Chang forwarded a compromise in recognition that the UN's two most powerful members were adamantly opposed to any form of legally binding and enforceable international bill of rights.[153] He proposed a way out: the bill of rights would take a tripartite form, comprising a general declaration, a legally binding covenant, and measures for implementation as three separate but interdependent components of the broader human rights concept—a "triptych," with the UDHR forming the central panel and the covenant and the measures for implementation forming the two side panels.[154] The first would be drafted immediately, with the other two to follow soon after. Other delegates reluctantly accepted the Soviet-U.S. demand that the convention be delayed (if not abandoned) but only if that action was accompanied by a clear commitment to adopt binding enforceable rights in the future. Chang's compromise proposal gave the superpowers what they wanted without dismissing the majority's expectation of a binding covenant. It was according to this understanding of the structure and timing of the international bill of rights that work on the UDHR moved forward. The pragmatic separation of principle, right, and remedy marked a major fragmentation of the universal human rights project.

The Fragmentation of the Bill of Rights

This decision, taken solely at the insistence of the CHR's two most powerful members against the wishes of nearly every other delegation, was highly unpopular among human rights advocates and in public opinion at large.[155] It meant that the major purpose of the human rights project was being postponed with no guarantee that it would ever be effectively addressed. To allay these concerns, Mrs. Roosevelt emphasized repeatedly that the problem was one of timing and did not reflect U.S. opposition to the concept of binding human rights.[156] The separation of principles and obligations was also seen by the U.S. delegation as a practical imperative to "reduce the risk that the Bill would be held hostage to ideological differences."[157] These rationales were misleading, to say the least, given that the State Department had already decided to oppose binding human rights principles.

The dangers of postponing enactment of a binding bill of rights were clear enough to many members of the CHR. They made sure to record their understanding that the fundamental work of the commission depended upon an integrated approach to the triptych and warned that the human rights idea itself would be negated if the declaration of principles alone was enacted. The British representative expressed this concern clearly. He declared that "the world should not receive the impression that the drafting of the Declaration will not be followed by a Convention until some time in the more or less distant future. The Commission should act quickly since the world expects some practical results from its deliberations. If the sole fruit of its labours are to be the draft of a Declaration, irreparable harm will have been done."[158]

Once the problem of implementation was removed, the drafting of the Universal Declaration moved ahead with alacrity, indeed with an "indecent haste," according to the British.[159] Throughout the process, Mrs. Roosevelt strove to emphasize its nonbinding nature while at the same time promoting its value as a form of global morality. In opening comments to the third session of the General Assembly, she asserted that the declaration would have "considerable weight" as "a statement of basic principles of inalienable human rights, setting up a common standard of achievement for all peoples and all nations," while at the same time emphasizing that it was "not a treaty or international agreement and did not impose legal obligations."[160] This bifurcated approach prompted a prescient warning from New Zealand's representative to the General Assembly during final debates on the declaration:

> It has frequently been emphasized that the declaration would not be legally binding. . . . If the declaration is adopted first, there is less likelihood that the covenant will be adopted at all; by the time it is ready for adoption, some States, having already accepted the declaration, might be unwilling to vote for it. . . . There is a real danger that, if the declaration is accepted without the covenant, undue importance might be ascribed to it.[161]

But this "danger" was precisely the goal of U.S. strategy toward human rights. The United States gave precedence to the UDHR not in spite of its status as a nonbinding statement of principles suitable for propaganda rather than legal implementation, but precisely because of it.[162] The fragmentation of the bill of rights did make it easier for the CHR and the General Assembly to press ahead with a holistic declaration combining civil and political rights with economic and social rights. Yet this separation also profoundly weakened the edifice of human rights at the United Nations, resulting in a 20-year lag between the UDHR and the covenants, ultimately exacerbating rather than reducing Cold War ideological divisions. U.S. championing of human rights was therefore a double-edged sword, ensuring a level of political success and public acclaim but also undermining the potential of human rights to make a difference in people's lives by reducing them to moral aspirations without legal effect.

It is useful here to recall the relationship between the shield of domestic sovereignty and the sword of human rights. While states often found it expedient to interpret the two concepts as contradictory, thereby elevating the former over the latter, many jurists and diplomats pointed out that the Charter could easily be read to prohibit interference in domestic affairs except to the limited extent necessary to accomplish the fundamental purposes of the organization, including promotion of human rights. Implementation of human rights did not require international interference in domestic law unless the domestic legal system broke down in a manner that threatened international peace and security. Lauterpacht's carefully worked out proposals envisioned that states, upon signing a binding bill of rights, would commit to incorporating human rights principles into their domestic laws rather than to surrendering jurisdiction to an international body.[163] International supervision would therefore be limited to monitoring domestic procedures to ensure adherence to human rights norms, and direct intervention would be a last resort in the most egregious cases. The advantage of this approach lay in promoting universal human rights principles without infringing on domestic legal systems, thereby allowing for diversity and autonomy within circumscribed international limits.

Futile Efforts at Implementation

Given the enormous pressure from the United States and Soviet Union to limit and effectively scuttle any proposals for human rights enforcement, it is not surprising that the third panel of the triptych, measures of implementation, turned out to be the least successful in terms of practical outcomes. The working group on implementation that was convened to study and make recommendations on the issue—Australia, Belgium, India, Iran, Ukraine, and Uruguay—disbanded without seeing any of its recommendations adopted by the CHR.[164] The United States, United Kingdom, and Soviet Union, along with the ILO, the Consultative Council of Jewish Organizations, and the World Jewish Congress, were present as observers. The working group experienced difficulties from the beginning; it would eventually fold its tent, having discussed many ideas over the course of three years but accomplishing little of substance. Decades later, some of the ideas would resurface during discussion of implementation measures under the two covenants.

At the working group's very first meeting, M. Klekovkin, the Ukrainian representative, opposed any enforcement measures, arguing that implementation was not necessary in his country given the "complete equality between citizens and national groups . . . assured by the new Stalin constitution."[165] Furthermore, he expressed doubt whether the group was in any position to draft implementation measures or agree on enforcement principles before the final contents of an international bill of rights had been decided: "The question of implementation demanded previous knowledge of the rules to be implemented."[166] Klekovkin's challenges occupied the working group for three entire days, during which other representatives made speeches and registered their own official statements denouncing him as "an obstructionist" and supporting consideration of implementation measures in their own right before other human rights instruments were finalized.[167]

The official Secretariat memorandum summarizing the first session of the CHR served as the basis for the discussions of the working group on implementation.[168] Various members had proposed a number of specific ideas. Hodgson supported the creation of an international court of human rights, distinct from the International Court of Justice (ICJ). Similarly, Rómulo envisaged that the CHR should in effect function as an international court of appeal.[169] Mehta suggested that the right of individuals and groups to petition should exist for the abolition of discrimination and protection of minorities.[170] Cassin recommended the post of an international attorney general for human rights to resolve disputes.[171] The working group compiled these and other proposals into a list for discussion and consideration by the full commission. The main proposals were:

1. The establishment of the right of the General Assembly and other organs of the United Nations, including possibly the Commission on Human Rights, to discuss and make recommendations in regard to violations of the covenant;
2. The establishment under the bill of rights of the right of individuals to petition the United Nations as a means of enforcing human rights;

3. The establishment of an international court of human rights with jurisdiction to supervise and enforce human rights *motu proprio*;
4. The establishment of jurisdiction in the CHR to consider cases of suspension of the bill of rights, either in whole or in part;
5. The establishment of local agencies of the United Nations in various countries with jurisdiction to supervise and enforce human rights therein.[172]

Group members agreed to postpone discussion of the last two proposals as premature until a covenant was established and in force; they had no way of knowing at the time that this would take almost thirty years. With respect to the right of the General Assembly and other organs to make recommendations regarding violation of the convention, the group felt that this was already vested in the assembly under Articles 10 and 12 of the Charter.[173] Similarly, this prerogative was granted to ECOSOC under Article 62,[174] but the working group felt that the CHR should request a formal delegation of this right from its parent body.

The right of individual petition was considered again based on proposals Hansa Mehta made on the issues of discrimination and protection of minorities.[175] The working group agreed that the right of petition should be open not only to states but also to individuals and groups and that provisions should be included in the proposed convention; the Secretariat was asked to draw up a full and detailed scheme of regulations and procedures regarding the right of petition. However, the United States objected to all proposals related to the petition on the grounds that the UN was not yet in a position to take effective action and that in any case the subcommission was the appropriate body for discussing complaints dealing with discrimination and minorities.[176] Expressing general skepticism regarding any form of implementation, the U.S. representative noted, "It is all very well to set up machinery for curing all ills which afflict human individuals, but it is another thing to see that this machinery will work."[177]

Along with the right of petition, the creation of an international court of human rights received strong support from most of the members. Hodgson warned the commission against postponing consideration of this question until after the covenant came into force, arguing that machinery for implementation should work automatically from the start and that the court should be distinct from the ICJ. Without an amendment to the Charter, the CHR had no mandate to seek the opinion of the ICJ, and in any case the ICJ procedure applied only to disputes between states. Hodgson's proposal received support from many members, including the three international lawyers on the commission. Malik argued strongly for the Australian proposal, remarking that "in his opinion the crux of the whole question of Human Rights lay in the implementation of measures for their protection."[178] He chastised the communist states for objecting based on national sovereignty: "The field of Human Rights was, in his opinion, outside that of national sovereignty. Firstly, their determination was not exclusive to any State. Secondly, their violation concerned not only the State but also the whole world."[179] Again the United States and Soviet Union combined to torpedo the proposal. The United States maintained that the idea could not be put into effect in the foreseeable future, at least until after the covenant was negotiated, and Soviets termed it an unacceptable intervention in the internal affairs of states.

Due to great power opposition, the working group on implementation was unable to implement any of its proposals. After meeting for several sessions, it decided in 1950 to cease activities until the covenant was drafted. The working group never did meet again; most of its ideas remained confined to the voluminous archives of the CHR's proceedings. The individual right of petition would eventually be attached to various human rights treaties, including the civil and political rights covenant, though not its counterpart for economic, social, and cultural rights. The petition procedure was not incorporated into the treaties, though; they were appended in the form of optional protocols. And there was no adjudicative body to issue, let alone enforce, meaningful decisions. One of the few ideas to succeed, at some level, was Cassin's proposal for an attorney general. The concept would periodically resurface in various guises over the years; in 1950, Uruguay and the Consultative Council of Jewish Organizations submitted an official proposal for the creation of a high commissioner for human rights.[180] Not until 1993, after considerable pressure from NGOs at the Vienna World Conference on Human Rights, would the idea be accepted by states through a landmark vote in the General Assembly.[181] However, the powers associated with the new position—coordination of UN programs and promotional role as spokesperson—were a mere shadow of Cassin's original vision of an international human rights champion authorized to receive petitions, mediate between states and the petitioners, and engage in fact-finding and diplomacy.

6

The Universal Declaration of Human Rights

Overview of the Drafting Process

Although numerous controversies and disputes marked the drafting of the Universal Declaration of Human Rights, the process nevertheless proceeded rapidly, especially given the complex and contentious nature of the task at hand.[1] The decisions to separate moral principles from binding laws and to forgo implementation cleared the way for approval of the UDHR; states were less likely to fight over provisions that did not have any legal weight or means of enforcement. Moreover, skillful bureaucratic operation by Mrs. Roosevelt and her team of advisors ensured that the process kept moving forward, all the while remaining in conformity with the U.S. vision of human rights.

The resulting document appears to present a cohesive and consensual elaboration of human rights, especially when compared to the ideological debates that would soon characterize all aspects of international relations during the Cold War. The appearance of consensus, however, did little more than paper over ideological cracks within the human rights idea. Fundamental philosophical questions about human rights were suppressed in favor of a dominant western paradigm of individual rights; practical disputes were resolved quickly and expediently on the basis of U.S. power and, when necessary, the vote. The most time-consuming discussions and debates centered on minor differences in wording once the basic framework of principles and articles had been accepted.

The task of drafting preparatory materials was given to John Humphrey in the Secretariat. The CHR initially requested that the Secretariat prepare a draft declaration, but ECOSOC later asked the Secretariat to prepare a draft outline first. Humphrey, who between 17 February and 15 March devoted himself to this challenge, chose to prepare a full draft declaration rather than an outline merely listing rights, although his draft would always be identified as the Secretariat outline.[2] In June 1947, a drafting committee of the CHR reviewed his declaration and assigned Cassin to prepare the next version. Cassin retained much of Humphrey's language and structure, keeping the original articles in the margins while adding three new articles: on the need of all citizens to take part in military service in states which recognize this institution, as the protection of human rights requires a public force; on provisions to establish the liability of public authorities or their agents; and on mothers and children as a special category deserving attention.[3] The drafting committee asked Cassin to further revise the declaration, and the new version, known as the Cassin draft, was presented at the second session of the CHR, along with the British draft of the covenant and measures of implementation.[4] It was later mistakenly identified as the original text of the declaration, leading Cassin to be dubbed the father of the UDHR. After this point, no particular member of the CHR was again associated with specific additions or deletions to the declaration.

At the second session of the CHR, the eight-member working group produced what became known as the Geneva draft. NGOs with consultative status also submitted their own drafts to the commission, and other NGOs and individuals submitted comments through the Secretariat. States were requested to submit written statements on the draft. The Secretariat compiled all comments from countries, NGOs, and individuals in a report that was the basis of discussion for the third session of the CHR in May and June of 1948.[5]

The third session was filled with tension; while the working group continued to plug away at the draft declaration, other members of the CHR were holding out for a binding legal covenant. However, no agreement could be reached because the communist countries and the Latin American states insisted on including economic and social rights in the covenant. Other European delegates such as Cassin and Dehousse also argued for the inclusion of rights of workers. It was at this stage that the CHR, under Mrs. Roosevelt's leadership, decided that it could only deliver a declaration at the fall General Assembly meeting of the Third Committee (social, humanitarian, and cultural).

The Third Committee met between September and December 1948, and even though the draft had cleared the CHR and ECOSOC (the latter simply transmitted the report of the third session of the CHR to the General Assembly), the delegates held eighty-five meetings to discuss the declaration and proposed 168 formal draft resolutions containing amendments to various articles.[6] On 30 November, a subcommittee was set up to examine the totality of the rights to ensure exact correspondence of the text in the five official languages of the UN.[7] After this review the draft declaration was put to vote and adopted by a roll-call vote of 29 to 0, with abstentions from Byelorussia, Canada, Czechoslovakia, Poland, Ukraine, the Soviet Union, and Yugoslavia (South Africa was absent on the day of the vote).

On 7 December, the Soviets complained that most of their amendments had been unfairly rejected and that the text adopted was practically identical with the original unsatisfactory draft. They submitted a resolution calling for "serious improvements in a whole series of articles" and requesting that the adoption of the Universal Declaration be postponed until the next assembly session.[8] This proposal was easily defeated.

The General Assembly discussed the report of the Third Committee on 9 and 10 December. Most representatives underlined the importance of the declaration, noting that its chief innovation was its universality.[9] Amid overwhelming support, there were several objections to particular provisions: the failure to refer to the divine origins of human dignity (Netherlands); imperfect ordering of the articles (Belgium); vague and imprecisely worded text (Canada); and lack of acknowledgement of Islamic practices (Egypt). Just before midnight on 10 December, the full declaration was put to vote and adopted by 48 votes to 0 with eight abstentions from the communist bloc, the Union of South Africa, and Saudi Arabia.

After this marathon effort, Mrs. Roosevelt felt compelled to remind the delegates that

> in giving our approval to the Declaration today, it is of primary importance that we keep clearly in mind the basic character of the document. It is not a treaty; it is not an international agreement. It is not and does not purport to be a statement of law or of legal obligation. It is a declaration of basic principles of human rights and freedoms to be stamped with the approval of the General Assembly by formal vote of its members, and to serve as a common standard of achievement for all peoples of all nations.[10]

The First Drafts of the Declaration

Between February and May 1947, Humphrey prepared four documents for the June meeting of the CHR's drafting committee: a draft declaration termed the Secretariat outline, a background document with 400 pages of commentary and attachments, a comparison of the Secretariat outline and the draft bill of rights submitted by the British,[11] and an outline listing various provisions that could be incorporated into a bill of rights.[12] Humphrey claimed to be most impressed and guided by the draft prepared by the American Law Institute.[13] In comparison to that draft, however, his version was long, unwieldy, and at times incoherent.[14] The American Law Institute bill included eighteen clear and concise articles;[15] the Secretariat outline contained a veritable laundry list of all possible rights with little organizing structure. Of the forty-eight articles Humphrey proposed, thirty-four covered civil and political rights; ten were on economic, social, and cultural rights; and four were on nondiscrimination, protection of minorities, duties of states, and the right to petition and UN jurisdiction.[16] The preamble contained four distinct ideas: (1) there can be no peace unless human rights are respected; (2) men and women have not only rights but also duties to society; (3) each person is not only of the state but also of the world; and (4) there can be neither human freedom nor human dignity unless war and the threat of war are abolished. Of these, only the first idea would be retained in the final declaration.

Humphrey's draft bill and accompanying materials were submitted for consideration to the eight-member drafting committee in June 1947. This was a crucial meeting, the first opportunity for the committee members to react officially to a draft document intended to be the cornerstone of the UN's human rights system. Members were generally appreciative of Humphrey's draft. Criticisms were reserved for issues of tone, language, length, and structure. Only Vladimir Koretsky, the Soviet representative, challenged its underlying philosophy and approach.

After a long speech detailing a litany of contemporary abuses, from the abusive treatment of Indians in South Africa to the ruthless U.S. campaign to eradicate feudalism from Japan, Koretsky turned to the basic assumptions of the Secretariat outline. First, he noted that it promoted the idea that the United Nations should intervene in the affairs of an individual country if a state had violated the rights of its citizens.[17] This was true; Humphrey's draft implied a level of enforcement by spelling out various rights with legal detail more typical of a convention than a declaration and including a right of individual petition (on the grounds that it would have been untenable to ignore the thousands of petitions already submitted to the commission). Second, Koretsky criticized the bourgeois political philosophy underlying the Secretariat draft, arguing that the intent of the draft was "to liberate man not from persecution but from his own government, from his own people. That meant putting him in opposition to his own government."[18] This reflected a traditional Marxist criticism of liberal individual rights as a war of all against all that disguised and enabled the exploitative rule of capitalist elites, in contrast to the Soviet model of rights as a means to both resist fascist and illegitimate governments and develop bonds of social solidarity beyond the alienation of class competition.

Koretsky also objected to the legalistic and uninspiring language of atomized rights as insufficient to awaken people's social and revolutionary consciousness. Instead he proposed that the declaration should be simple and decisive, that it should "imitate the style and manner of the old laws, especially their conciseness and clarity."

> It should have emotional appeal; conviction and provocative language; the clear fighting spirit of the U.S. Declaration of Independence and of the French Declaration of the Rights of Man. The Declaration of Human Rights should sound a bugle call and should state principles for which any man would be ready to stake his life.[19]

Koretsky did not attract support for his proposed reforms; even an avowed socialist like Santa Cruz was unwilling to align with the Soviet philosophy. After all, Humphrey's draft had incorporated a range of social and economic rights, albeit within a framework of western liberalism that granted individuals claims against their governments. It was clear from the outset that a majority of the CHR would reject any fundamental challenge to this paradigm and that ideological objections from communist delegates henceforth would be dismissed as obstructionist.

Cassin was given responsibility for incorporating comments and criticisms into a second draft. He restructured the document into eight chapters and forty-six articles, though the language was similar and in places identical to Humphrey's draft, which he duly noted in the margins. The draft still suffered from excessive length and detail.[20] Privately Humphrey criticized the modified document as too philosophical in nature, while the British Foreign Office lamented that Cassin was a "terrible draughtsman."[21] The expanded preamble included references to the tragedy of the two World Wars, the inspiration of the Four Freedoms, and the need for equal rights between men and women.[22] From the UN Secretariat draft, Cassin retained the idea that rights had to be protected by international as well as municipal law, although he avoided specific implementation mechanisms.

Chapter 1 of Cassin's draft set forth the general principles of liberty, equality, and fraternity as proclaimed in the French declaration and recognized "fundamental duties," including "obedience to law" and "sacrifices demanded for the common good." Chapter 2 elaborated the right to life. Chapter 3 recognized a set of personal freedoms, including privacy, due process, and the presumption of innocence. Chapter 4, on the legal status of rights, recognized the right to property. Chapter 5, on public freedom, asserted the rights of conscience, expression, and assembly. Here Cassin courted controversy by retaining an article from Humphrey's draft on the right to resist government oppression and tyranny. Political rights were included in Chapter 6, as well as the idea of military service as a national duty—"Each citizen should regard it as an honor to take part in military service"—an addition Britain and the United States later rejected.[23] Chapter 7 concerned the right to a nationality and protection of aliens. In Chapter 8, concerning social, economic, and cultural rights, Cassin dropped the rights to food and housing and, under social security, added the rights of mothers and children to special attention, care, and resources. He also included in Article 43 a new idea on intellectual rights for "the authors of all artistic, literary and scientific works."[24]

In the next twelve months, this draft would be debated and revised several times, becoming more concise and streamlined; detailed articles were shortened and the text took on the shape of a declaration of principles rather than a laundry list of articles. The general philosophy and principles set forth in the Humphrey and Cassin draft would be retained, and certain ideas, such as individual duties, were deemphasized and dropped down in the text. New ideas were added, such as Article 28: "Everyone is entitled to an international order in which the rights and freedoms set forth in this Declaration can be fully realized," a vague formulation that nonetheless is credited with serving as the basis for what became known as third-generation solidarity rights to peace, development, and environment.

Given Mrs. Roosevelt's guiding hand, the declaration was certain to be cast in a distinctly U.S. manner.[25] At the end of the first CHR session, a U.S. government report noted that its positions were accepted on all points. Later, at the end of the third session of the commission, another State Department memo noted that of thirty-three articles, twenty-four passed exactly or almost exactly to their specifications, seven passed in part, and only two failed to conform to U.S. wishes.

The UNESCO Interlude: A Human Rights Turf Battle

The difficulties inherent in defining human rights were further demonstrated in the CHR's reaction to a 1947 UNESCO project in which renowned scholars and public intellectuals worldwide considered the theoretical issues and dilemmas raised in producing a Universal Declaration of Human Rights that was equally applicable to all the peoples, nations, and cultures of the world.[26] Julian Huxley, director-general of UNESCO, had mentioned to Mrs. Roosevelt in 1946 that UNESCO would endeavor to establish certain shared principles of human rights. Unfortunately, he failed to officially inform the CHR about the project, violating a cardinal rule of bureaucratic turf.[27] CHR members were uniformly offended at being excluded from the process; rather than consider the wealth of valuable material in the UNESCO study, they did their utmost to ignore and bury it. This is especially regrettable given the caliber of the participants and the diversity and quality of their contributions, which covered cross-cultural issues that the CHR failed to address in the drafting of a supposedly universal moral ethic.

Responses to the UNESCO inquiry were received from a distinguished group, including British international theorist E. H. Carr; French Thomist philosopher Jacques Maritain; revolutionary leader of the Indian nonviolence movement Mohandas Gandhi; Italian philosopher and historian Benedetto Croce; British novelist Aldous Huxley; Indian poet and philosopher Humayun Kabir; U.S. philosopher Richard McKeon and political scientist Quincy Wright; and professor of philosophy in western China Chung-Shu Lo. Their essays addressed the fundamental differences in conceptions of rights, highlighted the incommensurable notions of the relationship between individual and state, and drew attention to both the necessity of and the inherent problems in any effective system of implementation.

The work undertaken by these scholars was perhaps less important in establishing which rights should be included in a declaration than it was in identifying and seeking a solution for the problem of reconciling opposing doctrinal conceptions of rights. The report stated that they hoped "not to set up an intellectual structure to reduce them [human rights] to a single formulation, but rather to discover the intellectual means to secure agreement concerning fundamental rights."[28] It acknowledged "the intellectual ramifications and implications of the problem of human rights in the modern world and in the international framework of the United Nations"[29]—a far more explicit admission of the enormity of the task facing the CHR than commission members themselves ever acknowledged. Warning that "we must not expect too much of an International Declaration of Human Rights," Jacques Maritain argued that the "ideological contrast [between rights theories] is irreducible and no theoretical reconciliation is possible."[30] His suggested solution to this incommensurability was based upon the recognition that theoretical agreement was not the same as practical agreement and that the one could be achieved without the other. UNESCO summarized the consensus of participants:

> The world of man is at a critical age in its political, social and economic evolution. If it is to proceed further on the path towards unity, it must develop a common set of ideas and principles. One of those is a common formulation of the rights of

man ... [that] must reconcile the various divergent or opposing formulations ... and be sufficiently definite to have real significance both as an inspiration and as a guide to practice.[31]

The views solicited ranged from Boris Tchecko's detailed analysis of the Soviet conception of the rights of man to the pithy statement of Gandhi, who wrote: "I learned from my illiterate but very wise mother that all rights to be deserved and preserved came from duty well done. Thus the very right to live accrues to us only when we fulfill the duty of citizenship of the world."[32] Croce was of the opinion that "a formal, public and international debate on the necessary principles underlying human dignity and civilization ... would no doubt formulate a declaration of certain historical and contemporary rights and needs, in some such form as the Ten Commandments."[33] John Lewis argued for a redefinition of rights and freedoms: "Liberty must be conceived in terms of the values of the masses who lack them and demand them. Hence the obstacles to the achievement of such aims become the centre of attention. The removal of such obstacles becomes the achievement of liberty and the vindication of human rights."[34] Chung-Shu Lo laid down three basic claims for every person in the world, namely the right to live at a biological and economic level, the right to self-expression on a political and social level, and the right to enjoyment on an aesthetic and spiritual level. He asserted:

> It is time for all nations and each individual in the world to be conscious of the following conditions, namely: (1) that the world is an organic whole, so we should work in cooperation to improve the lives of people as a whole; (2) that each individual is an end in himself, and all social institutions are the means to develop each individual as fully as possible; (3) that each individual or national group should respect the rights of others to the same degree as we treasure our own; and (4) that each, making the most of himself, can at the same time contribute best to the world at large.[35]

The final report set out a list of fundamental rights "on which all men are agreed."[36] This list contained the right to live; the right to protection of health; the right to work; the right to maintenance (in unemployment, sickness, infancy, and old age); the right to property; the right to education; the right to information; the right of self-expression; the right to justice; the right to political action; freedom of thought, speech, assembly, association, worship, and the press; the right to citizenship; the right to rebellion or revolution; and the right to share in progress. Its authors maintained that it emphasized the "dynamic character of the interrelations of human rights."[37] A declaration of human rights, they expressed, could be based on pragmatic consensus rather than philosophical unity:

It is related that at one of the meetings of a UNESCO National Commission where human rights were being discussed, someone expressed astonishment that certain champions of violently opposed ideologies had agreed on a list of those rights. *"Yes," they said, "we agree about the rights but on condition that no one asks us why."* (emphasis added)[38]

The members of the CHR rejected the findings of the UNESCO inquiry since they had not been consulted. Dehousse stated: "UNESCO's action was most regrettable. . . . In all its articles the Human Rights Commission of the United Nations was not mentioned once." He urged "that in future such incidents should be avoided."[39] Hodgson said that he personally "did not approve of the majority of the ideas put forward in the report and therefore saw no reason why the Commission should itself undertake public action."[40] This was important because the CHR had the power either to allow or block distribution of the UNESCO study to the member states of the UN.

Humphrey pointed out that the normal terms of agreement with a specialized agency like UNESCO were that documents ought to be reproduced and distributed in the same way as other documents sent to the CHR. However, Mrs. Roosevelt decided that the reproduction of the report should be put to a vote during the second session.[41] By a vote of eight to four the commission decided not to distribute the UNESCO report to all members of the UN.[42] The Secretariat was authorized to distribute the report to members of the CHR only; this valuable work would not be mentioned again in any subsequent proceedings of the commission.

Negotiating the Controversial Articles

In the second session in Geneva, the working group on the declaration spent long days on revisions, trying unsuccessfully to reconcile opposing ideological and practical differences through negotiations and consensus. In the end, these differences were either papered over or resolved in favor of the dominant view, generally the one backed by the United States. A number of the articles generated particular controversy as they made their way through the drafting process. The right to rebellion, for example, enjoyed widespread support among states, since most had attained independence through its exercise, but it ran into determined Anglo-American opposition. Both Humphrey and Cassin included the right in their draft declarations, based on the stirring language of the U.S. and French revolutions. Proposed by Humphrey as the right of an individual to resist oppression and tyranny, Cassin revised the text as a right to be exercised in the event of a grave crisis caused by human rights violations. Cassin felt that in less dire circumstances all citizens had a genuine duty to obey the law. The Latin American delegates supported the idea, and it enjoyed Soviet backing as legitimizing revolution in general and resistance to fascist tyranny in particular.[43]

The delegations of the UK and the United States, however, were dead set against recognizing the right, despite the historic role of revolution in defining their own national identities. Britain feared that it would provide legitimacy to armed insurrection in the colonies. The United States saw the right as undermining the fundamental purpose of the United Nations to promote global stability and peaceful resolution of conflict. Arguing that respect for human rights obviated the need for revolution, a State Department position paper explained:

> The purpose of the proposed bill of rights is to facilitate the task of the United Nations in promoting immunity from oppression and tyranny by peaceful means. Forcible resistance should be the last resort after it has become clear that no other means can be effective to achieve a just result. A man is arrested by a policeman for insufficient reason. This may well be a case of tyranny or oppression. Yet the proper course for the man is not to resist; it is to accept the arrest and get his remedy in law.[44]

The U.S. argument overlooked the problem that many existing countries, not to mention potential tyrannies, lacked functioning systems to protect the rule of law. It was also an ironic position for the United States to adopt after deliberately sabotaging the CHR's efforts to reach agreement on providing an enforceable "remedy in law" for human rights violations.

As the right enjoyed too much support to be deleted entirely, the U.S. and British delegations worked together successfully first to weaken the language and then to bury it in the preamble. The final text reflected U.S. concerns that rebellion not be recognized as an affirmative right but rather as a desperate measure applicable only in the absence of human rights protection. Thus, the preamble states: "Whereas it is essential, if man is not to be compelled to have recourse, as a last resort, to rebellion against tyranny and oppression, that human rights should be protected by the rule of law."[45]

Another controversial issue concerned the universal basis of human rights. While the delegates agreed that the qualities of reason and conscience were fundamental to human rights, they could not agree on the original source of these inherent values. Did they come from God, nature, or man? This was an existential question, eventually resolved by the tried-and-true method of agreeing to disagree and allowing silence to speak for all viewpoints. The Humphrey and Cassin drafts had avoided the issue altogether; however, the Geneva draft read: "All men are endowed by nature with reason and conscience."[46] Malik proposed that "by nature" be substituted with "by their

Creator," citing the U.S. Declaration of Independence; the Soviet delegate objected, on the basis that "the Declaration was meant for mankind as a whole, whether believers or unbelievers."[47] The commission dropped the reference to a deity, but it was resurrected by Brazil in the Third Committee, where a majority supported theistic language: "Created in the image and likeness of God, they are endowed with reason and conscience." The God and nature camps were too polarized to reach agreement, and the final compromise dropped reference to either. Thus, the origins of human reason and conscience remained undefined.

This left open the question of whether women were included in the term "men." According to Cassin's draft Article 1: "all men, being members of one family . . . shall regard each other as brothers." Koretsky challenged the view that "men" was synonymous with "people," arguing that this was "an historical reflection on the mastery of men over women."[48] While Mrs. Roosevelt professed indifference to the gendered use of language, Mehta objected strongly, as did Bodil Begtrup, chair of the UN Commission on the Status of Women.[49] There followed lengthy discussions in which different texts were translated in various languages. The word for "people" was not gender neutral in either Russian or French, so finally the delegates agreed to use the term "human beings." A number of delegates, Cassin among them, insisted on recognizing an equivalent English expression for the French concept of *fraternité*; the eventual compromise language referred to "the spirit of brotherhood." Thus the final language of Article 1 read: "All human beings are born free and equal in dignity and rights. They are endowed with reason and conscience and should act towards one another in a spirit of brotherhood."[50]

Despite a well-established history in international law, minority rights were not recognized in the UDHR; few states were willing to allow external scrutiny of such a sensitive domestic matter. Humphrey had included them in the original Secretariat draft, but the article gave rise to so much controversy that the issue was referred to the Sub-Commission on Prevention of Discrimination and Protection of Minorities for further study. Eventually the notion that minorities were entitled to international protection of their cultural identity was dropped in the draft declaration sent to the General Assembly in September 1948.[51] France attempted to restore the idea but found little support apart from the Soviet bloc. Latin American countries insisted that there were no minorities in their region and that the concept would prove divisive and political. As Humphrey noted, the Latin American assimilationist position also suited the interests of powerful states. Few nations were prepared to stand up for minority rights, and the demands of sovereignty won the day:

Any compromise between the views of the New World, where countries wanted to assimilate immigrants, and views held in Europe, where there were historical national minorities, would be impossible in the CHR in the views of the Americans and British. This was an oversimplification not only because there are in fact indigenous and other national minorities in the Americas but because most European governments are just as keen to assimilate their minorities as are governments on the other side of the Atlantic.[52]

Several other articles occasioned spirited debate between member states. The Soviet Union made a strong push to abolish the death penalty in peacetime, but the United States and European states rejected the proposal. Rather than defend their own practice of executions, they pointed out the hypocrisy of Soviet claims to have abolished the practice, noting that imprisonment in the gulag system often amounted to a death sentence.[53] The right to social security contained in Article 22 led to a debate between Muslim countries and France. The Syrian and Saudi delegates unsuccessfully attempted to replace social security with social justice, a broader concept that they felt conformed to the Islamic law of zakat, one of the five pillars of Islam, in which a voluntary tax is levied for the purpose of assisting the poor and unemployed.[54] The French delegate preferred the narrower conception of social insurance to ensure that governments would be bound by specific obligations, arguing "there could be no social justice without social security, as there could be no social security without social insurance."[55] Neither proposal was accepted.

Debating the Hierarchy in Universal Rights

One of the underlying points of contention throughout the drafting of the Universal Declaration was the status of economic, social, and cultural rights and their relationship to traditional western civil and political rights. The main debates were not over whether economic, social, and cultural rights should be included in the UDHR. On this there was a strong consensus; almost all delegations believed that they were an integral part of the human rights idea and that the declaration would be incomplete without recognizing the full array of human rights. The consensus was broken only by Britain, which at the outset had submitted a draft human rights treaty composed entirely of civil and political rights, and the United States, which opposed inclusion of economic, social, and cultural rights despite New Deal legislation entitling citizens to social security and welfare, not to mention former president Roosevelt's call for Four Freedoms.[56] But unlike the negotiations over the right to rebellion, in which the United States and Britain succeeded in substituting their view for that of the majority, Anglo-American unity was not sufficient in this case to override the rest of the CHR, especially given the strong support of the Soviet bloc, the Latin Americans, and influential representatives such as Cassin, Malik, and Chang.

Recognition of economic, social, and cultural rights alongside civil and political rights did not, however, mean that they were considered equal in status. Cassin, who so aggravated the U.S. and British delegations by fighting hard for economic and social rights, nevertheless perceived a hierarchy between them; economic, social, and cultural rights were "almost as important" as civil and political rights, representing a "logical development" from rather than an equal part of the human rights foundation.[57] He argued that economic and social rights "were different in character from any rights outlined in the earlier declarations of the rights of man. They all had in common the fact that national effort and international cooperation were needed for their very realization."[58] In contrast, traditional rights to life and freedom of conscience were more fundamental in nature and could be immediately safeguarded.[59] Although the distinction between cost-free "negative" civil and political rights and resource-intensive "positive" economic and social rights has been criticized and discredited, Cassin's view was widely shared on the commission.[60]

During discussions on the right to work, Malik raised the issue of the broader environment necessary to fulfill the right in addition to simply proclaiming the right itself. He proposed adding an article "calling attention to the need for establishing the kind of economic and social conditions that would guarantee this right"—a requirement that was not deemed necessary for civil and political rights.[61] A subcommittee was formed to draft an umbrella article similar to Article 3, which introduced civil and political rights with the definitive statement: "Everyone has the right to life, liberty and security of person." The proposed article for economic and social rights read: "Everyone has the right to a good social and international order in which the rights and freedoms set out in this Declaration can be fully realized."[62] The Soviet delegate objected to the insertion of the word "good"; it was not clear that even if all rights were to be achieved by an individual, it could be attributed to a "good" international system. He also derided the failure to mention concrete state obligations needed to achieve economic and social rights and dismissed the rhetorical language as "a far cry from real social justice and a really good social order."[63] Nevertheless the text, minus the word "good," was eventually accepted as Article 28 of the Universal Declaration. For forty years the article was ignored and forgotten, until human rights proponents reinterpreted it as providing the basis for a "third generation" of global solidarity rights to peace, development, and a healthy environment.[64]

The secondary status accorded to economic, social, and cultural rights was evident in the debates about the order of these articles in the overall Universal Declaration. Even sympathetic members of the CHR granted priority to civil and political rights, in terms of both the placement of the articles and their level of detail and elaboration. Cassin, Chang, Malik, Dehousse, and other influential members felt that economic, social, and cultural rights had emerged from modern economic and social realities confronting the individual and society as a whole, and thus they could be understood as "20th century grafts on an 18th century tree."[65] Chang argued that this historical development was properly reflected in the progression of articles in the Universal Declaration—they began with the traditional rights derived from European history and philosophy before recognizing the modern set of economic and social rights. The first three articles were intended to express the French ideals of equality, fraternity, and liberty;[66] Articles 4–21 covered the full spectrum of civil and political rights, with an emphasis on judicial process and protections; Articles 22–26 covered economic, social, and cultural rights in more general terms.

The communist delegates objected to this hierarchy of human rights. Mere chronology, in their view, did not justify downplaying those rights that reflected a twentieth-century consensus for social justice. On the contrary, they argued, the modern understanding was superior to an archaic model of rights developed in capitalist Europe in response to feudalism, royalism, and the power of the church.[67] Recognition of formal legal rights was meaningless without the social and economic means to fulfill them. Moreover, legal rights were themselves a product of social and economic conditions, as the Yugoslav delegate remarked:

> The economic factor has become decisive in the whole social development of the present time. Consequently, the social status of the individual is not based on juridical instruments but is the result of the social and economic conditions in which the individual lives. That means that the civil and political status of the individual has become in a very great measure dependent upon his social status.[68]

During discussions in the Third Committee, Alexei Pavlov, the Soviet delegate, insisted that the western liberal model inverted the true relationship between citizen and state, with the state seen in opposition to its citizens. Effectively governed modern states were not a threat to the rights of individuals but rather the means to the fulfillment of such rights.[69] The Soviets consistently opposed international implementation of human rights, but at the same time they championed recognition of state obligations at the domestic level. Pavlov accordingly proposed language requiring states to undertake all necessary measures, including legislation, to ensure enjoyment of economic and social rights.[70] Mrs. Roosevelt immediately responded with an ideological attack on economic, social, and cultural rights, particularly the idea that public action was necessary to fulfill them. While sharing Soviet opposition to UN enforcement of human rights, she also made it clear that economic, social, and cultural rights did not enjoy legal status even in the domestic context, remarking that the U.S. government "did not believe that the economic, social and cultural rights listed in the latter part of the declaration implied the need for direct government action."[71]

The General Assembly had the opportunity to debate the hierarchy of human rights prior to the adoption of the UDHR. Latin American countries in particular argued that the declaration should reflect the values of the American Declaration of the Rights and Duties of Man, which emphasized the full set of interdependent human rights.[72] They suggested two concrete amendments, both of which were eventually defeated. First, the delegate from Cuba, Guy Pérez Cisneros, noted that Article 3's reference to "security of the person" did not accurately reflect the economic and social aspects of security and proposed that the article be expanded to include the "physical integrity and legal, economic, and social security which is necessary to the full development of the personality."[73] The representative of Mexico emphasized the importance of genuine security for the American goal of "pursuit of happiness."[74]

The second amendment, which was sponsored by a number of countries including Uruguay, Cuba, Mexico, and Lebanon, sought to reverse the order of the thirty articles, placing economic and social rights in the beginning to lessen the apparent priority of civil and political rights. They recalled that just prior to the San Francisco conference, President Roosevelt had called on Congress to adopt a Second Bill of Rights focused on economic and social rights.[75] Cisneros urged other members to promote a progressive vision of human rights beyond the centuries-old traditional model:

> It must be borne in mind that man is no longer living in the eighteenth century. The twentieth century has witnessed the development of a new concept of liberty, which it is important to clarify in the declaration. . . . A new declaration of human rights will not be a slavish repetition of the 1789 declaration but will present the most lofty ideals of the current century.[76]

Despite enjoying the support of a majority of Latin American states and all nine communist states, these and other proposals to put the two sets of rights on more equal footing were defeated by the North Atlantic countries, their allies, and their former colonies.[77] Thus, at the very outset of the human rights project, the document considered to be the most holistic and integrated of all human rights instruments legitimized an implicit philosophical and practical ranking of human rights.[78] Soon the Cold War would exacerbate the division between civil and political rights and economic, social, and cultural rights, resulting in separate treaties for the two sets of rights and further fragmentation of the broader human rights concept.

Abstentions to the Universal Declaration

The Universal Declaration's "unanimous" approval by UN member states has been interpreted by human rights proponents and historians as a sign of its widespread appeal to the diverse peoples of the world. The General Assembly session in which it passed had all the markings of a publicity event; the assembled government representatives seemed to compete with one another to heap praise on the document, further burnishing its morally unassailable image. Their comments stand out for the manner in which they ignored or in effect rewrote the history of the drafting process. In one illustrative speech, the Ecuadorian ambassador claimed:

> Throughout many centuries of political struggle to bring about human unity, the climax had now been reached with the preparation of the document in which 58 nations had expressed their common ideal and their identity of thoughts regarding fundamental human rights. From time immemorial, man had sought an international standard which would make peace and the universal concept of human rights a reality.[79]

While it is a commonplace for politicians to play to popular expectations, the extent of the UN's embrace of the UDHR indicates both genuine appreciation for its achievement and the prevailing atmosphere of intense and seemingly exaggerated public hopes for human rights. People wanted something meaningful to come from the UN's commitment to human rights; they expected a new international morality, if not a new legality. Such public backing gave a measure of ideological "soft power" to human rights and raised the cost of opposing them, or even appearing to do so. Even states that perceived their fundamental national interests to be at odds with the new human rights regime were constrained from casting a negative vote; their opposition was expressed in their abstentions, which were ultimately subsumed within the declaration's image of universal acclaim.

Conventional wisdom dismisses the abstentions as defensive reactions by states with poor human rights records; however, many of the states that voted for the UDHR also committed violations as a matter of course. Among the abstaining countries, there were three distinct camps: South Africa stood alone in seeking to defend its apartheid regime; Saudi Arabia expressed what would eventually become a powerful developing-country critique of the secular Eurocentric basis of human rights; and the Soviet bloc assailed the western ideological bias toward individuals' rights against the state.

South Africa's withdrawal from the human rights project was inevitable, based on an irreconcilable conflict between legalized racial oppression and moral standards based on the equal dignity of each human individual. During discussions at the General Assembly, the South African representative, Eric Luow, justified abstention on the grounds that while the declaration was not binding, it could be interpreted to impose certain legal obligations as an authoritative definition of fundamental rights mentioned in the Charter—an accurate fear, given its eventual status as customary international law. He also criticized the declaration for recognizing rights far in excess of those "which were generally accepted all over the world," arguing that it was "not, after all, the function of the [Third] Committee to codify a whole philosophy of life" or to propagate a false notion of equality that "would not be in the interests of the less-advanced indigenous population." He also denounced the potential abuse of human rights as propaganda, warning, "It would be a tragedy if human rights became a *cliché* or developed into a political slogan."[80] His remarks drew outraged criticism from other members of the Third Committee, foreshadowing South Africa's eventual isolation from the world community as a human rights pariah.

Saudi Arabia's reasons for abstaining were based both on ideological and political grounds. That the declaration made no reference to God was seen to undermine the religious foundations of the Saudi state. The Saudi representative, Jamil Baroody, also denounced the failure of human rights to address issues of self-determination and colonialism as an indication of great-power politics and international racism. He argued that the supposed universality of the declaration only disguised the reality of a secular ideology based on "the unity of the European family."[81] He pointed out that the declaration was based largely on "Western patterns of culture, which were frequently at variance with the patterns of culture of Eastern states."[82] Compared to later remarks in the General Assembly with regard to western imperialism, Baroody's critique of human rights was relatively mild, but it laid the foundation for broader religious, cultural, and political critiques that would come to dominate UN discussions during decolonization.

The communist bloc had voiced objections throughout the drafting process, alleging that the declaration merely proclaimed rights without the means to fulfill them, failed to understand the interdependence between the citizen and the state, did not address the social and economic conditions necessary to realize human rights, and did nothing to keep the menace of fascism at bay. Explaining his country's decision to abstain, Andrei Vyshinsky argued that the Universal Declaration distorted the legal and philosophical basis for human rights by failing to recognize that rights "could not be conceived outside the State" and that "the very concept of right and law was connected with that of the State." Rights that were not protected and implemented by the state would become "empty illusions, easily created, but just as easily dispelled."[83]

The conclusion that the Soviet Union and its allies were the major losers in the human rights sweepstakes seems justified. Their goals of strengthening state sovereignty, gaining recognition for a materialist philosophy, and opposing fascist ideology were all rejected; on the contrary, the unique contribution of the UDHR was its affirmation of individual human rights transcending national boundaries. The only consolation for the Soviet Union was U.S. support for nonenforcement at the international level, but even that proved no defense against the moral force of human rights attacks during the Cold War.

Conclusion: Searching for the Universal in the Declaration

Was the UDHR truly universal in origin? The claim of universal consensus is a critical component of the ideological power of human rights, the very foundation of its status as the highest moral principle in international relations. The myriad human rights laws, treaties, agencies, and institutions that have arisen in the past half-century at the global, regional, and national levels, not to mention the ever-growing nongovernmental human rights movement, owe a large part of their appeal and authority to the presumed universality of the Universal Declaration.

Today the debate over universality continues to be polarized, with two opposing camps accusing each other of either cultural imperialism or cultural relativism. In the context of warnings of a looming clash of civilizations, it is important to clarify the historical basis of this debate. From the beginning, great-power politics and sovereign state interests were integral to the human rights story; the very meaning of the word universal must be interpreted in the context of a UN comprised of less than one-third of its current member states. Many countries were still under colonial rule; many states did not allow their citizens a democratic voice; minorities and indigenous peoples had few rights anywhere; racial oppression and segregation were the norm in many western democracies; and the Soviet gulag awaited political dissenters. The Soviet delegate to the Third Committee summed up the dilemma (while mistakenly exempting his own country from the list): "The relationship between the United Kingdom and Malaya, between the Netherlands and Indonesia, between different groups in Spain, between the rich and poor everywhere cannot be described as brotherly unless the brothers referred to are Cain and Abel."[84] For these countries to agree on a universal law was a tall order indeed.

There is little room for debating the simple historical fact that the Universal Declaration was based largely on western philosophical models, legal traditions, and geopolitical imperatives (although strangely enough, the conventional view of human rights has still not come around to acknowledging the full implications of this fact). The background materials used to develop the early drafts were, as Humphrey noted, "with two exceptions, all from English-speaking sources and all of them from the democratic West."[85] On the other hand, the political negotiations that produced the UDHR were lengthy and complex. Smaller states had opportunities to express views, assert agendas, and contribute to the development of the human rights system, leading some scholars to deny that "the international human rights project was an extension of U.S. and Western hegemony—or more precisely ... that it was only designed and promoted to serve such a purpose."[86]

While the exact extent of U.S. hegemony can be debated, it is a matter of historical record that the United States exercised predominant influence over all key decisions of the CHR, due to both the skills and resources of its drafting teams and its unparalleled ideological power in the postwar world. A few years after its adoption, Secretary of State John Foster Dulles told a group of U.S. lawyers that the Universal Declaration of Human Rights was not a mere statement of legal principles but America's "Sermon on the Mount" in the ideological struggle against the Soviet Union.[87] Similarly, it is also beyond reasonable dispute that the primary ideological model underlying the UDHR was western liberal individualism. Soviet and Latin American efforts to introduce alternative ideas of the relationship between rights, society, and the state were defeated, and economic, social, and cultural rights were included over Anglo-American objections, but in a secondary position. A valuable and far-reaching UNESCO study that both recognized and sought to reconcile diverse intellectual and cultural rights traditions (discussing, for example, the importance of duties and the role of group rights) was suppressed by the CHR.

The members of the commission were far from equal; a handful held disproportionate influence, in particular the "triumvirate" of Roosevelt, Malik, and Chang. The first was without doubt the leading and most influential personality on the commission; the latter two, while representing nonwestern traditions, were educated in a "European template," as more than one commentator has noted, and were understood at the time to be closely allied to the U.S. position.[88] Even language played a role. The UN procedure for translating papers between English and French—at that point the organization's two working languages—meant that drafts drawn up in English were often translated literally without due concern for the nuances of meaning, while the policy of consecutive rather than simultaneous translation left many delegates unclear as to what was being discussed or how they should vote on an issue. According to his biographer, René Cassin admitted that at certain times "I failed to understand, and thus let pass, proposals and resolutions that did not correspond to my own views."[89]

However, the most important obstacle to human rights universalism was not its decidedly Eurocentric and U.S. flavor; Latin American and Asian countries did contribute to the final product, albeit as role-players.[90] The major roadblock was the exclusive focus on the promotion of rights and the corresponding blackout on the protection of rights due to an unshakeable U.S.-Soviet axis that opposed any and all measures of enforcement. After World War II, different peoples of the world were perhaps more united than at any time before or since on the need for a practical enforceable international morality to avoid a recurrence of war and its accompanying mass atrocities. This is the reason that human rights held near-universal popular acclaim. But had the rights of the Universal Declaration included the means of implementation in accordance with public hopes and expectations, there would have been no "unanimous" approval, no declaration, no universal human rights at all; the price of great-power acceptance was the rejection of a system that might provide meaningful improvements in people's lives.

Nevertheless, the UDHR remains the most holistic and integrated statement of human rights. It has inspired generations of activists and movements to fight for justice. The real historical circumstances of its creation do not nullify its subsequent achievements; its appeal and ideological influence cannot be discounted simply because the most powerful nation-states were prepared neither to submit to international authority nor to hand sovereignty over to the rights-bearing individual. Reflecting in his diary on the regrettable gap between promotion and protection, Humphrey expressed a hope that may yet be fulfilled: "The distinction between moral force and legal binding force means little in the present state of international organization. . . . The Declaration will develop its own implementation."[91]

7

The Human Rights Covenants

- Human Rights Deadlock in the Cold War
- The Controversy over Economic and Social Rights
- Colonialism and Self-Determination
- Manipulations of Federal States
- The Colonial Clause
- Reservations against Universality
- Enforcement's Hollow Core
- The Legacy of Fragmentation

Human Rights Deadlock in the Cold War

At the first session of the CHR (January–February 1947), state representatives debated the scope and meaning of their mandate to draft an international bill of rights. Should it be a declaration of principles, a legally binding convention, a series of conventions, or some combination thereof?[1] A strong majority of members supported a single enforceable convention. This point of view was in line with public hopes that human rights would be the basis for a new system of global justice. But the United States and the Soviet Union joined forces to foreclose the possibility that they would have to subject their domestic policies to international standards, preferring that human rights remain subordinate to the prerogatives of great-power hegemony. The CHR was compelled to fragment the bill of rights into a triptych comprised of a declaration, a covenant, and measures of implementation, and three working groups were given the task of negotiating these documents. Members masked the political nature of this fragmentation behind professions of concern for procedural efficiency and division of labor.[2]

The three working groups were separate and unequal from the start. The United States pushed for quick action on the declaration; without it, the entire human rights project would be discredited. As a result, the CHR succeeded in overcoming numerous disputes to submit the Universal Declaration of

Human Rights to the General Assembly in only two years. In contrast, the working group on implementation disbanded after several years of fruitless negotiations without a single proposal that gained the CHR's approval; the United States and the Soviet Union were simply not willing to consider international mechanisms to implement human rights within national borders.[3] They shared similar concerns with respect to the covenant but faced strong countervailing pressures both within the CHR and General Assembly and among broader circles of civil society actors and international jurists. The wartime mobilization of public opinion and the proliferation of human rights proposals by states, regional groupings, and private legal associations created a common expectation that the UN would establish a bill of rights binding on all states. At the second session of the CHR (November–December 1947), Charles Malik gave voice to this prevailing sentiment, declaring the establishment of a legal treaty to be the "acid test" of the overall human rights project:

> It is imperative that the Commission's work should result in the drawing up of a Bill, a Convention or a Covenant, and not just a mere proclamation. . . . The real point at issue is whether there is in the world to-day an international moral sense, whose principles can be incorporated in national laws, or whether such anarchy exists in that field that only a vague proclamation of general principles can be achieved. If the latter is the case, the world is in very grave situation.[4]

The world, which had just emerged from a very grave situation, was on the brink of entering the Cold War. The hopeful postwar vision of a new world order with human rights providing universal standards of protection for all people, irrespective of nationality, was soon replaced by global conflict at all levels. The CHR became bitterly divided as rival states attacked each other on legal, moral, and ideological grounds. At the United Nations, progress on human rights agreements ground to a halt. It would take eighteen years of contentious negotiations to draft the bill of rights. Departing from the Universal Declaration's integrated approach, the bill of rights was split into two separate covenants, and the covenant on economic, social, and cultural rights was placed in an inferior position to the covenant on civil and political rights despite pious pronouncements of the "interdependence and indivisibility" of all rights.[5] It took another decade for the covenants to gain the thirty-five state ratifications necessary for them to enter into force. And even when they did so, implementation was weak and relied on self-reporting by states. Intended as the cornerstone of an enforceable system of international justice, the covenants instead reflected the further weakening and fragmentation of the original human rights project.

In retrospect, the Universal Declaration crowned a brief honeymoon period when it was still possible, albeit difficult, to bridge competing ideologies
of rights. By 1950, the Cold War had erupted into the open and the UN was
functioning as the diplomatic front line. When Mao Zedong's Communist
Party took power in China, the United States and its allies contrived to maintain the Kuomintang's seat at the Security Council and General Assembly,
prompting a brief Soviet boycott of the UN.[6] When the Soviets later vetoed
a Security Council resolution authorizing force in the Korean conflict, the
United States abrogated the great-power agreement that gave the council sole
responsibility for international security and instead persuaded a majority of
the General Assembly to adopt the resolution dubiously titled "Uniting for
Peace" that expanded the UN Charter's right of self-defense under Article
51 to allow for American military intervention.[7]

Throughout the 1950s, Cold War tensions, heightened by fears of nuclear
war, colored every aspect of international relations. The world was split into
two hostile camps with numerous points of conflict. Europe was divided,
Soviet tanks rolled into Hungary and Czechoslovakia, and the gulags filled
with political prisoners.[8] In the United States, Senator Joseph McCarthy's
anticommunist witch-hunts cowed liberal politicians and fostered national
hostility toward the United Nations, while the proposed Bricker Amendment
to the Constitution, which would have severely restricted domestic incorporation of international law and human rights, almost passed the Senate.[9]
Facing increased opposition both at home and at the UN, whose new members often favored the Soviet position, President Eisenhower signaled U.S.
withdrawal from its leading role in the CHR by replacing Mrs. Roosevelt with
Mary Lord, of whom René Cassin remarked that she conducted her business
"with a disinterest injurious to the Covenants."[10] Such conditions were clearly
not conducive to cooperative negotiation of human rights treaties.

The Security Council remained deadlocked in the 1960s while the balance of power in the General Assembly continued to shift sharply away from
western control. The war in Vietnam damaged U.S. standing in the world
body. The influx of newly decolonized states from Asia and Africa, whose
liberation struggles were backed by the Soviet Union and China, meant that
the United States could no longer dictate global policies, although by this
time the basic tracks of the human rights project had been laid down.[11] The
brutal and bloody wars of decolonization that devastated local economies
and claimed millions of civilian casualties were reflected in the diplomatic
jousting at UN bodies, making compromise elusive and consensus impossible to reach.

The protracted series of negotiations that finally gave birth to the covenants in 1966 mirrored this larger context of global conflict. UN delegates spent years fighting the same spirited battles over seemingly abstract legal issues: Were economic and social rights justiciable in the same manner as civil and political rights? Was self-determination a right or a principle held by individuals or national groups? Did the jurisdiction of human rights treaties extend to constituent states within federal systems and dependent dominions within colonial empires? Behind such debates, fundamental national interests were at stake that had implications in the fields of politics, economics, and war. These human rights conflicts were not trivial. It mattered to governments whether or not their ideological visions and legal systems—or those of their enemies—were validated in international law.

But where amid the cacophony of diplomatic disputes were the hopes and desires of ordinary people around the world for an approach to human rights that addressed the real problems of daily life? How many would choose political freedom for themselves and their children over economic security, or vice versa, rather than both together? Was it necessary to distinguish, morally or legally, between freedom from torture and freedom from starvation—particularly if both outcomes resulted from deliberate state policy? Such commonsense everyday concerns were largely absent from human rights debates at the world body. Indeed, nowhere was the gulf between "we the peoples" of the United Nations and the governments that purported to represent them more evident than in the global failure to develop a binding and effective system of human rights.

The Controversy over Economic and Social Rights

The core controversy of the bill of rights concerned the nature of legal obligations, which in turn implicated competing ideological visions of the respective roles of law and morality in both national government and global governance. A simplified understanding is that there were three primary groups of states at loggerheads in these human rights debates: the western bloc, led by the United States and UK; the communist countries, led by the Soviet Union; and the Third World countries, which served as an occasional buffer between Cold War antagonists. The western view held that only immediately realizable and justiciable rights—those rights capable of being adjudicated and enforced by domestic courts through traditional legal process—should properly be included in a bill of rights. The integrity of this position, however, was undermined by consistent Anglo-American efforts to deny enforcement measures and limit the jurisdiction even of civil and political rights in the colonial and federal contexts. The Soviets championed economic and social rights, minority rights, and the right of self-determination but only through enhancing the government's authority in these areas rather than accepting state accountability to individual rights; on the issue of international supervision and enforcement, the Soviets were equally if not more intransigent than the western powers. Below the surface of this human rights clash were competing ideologies of unfettered private market power versus centralized state planning. Third World countries generally did not act as a monolithic group, although they tended to support the interdependence of all human rights and oppose the superpower alliance against meaningful implementation.

At the CHR's second opening session in December 1947, the UK delegation submitted a draft convention of eighteen articles consisting solely of civil rights derived from English common law tradition; examples include the rights of personal liberty, due process of law, and freedom of religion and belief.[12] In this draft, the convention was accompanied by a broader, nonbinding resolution promoting "international cooperation to achieve the realization of the rights of all persons to work, to education, to social security and similar social and economic rights, which cannot by their nature be defined in the form of a legal obligation."[13] The British understood these rights as moral aspirations requiring social policy and government expenditure, and as such unsuited for inclusion in a legal treaty. René Cassin objected that certain political rights and economic rights related to workers were already well established in international law.[14]

A revised draft of the UK proposal, this one expanded to include political rights such as freedom from torture and slavery and the right to legal personality, was forwarded to the newly formed working group on the covenant, which met nine times in December 1947 during the CHR's second session.[15] The working group included Lord Dukeston of the UK as chair, Charles Malik as rapporteur, C. H. Wu of China, Omar Loutfi of Egypt, and Vladislav Ribnikar of Yugoslavia; in addition, many countries, including the United States, sent observers. These representatives advocated diverging visions of what constituted a bill of rights and recommended a wide range of specific rights. Yugoslavia proposed adding economic and social rights; Uruguay urged a ban on the death penalty; the UK wanted a colonial clause that exempted dominions from the jurisdiction of human rights treaties; the United States favored a federal clause that exempted constituent states within federal systems; and France suggested that not one but a series of covenants should be drafted.[16] Rather than trying to negotiate these various proposals, the working group produced a draft of twenty-seven articles based largely on the original UK version, adding the controversial federal and colonial clauses and two articles on the rights of workers.[17] Further work on the covenant was postponed for two years while the CHR focused on finalizing the Universal Declaration.

ECOSOC requested the CHR to reconsider the covenant during its fifth session (April–May 1949).[18] Chang was the chair and, as Humphrey observed, "having a very bad time of it."[19] Communist countries accused him of hiding behind American power and usurping the UN seat that rightfully belonged to Maoist China.[20] In fact, the formerly indispensable ally of Mrs. Roosevelt was growing increasingly bitter at what he perceived as America's arrogant and unprincipled human rights policy. He resigned from the UN in 1952, denouncing U.S. "dollar policy—all business and materialism without moral principles."[21]

The fifth session was taken up with heated and unproductive debates over the federal and colonial clauses and a U.S.-proposed general limitation clause that allowed states to disregard any articles that were inconsistent with domestic law. Humphrey interpreted the latter as a general escape clause that would have eviscerated the purpose of the covenant by leaving each state free to pick and choose which rights to recognize.[22] Members of the CHR were increasingly frustrated with Anglo-American efforts to undercut the scope and effectiveness of the covenants with procedural limitations and outright exclusion of substantive rights favored by most other members, in particular the economic, social, and cultural rights established in Articles 22–27 of the Universal Declaration. To help resolve controversies about these rights, the CHR decided to solicit the input of other UN bodies and outside experts.

Representatives of the ILO, UNESCO, and several specialized UN agencies as well as NGO observers attended the sixth session of the CHR (April–May 1950). The observers and most members favored including economic, social, and cultural rights and civil and political rights in a single covenant but decided to delay revising the current draft because of the Soviet boycott of the UN to protest the continued seating of the Kuomintang. At its eleventh session in Geneva (July–August 1950) ECOSOC deemed the CHR's draft covenant unsatisfactory and requested that the General Assembly resolve the major points of disagreement such as the federal and colonial clauses and the status of economic and social rights.[23]

When the Cold War began, the stage was set for vitriolic debate in the General Assembly. The leading issue of contention was whether the covenant should reduce the number and scope of rights the Universal Declaration recognized. The CHR's official rationale for separating the declaration and the covenant in the first place had been based not on a hierarchy of rights but on grounds of efficiency and timing. Latin American countries were particularly insistent that the Universal Declaration was only the first step toward achieving the legal enshrinement of the "conscience of mankind" and that the covenant was the logical next step in such development.[24] The representative of Argentina drew attention to the progressive revolution taking place throughout the world and maintained that the Universal Declaration's guarantee of economic and social rights was an advance that "kept abreast of the progress made by human aspirations in the preceding half-century."[25]

Lord MacDonald of the UK countered that "if the covenant is to be no more than a second edition of the Universal Declaration of Human Rights, it is a waste of time to try to cast it in the form of a legal document."[26] Mr. Azkoul, the Lebanese delegate, affirmed that "the difference between moral and legal obligation is the key to the form of the two instruments."[27] Demonstrating the colorful reasoning that flourished in these debates, he sought to clarify his position through analogy:

> The Declaration is the product of the intelligence of the United Nations, which has surveyed all the possible concepts of human rights. The covenant expresses the will of the United Nations, which decides which of the rights selected by the intelligence should be respected in law. The Declaration contains a larger number of rights than the covenant, since the intelligence acknowledges more rights than the will could undertake to apply.[28]

In discussions within the Third Committee, the majority of countries disagreed and favored revising the draft covenant to include the full range of rights in the Universal Declaration. They maintained that the draft covenant as it stood would be of little advantage because it contained rights already found in most constitutions but ignored recent legal trends that recognized basic human needs as human rights.[29] The representative of Mexico, noted that "as it stands, the covenant is at best a covenant regarding the political rights of the individual, and the exercise of those rights is generally assured; in that form it cannot contribute to the progress of humanity, particularly as it is considered that the problems requiring solution are essentially economic and social."[30]

Referring to decolonization struggles against European imperialism and the American civil rights movement, the Soviet delegate denounced the absence not only of economic and social rights but also the right to self-determination and protection for the rights of minorities, commenting that "the covenant contains serious defects and should be radically redrafted so that it will constitute a real guarantee of the implementation of the fundamental human rights and freedoms."[31] The Czech delegate observed that "if the covenant is accepted as it stands, it will be a hundred years behind the times."[32] This time frame was extended back another fifty years in an impassioned speech by the delegate from Yugoslavia:

> The Universal Declaration of Human Rights does not merely list certain economic and social rights; it includes those rights because it conceives of man as an integrated personality, which for its full expression and well-being requires the enjoyment of economic and social as well as political and civil rights. Such a conception is not fortuitous; it is the logical outcome of a hundred and fifty years of historical development. In the modern world, man's right to social and economic security is generally accepted; it has been recognized in the constitutions of a number of States with varying political, economic and social structures. The Universal Declaration on Human Rights has recognized it on the international plane, and it is for the covenant on human rights to transform that conception into an obligation. . . . It would be absurd if, through the elimination of economic and social rights, those two documents should present diametrically opposed conceptions of the human being and his rights.[33]

In its fifth session (October 1950), the General Assembly criticized the draft covenant because it included federal and colonial clauses and omitted "certain of the most elementary rights," failing to recognize that "when deprived of economic, social and cultural rights, man does not represent the human person whom the Universal Declaration regards as the ideal of the free man." It instructed the commission to submit recommendations to the next General Assembly session for extending provisions of the covenant to constituents of federal states and non-self-governing territories and to include "a clear expression of economic, social and cultural rights in a manner which relates them to the civic and political freedoms proclaimed by the draft Covenant."[34]

Establishing Hierarchy within Universal Rights

A solid majority in the General Assembly supported including economic, social, and cultural rights in the human rights covenant, and several western states changed course and offered a middle path out of the dilemma—include these rights but in a separate covenant. The Norwegian delegate reasoned that because disagreement might unduly delay the entire project, "it would be more practical to enunciate those rights in a separate covenant which would follow immediately upon the first."[35] The UK sought to reassure other delegates that "the inclusion of rights which gave rise to precise obligations together with rights which would not necessarily weaken any covenant."[36] Mrs. Roosevelt supported the French proposal that the two covenants be separated but drafted simultaneously, disingenuously claiming that this was justified "for the sole reason that the implementation of two separate covenants would be quicker than that of a single instrument."[37] All these arguments emphasized practical rather than political concerns, similar to the reasoning that had previously been used to justify splitting the bill of rights into a triptych of declaration, covenant, and implementation measures. In that case as well, delegates had insisted, falsely, as it turned out, that such expediency would not result in hierarchy and inequality between the separate instruments.

Bodil Begtrup, the Dutch delegate who had chaired the Commission on the Status of Women from 1946 to 1948,[38] also opposed including economic and social rights in the same treaty as civil and political rights, reminding delegates of earlier debates in which they had discussed the idea of not one but several covenants drafted on the basis of principles contained in the Universal Declaration.[39] The Polish delegate immediately countered, "The United Nations has taken no decision, nor does any document exist, to that effect. It is therefore necessary to draft a covenant on human rights embracing all the elementary rights."[40]

At the end of the session, the General Assembly adopted by a lopsided vote of 29 to 5, with 13 abstentions, a resolution recommending that the CHR include economic, social, and cultural rights in a single covenant and make proposals regarding each of the disputed issues, in particular the right to self-determination and the federal and colonial clauses.[41] But at the CHR's seventh session (April–May 1951), western states ignored these recommendations and continued to treat the two sets of rights differently. The United States and the UK proposed a resolution calling on the General Assembly to reconsider its decision about the unified covenant. After that resolution was defeated, the working group managed to draft fourteen articles on economic, social, and cultural rights and two separate umbrella clauses concerning obligations and limitations.[42] However, the United States and the UK flatly rejected the majority decision to treat all rights equally on the grounds that economic and social rights were not justiciable. As Humphrey noted, these ongoing efforts to prioritize civil and political rights turned the ostensibly single covenant into "a covenant within a covenant."[43]

Facing complete deadlock on implementation, the CHR sent the dispute back up to ECOSOC, where the United States, the UK, Belgium, India, and Uruguay submitted the resolution again, requesting that the General Assembly reconsider its decision to include economic, social, and cultural rights in a single covenant.[44] This time the resolution passed despite continued opposition from the Soviet bloc and the majority of Latin American states.

Several countries explained that their about-face was prompted by aggressive Anglo-American lobbying and concerns about losing U.S. support as chief backer of the human rights project.[45]

This set the stage for a series of procedural maneuvers throughout 1951 and 1952, when the issue bounced between ECOSOC and the General Assembly in the form of various resolutions and amendments. Countries that favored one covenant argued—ultimately in vain—that the original decision should not be reversed at the whim of several powerful members; countries that favored several covenants insisted that the CHR's inability to draft a single covenant was the result of legitimate and unbridgeable disagreements over means of implementation.[46]

Rejecting American pressure, the Third Committee of the General Assembly approved, by a vote of 29 to 21, with 6 abstentions, a joint resolution by Chile, Egypt, Pakistan, and Yugoslavia that called on the General Assembly to reaffirm a single covenant that included economic, social, and cultural rights.[47] But this was far from the end of the matter. In an interesting procedural tactic, Belgium, India, Lebanon, and the United States added an amendment to the resolution that once again asked ECOSOC to direct the CHR to draft two separate human rights covenants that would be approved by the General Assembly and opened for signature simultaneously.[48] Other countries objected that this was not an amendment but a nullification of the resolution, but Malik used his authority as chair to forward the amended resolution without further vote to the plenary session of the General Assembly.[49]

Chile sponsored a new amendment to delete the previous amendment and restore the unified covenant, but after intense U.S. lobbying it was defeated in the Third Committee by a vote of 29 to 25, with 4 abstentions.[50] Finally, after months of shifting fortunes, General Assembly resolution 543(VI), which requested ECOSOC to direct the CHR to prepare two separate covenants, passed by a vote of 27 to 20, with 3 abstentions.[51] Again the human rights project was fragmented; again the United States had succeeded in imposing its human rights vision on the United Nations despite majority opposition.

Language in the final resolution that called for the two covenants to share as many similar provisions as possible and be simultaneously presented for signature gave an appearance of unity to the world body's fractured human rights policy.[52] But this attempt to save face was belied by statements of record by the United States and western states as well some developing countries that indicated a strong bias against economic and social rights.

Once this major ideological dispute was resolved, the CHR made progress in its next two sessions toward completing the two draft covenants. Notwithstanding the mandate to treat the two sets of rights in an equal manner, the working group moved expeditiously along separate tracks, drafting civil and political rights as immediately realizable individual rights that impose absolute obligations on the state and economic and social rights as broad policy goals to be progressively realized according to each state's particular resource constraints.[53] Western states were comfortable modeling civil and political rights on justiciable constitutional rights, but Soviet and many Third World countries, which had championed the idea of a unified covenant, were reluctant to recognize government accountability for economic and social rights.[54]

The drafting history and plain language of the two texts reinforced the hierarchy within human rights.[55] Beyond the special case of the right to self-determination, the only common language was in the nonbinding preambles and the procedural and technical provisions.[56] The contrasting phrasing of crucial articles undermined the legal status of economic, social, and cultural rights and established a legacy of unequal treatment that continues to affect the human rights system today. Civil and political rights were expressed in classical rights terminology: "Every human being has the inherent right to life (Article 6). . . . No one shall be subjected to torture (Article 7). . . . Everyone has the right to liberty and security of the person (Article 9). . . . All persons shall be equal before the courts and tribunals (Article 14)."[57] But for economic, social, and cultural rights, the primary actor and agent was the state rather than the person: "The State Parties to the present Covenant recognize the right to work (Article 6). . . . The State Parties to the present Covenant undertake to ensure the right of everyone to form trade unions (Article 8). . . . The State Parties to the present Covenant recognize the right of everyone to an adequate standard of living (Article 11)."[58]

Compounding this disparate treatment, Article 2(3) of the civil and political rights covenant mandated effective remedies for violations, requiring states to "ensure that any person whose rights or freedoms as herein recognized are violated shall have an effective remedy . . . determined by competent judicial, administrative or legislative authorities . . . [and] ensure that the competent authorities shall enforce such remedies when granted."[59] In contrast, the economic, social, and cultural rights covenant not only omitted any mention of violations or remedies but also provided a broad escape clause in Article 2(1) that undermined the prospects for holding states accountable: "Each State Party undertakes to take steps, individually and through international assistance and cooperation, especially economic and technical, to the maximum of its available resources, with a view to achieving progressively the full realization of rights."[60]

The CHR submitted draft covenants to the General Assembly within two years of the decision to split the bill of rights. At its ninth session in 1954, the General Assembly undertook the first review of the two covenants, supplemented by a detailed reference document that summarized the drafting history of various articles.[61] But continued political polarization, particularly around the issues of the highly contested right to self-determination and western efforts to restrict the effect of the covenants in federal states and dependent territories, delayed agreement on the basic texts until 1962. Disputes about implementation added another four years to these negotiations and deepened the split between the two covenants. While the Soviet Union and its allies fought hardest against legal enforcement, most states were either hostile or indifferent to the idea of empowering citizens by giving them practical avenues to achieve their human rights, and the lowest common denominator won the day.[62]

The covenant on economic, social, and cultural rights was denied a monitoring body to ensure state compliance and a mechanism for reviewing individual complaints. Only in 1986 did ECOSOC agree to establish the Committee on Economic, Social and Cultural Rights, and that committee has no means to review individual petitions.[63] The civil and political rights covenant fared marginally better: Articles 28–45 established an expert monitoring body, the Human Rights Committee, but it has no capacity for independent investigation and therefore depends on self-reporting by states.[64] The committee was granted authority to review individual complaints, but only if states signed an addition protocol attached to the covenant.

The General Assembly approved the two covenants in December 1966. By 1976, each had gained the requisite number of state ratifications to come into force—almost thirty years after the peoples of the world had turned to the UN in hopes of establishing a new global code of universal rights.

The Political Ideology of Separation

The United States and a relatively small group of western states led the successful drive to divide the human rights covenant. Why was it so important for them to deny equal recognition of economic and social rights? American intransigence was especially puzzling due to its apparent contradiction of President Roosevelt's Four Freedoms speech of 1941, which had played a crucial role in raising the international profile of a broadly conceived vision of human rights that included economic rights. But the four freedoms were intended to entrench New Deal reforms in the domestic political landscape and provide a global platform for spreading American values.[65] President

Roosevelt and his State Department never seriously contemplated accepting international legal standards in the national sphere.[66] Once the McCarthyite right wing launched a sustained attack against the UN, Mrs. Roosevelt was given explicit written instructions by her State Department advisors to reject any moves toward recognizing the legal status of economic and social rights.[67]

Other western states did not face such virulent domestic opposition but shared a common legal heritage derived from the post-Enlightenment revolutions against feudal authority. In this tradition, individual rights were conceived as protection against state, and clerical power and property rights were limited to protection of private property. They did not recognize common rights to public goods like education and health care as enshrined in the constitutions of most communist and Third World states.[68] Conceding the equal value of economic and social rights at the international level, even without viable enforcement measures, posed an ideological threat to western legal and political traditions.

Proponents of civil and political rights offered several rationales for granting them a privileged position. They were conceived as "negative" rights that asked of power only to leave the free individual alone and therefore served as protection against government encroachment on liberty and integrity (i.e., torture, detention without due process, restriction on speech and belief). In this view, economic and social rights required "positive" state intervention to provide such public goods as health care, education, and housing. Civil and political rights were therefore considered absolute and immediately achievable through judicial means, whereas economic and social rights were relative and could only be gradually and progressively implemented through social policy. According to this paradigm, civil and political rights were virtually cost free, but economic and social rights required significant financial resources and national effort.

State representatives, primarily from western powers, put forward these ostensibly legal distinctions throughout the UN debates to justify subordinating economic and social rights in the covenants. Typical of this line of argument, the Canadian delegate explained the difference between the two sets of rights: "The former [civil and political rights] are primarily the rights of the individual with relation to others and to the State; the latter are only rights in so far as they are derived from the general duty of the State to work for the public good."[69] In his view, political systems might choose to confer material social advantages on citizens, but these were not legal rights. Rather, they were "declarations imposing moral obligations."[70] A number of communist and Third World countries agreed that the two sets of human rights were implicitly unequal, but they reversed the hierarchy. Insisting that economic and social rights should take priority, they critiqued the individualistic nature of civil and political rights and developed a normative model of "progressive" and "regressive" rights.[71] Such was the politicized rhetoric of universal human rights.

However, western states were not alone in their quest to privilege the legal status of civil and political rights. Several Third World countries, concerned about having to assume legal obligations to ameliorate the enormous crisis of domestic poverty, also preferred to downplay the validity of economic and social rights. The Indian delegate observed that while the two sets of rights had indeed emerged from the same root, "it would be imprudent to ignore" their differences.[72] He commented:

> It is, indeed, not necessarily axiomatic that the two groups of rights are equal in importance. Political and civil rights are of an absolute nature and, even making allowance for periods of national stress and emergency, governments are under the undeniable obligation of guaranteeing those rights to the citizens, and the citizen has an equal obligation to retain and exercise them . . . whereas the principle that the State should contribute to the welfare of the citizens by the provision of social and economic rights and amenities arose at a much later date. . . . Those rights are not absolute; it was impossible to lay down, for example, to precisely what standard or level of education a person has the right.[73]

At the end of the day, however, the decisive factor was the bare-knuckled American threat to scuttle the entire process unless economic, social, and cultural rights were treated differently. As the British representative pointedly cautioned, "It would be a tragedy if it [the covenant] were to remain a dead letter, either because States were unwilling to ratify it or because it was loosely drafted as to be capable of various interpretations."[74] His Belgian counterpart had earlier noted that "excessive perfectionism presents a danger which would be greater in the case of the single instrument than if two or more covenants were drawn up," the danger being that the covenant "might never see the light of day."[75]

These less-than-subtle warnings were enough to cow many states into accepting, however reluctantly, further fragmentation of the bill of rights.[76] The representatives of Pakistan and Chile took the optimistic view that the two covenants could be merged into one at a later stage if the General Assembly wished to reverse its decision.[77] But the Iraqi delegate made a more accurate prediction: "Mankind would not appreciate the—possibly very excellent—practical reasons underlying it but would conclude only that the United Nations had not considered that the two sets of rights were equally important for human progress."[78]

Because of the Cold War polarization of the human rights debate, there were few attempts to find a coherent conceptual basis for treating the two sets of rights alike. One such effort was made by the Israeli delegate, Mr. Najjar. Pointing out the fallacious reasoning behind the "absolute" nature of civil and political rights, he observed that implementing them required "a highly developed judiciary organization, which cannot be achieved at short notice."[79] In his view, the sharp distinction between immediately achievable civil and political rights and progressively realizable economic and social rights was artificial. Rather, he suggested, all human rights could be divided into two categories: those that could become an immediate reality because the structures necessary to implement them already existed and those that required additional time and resources to become a reality.[80] Because different states were at different stages in their development, they would necessarily place the same right in different categories.

The Israeli argument foreshadowed the UN consensus that emerged after the Cold War, although at the time it fell upon deaf ears. The primary justifications for separating the covenants have since been criticized as ideological and self-serving. For example, two human rights scholars have observed that the same western powers "that made the greatest effort to affirm the obligation of progressive realization [limited to economic, social, and cultural rights] are now often among those that cite the weakness of the obligation as evidence of the secondary, non-legal or non-binding nature of economic and social rights."[81] Similar circular reasoning that because western legal traditions recognize only civil and political rights, economic and social rights are therefore universally nonjusticiable has been disproved by the practical experience of constitutional adjudication in numerous jurisdictions, notably South Africa, India, Argentina, and several European Union countries.[82] Today most human rights scholars and practitioners dismiss sharp distinctions between the two sets of rights. Instead, it is understood that all rights have both negative aspects—the inclination of states to deprive disfavored individuals and groups of rights seems to apply equally to rights to health care and education and rights to free speech and due process—and positive aspects that require states to commit resources and build institutions.[83]

Irrespective of its motives or validity, the decision in 1952 to divide the bill of rights had important consequences that remain imprinted on the UN. This further fragmentation of the universal human rights project ensured that two distinct discourses of rights were developed almost independently of one another.[84] The broader disconnect between human rights and the fields of development, trade, and economic security had its roots in the long-standing neglect of economic and social factors within human rights. While the tangible impacts of this neglect are difficult to determine, it is clear that a more robust and integrated human rights approach could have mitigated the extremes of poverty and inequality evident throughout the world today.[85] The denigration of economic and social rights and consequent irrelevance of human rights in global socioeconomic policymaking was neither inevitable nor inescapable. On the contrary, the record of UN negotiations indicates the extent to which the fragmentation of human rights was closely contested and historically contingent.

Colonialism and Self-Determination

Judging by the terms of the covenants, self-determination appears to be the single issue that somehow bridged the partisan divisions that characterized the development of other human rights at the UN. It is the only substantive right affirmed in identical language in both covenants. Not only that, self-determination appears in front of all other rights, refers to the right of all peoples without distinction, requires states to promote and respect the right, and explicitly recognizes political, economic, social, and cultural aspects as an integrated whole. Because of its language and position in the covenants, UN human rights bodies typically describe self-determination as the foundation and cornerstone of the entire human rights framework.[86] Common Article 1 of the two covenants says:

1. All peoples have the right to self-determination. By virtue of that right they freely determine their political status and freely pursue their economic, social and cultural development.
2. All peoples may, for their own ends, freely dispose of their natural wealth and resources without prejudice to any obligations arising out of international economic co-operation, based upon the principle of mutual benefit, and international law. In no case may a people be deprived of its own means of subsistence.
3. The State Parties to the present Covenant, including those having responsibility for the administration of Non-Self-Governing Territories, shall promote the realization of the right to self-determination, and shall respect that right, in conformity with the provisions of the Charter of the United Nations.[87]

But the appearance of international agreement on the right to self-determination is highly misleading. It was one of the most divisive human rights issues at the UN, prompting contentious debates in the CHR that, according to Humphrey, nearly "torpedoed the covenant."[88] The consensus language on the right to self-determination masked a series of conflicts about its meaning and who was entitled to exercise it; these conflicts ran even deeper than the divide between the two covenants. The battle over splitting the human rights covenant concerned which of the Cold War's competing legal ideologies would receive international sanction and legitimacy. The battle over self-determination concerned which national groups would receive the fundamental rights of statehood and its accompanying political, economic, and military powers. The self-determination debate therefore affected the nature and composition of the United Nations itself and struck at the heart of the international system.

The UN was founded upon the primacy of nation-states and especially the hegemony of great powers. The global order established by the victorious powers after World War II maintained fundamental attributes of the colonial past; most of the world's peoples and territories remained dependent and subordinated. But the imperialist powers lacked the military and political capacity to maintain their dependent dominions. The increasingly forceful demands of unrecognized nations soon revealed that the international status quo was not sustainable.[89] The speed with which decolonization gained momentum around the world shocked western elites. UN membership doubled in the span of a decade, creating more new states than the aftermath of the two world wars combined.[90]

The human right to self-determination was inseparably linked to the geopolitical process of decolonization. As more states gained independence, the push for self-determination in the UN grew stronger. By the mid-1950s it was no longer possible for western powers to deny recognition of self-determination as a human right. The question became whether the right could be recognized without fragmenting the territorial basis of the UN's nation-state system.

Ironically, it was the newly established states that insisted on limiting the destructive potential of self-determination by rejecting its application to peoples struggling for self-expression outside the limited territorial context of decolonization. In the end, the right to self-determination in the covenants recognized the ground realities of decolonization without legitimizing rights to secession or internal democratic participation. Summarizing this broad historical trend, one legal scholar has observed that "in the second half of the twentieth century, a territorial right [limited] to independence for former colonies replaced the nineteenth century principle of allowing ethnic, linguistic, or religious groups to form various kinds of political units."[91]

Self-Determination in Modern History

Before turning to the specific UN debates about self-determination in the 1950s, it is useful to sketch its recent development in international law. When the UN was established, self-determination was a relatively new concept, having arisen in the nineteenth century in response to demands for political self-expression by ethnic and linguistic groups within larger European polities. It destabilized the traditional fortress-like concept of sovereignty that had prevailed in Europe since the Peace of Westphalia in 1648, in which states generally respected one another's territorial boundaries while competing to subjugate non-European peoples in the "great game" of imperial conquest.[92]

World War I delivered a deathblow to Westphalian sovereignty. President Wilson's stirring rhetoric proclaiming a new era of self-determination sparked nationalist movements not only in Europe but throughout Europe's far-flung empires.[93] The establishment of the colonial mandates co-opted these pressures within new legal and political structures, but the genie was out of the bottle. Nevertheless, the political principle of self-determination did not receive recognition in international law. Wilson's proposal to give the principle of self-determination legal status in the Covenant of the League of Nations was rejected not only by the European powers but also his own secretary of state, Robert Lansing:

> Fixity of national boundaries and of national allegiance, and political stability will disappear if this principle is uniformly applied. What effect will it have on the Irish, the Indians, the Egyptians, and the nationalists among the Boers? Will it not breed discontent, disorder and rebellion? Will not the Mohammedans of Syria and Palestine and possibly of Morocco and Tripoli rely on it? How can it be harmonized with Zionism, to which the President is practically committed?[94]

Lansing's fundamental concern resurfaced decades later during UN debates about self-determination as a human right.

World War II unleashed another wave of nationalist passions and again raised high expectations for self-determination worldwide, which were quickly dashed by the victorious powers once they established the United Nations. Behind the rhetoric of universality "the concept of sovereign equality remained confined to a few, the right of self-determination denied to large sections of the world's population."[95] The Atlantic Charter's recognition of "the right of all peoples to choose the form of government under which they will live" helped mobilize a powerful wartime coalition of diverse peoples.[96] But the UN Charter in Articles 1(2) and 55 downgraded this right to "the principle of equal rights and self-determination of peoples" and confined it to the context of developing "friendly relations among nations."[97] The *travaux préparatoires* from the San Francisco conference indicate that the concept of self-determination was left deliberately ambiguous to accommodate great-power tensions and that it was considered separate from and subordinate to the UN's overarching principle of sovereign equality between recognized nation-states.[98] At the time, the United States supported stronger language but the European powers insisted on a vague formulation to dampen agitation in their colonies; Churchill was deeply suspicious that the United States intended to dismantle the British empire and bring the new states into its economic orbit, similar to the nineteenth-century U.S. strategy of backing Latin American independence movements against Spain under the rubric of the Monroe Doctrine.

By the time the CHR commenced serious discussions on self-determination, however, the global tide had turned. Many liberation movements were finding inspiration and material support from the Soviet Union and China, and the United States had moved toward Europe's position of rejecting self-determination as a human right. Communist and Third World states fought back, determined to remedy the Universal Declaration's failure to mention self-determination and reverse their defeat over economic, social, and cultural rights. They defined self-determination to include economic, social, and cultural as well as political independence, prompting a U.S. State Department legal expert to complain that "the term self-determination was crowded into Article 1 of the Charter without relevance and without explanation; and upon that basis delegates today are making fantastic claims . . . not merely [for] independence . . . but perfect satisfaction for all human desires."[99]

In effect, the UN negotiations about self-determination served as a diplomatic proxy for the conflicts raging across the globe. Each of the major issues CHR faced had a practical counterpart outside the walls of the UN. In this charged context UN representatives in the CHR and General Assembly negotiated the key questions: Was self-determination a human right or a general principle? Did it implicate economic as well as political independence? Did it encompass the right to internal democratic participation? Did it apply only to colonized and non-self-governing territories, or did it also apply to national groups seeking to secede from recognized states?[100]

As with all human rights issues at the UN, Cold War animosity colored the debates. Soviet delegates accused the United States of pursuing imperialist policies in an era when more nations were demanding independence:

> The United States Government's aggressive and imperialist plans are forcing it to become more and more involved in the colonies and spheres of influence of its allies, who are having to yield part of their privileges to it. Thus the United States has become the leader of the resistance to the oppressed people's movement towards liberation. It is waging war on the Korean people; it is financing the war which France is waging against the people of Vietnam.[101]

The United States responded by pointing to the condition of nations denied sovereign rights and independence within the Iron Curtain and denouncing Soviet hypocrisy and double standards: "The Soviet Union has deprived a large number of countries of the right to self-determination by its resort to force and subversive activities. . . . The government and people of the United States are traditionally devoted to the principle of self-determination."[102] What was unusual about the conflict over the right to self-determination was that, for the first time, the United States and western allies were unable to impose their stamp on the human rights regime, in part because many new states perceived the issue as fundamental to their national identity and voted with the Soviet bloc.

In the first few sessions of the CHR, western states blocked efforts to discuss self-determination. In response, the General Assembly directed it in 1950 "to study ways and means to ensure the right of peoples and nations to self-determination, and to prepare recommendations for consideration by the General Assembly."[103] The CHR remained deadlocked in its 1951 session as western states offered numerous procedural objections and resisted majority proposals to include economic self-determination and emphasize the responsibility of colonial powers. Thereupon the General Assembly took the unusual step of insisting that the CHR include an article in the draft covenant using the language: "all peoples shall have the right to self-determination."[104]

The CHR spent most of its eighth session (April–June 1952) debating the issue. Humphrey attributed the actual drafting of the article to Hernán Santa Cruz of Chile and noted how annoyed Mrs. Roosevelt appeared to be when language was introduced that not only asserted that self-determination was a right, not a principle, but that it also had economic as well as political components.[105] She attacked the concept of economic self-determination in her regular newspaper column:

> The sins of the past are rising up to make life difficult for us in many ways! The delegate from Chile presented an article that . . . stated [that] the right of people to self-determination included the economic right to control all of their natural resources and not be deprived of their use or their means of existence by the action of any outside power. It amounts practically to confiscation of property of foreigners without compensation being legalized by a treaty.[106]

This issue was of fundamental importance to western states, which feared that recognition of economic self-determination would give countries a legal mechanism for altering terms of trade and imposing new regulations on private corporations. In view of the bitter legacy of economic exploitation colonialism had wrought, communist and Third World states were adamant that sovereign independence required national control over both economic and political life. Responding to Mrs. Roosevelt's critique, the Chilean delegate asserted:

> There is no question of authorizing States to denounce international agreements arbitrarily, rather is it a matter of settling relations between nations and foreign private undertakings, which made large profits by exploiting a country's natural resources without in most cases being affected by its legislations. The realization of the right of peoples to self-determination in accordance with United Nations principles should enable any State in a condition of economic subordination to recover full sovereignty by acquiring complete control of its own natural resources and should place that State in a position to apply its own national legislation to any private industry.[107]

During its eighth session, the CHR recommended that the General Assembly adopt a resolution calling for states to recognize "the right of self-determination of the people of Non-Self-Governing and Trust Territories who are under their administration; and grant this right on a demand for self-government" ascertained through a UN plebiscite.[108] Western states argued against focusing only on the colonial context and backed a U.S. amendment to extend the right to "all territories," including dependent territories—an ironic position for countries that in other settings continued to reject the right itself.[109] This amendment did not succeed; the original resolution passed over strong western objections.[110]

Negotiations over the scope and content of the right to self-determination continued for several years as draft articles and resolutions shuttled between the CHR and the Third Committee of the General Assembly. Throughout these debates, the United States, the UK, France, and other western powers fought hard against recognizing self-determination in the human rights covenants, fearing that UN endorsement would strengthen nationalist movements and impinge on decisions they believed fell properly within the mandate of the UN Trusteeship Council. The comments of New Zealand's delegate in response to Western Samoa's declaration of independence are indicative of western attitudes at the time: "In the opinion of the New Zealand delegation, an obligation to grant self-government whenever a demand is made would be in direct conflict with the Charter and the Trusteeship Agreements. . . . The findings of the [New Zealand] Mission, later endorsed by the Trusteeship Council, were that Western Samoa was not yet ready for self-government."[111]

Such statements elicited sharp rejoinders from Soviet-bloc countries, who found in the anticolonial argument a powerful diplomatic tool to attack the West and win favor with the emerging UN majority. The Soviet representative stated that "alleged lack of political maturity cannot serve as a ground for disregarding the national rights of any group. . . . Indeed, arguments to the contrary prove the desire of certain States to achieve world hegemony."[112] Complaining of "outworn" arguments, the Indian representative asserted the immediate right of all colonized peoples to self-determination: "India, speaking for all those countries in Asia which have so often been told that they would have to be patient and wait for the day when, after a gradual evolution, they would be able to achieve autonomy, wishes to state that at that moment all peoples, whatever stage of development they have reached, have the right to govern themselves."[113]

As was the case with economic and social rights, western opposition to self-determination was often couched in technical and procedural concerns. A number of states pointed to ambiguities of definition as they warned of the dangers of recognizing so broad and malleable a concept. The delegate from the Netherlands cautioned the General Assembly that the idea of self-determination was controversial and not susceptible to the kind of interstate consensus that was necessary to reach agreement on fundamental human rights. In his view, self-determination "is a complex set of ideas, rather than a single concept."

> The principle of internal self-determination, or self-determination on the national level, should be distinguished from that of external self-determination . . . the right of a group which considers itself a nation to form a State of its own. . . . So complex a problem must be approached cautiously, the more so because the adoption of too far-reaching a resolution might arouse unjustified expectations and still further increase confusion in a world that so greatly needs peaceful evolution.[114]

Mrs. Roosevelt issued a similar warning about expanding the legitimate principle of self-determination into a right that might wreak havoc on the established tenets of international order: "The concept of self-determination is a vital principle, and like all principles it cannot be applied absolutely or rigidly. . . . Just as the concept of individual liberty . . . carried to its logical extreme would mean anarchy, so the principle of self-determination given unrestricted application can only result in chaos."[115]

These concerns were not solely (even if largely) pretexts for resisting decolonization, nor were they merely academic. Newly established multi-ethnic states such as India, Indonesia, and almost all the African nations included dozens of subgroups with different languages, histories, and cultures; none of them conformed to Stalin's famous objective definition of a nation for purposes of self-determination: "A nation is a historically evolved, stable community of language, territory, economic life, and psychological make-up manifested in a community of culture."[116] These states were vulnerable to claims by internal groups for self-determination or secession. These two terms potentially described identical facts but carried vastly different political significance; the former was sanctioned by international law and the latter was disallowed.[117] Such concerns were heightened by the publication of an influential book by international jurist Georges Scelle arguing that the right to self-determination could force governments to renounce their right to resist secession.[118]

The fundamental dilemma most anticolonial movements faced was that their struggles were demarcated by the imperialist objectives of their former colonial masters. The era of colonialism divided and carved up peoples and their territories for a variety of reasons—competition between imperial powers, maximum exploitation of local resources, policies of divide, conquer, and rule, and so forth—that disregarded previous national, cultural, and historical continuities.[119] Different ethnics groups were divided, merged, and lumped together, in the process acquiring new and unstable national identities. Liberation movements resisted and yet were defined by these injustices. They created new states within the confines of foreign-imposed borders and rejected the threat to their political power and potential destabilization that would have accompanied a revisitation of those territorial realities.[120] Drawing on the precedent established by Latin American independence movements in the nineteenth century, the Organization of African Unity officially adopted the legal principle of uti possidetis and accepted the former colonial lines as the official borders of the new multi-ethnic states.[121]

The French delegate had in mind this vulnerability to secession when he observed that "self-determination is a double-edged sword which often wounds those who use it."[122] Explaining France's opposition to the right, he pointed to the conflicting and incompatible positions of different countries:

> There is no general agreement in the Committee either on the content of the principle or on the areas of the world in which it should be applied. In the view of some, the right of peoples to self-determination is largely equivalent to democracy, since no people living under a dictatorship can make its own decisions; to others it means political independence, while still others treated it as the equivalent of economic independence. Similarly, some think its application is most called for in Eastern Europe, whereas to others it evokes African or Asian countries. Such

lack of agreement is only natural, since the principle of self-determination has never been defined in positive law and no one knows when, by whom and how it can properly be applied.[123]

Such arguments, while accurately highlighting significant areas of ambiguity and uncertainty, were unconvincing to a majority of UN members for whom the basic necessity of validating liberation struggles was far more important than technically defined legal terminology. In matters of national independence, the western powers had little credibility with states that had suffered from foreign domination and exploitation. The Chinese delegate expressed a widely held view when he demanded legal status for the right to self-determination and rejected efforts to limit its scope:

> The States that were exploiting the human and natural resources of dependent countries want to convince the Commission that they favor the right of self-determination. In actual fact, their sole desire is to specify exactly what is to be understood by that right and the French representative has even declared that in no circumstances would he be able to advise his Government to agree to the insertion in the covenant of an article affirming that right, since that would be tantamount to adopting a hostile attitude towards the Administering Powers. . . . An article, however imperfect, affirming that right would enable a recognized moral principle to be transformed into a legal obligation. The exact meaning of the terms in which the article is to be couched is not so important as the spirit to which it would be applied.[124]

By the time the CHR submitted draft covenants to the General Assembly, a majority had overcome objections by its most powerful members to place the right to self-determination, including its political and economic aspects, as common Article 1 in both covenants. At that point negotiations shifted to the Third Committee, which held twenty-six meetings to discuss self-determination at its tenth session in 1955; it debated the issue at several subsequent sessions as well.[125]

The UK, France, Australia, and the Netherlands were among the countries that argued that Article 1 should be deleted from the covenants.[126] Belgium argued that it actively encouraged secession: "As it stands, leaving the article is tantamount to an incitement to insurrection and separatism."[127] But increasingly large margins in the Third Committee rejected attempts to remove self-determination from the covenants as the process of decolonization gathered momentum.[128]

Western states adopted several tactics to forestall recognition of an expansive right to self-determination in both covenants. They proposed splitting the article into separate political and economic components attached to their respective covenants, which would have diminished the legal authority of economic self-determination, but this idea rekindled the bitter disputes over splitting the covenants and was easily voted down.[129] Also rejected was a western proposal to recognize the right to self-determination in a General Assembly declaration rather than in the covenants; according to the Egyptian representative: "A mere declaration would be nothing more than a hazy shadow of existing realities. . . . It is difficult to see how the United Nations can be so lukewarm and reduce its obligations to a mere declaration which would have no binding force."[130]

Another recurring debate centered on including the right of democracy and political participation within the larger framework of self-determination. In the early negotiations of 1950, the United States had tried without success to include the right to participate in one's own government within the ambit of self-determination; this attempt was primarily backed by western states that were otherwise opposed to the right itself.[131] The United States in particular continued to promote the concept of internal and well as external self-determination at every opportunity as a lever against Soviet domination of Eastern Europe. Mrs. Roosevelt argued that "self-determination is a right which belongs to all peoples without distinction; the United Nations should not . . . refer only to peoples which have never exercised the right of self-determination . . . [and not] peoples which have once exercised the right and had it snatched from them."[132]

A number of Third World states, especially from Latin America, supported this idea as a check against domestic tyranny, and reintroduced the proposal at the Third Committee. The Costa Rican delegate pointed out that peoples living under the yoke of dictatorship could not enjoy the right to self-determination any more than those living under foreign domination.[133] The majority rejected this view, fearing that it would provide powerful states a legal justification for intervening in the domestic affairs of other nations. The delegate from Ceylon remarking that "it is dangerous to confuse political freedom with national independence. . . . The right of peoples and nations to self-determination is simply their right to establish their own political institutions, to develop their economy and to direct their culture and social evolution without any foreign intervention."[134] The Ghanaian representative expressed the predominant view in the General Assembly that self-determination should be restricted to the decolonization struggle: "There is no doubt whatever [that] the right of self-determination applies first and foremost to those who have never had the opportunity of exercising it in the past, that is to say, the peoples of the colonies and the Trust Territories. Refinements only obscure the discussion and raise insoluble questions."[135]

Leaving Peoples Undefined

Once the text of the article was completed, albeit still disputed, attention turned to the proverbial bull in the china shop, the debate over who constituted a people eligible to exercise the right of self-determination. States held conflicting views; those for whom the issue implicated national identity and territorial integrity were adamantly opposed to extending self-determination to minorities and secessionist movements. The Belgian delegate remarked that before accepting self-determination as a human right, "the first thing to be settled is the meaning of the word 'peoples.' Common sense indicates, however, that not every group regardless of its nature can be taken into consideration."[136] But common sense alone was not enough to resolve the powerful and conflicting interests at stake in defining the term.

Intent on denying legitimacy to separatist movements, the Indian delegate asserted that the term peoples referred "only to large compact national groups."[137] She argued strongly against considering ethnic groups and minorities within established states as peoples for purposes of self-determination, insisting that "the question of minorities and of the self-determination of peoples should not be confused."[138] China agreed that "the two problems were distinct and required different solutions. Furthermore the concept of secession should not be allowed to enter into the consideration of the question."[139] The Soviet Union and most Third World states strongly supported this view. Western states opposed it with equal force; they insisted that the right should not be restricted to the context of decolonization. The Irish delegate observed that the failure to address the legitimate claims of ethnic groups "always leads to violation of fundamental human freedoms, and even to bloodshed."[140] The UK asserted that certain minorities fit the criteria of a people and therefore were entitled to self-determination, while the delegate from New Zealand went further, insisting that the right to self-determination "should include the right of secession."[141]

The weight of historical evidence supports the conclusion that, although it is formulated broadly with reference to "all peoples," the right belongs only to non-self-governing territories.[142] In Humphrey's view, self-determination "would be understood in United Nations doctrine as a right belonging only to colonial peoples, which once it had been successfully exercised cannot be invoked again, and it would not include a right of secession except for colonies."[143] His view is supported in the General Assembly's 1960 Declaration on the Granting of Independence to Colonial Countries and Peoples, which, despite vague and at times contradictory language, includes a limiting clause that rejects the right of secession and upholds the sanctity of state sovereignty: "Any attempt aimed at the partial or total destruction of the national unity and the territorial integrity of a country is incompatible with the purposes and principles of the Charter of the United Nations."[144]

The final text of common Article 1 does not resolve this fundamental dispute about the definition of self-determination. One of the foremost legal authorities on the right of self-determination believes that states left the term deliberately vague to enable them to reach the appearance of consensus, and as a result, "no contemporary norm of international law has been so vigorously promoted or widely accepted. . . . Yet the meaning of that right remains as vague and imprecise as when it was first enunciated by President Woodrow Wilson and others at Versailles."[145] India, for example, ratified the covenants with a reservation to common Article 1: "The Government of India declares that the words 'the right of self-determination' apply only to peoples under foreign domination and that these words do not apply to sovereign independent states or to a section of a people or a nation—which is the essence of national integrity."[146] France, the Netherlands, and Germany each formally objected to India's reservation, with the latter stating: "The right of self-determination applies to all peoples and not only those under foreign domination. . . . Any limitation of their applicability to all nations is incompatible with the object and purposes of the Covenants."[147]

Unable to reach decision, states agreed to disagree, leaving the term "peoples" undefined and subject to contradictory interpretations. As a weapon in the field of ideological warfare, self-determination was flexible and served on multiple fronts. Communist and Third World states used it to denounce western imperialism, focusing on Israel and apartheid South Africa once the period of decolonization was over; western powers used it to pressure and help dismantle the Soviet Union and multi-ethnic states like Yugoslavia; and secessionist movements used it with varying degrees of success largely determined by their military strength and the power of their external sponsors.[148] The Indian delegate may have anticipated such an outcome back in 1955; dismissing as "exaggerated" concerns that the open-ended definition of self-determination would unleash dire consequences, he observed that "if an ethnic group which was claimed to be a minority was actually a people or a nation, it would succeed in achieving its independence whether or not the covenant contained an article on the right of self-determination."[149]

Self-determination has made only a limited appearance in the UN's human rights covenants. The treaty bodies monitoring compliance with the covenants have rarely addressed issues arising from Article 1 because state parties have largely ignored self-determination in their reporting. The Human Rights Committee further limited the relevance and use of Article 1 by deciding that only states have the right to complain about violations of the right to self-determination on behalf of a "people"; individuals cannot petition to bring self-determination claims under the Optional Protocol.[150]

With the benefit of hindsight, the charged and bitter arguments over the legal scope of self-determination look like much ado about nothing, although at the time they reflected the shifting fortunes of bloody wars fought for control of peoples, lands, and resources throughout the world. During one of the UN's heated human rights debate, the delegate from the Philippines reminded his colleagues of the relative unimportance of abstract legal interpretations in the broader sweep of history:

> History is full of examples of attempts to secede, some of which, like the secession of the American colonies from the British empire, succeeded and others, like that of southern states during the American Civil War, and more recently that of the Moslem Filipinos, did not. It might almost be said that self-determination is justified when it succeeds, and unjustified when it fails. The same idea is reflected in the use of the word "revolution" for a freedom movement that succeeds and the word "rebellion" for one that does not.[151]

Manipulations of Federal States

Another important front in the human rights debate concerned limitations on the scope and effect of the covenants. A number of states sought to constrain the potential impact of human rights through procedural means that either denied the applicability of the covenants in federal states and colonial territories or allowed states to place "reservations" on particular rights they did not wish to recognize, generally because they conflicted with domestic law and practice.[152] As might be expected, federal states supported limitations in the federal context and colonial empires supported them in the colonial context, while a number of states, led by the United States and Soviet Union, favored a broad right to make reservations.

All such efforts shared a common objective—to ensure that human rights did not infringe on national priorities and domestic legal orders in ways that might call into question a state's treatment of its citizens or people living under its control. In effect, these procedural limitations were another manifestation of the underlying paradox of announcing a new world order based on universal human rights without mechanisms to pierce the shield of state sovereignty. This could be justified in the first step of the human rights journey—the Universal Declaration of Human Rights established universal principles but lacked means to enforce them. The covenants, on the other hand, were meant to establish legal rights that were binding on all ratifying states for the purpose of encouraging, if not compelling, them to respect and incorporate the new legal standards.

It is commonplace nowadays to disparage the legal status of human rights because they lack the classical attributes of law—well-defined duties with predictable implementation and effective remedies—especially when viewed through the lens of the stark disparity between promotion and protection, between widely shared principles and realpolitik. But this was the outcome of a gradual series of diplomatic negotiations whose cumulative effect was the conceptual and bureaucratic fragmentation of human rights as institutionalized at the UN. During the early human rights debates, most states expected that human rights would be invested with some measure of legal force at the domestic and even international levels to deter abuses and improve people's lives. That this promise turned out to be largely illusory indicates the extent to which certain states, especially powerful states, understood human rights to threaten to their sovereign prerogatives and therefore acted to restrict their application and implementation.

In the second session of the CHR, the United States proposed a federal clause limiting the ability of federal states to bind their constituent states, provinces, or cantons.[153] The draft clause provided that a federal government could bring articles in the covenant that presumably fell within the local jurisdiction of constituent states to their attention with favorable recommendations, but the individual states would decide whether they would accept and implement them through legislative and other means. Since the prospects of a particular state incorporating an international human rights treaty into local law were slim, the clause would have enabled a federal state to ratify the covenant with no practical effect in vast areas of its domestic legal system.

It is interesting to note that one of the strongest opponents of the federal clause was America's closest ally on the CHR, the UK. This reflected the diametrically opposed views of the two Atlantic powers regarding the fundamental purpose of human rights. The UK favored a legal convention from the outset, modeled of course on English common law, and scorned the idea of a rhetorical proclamation of unachievable moral goals, preferring that a small number of states adhere to a binding treaty that would gain increasing support over time. The United States held an opposite view, seeking an ideological platform to spread its values worldwide and denounce its enemies without incurring any legal obligations that might enrage conservative domestic forces and invite international scrutiny of its practices at home. When James

Hendrick, one of Mrs. Roosevelt's key State Department advisors, informed Paul Gore-Booth, his British counterpart in the Foreign Office, that the U.S. government might not sign a convention absent a federal clause in late 1947, Gore-Booth reportedly responded that "opinion in the U.K. was frankly a little tired of Declarations which provided insincere Governments with an easy passport for virtue without the assumption of any of the obligations, and that we were not interested in a Declaration unless we could get a proper Convention to supplement it."[154] A historian of British human rights policy states that "the US proposal confirmed all the doubts of the UK delegation as to the sincerity of the State Department, which, British officials believed, wanted a text which committed nobody to anything."[155]

Most countries agreed with the British that allowing federal governments to limit the domestic applicability of human rights would undermine the basic purpose of the covenant and allow such states to ratify without meaning or effect. "It is unthinkable," declared the Czechoslovakian representative, "that sovereign States, under the pretext of showing their progressive and humanitarian spirit, should restrict themselves to assuming responsibility only for the acceptance of a covenant and evade responsibility for implementing it."[156] Malik also chastised his erstwhile friend and patron, Mrs. Roosevelt, advising that the United States "should adapt its federal system to the requirements of human progress and prevent its own internal conditions from impeding the ratification of a Convention on Human Rights."[157]

The United States nevertheless had strong support from other federal countries and succeeded in adding a draft article to the British convention that was being revised by the drafting committee of the working group.[158] Australia and Canada were particularly vocal in stating that the covenant could not be reconciled with their domestic legal arrangements without a federal clause even though, as was the case with the United States, most civil and political rights were already constitutionally binding throughout their territories. They argued that imposing the covenant on their constituent states "would be a breach of the whole spirit of federation" because certain issues covered by the covenant were subject to local rather than federal jurisdiction, particularly with respect to economic and social rights.[159] That the countries that insisted on a federal clause were also the countries that were most strongly opposed to including economic and social rights in the covenant was not deemed relevant; principled consistency was not a hallmark of UN debates on human rights.

The constitutional necessity for a federal clause was extremely dubious on legal grounds. Under the supremacy clause of the U.S. Constitution, when international treaties are ratified, they rank with the Constitution and federal statutes as the "supreme law of the land."[160] It is true that there is still a legal issue as to whether a treaty is self-executing, in which case it automatically becomes the law of the land upon ratification, or whether it is non-self-executing and requires implementing legislation to come into effect. But there was no legal justification for the position that the federal government lacked power to bind states to international law. The critical factor behind the federal clause was politics, not law.

The United States and its allies fought hard for the federal clause, while many states viewed it as a threat to the viability of the covenant. The Indian delegate sought to address the ostensible legal concerns of federal states through analysis of the U.S. Constitution. She observed:

> The United States of America should abandon all its fears. The Supreme Court of the United States has, in recent decisions, given so wide an interpretation to the term "privileges and immunities" . . . as to include a great variety of freedoms. The same liberal and progressive tendency is to be noted in recent decisions by the Oklahoma and California courts, one regarding the admission of Negroes to state colleges, the other invoking the Charter of the United Nations as superseding state legislation restricting fundamental human rights. Those decisions are encouraging signs for those who believe in the flexibility and adaptability of human institutions.[161]

Other states pointed out the double standard implicit in singling out human rights as the only area of international law where federal governments lost their representative authority. The Belgian representative noted that "it is equally possible, from the constitutional point of view, for the federal States which are members of the United Nations to bind their constituent states by a convention, such as the covenant on human rights, just as they have been able constitutionally to bind those states by the United Nations Charter. There is no doubt that the Charter is completely binding on both the federal States and each of their constituent states."[162]

The Pakistani delegate pointed to the disingenuous nature of the "more or less imaginary difficulties" created by certain member states that could not ratify a human rights covenant unless it contained a federal clause:

> Each member of the Committee represents a sovereign State able to assume international obligations, and not a federal or central government . . . but they change themselves into federal governments when it is a question of signing the covenant. . . . It would be unjust for some powerful States to hide behind the federal clause, thus depriving their signatures and even the covenant of any meaning. . . . Think of the unhappy moral consequences which the inclusion of that clause would have: it would encourage the adoption of the colonial clause which is even more open to criticism.[163]

Humphrey noted that a majority of states agreed with the Pakistani delegate's "brilliant" speech, creating "serious difficulties for countries like the U.S. and Canada."[164]

There was an important precedent in international law for a federal clause. In 1919, largely at the insistence of the United States, the International Labour Organization inserted a federal clause into its constitution: "It shall be at the discretion of the Government of such [federal] State to treat a draft convention . . . as a recommendation only."[165] The Australian delegate cited this example to critique the UN majority's uncompromising approach, and Mrs. Roosevelt suggested that federal states would be far more likely to ratify the covenant if it contained a similar clause.[166] The Polish representative questioned her assertion, observing that its presence had not encouraged the United States to ratify ILO treaties: "An ILO tabulation shows that out of a total 98 ILO conventions, only 6 have been ratified by the United States, in spite of the presence of a federal clause."[167]

The Soviet bloc used the opportunity to attack American human rights violations, arguing that the federal clause was just a cover to shield its policies of racial segregation and discrimination from international attention. The Polish delegate asked "what the consequences would be, if, for example, in the United States of America, such southern states as Georgia, Mississippi, and South Carolina known for their racial legislation and for their racial discrimination are not obliged to implement the draft covenant when it is of utmost important that those states in particular should be bound by that instrument."[168]

Faced with adamant opposition, the strongest weapon in the U.S. arsenal was the threat to withdraw support from the UN's human rights work. With the exception of the communist countries, most states viewed U.S. participation as central to the legitimacy and success of this endeavor. But the federal clause was too bitter a pill for them to swallow, although some did bend to the U.S. view. The Brazilian representative, for example, pointed out that "if a federal clause is omitted, the United Nations would be confronted with the paradoxical situation that precisely the countries which had proved to be the strongest defenders of human rights and individual freedom might be precluded from adhering to the very instrument setting forth those rights and freedoms."[169]

The paradox was not long in coming, but it was domestic factors that drove the United States to abandon its engagement with human rights at the UN. By 1953 American policy had become increasing hawkish and contemptuous of international cooperation under the influence of growing pressure from the reactionary right wing. McCarthy's anti-communist witch hunts had entered the halls of the UN. Dozens of employees with liberal leanings were purged; even Ralph Bunche, assistant secretary-general and Nobel Peace laureate, was dragged before Congress on false charges of communist affiliation.[170] Administration officials justified such actions by referring to "domestic political forces [that] aroused large-scale opposition to the conclusion of treaties in the field of human rights."[171] The opposition was led by the Committee on Peace and Law of the American Bar Association, which under the presidency of Frank Holman used every available legal and political forum to denounce human rights, especially economic and social rights, as communist-inspired and un-American, and which drafted the proposed constitutional amendment limiting U.S. treaty-making powers that was later popularized by Senator John Bricker.[172]

The State Department's growing intransigence was such that even P. C. Chang and Charles Malik, Mrs. Roosevelt's staunchest allies on the CHR, grew disillusioned with the inflexible and heavy-handed American approach to human rights. Things went from bad to worse when President Eisenhower replaced Mrs. Roosevelt with Mary Lord, who, according to René Cassin, at times acted with overt hostility to the human rights project.[173]

Public disclosure of the United State's withdrawal from human rights was made explicit in 1954, when the new secretary of state, John Foster Dulles, announced to Congress that the president was "committed to the exercise of the treaty-making power only within traditional limits" and had no intention of asking it to ratify a treaty on human rights.[174] Lord duly relayed this decision to the ninth session of the CHR: "The climate of world opinion does not yet seem favorable to the conclusion of the Covenants in the United Nations. The Covenants will not have the expected effectiveness in the field of human rights. For these reasons, my government has concluded that in the present stage of international relations it would not ratify the Covenants."[175] From this point forward, the relationship of the United States with the UN human rights project alternated between disengagement and obstruction.

This was the impetus for the United States to withdraw sponsorship of and abstain from voting on the federal clause. Humphrey reports that this abstention was interpreted throughout the UN as signaling a desire "to encourage the drafting of a Covenant so unacceptable to the U.S.A. that even a Democratic Senate would not ratify it."[176]

After more than a decade of negotiations, the federal clause was finally dropped.[177] The final text of the article in both covenants reads: "The provision of the Covenant shall extend to all parts of federal States without any limitations or exceptions."[178] Most federal states, including Australia and Canada, have nevertheless ratified both covenants. The United States has ratified only the Covenant on Civil and Political Rights.[179]

The Colonial Clause

The UK's "principled" opposition to the federal clause was called into question when it sponsored a similar provision, known as the territorial or colonial clause, for non-self-governing and trust territories.[180] The colonial clause would have permitted ratifying states to determine to what extent, if at all, the covenants should apply to their dependent territories.[181]

Even after the states of the South Asian subcontinent won independence in 1947, the British empire included thirty-seven territories worldwide with a combined population of more than 60 million people. The UK, however, stood alone in confronting a UN consensus that was hostile to the proposed clause; the number of European empires was diminishing, and the political power of the decolonization movement was growing. General Assembly resolution 422(V) of 1950 reflected this consensus in demanding that the provisions of the covenant be equally applicable to metropolitan states and territories, colonial, trust, and non-self-governing alike.[182] The firestorm of global protest against the colonial clause damaged the UK's standing as the only great power to support legally cognizable human rights. The issue exacerbated internal tensions between the UK's Foreign and Colonial Offices and caused the government to back down within a few years of introducing the measure.

It was the British understanding of the covenant as legally binding that prompted the Colonial Office, which had supported the Universal Declaration, to insist on a specific exemption to "exclude any provisions which Colonial Governments would not be able to implement. . . . It is clear that the acceptance of certain of these articles as they stand would involve the amendment of legislation in certain territories which has hitherto been considered essential."[183] Internal memoranda noted that such common practices as forced labor, restraints on free movement, and detention without trial were still lawful throughout the colonies.[184]

These concerns were heightened by the UK's experience with the UN Trusteeship Council, which had power to receive individual petitions from residents of trust territories that alleged abuse by colonial authorities. From 1947 to 1959 the council adopted an increasingly anticolonial position as it received and addressed over 16,000 such complaints.[185] The British Foreign Office recognized the danger that colonial policy would be criticized on human rights grounds but nevertheless favored the U.S. view that human rights served a more important geopolitical function of discrediting ideological enemies and maintaining the moral high ground. As a historian of British human rights policy has observed, "The real source of the disagreement was that the Foreign Office wanted an effective stick with which to beat the Soviets, whilst the Colonial Office feared the application of the same stick to its vulnerable posterior."[186]

As with the federal clause, the colonial clause provided ample opportunity for the Soviet bloc to ally with nonwestern states and score political points. The Polish representative remarked on the inconsistent arguments and hypocritical motivations behind the colonial clause: "Whenever a colonial Power has to transfer some of its power or grant certain rights, it claims that it does not have the consent of the population concerned; conversely, decisions binding those same people are taken without any attempt to secure their agreement." He went on to criticize the political basis of colonialism in terms that resonated with the newly empowered UN majority:

> History is repeating itself: the most ardent defenders of human rights are forgetting those rights when they affect the colonial question. They press for inclusion of the colonial clause because they wish to perpetuate a position of inferiority, oppression, and arbitrary exploitation in their colonies. It is a joke in bad taste to say that it is necessary to await the opinion of the peoples of the Non-Self Governing Territories as to whether or not they wish to be granted human rights.[187]

Lord MacDonald attempted to ignore the political context and focus on the technical legal difficulty of administering dependent territories. He argued that the UK was a driving force in support of the covenant but that allowance had to be made for the inherent complexities of extending human rights guarantees uniformly to vastly different territories.[188] He insisted that his government "is not seeking to provide itself with an excuse for not applying the provisions of the covenant in the territories which it administered. . . . The question before the Committee is not whether it is right or wrong that a colonial system should still exist in the twentieth century but merely whether, with such a system in existence, a colonial clause should be incorporated into the Covenant."[189]

For most other states, however, whether the colonial system should remain in existence was precisely the question. They viewed the UK's attempt to limit the universal provisions of the covenant on grounds of its legal and administrative burdens as paternalistic and unjustified. Chang pointed out that the responsibility of colonial administration "cannot be so very heavy, however, for all the nations concerned have been most anxious to assume it."[190] The Philippines condemned justifications for a colonial clause as "specious arguments."[191] The representative of Chile asserted that it was time that the West's "civilizing mission" come to an end.[192] Syria's delegate accused the colonial powers of crass self-interest: "Their only purpose, of course, is to prevent the application of the covenant on human rights to colonial territories."[193] States also attacked the British rationale that colonial territories needed to achieve a greater degree of development before they could enjoy the benefits of the covenant, arguing instead that applying the covenant was a fundamental prerequisite for their future development.

The overwhelming opposition to the colonial clause put the UK in an untenable position and forced its representatives to make increasingly insincere and unconvincing statements that supported the extension of human rights to the dependent territories.[194] Ultimately the Foreign Office won the internal policy battle and the Colonial Office conceded the point. Sir Thomas Lloyd, permanent undersecretary of the Colonial Office, recognized that continuing to push for the colonial clause would only further undermine the (threadbare) legitimacy of the empire: "The United Kingdom and the Colonial Empire as a whole would be exposed to most damaging criticism, on the score that it is our policy to deny fundamental human rights to colonial peoples."[195]

Reservations against Universality

The issue of reservations posed a greater challenge to the universal application of the covenants. Unlike the federal and colonial clauses, reservations were potentially available to all UN member states. Reservations allowed a state to adopt an international treaty while rejecting specific articles it deemed incompatible with its national laws through a formal process of written objection attached to its statement of ratification.[196] A major rationale for allowing reservations was to attract the maximum number of state ratifications by allowing objections to specific provisions rather than the entire treaty. But reservations damaged the universality of human rights principles. The Soviet Union's strong support for reservations, consistent with its demand for absolute sovereign authority over domestic affairs, tipped the balance of forces in this debate.[197] Facing an uphill battle against the united front of great powers, states opposed to reservations, primarily Third World countries with some European support, sought to uphold the central premise of the human rights regime—that all states were obligated to adhere to a codified set of fundamental legal principles applicable to all peoples. These states pointed out that inconsistent domestic laws were meant to be harmonized with, not shielded from, universal human rights.[198]

In 1947, Mrs. Roosevelt tried to preempt the need for reservations by requesting, on instructions from the State Department, that the working group insert a general limitation clause rather than "try to spell out every possible limitation in each article."[199] This would have given states room to interpret, and potentially negate, each article in light of domestic law. One version the United States proposed under the heading "Limitations on Exercise of Rights" provided that "in the exercise of his rights every one is limited by the rights of others and by the just requirements of the democratic state."[200] The entire U.S. delegation fought hard for this exception, pressuring the CHR and threatening the British representative "to have nothing to do with the covenant unless their ideas are accepted."[201]

This clause provoked widespread opposition. Malik argued that such a clause "might afford opportunities for abuse" by allowing states to limit rights in an arbitrary manner, pointing out that colonial powers might nullify the right to self-determination for non-self-governing territories.[202] The British Foreign Office again was staunchly opposed to U.S. efforts to undermine its cherished legal convention, calling the clause a "monstrosity" and writing that "we consider that nothing is more likely to bring the United Nations into discredit than the production of a Convention rendered innocuous by the general reservations [i.e., limitations] clause which would permit any signatory to continue all the abuses at present existing in its country."[203] In light of the broad consensus against a general limitations clause, the working group submitted the first draft of the covenant to ECOSOC with only the standard derogation clause limiting the exercise of rights in times of public emergency or war.[204]

The General Assembly turned to the issue of individual reservations in 1950 and 1951. Discussions focused on the controversy that resulted when four Soviet countries adopted the Convention on the Prevention and Punishment of Genocide with a series of reservations against specific language.[205] Based on this precedent, Bulgaria, Hungary, the Philippines, Poland, and Romania also ratified the treaty with reservations. A number of other countries objected, and the General Assembly referred the issue of reservations to the International Court of Justice for an advisory opinion and the International Law Commission for a study. The ICJ confirmed that a state could be a party to a treaty with reservations on condition that such reservations were compatible with the purpose of the treaty.[206]

With the ICJ precedent in mind, the General Assembly again debated the issue of reservations in 1952. States were split. The Soviet bloc insisted on the right to make reservations without any limitations. The Ecuadorian delegate concurred, remarking that "the principle of national sovereignty of States confers the right to formulate reservations to any international convention."[207] A larger group of countries took the opposite position and rejected reservations as inappropriate in the case of human rights treaties. Lebanon and Ethiopia, for example, took the view that the special universal character of the international bill of rights required states to accept all its articles.[208] The Iraqi representative argued that accepting reservations "would be tantamount to compromising the international conscience."[209] The Chilean representative expressed the concerns of most Latin American states that a reservations clause would drastically reduce the legally binding character of the covenants.[210] Another group of states supported allowing reservations but only in limited circumstances, in keeping with the ICJ precedent. Prominent legal authorities, including Hersch Lauterpacht, backed this approach.[211] A majority of states found reservations permissible with regard to economic and social rights but not with regard to civil and political rights. Expressing this view, the Syrian delegate commented that reservations "should apply only to articles on implementation," not substantive rights; were applicable only to economic, social, and cultural rights; and in "no way should refer to civil and political rights that are immediately justiciable."[212]

Unable to reach consensus, the General Assembly instructed the CHR to include "one or more clauses relating to the admissibility or non-admissibility of reservations" in the draft covenants without advising whether reservations should be allowed or prohibited.[213] In 1954, during its tenth session, the CHR held a series of heated debates on the issue of reservations.[214] Opponents of reservations held the view that the unity of universal human rights was nonnegotiable and that reservations would render the covenants meaningless. States would be at liberty to disengage themselves from any obligations that conflicted with their domestic policies and priorities, for whatever reason, just or unjust. They denounced the political machinations of the great powers in particular as contrary to the letter and spirit of the human rights idea, warning that their narrowly conceived self-interests would destroy the human rights project in which the peoples of the world placed such faith. The Secretary-General's report summarized this view: "It is unacceptable that the United Nations itself, after proclaiming that human rights are inherent in the human person and therefore inalienable, should at the same time admit that any rights can be legitimately disregarded by means of reservations."[215] Backed by a majority of states, Chile and Uruguay submitted a simple article stating that no state party could make reservations in respect to the covenants.[216]

Those in favor argued that failure to provide for the possibility of reservations would drastically reduce the number of ratifications and consign the covenants to political and legal oblivion. States who took this position felt it was more important that many states accept some provisions than that some states accept all. China, Egypt, Lebanon, and the Philippines proposed that any state could make a reservation compatible with the objective of the covenant and that any dispute that arose would be referred to the ICJ if it was not settled by the parties involved.[217] The United States and the UK agreed on the necessity for reservations in cases of conflict with domestic law but preferred to let the Soviet Union play the public role of heavy. The Soviets did not disappoint, declaring that "each State has the sovereign right to decide for itself whether or not it wishes to make reservations. . . . That is a matter for the domestic jurisdiction of each State concerned."[218] The representative of Czechoslovakia insisted that such fundamental state interests were not subject to a popular vote: "A purely fortuitous majority cannot be allowed to restrict the sovereign right of States to formulate such reservations."[219]

Over the next twelve years, the CHR debated the issue of reservations without reaching a decision, despite several additional instructions from the General Assembly. The battle lines were too sharply drawn: the great powers would not compromise in their demand for reservations, whereas the majority of states were not willing to endorse what they viewed as a fatal compromise of universality. The covenants therefore did not specifically address the permissibility of reservations, and the issue has been treated in accordance with the Vienna Convention on Multilateral Treaties, which provides that reservations are lawful so long as they do not conflict with the "object and purpose" of the covenants and are considered to be accepted by other states unless an objection is lodged within twelve months of their advertisement.[220]

Sixty-one of the 160 state parties to the International Covenant on Civil and Political Rights have made declarations of reservations, as have forty-four of the 155 state parties to the International Covenant on Economic, Social and Cultural Rights.[221] With one-third of states parties disavowing elements of the covenants to varying degrees, the claims of the international bill of rights of universality, even at the procedural level of ratification, stands on shaky ground.[222]

Enforcement's Hollow Core

Multiple disputes between states during the process of negotiating the international bill of rights resulted in a series of decisions that fragmented the initial vision of an integrated human rights corpus and imposed various limitations on the scope and applicability of specific rights. But all these debates paled in comparison to the fundamental question of how, if at all, human rights were to be made meaningful in people's lives. This was the core issue of the UN's human rights project. Legal experts and public opinion assumed that human rights required implementation to have a practical effect beyond words on paper. But for that to happen, states had abandon elements of national sovereignty enshrined in Article 2(7) and vest in external agencies the power to review their domestic laws and practices.

The vast majority of UN member states favored meaningful enforcement measures, even while disagreeing over which specific tools would best accomplish that purpose. In the opinion of most countries from Asia, Africa, and Latin America, the purpose of the human rights system was to protect individuals and groups against the abuse of state power, and protection required effective implementation. At its first meeting in 1947, the CHR working group on implementation considered a series of measures for achieving the realization of human rights. The working group was unanimous in the view that if human rights were to mean anything, the right of individuals and associations to petition the UN had to be provided for. The members reasoned that "the victims of the violations are individuals. It is therefore fitting to give them access to an international organ (to be determined) in order to enable them to obtain redress."[223] The working group proposed several other ideas, including an international court of human rights and a high commissioner. The United States and the Soviet Union rejected all of them.

Forceful speeches by delegates warning that failure to adopt enforcement measures would destroy the purpose and integrity of the human rights system are scattered throughout the summary records of the CHR and the Third Committee.[224] The General Assembly passed numerous resolutions urging the CHR to incorporate enforcement measures into the covenants. For example, resolution 421(V), passed in late 1950 after the United States and Soviet Union had blocked every proposal put forward by the working group on implementation, requested the CHR to consider specific mechanisms proposed by Chile, Ethiopia, France, Israel, and Uruguay and reaffirmed that it was "essential that the Covenant should include provisions rendering it obligatory for States to promote the implementation of the human rights and fundamental freedoms proclaimed in the Covenant and to take the necessary steps, including legislation, to guarantee to everyone the real opportunity of enjoying those rights and freedoms."[225]

The fundamental problem the UN majority faced was a lack of power to confront the three hegemonic states of the global system: the United States, the Soviet Union, and the United Kingdom. Despite disagreements on rationales and details, which often assumed the appearance of genuine conflict when framed in polarizing Cold War rhetoric, the great powers presented an immoveable, implacable, and ultimately united front against any advances toward the implementation and protection of human rights. They had won World War II at great cost and established a world organization in which international power was monopolized by a Security Council firmly under their control. They exercised effective authority and jurisdiction, in the geopolitical if not the legal sense, over large areas of the globe. They were not prepared to sacrifice national powers and interests on the altar of human rights.

The Soviet bloc countries stated their opposition to enforcement in the most forthright and unequivocal manner. Against any proposal put forward by the working group on implementation they raised the same shield of national sovereignty. A typical example was the caustic comment of Mr. Koretsky, the Soviet representative to the early sessions of the CHR, responding to a proposal to include a mechanism for reviewing individual petitions in the covenant: "The [Working] Group should bear in mind that there does not yet exist such a thing as world government. . . . The United Nations Charter does not allow interference in the domestic affairs of a State." He added that "this is not the way to deal with independent peoples. All disputes between peoples and their governments should be settled by their respective governments."[226] Expressing a frustration shared by most of his colleagues, the Panamanian delegate denounced Soviet-bloc countries for "the oft-repeated sophistry" of invoking domestic jurisdiction under Article 2(7) to justify not implementing human rights.[227]

Ironically, similar fears of world government lay behind the McCarthyite attacks on human rights in the 1950s.[228] However, it would be incorrect to assign blame for American rejection of human rights enforcement to the conservative right wing of the Republican Party; the track was laid down by President Roosevelt's State Department well before the San Francisco conference to establish the UN. Throughout her tenure at the CHR, Mrs. Roosevelt was consistently instructed to avoid any measures of implementation that might conflict with domestic law. Her State Department advisors warned her that human rights principles were a hard sell in an "office honeycombed with aged lawyers who have been there for years and . . . are very much opposed to the covenant" and that "the establishment of machinery for their international supervision and enforcement is not an immediate, practicable objective."[229]

Unlike the Soviet approach, the U.S. approach was nonconfrontational; instead, the United States used technical legal arguments and procedural delaying tactics. A State Department memo approved by both President Truman and Mrs. Roosevelt spelled out this method with respect to individual petitions (at a time when the NAACP petition alleging racial discrimination was making the rounds at the UN):

> With respect to complaints by individuals, the United States believes in taking things one by one, within the limits of foreseeable accomplishment. To provide forthwith for the right of petition would be a deception. We have not yet worked out the international machinery for the consideration of petitions, nor is it believed practicable or desirable in advance of the approval of the proposed Covenant by a substantial number of states to spell out such machinery.[230]

Of the superpowers, only the UK took implementation seriously. The government was pulled between the Foreign Office's view of human rights as a binding code of law that was helpful in establishing the superiority of British governance and the Colonial Office's fear of legal vulnerability. The latter complained that the Foreign Office was excessively attached to the legal status of the covenant and "very reluctant to accept any modification of it which . . . would weaken it as an international binding Covenant."[231]

The issue of petitions brought this internal conflict to a head. The Foreign Office was inclined to join the vast majority of states in supporting the right of petition for individuals and associations within ratifying states, arguing that "opposition would be harmful to the prestige of the United Kingdom . . . in influencing the deliberations on the United Nations on the whole principle of Human Rights."[232] Against this position, the Colonial Office stated that "the Slav States and the USA are reported to be opposed to the institution of any procedures for handling petitions. The Colonial Office fully shares their misgivings." In the event that the right of petition could not be eliminated, "our overriding object must be to remove so far as possible all teeth from the petition procedure and make it as innocuous as we can."[233] The issue was resolved when Foreign Secretary Ernest Bevin decided against the right of petition but adopted a compromise policy of "fence-sitting"—waiting to see whether joint U.S.-Soviet opposition was sufficient to remove the clause from the draft covenant without necessitating UK intervention. It did prove sufficient, thereby saving the British the embarrassment of having to undermine the legal status of their "binding" covenant.

The question of implementation continued to be discussed at the CHR and Third Committee throughout the 1950s. The United States and the Soviet bloc argued that alleged human rights violations should be settled by diplomatic negotiations between states and referred to an ad hoc fact-finding committee if negotiations failed. They were unwilling to consider the CHR's proposal to establish a permanent human rights committee with fact-finding and conciliation powers that could also review complaints from states, individuals, and civil associations.[234]

Having abandoned more ambitious ideas like a human rights court or a high commissioner, most states continued to push for some form of right to petition. This was widely seen as a bottom-line demand; without it there would be little prospect that domestic abuses would reach the attention of the UN human rights system. Responding to various arguments that had been raised against the right to petition, the Brazilian representative remarked:

> The eminent jurist [Lauterpacht] considers as unfounded the fear that the right of individual petition will release a flood of malicious or groundless complaints which will overwhelm the qualified international bodies and paralyse their action. The example of the Trusteeship Council is enough to prove that difficulty can be overcome. . . . For a bill of human rights which fails to recognize the right of individual petition will be an instrument devoid of any moral authority and will not live up to the expectations of the contemporary world.[235]

With the right to petition blocked, the CHR developed the idea of a human rights committee of independent experts to monitor state compliance with the covenants. The United States was amenable to this idea as long as the committee was stripped of any power to investigate in-country conditions and review complaints; its role was strictly limited to receiving periodic reports and working constructively with states to enhance compliance with the covenant.[236] Many states, however, did not believe that even a toothless monitoring committee was appropriate with respect to economic and social rights, given the difficulty of evaluating violations. The Dutch delegate proposed that the UN's existing humanitarian wing take on the job, pointing out that "the survey of the activities of the specialized agencies [i.e., the World Health Organization, UNICEF, the Food and Agriculture Organization] prepared by the Secretariat, reveals that they cover every field referred to in the articles concerning economic, social and cultural rights. It is therefore clear that machinery for the achievement of the aims of the draft Covenant already exists."[237] This proposal was abandoned when the specialized agencies themselves showed a distinct lack of interest in performing such roles.

Little progress was made on implementation until 1963, when the Third Committee revisited the issue in light of the embarrassing fact that both the European and Inter-American regional human rights systems had adopted petition mechanisms, whereas the UN had not even finalized the covenants. The United States softened its opposition to implementation provided that the means were ineffective. With a full-fledged right to petition still out of the question, the CHR turned to an optional protocol that would allow

state parties to choose whether their citizens would be eligible for this privilege—but only in the case of civil and political rights. Economic, social, and
cultural rights were deemed unsuited for even a quasi-judicial process.[238]
States also agreed to establish a Human Rights Committee that had weak
powers to oversee a system of periodic (and voluntary) state reporting under
the civil and political rights covenant.[239] The committee has since developed
an impressive body of jurisprudence by issuing decisions on petitions and
general comments clarifying broader points of law, but its overall impact
remains negligible and almost entirely dependent on the intervention of
powerful international NGOs such as Amnesty International and Human
Rights Watch to publicize instances of violations.[240]

Implementation under the Covenant on Economic, Social and Cultural
Rights was even more threadbare. State parties were requested only to send
periodic reports to an ad hoc committee of experts working with ECOSOC.
The system was a dismal failure. Most states did not bother to submit reports;
those that did rarely provided information that was relevant for evaluating
human rights.[241] Only in 1985 was an expert committee formed with similar
functions as the Human Rights Committee.[242] In view of its limited powers,
the Committee on Economic, Social and Cultural Rights has been extremely
effective in giving normative content to the rights and elevating them, conceptually and legally, to the same level as civil and political rights through
innovative use of general comments and concluding observations to state
reports.[243] The committee has even developed a jurisprudence of violations
by states that focuses on discrimination, retrogressive measures by the state,
and failure to meet the minimum core content of a right.[244]

While these human rights bodies have made important strides, they are
swimming against a strong tide. In effect, the human rights system was denied the most minimal tools of enforcement necessary to give legal status to
the rights set forth in the covenants. They have no power of investigation,
no capacity for independent monitoring, no judicial authority, no ability to
impose even symbolic penalties, no resources for research to verify state
reporting, and no authority to compel states to submit reports every five
years as required. What limited impact the committees have had is due to an
activist approach by a handful of its experts and a strategic partnership with
human rights groups capable of disseminating and publicizing their work.

The Legacy of Fragmentation

Thirty years passed between the adoption of the Universal Declaration
of Human Rights and the coming into force of two separate, unequal, and

relatively toothless human rights covenants that marked the completion of the international bill of rights, the foundation of the UN human rights regime. Widespread popular expectations in 1945 that the CHR would draft a single human rights bill, as specifically written into the UN Charter, proved to be a short-lived illusion. That it took so long for the CHR to accomplish its primary task indicates the difficulties in establishing an agreed code of binding universal principles in an international system of sovereign nation-states dominated by a handful of major powers. It also demonstrates the increasingly divided global context of the Cold War and the wars of decolonization in which these negotiations took place.

The fragmentation of the human rights system reflected the fragmentation of world politics or, more accurately, the reemergence of competing national interests after a brief period of comparative consensus following the military defeat of the Axis powers and their totalitarian ideologies. The rapid escalation of conflict between liberal and communist states during the 1950s, dominated by the threatening shadow of U.S.-Soviet nuclear confrontation, created an environment of intense ideological polarization that colored every aspect of international affairs. The incorporation of Eastern European states into the Soviet Union, the establishment of the North Atlantic Treaty Organization, the communist revolution in China, the Korean and Vietnam wars, and the rise of Third World nationalism all combined to produce an antagonistic context for diplomatic discussions aimed at reaching agreement on fundamental human rights. Rather than serving as a platform to address and overcome ideological and legal differences, as seemed possible after World War II, human rights became a form of bare-knuckled politics by other means, a propaganda contest in which dogmatic oppositions were only sharpened.

Given these various divisions, perhaps the most surprising aspect of this history is the extent to which most UN members developed genuine consensus positions on human rights principles and enforcement. The covenant was split only after a protracted struggle in which western states under Anglo-American leadership managed to overcome the majority view through broken promises that the two sets of rights would be given equal treatment. Had the debate occurred after the wave of decolonization several years later, the result would certainly have been different. The consensus in favor of implementation was even stronger; it took adamant unified opposition by the otherwise rival superpowers to degrade human rights of all meaningful enforcement measures. Had the global civil society movements which developed in the 1970s and influenced human rights treaties on such issues as women's rights and child rights been around to participate in the earlier UN debates, it is likely that the human rights covenants would have taken a different shape. But as it happened, the fragmentation and weakening of the international bill of rights took place in spite of strong state and public support for a more integrated approach. This had dire consequences for human beings seeking international protection for violations of their rights and dignity.

It is generally not considered useful in historical analysis to speculate about what might have been under various hypothetical scenarios. The point to bear in mind, however, is that the modern human right system was shaped far less by philosophical or legal theories than by the contingencies and expediencies of historical, political, and ideological circumstance. Human rights were contested terrain; outcomes which appear inevitable from today's perspective were often in doubt during the bitter debates of earlier times. The implications of this view are important for understanding the possibilities of the future.

Part 3. The Impact of Civil Society and Decolonization

This section focuses on the changing dynamics at the UN in the 1960s and 1970s, which gave rise to efforts by groups excluded from the original human rights project to air their grievances and fight for their rights. The explosive growth in UN membership from newly independent states in Africa and Asia highlighted a new set of issues focused on colonialism's legacy of poverty and inequality, which afflicted the majority of the world population. Demands for racial equality were framed as human rights challenges to the exclusive focus on individual rights that characterized the UN system. The success of decolonization also gave rise to the self-determination claims of minorities and indigenous peoples. However, their demands faced an uphill struggle at the UN, as they were viewed skeptically by almost all states, including developing countries that feared that secessionist movements could destroy their fragile borders. The women's movement had greater success in framing women's issues as human rights deserving of recognition and protection at the international level. The ratification of the Convention on the Rights of the Child by every state except the United States and Somalia marked a high-water mark for universal recognition of human rights, although many states adopted limiting reservations. In addition to group rights, this section describes the journey of the right to development from a radical demand for economic justice and redistribution following decolonization to a more limited human right to procedural recognition of the centrality of rights in the development process.

Chapter 8 describes the enormous challenges these groups faced in bringing their issues before the UN. Few member states were sympathetic to group rights for fear that recognition would open the door to self-determination of national groups within state borders. Moreover, the liberal ideology of the human rights paradigm was itself hostile to extending rights from individuals to groups; many meetings were occupied with theoretical debates about whether group members held rights as individuals or through their membership in a collectivity. In general, states sought to frame group issues in terms of discrimination rather than equality. To the extent equality was discussed, the focus was limited to formal equality before the law rather than substantive equality of outcome. States also preferred a policy of assimilation to one recognizing cultural diversity. This led them to deny legal protections for minorities; UN activities were restricted to reports by experts and rapporteurs and vague resolutions by the General Assembly. Fear of self-determination was so great that the only recognition of minority rights in treaty law was a single mention in Article 27 of the Covenant on Civil and Political Rights that minorities "not be denied" their culture, religion, and language. The failure to address the rights of minorities living in majority states is a factor in the persistence of violence against minorities, which in its worst manifestations can erupt into genocide, as in Rwanda.

Groups advocating for racial equality fared better, as the issue of race was more amenable to treatment through nondiscrimination. Especially after concerns about rising fascism and anti-Semitism in the 1960s, advocates were able to make rapid progress drafting the International Convention on the Elimination of All Forms of Racial Discrimination, which came into force in 1969, before even the two international covenants. African and Asian states were strong supporters, although the provisions did not address the issue of substantive equality beyond an allowance for affirmative action measures. Moreover, the implementation committee was designed with minimal powers of enforcement limited to receiving and responding to voluntary state reports through a process of constructive dialogue. It is thus subject to question how much impact the Committee on the Elimination of Racial Discrimination has had in the practical arena of eliminating racial discrimination.

Indigenous peoples faced the same dilemma as minorities—how to advance their cause in a state-based system that feared secessionist movements above all. Their cause was particularly urgent, as many indigenous groups in the latter half of the twentieth century faced threats to their continued physical existence and cultural survival. Given the opposition of most states, it was considered a triumph simply to place the issue on the UN agenda through the establishment of a working group and the negotiation, through the CHR, of a draft Declaration on the Rights of Indigenous Peoples. However, widespread state resistance has ensured that the declaration remains a draft and that recommendations by the working group and special rapporteur remain unimplemented. Denial of indigenous rights is so entrenched that states at the Vienna 1993 World Conference on Human Rights by consensus refused to acknowledge that indigenous peoples in different parts of the world with different histories, cultures, and languages constitute separate nations rather than a monolithic whole. Thus they were called indigenous "people" rather than "peoples" in all relevant UN documents.

Advocates of women's rights were more successful pushing their cause at the world body. The presence of a well-organized global movement and the strong support of the Commission on the Status of Women eventually culminated in the adoption of the Convention on the Elimination of All Forms of Discrimination against Women (CEDAW) in 1979. CEDAW is lauded as the first treaty to break down the artificial distinction between civil and political rights and economic, social, and cultural rights, although the latter receive comparatively little attention despite the disproportionate impact of poverty and economic inequality women face worldwide. Furthermore, CEDAW started a process of questioning the distinction between public and private spheres in terms of rights abuses, eventually leading to a UN focus on domestic as well as state violence against women. While CEDAW has been criticized as putting women's rights in a ghetto rather than mainstreaming them in all human rights treaties, the fact is that women's rights received very little attention in the Universal Declaration. At the same time, CEDAW suffers the same flaw of all human rights treaties—inadequate enforcement measures. This weakness channels its impact toward moral slogans rather than legal measures to protect women's rights.

The Convention on the Rights of the Child (CRC), which has been ratified by 192 countries, appears to be the least controversial treaty in the human rights repertoire. Unfortunately, this impressive support is mitigated by reservations by one-third of the signatory states, which have limited the scope of their obligations. A large number of reservations have to do with cultural and religious values. Only two UN member states, the United States and Somalia, have failed to ratify the treaty. The United States is opposed to the CRC's prohibition on the execution of juveniles, among other provisions deemed inconsistent with domestic law and practice. Somalia lacks a functional government that could consider ratification. Detractors of the treaty identify two other troubling aspects. First, the CRC merely duplicates the language of preexisting instruments in many provisions, and second, certain articles fall short of preexisting standards due to compromises necessary to reach a consensus between states with diverse views. Nonetheless, the involvement of nongovernmental agencies in its drafting and adoption and the UN Children Fund's application of the CRC can be described as a highly promising exercise.

In Chapter 9, we discuss how the right to development arose out of the economic challenge developing countries posed to their former colonial masters. The right to development is an outgrowth of the decolonization process, which shifted the center of gravity at the UN from an exclusive focus on civil and political rights to an increased concern with economic, social, and cultural rights and eventually to recognition of a third generation of solidarity rights to development, peace, and a sustainable environment (albeit with even less enforcement potential than previous toothless human rights instruments).

The devastating legacy of colonialism prompted the new states of Africa and Asia to join together in a Third World movement demanding reparation, transfer of wealth and technology, and other forms of redistributive justice under the rubric of the New International Economic Order. The NIEO championed new theories of development that linked poverty to economic policies carried out in the developed North. However, when the rich countries refused to consider economic redistribution, the UN's focus shifted to efforts to close the development gap through a mix of aid, trade, enormous loans, and the rhetorical promotion of development "decades." When these efforts also failed, eventually culminating in the Third World debt crisis, states and international jurists turned to the right to development.

First coined by an African jurist, the right to development was said to derive from the integral link between rights and development that had been frequently proclaimed in various UN instruments but never acted upon. The North suspected that it was simply an attempt to resurrect the failed NIEO in the guise of human rights and therefore was initially strongly opposed to the right to development. Developing countries tended to perceive the right to development as requiring the channeling of aid and resources from North to South, although the language used stressed cooperation. Many of the familiar human rights debates were played out in the right to development. Was it an individual or collective right? For people or states? A new right or simply a restatement of human rights as applied to the development process? Did it imply concrete obligations on the part of the international community?

These controversies slowed progress in defining the right; indeed, it took a working group ten years of laborious interstate negotiation before it could present the Declaration on the Right to Development to the General Assembly for approval in 1986. During these negotiations, the right was watered down and western opposition softened once it became clear that there would be no legal obligation to transfer a single dollar. The declaration is a confusing document, but it does not seem to impose any duty beyond that of respecting people's human rights in all aspects of development. The declaration has encouraged the mainstreaming of rights in development at the UN, and at the practical level it gave impetus to activists seeking to hold nonstate actors accountable for their policies. But it remains a far cry from the original Third World demand for economic justice that gave rise to the NIEO.

8

The Human Rights of Special Groups

- Rights of Minorities
- Race and Nondiscrimination
- The Quest of Indigenous Peoples
- The Commission on the Status of Women and Women's Equality
- The Rights of the Child

In San Francisco, the great powers had dismissed the problems associated with the protection of special groups, particularly minorities, on the pretext that if human rights of the individual were protected, then nothing else needed to be done. The UN therefore avoided conferring special rights and protections to members of a particular group, regardless of whether its members faced oppression or disadvantages by virtue of such membership. In drafting the Universal Declaration of Human Rights, the Human Rights Commission also circumvented the issues, recognizing the rights of individuals belonging to a particular group only through nondiscrimination clauses rather than by recognition of the group itself.[1] In explaining Yugoslavia's abstention to the UDHR, Vladislav Ribnikar decried this exclusive focus on the rights of isolated individuals:

> The strictly individualistic attitude of the majority of the Third Committee—which is also the fundamental characteristic of the declaration—has led to another important shortcoming, namely, the absence of provision to protect different communities, such as national minorities. . . . The well-being of man depends in a very great measure on the conditions existing in the community to which he belongs, and therefore, the protection of that community, whether social, religious or any other character, ought to have been included among human rights.[2]

This framework did not grant the rights of collectivities whose members were linked by cultural, physical, social, racial, religious, or other characteristics.[3] Member states perceived that granting rights to groups would highlight the social and economic inequities that existed between national communities, particularly between blacks and whites in the United States. Later, states that were engaged in throwing off the yoke of colonialism felt that granting group rights would undermine national self-determination and permit internal secession on the basis of ethnic, linguistic, or other cultural differences within state borders. Even more troubling was the demand for special privileges by minorities when national leaders wanted such groups to submerge differences within the national identity. Collective or group rights was a Pandora's box that few states wanted to open, as it implied broadening the definition of self-determination beyond the terms established by the UN.[4] Internal secession of groups seemed to be a vexing problem for states, as it raised the question of "where to draw the line between the sovereign rights of the Government of a multiracial State and the right of self-determination of its component ethnic groups." The right of secession was one part of the very important question of minorities. If the right of self-determination was to be exercised without the right of seccession, it was difficult to see where to draw the line between a policy of national integration through the inculcation of a common language or the imposition of a centralized political and economic system, and a policy of respecting and preserving the language, culture, and way of life of minority groups.[5]

The popular state paradigm at the time favored assimilation: minorities would eventually become more like the majority, women would gain equality with men, and peoples of color would achieve parity with whites. The fact that these groups might require protection or want to maintain their distinctiveness was not a pressing concern, especially for states engaged in the fight for self-determination against colonial occupiers, as each person was first a citizen of the state and then viewed as belonging to a distinct national community.[6] Self-determination for these groups remained off the UN agenda, and self-determination became one of the most politically loaded terms, stripped of the principle of equality before the law.[7] The politicization was about agreement over legal definitions of human rights, individual autonomy, and discrimination against certain groups or collectives such as children, women, refugees, migrant workers, indigenous peoples, and members of racial, ethnic, and religious minorities.[8]

The issues of the rights of minorities, races, indigenous peoples, and women were present at the UN from the beginning and raise some of the most difficult questions for its members regarding the self-determination, equality, nondiscrimination, and justiciability of group rights.[9] As each topic cannot be fully explored in the space of a chapter, we examine the basic developments and parameters of efforts to achieve the recognition of and protection for the rights of these four groups.

Rights of Minorities

After World War II, evidence regarding the repression of groups pointed to the need to create special protective measures for minorities not only in Europe but worldwide, especially in the Arab world, South Asia, and Southern Africa.[10] Although no article on the protection of minorities was included in the UN Charter or the Universal Declaration of Human Rights, the UN recognized that the problems of minorities had to be addressed. Therefore, as part of its mandate, the CHR was empowered to make recommendations on the topic of special protections for minorities and, if necessary, set up subcommissions for that purpose.[11] The Soviet Union argued that two separate subcommissions should be set up: one on minorities and the other on nondiscrimination. It noted that the protection of minorities was distinct from prevention of discrimination against individuals as part of a group. The discussions about whether two separate bodies on minority protections and nondiscrimination should be created or whether both issues should be assigned to a single institution were heated, with the United States and the United Kingdom arguing for one body and the Soviet Union and India arguing for two separate subcommissions.[12] ECOSOC authorized the establishment of three separate subcommissions—one on the freedom of information and the press, one on protection of minorities, and one on the prevention of discrimination.[13] But in the CHR, the United States and United Kingdom continued to push for a single subcommission on the protection of minorities and the prevention of discrimination, and this effort eventually succeeded.

Humphrey observed that the decision to collapse these two disparate topics was unfortunate and provided for a slow start "on what was to become its most important contribution, the prevention of discrimination; and it also made it easier for the United Nations to dodge responsibility for the protection of minorities."[14] Humphrey also noted that apart from the formal decision to create a body that has the protection of minorities in its mandate, the UN showed limited interest in the workings of the subcommission. However, the Sub-Commission on Prevention of Discrimination and Protection of Minorities was a unique organ within the UN, as it consisted of an independent body of twelve experts who were not appointed as spokespersons for their governments even though often they acted as such.[15] Over the years, the subcommission has done excellent work on the issue of discrimination, but, because of larger political constraints, has made little contribution in the area of protection of minorities.

Setback in 1948

The greatest setback for protection of the rights of minorities took place in 1948. The Convention on the Prevention and Punishment of the Crime of Genocide was adopted by the General Assembly on 9 December 1948, the day before the Universal Declaration was adopted.[16] Both documents fail to contain any provisions, even in principle, for the protection of the rights of minorities. Although the genocide convention was a step forward in criminalizing the systemic killings of peoples, it omitted the prevention of the physical and cultural destruction of groups as an important concept in the protection of minorities.[17] The UDHR also does not contain any text on protection of minority rights.[18] How this failure to include rights of minorities in two seminal documents that laid the foundation for human rights ideas came about is an insightful story about power politics and the fear of western states about developing a meaningful mechanism for the protection of minority rights.

The term "genocide"—from the Greek *genos* meaning race, nation, or tribe and Latin *cide* meaning killing—was coined by Raphael Lemkin, a Jewish lawyer who fled Poland for Sweden in 1939 and came to the United States, teaching at Duke University and at Yale. In 1933, Lemkin envisioned the creation of two new international crimes: the crime of barbarity, consisting of extermination of racial, religious, or social collectivities; and the crime of vandalism, consisting of destruction of cultural and artistic works of these groups.[19] He argued that genocide during World War II was a direct result of the failure to punish states for gross human rights violations under the system of Minorities Treaties of the League of Nations, creating a sense of impunity that empowered states to engage in planned annihilation of a national group.[20]

In Lemkin's definition, genocide was a coordinated plan aimed at destroying "the essential foundations of the life of national groups. . . . The objective of such a plan would be disintegration of the political and social institutions of culture, language, national feelings, religion, and the[ir] economic existence."[21] He defined two phases: the obliteration of the national pattern of the oppressed group and the imposition of the national pattern of the oppressor group. His analogy was based on Nazi Germany and Hitler's plans to "Germanize" some groups and exterminate others. Lemkin's definition also included state culpability in carrying out the crime of genocide. He intended to declare both crimes punishable regardless of where the culprit might be caught and where the crime was committed.[22]

Ernesto Dihigo of Cuba, joined by delegates of India and Panama, requested that genocide be put on the agenda of the General Assembly and later submitted a draft resolution to that effect.[23] The United Kingdom had proposed that the resolution include the criminal responsibility of states along with that of individuals, but it joined France and the United States in opposed the drafting of a convention. However, in the course of the debate on the resolution, the idea to develop a full-blown convention began to circulate and gain support.[24]

The Secretariat, or more precisely the director of the Human Rights Division, John Humphrey, prepared the initial draft. He took an approach similar to the approach he used in the formation of the UDHR by including as many ideas as possible and then allowing the competent body at the UN, in this case the Sixth Committee (Legal), to eliminate the articles it did not want to include.[25] A team of outside experts, including Lemkin; Vespasian V. Pella, a Romanian law professor; and Henri Donnedieu de Vabres,[26] a former judge of the Nuremberg Tribunal, reviewed the draft. In May 1948, the General Assembly discussed the draft text of the genocide convention, which included prohibition of cultural, physical, and biological genocide, based on Lemkin's definition of genocide as:

> a co-coordinated plan of different actions aiming at the destruction of essential foundations of the life of national groups, with the aim of annihilating the groups themselves. The objective of such a plan would be disintegration of the political and social institutions of culture, language, national feelings, religion, and the economic existence of national groups and the destruction of the personal security, liberty, health, dignity and even the lives of the individuals belonging to such groups. Genocide is directed against the national group as an entity, and the actions involved are directed against the individuals, not in their individual capacity, but as members of the national group.[27]

For Lemkin, safeguarding against the destruction of art and culture was especially important, as these objects belonged to the whole of humanity and thus the international community as a whole should have an interest in protecting them.[28]

ECOSOC created an ad hoc drafting committee for the genocide convention that met twenty-eight times in April and May 1948.[29] Several issues remained sore points with governments. The first was the reference to cultural genocide; second, the issue of state responsibility; and third, the creation of an international criminal court,[30] which many felt ran counter to the principle of protection of domestic jurisdiction in Article 2(7) of the UN Charter. Although the United States opposed the idea of cultural genocide, it supported the focus on state involvement, "as genocide could not be an international crime unless a government participated in its perpetration, either by act or by omission."[31] All along, the U.S. government was enthusiastic about the convention but the American Bar Association saw in the text serious constitutional and legal problems. However, the U.S. delegate noted that the problem of cultural genocide was linked with that of protection of minorities and would be more appropriately dealt within the Commission on Human Rights. Both of the other experts, de Vabres and Pella, were also of the opinion that implementing agreements to prevent cultural genocide—the destruction of specific characteristics of groups—amounted to reconstituting the former protection of minorities and overextending the concept of criminalization of genocide.[32] The UK delegate commented that the Allies had rejected Lemkin's definition and instead adopted the definition as defined in the term "crimes against humanity" in the Charter of the International Military Tribunal for the Nuremberg trials.[33] In this definition, genocide encompassed persecution and extermination on political, racial, or religious grounds but not with respect to culture and minorities.[34] Similar debates on definitions surrounded the issue of protection of political groups, a concept which also did not make it into the convention.

States that supported the idea of including cultural genocide in the convention argued that destroying a group's culture, in particular the culture of a minority group, was a preparatory step toward physical genocide. Sixteen countries, primarily communist and Arab states, and Ecuador, Mexico, Pakistan, and the Philippines were strongly committed to including minority rights in the convention.[35] While the idea survived in the drafting committee, it was defeated in the General Assembly's Sixth Committee. In the Sixth Committee (Legal Committee), which was responsible for the final text of the Genocide Convention, the majority bloc of states of the Americas and Europe denied any kind of minority problem within their borders as they supported a national policy of assimilation.[36]

The United States argued that only acts directed toward physical destruction of the designated group should be included and moved to eliminate any reference to the destruction of cultural and educational institutions from the text.[37] This omission was conceptually and politically very important because the genocide convention differed from declarations (considered at the time to be international hortatory documents of moral principles) in its criminalization of the mass-scale destruction of groups and their institutions. By focusing only on physical aspects, the actual destruction of the group instead of their institutions or way of life, the genocide convention set back the framework of protection of group rights of minorities.[38]

The Indian delegate, representing a multicultural state which had recently become independent and was striving to build a national Indian identity, commented: "The protection of cultural rights of a group should be guaranteed not by the convention on genocide, but by the declaration on human rights."[39] The European states held the pivotal votes. Even though they had experienced acts of ethnic cleansing at first hand and understood the arguments of communist and Arab states about the connection between means and ends with regard to cultural and physical genocide, they noted that full protection for minorities would be considered under the international bill of rights being prepared by the CHR.[40] Yet they failed to deliver on their promise in the Third Committee discussions on the Universal Declaration of Human Rights, which also excluded minority rights.

In the original Secretariat draft of the UDHR, Humphrey had included the rights of minorities.[41] Article 46 discussed positive actions to protect minorities as distinct from the negative action of nondiscrimination, which was dealt with in Article 45.[42] Humphrey had proposed that a certain amount of public funds be used to create and maintain cultural and religious institutions and schools for minorities. Cassin, working from the Secretariat draft, removed the idea of equitable allocation of funding for minority institutions as an unnecessary specificity. Humphrey viewed this deletion as further proof of bias in the United Nations against any scheme to protect minorities.[43] The text was then referred to the Sub-Commission on Prevention of Discrimination and Protection of Minorities, which was also meeting in December 1947. The subcommission came up with a rather complete definition with respect to minorities:

> Protection of minorities is the protection of non-dominant groups which, while wishing in general for equality of treatment with the majority, wish for a measure of differential treatment in order to preserve basic characteristics which they possess and which distinguish them from the majority of the population. The protection applies equally to individuals belonging to such groups and wishing the same protection. It follows that differential treatment of such groups or of individuals belonging to such groups is justified when it is exercised in the interest of their contentment and the welfare of the community as a whole. The characteristics meriting such protection are race, religion and language. In order to qualify for protection a minority must owe undivided allegiance to the Government of the State in which it lives. . . . If a minority wishes for assimilation and is debarred, the question is one of discrimination and should be treated as such.[44]

Despite this clarity in understanding and definitions with respect to minorities, CHR delegates continued to stress their preference for assimilation: "The persistence of a minority represents a transitional and rather anomalous status, and every effort should be made to accelerate their natural trend for assimilation."[45] The Ecuadorian delegate commented: "The various cultures within a Nation must be given every opportunity to develop and expand, reveal their innate qualities and contribute to the larger group in order to promote the creation of such conditions as will permit their fusion into a single common culture under the individual sign of a single national ideal."[46] The delegates from the United States and Latin America denied the cultural identities of their indigenous populations and focused on assimilating them and immigrants from other countries.[47]

Cassin's article on minorities was the basis of discussion in the CHR's working group on the declaration in December 1947.[48] Rights of minorities were acceptable as long as protecting them did not conflict with the territorial integrity of the state. Minority groups owed individual allegiance to the government of the state in which they resided, and in the event they desired to become assimilated with the majority and were prevented from doing so, this would constitute discrimination. Humphrey felt that the subcommission had refined the concept by introducing the idea that "minorities, to be protected, must *want* differential treatment."[49] This insertion was made to allay the fears of certain minorities, in particular blacks in the United States, who reject the idea of differential treatment.[50] In the working group, the two communist members (the representatives of Byelorussian Soviet Socialist Republic and the Soviet Union), Rómulo of the Philippines, and Cassin were strong supporters of the article on minority rights; the only Latin American voice in the group, Panama, was muted, and the sole opposing voice was that of Mrs. Roosevelt of the U.S. delegation. In the very first meeting of the CHR, Mrs. Roosevelt had declared that despite the different ethnic and linguistic groups in the United States, "there was no minority problem."[51]

The issue of nonresident aliens and their rights also stemmed from discussions on the rights of minorities. Mehta, in referring to Indians residing in South Africa, commented that efforts must be made to define in precise, legal, and practical terms what a minority is and what discrimination is. She felt that a definition needed to be made immediately available regarding what specific safeguards had to be incorporated in the proposed bill of human rights to prevent the assimilation of minorities where they existed.[52] The Belgian representative felt that any rights accorded to a minority group should not be extended to apply to aliens, especially if those individuals had moved voluntarily.[53] Cassin, sensing the differences between delegates, felt that the article had not been finalized and should be held over. The decision was taken to send the amended article to ECOSOC with a note about the lack of agreement in the CHR and request further study.[54] The article was placed in limbo, and at the CHR third session in May 1948, members, who were mostly from the Americas and Europe, voted not to include an article on minority rights.[55] Both the Soviet Union and Yugoslavia attempted to include a minority rights article in the Third Committee meetings on the Universal Declaration.[56] The Yugoslav article stated:

> the problem of national minorities is one of protecting small national groups which are scattered like islets in the midst of the territory of a nation.... In order to ensure the protection of the individuals who form a community, that community must first of all be recognized and protected. Thus the principle of the recognition and protection of national minorities as communities must appear in the Declaration of Human Rights.[57]

They were joined by a proposal from the delegate from Denmark, "All persons belonging to a racial, national, religious or linguist minority have the right to establish their own schools and receive training in the language of their choice."[58] This was the only attempt to redeem the promissory note on the exclusion of minorities from the genocide convention. However, these efforts were not well coordinated and the three delegates made no attempts to lobby other nations.[59]

The United States again opposed this article, noting that minorities, particularly immigrants, who wanted to avail themselves of the right to separate schools, might threaten the unity of their country.[60] Latin American states supported the U.S. view. Belgium representative Dehousse, challenging the fallacious reasoning, observed that the issues related to immigrants and immigration were not the same as the rights of minorities. But the international momentum at the time was driven by the United States and immigrant-receiving countries in Latin America, which favored replacing "protection of minorities" with "prevention of discrimination."[61]

The Third Committee could not agree about including any article on minorities in the Universal Declaration and eventually dropped the amendments to include such text without a vote. The communist countries, along with China, Haiti, and the Philippines, therefore turned to the genocide convention to make a case for reinstating the idea of cultural genocide. But given that the right was blocked in a mere declaration, it had little chance of being included in a legally binding covenant. The protection of minorities and their cultures failed to materialize in either document. Thus it was no great surprise that after a short and somewhat unsuccessful interlude with the issue of protection of minorities, the subcommission maintained its distance from the topic.[62]

Rights of Minorities in the Civil and Political Covenant

For the next few years, the subcommission engaged in discussions on the question of minorities. James Green, member of the U.S. delegation to the CHR, commented that "by the summer of 1950, when the Economic and Social Council held its eleventh session, considerable dissatisfaction had developed over the work of the Sub-commission," and although a meeting was held in October 1951, ECOSOC discussed liquidating the body altogether.[63] Humphrey felt that it was because the subcommission had taken seriously the issue of rights of minorities, which key UN members meant to bury. He observed, "1951 had indeed been a critical year in its history. One might even say that its [the subcommission's] effective history began as of then."[64] The subcommission endorsed the Secretariat memorandum, which concluded that protection of minorities required positive action consisting of enforced distinctions voluntarily maintained by the group.[65]

Once the decision was made to draft two covenants, the subcommission submitted a substantially weaker article, Article 27, for the Covenant on Civil and Political Rights than the one it had proposed for the UDHR on the protection of minorities.[66] The discussion about this article focused on what constituted a minority and the issue of differential treatment (even though it had been defined earlier by the subcommission). CHR members agreed that minorities covered separate and distinct groups that had been long established in the territory of a state. Initially, this meant ethnic, religious, linguistic, and national (in the sense of an origin linked closely with race) minorities, but later "national" minorities were excluded, as they did not constitute a distinct group. With the exception of communist states, almost all countries rejected a proposal for minorities to build and manage their national schools, libraries, museums, and other institutions.[67] Most states held that the rights of minorities should not obstruct the process of assimilation or impair national unity or security (an emerging area of concern for recently decolonized countries).

With respect to the civil and political rights covenant, communist states again argued that differential treatment should be granted to minorities in order to ensure them real equality of status with others in the population. The covenant's general article on discrimination, Article 2(1), was deemed insufficient.[68] Therefore, Article 27 phrased the protection of minorities at the individual level and not as a group right:

> In those States in which ethnic, religious or linguistic minorities exist, persons belonging to such minorities shall not be denied the right, in community with the

other members of their group, to enjoy their own culture, to profess and practice their own religion, or to use their own language.[69]

The negative phrase "shall not be denied" was different from other positively worded articles in the covenant. Once the article was drafted, not many changes were made to the text. To date, it is the only whole and general statement of the treaty rights of minorities in modern international law.[70]

In January 1954, the subcommission made one last effort to initiate a study of the position of minorities in the world and requested that the CHR appoint an expert, but this proposal was not approved.[71] For the individually oriented western states, collective rights were vague and Marxist-inspired and could undermine individual freedom. The western position coincided with the political interests of African and Asian states undergoing the process of decolonization. The few newly independent states preferred to focus on the national identity of their citizens rather than address the ethnic, linguistic, religious, and racial diversity of groups within their borders. For them, territorial integrity was all important; minority characteristics would gradually disappear as the citizen's national identity emerged.

For the next seventeen years, the CHR and its subordinate body remained silent on the rights of minorities. In 1971, Francesco Capotorti[72] was appointed as the special rapporteur on discrimination against minorities and asked to study the implications of Article 27 of the Covenant on Civil and Political Rights.[73] He proposed a definition of a minority as "a group numerically inferior to the rest of the population of a State whose members—being nationals of the State—possess ethnic, religious or linguistic characteristics differing from the rest of the population and who, if only implicitly, maintain a sense of solidarity, directed towards preserving their culture, traditions, religion or language." The Capotorti study is still one of the most thorough UN reports on the subject of minorities.

Asbjørn Eide, legal advocate and member of the subcommission, summarized Capotorti's results regarding special protection of minorities:

1. Any international system may be viewed as a pretext for interferences in States' internal affairs;
2. The usefulness of a uniform approach in such profoundly different situations is questionable;
3. Preservation of the identity of minorities is seen as a threat to State unity and stability; and
4. The need for special protection could be used to justify reverse discrimination.[74]

Capotorti concluded that governments would prefer to have a free hand in the treatment of minorities. Comparing Article 27 to Articles 13–15 (on education and culture) in the Covenant on Economic, Social and Cultural Rights, he observed that appropriate state measures were needed for its realization:

> Only the effective exercise of the rights set forth in Article 27 can guarantee observance of the principle of real, and not only formal, equality of the persons belonging to minority groups. The implementation of these rights calls for active and sustained interventions by States. A passive attitude on the part of the latter would render such rights inoperative.[75]

After reviewing the special rapporteur's reports, and given the seriousness of the topic, the CHR recommended that a special working group be established.[76] One of its mandates was to draft a declaration of principles on the rights of minorities; by that point, drafting a declaration was a fairly standard UN response demonstrating that the issue was of critical importance and that work under way would eventually produce a legal document. The declaration on minorities, adopted in 1992, is the first exclusively devoted to the subject of minorities.[77]

Conclusion

Minorities are found in every part of the world, and the highest concentration (and this is partly a reflection of arbitrary boundaries) is located in Africa, one of the most conflict-ridden continents.[78] During the Cold War, the UN did virtually nothing to prevent genocide, and as a result genocide was committed with impunity.[79] The end of the Cold War triggered optimism that there would be an active role for the UN in averting crisis. The Security Council requested that Secretary-General Boutros-Ghali develop an agenda for peace. His report argued that it was time to reinvigorate UN enforcement measures and bring to fruition its envisioned role of safeguarding world peace.[80] However, shortly after the adoption of *An Agenda for Peace*, genocide raised its ugly face, in Rwanda and in the former Yugoslavia. In both instances, the UN failed to effectively protect minorities, further demonstrating that it was not up to the task of acting decisively or boldly.

The UN's response to Rwanda was abysmal, as various experts have noted, particularly because it took place under the watchful eye of the newly created post of the UN commissioner for human rights.[81] While the initial pullout of UN forces from the country was a mistake, many considered the failure to immediately deploy UN human rights monitors—"a useful face-saving tool in the UN armoury"—to be criminal. Moreover, former UN commissioner for human rights Jose Ayala Lasso's suggestion that "the Commission . . . should consider appointing a special rapporteur to examine all human rights aspects of the situation, including causes and responsibilities" was patently inadequate. The response of the UN's chief human rights officer to the swiftest genocide in the history of the planet was to dispatch one man to "examine" the situation. In the seven weeks it took Mr. Lasso to come to this conclusion, 750,000 Rwandans were murdered.[82]

On the other hand, there are longstanding structural reasons why the UN and its public servants act—and fail to act—in the way they do. For one, there are no enforcement mechanisms or effective measures to protect victims unless states—in this case, members of the Security Council—authorize action. Only then can the UN initiate peacekeeping operations or in cases of gross violations set up special tribunals to punish the perpetrators.[83] In fact, when Serb forces overran the UN-declared safe havens and massacred civilians in 1995, the best the CHR could do was to study the situation and make recommendations.[84]

Prosecution is often treated in a separate manner under criminal international law. In the case of the former Yugoslavia and Rwanda, two ad hoc international courts were established under the Security Council for the express purpose of trying those indicted for genocide, crimes against humanity, and war crimes.[85] These international tribunals, however, have not been successful in addressing the gross human rights violations in these two states.[86]

To prove that impunity is no longer an option for the perpetrators of genocide, the Rome Statute of the International Criminal Court (ICC) was finally adopted in July 1998, fifty years after Pella had emphasized the need to set up an international criminal court.[87] However, in 1950 the Cold War was already in full swing, and it was impossible to consider Pella's proposal. After the fall of the Soviet Union and the emergence of a strong NGO lobby for an international court, it was possible to discuss this option. The ICC became operative in the summer of 2002, after a minimum of sixty countries had ratified it. The longest holdout was the United States, which repeatedly attempted to undermine the provisions of the ICC. It finally signed the ICC treaty after the UN agreed that U.S. citizens serving in UN field operations were outside the court's jurisdiction. The George W. Bush administration later unsigned the ratification, once again demonstrating U.S. "exceptionalism" to human rights enforcement measures.[88]

The fourth high commissioner for human rights, Louise Arbour, highlighted the gap in protection of minorities in a 2005 report to the CHR.[89]

The report stressed the importance of conflict prevention with regard to minorities and the role of NGOs in pointing out the limitations of the Working Group on Minorities and the insufficiency of protection measures.[90] In December 2004, the subcommission proposed that the Secretary-General create a post of special representative on minority issues with a focus on country fact-finding missions and preventative diplomacy. The post was not created, but an independent expert on minority issues was established under the offices of the UN high commissioner for human rights.[91]

Many human rights violations of a communal and ethnic nature have turned into conflict and genocide.[92] How are these crimes continuously perpetrated almost sixty years after the genocide convention?[93] This reality can be attributed to fact that the very states that created the system also acquiesce or condone and even at times officially sponsor the removal of unwanted people (minorities and immigrants) from their territories and therefore are not in a position to take any action to protect such individuals or prevent abuses. Therein lies the dilemma for minorities: the protectors are often the perpetrators. A proper legal framework that addresses rights of minorities, in particular the right to self-determination, is needed. As one expert notes:

> Those in a majority community can insist on individualism and the nondiscriminatory treatment of individuals, and can decry any differentiation based on race, language or religion, knowing that this formula assures their dominance. If the less numerous ethnic communities are to preserve their identity and their culture, and even if they are to simply be assured of fair considerations of their interests, it may well be imperative to grant them special rights as collective entities.[94]

Race and Nondiscrimination

On 21 December 1965, the General Assembly unanimously adopted and opened for signature and ratification the International Convention on the Elimination of All Forms of Racial Discrimination (ICERD).[95] The convention was finalized with record speed; the drafting process began in January 1964, and it was adopted in December 1965.[96] The speeches in the assembly's twentieth session (1965) were overwhelmingly positive. The French representative observed that no convention of equal scope had ever been adopted before, and the great powers all expressed their satisfaction and support. Many delegates expressed the urgent need for a legal means to combat racism. The Polish delegate observed that "what was really needed was a legal tool for fighting racial discrimination, which would define precisely not only general aims but also means of implementation."[97] At the time, the implementation mechanisms of the two international covenants as part of the international bill of rights appeared to be a dead letter.

What chain of events resulted in all countries agreeing so quickly on a topic that in the past had been so contentious? The immediate impetus to address race-based discrimination was triggered by an epidemic of swastika-painting and other anti-Semitic acts and racial and religious prejudices in the Federal Republic of Germany in the winter of 1959–1960.[98] The fear was that less than twenty-years after Hitler, neo-Nazi sentiments were brewing once again in Europe, manifesting in the form of racial and religious hatred. At the time, the Sub-Commission on Prevention of Discrimination and Protection of Minorities was in session. It adopted a resolution condemning these actions as violations of principles in the Charter and the UDHR and requested that facts about the events and their underlying causes and motivations be collected so effective measures could be taken.[99] This trigger sparked discussion at the UN about a legal treaty to prohibit discrimination.

From 1960 to 1963, Africa became one of the largest continental presences at the UN—thirty-four out the 113 states were from new and recently independent African countries.[100] Although African countries continued to have limited representation on the CHR and exerted almost no influence there, in the General Assembly they were able to change priorities.[101] Given the practice of apartheid, it was not surprising that the issue of race-based discrimination for Africans and generally for other Third World countries was considered an overriding human rights problem. The African countries in the 1962 assembly argued for the immediate adoption of a convention on racial discrimination but agreed to a compromise in which a declaration would be prepared and a convention would follow.[102] Western states wanted to include religious discrimination as part of the document, but after significant opposition from Arab countries on definitions of anti-Semitism and Zionism as racism, the decision was taken to separate racial discrimination from religious discrimination.[103] The grand alliance on racial discrimination would eventually unravel, but during the UN's "finest hour,"[104] it drafted a legally binding document on the elimination of race-based discrimination.

The International Convention on Elimination of Racial Discrimination

The subcommission was the first stop for discussions on ICERD. The Polish delegate felt that "their function was to go to the root of the problem without worrying too much about the reaction of countries to their work. Otherwise, they might easily produce a weak and insipid text."[105] Others expressed the purpose of ICERD as building upon the principles in the UDHR: "[Racial discrimination] practices will continue unless pressure is exerted in the form of enlightened international opinion, and the draft Declaration will establish a framework that makes it easier to enforce the principle of the equality of all human beings and to make the Universal Declaration of Human Rights a living and meaningful instrument."[106] But the subcommission's members had decided early on to base their discussions on a fleshed-out version of the Declaration on the Elimination of Racial Discrimination[107] that the United States had submitted.[108]

After twenty-one meetings on the subject, the subcommission sent a draft to the Commission on Human Rights, which discussed and revised the ICERD draft over the course of thirty-five meetings before sending its version on to the Third Committee of the General Assembly. The Third Committee discussed the draft over forty meetings before finally submitting it to the plenary session of the assembly for approval.

The convention is divided into three parts. Part I is on substantive law and fundamental obligations of state parties (Articles 1–7). Part II introduces the creation of international supervisory machinery, in particular the Committee on the Elimination of Racial Discrimination, an innovative idea in and of itself (Articles 8–16). Part III contains the general procedural issues of accession by states and entry into force (Articles 17–25). Article 21 of the convention introduces an unprecedented innovation in its provision regarding reservations: state parties have an unrestricted right to denounce the convention, meaning that they can withdraw from the treaty after written notification.[109]

From the beginning, the issue of the so-called scientific theories of racial superiority was considered politically incorrect and morally repugnant. It was observed that these explanations had been used against peoples of color to confer racial superiority on whites and were characteristic of the anti-Semitic actions underlying neo-Nazism. Delegates from developing countries felt that this erroneous way of thinking should be pointed out in the convention. The Soviet delegate observed:

> It is a fact that so-called scientists in the pay of fascist and racist organizations are still disseminating false racial theories. Such theories are especially dangerous to youth and could do extensive harm when supported by Governments. The preamble of the convention should therefore contain a general statement to the effect that racial superiority and racial discrimination are false in theory, socially dangerous and unjust and cannot be tolerated either in theory or in practice.[110]

In the subcommission, differences over the "separate but equal" doctrine was the subject of a heated dispute between the United States and Poland; the U.S. process of gradually desegregating public facilities in the 1950s was moving very slowly on a case-by-case basis.[111] In the subcommission, U.S. delegate Morris Abram wanted to change condemnation of doctrines based on "racial differentiation or superiority" to condemnation of doctrines "of superiority based on racial differentiation."[112] Poland challenged Abram on this: "Racism is not based merely on the doctrine of superiority," the Polish representative said that "it frequently finds its justification precisely in the differences between individuals or groups." He noted that Abram's amendment "would tend to support the argument that there was no discrimination so long as all racial groups enjoyed 'separate but equal' treatment."[113] Abram countered that "on the contrary, the whole purpose of the effort to eliminate racial discrimination is to protect the differences between races apparent to any observer; those differences are indeed among the beauties and glories of the human race."[114] The subcommission, which tackled the question of differential treatment first, decided to put in a paragraph stating that measures preferring certain racial groups were not "racial discrimination" when they were "for the sole purpose of securing adequate development or protection of individuals belonging to them."[115] The exception did not apply if the measures led to unequal or separate rights. The CHR wanted to make sure that extra measures given to people who had suffered past discrimination did not turn into unequal privileges. The discussion focused on specific obligations for states under the convention, and the commission decided to delete the obligation of a state party to ensure "full enjoyment" of economic and social rights to its "under-developed" groups. As the Lebanese representative stated, this obligation was "tantamount to discriminating against the rest of the population" since in developing countries, it was impossible to guarantee economic and social rights to all their nationals.[116]

The Third Committee returned to a broader debate about substantive and procedural rights. The Ivory Coast pointed out that not only had the principle of developing or protecting underdeveloped groups been used to justify colonialism but it "still represented discrimination, even though the aims might be good and even though limits were set for the length of time such special measures would be in effect."[117] In the end, the committee created a thorough, if wordy, reincarnation of the subcommission's stab at substantive equality and deleted contentious words such as "underprivileged."[118] Article 1.4 of the convention states:

> Special measures taken for the sole purpose of securing adequate advancement of certain racial or ethnic groups or individuals requiring such protection as may be necessary in order to ensure such groups or individuals' equal enjoyment or exercise of human rights and fundamental freedoms shall not be deemed racial discrimination.

The convention is ambiguous about the issue of group rights. Several delegates argued that the convention should include group rights in addition to rights of individuals. Ecuador and Lebanon were particularly vocal on this point during the CHR's discussions. Ecuador pointed out that in Latin America, members of the large indigenous population were "more aware of their existence as members of a group than of their existence as individuals."[119] Lebanon, too, argued that the convention should protect "not only individuals belonging to certain racial groups, but those racial groups as such."[120] These proposals regarding group rights were voted down. Italy and other western states felt that the idea of group rights was "a new one which puzzled this delegation. The Commission should not seek to emphasize the distinctions between different racial groups but rather to ensure that persons belonging to such groups could be integrated into the community."[121] Others emphasized that the convention was "designed to protect the rights of the individual, which was the purpose of all United Nations conventions in the field of human rights."[122] Yet the convention provides special protection for groups that are victims of past discrimination.

Another issue of confusion was whether to include nationality as a form of discrimination banned by the convention.[123] The issue arose over the use of nationality as a politico-legal term denoting membership of a state or as a historical-biological term denoting membership in a nation (i.e., an ethnic community or minority). The example was given of citizens with cultural traditions different than those of the majority in the state, against whom discrimination was exercised on the basis of this difference. The initial draft had a rather cumbersome sentence stating that when countries had multiple nationalities (or ethnic origins), there should be "no discrimination based on such differences."[124] The following article stated that no state shall discriminate "on the basis of 'nationality' or national origin."[125] Although nobody liked putting "nationality" into quotation marks in the text, and despite the general complaints about word usage, most delegations agreed that the term "nationality" should be part of the definition of racial discrimination. Finland pointed out that "in international law, the term 'nationality' was frequently used to mean 'citizenship.' . . . The use of the term 'national origin' would avoid ambiguity."[126] The subcommission eventually adopted a hybrid definition that included both the term "national origin" and the wordy explanation about countries with different nationalities.[127]

The definition of racial discrimination in ICERD is narrower than in other UN instruments. Article 26 of the International Charter on Civil and Political Rights proscribes distinction on the basis of race, sex, language, or religion. The civil and political rights covenant adds color, political or other opinion, national or social origin, property, and birth or other status to the list in the Charter. Article 1 of ICERD bases racial discrimination on any distinction, exclusion, restriction, or preference based on race, color, descent, or national or ethnic origin, "which has the purpose or effect of nullifying or impairing the recognition, enjoyment or exercise, on an equal footing, of human rights." There was discussion about nationality as a type of racial discrimination in lieu of national origin. On one side of the argument were countries such as the Philippines, which noted that "failing to mention discrimination based on nationality or national origin would mean ignoring the existence of a form of discrimination . . . as serious as racial discrimination."[128] Some countries pointed out that while discrimination on the basis of nationality was serious, it should not be included in a convention on racial discrimination, since, as the representative of Lebanon put it, "the notions of race and of nationality might sometimes coincide, but nationality could also be determined by other factors, such as language or culture. Individuals of the same race might be of different nationalities."[129] But the commission by a narrow vote of 10 in favor and 9 against decided to keep the reference to national origin in the definition.

Given the confusion about definitions, the topic rose again during Third Committee discussions, as some countries suggested deleting the term "national origin" because it was an implied part of "ethnic origin."[130] The United States and France proposed keeping "nationality" as a form of racial discrimination[131] but including a second paragraph to explain that countries were certainly able to have different policies for citizens and noncitizens. According to France, the point was to "ensure that no difficulties would be created in France and other countries using similar definitions by mistaken interpretation of the word 'nationality.'" In French legal terminology, he explained, the term "nationality" covered the rules governing acquisition or loss of nationality and the rights derived therefrom.[132]

There was a fair amount of protest and some confusion over using "national origin." The representative from Cameroon argued that since people can choose their nationality, it "did not imply that element of non-responsibility which made racial discrimination particularly odious."[133] Greece wanted to delete either "national" or "ethnic" because the words have the same meaning in Greek.[134] The actual compromise was crafted during informal discussions. It essentially followed the U.S. and French suggestion but cleaned up the explanatory second paragraph, which was rather wordy in the draft amendment. The final text includes national origin as a banned form of discrimination but also includes a provision permitting governments to treat citizens and noncitizens differently.[135]

Freedom of speech was a controversial topic that triggered a Cold War battle even before the subcommission had made any headway. The U.S. draft text laid out a fairly detailed article that specified that organizations that received government funding were prohibited from any racist activities but did not seek similar regulation of private actors.[136] The UK delegate pointed out that although organizations inciting acts of violence on racial grounds were deplorable, it was important that the convention prosecute individuals "on the grounds of what they did rather than what they thought."[137]

The Soviet Union proposed an amendment outlawing all organizations that promoted or incited racial discrimination (instead of "*and* incited racial discrimination").[138] Poland, meanwhile, suggested adding "and shall declare participation in such organizations or activities to be an offence punishable by law."[139] The Polish delegate noted that the U.S. and British views were inadequate, for they "might be construed as giving the State the right to intervene only when an act of violence was committed or was likely to be committed."

> Thus State intervention would be delayed, and at times difficult or impossible. But a State should take forceful and long-term measures against persons advocating racist doctrines; racist activities should not be permitted to reach the stage of imminent violence. Hitler . . . advocated racist doctrines long before he . . . passed to action, and when at last he resorted to violence, the Weimar Republic, which had failed to take measures against him earlier, fell.[140]

An intense disagreement took place in the CHR when the Soviet Union, building on the Polish proposal, submitted an amendment outlawing any contribution or assistance to such groups.[141] The U.S. delegate, noting that America was built on certain principles of freedom, responded that "under the law of the United States and other countries, organizations as such could not be prohibited, although persons who engaged in illegal activities could be prosecuted for their actions"[142] and offered a proposal limiting the clause to the "activities of" organizations rather than the organizations themselves.[143] The Soviet Union protested strongly, saying the U.S. amendment was "based on an entirely misunderstood conception of freedom of association" and that the U.S. government was "proposing that States parties . . . stand idly by while fascist organizations secured financial support, solicited members, and planned their activities, until they became so powerful that they could not be repressed. . . . Nobody could grant such freedom of association to Nazi, fascist and neo-colonialist organizations dedicated to activities prohibited by the convention itself." The Soviet Union contended that "not only the persons who actually perpetrated the prohibited acts but also the leaders of the organization and its financial backers should be held responsible," and "if its laws did not provide for prohibiting racist organizations, the United States would simply have to revise its legislation to bring it into line with the convention: that was an obligation which would devolve on all contracting states."[144]

The CHR eventually voted down all the Soviet and Polish amendments. The votes were close and fell along Cold War lines, although some countries (Ecuador and Lebanon) abstained repeatedly. The paragraph that was adopted outlawed "the activities of organizations" instead of the organizations themselves.[145] (It is interesting to note today that under the rubric of the war on terror, the United States has banned certain organizations and prohibited all financial contributions to them.) The Third Committee's discussions on this issue were no less controversial and more polemical, but eventually it adopted a compromise text that paid due regard to principles of free speech by referring to the Universal Declaration in the article's chapeau[146] and condemned all propaganda and organizations, including a provision requiring states to declare illegal organizations that incite racial discrimination.[147]

Throughout these discussions, delegates wanted to include references to specific forms of racism. Most frequently, delegations gave impassioned speeches naming Nazism as a particularly virulent form of racism and one that should be included by name in the convention. The Polish delegate summarized this viewpoint:

> Fascism is still very much alive. It is a doctrine of oppression and hatred, of the domination of the weak by the powerful; it is the common denominator of all the racists of the world. The racists of South Africa, of the Portuguese colonies and of the southern states in the United States of America are all influenced by fascism. In view of fascism's sinister history, the inclusion of the word "fascist" beside the word "racist" in the draft convention is a political necessity.[148]

The French delegate retorted that by fascism, the Polish actually meant national socialism but that in any event "there is nothing to prove that fascism and racism always go hand in hand." Indeed, he said that "in some countries which have proclaimed themselves as anti-fascist or anti-totalitarian, there have been manifestations of racial discrimination."[149] Other delegates expressed an optimistic view that the convention should not include references to contemporary forms of discrimination, because "although such phenomena are obviously in everyone's mind . . . it is to be hoped that the convention will stand for all time, whereas transient current practices might be expected to disappear."[150] However, this viewpoint was frequently drowned out by impassioned speeches about particular types of racism.

Anti-Semitism was a particular sticking point. In the CHR, the United States introduced a new article specifically condemning anti-Semitism, saying by way of introduction that "Anti-Semitism was an evil which should be mentioned side by side with *apartheid* and which was far from having disappeared after the Second World War."[151] For a change, the Soviet Union and United States worked together on this issue. The Soviets proposed a few modifications to the U.S. text, essentially adding additional forms of racism alongside "anti-Semitism," and the commission agreed to forward the proposal to the Third Committee for final decision. Saudi Arabia commented early on that the term was being used incorrectly:

> The note by the Secretary-General (A/5129) ... repeats, in good faith, terms wrongly used by other bodies. Anti-Semitism is a misnomer; the real Semites are the Arabs, and the Jews properly so-called represented hardly two per cent of what can be termed the Semitic race. Reference should be made to either the anti-Zionist or the anti-Jewish movement and care must be taken not to confuse the two. The former indisputably exists in the region to which Saudi Arabia belongs and the latter, which is deplorable, is still in evidence here and there throughout the world.[152]

Baroody's remarks did not preclude repeated attempts to include anti-Semitism in a way that was meant to refer to racism against the Jewish people in the convention. In the Third Committee, debates on the meaning of each term were repeated once more. Poland insisted on including Nazism,[153] and the United States and Brazil wanted anti-Semitism.[154] Saudi Arabia once again suggested deleting references to any particular form of racism, "not because it is unaware of the horrors of Nazism or of the suffering which countries like Poland have undergone at the hands of the Nazis, but because there are countless 'isms' which will have to be enumerated if any one is."

> For example, while the greatest recent affliction of Europe has been Nazism, for the rest of the world it has no doubt been colonialism, and it could be convincingly argued that colonialism is a cause of racial discrimination. Arabs have suffered owing to a certain ism, yet no delegation has asked that it should be mentioned in the draft Convention. It is not the purpose of the convention to revive memories of past evils, particularly at a time when the countries of the world seem to be striving towards new ideals.[155]

Other delegates agreed with Baroody that no mention should be made of specific forms of racism. The Turkish delegation pointed out, "Since it is impossible to include in the draft Convention an exhaustive list of specific forms of racial discrimination, and since the omission of some forms might give the impression that they are acceptable, his delegation preferred that the text should be drafted in general terms."[156] A joint Greek/Hungarian resolution[157] passed that stated simply that the Third Committee had decided not to include any reference to a specific form of racism other than apartheid.[158]

The substance of the convention was aimed at putting an end to discrimination, a tall order, and had the support of African, Asian, and other developing countries.[159] The convention promotes the idea that states can eliminate racially based discrimination and disparities and secure de facto equality.[160] But this goal was hampered by the priority the convention placed on equal treatment (obligations of means, or formal equality) as opposed to equal outcome (obligations of results, or substantive equality).[161] That is, the convention fails to address discrimination and discriminatory practices resulting from structural inequality built in over centuries. Policies or practices that seem neutral may not actually change discriminatory practices and outcomes but can still be consistent with the convention's purpose of attaining formal equality. Nonetheless, the issue galvanized state representatives over a short period into a consensus to draft and adopt the convention.

Conclusion: Measures of Implementation

The most innovative contribution of ICERD was its development of complaint mechanisms, which influenced the complaint mechanism for the civil and political rights covenant and subsequent treaties. The original proposal submitted by the Philippines delegate in the subcommission built upon established procedures for implementing conventions and recommendations of the draft international covenants on human rights, the ILO Convention on Discrimination in Respect of Employment and Occupation, and the UNESCO Convention against Discrimination in Education.[162] The Philippine representative explained, "The Sub-Commission should provide a similar procedure for the draft convention, so that the latter will not be less strictly enforced than the conventions on discrimination produced by those agencies."[163] He then produced a draft that essentially required states to submit periodic reports and created a committee to review the reports and deal with any problems that could arise under the convention.[164]

There was little substantive discussion on the Philippines proposal. All the delegates understood these measures to be weak and ineffectual; there was no enforcement, and state compliance with reporting obligations was strictly voluntary. Paradoxically, the only recorded protest to implementation was from the Polish representative, who had been the strongest proponent of strict substantive articles. He commented:

> It is a fundamental principle of international law that by ratifying a treaty, conven-
> tion or agreement States undertake to implement all its provisions and to bring
> their national laws into conformity with the instrument. It is not the practice to
> provide for special implementation machinery in every case, since there are already
> enough suitable organs, both in and outside the United Nations. Furthermore, the
> provisions of the Charter and other treaties can be invoked in cases of violation.
> . . . It is impossible to decide beforehand what would be the most suitable proce-
> dure in any dispute that might arise in connection with the elimination of racial
> discrimination. In some cases negotiation might be sufficient; in others arbitral or
> judicial procedure might be necessary; in yet others action by the Security Council
> might be called for.[165]

The subcommission failed to develop a mutually satisfying text on implementation that could be forwarded to the CHR, which in turn accomplished even
less because it ran out of time before the agenda item could be discussed.[166]
The Philippine proposal from the subcommission was simply forwarded to
the Third Committee for discussion.[167]

In addition to the Philippine proposal, several Latin American countries
submitted suggestions for implementation that would allow complaints from
individuals and NGOs.[168] The Netherlands included a similar proposal.[169]
The United States made a proposal to replace the General Assembly with
the International Court of Justice as the body responsible for choosing committee members,[170] and there was a Tunisian amendment that would allow
state parties to report violations by other state parties,[171] and a lengthy Ghanaian text that would replace the entire human rights machinery.[172] These
proposals launched a protracted debate in the Third Committee. European
delegates, given the functional European system on human rights, felt that
proclamations regarding international instruments and standards on human
rights were "not generally considered to provide a sufficient guarantee of
their observance." They also argued that "the creation of effective safeguards
to ensure the protection and enjoyment of the rights proclaimed is recognized as an indispensable part of the task of the United Nations in the fields
of human rights and fundamental freedoms."[173] Others picked at the text,
focusing on concerns over freedom of speech and sovereignty with respect
to a mechanism for interstate complaints and an optional mechanism for
individuals and groups.

The United Kingdom led the charge on freedom of speech, stating color-
fully that it "considered legislation alone to be of doubtful value in eradicating [racial discrimination, because that] . . . is like cutting down a noxious
weed above the ground and leaving the roots intact. Moreover, there comes
a point when legislation encroaches on freedom of speech and association.

The United Kingdom has always sought to keep a balance between repressive legislation and freedom of expression."[174] The Tanzanian representative identified legal problems of domestic jurisdiction with the complaints mechanism proposals because "he did not see how the Committee could accept a provision under which one State could lodge a complaint against another State concerning internal practices."[175] He also chastised the UK and Canadian delegates for using the discussion on measures of implementation "as an opportunity for gaining political advantage over other delegations. ... Surely no one can accept the thesis that the representatives of developing countries who attack colonialism and apartheid but who advocate prudence in dealing with the question now before the Committee are opposed to the effective implementation of the draft Convention."[176]

The delegate from Belgium observed that "it is . . . surprising that the question of the sovereignty of States should so often be raised. It seems . . . obvious that their sovereignty must be respected and that accession to the Convention is in itself an act of sovereignty. Under the pretext of sovereignty, are individuals to be left at the mercy of arbitrary government action?"[177] Baroody, reflecting some of the frustration over these polemical debates, suggested implementation by a national tribunal rather than an international committee.[178] This proposal fell by the wayside when the Philippines and Ghana finally managed to come up with a compromise text that recommended a committee of eighteen experts of high moral standing who would serve in their personal capacity and would acknowledge impartiality.[179] The Ghanaian representative remarked that "the sponsors . . . have never intended the creation of a United Nations committee because they do not expect the entire membership of the United Nations to become Parties to the Convention. The General Assembly should, however, consider reports of the proposed committee, first, because the Convention has been negotiated under the auspices of the United Nations and, secondly, because the subject of the Convention is human dignity, the most important principle of the Charter."[180]

Eventually, the situation calmed down in the Third Committee. The concerns about freedom of speech were relatively irrelevant and were dropped. The concerns about sovereignty were more serious but were finally addressed by the special permission a state had to give to allow its nationals to submit individual communications (the term "petition" was dropped in the face of U.S. and Canadian opposition) to the Committee on the Elimination of Racial Discrimination.[181] However, the person from whom the communication originated was recognized as the petitioner. The provision allowing states to lodge complaints against each other remained in Article 11, but the article required the committee to make sure that "all domestic remedies are exhausted" before proceeding to hear such complaints.[182] The specter of domestic jurisdiction continued to hang over protection of the rights of individuals, but the human rights project had taken some limited steps on enforcement and made a minor dent in the armor of state sovereignty.

A final question was raised in the debate over ICERD: Was it desirable to create several similar institutions to ensure the implementation of each separate international instrument or should implementation be streamlined through one body? Norway and the Scandinavian countries felt that it was preferable to construct only one machinery for implementation. They warned of the dangers of fragmentation in implementation if every new convention adopted by the UN had its own separate mechanism; the proliferation of instruments would lead to complications.[183] The CHR decided that however desirable a common machinery might be in practice, it might not be attainable because at the time the implementation mechanisms for the two covenants had not been finalized.

The International Convention on the Elimination of Racial Discrimination and its mechanism of implementation were far more advanced than the mores of the international community of states at the UN at the time.[184] The convention was also the first of the international instruments to bridge the artificial divide between civil and political rights and economic, social, and cultural rights that had been created as a result of the polarization over the international bill of rights.[185] The Committee on the Elimination of Racial Discrimination, however, has been very cautious in reviewing individual communications and first tries to establish whether discrimination as defined in the convention has taken place.[186] And despite the far-reaching complaints mechanism under the convention, only a few dozen complaints have ever been registered with the Committee on the Elimination of Racial Discrimination because individuals or groups must first overcome the criteria. Even after the committee receives a complaint communication, the best it can do is make recommendations to the state party concerned, contributing to the sense of futility and cynicism regarding human rights efforts at the UN.[187]

The Quest of Indigenous Peoples

Petitions from indigenous peoples in the Americas have been sent to the CHR every year since its establishment, as Humphrey's personal papers record.[188] But because the CHR had denied itself authority to take any action, these petitions were tabled. Bolivia had proposed that the Sub-Commission on

Prevention of Discrimination and Protection of Minorities study the special problems of poverty among indigenous populations in the Americas.[189] The proposal discussed at the third session of the CHR (1951), unfortunately, coincided with general opposition to the Sub-Commission on Prevention of Discrimination and Protection of Minorities and an attack on its experts for failing to fulfill their mandate, resulting in the termination of the inquiry.[190] For twenty-five years there was no recorded activity with regard to indigenous peoples at the United Nations, with the exception of the ILO, which in 1957 adopted Convention No. 107 on Indigenous and Tribal Populations. The convention, while recognizing indigenous peoples as a separate group, also saw them as economically exploited rural laborers and emphasized that they should be integrated into the modern economy.[191]

In the mid-1960s, when racial discrimination issues, in particular the apartheid policies of South Africa, were occupying the subcommission and the CHR, a Protestant group of linguist-missionaries published a report on the dire conditions of Amazonian Indians. This study, along with substantive evidence from two NGOs, western anthropologists, and the indigenous people themselves confirming that the indigenous peoples of Brazil faced an imminent threat of cultural extinction or ethnocide in the name of economic progress, received attention in a series of *New York Times* articles.[192] The other development affecting the status of indigenous peoples was decolonization and self-determination.[193] The Declaration on the Granting of Independence to Colonial Countries and Peoples fit well within the concept of self-determination and associated it with the idea of statehood, stressing nonintervention and preserving territorial integrity.

The rights of indigenous peoples had been tacitly avoided in the drafting of the two international conventions and ICERD because of assimilationist tendencies among state representatives.[194] Article 27 of the International Covenant on Civil and Political Rights had addressed the rights of individuals as ethnic, religious, or linguistic minorities but not as members of a group or a collective. Augusto Willemsen Diaz, a lawyer from Guatemala on the UN Secretariat staff, took a strategic decision to address the rights of indigenous peoples using the issue of racial discrimination. He noted that racial discrimination was just one of many issues affecting indigenous peoples, but it was the only way available to address their rights at the world body.[195] In 1971, the subcommission appointed Mexican ambassador José R. Martinez Cobo as the special rapporteur to study discrimination against indigenous populations. Cobo, however, did very little substantive work on the issue, and it was left to Diaz to prepare the studies of the special rapporteur.[196]

By the late 1970s, Nordic countries and the United Nations Centre for Human Rights, headed by Theo Van Boven of the Netherlands, were supporting indigenous groups.[197] Norway had begun to identify indigenous peoples in its foreign aid policies and urged other countries with indigenous peoples to do the same. Three international conferences had been held to draw attention to the discrimination, including the international NGO Conference on Discrimination against Indigenous Peoples of the Americas, held in 1977 in Geneva, which had set forth a draft Declaration of Principles for the Defense of the Indigenous Nations and Peoples of the Western Hemisphere.[198] In 1978, when the first UN World Conference to Combat Racism and Racial Discrimination was held in Geneva, Norway included a Sami leader in its delegation.[199]

The Cobo study on indigenous peoples was finally completed and made available in 1983.[200] It had taken twelve years to complete, and Cobo had concluded that "self-determination, in its many forms, must be recognized as the basic precondition for the enjoyment by indigenous peoples of their fundamental rights."[201] He further concluded that indigenous peoples have an inalienable right to their territory and can claim lands that had been taken from them. He asserted that a declaration leading to a convention was required.[202] The study received a lukewarm reception from states. North American indigenous groups[203] were frustrated with delays in the completion of the study; even before the formal release of the report, these groups began to actively lobby the UN to establish a working group on indigenous issues.[204] The Nordic states and the United Nations Centre for Human Rights supported these efforts.

In 1983 the UN established a Working Group on Indigenous Populations, and for the first time indigenous groups had official access to an international forum at the world body exclusively devoted to their concerns.[205] It was both a dramatic and modest breakthrough; it was established at the lowest political level in the UN system. Any recommendations or declarations coming from it would have to go through the Sub-Commission on Prevention of Discrimination and Protection of Minorities, the CHR, ECOSOC, the Third Committee, and the plenary session of the General Assembly for approval. The group consisted of five members from the subcommission, representing the five regions. Asbjørn Eide from Norway was the group's chair.[206]

Eide was already familiar with and concerned about indigenous rights in his own country. In a domestic trial about a proposed hydroelectric project, he had testified that Article 27 of the International Covenant on Civil and Political Rights, which protected minorities from discrimination, also protected their cultural rights. Eide had argued that the hydroelectric project would threaten the cultural survival of the Sami.[207] Under his leadership, the Working Group on Indigenous Populations became one of the most transparent bodies in the UN system, allowing open access to NGOs. It became a forum for indigenous complaints, and as such it was viewed by states as undermining their power at a time when they were trying to address grievances from indigenous peoples within their own borders. When Eide publicly expressed grave concern over an alleged threat concerning a leader of an indigenous (Dalit) movement in India, India's representative lobbied successfully against the renewal of his term in the 1984 election.[208] For a year, there was a lull in activities of the Working Group on Indigenous Populations until, under the new leadership of Erica-Irene Daes of Greece, the group began to work on a draft declaration.

The Draft Declaration on the Rights of Indigenous Peoples

The drafters of the declaration faced major obstacles as they tried to reconcile the interests of states who opposed the declaration and those of indigenous peoples.[209] After twenty years it has still not been finalized. The main resistance came from Latin American and Asian states. African states, in general, did not appear at most sessions until after the Rwandan genocide, and the United States never took the group seriously. Canadians and Europeans joined the Soviet Union and its allies as major supporters of indigenous claims.

The main political obstacle to agreement has been the inclusion of the principle of self-determination. Already one of the most hotly debated topics within the UN, self-determination became even more bitterly contested after decolonization.[210] Chile argued that self-determination ought to be subordinated to the territorial integrity of existing states. The U.S. representative objected to any inclusion of self-determination language on the grounds that it was an excuse for secession in all corners of the world.[211] There were also objections to the recognition of collective political rights. Australia, Canada, Finland, and the Russian Federation recognized the right without explicit limitations,[212] but Australia noted that indigenous peoples' self-determination needed to be an integral part of national reconciliation.[213]

The final draft text accepted by all parties in 1992 was taken from the definition of self-determination in the Declaration on the Granting of Independence to Colonial Countries and People, granting indigenous peoples political rights and free pursuit of economic, social, and cultural development.[214] Despite its origins, it was claimed that the right of self-determination as defined by indigenous groups expanded the idea beyond decolonization. States such as the United States, India, and Brazil continued to object to the definition, noting that the right to self-determination was subject to the previously existing political and legal systems of the state. The issue remains unresolved today; many governments still object to the expansive definition of self-determination because of the critical issue of territorial integrity, while indigenous groups insist that their rights should be read in conjunction with the right to self-governance.[215]

The 1993 Vienna World Conference on Human Rights raised a red flag over the use of the term "peoples." Indigenous groups did not view themselves as one monolithic entity but as separate nations and therefore preferred the term "peoples." In 1992, the special rapporteur of the CHR proposed that 1992 be proclaimed the International Year of the World's Indigenous Peoples.[216] States, in particular Canada and Brazil, objected in the CHR to the term "peoples," fearing that it implied self-determination, and insisted on the singular term "people." This battle over the inclusion of "s" reached its peak in Vienna. Many state representatives were unwilling to accept the plural term as it could be interpreted to include group rights to self-determination. Despite the active advocacy of indigenous groups and the special rapporteur and the support of African states, the final Vienna Declaration and Programme of Action, which was negotiated in closed-door sessions, chose by consensus to adopt the term "people" to refer to indigenous groups.[217] The document also classified indigenous groups under the section on minorities—"persons belonging to national or ethnic, religious and linguistic minorities."[218] These were major symbolic defeats in terms of recognition for indigenous peoples. At the beginning of the 1993 session of the Working Group on Indigenous Populations, Mrs. Daes referred to the conference as a defeat for indigenous peoples.[219]

The First International Decade of the World's Indigenous People ended in 2005 without the adoption of the draft declaration by the commission.[220] Instead, a Second International Decade of the World's Indigenous People has been proclaimed.[221] The debate on self-determination has yet to be resolved; the current focus is on technical aspects of the perceived limitations on such a right.[222] The definition of "indigenous peoples" has also been a source of contention.[223] There is no "commonly accepted definition of the term indigenous in international law," but indigenous peoples have been defined as separate from minorities.[224] With the emerging environmental movement of the 1970s, their very survival was highlighted as a key issue as well as the survival of their traditional cultures and systems of knowledge.[225]

Conclusion: Triumph or Tragedy?

The rights of indigenous peoples raise the paradox that is an inherent part of the UN—no matter how strong a lobby of outside groups may be, it is states that have the final word in the United Nations. States' fears that anarchy and secession will undermine their authority, not to mention their economic interests, prompted them to co-opt the idea of indigenous rights, even at the rhetorical level. Even in documents of principle, the value of words is immense because of the fear that these documents might one day be turned into a legally binding treaty. Whether indigenous claims to self-determination will succeed in breaking out of this paradigm to give further validity to the concept of group rights and improve the economic, social, and political circumstances of indigenous peoples remains to be seen.[226] Nevertheless, indigenous peoples and their views have gained greater visibility, even if they often appear illusory, through the UN Working Group on Indigenous Populations and the Permanent Forum on Indigenous Issues.[227]

The Commission on the Status of Women and Women's Equality

This chapter on group rights would not be complete without mention of women and human rights ideas.[228] Two ideas regarding women's human rights were included from the beginning at the UN: the concept of equality between the sexes and the concept of nondiscrimination. Equality between the sexes is mentioned in the preamble of the UN Charter—"to reaffirm faith in fundamental human rights, in the dignity and worth of the human person, in the equal rights of men and women"[229]—as well as in Article 8 of Chapter III—"The United Nations shall place no restrictions on the eligibility of men and women to participate in any capacity and under conditions of equality in its principal and subsidiary organs."[230] The latter article, even though some delegates considered the need to include it to be self-evident and others saw it as irrelevant, was included at the insistence of the Committee of Women's Organizations at the San Francisco conference.[231] It has turned out to be of great importance and has given women access to and representation within UN bodies.[232]

The Commission on the Status of Women

The first General Assembly meeting in 1946 easily passed a Danish-sponsored resolution asking member states to adopt measures necessary to fulfill the aims of the Charter by granting women the same political rights as men.[233] As a result, ECOSOC requested that the CHR form a Sub-Commission on the Status of Women; it was the only named subcommission.[234] But the subordinate relationship did not last, and at the second session of ECOSOC, the Commission on the Status of Women was established. Its primary functions were to prepare recommendations and reports for ECOSOC on promoting women's rights in political, economic, civil, social, and educational fields and to implement the principle that men and women shall have equal rights.[235] Humphrey noted that by separating the women's commission from the CHR and giving it equal status, "the organic link between the two bodies was severed."[236]

At the time, there were two schools of thought about whether the CHR could take care of the special problems of women.[237] On one side, some experts believed that it was disadvantageous "to set women and women's interests apart from the main stream of contemporary political life and thought in which they were now so triumphantly emerging."[238] Others agreed that segregation was a danger to be avoided, but "they argued that the time had not yet come for women to lose themselves wholly in the stream, that habits of centuries did not change so quickly, and that what was still needed was a spark plug to watch out for women's interests."[239] In their opinion, a separate body would ensure that women's issues were at the forefront of all UN activities, including the specialized agencies. Bodil Begtrup, representing Denmark at the UN and one of a handful of women delegates, also noted that "women did not want to be dependent on the pace of another commission."[240]

Mrs. Roosevelt, as chair of the CHR, had made little effort to include Begtrup in CHR activities and did not actively seek out the opinions of the CSW in drafting the international bill of rights. At the very first session of the CHR, Mrs. Roosevelt pointed out that because the parallel body existed, perhaps it would be best to exclude women's issues altogether from the work of the CHR. The Soviets and the Indian delegates responded that the status of women was an essential part of the international bill of rights and that it needed to continue to be part of the CHR mandate.[241] Despite the differences between the two women, Begtrup attended most sessions of the CHR,[242] and the absence of sexism in the UDHR is often attributed to her interventions.[243]

The UDHR does not have any explicit articles on women, although the preamble reaffirms the Charter language of "equal rights of men and women" and Article 2 prohibits discrimination based on sex. Article 16 is controversial in terms of its stand on women. On one hand it provides for equal marital rights and on the other it implies that women's primary roles are those of mothers and caregivers within the family.[244] The CSW, which was composed solely of women and was dominated in representation by western states, had proposed full equality of civil rights and further stressed that the CHR abolish polygamy through the international bill of rights.[245] While the CHR did not outlaw polygamy, the Covenant on Civil and Political Rights provided that "no marriage shall be entered into without the free and full consent of intending spouses."[246]

In 1947, the CSW adopted its own guidelines and affirmed its intent to raise the social, legal, and political status of women to that of men and to eliminate all discrimination.[247] With these aims, the CSW drafted various measures, including several conventions on the political rights of women and on marriage.[248] In 1946, a British NGO had suggested to the General Assembly that a UN convention on discrimination against women was called for, but it was not taken up until 1963, when the Soviet Union and developing countries introduced an assembly resolution calling for a declaration on the issue. The Declaration on the Elimination of Discrimination against Women took four years to complete.[249]

The following year, 1968, the CSW launched a long-term program for the advancement of women in which all UN agencies were to participate. The usual step of having a convention follow the declaration was lost in the excitement of the proposal by the communist states and Latin America for a world conference on women to be held in Mexico City in 1975.[250] The process was viewed as a validation of women's struggle for inclusion at the UN.[251] The World Conference of the International Women's Year was marred by contentious divisions between representatives of developing countries who wanted to focus on economic and political equality in the context of the New International Economic Order and western states who felt that sex-based discrimination was the issue in their countries.[252] Nevertheless, the conference managed to come up with a fourteen-point list of goals to be achieved within five years.[253] They also agreed to draft a convention and declare 1975 to 1985 the United Nations Decade for Women.[254]

The Drafting of CEDAW

The CSW appointed a special working group to prepare the draft convention on the elimination of discrimination against women with the idea that it would be ready in 1980 for the world conference on women's rights in Copenhagen. Controversial issues included those associated with religion and culture, equality under the law and in marriage, and equal treatment with men versus special protections as women.[255] Implementation measures for the convention also proved tricky, as a specific body already existed on women's issues. Should the convention establish an independent expert body or should the CSW monitor the convention? The drafters opted for an independent body and referred the proposed convention to the Third Committee in 1979. After a contentious debate on several issues—the preamble (which included clauses on nondiscrimination in religion or belief), Article 9 (on the right of women to convey nationality to their children), and Article 16 (on marriage and family law, which was opposed by Arab countries)—it was hastily adopted on 19 December[256] in time for the opening ceremony at the World Conference of the United Nations Decade for Women at Copenhagen.[257]

CEDAW was a turning point, as it elevated women's rights on the international agenda on par with other human rights and had its own supervisory machinery.[258] The ideas contained in it go further than equality of opportunity; they focus also on equality of result. CEDAW also began to break down the artificial divide between private and public spheres in international law.[259]

CEDAW, however, is not without its critics. Women advocates from developing countries perceive a western liberal bias in the casting of women's rights with a focus on nondiscrimination and civil and political rights.[260] Critics argue that the issue of equality, defined as sameness with men, ignores the reality that the two sexes are separate and that males have historically been in a position of power vis-à-vis women.[261] They feel that the convention reinforces the malecentric view, focusing on public life, the law, and education, with only limited recognition of oppression within the private sphere.[262]

International human rights law, in general, marginalizes the rights of women. One western expert argues that international human rights law has made women's rights invisible:

> The narrow definition of human rights, recognized by many in the West as solely a matter of state violation of civil and political liberties, impedes consideration of women's rights. In the United States the concept has been further limited by some who have used it as a weapon in the cold war almost exclusively to challenge human rights abuses perpetrated in communist countries. Even then, many abuses that affected women, such as forced pregnancy in Romania, were ignored.[263]

Another criticism of CEDAW has been the issue of reservations or derogations, which are permitted under Article 28(1) as long as they are not incompatible with the object and purpose of the convention. Incompatibility, however, is not defined, and no criteria are even suggested for its determination. One-third of the ratifying states, 162 as of March 2006, have made a significant number of reservations,[264] many of which are motivated by religious prohibitions on gender equality.[265] Others focus on women's inheritance and property rights, nationality laws, and limitations on women's economic opportunities.[266] The situation reflects the general problem that states can ratify human rights treaties without having to change their political and social patterns of behavior. Through reservations, states can technically evade responsibility and continue patriarchal practices that undermine women's rights and subordinate women.

Conclusion: Violence Against Women

The CSW has been most successful in mobilizing women from different walks of life on the issue of violence against women. There is unanimity on the principle that sexism kills, with increasing examples of the many ways in which being female is potentially life-threatening.[267] The campaign on violence against women has also been successful in bridging the Covenant on Civil and Political Rights and the Covenant on Economic, Social and Cultural Rights by recognizing that it is not only women's lack of political power but also the absence of socioeconomic power that makes them vulnerable to abuse in society.[268] Violence against women is not specifically included in CEDAW, but in 1989 the Committee on the Elimination of Discrimination against Women adopted a resolution on this issue instructing states to include this information in their periodic reports.[269]

The issue was raised in 1985 in Nairobi at the World Conference to Review and Appraise the Achievements of the United Nations Decade for Women in the context of health, specifically in the context of traditional practices on female circumcision.[270] The adopted paragraph in the Nairobi Platform stated:

> Violence against women exists in various forms in everyday life in all societies. Women are beaten, mutilated, burned, sexually abused and raped. Such violence is a major obstacle to the achievement of peace and the other objectives of the Decade and should be given special attention. Women victims of violence should be given particular attention and comprehensive assistance. To this end, legal measures should be formulated to prevent violence and to assist women victims. National machinery should be established in order to deal with the question of violence against women within the family and society. Preventive policies should be elaborated, and institutionalized forms of assistance to women victims provided.[271]

Female genital mutilation was not mentioned directly in the text, but the concept of domestic violence was discussed at the world conference in Nairobi. The women's lobby advocated for a declaration on the elimination of violence against women. One of the main areas of disagreement between northern/western and southern delegates was about recognizing the importance of economic and social disempowerment as a basis of gender-based violence.[272] In 1993, at the World Conference on Human Rights, women's groups united and were able to restore the link between women's rights and human rights and recommend that they be mainstreamed throughout UN programs and institutions.[273]

Over the last two decades the efforts of the CSW and subsequently the CEDAW committee have made great strides in shaping worldwide understanding of violence against women; their arguments support the proposition that women's rights are human rights.[274] The fear that creating a separate stream on women's issues would result in a women's ghetto has proven to be exaggerated. The main concern for women activists has been the lack of enforcement capacity of these bodies, especially during civil strife and war. In October 1999, in a landmark decision for women's rights, the General Assembly, acting without a vote, adopted an Optional Protocol to CEDAW,[275] putting it on an equal footing with the International Covenant on Civil and Political Rights, the Convention on the Elimination of All Forms of Racial Discrimination, and the Convention against Torture and other Forms of Cruel, Inhuman or Degrading Treatment or Punishment, which all have communications procedures. The protocol allows for a complaints procedure for individual women or groups of women and creates an inquiry mechanism that enables the CEDAW committee to initiate studies of situations of grave or systematic violations of women's rights. However, similar to other mechanisms, all domestic remedies must be exhausted first, and states have the option to be party to the protocol. Moreover, there is an opt-out clause allowing states upon ratification or accession to declare that they do not accept the inquiry procedure.

Despite this progress and the fact that women constitute over 50 percent of the population, securing women's equal representation in a largely patriarchic system of family, national, and international decision-making processes continues to be a formidable task, and women's concerns are often relegated to the status of group interests.[276] As is the case with other group rights, the issue of women's self-determination needs to be further advanced. The UN has provided an effective arena for airing views and negotiating rights principles, but its impact on the daily lives of women and men remains limited.[277]

The Rights of the Child

The idea that children are indeed a special group requiring the UN's attention emerged in response to the devastating impacts of World War II. In 1947, the General Assembly and ECOSOC established the International Children's Emergency Fund to meet the needs of some 30 million children in Europe who were undernourished. At the time, the activities of the United Nations Relief and Rehabilitation Administration (UNRRA) were winding down because of the refusal of the United States to channel relief to Western and Eastern Europe after the Iron Curtain had descended. European delegates emphasized that the well-being of the entire next generation was at stake.[278] The Polish delegate, Ludwik Rajchmam, was particularly vocal about the need to protect the fate of Europe's children through the residual resources of UNRRA.

Western states through the UN embraced a new central principle that children were above the political divide of the Cold War when it came to humanitarian assistance.[279] Although the United Nations Children's Fund (UNICEF) was established to assist children affected by war (the original resolution included the phrase "for child health purposes generally"), it survived the postwar emergency. This became the legal niche—after passionate lobbying, especially by delegates of developing countries—through which the organization sustained itself, even though the UN had established the World Health Organization. In 1953, UNICEF became a permanent member of the growing UN family of special organizations, focusing on the needs of children.

The winds of change blew for UNICEF in the late 1950s and the 1960s. Rapid decolonization along with the U.S. emphasis on economic growth with the aim of ending poverty redefined UNICEF's purely humanitarian focus with respect to children to a focus on broader issues of development. This made the prime objective of the organization murky and less clear, as it involved issues that affected whole communities and the countries in which they were situated. Maurice Pate, executive director of UNICEF from 1947 to 1965, noted that children were on the front line in the war on poverty, as they were most acutely affected by it. NGOs also urged the General Assembly to endorse the 1924 League of Nations World Child Welfare Charter, which asserted that the child had rights to special protective measures. This effort culminated in the form of a ten-point Declaration of the Rights of the Child adopted in 1959.[280] For the next two decades, issues concerning children were not a central focus within the UN's work on human rights. In 1978, searching for a weightier international instrument, Poland sent the CHR a proposal to establish a convention on the rights of the child as one of the suggested initiatives for celebrating the 1979 International Year of the Child.[281]

On 20 November 1989, the General Assembly adopted the Convention on the Rights of the Child, which as of May 2006 had 192 state parties, far more than any other human rights treaty.[282] The final text of fifty-four articles was a culmination of eleven years of hard work and was considered a watershed in the long history of the exploitation of children, as it definitively established the principle of child rights. Taking its place in the growing line of human rights treaties, it builds upon the two international covenants, ICERD, CEDAW, and the Convention against Torture and Other Cruel, Inhuman or Degrading Treatment or Punishment. Yet detractors often raise two questions. First, did the CRC add anything new to the existing set of human rights treaties? And second, are children better off today than they were before as a result of the treaty?

The Drafting Process

The original Polish draft of the CRC drew upon the 1959 Declaration on the Rights of the Child, but it was considered incomplete by developing countries because it did not take into account many of their priorities.[283] An open-ended working group was established at the CHR. The drafting process of the CRC included developing a new conceptual framework for understanding children's rights. The exercise was unique inasmuch as it was not only an attempt to build consensus between states but was a consciousness-raising effort as well. It involved the dynamic participation of NGOs at every stage and developed new means of advocating for the rights of the child.[284] NGOs, while injecting an element of creativity and progress in the drafting process, were also viewed in the eyes of delegates as often acting only on single issues.[285] The UN specialized agencies were heavily criticized for not being more involved in shaping the provisions contained in the final draft, including UNICEF, which did, however, contribute a significant amount of funds for the preparation of the convention.[286] For the first time ever, UNICEF, other specialized agencies, and other competent bodies (NGOs) were mentioned in an international human rights treaty as providing expert advice on implementation.[287]

The CRC is premised on the idea that it serves "the best interests of the child," recognizing children as human beings of equal value and marking the end of the age-old era when children were considered as possessions of their guardians.[288] The forty-one substantive articles address a wide range of human rights from the two international covenants on civil and political rights and economic, social, and cultural rights. However, very little on political rights is included in the CRC. According to one expert, articles in the CRC can be grouped into the "three Ps"—provision, protection, and participation—and the convention is stronger on the first two.[289] Provision implies the right to fulfill the child's basic needs; protection indicates that the child has the right to be shielded from harmful acts or practices (including warfare); and participation includes the right of children to be heard on decisions affecting their own lives. Although the CRC declares that the dignity of the child should always be respected and the child's interests should be the main consideration, in reality there is an inherent tension between parents' rights and children's rights. While formulating the articles, states recognized the conflict and attempted to triangulate the relationship between child, parent, and the state.

One interesting battle was over the rights of the unborn child. Certain states, including the Holy See, proposed including the language "before as well as after birth" in the preamble to qualify the care and assistance due to children.[290] While previous texts include similar language, the debate that ensued quickly divided into two camps: those who were pro-choice and those who were anti-abortion. The only NGO to touch upon the issue was the International Humanist and Ethical Union, which expressed the idea that every child has a right to be born a wanted child.[291] Given the religious differences, in the end nothing was included in the final text that requires state parties to draft legislation protecting the rights of the fetus.[292]

Another highly controversial issue was the death penalty, chiefly because the United States objected to the prohibition of capital punishment for offenses committed by persons below the age of eighteen. However, Article 37(a) unequivocally states: "Neither capital punishment nor life imprisonment without the possibility of release shall be imposed for offences committed by persons below eighteen years of age."[293] The United States exerted pressure to weaken the article on children in armed conflict even though twice it had agreed to the formulation that no child would take part in direct hostilities.[294] The age limit for recruitment was set at fifteen. This was a major setback for NGOs that were advocating for an age limit of eighteen.

There was also an extensive debate over articles concerning health care. The Soviet Union and socialist states proposed that health care should be provided free of cost to children, and the United States objected that this was not possible and that the convention could only require states to provide health care "in case of need."[295] The U.S. delegate voiced the fear that free health care might result in the misappropriation of funds. In the end, a compromise was reached. Article 24 recognizes the right of the child to enjoy the highest attainable health and prohibits states from depriving access to health care services. Part two of Article 24 notes that state parties should "take appropriate measures" to diminish child and infant mortality, ensure provision of necessary services, combat disease within the primary health care framework, and ensure prenatal and postnatal care for mothers. Part three states that practices prejudicial to the health of children should be abolished.

Moreover, in Article 24—as well as in Article 28 dealing with education—state parties agreed "to promote and encourage international cooperation with a view to achieving progressively the full realization of the right[s] recognized in [these] article[s]"; it gives particular attention to "the needs of developing countries." This recognition of the special needs of poorer countries for international support is significant and differs from most other conventions.

While certain principles in the CRC are already reflected in international instruments, some new rights were also created,[296] such as Article 8 on the preservation of the identity of the child and Article 21 on intercountry adoption.[297] However, the CRC includes some text that falls short of preexisting standards. For example, it is not clear whether the convention's omission of certain rights that are included in other treaties implies that children are not entitled to these rights.[298] A much more troubling aspect is an article on the issue of state derogations or reservation that seriously weakens the convention. For example, a large number of states expressed reservations to an article that recognized or permitted adoption.[299] Similarly, at ratification, Myanmar made a reservation regarding the juvenile death penalty, which clearly violated the purpose of the CRC. It eventually withdrew its reservation. The CRC, unlike ICERD, for example, is silent about suggesting a mechanism for determining whether or not a reservation is valid. It has been suggested that the issue of reservation with respect to substantive provisions of the CRC may not be valid since obligations assumed under the convention aim to protect the child and are not concerned with reciprocity of obligations between contracting parties.[300]

Finally, like other international conventions, the CRC also has a committee and reporting requirements, which adds to the growing list of reports each committee is producing that is attached to a human rights treaty. The CRC does not create any implementation mechanisms or concrete means of enforcement through the Committee on the Rights of the Child. Its one hope for implementation is the involvement of UN specialized agencies, in particular UNICEF. These organizations could aim to accomplish some of the content laid out in the convention. The mainstreaming of human rights into all UNICEF programs suggests that efforts are being extended into this area.[301]

Conclusion: Impact on Children's Lives

The CRC, the magna carta for children, contains important principles regarding the survival, well-being, and development of children and the protection of children from abuse. In addition, it involves UNICEF and other agencies, including NGOs, in its implementation. It has the most state signatories and is perhaps the most widely known and least controversial of all the human rights treaties. The situation for children, however, remains dire. According to the 2005 UNICEF report *State of the World's Children*, 1 billion children worldwide are deprived of any semblance of a normal childhood, facing instead the effects of poverty, war, and AIDS.[302] The director of UNICEF has stated:

> Too many governments are making informed, deliberate choices that actually hurt childhood. When half the world's children are growing up hungry and unhealthy, when schools have become targets and whole villages are being emptied by AIDS, we've failed to deliver on the promise of childhood.[303]

In 2003, 10.6 million children died before the age of five—the equivalent of all of the children in France, Germany, Greece, and Italy. This is an improvement compared to the 1996 mortality statistics of 12.5 million child deaths, but nowhere close to target figures. Some children are excluded or invisible, meaning that their births are never registered with the authorities. UNICEF has estimated this figure to constitute at least 30 percent of births in developing countries; in nineteen cases, the estimate was as high as 60 percent. These figures illustrate that CRC Article 7, which states that "the child shall be registered immediately after birth and shall have the right from birth to a name, the right to nationality" and that "State Parties shall ensure the implementation of these rights in accordance with national law," is not being enforced. Despite the failure of states to register approximately 50 million births, the Committee on the Rights of the Child has no recourse against state parties to the convention.[304] Similar problems prevail in other areas such as the trafficking of children, children in armed conflict, and child labor.

The goal of the 1978 conference held at Alma-Ata in the Soviet Union was "Health for All by the Year 2000."[305] This was a revolutionary concept, as it was elaborated through the delivery of primary health care, a bottom-up approach concentrating on low-cost prevention rather than high-cost cure. Most important, it engaged people in defining their own health priorities. With a huge boost from the World Health Organization and UNICEF, the

Declaration of Alma-Ata was intended to be an important trigger of change, combining principles adopted at the international level that then had to be transformed into national efforts. Yet planners soon discovered that building a consensus around ideals, difficult as it may be, was easier to achieve than implementation. There was a lack of political will on the part of political figures to support the Alma-Ata vision. Furthermore, the goals were never linked to the Covenant on Economic, Social and Cultural Rights or to principles in the drafting of the Convention on the Rights of the Child.

The Millennium Development Goals (MDGs) have been formulated to deal explicitly with improving the lives of children and reducing the mortality of children under five, but they do not acknowledge a human rights framework, including principles in the CRC,[306] although human rights featured prominently in the Millennium Declaration. Efforts are being made to ensure that the MDGs are implemented with human rights norms and techniques in mind. Yet these linkages are often missing in actual practice. While UNICEF is beginning to mainstream human rights and the CRC in its own programmatic work, it has not explicitly established any links with the MDGs.[307] Moreover, the prevailing school of thought among political figures, who make statement after statement of support, continues in the same vein as the thinking about implementation of the Alma-Ata goals—such matters cannot be seen as subject to human rights because a government cannot command resources and guarantee that each of the goals will be met. Thus, the chasm between rhetoric and practice continues to be wide, despite various commitments to improving the lives of children and protecting their rights.

9

The Right to Development

- The North-South Divide on the Right to Development
- The Third World Confronts Economic Colonialism
- The Failure of the Development Decades
- The Turn to Human Rights
- The Question of Rights-Holders
- The Question of Duty-Holders
- Content and Implementation
- The Legacy of the Right to Development

The North-South Divide on the Right to Development

The right to development, considered a significant milestone in the intellectual history of human rights at the United Nations, arose out of contentious global debates about the meaning of economic justice. It was first proposed in 1972 by Kéba Mbaye, who was concurrently a member of the CHR, president of the Senegalese Supreme Court, and judge with the International Court of Justice.[1] The right brought within its broad ambit a number of controversial ideas: the nexus of human rights and development; the link between civil and political rights and economic, social, and cultural rights; the right of states to economic self-determination; the right of individuals to participate in national economic decision-making; the duty of states to cooperate in fostering local and international development; and the obligation of wealthy countries to transfer resources and technology to poor states. These distinct and often contradictory concepts did not fit comfortably within a coherent legal philosophy; in fact, behind the bitter UN debates were two diametrically opposed ideas of the purpose and meaning of the right to development.

According to a majority of UN states, most of which are from the Third World, the right to development expresses the legal duty of former colonial powers to make compensation for centuries of pillaging and depredation through reparations, favorable terms of trade, direct aid, and other redistributive measures aimed at rectifying structural economic disparities in the global economic system. In short, it reflected the rich North's obligation to repay the deprived South for the legacy of colonial exploitation. These latter countries, organized at the UN as the Non-Aligned Movement, hoped that enshrining development as a human right would lead to a more just international order as called for in both the UN Charter and the Universal Declaration of Human Rights.[2] The NAM's vision of development, outlined in its demands for a New International Economic Order, initially did not embrace human rights; this language was adopted as a strategy only after the NIEO's economic demands were defeated on the political front.

According to western states, the right to development the NAM asserted simply did not exist; broad language promoting international cooperation could not be stretched and distorted into the right of poor states to development aid and a corresponding duty of rich states to provide it. They were willing to accept a moral (i.e., unenforceable) commitment to development but not a legal obligation to transfer resources. They further argued that such an approach would confuse and undermine the existing human rights system of individual rights. Western states understood the right to development to be limited to promoting the right of citizens to democratic participation in national development policy and requiring governments to respect individual human rights in the development process. Third World efforts to redress economic inequity through international redistribution were seen as an attempt to divert attention away from national corruption and mismanagement and justify the subordination of civil and political rights to centralized development planning. Not surprisingly, the strongest opposition to the NIEO and the right to development came from the United States, which perceived a challenge to the global economic order it had shaped and dominated since World War II.[3]

As the debate about the right to development dragged on over the course of a decade through various UN meetings and committees, radical demands for economic redistribution gave way to the realities of northern rejection. With power only to pass nonbinding General Assembly resolutions, the NAM ultimately had little choice but to accept a watered-down formulation of the right to development that paid lip service to international cooperation and collective rights without defining these terms or establishing specific legal obligations, let alone implementation mechanisms. As happened so often with human rights agreements, the text of the 1986 Declaration on the Right to Development reflected a broad compromise stated in language that was elastic enough to hold conflicting interpretations.[4] Thus, the right to development is considered both an independent human right and a precondition for other rights, a collective and an individual right, a right to both a process of participation and an outcome of that process. As defined in Article 1.1 of the Declaration on the Right to Development (1986), it is "an inalienable human right by virtue of which every human person and all peoples are entitled to participate in, contribute to, and enjoy economic, social and cultural and political development, in which all human rights and fundamental freedoms can be fully realized."[5]

The Third World Confronts Economic Colonialism

The right to development emerged from the legacy of colonialism and Third World demands for economic self-determination and equality. At the birth of the UN, large parts of Asia and almost all of Africa were under European domination.[6] Latin American states were politically independent but economically dominated by the United States.[7] Although the ruling indigenous elites of many colonies received better health care, education, and income than their co-nationals and the larger society gained some benefit from modern transportation and communications infrastructures, the imperial powers were loath to undertake deeper structural modifications that might enable these regions to challenge their political subordination and economic exploitation.[8] As a result the colonies developed a dual economy consisting of an export-oriented sector that supplied Europe with forced labor and cheap natural resources and a subsistence-oriented agricultural economy for the local population.

After the avalanche of decolonization, the new states joined their well-established and powerful former masters at the UN as they faced the daunting responsibility of rebuilding the political, economic, civil, social, and cultural lives of their citizens.[9] Economic self-determination was a central challenge in light of the concentration of national wealth, expertise, and production in the hands of foreign companies and European residents. Confronted with economic crises and an international balance of power tilted sharply against them, the new states began to call for compensation and assistance to redress the decades and centuries of exploitation.

The 1955 Asian-African Conference in Bandung, Indonesia, marked a watershed in the development of Third World identity and voice. It brought twenty-nine nations that shared a legacy of colonialism and the ongoing problems of global economic disparity together to demand an equal footing in the international order.[10] In the conference's Final Communiqué, the assembled states issued "a renunciation of colonialism and demands for decolonization; a call for dialogue between North and South in relation to

economic issues, with an emphasis on the need to promote economic development; [and] an assertion of the need to avoid military alliances with the
superpowers."[11] This opening shot in the formation of the NAM emphasized
the need to establish a collective position on economic justice and avoid Cold
War entanglements. It reflected a pragmatic understanding that while the
Soviet Union and China had provided military and ideological support to
anticolonial liberation movements, it was the West, and primarily the United
States, that held the keys to international trade and finance.

The development agenda of the NAM was promoted at the intellectual
and conceptual level by a group of prominent Third World economists. Many
senior figures associated with the UN and multilateral organizations, who
had been involved with national development planning, were dismayed by
the reigning economic paradigm of growth without equity. These economists, including Samir Amin of the UN Institute for Development Planning,
Mahbub ul Haq at the World Bank, Gamini Corea at the UN Conference on
Trade and Development (UNCTAD), and Enrique Iglesias at the Economic
Commission for Latin America, formed the Third World Forum with the aim
of establishing a new development model based on economic redistribution
within states and greater equity between rich and poor countries.[12] Samir
Amin recalled:

> I was among those who saw in this period a turning point in history that would
> lead . . . to a major opportunity for development, for an affirmation of a will to
> develop. Of course, the term was very general, very vague—and thus inevitably
> took on varying connotations depending upon the internal political considerations
> of each liberation movement.[13]

In 1960, forty-three Asian and African states sponsored General Assembly
resolution 1514, the Declaration on the Granting of Independence to Colonial
Countries and Peoples, which asserted that "alien subjugation, domination
and exploitation constitutes a denial of fundamental human rights, is contrary
to the Charter of the United Nations and is an impediment to the promotion of world peace and co-operation."[14] That same year, an ECOSOC report
reflected the new development paradigm of the NAM and its intellectual
supporters. Delivering an implicit rebuke to the U.S. and Soviet penchant
for measuring development strictly in terms of material growth, the report
sought to place human beings at the center of economic life:

> One of the greatest dangers in development policy lies in the tendency to give to
> the more material aspects of growth an overriding and disproportionate emphasis.
> The end may be forgotten in preoccupation with the means. Human rights may
> be submerged and human beings seen only as instruments of production rather

than as free entities for whose welfare and cultural advance the increased production is intended. . . . Even where there is recognition of the fact that the end of all economic development is a social objective, i.e., the growth and well-being of the individual in larger freedom, methods of development may be used which are a denial of basic human rights.[15]

Most postcolonial states, however, were not willing or able to implement these development theories. Throughout the Third World, the development crisis deepened during the 1960s. Outside of the success of the East Asian "tigers," whose economies had suffered comparatively less damage from foreign intervention, the newly independent states were locked into an economic model focused on gross domestic product (GDP) growth and were overly dependent on the export of raw commodities.[16] Government-led five-year plans to develop industrial capacity foundered on a lack of expertise, corruption and waste, volatile commodity prices, mounting debt, increasing inflation, trade barriers imposed by the industrialized North, and a general lack of power to influence the global capitalist system.[17]

The growing numerical strength of Third World countries within the UN prompted them to launch a formal campaign for economic justice at the Sixth Special Session of the 1974 General Assembly, resulting in the Declaration on the Establishment of a New International Economic Order.[18] The declaration emphasized that existing international economic relations had become anachronistic since they were institutionalized at a time "when most of the developing countries did not even exist as independent States." It called for a new order "based on equity, sovereign equality, interdependence, common interest and co-operation among all States, irrespective of their economic or social systems, which shall correct inequalities and redress existing injustices," especially with respect to aid, trade, and foreign investment.[19]

Amid confrontation with the West, the NAM pushed a parallel resolution though the General Assembly that adopted an NIEO program of action proposing a fundamental restructuring of the international economic, financial, and political systems.[20] Its main ideas included direct restitution for the damaging effects of colonialism, stabilization of the prices of raw materials, removal of tariffs on exports from developing countries, reform of the international financial sector to control inflation, stabilization of the exchange rate, the creation of links between assistance and rights, the establishment of a code of conduct for transnational corporations, the creation of specific targets for economic assistance, and an increased role for the UN and its specialized agencies in implementing the NIEO agenda.

While the declaration was generally not phrased in rights terminology, it contained a specific legal obligation regarding the controversial issue of restitution; it recognized "the right of all States, territories and peoples under foreign occupation, alien and colonial domination or apartheid to restitution and full compensation for the exploitation and depletion of, and damages to, the natural resources and all other resources of those States, territories and peoples."[21] The concept of legal obligation also formed the basis for a related General Assembly resolution adopted later in 1974. The Charter on the Economic Rights and Duties of States, which passed by an overwhelming margin of 120 to 6, with 10 abstentions, was drafted by a NAM-dominated working group of thirty-one state representatives under the auspices of UNCTAD.[22] It asserted that colonial powers were required under the "duty to cooperate" to assume greater responsibility for the elimination of poverty in the Third World, to cease discrimination in trade, and to recognize unfettered economic sovereignty.[23]

Needless to say, western states viewed the NIEO with extreme antagonism, irrespective of the strong support from a vast majority of UN members. The U.S. representative spoke for the handful of powerful industrialized nations in flatly declaring: "We are not willing to lend our support to the creation of the kind of New International Economic Order envisaged by the Program of Action adopted by the Sixth Special Session."[24] Unable to block the resolutions through voting, these countries rejected the means of implementation, in particular any legal obligation to provide economic assistance through direct North-South financial transfers. Western nations could accept moral arguments promoting development cooperation on a voluntary basis but adamantly denied the existence of a right to reparations or aid.[25]

One international lawyer has observed that the demand by Third World states for legal recognition of a right to economic redistribution appeared to rest upon a contradiction between asserting independent sovereign status on the one hand while claiming redress for subordinated economic status on the other.[26] But the real contradiction involved political authority, not legal theory. It was not inconsistent for postcolonial states to retain political independence while expecting reparations on the grounds that they had been robbed and abused by western powers. Even if imperialism could be recognized as a crime with measurable economic costs to the wronged nation, there were few means for the colonialist state to correct any part of the damage save through financial restitution and more favorable economic relations. The dilemma for Third World countries was that they had sufficient power to force western states to withdraw their occupying armies but no means to compel them to provide reparations, let alone reform the global economic system to balance the playing field. Economic redistribution required cooperation and agreement; even unilateral acts such as nationalizing foreign-owned assets would provoke damaging countermeasures given the fact that Third World economies were integrating into global markets dominated by the United States and its European allies.[27]

Thus, the NAM had the ability to pass UN resolutions with strong rhetorical pronouncements that demanded concrete measures to advance economic equity, but the western countries had the ultimate power to refuse. The U.S. representative expressed this reality when he declared that the various NIEO initiatives were "meaningless without the agreement of those countries which might be small in number but whose significance in international economic relations and development could hardly be ignored."[28] To preempt increased opposition to the global economic order over which they presided, the United States and its allies proposed an alternative model for Third World development: voluntary trade and investment targets promoted through the UN development decades.

The Failure of the Development Decades

Seeking to contain the radicalization of the NAM and forestall demands for legalized redistribution, the United States designated the 1960s as "the crucial decade for development" and launched the First Development Decade (1960–1969) at the UN with great fanfare.[29] The well-publicized campaign used similar market-based incentives as the Alliance for Progress, which was simultaneously implemented in Latin America to blunt the appeal of communism after the Cuban revolution.[30] Appearing to adopt the slogans of the NIEO, U.S. president John F. Kennedy declared to the General Assembly:

> Political sovereignty is but a mockery without the means of meeting poverty and illiteracy and disease. Self-determination is but a slogan if the future holds no hope. That is why my Nation, which has freely shared its capital and technology to help others help themselves, now proposes officially designating the decade of the 1960s as the United Nations Decade of Development.[31]

The United States understood the problem of development through the lens of free market growth, based on the prevailing economic theory that increased GDP would benefit the entire society, including the poorest sectors.[32] The First Development Decade's primary goal was therefore to achieve a "minimum annual rate of growth of aggregate national income of 5 per cent at the end of the Decade" through increased exports and domestic reforms to attract foreign investment.[33] Social development goals were viewed not as human rights but rather as means to increase economic growth through taking "measures to accelerate the elimination of illiteracy, hunger and disease, which seriously affect the productivity of the people of the less developed countries."[34]

The First Development Decade was universally acknowledged as a failure; the policies did not measurably improve economic performance in developing countries. After 1965, aid flows from the North to the South began to decline, especially once western countries experienced economic recession at the end of the decade.[35] The General Assembly declared that the strategy of focusing on economic growth through export-led trade and investment was insufficient to alleviate poverty or address the growing gap in income and wealth between the Third World and industrialized countries.[36] The authors of the UN's global poverty report in 1968 were "deeply concerned that the world social situation has continued to deteriorate, that the persistence of poverty, unemployment hunger, disease, illiteracy, inadequate, housing and uncontrolled growth of population in certain parts of the world has acquired new dimensions."[37] Nevertheless, the publicity around the campaign raised expectations that the North would take concrete measures to increase its commitment to address the development crisis in the South.

The Second Development Decade (1970–1979) was launched with less fanfare and a more direct orientation toward social welfare.[38] Rather than strict economic growth targets, the UN highlighted the need to address growing problems of unemployment, poverty, and worsening income distribution.[39] But the same problem remained: there were no means to implement these recommendations, and the moral appeal that western states should assist Third World development from generosity alone proved inadequate. These problems were exacerbated by the prevalence of authoritarian regimes (generally backed by one of the superpowers) which lacked competence to meet the multiple economic challenges posed by low commodity prices, high inflation, a strong dollar, high rates of interest, oil-price shocks, and easily available credit from recycled "petrodollars."[40] The fundamental problem was a burgeoning debt load that compelled governments of developing countries to cut back on social spending, lower barriers to foreign investment, and give top priority to exporting natural resources.

Even when Third World governments took these measures, debt servicing as a proportion of exports of goods increased 30 percent from 1975 to 1980.[41] Between 1975 and 1982, the debt ratio of Latin American nations doubled to an astonishing 40 percent of exports.[42] The NIEO's rhetorical demand for resource transfers was reversed, as an estimated $100 billion flowed from Latin American treasuries to banks in the North.[43] Industrialized countries of the Organisation for Economic Co-operation and Development (OECD) roundly ignored the nonbinding suggestion of the World Bank's Brandt Commission that they increase development assistance from an average of 0.35 percent of GDP in 1977 to 1 percent by 2000; by 2000 the actual OECD figure had dropped to 0.22 percent.[44]

UN assessments of the Second Development Decade showed stagnating social and economic conditions throughout the Third World.[45] A delegate to the CHR noted the precarious economic situation of the Third World in this period:

> The persistence of protectionist policies in many industrialized countries, the problem of falling prices of raw materials due to factors beyond the control of the producing countries, the resistance to the transfer of financial resources to developing countries, the delay in establishing a new economic order, the deterioration of the terms of trade, and the defense of maritime sovereignty and jurisdiction are all problems common to the whole developing world.[46]

Faced with this legacy of failure, the Third Development Decade (1980–1989) shifted gears once again and adopted what was termed the basic-needs approach, focusing on addressing the plight of the most vulnerable and poor populations through designating specific targets for employment, hunger, literacy, infant mortality, water, sanitation, and primary health care.[47] Spurred by concerns over growing inequality, the basic-needs approach sought to ensure universal access to a minimum of basic goods and highlighted the importance of participatory governance in an integrated development strategy.[48] It reflected the increasing nexus between human rights and development that was promoted by states, scholars, and civil society movements, and articulated at various world conferences in the 1970s.[49]

Robert McNamara, president of the World Bank from 1968 to 1981, expounded a more conservative rationale for the basic-needs approach, warning of the radicalizing effect of extreme poverty:

> When the highly privileged are few and the desperately poor are many—and when the gap between them is worsening rather than improving—it is only a question of time before a decisive choice must be made between the political costs of reform and the political risks of rebellion. That is why policies specifically designed to reduce the deprivation among the poorest 40 percent in developing countries are a prescription not only of principle but of prudence.[50]

Regardless of motivation, the laudable goals of the third and last development decade never had a chance to take effect. According to two experts of UN development policy, by 1981 the much vaunted North-South dialogue that underlay the concept of the development decades was dead for all intents and purposes, a victim of both polarization around the NIEO and the onset of a full-fledged debt crisis that swept through Latin America and then the rest of the developing world.[51] In many countries, the 1973 spike in oil prices drained foreign exchange reserves and precipitated a "borrowing binge" to make up for falling commodity prices.[52] The second round of oil-price shocks in 1979–1980 plunged the world into recession, burying developing countries deeper into debt and rendering them unable to make payments on the accumulated loans.[53] Suddenly the same countries that had called for complete sovereignty over natural resources in the NIEO were forced to compete for foreign investment to repay mounting debts. Facing economic collapse, they came under unbearable pressure from the Bretton Woods institutions to "restructure" their economies by reducing social expenditures, removing price controls, liberalizing trade, and privatizing the economy.[54] This neoliberal shock treatment aggravated poverty and inequality, resulting in what has been called the "lost decade" for Latin America, Africa, and parts of Asia.[55]

The UN development and humanitarian apparatus essentially sat powerless on the sidelines throughout the entire debt crisis and the imposition of structural adjustment programs, its role limited to issuing studies and reports highlighting the disturbing nexus of neoliberal policies and increasing poverty. The specialized agencies, led by UNICEF, began at this time to promote a human-centered approach to development and calling for "adjustment with a human face."[56] It was against this backdrop of economic meltdown, marked by the defeat of the main pillars of the NIEO's economic agenda, that the Third World countries that by this time dominated the CHR took up the right to development in earnest.

The Turn to Human Rights

Stymied in the political and economic arenas of the UN, the NAM turned to the human rights system to advance its economic agenda. In 1967, ECOSOC expanded the membership of the CHR from twenty-one to thirty-two. Occupying two-thirds of the seats, developing countries had the power and means to direct the CHR to promote economic self-determination through the right to development.[57]

Previous UN reports, declarations, and resolutions provided conceptual support for the right to development. In 1957, a General Assembly resolution affirmed "that a balanced and integrated social and economic development would contribute towards the promotion and maintenance of peace and security, social progress and better standards of living . . . and respect for human rights."[58] The final declaration of the 1968 International Conference on Human Rights in Teheran noted the "profound interconnection between the realization of human rights and economic development."[59] The 1969 Declaration on Social Progress and Development called for the international community to take specific steps to mitigate poverty and guarantee basic economic and social rights, linked disarmament with development, and identified protection of the human environment as an important element in development.[60]

In 1977, over strong western opposition, the NAM sponsored a General Assembly resolution directing UN human rights activities to take into account the NIEO and give priority to "flagrant human rights violations" resulting from apartheid, colonialism, racial discrimination, and foreign appropriation of sovereign resources.[61] The resolution included a set of principles to establish accountability for violations and specific proposals for enforcement.[62] Industrialized nations accused developing countries of conspiring to weaken traditional human rights mechanisms and justify dictatorial practices and in turn were accused of continuing to behave like colonial masters while pretending to champion human rights.[63] Such recriminations would set the tone for the CHR debates about the right to self-determination.

At the intellectual level, the CHR's effort to inject human rights content into the NIEO agenda was supported by the elaboration of "third generation" solidarity rights to peace and development, based loosely on the Universal Declaration's call for a just international order.[64] Solidarity rights are the collective rights of peoples that require international as well as national efforts for their realization. The concept of solidarity rights, in particular the right to development, provided a framework that linked fulfillment of economic and social rights at the national level to reforms in the global economic system. The CHR discussed incorporating solidarity rights within its mandate in the context of a UN special rapporteur's report in 1976 on economic, social, and cultural rights in developing countries.[65] Despite objections by northern members, the CHR decided to formalize the right to development in international law. The Peruvian delegate articulated the consensus view: "The right to development is an inalienable and universal human right . . . reflecting the aspiration of peoples to live in a world of well-being, peace and social justice."[66] The foundation was in place for the CHR to transform this consensus into the human right to development.

Kéba Mbaye, the distinguished African jurist who first gave intellectual content to the right to development, was the driving force behind the CHR's decision to elaborate its scope and content in an international instrument.

Serving on the CHR from 1972 to 1987, he waged a determined campaign to overcome western resistance and activate the UN human rights machinery. Mbaye was adamant that the right to development was a legal right, grounded in the duty to cooperate in achieving the UN's fundamental purposes and principles as set forth in its Charter, the economic and social rights provisions of the Universal Declaration and the covenants, relevant resolutions of the General Assembly, and the statutes of the specialized agencies.[67] He argued that the right included both the negative duty not to impede development and the positive duty to fulfill it. He did not shy away from asserting that industrialized states and former colonial powers shared a responsibility to remedy the development crisis in the Third World:

> They decide on peace and war, the international monetary system, the conditions governing business relations; they impose ideologies, and so on. What could be more natural than that they should assume responsibility for the consequences of events and circumstances that are their own doing? . . . The responsibility for the harm inflicted should be shouldered by those who caused it; it is a matter of elementary justice.[68]

During its 1978 session, the CHR debated the content of a report by the special rapporteur on economic, social, and cultural rights, which argued in favor of overcoming the artificial divisions within human rights in light of the new realities of decolonization and the NIEO.[69] Western states objected to any move that questioned the superior legal status of civil and political rights, but the balance of forces within the CHR was now tilted in favor of the NAM countries, which saw the right to development as a major breakthrough that corrected the overtly individualistic bias of the human rights system. As an indication of this shift in attitude, India, which had previously supported separating the covenants, actively promoted the right to development as a means to bridge the "artificial" split:

> Any approach that seeks to divide human rights into civil and political rights on the one hand, and economic, social and cultural rights on the other, will lead to an artificial compartmentalization which will not serve the cause of promoting the full enjoyment of human rights. The right to development is also a human right, and one that cannot be implemented without narrowing the gap between the standard of living of the developed and the developing countries. For the poor, human rights remain an abstraction, and bread without freedom is as much an affront to human dignity as freedom without bread.[70]

With strong majority support, the CHR recommended that ECOSOC invite both the Secretary-General and UNESCO to study the "international dimensions of a right to development as a human right in relation with other human rights based on international cooperation, including the right to peace, taking into account the requirements of the New International Economic Order and fundamental human needs."[71] This was the crucial first step in the international formulation of the right to development.

The Secretary-General's report of 1979 surveyed the spectrum of state opinions "ranging from the relatively pragmatic view that it is in the best interests of all States to promote the universal realization of the right, to the view that there are fundamental philosophical values which can be said to underlie the right," while noting that only a small number of states rejected it outright.[72] Recognizing that the concept was still evolving, the study concluded that the human rights aspects of development were gaining increasing prominence and acceptance and noted that "recent developments have tended to emphasize the human significance of the new order rather than its strictly economic dimensions. It is in this light that the relationship between the New International Economic Order and the human right to development assumes its fullest significance."[73] The study concluded that the legal status of the right to development was based on the UN Charter and the international bill of human rights. A parallel report by the Secretary-General in 1980 highlighted the specific obstacles faced by developing countries in securing human rights in the economic and social spheres.[74]

In 1978, UNESCO brought together a number of prominent international jurists, including Mbaye, for a Meeting of Experts on Human Rights, Human Needs and the Establishment of a New International Economic Order. The meeting began with the premise that it was necessary to study the issue of development in a legal manner. Focusing on its status as a human right, participants discussed three important elements of the right: first, that it confirmed power to a rights-holder; second, the need for a determinate content that defined the scope of that power; and third, that it imposed either a positive obligation on the part of duty-holder toward the rights-holder or a negative obligation to abstain from interference in that right.[75] UNESCO's report on the meeting spelled out a range of options for codifying a set of specific rights, duties, and obligations in international law.[76]

The CHR reviewed the Secretary-General's report and the work of UNESCO and recommended that a working group with fifteen members representing each geographic region be established to draft an international document that defined the right to development.[77] The Working Group of Governmental Experts on the Right to Development was the first such group to be authorized since the original three that had drafted the instruments of the international bill of rights. It became one of the CHR's costliest undertakings ever, meeting in regular sessions from 1981 until 1986, when the General Assembly voted overwhelmingly to approve the Declaration on the Right to Development.[78]

As expected, the debates were highly contentious; the working group faced a monumental challenge in seeking to bridge fundamentally opposing views on the basic legitimacy of the prevailing international economic order. A large majority of members sought fundamental change in line with the NIEO framework but faced determined opposition from a handful of powerful states, led by a conservative U.S. government under President Ronald Reagan that was increasingly hostile to international law. Recognizing that without some measure of western consent the right to development would arrive stillborn, the united front of Soviet-bloc and NAM countries was eventually forced into a series of compromises that weakened the legal status of the right and removed all obligatory implementation measures.[79]

Members of the working group initially adopted the language of the NAM and the NIEO, emphasizing the need to overcome "the after-effects of colonialism, neo-colonialism, racism, apartheid, racial discrimination, unjustified economic sanctions and all forms of foreign aggression and interference in the internal affairs of States . . . [and] the need to establish a new international economic order and to make relations among States more democratic through the just and equitable participation of all in taking decisions on development."[80] However, members soon had to confront vexing legal questions about the scope and parameters of the right to development that did not lend themselves to straightforward answers even in the absence of ideological disagreement: Whose rights? Whose duties? Entitlements to which benefits? Obligations to perform which acts? How to implement the right? How to measure and enforce compliance?

Consistent with the NIEO agenda, developing countries focused on the collective dimension of national rights, the duties of rich countries and the international community as a whole, and implementation and compliance by meeting agreed benchmarks of mandatory aid to foster economic parity between states. Consistent with their desire to maintain economic hegemony and avoid redistribution, western states focused on individual rights, rejected state and international obligations, and stressed individual political participation aimed at holding national governments accountable for development performance. The ideological divide was so great that developing countries prepared one draft while western states prepared a separate one.[81] The only point of agreement was that the end product of the drafting process would be a declaration rather than a binding convention. This reflected the understanding that a convention that leading industrialized countries did not ratify would have little legal value and no concrete effect, whereas a declaration would have a greater likelihood of gaining consensus (and perhaps eventual implementation) through use of the time-honored trick of "agreeing" to broad language as a cover for contradictory interpretations and ongoing disagreements.

The Question of Rights-Holders

For western states, the biggest obstacle to accepting the right to development was its proposed status as a collective national right. This struck at the post–World War II liberal ideal of a limited representative government that is accountable for protecting the rights of its citizens.[82] Even worse, from the perspective of western states, it could even legitimize a duty to fund Third World development and call into question the reigning neoliberal paradigm that had secured a predominant place in the global economy for the United States and its allies. They consequently rejected any recognition of a sovereign basis to the right to development even in a nonbinding declaration and instead insisted that governments had the ultimate responsibility for ensuring the economic welfare of their citizens.[83] The U.S. delegation in particular vehemently rejected recognition of any collective rights: "The view that States have the right to development is unacceptable. States are merely instruments created by citizens to protect their rights. It has already been pointed out that, in the matter of development, individuals have rights whereas States have obligations. Development therefore implies a limitation on the right of States."[84]

Experts in the working group sought to overcome these objections by referring to the principles of solidarity and interdependence between countries and noting that the right to development had a dual nature that included both collective and individual dimensions.[85] Developing countries argued that the supposed contradiction between the rights of states and the rights of citizens was illusory, pointing out that certain collective rights, such as self-determination, sovereign equality, and territorial integrity were already recognized in the UN Charter as the foundation of human rights.[86] In this view, collective rights were a necessary precondition for the realization of individual rights, especially with respect to economic and social rights: the right to development did not trump people's rights but rather formed the basis for their economic self-determination. Their position was later supported by the UN's independent expert on the right to development, who observed that "logically, there is no reason to take the rights of a group or a collective (people or nation, ethnic or linguistic group) to be fundamentally different in nature from an individual's human rights, so long as it is possible to define the obligation to fulfill them and for duty-holders to secure them."[87]

But it was precisely the ill-defined and ambiguous legal character of the right to development that caused the CHR's U.S. representative to object that it would demean genuine individual rights, dilute and confuse the human rights framework, and prevent the UN from addressing existing violations (particularly in the Soviet bloc).[88] Reagan administration human rights officials argued that economic and social issues were simply not "rights—at least not in the traditional, Lockean sense of the word. . . . Unlike political rights, which are realized the moment the government stops infringing upon them, it is never clear when, if ever, governments will realize the right to education, the right to social security, or the right to development."[89]

This argument raised a broader concern that recognizing a state's right to development could empower authoritarian governments, many of which already had atrocious human rights records, to deny citizens their civil and political rights.[90] The delegate from the Netherlands cautioned that "the right to development should never serve as a basis for strengthening the position of a ruling elite who exploits the popular masses."[91] Along these lines, western states voiced suspicion that certain countries were seeking to enhance centralized authority, justify repressive development policies, and circumvent the established human rights system.[92] The United States warned that "enumerating endless 'rights,' such as the 'right to development,' which still has to be defined, demeans and threatens rights protecting the individual from official abuse without fostering economic and social development. The totalitarian nations often have recourse to the creation of new rights in order to hide the fact that their peoples have no political, civil, economic or social rights."[93] The Finnish delegate, speaking on behalf of Denmark, Iceland, and Sweden, agreed with this claim and asserted:

> We are of the opinion that the questions of human rights will be distorted if the rights of States are dealt with under this label. The question of safeguarding the integrity of the human person against oppression and abuse of power by State authorities should be our main concern. We are worried that by elevating the right to development to a human right, the protection of the human person against oppression by State authorities may be jeopardized.[94]

Developing countries ridiculed this line of argument as a smoke screen that would enable the West to keep developed countries in economic subjugation and pointed out that the most corrupt and repressive anticommunist regimes counted on unstinting American support. The delegate from Mozambique declared that "by extending economic, financial, diplomatic and military assistance, the imperialists are keeping the developing countries in a permanent state of underdevelopment while aggravating their savage exploitation of the peoples of African, Asian and Latin American countries."[95] The Colombian representative denounced the pretext of using human rights concerns to reject the right to development: "Unfortunately some countries, very few, and strangely enough precisely those who claim a special right to make protestations about human rights violations throughout the world, without looking very far into possible causes—perhaps in order to avoid acceptance of any responsibility for such violations—are unable to recognize the right to development. Some of them even go so far as to oppose recognition of such a right."[96]

Concerns about individual participation in national decision-making were not limited to western governments seeking to undermine the right to development and preserve their privileged economic position. The Secretary-General's office prepared a study on the connection between human rights and citizens' participation in formulating national development policy.[97] The study considered the right of political participation to be necessary for the realization of the right to development—"both for the transfer of political power to underprivileged groups and for economic and social development."[98] A growing activist movement was beginning to criticize development mega-projects that were imposed on local communities without their consent, denouncing both authoritarian national governments and unaccountable international funding agencies.[99]

During the same period as the declaration on the right to development was being drafted, group rights, in particular the rights of indigenous peoples, were emerging on the UN's agenda, despite opposition from the vast majority of states. Minorities and indigenous peoples in the Third World were making the same claims of exclusion and exploitation against their own governments as developing countries had made against the North, particularly with respect to damages resulting from large-scale development.[100] NGOs present at the CHR during discussions on the right to development brought these issues to the attention of member states and government experts: "Important as the international aspect was, it was surely at least equally important to ensure that the right to development of the individual and of the disadvantaged communities in a society should receive equal emphasis."[101] But most states, including NAM countries, suppressed consideration of democratic participation and group rights. As the Greek representative emphasized, collective rights referred only to states, not minorities or indigenous groups.[102]

The Question of Duty-Holders

Western states were especially resistant to language that might trigger legal obligations to provide resources to the South. The Working Group of Governmental Experts on the Right to Development tried to legitimize the duty of international cooperation by using the latest language of development discourse; its report stressed "the principles of solidarity and interdependence uniting developed and developing countries" and urged "as far as possible, non-reciprocal preferential treatment to developing countries in all areas of international co-operation."[103] While some Third World countries continued to make extravagant demands for not only aid and technology transfer but also reduced western consumption and a halt to the arms race, the working group reports were already several rhetorical notches below NIEO standards. The longer the negotiations dragged on without results, the more accommodating the working group became.[104]

Industrialized states maintained that the duty to cooperate under the UN Charter and related international instruments referred strictly to voluntary acts by sovereign states and could not be invoked as the basis for legal obligations.[105] The UK representative observed that "her Government, as one of the largest donors of development assistance, agreed that States should take steps to promote development, including that of the developing countries, but could not agree that that should become an obligation under international law."[106] The U.S. representative also downplayed the duty of international cooperation, observing that "of course the international community had a role to play, but the solution of social and economic problems was primarily the responsibility of Member States."[107] The Italian delegate rejected the exclusive focus on the Third World, noting that development was a continuous process that applied to industrialized countries as well.[108]

For most poor countries, the duty to remedy past and ongoing economic injustice was the crux of the right to development. Mired in debt, lacking an industrial infrastructure, without enough technologically trained citizens, these states needed major capital transfers, that is, "non-reciprocal preferential treatment," to help them climb out of the poverty trap.[109] The situation in Africa, which was suffering from civil wars, political turmoil, and famines after having endured the most devastating forms of colonialism, was particularly desperate.[110] African countries were consistent proponents of an enforceable duty to aid; Senegal advocated that "to ensure the effective enjoyment of the right to development, the developed countries should accelerate the transfer of resources to the developing countries and guarantee them favorable treatment in the economic, trade and technological sphere."[111]

The Soviet delegate cited figures that the United States received $80 billion a year from Third World countries during the period 1980 to 1984, dwarfing its direct aid budget, and asserted that "those facts cast a different light on the position of the United States delegation and the selfish reasons which really prompted the adversaries of the right to development."[112] He insisted that in light of the unjust economic order, "the international community," meaning western governments, "has a duty to help the developing countries to escape from their disastrous economic situation, to free themselves from neo-colonial exploitation, to stem the outflow of their financial resources, to protect themselves against the plunder of transnational corporations and to resolve the serious problem of their external debt."[113]

The working group also identified transnational corporations as key players in guaranteeing the right to development. Many countries spoke out in the CHR against the role of foreign corporations not only in dictating economic policies but also, in the case of U.S. transnationals, in fomenting CIA-backed coups against popular governments seeking control over their own economies: Iran in 1953, Guatemala in 1954, and Chile in 1973.[114] The Egyptian representative, who noted that transnational corporations had replaced colonial powers in exploiting the resources of developing countries, stated this common sentiment:

> The inability of developing countries to guarantee the economic rights of their people is neo-colonialism, in the form of the monopoly exercised by the transnational corporation, which continues to play a dominant role in the world market, in the transfer of technology, in fixing the prices of raw materials produced by developing countries—which are kept at the lowest possible level—and the prices of manufactured goods from the industrialized countries, which are increasing every year.[115]

While the CHR provided a forum for Third World countries to denounce the injustices of the global economy, reaching agreement on the specific modalities of the right to development proved more challenging. Developing countries faced the paradox of having to convince the United States and its western allies to acknowledge that the postwar economic system they had carefully constructed was structurally biased and in need of reform or, failing that, convincing them to part with a small measure of economic advantage as the price for leaving the system intact. The Pakistani representative summarized the majority view in the CHR:

> The facts justify such an approach; the political independence to which developing countries have acceded during the past 30 years have not been accompanied by genuine economic development. Those countries, by dint of great sacrifices, have achieved growth rates of over 6 per cent; but their economic position in relation to other countries is worsening year by year, because they are caught up in an international economic system created by a small number of economically strong

countries, a system in their own image that serves their own interests. As long as that system continues the developing countries cannot develop in the full sense of the term. The right to development must therefore take account of that situation and postulate the necessity of reordering international economic relations on a just and equitable basis.[116]

But what leverage existed for demanding such reform? NAM countries had collective diplomatic strength only outside of global decision-making structures. They were relatively powerless in the Security Council, the Bretton Woods institutions, and other western-dominated international financial agencies; the Soviet Union presented an alternative only in the military sphere.

One way the CHR attempted to overcome northern objections to resource transfers was by linking disarmament and development.[117] Members of the working group advanced the argument that the arms race not only multiplied conflicts around the world and thereby exacerbated poverty but also squandered enormous resources that could be used to overcome the financial obstacles Third World development faced.[118] They therefore proposed that disarmament funds be used to fulfill the right to development.

This proposal drew on a long history of failed UN initiatives to fund development through disarmament. After the 1962 Cuban missile crisis alerted the world to the imminent threat of nuclear war, ECOSOC released an influential report on the potential social and economic benefits of disarmament, and the UN secretariat reported that rapid growth in developing countries could be financed with just 10 percent of the savings generated by halving global arms purchases.[119] Secretary-General Kurt Waldheim's 1980 report to the General Assembly noted that the basic needs of global society were held hostage to a spiraling arms race whose annual costs exceeded $500 billion.[120] The Secretary-General's preparatory study on the right to development reaffirmed that that the purchase of arms bore little relation to actual national security interests, damaged human development, and increased national debt burdens.[121] In 1987, just after the declaration on the right to development was adopted, the Secretary-General convened a seminar titled "The Relationship between Human Rights, Peace and Development."[122]

However, the early 1980s was not an auspicious time for such ideas. In 1983, President Ronald Reagan delivered his speech describing the Soviet Union as "the focus of evil in the modern world" and announced a new military program to weaponize space that was aptly titled Star Wars.[123] Soviet representatives responded with furious attacks in all UN bodies: "The role of the State is being strengthened as an instrument of monopolistic and militaristic totalitarianism, which exacerbates the arms race and mortgages the future of mankind by introducing nuclear weapons in space. That militaristic machine provides its own people with disinformation and tries to enslave others."[124] The arms race escalated to new heights, and CHR discussions on disarmament and development broke down amid renewed Cold War antagonism.

Content and Implementation

In 1985, the Working Group on the Right to Development presented a draft of the Declaration on the Right to Development to the CHR.[125] The final set of ten articles had something for everyone; it was broad enough to justify support by states yet included opposing views on almost every aspect of human rights and development. As framed in the declaration, the right to development was not so much a new human right as an affirmation of existing rights in the particular context of development with an emphasis on its social and economic aspects. Skeptics have noted that the outcome "reflects a range of compromises hammered out over a five year period and has succeeded more in restating and enshrining the competing and often contradictory visions of the different groups than in resolving them."[126]

This was the price of consensus. The working group hoped to establish a precedent similar to the Universal Declaration whereby a nonbinding statement of principles by the international community would gain legal effect over time through unanimous endorsement and eventual recognition in customary international law. But to ensure that western states did not vote against it, the draft softened the common demands for reparations and economic parity that once characterized the NIEO into toothless pleas for cooperation. While most developing countries were disappointed by the outcome, some, like the Chilean representative, preferred to look toward the future for a silver lining: "The situation was similar to that of the concept of a 200-mile limit for territorial waters, which had been launched in 1947 and which, 50 years later, had become an accepted norm of public international law."[127]

Yet even with its greatly watered-down final content, the Declaration on the Right to Development failed to achieve the unanimous endorsement on which the working group had placed high hopes. The final General Assembly resolution was adopted on 4 December 1986 by a vote of 146 to 1, with 8 abstentions: Denmark, Finland, West Germany, Iceland, Israel, Japan, Sweden, and the United Kingdom.[128] The United States cast the sole dissenting vote after lobbying harder than any other country to remove objectionable ideas and force the final draft toward its image of individual rights. This effort was remarkably successful because of the working group's desire to bring the superpower on board. One human rights scholar describes this strategy as "bait and switch" and argues that it has long been a defining characteristic of U.S. human right policy.[129]

Many ideas the NAM favored find some mention in the final declaration. Article 1 refers to the rights of "peoples," although Article 2 makes clear that individuals are the main beneficiaries of the right to development.[130] Article 3 declares that "states have the duty to co-operate with each other" but also that "states have the primary responsibility" for "the realization of the right to development."[131] Article 6 insists that all human rights are "indivisible and interdependent" and that states should ensure the realization of both sets of rights in the development process.[132] Article 7 urges states to "do their utmost to achieve general and complete disarmament."[133] Throughout the declaration, provisions are framed in the language of aspiration rather than obligation. Thus, states "should undertake necessary measures" to involve women in development (Article 8), and "steps should be taken" to enhance the right to development through policy and legislative measures (Article 10).[134]

On the critical issue of legal obligation, however, the northern countries won the day. The declaration is littered with references to rights and duties of all kinds, often in conflict with one another, but nowhere is it mentioned that former colonies or poor countries have specific rights to aid, trade, or any form of economic benefits or that industrialized states have any obligation to provide such benefits. If a single theme could be extracted from the confusing verbiage surrounding the right to development, it would probably be that national governments are obligated to respect the full range of human rights during the development process, whereas states in general have only nonbinding duties to help each other overcome obstacles to development.[135]

Pakistan, which had been among the staunchest advocates of mandatory "non-reciprocal" aid and trade benefits for developing countries, recognized the essential weakness of the text: "Efforts to draft a consensus text of the Declaration have entailed the dilution and, indeed, the erosion of the normative positions justifiably adopted by the non-aligned and the developing countries. Pakistan hopes that this demonstration of flexibility will not be construed as a sign of weakness and will be reciprocated by commensurate goodwill and co-operations."[136]

A number of western scholars have attacked the right to development as an affront to the integrity of individual justiciable human rights despite its broad, nonbinding, and surprisingly noncontroversial character.[137] Others argue that its vague content and lack of clear definitions make enforcement highly problematic.[138] But the main contribution of the right to development was that it overcame the divide between the political and economic dimensions of human rights and opened new spaces within and beyond the UN for placing human beings at the center of the development paradigm. Notwithstanding the bitter ideological disputes that marked the birth of the right to development, it was important because it returned human rights to the more holistic and integrated approach of the Universal Declaration.

Once the General Assembly passed the declaration, the CHR turned to the issue of implementation. To prepare a study and make recommendations, the working group solicited the views of governments, specialized agencies, and NGOs. But after three annual sessions marked again by North-South divisions, members could not reach agreement on next steps and failed to adopt any concrete recommendations for implementation,[139] and they requested through the CHR that the Secretary-General organize a global consultation.[140] In January 1990, the Global Consultation on the Right to Development as a Human Right convened in Geneva with a focus on integrating the right to development into the UN's operational programs.[141] The global consultation's report noted that the main obstacle to development was "the concentration of economic and political power in the most industrialized countries perpetuated by the non-democratic decision-making processes of international economic, financial and trade institutions."[142] It endorsed the participation of individuals and groups in the development process and emphasized the need to involve indigenous peoples who were traditionally deprived of any role in decision-making with respect to their territories.[143]

The global consultation's most controversial and ambitious recommendation was that a high-level committee of experts be appointed that was mandated to conduct research on implementing the right to development through all UN programs concerned with human rights, development, and humanitarian affairs.[144] To accomplish this, a network of liaison officers would be established within these programs with the aim of mainstreaming the right throughout the UN system. However, the high-level committee and its liaison officers were never established. The United States, the United Kingdom, West Germany, and Japan reaffirmed their view that the right to development concerned only the relationship between governments and their citizens and that the CHR was exceeding its mandate by addressing economic questions.[145] Developing countries were not prepared to challenge this position and instead held out for a gradualist strategy in the hope of achieving consensus, which never materialized.[146]

After this setback, the prospects for implementing the right to development dimmed considerably. During the 1990s, the CHR formed several more working groups to examine various aspects of the right to development that added to the extensive literature on the topic but never successfully overcame western objections to implementation or moved the UN bureaucracy toward adopting significant programs. In 1998, ECOSOC appointed an independent expert, Arjun Sengupta, to report on progress in implementing the right to development.[147] Sengupta prepared a series of comprehensive reports in an effort to overcome the continuing divide between the world's most powerful industrialized nations and the vast majority of UN member states, to little avail.[148]

The Legacy of the Right to Development

While the right to development stalled at the level of implementation, it made a high-profile appearance during the landmark 1993 World Conference on Human Rights in Vienna, where it was affirmed as a fundamental right in the final declaration.[149] But this affirmation came only after a showdown with Asian states that three months earlier, at a preparatory meeting in Bangkok, had declared the right to development as a collective right of states that could in certain circumstances trump individual civil and political rights.[150] Western states, and many in the human rights movement, took the Bangkok Declaration to be a thinly veiled attack on the universality of human rights in the name of "Asian values" and denounced the misuse of the right to development.[151]

Relative to the old NIEO rhetoric, the Asian statement was mild, identifying international macroeconomic policies as the underlying cause of economic inequity and poverty and inviting all countries to establish a just world order through international cooperation.[152] Nevertheless, the Vienna Declaration emphatically rejected the implicit message of Bangkok: "While development facilitates the enjoyment of all human rights, the lack of development may not be invoked to justify the abridgement of internationally recognized human rights."[153] It urged "comprehensive and effective measures to eliminate obstacles to the implementation and realization of the Declaration on the Right to Development and recommend ways and means towards the realization of the right to development by all States."[154] In this way, the West's perception that the right to development posed a threat to its agenda ended up enhancing its status internationally.

The major success of the right to development, albeit mostly at the level of theory, has been its role as a bridge between the increasingly close disciplines of human rights and development. The pioneering work of Indian economist Amartya Sen was crucial in establishing this nexus both in academic discourse and at the UN. His concept of human capabilities wedded rights values of individual empowerment and public accountability with a human-centered approach to development.[155] A new generation of development economists advanced these ideas in a multidimensional paradigm that linked development with human rights and environmental concerns. This prompted the UN to adopt a strategy of "sustainable human development" that had important implications for development practice and field work.[156] In 1990, the United Nations Development Programme (UNDP) published a series of Human Development Reports popularizing a people-centered view of the development process.[157] In 2000, UNDP chose "human rights and human development" as the annual theme of the Human Development Report.[158] The report concluded that while human rights values were pushing development theory and practice to focus on vulnerable groups and recognize the importance of accountability, such advances were not yet having a measurable impact on the lives of the poor.[159]

The right to development has had markedly less success penetrating the citadels of global economic power: the Bretton Woods institutions and the WTO.[160] The international financial institutions, which have predominant influence among national executives and in ministries of finance and planning, where development policy is actually designed and carried out, rarely use human rights language, ideas, or practices.[161] Dialogues about human rights and development generally take place among UN officials and their counterparts at ministries of foreign and humanitarian affairs without leading to meaningful results.[162] In practice, the relationship between national governments and human rights institutions is still tangential to development policy.

This can be seen most clearly in the latest international effort to combat poverty and promote human development. Announced with great fanfare by Secretary-General Kofi Annan, the Millennium Development Goals set benchmarks for states to achieve measurable progress in key social and economic sectors: eradicating extreme poverty; achieving universal primary education; promoting gender equality; reducing child mortality; improving maternal health; combating HIV/AIDS, malaria, and other diseases; ensuring environmental sustainability; and developing a global partnership for development.[163] The MDGs cover topics squarely within the human rights framework at a time when the UN is ostensibly committed to mainstreaming human rights throughout all its programs. Goal number 8, for example, relating to a global partnership for development, has set seven targets and fifteen indicators relating to economic cooperation, debt, subsidies and tariffs, and access to drugs and technology.[164] Yet somehow the MDGs manage to disregard rights altogether, including the right to development, even as they set specific development goals and seek state accountability for meeting them.[165]

The CHR working group on the right to development has tried without success to involve itself in the MDG process, particularly around goal 8.[166] But the Bretton Woods institutions have been given the lead role in implementing the goals and meeting the targets and indicators.[167] Midway toward the target date of 2015 for achieving the MDGs, it is already clear that most targets will be missed.[168] Philip Alston, an independent expert on human rights and development, comments that while the MDGs and the human rights agenda have a great deal in common, "neither the human rights nor development communities has embraced this linkage with enthusiasm or conviction," instead appearing to "resemble ships passing in the night, even though they are both headed for very similar destinations."[169]

The trajectory of the right to development mirrors the broader trajectory of human rights as a whole. It burst into prominence with high expectations but quickly ran aground in the face of opposition from the world's most powerful states. Just as human rights impinged on the sovereign prerogatives of the great powers and their hegemony over the new world body, the right to development threatened the economic order the United States and Europe constructed to maintain their dominant global position. The Third World majority turned to human rights only after their bold ideas for a New International Economic Order stalled at the rhetorical level in the UN General Assembly and collapsed at the material level with the onset of the global debt crisis. They demanded enforceable legal remedies to undo the scourge of colonialism and to offer protection from an unjust economic system.

They obtained neither through the right to development, and from that perspective it must be judged a failure. The right was allowed to come into being only in a muddled state and lacking strength. In the twenty years since the Declaration on the Right to Development, inequalities between and within countries have literally exploded, creating unprecedented social and economic stratification between peoples and individuals. In 1999, UNDP revealed the astounding statistic that the assets of the three richest people in the world surpassed the combined gross national product of all least developed countries, home to hundreds of millions of people struggling to survive in extreme poverty.[170]

There is another side to the story of the right to development: its value as a reflection of popular struggles for a better life yet unrealized. Lacking power, for the most part, to change people's material conditions, it still stands opposed to the global economic forces that produce such egregious forms of inequality and poverty. In so doing it represents the will of most of humanity. The history of the right to development makes plain that the most powerful nations are prepared, grudgingly, to recognize but not implement the right of everyone to a minimal (if not just) portion of the world's riches. However, the principle itself can no longer be denied; despite many obstacles it has gained prominence inside and outside the United Nations. It remains available for the day when enough forces are gathered to make the promise of human rights real to human beings.

10

Human Rights after the Cold War

- The Hollow Image of Success
- Globalization and Free Trade
- War on Terror or War on Rights?
- Repairing a Sinking Ship
- The Final Word?

In this concluding chapter, we examine the broad trends that have affected human rights since the 1990s. In particular, we consider the latest and most troubling human rights paradox: Why does the overall system face a grave threat to its relevance under world conditions that, on the surface, appear to be more conducive than ever to cooperative conflict resolution and the implementation of a universal legal ethic?

On the positive side of the ledger, the end of the Cold War and the rise of global communications and exchange have spurred significant advances in human rights. The apparent unconditional triumph of democracy put an end to a conflict that had distorted all areas of international relations. At the level of states, the end of ideological deadlock opened new possibilities to advance global peace and security through an enhanced commitment to international law. Human rights seemed a logical foundation upon which to build a more cooperative world. The conceptual unity of human rights was reinforced; it was again possible to return to the original holistic idea of human rights, linking notions of freedom and social justice. At the level of civil society, the new ideological space was filled by a veritable explosion of human rights discourse and activism. In every corner of the world, NGOs were established to fight for a broad range of rights, notably economic and social rights and women's rights. At the United Nations, human rights were operationally "mainstreamed" throughout various programs and agencies in an effort to address the long-standing institutional weakness of human rights implementation. The traditionally distinct fields of human rights, development, and security found a common language and common platforms; human development and human security became the buzzwords of the day, promoted at the conceptual level through the UNDP's influential Human Development Reports. In short, with the demise of superpower rivalries and the unleashing of civil society energies, the world finally seemed prepared to advance the human rights system through the development of meaningful enforcement measures to protect the full range of people's rights.

From today's perspective, this optimistic scenario tells only part of the story. The end of the Cold War did not, as it turns out, resolve the long-standing tensions and structural weaknesses that have bedeviled the human rights framework since its inception. The perennial obstacles of superpower manipulation and the shield of sovereignty in a state-based world system continued to thwart meaningful human rights advances. Even though human rights was given higher priority at the UN, human rights remained dependent on voluntary state compliance with soft norms and policy targets. Moreover, the UN's rhetorical commitment to human rights mainstreaming was not matched by necessary changes in bureaucratic operations. Even the proliferation of NGOs had mixed results, giving rise to questions about representation, transparency, and governance in civil society movements.

In our view, these problems do not, on their own, pose a major threat to the overall human rights paradigm or the prospects for its continued development. The emergence and consolidation of two new trends—neoliberal globalization and the war on terror—raise fundamental questions for the future.

The rapid spread of economic globalization has shifted the predominant influence over social and economic policy from the state—where such policies were in principle subject to democratic control—to international institutions and transnational corporations. Neoliberal economic policies have increased the already wide gulf between rich and poor, while the WTO has explicitly excluded human rights values from the dominant global trade system. Thus, at the very moment when economic and social rights came to be accepted as a valid international concern, the means for their realization was ceded to nonstate actors that were relatively immune to political pressure and accountability. Enforcing these rights against state power had already been an uphill battle; now the obstacles were multiplied.

The second major challenge has come through the war on terror, which reinforced the argument for the national security state. In many parts of the world, the trend toward democratic rights was undermined, decades of progress in advancing civil liberties were reversed, and the overall framework of human rights was attacked as irrelevant to modern conflict—not only by authoritarian regimes but also by the United States and its western allies, upon whose financial and political support the UN depends for its very survival. The simultaneous weakening of state power to protect economic and social rights and the strengthening of state power to abuse civil and political rights raises a dark cloud over the capacity of the UN human rights system to secure its fundamental objectives. This has led to more open questioning, by states and NGOs alike, of the universality and efficacy of the overall human rights paradigm. As might be expected, popular support for the human rights idea, the bedrock of its enduring ideological power, has suffered as a result. This trend is especially pronounced in the Islamic world and the South as a whole.

Predicting the future of human rights, or even assessing whether the human rights glass is half full or half empty, is ultimately a matter of perspective. Our goal is not to be alarmist; there is a German expression, *die lage war immer so ernst,* that roughly means the sky is always falling. Nevertheless, it is our assessment that the human rights system, as currently organized, faces existential issues that must be squarely confronted. The universal human longing for justice will not disappear; indeed, the need for a system of rules to resolve global conflicts seems more urgent than ever. However, the current human rights system may not be capable, at the most practical level, of fulfilling its raison d'être under international conditions that are marked, on the one hand, by economic interdependence that transcends the borders of nation-states, and on the other, by growing ideological and military conflict between these territorial polities. Whether the system will be reformed, replaced, or abandoned remains an open question.

This conclusion covers five main issues: cracks in the 1990s image of human rights success, the human rights implications of globalization, the attack on human rights associated with the war on terror, the recent establishment of the UN's Human Rights Council, and future prospects for the human rights paradigm. Limitations of space and scope allow us to sketch these issues only briefly, with little historical detail or analytical depth. Moreover, topics such as globalization and the war on terror are inherently contentious and do not lend themselves to glib political consensus. Yet these are the defining forces of present times; it is not possible to assess the prospects for human rights without taking them into account.

The Hollow Image of Success

The end of the Cold War seemed to herald an auspicious period for human rights. The spread of ostensibly democratic governments throughout the former Soviet bloc brought immense changes to the entire globe. In western political and intellectual circles, the feelings of euphoria unleashed by the stunning and unexpected victory over Soviet ideology and practice were expressed in popular arguments about the "end of history," premised on the irrevocable spread of democracy, rule of law, and human rights.[1] The UN system in particular was gripped by a new sense of hope that the deadlock and paralysis characteristic of Cold War tensions might finally be lifted, allowing for a renewed commitment to the original principles and purposes of the international organization. Buoyed by the revitalization of democratic principles among its member states, Secretary-General Boutros-Ghali proclaimed that "democracy is a thread that runs through all the work of the Organization" and that "human rights, equal rights and government under law are important attributes of democracy."[2] An international policy based on the merging of these principles seemed at last to be within the UN's reach.

With democracy as an overarching framework, the stage was set to integrate the political and economic faces of human rights, long divided by ideology. For decades, the idea of human rights as an integrated paradigm had been frustrated by ideological divisions, among other factors. Yet the connection between human rights and development was a central, albeit unrealized, principle of the United Nations. The Charter linked "universal respect for, and observance of, human rights" with "economic and social progress and development" as fundamental concerns of the entire UN system.[3] The Universal Declaration linked civil, political, economic, social, and cultural human rights as "the foundation of freedom, justice and peace in the world."[4] After a long period of neglect, the fractures within human rights could be redressed by all three levels of the United Nations: the peoples of international civil society; the agencies, institutions, and operational programs of the organization itself; and the community of states.

As the debate over capitalism versus communism waned, interest in human rights as a bridging ideology exploded, much as it had immediately after World War II. The number of human rights and advocacy groups, both international and local, increased exponentially. Through the activities of these groups, human rights became part of the local milieu in countries around the world—covered by the media, contested in political circles, and discussed by the general public. International instruments such as the Convention on the Rights of the Child and CEDAW were taken off the shelves, so to speak, and brought to bear on policy debates concerning an increasing range of issues, from child soldiers to domestic violence against women. The rise of civil society activism had a direct impact on international standard-setting at the UN, not only through interventions with specialized agencies and human rights treaty bodies but also at the landmark global gatherings of heads of state throughout the 1990s. Mobilizing thousands of representatives from around the world, NGOs established a forceful parallel presence to states at the world conferences on environment and development at Rio, human rights at Vienna, population at Cairo, social development at Copenhagen, women's rights at Beijing, housing at Istanbul, and food security at Rome.[5] While these world summits have been criticized for emphasizing pomp and ceremony over substance, they did raise the global profile of human rights. This was due largely to the interventions of members of civil society groups, who proposed alternative texts, buttonholed state delegates, and lobbied for stronger human rights protections. Public pressure was particularly effective at the World Conference on Human Rights in Vienna; the final declaration affirmed the interdependence and indivisibility of all human rights, linking them to other core UN principles on the grounds that "democracy, development and respect for human rights and fundamental freedoms are interdependent and mutually reinforcing."[6] It was also at Vienna that states agreed to establish the Office of the High Commissioner for Human Rights to coordinate UN human rights activities and programs, finally bringing to life an idea that René Cassin had proposed almost fifty years earlier.

The new human rights–friendly atmosphere enabled Secretary-General Kofi Annan to take steps to address the critical gap between promotion and protection, requiring all departments to mainstream human rights throughout operational programs and making economic, social, and cultural rights a primary area of concern after decades of neglect. In 1997, he designated human rights as a cross-cutting issue in the overall reform of the UN system as a whole, declaring that "a major task for the future will be to enhance the human rights programme and integrate it into the broad range of activities."[7] The recognition that human rights was an overarching principle for all UN programs was meant to overcome the isolation of human rights institutions in a series of underfunded and undervalued UN outposts.

The United Nations Development Group (UNDG), whose representatives come from a cross-section of UN agencies, was placed at the center of reform initiatives aimed at strengthening cooperation for development and implementing the right to development at the country level. Under the UNDG, interagency country teams have sought to ensure that operational programs emphasize human rights, promote awareness of human rights among the general public, encourage cooperation between governments and civil society, and propose legislative and judicial reforms. An enormous number of policy briefs, reports, and program guidelines have been published by the various agencies to highlight their commitment to and progress in mainstreaming human rights. It seems that no document is now complete without reference to human rights:

UNDP expresses its commitment to strengthen its support for all human rights—civil, cultural, economic, political, and social—in a holistic way, and to mainstream human rights into its work in support of sustainable human development.[8]

The FAO strategy takes the right to food as its point of departure, stressing the importance of human rights, democracy, peace, and good governance, including effective decentralization, as essential to achieving long-term food security.[9]

UNICEF is mandated by the General Assembly to advocate for the protection of children's rights, to help meet their basic needs, and to expand their opportunities to reach their full potential.[10]

The Office of the High Commissioner for Human Rights was given responsibility for spearheading the integration of human rights into the work of constituent agencies and programs. By 2000, it found much to be pleased with: "Today, the entire UN system is committed to integrating human rights in development work, and every major donor and aid agency (bilateral, multilateral and private) has publicly committed itself to doing the same."[11] In a similar vein, the fiftieth anniversary of the Universal Declaration of Human Rights on 10 December 1998 was an occasion for celebration at the United Nations. From its modest beginnings in a nonbinding declaration of principles, the human rights system had expanded with astonishing rapidity, engendering a diverse global movement of activists, intellectuals, and civil society organizations in virtually every country.

However, there was a significant flaw in this rosy assessment: If civil society, the UN, and even states were intensifying their commitments to human rights, where was the evidence in people's lives? To what extent did the heightened prominence of human rights in global discourse enhance the well-being of people, especially those at the bottom rungs of society? In other words, do human rights matter, in the most practical sense? The two sides of this dilemma are illustrated in this UNICEF statement:

Children's rights are now higher on public and political agendas than ever before. . . . Non-governmental organizations and other actors in civil society have emerged as innovative and powerful voices for children's rights. . . . States have acquired new impetus to achieving child survival and development goals. However, many children in developing countries are not in primary school and the majority of them are girls. Millions of children are severely or moderately malnourished or die every year of easily preventable causes. Hundreds of millions of children . . . lack access to safe water [and] are engaged in some form of labour.[12]

The point is not that the mere presence and persistence of human rights violations automatically condemns the human rights paradigm but rather that the relationship between ideals and outcomes is fundamental in assessing the value of human rights as a program of human emancipation, albeit a gradual and progressive one. And from that perspective, it is hard to argue that the dramatic advance in commitments on paper has been matched by even marginal improvements in human rights conditions. In the rest of this conclusion, we will examine why this has been the case. Before turning to the key trends of globalization and the war on terror, we will discuss how the post–Cold War promise of human rights was undermined by the geopolitics of a unipolar world order and the recurrence of global ideological divisions, this time along North-South lines.

Unipolarity

The UN's ambition to mainstream human rights was destined from the start to generate more rhetoric than effect. The UN bureaucracy was simply ill suited to implement the myriad policy declarations in concrete programs on the ground. But even had the agencies been capable of transforming their field operations, they possessed little in the way of incentives to induce state compliance with human rights. While the Bretton Woods institutions could impose a raft of conditions on indebted countries before approving new loans, what measures were available to the UN agencies? This again highlights the problem of implementation: the human rights system was designed from the start to not be enforced except through political means at the behest of powerful states.[13] Under this arrangement, only changes at the level of states at the first UN could secure meaningful improvements in respect for human rights.

This is why the end of the Cold War and its ideological divisions initially raised such high hopes inside and outside the UN. The apparent global consensus in favor of democracy and rule of law augured well for reforming the UN system to redress the lack of state accountability. But enthusiasm for tying the success of human rights to a unipolar world proved to be short-lived; the deadlock of superpower rivalry was replaced by the runaway geopolitical interests of one hegemonic power. In fact, the role of power politics as the final arbiter of human rights was, in certain respects, enhanced rather than diminished by the fall of the Soviet Union. U.S. support became the sine qua non for effective UN action on human rights, irrespective of considerations of impartiality. The contrasting treatment of Iraq and Rwanda illustrates this point.

In retrospect, it should have elicited far more concern that the first major act of a Security Council "liberated" from Cold War paralysis and human rights politics was to authorize military force against Iraq. The war resolution was produced after intense and open U.S. pressure on the Security Council, candidly described as bullying and bribing by Secretary of State James Baker.[14] Evidence purporting to show an Iraqi threat to Saudi Arabia was falsified and the size of its military exaggerated.[15] Diplomacy was discouraged and UN resolutions were enforced aggressively, in marked contrast to U.S. disregard of international law violations committed by its regional allies, Israel in particular. For twelve years after the war, the United States and Britain effectively held the rest of the UN hostage to the Security Council's policy of maintaining sanctions against Iraq—despite systematic impoverishment of the entire population—until Saddam Hussein's regime was toppled by a second invasion in 2003. One can only wonder what precedent might have been set for the new world order had the UN instead been empowered to pursue a multilateral diplomatic solution to the restoration of Kuwaiti sovereignty.

The contrast with Rwanda could not be more pronounced. In the face of a deluge of credible intelligence from UN and other sources on the ground, both before and during the genocide, the Security Council refused to take action. The United States set the tone by deliberately refraining from using the term "genocide" during council discussion so as to avoid triggering a legal obligation to act under the genocide convention.[16] Bowing to U.S. pressure, the UN Secretariat soft-pedaled the increasingly frantic calls for military intervention from its field staff, despite indisputable evidence of organized massacres. UN peacekeeping forces were denied the right to intervene to prevent mass killings, despite public appeals by its top commanders on the ground.[17] U.S. inaction was blamed on mission fatigue after the debacle of humanitarian intervention in Somalia. The killing did not end until the Rwandan government was ousted in a civil war, by which time the reputation of the UN had suffered another blow. The Rwandan genocide was the first to take place under the watchful eye and with the full knowledge of the international community.

The North-South Divide

Even at the ideological level, the post–Cold War euphoria for human rights was short-lived; from many quarters, fundamental questions began to be asked about alleged imbalance in the human rights paradigm. China, Malaysia, Singapore, and other governments raised the "Asian challenge": the proposition that development should be prioritized over political freedom.[18] Western states and human rights activists alike dismissed this argument as a rationale for state repression—which it often was. At the same time, the Asian challenge called into question the western bias in favor of civil and political rights that had long defined the human rights system at the UN. Despite repeated commitments to the interdependence of all rights, UN agencies and international NGOs focused their criticism almost exclusively on political rather than economic oppression. The contrast between the economic success of the politically autocratic Asian tigers and the economic debacle of most developing countries locked into the model of formal democracy and neoliberalism has been dismissed as irrelevant by the conventional human rights paradigm. This raises the question of whether China should continue to be singled out as one of the world's worst human rights violators when its economic and social policies have raised hundreds of millions of people out of poverty. Is this exclusive emphasis on political freedom and progress an accurate or distorted reflection of most people's core values and beliefs?

A similar ideological challenge arose from within the human rights movement. NGOs and activists from the South decried the Eurocentric origins of human rights and domination of the field by northern-based international NGOs.[19] Many had first turned to human rights to fight local forms of tyranny and hypocrisy, only to grow disappointed and disillusioned by double standards within the human rights movement. They called for cross-cultural dialogue, if not radical transformation, to rescue the universal basis for human rights from overt Eurocentric biases.[20] The rise of activism in developing countries helped break the northern stranglehold on human rights discourse and practice, but neither compelled significant changes in the human rights system nor led to a process of meaningful reevaluation. Instead, northern funding agencies and international NGOs discovered the virtues of North-South partnerships while failing to address the deeper critiques.

In our view, this reflected a form of myopia within the human rights movement, an excessive instinct for self-preservation. There was a sense that the future of the human rights paradigm rested on touting the success, such as it was, of the existing model without taking into account growing doubts about its hollow core that were expressed by well-wishers and detractors alike. The concrete historical and political processes underlying the development of human rights at the UN remained largely hidden from view and effectively forbidden from discussion. In particular, the question of "design flaws"—structural weaknesses in the UN's human rights model—were not part of the accepted discourse. Protecting the image of universality and impartiality became more important than addressing and incorporating legitimate concerns about the reality of these concepts.

Globalization and Free Trade

Perhaps the fundamental critique of the existing human rights paradigm, which has been leveled primarily but not exclusively by states and activists from the South, has been its failure to seek the social and economic justice that was promised in the Universal Declaration and a host of subsequent instruments. The recent acceptance of human rights mainstreaming has operated at the rhetorical level without impacting the lives of the vast majority of humanity. In particular, the neoliberal economic model—the Washington consensus—that has transformed the global economy appears at best indifferent and at worst hostile to a human rights approach.[21] In this context, it is important to examine the human rights implications of globalization in its most practical manifestations. Two broad trends suffice to present the main human rights dilemma. The first trend concerns the ideological and historical expansion of the Washington consensus, initially imposed on indebted counties by the Bretton Woods institutions, and the second concerns the recent development of binding international free trade law enforced by the WTO in disregard of human rights values and norms.

While globalization is a term that means many things to many people, we understand it as the process of integrating local economies into a global economic system with relatively unimpeded capital and trade flows spurred by new communications technologies and a framework of international law that promotes free and open access to the market.[22] This is not a neutral process guided by the invisible hand of the global market; its expansion was made possible only through the direct intervention of the richest countries of the world.[23] Indebted countries were required to adopt a uniform package of neoliberal policies aimed at privatizing local industries, opening markets to unregulated foreign competition, and eliminating social subsides.[24]

This phenomenon has impacted the realization of human rights, particularly economic and social rights and the right to development. Yet human rights, which are meant to represent the highest normative values of global society, are explicitly excluded from the legal and policy frameworks of globalization.[25] In effect, human rights are considered irrelevant to a process that has a decisive impact on the socioeconomic well-being of virtually all human beings. Thus, at the very time that the UN has taken steps to interlink rights and development, the global forces that shape economic policy at national and local levels have imposed a separation between the two.

If human rights are to have any meaning in social and economic affairs, how can their exclusion from global policy be understood and justified? In our view, the only legitimate rationale for such separation is the argument

that the Washington consensus is the only viable economic model for securing growth and development and the consequent realization of human
rights in the global economy.[26] In other words, in this rationale, human
rights do not have to be taken into account because proper application of
the Washington consensus will automatically produce outcomes consistent
with human rights.

There are several difficulties with this position. For one, it contradicts
the well-established historical record of national growth and development,
even in the latter part of the twentieth century. It is beyond dispute that the
successful economies of Europe and the United States have relied on a high
degree of state management and protection of national industry—not to
mention outright expropriation of foreign assets during centuries of slavery,
imperialism, and colonialism. The recent example of the East Asian "miracle"
is even more telling. A substantial body of academic work demonstrates that
the industrialization achieved in recent decades by Japan, Taiwan, Hong
Kong, Singapore, South Korea, and now China was the result of policies that
are completely antithetical to the Washington consensus.[27] These policies
included tariff and trade barriers to protect local industry; heavy investment
in human capital and social sectors, especially public education and housing;
regulations to boost technology transfer and channel credit toward favored
industries; high enforced savings rates; and laws to discourage short-term
speculative domestic or overseas investment.[28] For example, South Korea
in the 1960s prohibited exports of more than 1 million U.S. dollars without
government permission on pain of penalties ranging from ten years' imprisonment to death, while the government of Hong Kong used state ownership of land as a budgetary mechanism to enable the delivery of a relatively
extensive welfare system based on access to public housing.[29]

Another difficulty with the Washington consensus is inconsistent application. Wealthy and powerful countries have insisted on forcing open global
markets in those areas in which they enjoy a competitive advantage (i.e.,
manufactured goods and merchandise, intellectual property and services)
while retaining trade barriers and national subsidies in areas in which they are
at a competitive disadvantage (i.e., agriculture and textiles).[30] Poor developing
countries are thus doubly disadvantaged. Such hypocrisy in practice, which
continues to distort the free trade system even today, has no principled basis
outside of power politics. It is difficult to escape the conclusion that the ideology of free trade masks the underlying reality of economic exploitation, with
powerful countries deploying the Washington consensus to impose favorable
terms of trade without having to use gunboat diplomacy.[31] As Joseph Stiglitz,
former chief economists of the World Bank, has observed: "The critics of
globalization accuse Western countries of hypocrisy and the critics are right.

The Western countries have pushed poor countries to eliminate trade barriers, but kept up their own barriers, preventing developing countries from
exporting their agricultural products and so depriving them of desperately
needed export income."[32]

The most damning indictment of the Washington consensus lies in its
impact. The failure to deliver sustainable or equitable growth in countries
that have adopted structural adjustment is well known and well documented
in development literature, though acceptance of this evidence is still resisted
in neoliberal policymaking circles.[33] Stiglitz has accused the Bretton Woods
institutions of denying the extent of these failures in order to maintain the
stability of the global system.[34] In Sub-Saharan Africa, which has been forced
to adopt an extreme form of neoliberal restructuring, the results have been
dismal: an annual loss of $6.5 billion during the 1980s, which is more than 10
percent of regional GDP, and rapidly declining terms of trade under a strict
commodity-export model.[35] These trends can be seen in global statistics as
well. In the twenty years since the Washington consensus emerged as the
unchallenged economic paradigm, there has been an unprecedented concentration of wealth and power in the hands of a small minority of humanity,
an unprecedented explosion of inequality between rich and poor nations as
well as within nations.[36] The facts and figures are difficult to reconcile with
an economic model meant to advance development and human rights for
all. According to the UNDP's 2005 *Human Development Report* on globalization and inequality, "The world's richest fifty individuals in the world have a
combined income greater than that of the poorest 416 million. The 2.5 billion
people living on less than $2 a day—40% of the world's population—receive
only 5% of global income. The richest 10%, almost all of whom live in high
income countries, account for 54%."[37]

Perhaps the greatest irony of the Washington consensus is that what is
called free trade was literally forced on poor nations through economic
coercion: governments faced the "choice" of submission to structural adjustment or economic collapse. Postcolonial states that won independence
through national struggle inherited economies damaged by colonialism
and war. After failing to win reparations at the UN, secure a legal obligation
from the North to assist them economically, or establish a New International
Economic Order, they turned to the international financial system for help.[38]
The loans they obtained were often squandered by corrupt and authoritarian
regimes on ill-conceived development projects. The oil-price shocks and
falling commodity prices of the 1970s triggered a debt crisis in the 1980s,
but it was the response of the Bretton Woods institutions that ensured the
globalization of an extreme neoliberal economic model.[39]

Rather than accept a measure of responsibility for channeling huge loans into bad projects with no accountability, the international financial institutions adopted the policies of "good governance" and "structural adjustment." This approach required all governments, regardless of whether they were in power during the years of profligate borrowing, to accept a standard package of political and especially economic "conditionalities" to avoid bankruptcy: eliminate barriers to foreign investment and free trade; end industrial protectionism; deregulate price and wage controls; reorient agriculture and raw materials toward export; tighten credit and money supplies; slash public spending; eliminate social subsidies in food, health, education, and housing; and, of course, prioritize the servicing of debt.

Governments had no leverage to refuse; without additional credit, their heavily indebted economies would collapse. The disintegration of the Soviet Union and the wave of privatization that swept across Eastern Europe in the early 1990s reinforced the Washington consensus as the only game in town. The growing international acceptance of economic and social rights and the right to development, epitomized by the UN's efforts to mainstream human rights in development, were thereby consigned to practical irrelevance. Jan Pronk, former Dutch minister for development cooperation and UN assistant secretary-general, aptly described the marginalization of rights within globalization:

> The forces of globalization have become so strong that this paradigm [the rights-based approach to development] eroded. The idea of good governance came instead: good governance as defined by the West again on the basis of the Washington consensus, everywhere in the world the same, irrespective of the specific circumstances of the country concerned. Good governance also was a precondition for development and as a precondition for development assistance rather than as an objective and as a possible outcome of development policies assisted from outside.[40]

As Pronk observed, it is not simply that human rights were violated under neoliberal globalization but that the overall concept of human rights was superseded and, in effect, "disappeared." Victims of globalization were deprived of the ideological and moral force of human rights as a tool to change their conditions. The accumulated injustices associated with globalization eventually gave rise to various forms of organized resistance, including human rights activism, compelling the Bretton Woods institutions to address environmental and social impacts.[41] They were less accessible and accountable to popular pressures than states, though, having been deliberately separated from the UN in 1947 precisely as a shield against such pressures.

However, it was not until the establishment of the WTO following the 1994 Uruguay Round of the General Agreement on Tariffs and Trade (GATT) negotiations that the divide between human rights and global economics became an entrenched feature of international law. The Bretton Woods institutions imposed the Washington consensus on poor countries through bilateral arrangements and contractual agreements: in the 1980s, the number of structural adjustment loans increased from 7 to 187.[42] In contrast, the WTO rules applied automatically to all member states; this was a truly global system of international economic law with powerful mechanisms of implementation. Until 1999, when the political emergence of mass anti-globalization protest at the "Battle of Seattle" slowed the incorporation of various trade agreements within the WTO mandate, many aspects of neoliberal trade, finance, and investment became enforceable international law.[43] As an international jurist comments: "From its imperfect beginning in the GATT 1947 to its current apotheosis in the WTO, the revolution in international economic law means that more aspects of the international economy are regulated through treaty-based rules than at any previous time, rules with less room for state discretion and unilateral action than at any prior time, and under the adjudicative supervision of stronger institutions than at any other time."[44]

The conflict between human rights and trade arises from a fundamental divide in their respective values, laws, and means of implementation in the current international system. The philosophical basis of human rights is deontological. In other words, human rights are ends in themselves; they do not derive their value from a utilitarian or instrumentalist calculus. As one commentator explains, "What is central about human beings is not their tendency to rationally maximize their self-interest, but their intrinsic human dignity and worth."[45] In contrast, the neoliberal model of economics is based on achieving maximum economic efficiency through the specific mechanism of removing barriers to the free flow of capital and goods (even though labor remains imprisoned within the nation-state, contradicting one of the essential pillars of capitalism as theorized by Adam Smith and David Ricardo).[46] Values that do not relate to efficient commercial exchange are viewed as outside the scope of, and even hostile to, the purposes and vision of trade law; they therefore find no formal recognition in the regulatory framework of international trade. In theory, defenders of free trade insist that human rights and environmental concerns will be achieved as automatic results of trade liberalization and free markets, assuming that people vote with their pocketbooks to prioritize these values. But in practice, the evolving free trade jurisprudence has consistently overturned democratically enacted human rights, labor, and environmental laws.[47] The exclusion of so-called nontrade values from international trade law would not be so significant if it were not for the fact that the reach of trade law has effectively superseded major areas of public interest law.[48]

From 1995 to 2000, 170 cases were brought to the WTO dispute settlement process, virtually all by the United States or Europe. In every case challenging environmental, human rights, or labor regulations, WTO panels have struck down these regulations for violating trade laws.[49] The legal playing field is far from level: WTO judicial procedures are confidential and closed to everyone except disputing state parties, and WTO judges have no training in human rights or environmental law. The following examples demonstrate how the WTO rejects as disguised protectionism any efforts to promote "nontrade values" through national law, even if such laws are enacted in response to pressure from citizens' groups with no interest in protecting industry.[50]

A Massachusetts law to deny public contracts to companies that do business with Burma, modeled on anti-apartheid laws, was held to violate WTO restraint-of-trade principles. Because WTO rules recognize only federal state parties, Massachusetts was represented before the panel by the U.S. government, which opposed the law in the first place. In 1996, Venezuela brought a case against the U.S. Clean Air Act to the WTO after the Venezuelan oil industry had failed in a similar challenge in U.S. domestic court.[51] The WTO upheld Venezuela's argument that U.S. emissions standards put Venezuelan domestic refineries at an unfair disadvantage because their gas was not as clean as that produced in U.S. refineries. The fact that U.S. law reflected a democratic consensus to prioritize health and environmental concerns over cheaper gas was not deemed relevant by the WTO panel. Rather than face $150 million in trade sanctions, the U.S. changed its law to allow dirtier gas to come into the country. Another case with human rights implications was the Caribbean banana case, in which the United States challenged the European Union's policy of granting trade preferences to bananas grown by former colonies.[52] The WTO authorized the United States to impose $200 million in countervailing duties, and the EU dropped its policy, resulting in loss of livelihood for thousands of Caribbean workers. In the beef hormone case, a WTO panel supported a U.S. challenge to the EU's ban on the sale of beef with artificial growth hormones. Finding the ban an unfair restriction on trade in the absence of clear scientific evidence of the danger, the panel required the EU to open its markets to hormone-treated beef or face countervailing duties amounting to over $500 million. This ruling directly reversed the precautionary principle, a key environmental norm that permits restrictions on potentially harmful products unless there is clear scientific evidence that they do not pose a danger.

From this brief survey, it can be seen that the UN human rights system and the institutions of globalization appear to occupy parallel universes.

Human rights make states the locus of accountability, at least in theory, but trade law has stripped states and their constituencies of the ability to exercise control over many aspects of socioeconomic policies. Human rights enjoy strong public support but few institutional means for implementation unless they have political backing from powerful states. Globalization and trade law have minimal public support yet enjoy extremely powerful enforcement mechanisms. Most important, globalization has played a decisive role in shaping socioeconomic conditions, whereas human rights remain sidelined and ineffective. Unless the human rights paradigm begins to systematically challenge the well-documented shortcomings of globalization and free trade, if only at the conceptual level of delegitimizing violations, it will continue the slide into irrelevance.

War on Terror or War on Rights?

The human rights system was already subject to increasing criticism when the attacks of 9/11 transformed the geopolitical landscape. The discourse of global security shifted almost overnight from a theoretical commitment to human rights and human development to one stressing the impending clash of civilizations. The international press carried predictions of a new world war between competing cultures and ideologies—theories put forward not by fringe elements but by the political, military, and intellectual leaders of the world's most powerful nations, the United States in particular.[53]

Ideas of justice have always been transformed in times of war. Human rights are no exception; they were incubated in the crucible of World War I and burst onto the scene during World War II. Throughout history, major military conflicts have not only redrawn geographic boundaries but have reshaped ideological lines as well. According to the script, victorious powers put forward their moral ideology as the true universal standard that is intended to ensure that never again will atrocities be allowed to take place . . . until the next global conflict.

This dynamic seems to be operative in the early stages of what former U.S. secretary of defense Donald Rumsfeld called the "long war" and the Pentagon terms the GWOT—Global War on Terror.[54] This phrase encapsulates three key themes of the new conflict: it is global and unconstrained by the traditional boundaries of state sovereignty; it is a war requiring the mobilization of vast resources; and the "enemy" is an ideology and mindset rather than a territorial state, impossible to defeat by conventional military means. This indicates an ambitious transformation of the nature of war, which has a number of dramatic consequences for human rights.

First, human rights ideas were enlisted in the war effort. As a result, the meaning of concepts such as freedom and democracy became even more polarized. After 9/11, the axiom that one person's terrorist is another person's freedom fighter came to symbolize a fundamental ideological divide, a gap that threatened not only the universality of human rights but the integrity of the UN as a whole. Second, human rights groups have reported significant increases in violations throughout the world in the name of counterterrorism by greater and lesser powers alike. The United States, for example, has openly justified abuse of even previously sacrosanct rights such as freedom from torture and judicial due process.[55] Emboldened by the superpower's example, many states have ramped up their own repressive apparatuses, restricted civil liberties, clamped down on domestic opposition, and prepared their militaries for the predicted conflict.[56] Third and most important, the entire human rights framework, and international law more broadly, has been attacked and undermined as irrelevant and incapable of dealing with the exigencies of the new war against terror.[57] The paradigm shift was so sudden and dramatic that human rights advocates began to pose fundamental questions about the nature of these changes: "Did the events of September 11, 2001 change the world forever? Is the possibility that a terrorist cell will detonate weapons of mass destruction in a large city so imminent a threat that the entire structure of international law and society must bend to the imperative of doing whatever is necessary to meet this threat regardless of the human rights consequences?"[58]

The ideological tone of the war on terror was set within hours of the 9/11 attacks. In an address to the nation that evening, President George W. Bush declared that "America and our friends and allies join with all those who want peace and security in the world, and we stand together to win the war against terrorism."[59] It was not self-evident at the time that the attacks should be classified as war at a global scale; the UN and world opinion in general preferred to classify 9/11 as a crime against humanity prosecutable under existing international law.[60] Compared to the power of Nazi Germany or the Soviet Union, Al Qaeda had virtually no operational capacity to inflict serious damage on either the United States or its allies, who together accounted for most of the world's military might. On the contrary, in an age of "information war," the reach of Al Qaeda was and remains a product not of its actual and extremely limited military ability to strike targets but of a distorted perception of its power magnified by fear.[61] This perception has been blown out of proportion by war rhetoric of the United States, whose access to and influence over global media dwarfs that of the militants.

In addition to hyping the threat of terrorism, the U.S. government defined the conflict as a grand moral crusade. While warning that states "harboring" terrorists were subject to attack—a dramatic departure from the traditional concept of sovereignty—the broader war was aimed not at states but at an abstract ideology. President Bush made frequent use of religious symbols, defining the conflict as a "monumental struggle of good versus evil," thereby echoing the apocalyptic perspective of Al Qaeda.[62] The use of theological language and the goal of eliminating evil reinforced the concept of an "endless" war. Accordingly, the campaign against Afghanistan was initially termed "operation infinite justice."[63] Such appeals for a modern form of holy war have created an atmosphere entirely inhospitable to respect for human rights.

The phenomenon of increasing rights violations arising from counter-terrorism operations has been thoroughly documented by human rights groups.[64] Most disturbing is the increasing use of domestic law to legitimize such violations—the legal model of a national security state.[65] Many states have adopted legislation similar to the USA Patriot Act that expands the reach of government surveillance and monitoring; authorizes or condones interrogation methods that fall squarely within accepted definitions of torture and inhumane treatment; criminalizes previously acceptable forms of political opposition, including peaceful dissent; restricts civil liberties, in particular the rights to free speech and free association; discriminates against noncitizens and minority groups, especially Muslims; eliminates or limits rights of habeas corpus and due process; and authorizes indefinite detentions without charge or trial, thereby establishing a presumption of guilt for anyone suspected of terrorist activities.[66]

Some of these security policies are enacted openly through parliamentary process and legislation; others are conducted by intelligence agencies operating without democratic oversight or public accountability. The special rapporteur for the Council of Europe has recently reported the existence of a "spider web" of secret relations between states in Europe, Asia, and the Middle East to facilitate a covert U.S. program of capturing, transporting, torturing, and detaining alleged terrorist suspects.[67] Such detainees are effectively "disappeared" without legal process, deprived of all rights, and stripped of their identities. These legislative restrictions and secret policies strike at the heart of the universal human rights corpus, undermining civil and political rights that have traditionally enjoyed the most protection in both international and constitutional law, especially among western governments and public opinion. Commenting on U.S. torture and detention policies, a British judge has written: "It is a recurring theme in history that in times of war, armed conflict, or perceived national danger, even liberal democracies adopt measures infringing human rights in ways that are totally disproportionate to the crisis."[68]

It is often argued that sanctioning such abuse feeds the conditions and grievances that fuel terrorism in the first place, making the prophecy of the "long" war on terror a self-fulfilling one. But the damage is even more profound than that. Empowering governments to strengthen their repressive apparatus without legal constraint inevitably leads to their casting an ever wider net of repression, alienating previously law-abiding sectors of society and mobilizing popular opposition, which in turn requires ever greater measures of state control and repression—a familiar pattern of escalating violence.[69] But even these patterns of abuse are not the gravest challenge to human rights today. That honor is reserved for U.S.-led efforts to undermine the institutions, principles, and values of international law itself, based on the argument that the new global war is so threatening and the new enemy so evil that traditional legal protections must be discarded if ultimate victory is to be achieved. Understanding the roots of this profoundly ideological worldview is one of the keys to assessing the future prospects of human rights and the UN itself.

It is now commonplace in intellectual and public circles to discuss the United States as a global empire, for better or worse.[70] Such open discussion of a previously discredited mode of geopolitics is the legacy of an influential group of "neoconservative" think tanks, diplomats, and intellectuals. After the Cold War, they proposed through a series of policy papers, research reports, and conferences that the U.S. monopoly on military might, buttressed by economic and ideological power, should be aggressively and openly deployed to reshape the world according to a "new American century."[71] The main geographic arena for extending the U.S. empire was the Middle East, the fulcrum for consolidating control over the Eurasian land mass.[72] This worldview saw Israel as the crucial strategic ally for transforming the region through a policy of regime change in such countries as Iraq, Iran, and Syria.[73] Even moderate "realist" political theorists, such as Zbigniew Brzezinski, advocated U.S. domination of Eurasia, albeit through international alliances and the tactical use of "soft power" like human rights in addition to direct military interventions.[74]

The U.S. presidential elections in 2000 provided the opening for political theory to become political reality. Once in power, President Bush appointed partisans of the neoconservative doctrine of U.S. empire to key positions throughout the defense, intelligence, and security establishments. Under Defense Secretary Rumsfeld, the doctrine became official Pentagon policy, outlined in a public and controversial strategy to exercise "full-spectrum dominance" aimed at preventing any rival power or group of powers from challenging U.S. "unipolar hegemony" through tactics that include preventive war to eliminate threats before they gather momentum and the use of nuclear first strike in a wide range of scenarios.[75] The relevant policy document declared: "Given the global nature of our interests and obligations, the United States must retain its overseas presence forces and the ability of rapidly projecting power worldwide in order to achieve full-spectrum dominance."[76]

However, the established UN system of collective security and the legal regimes of humanitarian law and human rights stood in the way of U.S. designs. Apart from self-defense, military interventions required, in theory, Security Council approval based on legal norms that limit war to a measure of last resort.[77] Ever since the Nuremberg Tribunal, aggressive war has been prohibited and stigmatized as "the supreme international crime."[78] This is why many neoconservative legal theorists, including John Bolton, former ambassador to the UN (not to mention President Bush himself), have attacked the overall concept of international law and derided the UN itself as a useless anachronism unsuited for decisive actions in a dangerous world.[79]

It is no secret that the U.S. government is pursuing major changes in international law. Even before 9/11, the United States had a track record of "exceptionalism"—standing outside the global legal consensus on such issues as the international criminal court, environmental protection and climate change, halting the spread of unconventional weapons, and arms control in general.[80] The war on terror has provided a conceptual and ideological justification for directly attacking the laws of war and peace. President Bush remarked that "this new paradigm—ushered in not by us, but by terrorists—required new thinking in the law of war."[81] The new thinking included rejecting the accepted definitions of torture, denying the application of the Geneva Conventions to suspected terrorists, and dismissing the laws of war as, in the words of the nation's highest law enforcement official, "quaint," "undefined," and "obsolete."[82]

The high-level Schlesinger panel, appointed in May 2004 by Rumsfeld to review the Pentagon's detention operations, explicitly recommended dropping adherence to these laws: "The United States needs to redefine its approach to customary and treaty international humanitarian law, which must be adapted to the realities of the nature of conflict in the 21st Century. In doing so the United States should emphasize the standard of reciprocity."[83] Under reciprocity, the United States presumably would be justified in summarily executing civilians. The ICRC issued an unusually sharp response: "The standard of reciprocity cannot apply to fundamental safeguards such as the prohibition on torture without accepting the risk of destroying not only the principle of law, but also the very values on which it is built."[84]

The United States is certainly not alone in seeking to shake off the constraints of human rights and international law. China, Russia, Israel, Pakistan, and a host of other countries have systematically violated rights in pursuing their domestic variants of the war against terror.[85] This trend is not necessarily destined to continue; a change in U.S. government could end the direct assault on the UN and its principles of collective security. But an enormous amount of damage has already been done to the reputation and prospects of the global organization. As at the height of the Cold War, human rights are again an ideological battlefield, and the UN is again a forum for sharpening rather than resolving these conflicts. Moreover, the bipartisan consensus in the U.S. political establishment to continue the war on terror rather than question its basic assumptions does not augur well for the future. While it is too early to write a eulogy for the human rights paradigm, its value and relevance have been profoundly challenged. The fallout at the UN can be seen in the increasingly politicized debates concerning human rights reform.

Repairing a Sinking Ship

On 15 March 2006, the General Assembly resolved to replace the Commission on Human Rights, the principal UN human rights organ for the past sixty years, with a new Human Rights Council in order "to further strengthen the United Nations Human Rights machinery."[86] The General Assembly vote followed the recommendation of a high-level panel on UN reform convened by Secretary-General Annan. The panel reported in December 2004 that the commission had lost "credibility and professionalism by maintaining double standards in addressing human rights concerns," and it concluded that many states had joined the commission "not to strengthen human rights but to protect themselves against criticism or to criticize others."[87]

The panel echoed a critique of the CHR made by the United States, other western states, and most human rights NGOs. Especially after being voted off the commission for the first time ever in May 2001, the United States develop an aggressive position that only "real democracies" should serve on the human rights body to prevent it from "becoming a protected sanctuary for human rights violators who aim to pervert and distort its work."[88] The U.S. reform priority focused on introducing criteria to exclude states with bad human rights records. According to this view, the CHR was a victim of its own success; since the Cold War, it had become more bold and effective in issuing country-specific condemnations of human rights abuses, taking "strong stands against abusers, both north and south . . . [and] establishing a system of independent monitors to probe torture, political killings and violence against women."[89]

While this position exaggerates the CHR's actual impact, given the lack of penalties or enforcement as such, it is true that targeted states developed counterstrategies. In response to the political stigma of being labeled actual or potential violators, the so-called like-minded group of countries, led by China, Pakistan, Cuba, Indonesia, and others, entered the commission in recent years and blunted its critical edge. These countries were able to win seats due to the policy of regional bloc voting, in which regions forward one name for every pre-allotted slot and the uncontested candidates receive rubber-stamp approval from ECOSOC.

On the other hand, the like-minded group blamed the western countries for manipulating and politicizing the commission, turning it into "an inquisition tribunal for the rich" to judge and condemn southern countries. They denounced the double standards of their accusers for using the CHR to attack ideological enemies and defend allies, all the while enjoying the immunity of strong national powers. After all, apart from U.S. influence, it is hard to explain and justify the ritual condemnation of Cuba as among the most egregious violators in a world rife with repression and atrocities. China condemned the "intense politicization and confrontation" of human rights at the commission and called for "more soul-searching and less finger-pointing." Cuba termed the CHR "a sinking ship, wrecked because of its growing lack of credibility and prestige" and accused the West of "the pernicious practice of imposing unjust resolutions against countries" that reflect "double standards and the impunity of the powerful."[90]

It is noteworthy that both sides in the debate accuse the other of politicizing human rights in apparent disregard of the fact that the UN system has been political from its inception; powerful states established human rights as moral principles useful for ideological attack rather than as legal standards enforceable through impartial institutions. After 9/11, the propagandistic use of human rights to support military actions further undermined the presumed neutrality of the human rights idea. The failure of the international community to address human rights violations due to economic globalization and the war on terror further polarized the human rights debate, leading to open warfare on the CHR.

For most human rights proponents, the attempt to establish higher human rights standards for commission members is inherently appealing. However, it also exposes the contradiction of seeking political impartiality and consistency in a human rights system fully subordinated to the interests of sovereign states ranked in an implicit hierarchy of geopolitical power. Moreover, using respect for human rights as a meaningful filter would exclude most UN member states outside of a handful of largely European countries and would also invite debates about what constitutes respect for human rights. For example, the Asian Centre for Human Rights recommended that not only standard targets of the West such as China, Cuba, Nepal, Russia, Sudan,

Zimbabwe, and Saudi Arabia be excluded but also the United States and the United Kingdom for illegally invading Iraq and other violations associated with the war on terror.[91]

Based on a political acceptance that "there's no way in the UN context that governments are going to impose [strict] criteria on themselves," Human Rights Watch has proposed "softer alternative" criteria: ratification of core treaties, timely human rights reporting, standing invitations to UN investigators, and promises to vote in accordance with human rights principles.[92] Yet one human rights scholar concluded that few states would pass even these limited tests.[93]

After significant interstate debates, disputes, and negotiations, the actual reforms embodied in the new Human Rights Council were rather modest, reflecting a series of back-door compromises. The body was made subsidiary to the General Assembly rather than to ECOSOC, giving it a somewhat higher political profile. Its size was reduced from fifty-three to forty-seven members, although the United States advocated a reduction to twenty-five to thirty members. Each candidate must garner an absolute majority of votes in the General Assembly, although standard behind-the-scenes politicking by regional blocs could undermine this procedure. Members are limited to two consecutive three-year terms rather than the de facto lifetime membership powerful states enjoyed in the CHR. It has the ability to convene year round and respond to emergencies rather than sitting for one fixed annual session. And finally, members can be suspended for "gross and systematic violations of human rights" by a two-thirds majority of the General Assembly.[94]

The proposal for the council passed the General Assembly with an overwhelming majority, 170 in favor and 4 opposed (the United States, Israel, the Marshall Islands, and Palau). Most human rights NGOs supported the change as a marked improvement over the "regional politics and horse-trading" of the increasingly dysfunctional commission.[95] These undeniable improvements are largely procedural, however, and do not address the deeper problems with the human rights system at the UN—the imbalance between state sovereignty and the rights of individuals and groups, the lack of meaningful enforcement, the overall politicization of human rights by competing states, the lack of accountability for the institutions of globalization, and the growing repressive power of the national security state. While marginal improvements can be expected under the Human Rights Council, it is hard to escape the impression that too much attention is being paid to rearranging the deck chairs on the Titanic.

Of far greater historical significance than minor shifts in the UN bureaucracy is the position of the United States toward the new human rights body. Explaining his negative vote, Ambassador Bolton argued that the resolution did not go far enough in reforming the system and failed to impose membership criteria to ensure that human rights violators would be excluded.[96] He then dropped a bombshell in announcing that the United States would not run for a seat on the new council, "the first time in more than half a century that the United States has chosen not to pursue membership in the United Nations' principal rights organization."[97] Bolton's rationale—"our leverage in terms of the performance of the new council is greater by the U.S. not running"—was implausible given that the first council would set the procedures and policies for future sessions.

It may be, as most commentators assume, that the real reason was that the United States feared it would not be elected to the Human Rights Council.[98] But it also may signal a decisive shift toward U.S. withdrawal from, and perhaps ultimately rejection of, the UN human rights project. Current U.S. foreign policy has already necessitated open rejection of fundamental human rights and humanitarian law principles. This trend is likely to continue unless the U.S. government backs away from its strategy of seeking unipolar global hegemony and extending direct military control throughout the Middle East and Central Asia.

At the first election of the new council, on 10 May 2006, China, Russia, Cuba, Pakistan, and Saudi Arabia all won seats despite their dubious human rights records.[99] This was widely seen as defiance of U.S. pressure to exclude such countries.[100] Political and editorial opinion in the United States was negative.[101] Cuba, on the other hand, declared "a victory against the U.S. and against those who did not want Cuba to be elected. . . . The U.S. and some Western countries make judgments about human rights but they don't look at their own human rights records."[102]

How might the United States react if countries such as China and Cuba seek to subject U.S. policies, for example the unlawful detentions at Guantanamo Bay, to scrutiny by the Human Rights Council? Under such a scenario, the United States could choose to make a clean break with a UN human rights system already denounced as corrupt and unable to reform itself. The impact on human rights more broadly would be enormous, potentially spelling the demise of the current paradigm or, conversely, freeing it from state domination to develop into a more popular constituency-based expression of universal justice.

The Final Word?

The creation of a human rights system founded upon the equal and inalienable rights of each and every human person (both as individuals and members of recognized groups) carried within it the potential to transform the world. People have always yearned for freedom, security, and social justice; the modern human rights system was the first to assert these values as the birthright of everyone everywhere. When the UN was first established amid a groundswell of public enthusiasm and interstate cooperation, it appeared that an enforceable system of global morality was within reach. Hersch Lauterpacht, one of the most renowned legal minds of the time, expressed a common hope that the time had finally come for all states to accept legal obligations to uphold the rights of humanity. He wrote in 1943:

> The sovereign national State, whether or not it be the permanent form of the political organization of man, is not an end unto itself, but the trustee of the welfare and the final purpose of man. In that scheme of things it would be for the international society to ensure the fulfillment of that trust through a fundamental enactment—an International Bill of the Rights of Man—conceived not as a declaration of principles, but as part of positive law, and part of the constitutional law both of States and of the society of States at large.[103]

From the outset, human rights ideas have confronted the age-old dilemma of how to protect ethical principles in a world characterized by hierarchies and power imbalances both between and within states. Genuine realization of human rights beyond mere formal recognition would have required substantial transformation not only in the international system but within the domestic orders of every nation. Instead, human rights were built on a foundation of territorial nationalism and the supremacy of domestic jurisdiction. Ostensibly based on the four pillars of peace, security, development, and human rights, the UN structure in fact protected state sovereignty and enabled the victorious powers to dominate the organization. As one observer commented, "The League of Nations and the United Nations were based on the meaningless Austinian fiction—the sovereign equality of all states—though the quantum of sovereign power in the present day world has become a 'function' of military resources."[104]

Viewed through the lens of gross violations by states and nonstate actors of every stripe, it is tempting to conclude that the human rights idea has failed. In this perspective, the twin forces of globalization and the war on terror have merely exposed the flaws of a system that was bound, sooner or later, to crumble under the weight of internal contradictions. But the final balance sheet is not yet written. The rapid spread of human rights ideas, even if they lack effective means for enforcement, has changed the discourse of international relations and succeeded in creating a new consciousness and awareness throughout the world. While the proliferation of human rights instruments and institutions have not, in themselves, made a significant mark on most people's daily experience, the gap in enforcement has been taken up by civil society organizations and, more cautiously, by social movements representing mass constituencies. If we consider the extent to which human rights have "colonized" the globe in the span of just sixty years, it would be too early to discount the possibility that this ethical consensus, as close to a universal ideology as yet exists, might be reformulated to better reflect the cultural strengths and diversity of our interconnected planet.

Through this book, we are adding our voices to many others that call for a more critical examination of the historical origins and impact of human rights at the United Nations—not to hasten their demise but to consider whether they can be reestablished on firmer footing in the future. In this way, we may still succeed in producing human rights principles, laws, and institutions capable of realizing people's hopes and expectations for a better life.

Notes

Series Editors' Foreword

1. Craig N. Murphy, *The United Nations Development Programme: A Better Way?* (Oxford: Oxford University Press, 2006).

2. D. John Shaw, *UN World Food Programme and the Development of Food Aid* (New York: Palgrave, 2001).

3. Maggie Black, *The Children and the Nations* (New York: UNICEF, 1986); and *Children First: The Story of UNICEF* (Oxford: Oxford University Press, 1996).

4. Thomas G. Weiss and Sam Daws, eds., *Oxford Handbook on the United Nations* (Oxford: Oxford University Press, 2007).

5. Louis Emmerij, Richard Jolly, and Thomas G. Weiss, *Ahead of the Curve? UN Ideas and Global Challenges* (Bloomington: Indiana University Press, 2001), xi.

Preface

1. The organization is called the Center for Economic and Social Rights. For information on its programs and projects, see http://www.cesr.org.

2. A number of reports and articles on the humanitarian impact of sanctions may be noted: Joy Gordon, "When Intent Makes All the Difference in the World: Economic Sanctions on Iraq and the Accusation of Genocide," *Yale Human Rights and Development Law Journal* 5 (January 2002): 57; H. C. Von Sponeck and C. N Amorim, *A Different Kind of War: The UN Sanctions Regime in Iraq* (Oxford: Berghahn Books, 2006); Geoffrey L. Simons, *The Scourging of Iraq: Sanctions, Law, and Natural Justice* (New York: St. Martin's Press, 1996); "When Sanctions Don't Work," *Economist* 355, no. 8165 (8–14 April 2000): 23–25; "Iraq Sanctions: Humanitarian Implications and Options for the Future," *Global Policy Forum* (6 August 2002), available online at www.globalpolicy .org/security/sanction/iraq1/2002/paper.htm; and David Rieff, "Were Sanctions Right?" *New York Times,* 27 July 2003.

3. These missions took place in March and August 1991, August 1996, and January–February 2003. The reports and findings cited in this section are available at www .cesr.org.

4. Sarah participated in three missions with the United Nations Food and Agriculture Organization in 1993, 1995, and 1997.

5. See Mohamed M. Ali, John C. Blacker, and Gareth Jones, "Annual Mortality Rates

and Excess Deaths of Children under Five in Iraq 1991–98," *Population Studies* 57, no. 2 (2003): 217–226; Mohamed M. Ali and Iqbal H. Shah, "Sanctions and Childhood Mortality in Iraq," *The Lancet* 355, no. 9218 (27 May 2000): 1851–1857.

6. Lesley Stahl, "Punishing Saddam," transcript, *60 Minutes,* broadcast of 12 May 1996.

7. Center for Economic and Social Rights, "Unsanctioned Suffering: A Human Rights Assessment of United Nations Sanctions on Iraq," May 1996, available online at http://cesr.org/node/393.

8. Out of ninety-six reports on Iraq since 1993 listed in Amnesty International's Web site library archive, not one discusses the human rights implications of sanctions. (See http://web.amnesty.org/library/eng-irq/reports&start=1.) Similarly, Amnesty USA does not list any such reports on its Web site. (See http://www.amnestyusa.org/countries/iraq/reports.do?page=1). The Human Rights Watch Web site lists only two letters, both from 2000, that refer to the impact of sanctions. These letters are phrased in mild terms, referring to humanitarian principles rather than human rights violations. A letter from Human Rights Watch to Iraqi ambassador Ouane dated 20 September 2000 noted that "Human Rights Watch strongly urges the Council once again to address in a more satisfactory way the humanitarian consequences of the sanctions it has authorized in Iraq, and to take into account the most basic humanitarian principles when applying coercive measures that affect the well-being of the civilian population." (See http://www.hrw.org/press/2000/09/ouaneltr.htm).

9. For recent reports on the crisis in Iraq, see Human Rights Watch, "Reverse Decision to Execute Saddam: Appeals Chamber Should Review Flawed Verdict," *Human Rights News,* 26 December 2006, http://hrw.org/doc/?t=mideast&c=iraq; Human Rights Watch, "Getting Away with Torture? Command Responsibility for the U.S. Abuse of Detainees," *Human Rights Watch Report,* 25 April 2005, available online at http://www.hrw.org/reports/2005/us0405/; International Crisis Group, "Afghanistan's Endangered Compact," International Crisis Group Policy Briefing 59, 27 January 2007, available at http://www.crisisgroup.org/library/documents/asia/south_asia/b59_afghanistans_endangered_compact.pdf; International Crisis Group, "Afghanistan: The Problem of Pashtun Alienation," *Asia Report* 62 (5 August 2003), available online at http://www.crisisgroup.org/home/index.cfm?id=1266&l=1.

10. Ahmed Rashid, *Taliban: Militant Islam, Oil, and Fundamentalism in Central Asia* (New Haven, Conn.: Yale Nota Bene, 2001); Nafeez M. Ahmed, *The War on Truth: 9/11, Disinformation, and the Anatomy of Terrorism* (Northampton, Mass.: Olive Branch Press, 2005).

11. Center for Economic and Social Rights, *Human Rights and Reconstruction in Afghanistan* (Brooklyn, N.Y.: Center for Economic and Social Rights, 2002), 2, available online at http://cesr.org/node/499.

12. *Human Rights and Reconstruction in Afghanistan,* 3.

13. Roger Normand, "Separate and Unequal: Trade and Human Rights Regimes," January 2000, background paper for UNDP-HDR, *Human Development Report: Human Rights and Human Development* (New York: Oxford University Press, 2000).

Introduction

1. "General Assembly Establishes New Human Rights Council by Vote of 170 in Favor to 4 Against, with 3 Abstentions," General Assembly document GA/10449, 15 March 2006, available online at www.un.org/News/Press/docs/2006/ga10449.doc.htm.

2. The NAM currently has 110 members, constituting a majority of the UN's 192 member states. Yet its influence, like that of the General Assembly as a whole, is largely limited to making rhetorical pronouncements. This raises questions about the meaning of global democracy in an anti-democratic and hierarchical organization such as the UN. It is an irony that the minority of rich states that are widely recognized to adhere most closely to democratic principles of governance at the domestic level insist on wielding disproportionate global power through the Security Council and control over the Bretton Woods institutions.

3. On import of "soft power," see Joseph Nye, *The Paradox of American Power: Why the World's Only Superpower Can't Go It Alone* (New York: Oxford University Press, 2002).

4. The report "The Human Rights Record of the United States in 2005" was released by The Information Office of the State Council of the People's Republic of China on 9 March 2006. It is available online at news.xinhuanet.com/english/2006-03/09/content_4279287.htm.

5. Thalif Deen, "UN Defies West in Vote for Human Rights Council," *Inter Press Service,* 9 May 2006.

6. For obvious reasons, countries such as China and the United States do not face the same possibility of military pressure as countries such as Cuba and Iran do, regardless of the nature of alleged violations.

7. The commission was formed under Article 68 of the UN Charter, which required ECOSOC to "set up commissions . . . for the promotion of human rights."

8. Despite having unsuccessfully pushed for stricter membership criteria, the major international NGOs have cautiously welcomed the council as an improvement over the commission. See Human Rights Watch, "U.N.: New Council Must Champion Fight for Rights," *Human Rights News*, 10 May 2006, available online at http://hrw.org/english/docs/2006/05/10/global13343.htm. See also Amnesty International, "UN Human Rights Council: The Promise of a New Beginning," 19 June 2006, available online at web.amnesty .org/library/Index/ENGIOR400232006.

9. There are, of course, exceptions, individuals who take a more critical view. See, for example, Makau Mutua, *Human Rights: A Political and Cultural Critique* (Philadelphia: University of Pennsylvania Press 2002).

10. Walt Whitman, *Leaves of Grass* (Philadelphia, Pa.: David McKay, 1900).

11. Joseph Campbell, *The Hero with a Thousand Faces* (Princeton, N.J.: Princeton University Press, 1972).

12. Louis Henkin, *The Age of Rights* (New York: Columbia University Press, 1990).

13. R. Steel, "Motherhood, Apple Pie and Human Rights," *The New Republic,* 4 June 1977, 14.

14. See UNDP, *Human Development Report 2005: International Cooperation at a Crossroads: Aid, Trade and Security in an Unequal World* (Oxford: Oxford University Press, 2005).

15. Mark Mazower, "The Strange Triumph of Human Rights, 1933–1950," *The Historical Journal* 47, no. 2 (2004): 380.

16. These are the opening words of *International Legal Protections for Human Rights* (Washington, D.C.: World Peace Through Law Center, 1977), 17, quoted in Elaine Pagels, "Human Rights: Legitimizing a Recent Concept," *Annals of the American Academy of Political and Social Science* 442 (March 1979): 58.

17. Paul Gordon Lauren, *The Evolution of International Human Rights: Visions Seen* (Philadelphia: University of Pennsylvania Press, 1998): 28–33.

18. See Pagels, "Human Rights: Legitimizing a Recent Concept."

19. Lauren, *The Evolution of International Human Rights*, 5–7.

20. Louis Henkin, "Judaism and Human Rights," *Judaism: A Quarterly Review of Jewish Life and Thought* 25, no. 4 (1976): 436–437.

21. Lauren, *The Evolution of International Human Rights*, 10.

22. Pagels, "Human Rights: Legitimizing a Recent Concept," 59.

23. Ibid., 58.

24. Lauren, *The Evolution of International Human Rights*, 14.

25. Locke further argued that all humans possess "a title to perfect freedom and uncontrolled enjoyment of all the rights and privileges of the law of nature and have by nature a power not only to preserve his property—that is his life, liberty and estate—against the injuries and attempts of other men, but to judge and punish the breaches of that law in others"; quoted in Lauren, *The Evolution of International Human Rights*, 15.

26. Peter C. Myers, "Between Divine and Human Sovereignty: The State of Nature and the Basis of Locke's Political Thought," *Polity* 27, no. 4 (1995): 633–636.

27. Louis Henkin, *Human Rights* (New York: Foundation Press, 1999), 35–36.

28. Thomas Paine, "The Rights of Man," quoted in ibid., 36.

29. "A constitution is a thing antecedent to a government and a government is only the creature of a constitution. The constitution of a country is not the act of its government but of the people constituting a government"; ibid., 36.

30. Paul Marshall, "Two Types of Rights," *Canadian Journal of Political Science* 25, no. 4 (December 1992): 670.

31. Burke believed that this fiction would "inspire false ideas and vain expectations in men destined to travel in the obscure walk of laborious life." Lauren, *The Evolution of International Human Rights*, 21–22.

32. Cited in Henkin, *Human Rights*, 50–52.

33. Lauren, *The Evolution of International Human Rights*, 22.

34. Marx most famously elaborated his critique of liberal rights in an essay titled "On the Jewish Question," cited in Henkin, *Human Rights*, 54–59. For a general discussion of Marxism and rights, see Kenneth Baynes, "Rights as Critique and the Critique of Rights: Karl Marx, Wendy Brown, and the Social Function of Rights," *Political Theory* 28, no. 2 (August 2000): 451–468.

35. Abdullah An-Naʿim, ed., *Human Rights and Cross Cultural Perspectives: A Quest for Consensus* (Philadelphia: University of Pennsylvania Press, 1992); Makau Mutua, *Human Rights: A Political and Cultural Critique* (Philadelphia: University of Pennsylvania Press, 2002).

36. This conception of three UNs has been discussed in other volumes of the United Nations Intellectual History Project. See, for example, Louis Emmerij, Richard Jolly, and Thomas G. Weiss, *Ahead of the Curve? UN Ideas and Global Challenges* (Bloomington: Indiana University Press, 2001); and Thomas G. Weiss, Tatiana Carayannis, Louis Emmerij, and Richard Jolly, *UN Voices: The Struggle for Development and Social Justice* (Bloomington: Indiana University Press, 2005).

37. George Orwell, *Nineteen Eighty-Four* (London: Penguin, 1989).

38. See Donald H. Rumsfeld, "War in the Information Age," *Los Angeles Times,* 23 February 2006.

39. James Reston, "The Critic Turns Actor," *Foreign Affairs* (October 1945): 50.

40. This refers to Howard Zinn's populist treatment of American history, *A People's History of the United States* (New York: Harper & Row Publishers, 1980). For books that emphasize the contribution of popular struggles in the development of human rights, see Micheline Ishay, *History of Human Rights: From Ancient Times to the Globalization Era* (Berkeley: University of California Press, 2004); Lauren, *The Evolution of International Human Rights*; and William Korey, *NGOs and the Universal Declaration of Human Rights* (New York: St. Martins Press, 1998).

41. Philip Alston, "Critical Appraisal of the U.N. Human Rights Regime," in *The United Nations and Human Rights: A Critical Appraisal* (New York: Oxford University Press, 1992): 1–22, esp. 5.

Part 1. Human Rights Foundations in the First Half of the Twentieth Century

1. One historian who researched the influence and prevalence of human rights ideas in the early twentieth century was surprised by the paucity of references to human rights during this period even among international law circles. See Jan H. Burgers, "The Road to San Francisco: The Revival of the Human Rights Idea in the Twentieth Century," *Human Rights Quarterly* 14, no. 4 (November 1992): 447–477.

2. While there is broad scholarly agreement that human rights derived, philosophically and legally, from European, especially Anglo-American, political and legal traditions of the seventeenth and eighteenth centuries, there are different views about the earlier origins of the human rights idea in religious and moral systems. Many commentators trace human rights to the earliest ethical traditions of humanity, including religious ideas. See Misheline R. Ishay, *A History of Human Rights: From Ancient Times to the Globalization Era* (Berkeley: University of California Press, 2004), 15–69; Paul Gordon Lauren, *The Evolution of International Human Rights: Visions Seen* (Philadelphia: University of Pennsylvania Press, 1998), 4–36; Burns Weston, "Human Rights," *Human Rights Quarterly* 6, no. 3 (August 1984): 258–262. Others disagree, noting that human rights is a modern

concept based on individual rights to freedom from oppression by the organized power of church and state, whereas previous ethical and religious traditions generally emphasized the divine rights of the sovereign and the duties individuals owed to God and state rather than entitlements held by virtue of one's humanity. See Elaine Pagels, "Human Rights: Legitimizing a Recent Concept," *Annals of the American Academy of Political Science* 442 (March 1979): 57–62.

3. The classic counterfactual scenario is victory by Germany in World War II and the extraordinary ideological as well as geopolitical transformation this would have entailed for Europe and the rest of the world. Such a scenario is not at all far-fetched; many historians believe that Hitler's obsession with race caused him to invade the Soviet Union prematurely, against the advice of his professional military staff, and later to divert scarce military resources to the war of extermination against Jews, gypsies, and homosexuals. As Eric Hobsbawm notes, after sweeping through Western Europe and isolating Great Britain, "the war was revived by Hitler's invasion of the USSR on 22 June 1941, the decisive date in the Second World War; an invasion so senseless that Stalin simply would not believe that Hitler could contemplate it. But for Hitler the conquest of a vast eastern land-empire, rich in resources and slave labour, was the logical next step. . . . [Another] mystery is why Hitler, already fully stretched in Russia, gratuitously declared war on the U.S.A., thus giving Roosevelt's government the chance to enter the war on the British side without meeting overwhelming political resistance at home"; Eric Hobsbawm, *The Age of Extremes: A History of the World, 1914–1991* (New York: Random House, 1994), 39, 41.

4. Francis Fukuyama's famous essay celebrating the "end of history" after the fall of the Soviet Union is the best known, but by no means only, example of this kind of shortsighted, triumphalist, and ahistorical thinking. See Francis Fukuyama, "The End of History," *The National Interest* (Summer 1989): 3–18. As one historian of Europe notes, "What all ideologies have in common is that they like to present their own utopia as an End to History—whether in the form of universal communism, global democracy or a Thousand Year Reich. They share what Ignazio Silone once described as 'the widespread virtue that identifies History as the winning side'"; Mark Mazower, *Dark Continent: Europe's Twentieth Century* (New York: Alfred Knopf, 1999).

5. Compare Samuel P. Huntington, *The Third Wave, Democratization in the Late Twentieth Century* (Norman: University of Oklahoma Press, 1991), which argues that the present age is characterized by an irresistible wave of democratization, with Samuel P. Huntington, "The Clash of Civilizations?" *Foreign Affairs* 72, no. 3 (1993): 22–49, which predicts an inevitable global conflict between western democracy and Islamic fundamentalism.

6. President Bush, Vice-President Cheney, Secretary of Defense Rumsfeld, and Secretary of State Rice all made public declarations warning the United States, and the world, to prepare for a long, drawn-out war against the "enemies of freedom." The Pentagon's new counterterrorism strategy document asserts that success in this war will be achieved only when "violent extremist ideology and terrorist attacks . . . [are] eliminated as a threat to the way of life of free and open societies"; Thom Shanker, "The Pentagon Hones Its Strategy on Terror," *New York Times*, 5 February 2006.

7. For a comprehensive and illuminating assessment of the weakness of liberal ideology relative to communism and fascism during this period, see Mazower, *Dark Continent*, 3–40, 104–181. He writes, "Today it is hard to see the inter-war experiment with democracy for the novelty that it was. . . . Though we may like to think democracy's victory in the Cold War proves its deep roots in European soil, history tells us otherwise. Triumphant in 1918, it was virtually extinct twenty years on" (5).

8. Military, political, and economic factors were, of course, predominant in the breakup of old empires and emergence of new states after World War I. However, President Wilson's rhetoric also played a role, to the dismay of European powers and his own State Department. See Margaret Macmillan, *Paris 1919: Six Months that Changed the World* (New York: Random House, 2003), 3–17.

9. There has been an ongoing debate in historiography and the social sciences, at least since the writings of Karl Marx, on the relative roles of ideas and material factors in shaping human history. We do not intend to resolve that debate, but based on our reading of the history of human rights, we take the view that the two forces are mutually reinforcing and interdependent: ideas have a concrete impact in shaping the material environment, just as the material environment helps shapes consciousness itself.

10. Cordell Hull, quoted in Lauren, *The Evolution of International Human Rights*, 165.

1. First Expressions of Human Rights Ideas

1. Prominent international jurist Hersch Lauterpacht maintained that "we shall utterly fail to understand the true character of the law of war unless we are to realize that its purpose is almost entirely humanitarian in the literal sense of the word"; Hersch Lauterpacht, "The Problem of the Revision of the Law of War," *British Year Book of International Law* 360 (1952): 363–364.

2. Josef L. Kunz, "The Laws of War," *American Journal of International Law* 50, no. 2 (1956): 313, 322.

3. French field marshall Foch, quoted in Jean Pictet, *Development and Principles of International Humanitarian Law* (Dordrecht: M. Nijhoff Publishers, 1982), 24.

4. The nineteenth century saw the end of *kreigsspeil,* or "play war," as von Clausewitz derisively termed the "dynamistic jousting" between small professional armies that occurred between 1648 and 1792. Quoted in William V. O'Brien, "The Meaning of Military Necessity in International Law," *World Polity* 1 (1957): 109, 132. In modern wars, enormous conscript armies replaced the small ranks of professionals and casualty rates skyrocketed for noncombatants. Those who stayed home were no longer safe from war's destructive reach. Quincy Wright, *A Study of War,* 2nd ed. (Chicago: University of Chicago Press, 1965), 291–328.

5. While the Peace of Westphalia established the principle of equal rights for Catholics and Protestants in Germany, such tolerance did not extended to the non-Christian world. Over the next several centuries, Europe used the issue of religious rights to engage in "humanitarian" military interventions, especially in the Ottoman empire and China, ostensibly to protect the rights of Christian minorities but invariably achieving imperialist objectives. One historian of human rights notes, with understatement, that under this

principle, "numerous military operations and diplomatic representations" were undertaken, "not all with the purest of intentions"; Burns H. Weston, "Human Rights," *Human Rights Quarterly* 6, no. 3 (August 1984): 257–283.

6. See Andre Durand, *From Sarajevo to Hiroshima: History of the International Committee of the Red Cross* (Geneva: Henri Dunant Institute, 1984); John Hutchinson, *Champions of Charity: War and the Rise of the Red Cross* (Boulder, Colo.: Westview Press, 1996).

7. The research for this section is largely derived from Chris Jochnick and Roger Normand, "The Legitimation of Violence: A Critical History of the Laws of War," *Harvard International Law Journal* 35, no 1. (1994): 49.

8. Frederick W. Holls, *Peace Conference at the Hague and Its Bearings on International Law and Policy* (New York: Macmillan, 1900), 8–10; James B. Scott, ed., *The Proceedings of the Hague Peace Conferences* (New York: Oxford University Press, 1920), 14–15. Several months later, Russia's foreign minister distributed another letter detailing a proposed agenda for the conference. The letter divided the agenda into eight basic proposals, including freezing land and sea forces at existing levels, declaring a moratorium on weapons development, restricting the use of current means and methods of warfare, and establishing an international court of arbitration to assist in settling disputes. These proposals were unprecedented insofar as they sought international agreement to restrict weapons of vital importance. See James B. Scott, *The Hague Peace Conferences of 1899 and 1907* (Baltimore, Md.: Johns Hopkins Press, 1909), 15; Joseph Hodges Choate, *The Two Hague Conferences,* 2nd ed. (Princeton, N.J.: Princeton University Press, 1920), 9.

9. See Calvin DeArmond Davis, *The United States and the First Hague Peace Conference* (Ithaca, N.Y.: Cornell University Press, 1962), 54–63; G. H. Perris, ed., *A History of the Peace Conference at The Hague* (London: International Arbitration Association, 1899).

10. Perris, *A History of the Peace Conference at The Hague.*

11. For a survey of press coverage of the announcement of the Hague conference, see William Hull, *The Two Hague Conferences and Their Contributions to International Law* (New York: Garland Publishing, 1972), 21–27; Andrew Dickson White, *The Autobiography of Andrew Dickson White* (New York: Century, 1906), 251–252.

12. See Emile J. Dillon, *The Eclipse of Russia* (New York: George H. Doran Company, 1918), 276–278; Thomas K. Ford, "The Genesis of the First Hague Peace Conference," *Political Science Quarterly* 51 (September 1936): 354–364.

13. Davis, *The United States and the First Hague Peace Conference,* 46.

14. Paul Cambon, *Correspondence 1870–1914* (Paris: Bernard Grasset, 1946), 438.

15. Quoted in Prince von Bülow, *The Memoirs of Prince von Bülow* (Boston: Little Brown and Co., 1931), 321.

16. Statement by Japanese prime minister in *British Documents on the Origins of the War, 1898–1914* (London: C. P. Gooch & Howard Temperly, 1926), 221–222.

17. Austria-Hungary, Belgium, Bulgaria, China, Denmark, France, Germany, Great Britain, Greece, Italy, Japan, Luxemburg, Mexico, Montenegro, Netherlands, the Ottoman empire, Persia, Portugal, Romania, Russia, Serbia, Siam, Spain, Sweden and Norway, Switzerland, and the United States sent government representatives.

18. See Perris, *A History of the Peace Conference at the Hague,* 6–7; Geoffrey Best,

Humanity in Warfare: The Modern History of the International Law of Armed Conflict (London: Methuen, 1983), 139.

19. Jochnick and Normand, "The Legitimation of Violence."

20. Andrew D. White, *The First Hague Conference* (Boston: World Peace Foundation, 1912), 63.

21. Davis, *The United States and the First Hague Peace Conference,* 88.

22. White, *The Autobiography of Andrew D. White,* 256. Ambassador White reports encountering tremendous doubt among the European diplomatic corps about Russia's motives. He noted that "among all these delegates acquainted with public men and measures in Europe, there is considerable distrust of the intentions of Russia; and, naturally, the weakness of the Russian Emperor is well understood, though all are reticent regarding it"; White, *The First Hague Conference,* 8.

23. See U.S. Department of State, "Instructions to the American Delegates to the Hague Conference of 1899," reprinted in Scott, *The Hague Peace Conferences of 1899 and 1907,* 6–7; Michael Howard, "Temperamenta Belli: Can War Be Controlled?" in *Restraints on War: Studies in the Limitation of Armed Conflict,* ed. Michael Howard (New York: Oxford University Press, 1979), 60–61.

24. One survey of the negotiations concludes that they were "characterized by the self-interested maneuverings of large and small powers intent on retaining those means and methods of warfare in which they were superior and limiting those in which they were inferior"; Jochnick and Normand, "The Legitimation of Violence," 77.

25. See Morton W. Royse, *Aerial Bombardment and the International Regulation of Warfare* (New York: H. Vinal, 1928), 7–9. For records of these debates, see Scott, *The Proceedings of the Hague Peace Conferences,* 367–369.

26. Colonel von Schwarzhoff, quoted in Scott, *The Proceedings of the Hague Peace Conferences,* 308–309. Von Schwarzhoff also rejected limitations on weapons development, arguing that "we cannot tie our hands in advance for fear of neglecting more humanitarian methods which may be invented in the future"; quoted in Frits Kalshoven, *Constraints on the Waging of War* (Dordrecht: Martinus Nijhoff Publishers, 1987), 372.

27. See Jochnick and Normand, "The Legitimation of Violence," 72–73. For a summary of the debate on these bans, see Scott, *The Proceedings of the Hague Peace Conferences,* 365–367.

28. Captain Mahan, the chief U.S. military delegate, dismissed the humanitarian motives of his opponents, arguing that new weapons were always denounced as barbaric until proven militarily useful, at which point all pretense was dropped and they quickly entered the arsenals of all nations. He explained, "The reproach of perfidy and cruelty, addressed against these supposed [gas] shells, was equally uttered formerly against firearms and torpedoes, both of which are now employed without scruple"; quoted in Scott, *The Hague Peace Conferences of 1899 and 1907,* 37.

29. Explaining UK opposition to the ban, Sir John Ardagh reminded his colleagues that ordinary bullets did not work against "savages": "In civilized war a soldier penetrated by a small projectile is wounded, withdraws to the ambulance, and does not advance any further. It is very different with a savage. Even though pierced two or three times, he does not cease to march forward, does not call upon the hospital attendees, but continues on,

and before anyone has time to explain to him that he is flagrantly violating the decision of the Hague Conference, he cuts off your head"; quoted in Scott, *The Proceedings of the Hague Peace Conferences,* 343.

30. This marked a continuation of the trend that started with the 1864 Geneva Convention for the Amelioration of the Condition of the Wounded in Armies in the Field, the first multilateral treaty in history to offer explicit protections for individuals during war.

31. "Convention with Respect to the Laws and Customs of War on Land, July 29, 1899," Article 22, available online at http://www.yale.edu/lawweb/avalon/lawofwar/hague02 .htm.

32. Ibid., Article 23.

33. Ibid., Preamble.

34. See Johannes Philippus Suijling, *The Hague Peace Conferences of 1899 and 1907: The Results Obtained, the Principles Applied and the Influences Felt* (The Hague: M. Nijhoff, 1910), 13–14; Jochnick and Normand, "The Legitimation of Violence" 76–77.

35. White, *Autobiography of Andrew D. White,* 100. Another U.S. delegate, Frederick Holls, remarked that "it is a matter of history that immediately after the adjournment of the Conference, this alleged failure to agree, even upon a limitation of present armaments, was made the text of numerous unfavorable comments upon the Conference as a whole"; Holls, *Peace Conference at the Hague,* 14.

36. Quoted in Choate, *The Two Hague Conferences,* 56.

37. See Royse, *Aerial Bombardment and the International Regulation of Warfare,* 49–55.

38. See Merze Tate, *The Disarmament Illusion: The Movement for a Limitation of Armaments to 1907* (New York: Macmillan Company, 1942), 324–327.

39. Royse, *Aerial Bombardment and the International Regulation of Warfare,* 131–132.

40. But if viewed as the first step in a long journey toward human rights, it can be argued that the Hague conferences contributed to developing principles of international justice. The laws of war would be revisited, first after World War II, resulting in the adoption of the 1949 Geneva Conventions, and again after the wars of decolonization, resulting in the Additional Protocols of 1977. While these agreements can also be subject to critical historical analysis, they represent a progression in lawful restrictions on war.

41. The absence of an "international society" is seen as one of the fundamental obstacles to the development of international organization, especially global morality that presupposes the existence of universal values across nations and cultures. According to Hedley Bull's classic definition, an international society is said to "exist when a group of states, conscious of certain common interest and common values, form a society in the sense that they conceive themselves to be bound by a common set of rules in their relation to one another"; Hedley Bull, *The Anarchical Society: A Study of Order in World Politics* (New York: Columbia University Press, 1977), 13.

42. See Martin Gilbert, *History of the Twentieth Century,* concise ed. (New York: William Morrow, 2001), 53–80.

43. For a survey of the social, political, and economic conditions that precipitated World War I, see Wright, *A Study of War,* 300–303, 338–341, 725–727.

44. See Elbridge Colby, "Laws of Aerial Warfare," *Minnesota Law Review* 10 (1926): 207–227.

45. Air power enabled belligerents to attack an enemy's weaponry at the source of manufacture before it could be deployed in battle. One military historian concluded: "By no process of reasoning could a belligerent be persuaded that the makers of armaments in his enemy's country were less his active enemies than the men who wore uniforms and opposed him in the field. They had been spared so far because they could not be got at and for no other reason"; James M. Spaight, *Air Power and War Rights* (New York: Longmans, Green, 1947), 43–44.

46. British officer quoted in James M. Spaight, *Air Power and the Cities* (New York: Longmans, Green, 1930), 117. Italian general Giulio Douhet, a leading proponent of attacks on morale, argued that "people who know they will be bombed again tomorrow, and see no end to their martyrdom, are bound to call for peace at length"; quoted in Stefan T. Possony, *Strategic Air Power: The Pattern of Dynamic Security* (Washington, D.C.: Infantry Journal Press, 1949), 146.

47. O'Brien, "The Meaning of Military Necessity in International Law," 134.

48. A. J. P. Taylor, *The History of World War I* (London: Octopus, 1974); Mazower, *Dark Continent,* ix.

49. The Austro-Hungarian, German-Hohenzollern, and Russian empires were divided into Albania, Austria, Bulgaria, Czechoslovakia, Estonia, Finland, Germany, Greece, Hungary, Latvia, Lithuania, Poland, Romania, and Yugoslavia. See Lucy P. Mair, *The Protection of Minorities: The Working and Scope of the Minority Treaties under the League of Nations* (London: Christophers, 1928); C. A. Macartney, *National States and National Minorities* (Oxford: Oxford University Press, 1934).

50. Hobsbawm, *The Age of Extremes,* 45.

51. Paul Gordon Lauren, *The Evolution of International Human Rights: Visions Seen* (Philadelphia: University of Pennsylvania Press, 1998), 96.

52. Arthur Marwick, *Women at War, 1914–1918* (London: Fontana, 1977).

53. Woman suffrage movements scored a rapid strong of successes during these years. Women won the right to vote in Denmark and Iceland in 1915; in Russia in 1917; in England, Ireland, and Australia in 1918; and in the United States in 1919; Lauren, *The Evolution of International Human Rights,* 88.

54. Woodrow Wilson uttered his famous phrase "the world must be made safe for democracy" in an address to Congress on 2 April 1917, after several U.S. ships had been sunk by German submarines. Four days later, the United States declared war against Germany; Gilbert, *History of the Twentieth Century,* 98.

55. See Arno J. Mayer, "Post-War Nationalisms 1918–1919," *Past and Present* 34 (July 1966): 114–126.

56. The recruitment of these soldiers would come back to haunt the imperialist powers. "This extensive participation of non whites and non-westerners in the combat of World War I proved to be of extraordinary importance in the subsequent development of African and Asian nationalisms and visions of human rights, including that of self-determination. It helped destroy the myth of 'superior' and 'invincible' whites, accelerated discussions about the meaning of rights beyond national borders, struck blows that shook the existing

imperial system, and greatly politicized many of those who survived by heightening their collective sense of confidence and entitlement"; Mayer, "Post-War Nationalisms," 85.

57. W. E. B. Du Bois, "Close Ranks," *Crisis* (July 1918), quoted in W. E. B. Du Bois, *Dusk of Dawn* (New York: Harcourt Brace, 1940), 254.

58. Many returning soldiers spoke and wrote about how their wartime experiences heightened their bitterness about U.S. racism. One former soldier, Kelly Miller, chronicled these emotions in several books; see Kelly Miller, *An Appeal to Conscience* (1918; reprint, Miami: Mnemosyne, 1969); and Kelly Miller, *The World War for Human Rights* (1919; reprint, New York: Negro Universities Press, 1969). For an excellent account of the African American struggle for equality through human rights, see Carole Anderson, *Eyes Off the Prize: The United Nations and the African American Struggle for Human Rights, 1944–1955* (Cambridge: Cambridge University Press, 2003).

59. MacMillan, *Paris 1919,* 316.

60. F. C. Jones, *Extraterritoriality in Japan and the Diplomatic Relations Resulting in Its Abolition, 1835–1899* (New Haven, Conn.: Yale University Press, 1931).

61. Pekka Korhoren, "The Pacific Age in World History," *Journal of World History* 7, no. 1 (1996): 47–70.

62. W. E. B. DuBois, "Opinion," *Crisis* (May 1918): 7.

63. E. J. Dillon, *The Inside Story of the Peace Conference* (New York: Harper and Brothers, 1930), 5.

64. Harold Nicolson, *Peacemaking 1919* (New York: Grosset & Dunlop, 1965), 31–32.

65. Woodrow Wilson, quoted in Norman Graebner, "Human Rights and Foreign Policy," in *The Moral Imperatives of Human Rights,* ed. Kenneth Thompson (Lanham, Md.: University Press of America, 1980), 40.

66. Woodrow Wilson, 11 February 1918, quoted in *The Papers of Woodrow Wilson,* ed. Arthur Link (Princeton, N.J.: Princeton University Press, 1983), 46:321.

67. Wilson's secretary of state, Robert Lansing, counseled against open-ended promises concerning the right to self-determination, terming the concept "a loaded dynamite"; diary entries for 20 December and 30 December 1918, Reel 2, Robert Lansing Papers, Manuscripts Division, Library of Congress, Washington, D.C.

68. See Arno Mayer, *Wilson v. Lenin* (New York: World, 1964).

69. V. I. Lenin, "Imperialism, The Highest Stage of Capitalism," in V. I. Lenin, *Collected Works of V. I. Lenin* (New York: International Publishers, 1945), 18:367.

70. Lauren notes, "Lenin's initial actions in this regard appeared to lend credibility to his words, for almost immediately on seizing power his government issued the Declaration of the Rights of the Peoples of Russia, abolishing all privileges and disabilities based on nationality or religion and granting all the right of self-determination"; Lauren, *The Evolution of International Human Rights,* 91.

71. Mazower, *Dark Continent,* 50. Mazower further notes, "In the Ukraine, for instance, 97% of Ukrainian school children received instruction in their native language by 1929, something they could only have dreamed of before the revolution" (50).

72. See Woodrow Wilson, "The Fourteen Points," 8 January 1918, in *Essential Readings*

in World Politics, 2nd ed., ed. Karen Mingst and Jack Snyder (New York: W. W. Norton, 2004), 26.

73. Whatever may be one's personal views of diplomatic deception, it has been recommended as indispensable by a prominent line of theorists and practitioners, from Sun Tzu and Machiavelli to Leo Strauss and Henry Kissinger.

74. The story of European betrayal of promised Arab independence is discussed in MacMillan, *Paris 1919,* 381–409.

75. For an interesting summary of the domestic and international politics that led to Italy's walkout at Paris, see MacMillan, *Paris 1919,* 278–305.

76. Aldrovandi Marescotti, *Guerra Diplomatica,* 239, quoted in MacMillan, *Paris 1919,* 298.

77. The cosmopolitan character of Prince Saionji is discussed in MacMillan, *Paris 1919,* 306–310.

78. "Do to Others," *Japan Times,* 9 February 1919, quoted in Lauren, *The Evolution of International Human Rights,* 101.

79. MacMillan, *Paris 1919,* 319.

80. Ibid., 320.

81. Ibid.

82. Recueil des Actes de la Conference, "Secret, Partie 4, Passim," in *Commission de la Société des Nations* (Paris: Imprimerie Nationale, 1922), quoted in Lauren, *The Evolution of International Human Rights,* 101.

83. See "Peace Delegates Beat Japan's Proposal for Racial Equality," *Sacramento Union,* 13 April 1919, 1.

84. See William Tuttle, Jr., "Views of a Negro During the 'Red Summer' of 1919," *Journal of Negro History* 51 (July 1966): 209–218.

85. See Albert Memmi, *The Colonizer and the Colonized* (New York: Orion Press, 1965); Franz Fanon, *Black Skins, White Masks* (New York: Grove Press, 1967).

86. Many scientists drew on theories of race, notably the writings of Arthur Gobineau and his study *The Inequality of Human Races,* which provided pseudo-scientific justification for the subjugation of colored peoples across the world. Prominent scientists opposed these theories; see J. S. Huxley and A. C. Haddon, *We Europeans: A Survey of "Racial" Problems* (London/New York: 1936). For a survey of scientific attitudes about race during this time, see M. Kohn, *The Race Gallery: The Revival of Scientific Racism* (London: Jonathan Cape, 1995); and Elazar Barkan, *The Retreat of Scientific Racism: Changing Concepts of Race in Britain and the United States between the World Wars* (Cambridge: Cambridge University Press, 1992).

87. Mazower, *Dark Continent,* 100.

88. Support for the Japanese proposal for a racial equality clause "came from throughout the colonial world." Members of Asian, African, and Latin American nations "listened in horror as they heard many of the decision-makers at the Paris Peace Conference refer to them as 'primitive' and 'racially inferior' peoples, 'savage tribes,' and too 'backward' for self-government"; Lauren, *The Evolution of International Human Rights,* 101.

89. MacMillan, *Paris 1919,* 333–334.

90. Tse-Tsung Chow, quoted in *The May 4 Movement: Intellectual Revolution in Modern China* (Cambridge, Mass.: Harvard University Press, 1960), 93, quoted in MacMillan, *Paris 1919*, 340.

91. See Vera Schwartz, *The Chinese Enlightenment: Intellectuals and the Legacy of the May Fourth Movement of 1919* (Berkeley: University of California Press, 1986), 15–22.

92. After World War I, legislation was enacted across Europe limiting immigration based on the belief that new immigrants would dilute the superior racial stock. Later studies were conducted on the physical and physiological superiority as well as the psychological and mental advancement of the white race. See Helen V. McLean, "Racial Prejudice," *Phylon* 6, no. 2 (1945): 145–153; E. B. Reuter, "Racial Theory," *American Journal of Sociology* 50, no. 6 (1945): 452–461.

93. James Shotwell, a historian and member of the U.S. delegation to Paris who would later be involved with the United Nations, noted that the UK signed the treaty as the "British Empire" in recognition of its additional sovereignty among other sovereign states. James T. Shotwell, *At the Paris Peace Conference* (New York: MacMillan Company, 1937), 414–417.

94. Great Britain administered Iraq, Palestine and Transjordan, Tanganyika, British Togo and Cameroons, and Nauru; France administered Syria, Lebanon, French Togo, and Cameroons; Belgium administered Ruanda-Urundi; Australia administered New Guinea; New Zealand administered Western Samoa; South Africa administered South West Africa; and Japan administered the North Pacific Islands. By 1938 several treaties had been signed in support of emancipation of these territories, including Syria, Lebanon, and Iraq; Quincy Wright, "The Mandates in 1938," *American Journal of International Law* 33, no. 2 (1939): 342–349.

95. See Lucy P. Mair, *The Protection of Minorities: The Working and Scope of the Minority Treaties under the League of Nations* (London: Christophers, 1928); Macartney, *National States and National Minorities*.

96. See Richard Hovannisian, "Etiology and Sequelae of the Armenian Genocide," in *Genocide: Conceptual and Historical Dimensions*, ed. George Andreopolous (Philadelphia: University of Pennsylvania Press, 1994).

97. Mazower, *Dark Continent*, 57.

98. James W. Headlam-Morley, *A Memoir of the Paris Peace Conference, 1919* (London: Methuen, 1972), 112.

99. The ILO was set up under Part XIII of the Treaty of Versailles. For a contemporaneous account at the ILO's founding, see Sophy Sanger, "International Labour Organisation in the League of Nations," *Transactions of the Grotius Society* 5 (1919): 145–154.

100. Lauren, *The Evolution of International Human Rights*, 96.

101. Ibid.

102. Comments of Samuel Gompers and James Duncan in U.S. Department of State, *Foreign Relations of the United States: Paris Peace Conference, 1919* (Washington, D.C.: Government Printing Office, 1947), 11:71.

103. Details of the workings of the commission are drawn from Lauren, *The Evolution of International Human Rights*, 96–97.

104. The ILO depended initially on funding from the League of Nations, but it was seen as primarily an educational body, unlike the League, which was viewed as a political and diplomatic institution. The ILO gradually separated from the League and spent a portion of its funds to construct a building near Lake Geneva in Switzerland. See Edward M. Gilliard, "The International Labour Organization," *American Journal of Sociology* 36, no. 2 (September 1930): 233–240.

105. Its activities may have also been conceived from the beginning as a counterresponse to the ideology of communism; see Mark Mazower, "The Strange Triumph of Human Rights, 1933–1950," *Historical Journal* 47, no. 2 (2004): 379–398.

106. C. Wilfred Jenks, *Human Rights and International Labor Standards* (London: Stevens, 1960).

107. John Maynard Keynes, *Economic Consequences of the Peace* (London: Macmillan, 1919).

2. The Decline of Human Rights between World Wars

1. Our use of the terms "liberal rights" and "liberal states" refers primarily to formal rhetorical adherence to liberal principles, regardless of the practical failure to recognize, let alone enforce, the universality of these rights. In practice it is clear that the European powers maintained an illiberal and openly racist relationship to colonies and non-Europeans.

2. Hobsbawm remarks, "The U.S.A. almost immediately contracted out, and in a world no longer Euro-centred and Euro-determined, no settlement not underwritten by what was now a major world power could hold"; Eric Hobsbawm, *The Age of Extremes: A History of the World, 1914–1991* (New York: Random House, 1994), 34–35.

3. Margaret Macmillan, *Paris 1919: Six Months that Changed the World* (New York: Random House, 2003), 488–492.

4. Stephen C. Schlesinger, *Act of Creation: The Founding of the United Nations* (Boulder, Colo.: Westview Press, 2003), 22–25.

5. Senator James Reed, as quoted in Ralph Stone, *The Irreconcilables* (Lexington: University of Kentucky, 1970), 88.

6. Hobsbawm, *The Age of Extremes*, 35. When Germany and Russia did reappear, armed not only with mechanized forces but also with mass-based ideologies, they almost brought down the edifice of the liberal world order.

7. Mark Mazower, *Dark Continent: Europe's Twentieth Century* (New York: Alfred Knopf, 1999), 65–66.

8. John Basset Moore, U.S. representative and chair of the Commission of Jurists, stated that "the preservation of the distinction between combatants and non-combatants, especially as affected by aerial bombardment, looms larger in the public mind than any other question before the Commission"; John Bassett Moore, *International Law and Some Current Illusions* (New York: The Macmillan Company, 1924), 182. See also Morton W. Royse, *Aerial Bombardment and the International Regulation of Warfare* (New York: H. Vinal, 1928), 212n132.

9. C. P. Phillips, "Air Warfare and Law," *George Washington Law Review* 21 (1953): 395. This failure represents the flip side of what happened at the 1899 Hague conference. The 1923 conference ignored military considerations in favor of humanitarian principles and was subsequently rejected by states; the Hague conference ignored humanitarian principles in favor of military considerations and thus won the support of states. But in neither case were civilian interests protected.

10. W. Hays Parks, "Air War and the Laws of War," *Air Force Law Review* 32, no. 1 (1984): 35. According to Parks: "The 1923 Hague Air Rules suffered an ignominious death, doomed from the outset by language that established black-and-white situations in a combat environment permeated by shades of grey" (ibid).

11. Royal Institute of International Affairs, "The League of Nations and the Laws of War," *British Year Book of International Law* (London: Hodder and Stoughton, 1920), 1:116.

12. For an example of the suppression of nationalist movements in the interwar period, see Michael Cohen and Martin Kolinsky, eds., *Demise of the British Empire in the Middle East: Britain's Responses to Nationalist Movements 1943–1955* (London: Routledge, 1998). For a scathing critique of colonial repression, see Frantz Fanon, *Damnés de la Terre* (Paris: F. Maspero, 1961).

13. League of Nations, *Ten Years of World Co-operation* (Geneva: Secretariat of the League of Nations, 1930), 428 (Article 23) and 429–430 (Article 25). Establishing the mandates did almost nothing to change the military and administrative structures that governed the territories, despite the legal provisions that called for increased self-government and respect for a range of rights.

14. Many of these petitions concerned racial equality and protested overt legal and political persecution. When African American activists W. E. B. Du Bois and Marcus Garvey along with indigenous leaders from New Zealand traveled to Geneva to present their case in person, they were told that the rules of procedure did not allow for such direct forms of intervention. Regarding the flood of legal petitions, "influential members of the League insisted that such communications be regarded as simply reports rather than appeals, thus possessing no legal status, and that delegations of minority populations never be allowed to appear before the Council where only the accused state governments could be represented, and thus were not likely to call for punishment against themselves"; Paul Gordon Lauren, *The Evolution of International Human Rights: Visions Seen* (Philadelphia: University of Pennsylvania Press, 1998), 127.

15. This is the phrase infamously used by U.S. president George W. Bush to describe the UN Security Council after its hesitation to authorize unlawful force against Iraq in the lead-up to the U.S.-led invasion in March 2003. "Bush to UN: Be More Than a 'Debating Society,'" CNN, 22 October 2002. President Bush said: "The United Nations can't make its mind up. If Saddam won't disarm, we will lead a coalition to disarm him for the sake of peace. . . . [The United Nations] must resolve itself to be something more than the League of Nations, must resolve itself to be more than a debating society, must resolve itself to keep international peace"; "Remarks in Downingtown, Pennsylvania, October 22, 2002," *Weekly Compilation of Presidential Documents* 38, no. 43 (28 October 2002): 1820–1826, available online at http://www.gpo.gov/nara/nara003.html.

16. After the League's inability to condemn German and Italian intervention, the Spanish foreign minister complained of "a strange theory according to which the best method of serving the League was to remove from its purview all questions relating to peace, and the application of the Covenant"; quoted in Mazower, *Dark Continent*, 68.

17. George W. Baer, *Test Case: Italy, Ethiopia, and the League of Nations* (Palo Alto, Calif.: Hoover Institution Press, 1967), 296.

18. Mazower, *Dark Continent*, 55.

19. Ibid., 57.

20. See Vera M. Dean, ed., *New Governments in Europe: The Trend Towards Dictatorship* (New York: T. Nelson and Sons, 1934).

21. See Malbone W. Graham, Jr., *New Governments of Central Europe* (London: Henry Holt, 1924); Dean, *New Governments in Europe*.

22. Quoted in Mazower, *Dark Continent*, 6.

23. "Constitution of the German Federation," 11 August 1919 (Weimar Constitution), Section 1. Available online at http://web.jjay.cuny.edu/~jobrien/reference/ob13.html.

24. Quoted in Mazower, *Dark Continent*, 9.

25. Ibid., 25.

26. See Moritz J. Bonn, *The Crisis of European Democracy* (New Haven, Conn.: Yale University Press, 1925).

27. Mazower, *Dark Continent*, 23. The theories of Hugo Preuss and Hans Kelsen, two prominent European jurists, propelled the spread of legal positivism and formal constitutionalism. When the crisis of democratic governance hit Europe in the 1920s, they were blamed for naively introducing abstract legal principles into the hard-nosed job of politics. Kelsen, in particular, had disdained the compromises and blackmail of rough-and-tumble politics in favor of a constitutional legal theory "purified of all political ideologies" (ibid.).

28. Herbert Hoover, the future U.S. president, and Fridtjof Nansen, the famed Norwegian explorer, were two of the leading figures in postwar relief. Nansen described conditions in 1921 Russia in the following media dispatch: "Words cannot possibly describe the misery and horrors I have seen. People are dying in their houses and in the village streets in the pitiless cold of a Russian winter without food or fuel to feed them. Millions must unavoidably die"; quoted in Martin Gilbert, *History of the Twentieth Century*, concise ed. (New York: William Morrow, 2001), 133.

29. Richard Pipes, *Russia Under the Bolshevik Regime* (New York: Vintage Books, 1995); Gur Ofer, "Soviet Economic Growth: 1928–1985," *Journal of Economic Literature* 25, no. 4 (1987): 1767–1833.

30. Mazower, *Dark Continent*, 50.

31. "In the Ukraine, for instance, 97% of Ukrainian school children received instruction in their native language by 1929; something they could only have dreamed of before the revolution; Poland at the same time was busy shutting down its Ukrainian-language schools. . . . Only on the basis of this contrast can we understand why so many Ukrainians and Jews celebrated the downfall of the Polish republic and the arrival of the Red Army into Eastern Ukraine in the autumn of 1939"; Mazower, *Dark Continent*, 50–51.

32. Hobsbawm, *The Age of Extremes*, 56.

33. By the end of the Cold War, the life-and-death nature of the struggle had dissipated into a feeling of routine and stagnation. As Hobsbawm notes, "By the 1980s, this image of world politics as a duel between the forces of two rival social systems had as little relevance to international politics as the Crusades"; Hobsbawm, *The Age of Extremes,* 56.

34. Mazower, *Dark Continent,* 12–14.

35. Gilbert, *History of the Twentieth Century,* 113.

36. Mazower, *Dark Continent,* 4; Michael Mann, *Fascists* (Cambridge: Cambridge University Press, 2004).

37. Mazower, *Dark Continent,* xii.

38. Quoted in A. W. Brian Simpson, *Human Rights and the End of Empire: Britain and the Genesis of the European Convention* (Oxford: Oxford University Press, 2001), 227.

39. The figures in Eastern European states such as Poland, Estonia, and Latvia were generally even higher; Mazower, *Dark Continent,* 18.

40. Parliamentary instability led to public calls to strengthen executive power; ibid., 9.

41. Ibid., 19.

42. German legal theorist Carl Schmitt promoted the strategy of using presidential emergency powers to circumvent parliamentary paralysis instead of instituting a dictatorship. He went on to become the primary legal theorist for Hitler's Germany. See Joseph Benderesky, *Carl Schmitt: Theorist for the Reich* (Princeton, N.J.: Princeton University Press, 1983).

43. Hobsbawm, *The Age of Extremes,* 7.

44. The short-sighted preoccupation with the threat of communism blinded both the European states bordering the Soviet Union and the victorious powers of the United Kingdom and France to the more present danger of fascism. The victors "were concerned more about communism than dictatorship; so long as the new states of central-eastern Europe held communism at bay, they cared little about their domestic political arrangements"; Mazower, *Dark Continent,* 23.

45. Roger Griffin, *The Nature of Fascism* (London: Routledge, 1991); Stanley G. Payne, *A History of Fascism, 1914–1945* (London: UCL Press, 1995).

46. Benito Mussolini, *Le Fascisme: Doctrine, Institutions* (Paris: Denoël et Steele, 1933), 19.

47. Quoted in Mazower, *Dark Continent,* 27.

48. Ibid., xii–xiii.

49. The Nazis deemed equality historically and scientifically false. Marshal Petain described Vichy France as "a social hierarchy . . . rejecting the false idea of the equality of men"; Mazower, *Dark Continent,* 73.

50. See Mazower, *Dark Continent,* 98–100.

51. Ibid., 23.

52. Gilbert, *History of the Twentieth Century,* 248.

53. The Neutrality Acts were passed during the years 1935–1937. The 1935 Neutrality Act "prohibited American citizens from selling arms to belligerents in international war." Its 1936 counterpart prohibited trade in war matériel as well as loans or credits to belligerents. The Neutrality Act of 1937 tightened the restrictions on U.S. businesses and private individuals assisting belligerents, even prohibiting travel by U.S. citizens on ships

of belligerents; Edward Dumbauld, "Neutrality Laws of the United States," *American Journal of International Law* 31, no. 2 (1937): 258–270. A historical study of U.S. isolationism described the Neutrality Acts as "the very epitome of American isolationism, embracing every conceivable device to protect the country from the dangers to which it had been exposed in 1914–1917"; W. L. Langer and S. E. Gleason, *The Challenge to Isolation: The World Crisis of 1937–1940 and American Foreign Policy* (New York: Harper and Brothers, 1952).

54. Jan H. Burgers, "The Road to San Francisco: The Revival of the Human Rights Idea in the Twentieth Century," *Human Rights Quarterly* 14, no. 4 (1992): 450–464; Lauren, *The Evolution of International Human Rights*, 106–123.

55. Paul Gordon Lauren, "First Principles of Racial Equality: History and the Politics and Diplomacy of Human Rights Provision in the United Nations Charter," *Human Rights Quarterly* 5, no. 1 (1983): 1–26.

56. See Percy Martin, ed., *Who's Who in Latin America* (Stanford, Calif.: Stanford University Press, 1940), 19–20.

57. Alejandro Alvarez, quoted in Albert Verdoodt, *Naissance et Signification de la Déclaration Universelle des Droits de l'Homme* (Louvain-Paris: Editions Nauwelaerts, 1964), 41. Other examples of Alvarez's writings available in English include "Latin American and International Law," *American Journal of International Law* 3 (1909): 269–312; and "The New International Law," *Transactions of the Grotius Society* 15 (1929): 35–60.

58. For further discussion of Mandelstam's role in promoting human rights and the roles of Antoine Frangulis and the other personalities and initiatives mentioned in this section, see Burgers, "The Road to San Francisco," 450–454.

59. Mandelstam's personal views are expressed in A. N. Mandelstam, "La protection internationale des droits de l'homme," *Recueil des Cours—Hague Academy of International Law* 38 (1931): 125–232.

60. Burgers, "The Road to San Francisco," 451.

61. Ibid.

62. This would qualify the declaration as a source of international law under Article 38 of the Statute of the Permanent Court of International Justice.

63. See Mandelstam, "La protection internationale des droits de l'homme," 218.

64. This declaration was prepared under the direction of the Institut de Droit International, adopted by the International Law Institute on 12 October 1929 at a meeting where Mandelstam served as rapporteur. The declaration was financed by the Carnegie Endowment for International Peace and endorsed by a variety of other legal associations, including Frangulin's Academy; see Burgers, "The Road to San Francisco," 452–453.

65. French activist Victor Basch and German journalist Carl von Ossietsky formed the Fédération Internationale des Droits de l'Homme with fourteen other local human rights leagues. During World War II, Basch and von Ossietsky were assassinated by the Nazis and the organization was disbanded. It was reconstituted in October 1948, and René Cassin, the French representative on the UN's Commission on Human Rights, became one of its most prominent members; see Lauren, *The Evolution of International Human Rights*, 108, 113, and the website of the *fédération* at www.fidh.org, which includes a section on the history of the organization.

66. Quoted in Burgers, "The Road to San Francisco," 454.

67. The information in this section is based largely on Burgers, "The Road to San Francisco," 464–468. Burgers's article is based on H. G. Wells, *The Rights of Man, or What Are We Fighting For?* (Harmondsworth, Middlesex, UK: Penguin Books, 1940). See David C. Smith, *H. G. Wells: Desperately Mortal* (New Haven, Conn.: Yale University Press, 1986), 428–433, 442–449, 601–608; Vincent Brome, *H. G. Wells* (London: Longmans, Green and Co., 1951), 214–218; and Lord Ritchie Calder, *On Human Rights* (Edgware, Middlesex, UK: H. G. Wells Society, 1968).

68. H. G. Wells, *The New World Order* (New York: A. A. Knopf, 1940), 51.

69. Ibid., 45.

70. Burgers, "The Road to San Francisco," 465.

71. H. G. Wells, "Declaration of the Rights of Man," *Times* (London), 23 October 1939.

72. Ibid.

73. Burgers, "The Road to San Francisco," 465.

74. Ibid., 466.

75. Compare Ruth Nanda Anshen, ed., *Freedom: Its Meaning* (London: George Allen & Unwin, 1940), which does not mention the term human rights, with UNESCO, ed., *Human Rights: Comments and Interpretations* (London: Allen Wingate, 1949).

76. Burgers, "The Road to San Francisco," 460. Burgers notes that not even prominent postwar human rights advocate René Cassin mentioned human rights in his prewar writings, despite his familiarity with the concept and with the draft declarations Mandelstam and others circulated.

77. Mazower, *Dark Continent,* 184.

78. Ibid., 185.

79. E. Ranshofen-Wertheimer, *Victory Is Not Enough: The Strategy for a Lasting Peace* (New York: W. W. Norton, 1942), 122–123.

80. Mazower, *Dark Continent,* 24.

81. Franklin D. Roosevelt, *Looking Forward* (New York: John Day, 1933), 254.

82. Norman Rich, *Hitler's War Aims: Ideology, the Nazi State, and the Course of Expansion* (New York: W. W. Norton, 1973).

83. The list of world events that the League had no power to challenge is lengthy, including Joseph Stalin's purges that sent thousands to the Siberian Gulag, Mussolini's invasion of Ethiopia to civilize an inferior race, the United Kingdom's suppression of its colonies, and Franco's rise to power in Spain by defeating democratic forces; Lauren, *The Evolution of International Human Rights,* 120–123, 134.

3. The Human Rights Crusade in World War II

1. Chris Jochnick and Roger Normand, "The Legitimation of Violence: A Critical History of the Laws of War," *Harvard International Law Journal* 35 (1994): 85–89.

2. Bradley Lightbody, *The Second World War: Ambitions to Nemesis* (New York: Routledge, 2004); Gerhard L. Weinburg, *A World at Arms: A Global History of World War II* (Cambridge: Cambridge University Press, 1994), 895.

3. Quoted in Mark Mazower, *Dark Continent: Europe's Twentieth Century* (New York: Alfred Knopf, 1999), 193.

4. Eric Hobsbawm, *The Age of Extremes: A History of the World, 1914–1991* (New York: Random House, 1994), 171–175.

5. According to a British historian, "Unlike Woodrow Wilson, Roosevelt, for whom deviousness was a way of life, wanted planning to take place in secret"; A. W. Brian Simpson, *Human Rights and the End of Empire: Britain and the Genesis of the European Convention* (Oxford: Oxford University Press, 2001), 175.

6. Ibid., 176.

7. See, for example, Stephen C. Schlesinger, *Act of Creation: The Founding of the United Nations* (Boulder, Colo.: Westview Press, 2003); Robert C. Hilderbrand, *Dumbarton Oaks: The Origins of the United Nations and the Search for Postwar Security* (Chapel Hill: University of North Carolina Press, 1990); Peter Gowan, "US: UN," *New Left Review* 24 (November–December 2003): 5–28.

8. See C. D. O'Sullivan, *Sumner Welles: Post-War Planning and the Quest for a New World Order* (New York: Columbia University Press, 2004), 4. This source is available online at www.gutenberg-e.org/osco1/.

9. Ibid., 1.

10. Gowan, "US: UN," 7.

11. O'Sullivan, *Sumner Welles*, 9–10. On Latin America, "Welles saw no contradiction between his opposition to European style colonialism and Washington's perpetuation of a virtual 'informal empire' in the Western Hemisphere" (172).

12. Ibid., 6. Welles's thinking was so closely aligned with the president's that O'Sullivan asks: "Which way did the influence flow, from Welles to Roosevelt or vice versa?" (4).

13. Quoted in Ruth B. Russell and Jeannette E. Muther, *A History of the United Nations Charter: The Role of the United States 1940–45* (Washington, D.C.: Brookings Institution, 1958), 32–33. At the same time, Welles's statement must be understood not as a plea for economic equality between peoples and nations but rather for a system of free trade in goods and resources under the hegemony of the United States, as opposed to the existing system of preferences between imperial states such as Britain and their dependent colonies.

14. The irony of Welles's speech is that the United States emerged in the years after World War II as the world's most dominant state, eager to protect its overwhelming advantages in military (including nuclear) and economic power. Before long, official State Department doctrine would seek to protect the very military monopolies and economic inequalities that Welles considered a threat to international peace when European powers pursued them.

15. See O'Sullivan, *Sumner Welles*, 5.

16. In some ways, Welles's liberal free-market ideology resembles Italian Marxist Antonio Gramsci's definition of hegemony as "consent ringed by the armor of coercion." Antonio Gramsci, *Selections from the Prison Notebooks of Antonio Gramsci*, ed. Quintin Hoare and Geoffrey Newell-Smith (London: Lawrence and Wishart, 1991), 2.

17. O'Sullivan, *Sumner Welles*, 5.

18. Ibid., 8.

19. Schlesinger, *Act of Creation,* 33. For more background on Pasvolsky, see 33–51.

20. Ibid., 35. In his memoirs, Hull wrote of Pasvolsky: "His capacities were splendid, his service exceedingly valuable"; Cordell Hull, *Memoirs of Cordell Hull* (New York: McMillan, 1948), 2:1626.

21. See Schlesinger, *Act of Creation,* 38.

22. The allegation that ended Welles's career was based on complaints by black male porters that he had aggressively solicited them during a train trip. Given prevailing attitudes toward sexuality and race at the time, these complaints were lethal to a public servant. Even though President Roosevelt and FBI director J. Edgar Hoover tried to protect Welles, Hull brought his conduct to the attention of the Senate Foreign Relations Committee in the summer of 1943, and Welles abruptly withdrew from public life at the age of fifty. O'Sullivan, *Sumner Welles,* 2–3.

23. Upon his death in 1961, the *New York Times* wrote that "few Americans were better known or more highly regarded in the chanceries of the world than he. There is no fear that he will be forgotten, for he made his mark on the history of the twentieth century"; Editorial, *New York Times,* 25 September 1961. Today few people associate Welles with the global institution he was so instrumental in creating.

24. See Schlesinger, *Act of Creation,* 40–42.

25. Quoted in Hull, *Memoirs of Cordell Hull,* 2:1647.

26. Franklin D. Roosevelt, "Annual Message to Congress," 6 January 1941 (the "Four Freedoms" address), in Franklin D. Roosevelt, *The Public Papers and Addresses of Franklin D. Roosevelt* (New York: Harper & Brothers, 1950), 10:672.

27. Byron W. Danes, William D. Pederson, and Michael P. Ricards, ed., *The New Deal and Public Policy* (London: Macmillan, 1998).

28. William E. Leuchtenberg, *The Supreme Court Reborn: The Constitutional Revolution in the Age of Roosevelt* (New York: Oxford University Press, 1995).

29. The most famous instance of executive bullying in the twentieth century is referred to infamously as Roosevelt's "court packing" plan by which the president attempted to increase the size of the Supreme Court bench. Although the Senate rejected his proposal, the Supreme Court eventually ruled in favor of his New Deal legislation. See Richard-Holder Williams, *The Politics of the United States Supreme Court* (London: George Allen and Unwin Ltd.: 1980).

30. Gowan, "US: UN," 8.

31. On the other hand, it must be noted that freedom from want, in Roosevelt's conception, had a commercial aspect that would be guaranteed by free trade and relations between states rather than a state obligation to provide every individual with certain socioeconomic guarantees. See Simpson, *Human Rights and the End of Empire,* 173. In response to a journalist's question about the nature of the third freedom, Roosevelt said: "Freedom from want: in other words, the removal of certain barriers between nations, cultural in the first place, and commercial in the second place" (ibid.).

32. Roosevelt, "Annual Message to Congress," 6 January 1941, in Roosevelt, *The Public Papers and Addresses of Franklin D. Roosevelt,* 10:672.

33. Ibid.

34. One British Foreign Office official worried that public enthusiasm and unofficial government reactions gave Roosevelt's words "an actuality which they would not otherwise have"; Simpson, *Human Rights and the End of Empire*, 209.

35. Ibid., 174.

36. Ibid.

37. Manfred Jonas, Harold D. Langley, and Francis L. Loewenheim, eds., *Roosevelt and Churchill: Their Secret Wartime Correspondence* (New York: Saturday Review Press, 1975).

38. Among Roosevelt's major postwar policy concerns were the promotion of freer trade and the need to control excessive overproduction of raw materials. The trade principle was at odds with that of the UK, which had a preferential system for purchasing from its colonies. See Simpson, *Human Rights and the End of Empire*, 177–182.

39. Ibid., 235–238. The United Kingdom fought a losing battle to avoid a trusteeship system for the mandates and, in Churchill's words, to allow "foreign powers [i.e., the United States] a means of expressing their reasonable and legitimate interest in colonial territories without affecting our sovereignty or exclusive authority, or establishing international bodies possessing powers of interference divorced from responsibility" (236).

40. O'Sullivan, *Sumner Welles*, 173.

41. Ibid.

42. J. Harvey, ed., *The War Diaries of Oliver Harvey* (London: Collins, 1978), 31.

43. Cited in Louise W. Holborn, *War and Peace Aims of the United Nations* (Boston: World Peace Foundation, 1948), 568.

44. "Against Naked Force the Only Possible Defence Is Naked Force," message to the National Convention of Young Democrats, 21 August 1941, in Roosevelt, *The Public Papers and Addresses of Franklin D. Roosevelt*, 10:334.

45. Churchill recognized this as a great improvement for a grand alliance; Winston S. Churchill, *The Grand Alliance* (Boston: Houghton Mifflin, 1951), 682–683.

46. Quoted in James Fredrick Green, *The United Nations and Human Rights* (Washington, D.C.: Brookings Institution, 1956), 14.

47. Simpson, *Human Rights and the End of Empire*, 185.

48. Atlantic Charter, in Roosevelt, *Public Papers and Addresses of Franklin D. Roosevelt*, 10:314.

49. Green, *The United Nations and Human Rights*, 14.

50. Franklin D. Roosevelt, "Annual Message to Congress," 6 January 1942, in Roosevelt, *Public Papers and Addresses of Franklin D. Roosevelt*, 10:42.

51. Russell and Muther, *A History of the United Nations Charter*, 76.

52. In *Fred Korematsu v. United States* (323 U.S. 214, 65 S. Ct. 193, 89 L. Ed. 194), the court ruled in favor of the federal government's decision to relocate citizens of Japanese descent on the basis of military necessity.

53. Simpson, *Human Rights and the End of Empire*, 182.

54. For a rather scathing critique by liberal groups, see Charles H. Thompson, "Editorial Comment: India: A Crucial Test of the War and Peace Aims of the United Nations," *The Journal of Negro Education* 11, no. 4 (1942): 435–443.

55. Simpson, *Human Rights and the End of Empire*, 193.

56. See Nehemiah Robinson, *The United Nations and the World Jewish Congress* (New York: Institute of Jewish Affairs, World Jewish Congress, 1955).

57. See Alexander. S. Kohanski, *The American Jewish Conference: Its Organization and Proceedings of the First Session, August 29 to September 2, 1943* (New York: American Jewish Conference, 1944).

58. Clyde Eagleton, "Organization of the Community of Nations," *American Journal of International Law* 36, no. 2 (1942): 229–241; Clark M. Eichelberger, "Next Steps in the Organization of the United Nations," *Annals of the American Academy of Political and Social Science* 228, no. 1 (1943): 34–39.

59. Robert Hillmann, "Quincy Wright and the Commission to Study the Organization of Peace," *Global Governance* 4, no. 4 (1998): 12–26.

60. Hans Kelsen had proposed this idea in 1920; see Danilo Zolo, "Hans Kelsen: International Peace through International Law," *European Journal of International Law* 9, no. 2 (1998): 306–324.

61. American Law Institute, *Report of William Draper Lewis on the Discussion of the International Bill of Rights Project at the Annual Meeting, May 12, 1943* (Philadelphia, Pa.: American Law Institute, 1943).

62. See Louis B. Sohn, "How American International Lawyers Prepared for the San Francisco Bill of Rights," *American Journal of International Law* 89, no. 3 (1995): 540–543.

63. American Law Institute, *Report to the Council of the Institute and Statement of Essential Human Rights by a Committee of Advisers, Representing the Principal Cultures of the World* (Philadelphia, Pa.: American Law Institute, 1944).

64. Canon John Nurser, "The Ecumenical Movement Churches, Global Order and Human Rights: 1938–1948," *Human Rights Quarterly* 25, no. 4 (2003): 841–881.

65. Charles A. Baylis, "Towards an International Bill of Rights," *Public Opinion Quarterly* 8, no. 2 (1944): 244–253.

66. "The International Law of the Future: Postulates, Principles, Proposals: A Statement of a Community of Views by North Americans," *International Conciliation* 399 (1944): 253. See also Josef L. Kunz, "International Affairs: The International Law of the Future," *American Political Science Review* 38, no. 2 (1994): 354–369.

67. Quoted in Mazower, *Dark Continent*, 188.

68. Ibid., 185.

69. See Jacques Maritain, *The Rights of Man and Natural Law*, in Maritain, *Christianity and Democracy; and, The Rights of Man and Natural Law* (San Francisco, Calif.: Ignatius Press, 1986).

70. For Lauterpacht's life and views, see Martti Koskenniemi, "Lauterpacht: The Victorian Tradition in International Law," *European Journal of International Law* 8, no. 2 (1997): 215–263.

71. In this article, Lauterpacht traces the history of the law of nature and its role in the creation of modern international law and the law of nations, noting that "each of the three has been, in relation to the two others, the recipient and the benefactor, the master and

the tool, the originator and the product"; Hersch Lauterpacht, "The Law of Nations, the Law of Nature, and the Rights of Man," *Transactions of the Grotius Society* 29 (1943): 2.

72. Hersch Lauterpacht, *An International Bill of the Rights of Man* (New York: Columbia University Press, 1945), later published as *International Law and Human Rights* (New York: F. A. Praeger, 1950).

73. This innovative proposal foreshadowed the present efforts of many human rights organizations and advocates to promote the "domestic applicability" of international human rights norms.

74. Mazower, *Dark Continent,* 186.

75. See Athol Fitzgibbons, *Keynes's Vision: A New Political Economy* (Oxford: Clarendon Press, 1988). Keynes's proposal to regulate international currency exchange was never adopted.

76. Ibid., 187.

77. Hobsbawm, *The Age of Extremes,* 270.

78. Hobsbawm credits this alliance with saving Europe from fascism: "Only the temporary and bizarre alliance of liberal capitalism and communism in self-defense against this challenger saved democracy, for the victory over Germany was essentially won, and could only have been won, by the Red Army"; *The Age of Extremes,* 7.

79. Mazower, *Dark Continent,* 191.

80. Roosevelt's idea of the "Four Policemen"—the United States, United Kingdom, Soviet Union, and China (whose role was largely symbolic)—was that they would provide globaly security and lesser powers would play a subsidiary role. He believed that the United States had an opportunity and an obligation to impose its vision of peace and justice on a war weary world.

81. The one supreme objective was "security," not just physical but also economic, social, and moral. Roosevelt felt that citizens could not be free from fear unless they had some minimal security in the form of adequate education and decent economic opportunity. See Cass R. Sunstein, *The Second Bill of Rights: FDR's Unfinished Revolution and Why We Need It More Than Ever* (New York: Basic Books, 2004).

82. Quoted in Gowan, "US: UN," 7.

83. Ibid., 8.

84. Russell and Muther, *A History of the United Nations Charter,* 323–329; Simpson, *Human Rights and the End of Empire,* 183–220.

85. This is discussed in detail in Sunstein, *The Second Bill of Rights,* 323–329.

86. Lauren, *The Evolution of International Human Rights,* 162–165.

87. These different proposals are discussed in Simpson, *Human Rights and the End of Empire,* 185–187.

88. On the role of the State Department, see Schlesinger, *Act of Creation,* 33–51. Pasvolsky and Welles also disagreed over power and representation in the new organization. Pasvolsky preferred an international decentralized organization, and Welles advocated for regional representation. Their differences were moot given that in Roosevelt's mind the four major powers would provide security for any world organization through their permanent seats and veto power on a supreme council.

89. Lauren, *The Evolution of International Human Rights,* 163–165.

90. Ibid.

91. "Policy Summaries, 1943–4," Records of Harley A. Notter, Advisor for United Nations Affairs, Box 156, General Records of the Department of State, RG59, NARA, Washington, D.C.

92. H. St. L. B. Moss, quoted in Simpson, *Human Rights and the End of Empire,* 212.

93. Quoted in Lauren, *The Evolution of International Human Rights,* 163.

94. Ibid., 165.

4. Human Rights Politics in the United Nations Charter

1. Peter Gowan, "US: UN," *New Left Review* 24 (November–December 2003): 9.

2. Cordell Hull, *Memoirs of Cordell Hull* (New York: McMillan, 1948), 2:1647–1648.

3. Harley A. Notter, *Post-War Foreign Policy Preparation: State Department Records of Harvey A. Notter, 1939–1945* (Bethesda, Md.: Congressional Information Service, 1949), 186–194.

4. United Nations, *Yearbook of the United Nations, 1946–47* (Lake Success, N.Y.: United Nations, 1947), 3.

5. U.S. Bureau of Public Affairs, Historical Office, *Foreign Relations of the United States: The Conferences at Cairo and Teheran, 1943* (Washington, D.C.: U.S. Government Printing Office, 1961), 552–555.

6. Robert C. Hilderbrand, *Dumbarton Oaks: The Origins of the United Nations and the Search for Postwar Security* (Chapel Hill: University of North Carolina Press, 1990), 30–34.

7. See Hilderbrand, *Dumbarton Oaks,* 67–69.

8. See Notter, *Post-War Foreign Policy Preparation,* chapters 12–14.

9. Hilderbrand, *Dumbarton Oaks,* 71. Another historian concluded that the U.S. proposal, "to a large extent, formed the basis of discussions"; Evan Luard, *A History of the United Nations: The Years of Domination, 1945–55* (New York: St. Martin's Press, 1982), 1:25.

10. Hull, *Memoirs of Cordell Hull,* 2:1684.

11. Quoted in Paul Gordon Lauren, *The Evolution of International Human Rights: Visions Seen* (Philadelphia: University of Pennsylvania Press, 1998), 170.

12. At Yalta, the spheres of influence of the great powers and the sensitive issue of the Security Council veto were agreed to by Churchill, Roosevelt, and Stalin. These agreements were then to be imposed on the members of the San Francisco conference in April–June 1945. See David Armstrong, Lorna Lloyd, and John Redmond, *From Versailles to Maastricht: International Organisation in the 20th Century* (New York: St. Martin's Press, 1996), 62–65.

13. Charles E. Bohlen, *Witness to History, 1929–1969* (New York: Norton, 1973), 181.

14. Churchill had opposed inviting China to the Dumbarton Oaks negotiations,

dismissing it as a nation that was not a world power or equal partner; Gabriel Kolko, *The Politics of War: The World and United States Policy, 1943–45* (New York: Random House, 1968), 266–267.

15. Gowan, "US: UN," 12.

16. Hilderbrand, *Dumbarton Oaks,* 229. As the Hilderbrand put it, the Chinese were present "to be blessed, not to reform the church" (239).

17. A. W. Brian Simpson, *Human Rights and the End of Empire: Britain and the Genesis of the European Convention* (Oxford: Oxford University Press, 2001), 242.

18. The UK delegation believed that the relationship with the colonies would not trigger legal sanctions under the racial equality clause in the same manner as U.S. discriminatory legislation in the southern states would. Seeming to forget its historical opposition to such clauses in previous contexts, it took the view that "it would be against our interests and traditions to oppose the insertion in the Charter of a provision on racial equality"; ibid.

19. Lauren, *The Evolution of International Human Rights,* 167.

20. Simpson, *Human Rights and the End of Empire,* 239–240.

21. Stephen C. Schlesinger, *Act of Creation: The Founding of the United Nations* (Boulder, Colo.: Westview Press, 2003), 50. As Schlesinger explains, Pasvolsky often wore down his opponents in these debates with his "sheer perseverance."

22. Gowan, "US: UN," 10.

23. Schlesinger, *Act of Creation,* 50.

24. The structure was similar to that of the League of Nations; Ruth B. Russell and Jeannette E. Muther, *A History of the United Nations Charter: The Role of the United States 1940–45* (Washington, D.C.: Brookings Institution, 1958), 421–477.

25. Russell and Muther, *A History of the United Nations Charter,* 240–242.

26. Cohen's initial attempt to include gender equality in the human rights clause was received negatively by both the UK and Soviet representatives, and the matter died quietly. Hilderbrand, *Dumbarton Oaks,* 91–93.

27. Simpson, *Human Rights and the End of Empire,* 244.

28. Ibid., 246.

29. Russell and Muther, *A History of the United Nations Charter,* 423.

30. Quoted in Simpson, *Human Rights and the End of Empire,* 244.

31. The United States and the United Kingdom felt that the concept of fascism was difficult to define, and in the end an agreement was reached that membership would be open to all peace-loving states; Hilderbrand, *Dumbarton Oaks,* 92.

32. Simpson, *Human Rights and the End of Empire,* 246.

33. Quoted in ibid., 246–247.

34. Ibid., 247.

35. Kristen Sellars, *The Rise and Rise of Human Rights* (Stroud, Gloucestershire: Sutton, 2002), xiii.

36. Dorothy B. Robins, *Experiment in Democracy: The Story of U.S. Citizen Organizations in Forging the Charter of the United Nations* (New York: Parkside Press, 1971).

37. See Lauren, *The Evolution of International Human Rights,* 173.

38. Quoted in Carol Anderson, *Eyes Off the Prize: The United Nations and the African American Struggle for Human Rights, 1944–1955* (Cambridge: Cambridge University Press, 2003), 37–38.

39. See Schlesinger, *Act of Creation*, 53–55.

40. Ibid., 67–68.

41. See Simpson, *Human Rights and the End of Empire*, 252.

42. Ibid., 252.

43. James T. Shotwell, *Autobiography* (Indianapolis: Bobbs-Merrill, 1961), 314. Historians have questioned the rather self-glorifying accounts of Shotwell, Proskauer, and other NGO consultants; they view their participation as an ingenious public relations strategy by the State Department to co-opt potential opposition.

44. Records from the British Foreign Office from officials who attended some of the same meetings as the NGO consultants assert that State Department officials essentially tricked the consultants into believing that their interventions were critical to advancing the human rights project, when in fact the State Department had already approved a set of human rights positions entirely consistent with the NGO interventions; Kristen Sellars, *The Rise and Rise of Human Rights*, 2–6.

45. Lauren, *The Evolution of International Human Rights*, 173–178.

46. Ibid., 175.

47. Ibid.

48. Ibid., 175–178.

49. See Manuel S. Caynes, "The Inter-American System and the Conference of Chapultepec," *The American Journal of International Law* 39, no. 3 (1945): 504–517.

50. Lauren, *The Evolution of International Human Rights*, 176–178.

51. Mary Ann Glendon, "The Forgotten Crucible: The Latin American Influence on the Universal Human Rights Idea," *Harvard Human Rights Journal* 16 (Spring 2003): 27.

52. Paolo G. Carozza, "From Conquest to Constitutions: Retrieving a Latin American Tradition of the Idea of Human Rights," *Human Rights Quarterly* 24, no. 2 (2002): 281–313.

53. Hector Gros Espiell, vice-president of the Inter-American Court of Human Rights, quoted in Glendon, *The Forgotten Crucible*, 28–29.

54. Gowan, "US: UN," 19.

55. Ibid., 18–19.

56. Peter Collier and David Horowitz, *The Rockefellers: An American Dynasty* (New York: Holt, Rinehart and Winston, 1976), 230.

57. Collier and Horowitz, *The Rockefellers*, 236.

58. James B. Reston, "U.S. Retains Right to Alter Oaks Plan," *New York Times*, 7 April 1945; Lansing Warren, "'Must Keep Peace for Own Sakes,' Says Stettinius, Back from Mexico," *New York Times*, 11 March 1945.

59. Schlesinger, *Act of Creation*, 57.

60. Anne O'Hare McCormick, "His 'Unfinished Business'—and Ours," *New York Times Magazine*, 22 April 1945, 71–72.

61. Ibid., 43–44.

62. Gowan, "US: UN," 9.

63. William Leuchtenberg, *In the Shadow of FDR: From Harry Truman to Ronald Reagan* (Ithaca, N.Y.: Cornell University Press, 1983), 14–15.

64. Schlesinger, *Act of Creation*, 62–63.

65. Stettinius had received mail critical of the fact that no women were present at Dumbarton Oaks. Durward Sandifer had drawn up a list of a dozen women, but many were rejected as being critical of the Dumbarton Oaks proposal. See Hilderbrand, *Dumbarton Oaks*, 82.

66. These countries had declared war against the Axis by March and were already members of the United Nations Relief and Rehabilitation Administration, the first operating agency of the United Nations created in Atlantic City in 1944. For more information on this administration, see Philip C. Jessup, "The First Session of the Council of UNRAA," *American Journal of International Law* 38, no. 1 (1944): 101–106. The delegates discussed and debated the blueprint of a new international peace and security organization. At the time it was felt that an international institution was needed to address international problems, an authority to prevent future aggression. Fifty-one countries eventually signed the Charter of the United Nations in San Francisco.

67. Virginia Gildersleeve, *Many a Good Crusade: Memoirs of Virginia Crocheron Gildersleeve* (New York: MacMillan, 1954), 316.

68. John Thomas Peters Humphrey, *The United Nations and Human Rights* (Toronto: Baxter Publishing Company for the Canadian Institute of International Affairs, 1963); "Millions Will Pray on April 21 and 22 for Delegates to San Francisco Parley," *New York Times*, 12 April 1945; James B. Reston, "The Critic Turns Actor," *Foreign Affairs* (October 1945): 50–61; "Views on Peace Sought; Leaders of Service Men's Wives Go to San Francisco," *New York Times*, 21 April 1945.

69. Details of the conference setup are described in Schlesinger, *Act of Creation*, 111–126.

70. Ibid.

71. Ibid., 112–116.

72. Gowan, "US: UN," 16.

73. Schlesinger, *Act of Creation*, 116.

74. Ibid.

75. One of the few developing-country perspectives at the time on human rights and the United Nations is Taraknath Das, "Human Rights and the United Nations," *Annals of the American Academy of Political and Social Science* 252, no. 1 (1947): 53–62.

76. Schlesinger, *Act of Creation*, 144–157.

77. Vijaya Lakshmi Pandit, who was not included in the Indian delegation, promoted the Indian amendment of "fundamental human rights for all men and women, irrespective of race, color or creed, in all nations and in international relations and associations of nations one with another" with great vigor; Lauren, *The Evolution of International Human Rights*, 190 n67. Another charismatic figure was Nigerian Kingsley Ozuombo Mbadiwe, founder of the African Academy for Arts and Research. For a review of Africans present at the founding conference, see Marika Sherwood, "There Is No Deal for the

Blackman in the San Francisco: African Attempts to Influence the Founding Conference of the United Nations, April–July, 1945," *The International Journal of African Historical Studies* 29, no. 1 (1996): 71–94.

78. Simpson, *Human Rights and the End of Empire,* 253.

79. Ibid., 251.

80. The most comprehensive account of the spying operation is found in Schlesinger, *Act of Creation,* 93–110; and Stephen Schlesinger, "Cryptanalysis for Peacetime: Codebreakers and the Birth and Structure of the United Nations," *Cryptologia* 19, no. 3 (1995): 217–235.

81. Schlesinger, *Act of Creation,* 331.

82. Ibid., 111–113, 251–252.

83. Ibid., 99–100.

84. Ibid.

85. Ibid., 101.

86. Ibid., 101–102.

87. See John Nurser, *For All Peoples and All Nations: Christian Churches and Human Rights* (Geneva: World Council of Churches Publications, 2005).

88. Charles DeBenedetti, "James T. Shotwell and the Science of International Politics," *Political Science Quarterly* 89, no. 2 (1974): 379–395.

89. Nurser, *For All Peoples and All Nations,* 109.

90. Schlesinger, *Act of Creation,* 53–54.

91. Quoted in Nurser, *For All Peoples and All Nations,* 111.

92. "Social Plan Vague, Jewish Groups Say," *New York Times,* 6 May 1945, 30. Stephen S. Wise (World Jewish Conference president), Israel Goldstein, Louis Lipsky, and Henry Monsky (American Jewish Conference co-chairs) and Selig Brodetsky (president of the Board of Deputies of British Jews) signed the memorandum, which also mentioned setting up a commission on human rights.

93. Russell B. Porter, "Jewish Groups Ask Hearing at Parley," *New York Times,* 29 April 1945.

94. "Three Faiths Map Ideas for Charter," *New York Times,* 5 April 1945, 14.

95. Simpson, *Human Rights and the End of Empire,* 251.

96. Lauren, *The Evolution of International Human Rights,* 176–178.

97. R. H. Hadow, quoted in Sellars, *The Rise and Rise of Human Rights,* 8.

98. C. K. Webster, "The Making of the Charter of the United Nations," *History* 32 (1947–1948): 16.

99. William Korey, *NGOs and the Universal Declaration of Human Rights: A Curious Grapevine* (New York: St. Martin's Press, 1998); Louis B. Sohn, "How American International Lawyers Prepared for the San Francisco Bill of Rights," *American Journal of International Law* 89, no. 3 (1995): 29–50.

100. For a complete account, see Korey, *NGOs and the Universal Declaration of Human Rights,* 29–42.

101. See for example, Frederick O. Nolde, *Free and Equal: Human Rights in Ecumenical Perspective, with Reflections on the Origin of the Universal Declaration of Human Rights*

by Charles Habib Malik (Geneva: World Council of Churches, 1968), 21–22; and Joseph M. Proskauer, *A Segment of My Times* (New York: Farrar, Strauss, 1950), 221–225.

102. Proskauer, *A Segment of My Times,* 221.

103. Nolde, *Free and Equal,* 21.

104. For a complete account, see Korey, *NGOs and the Universal Declaration,* 29–42.

105. Ibid., 37. Earlier Proskauer had written: "We emphasize our profound belief that while the peace conference will ultimately give attention to the wrongs which have been especially inflicted on the stricken Jews of Europe by the holocaust and the bestiality of Hitler, the ultimate safety of the Jewish populations of Europe will rest upon the international enforcement of justice and equality of treatment to all men of every race and creed"; quoted in "Jewish Group Asks World Rights Bill: Commission on Migration and Statelessness Also Suggested by Proskauer," *New York Times,* 29 April 1945.

106. Walter Kotschnig, quoted in Robins, *Experiment in Democracy,* 132.

107. A. M. McDiarmid, "The Charter and the Promotion of Human Rights," *U.S. Department of State Bulletin* 19 (1946): 212, 222.

108. See, for example, Robins, *Experiment in Democracy*; John P. Humphrey, *Human Rights & the United Nations: A Great Adventure* (Dobbs Ferry, N.Y.: Transnational Publishers, 1984); Felice D. Gaer, "Reality Check: Human Rights Nongovernmental Organizations Confront Governments at the United Nations," *Third World Quarterly* 16, no. 3 (1995): 389–406; Korey, *NGOs and the Universal Declaration*; Margaret E. Keck and Kathryn Sikkink, *Activists beyond Borders: Advocacy Networks in International Politics* (Ithaca, N.Y.: Cornell University Press, 1998).

109. Sellars, *The Rise and Rise of Human Rights,* 3.

110. Simpson, *Human Rights and the End of Empire,* 256.

111. Sellars, *The Rise and Rise of Human Rights,* 4.

112. Ibid., 200 n12.

113. Ibid., 5.

114. Gladwyn Jebb, quoted in ibid., 10.

115. The United States emerged as the most materially and militarily powerful state after World War II. It was intent on promoting human rights, securing its dominant economic position, and avoiding a return to isolationism; see Wilfried Loth, *The Division of the World, 1941–45* (London: Routledge, 1988); Noam Chomsky, *The Umbrella of U.S. Power: The Universal Declaration of Human Rights and the Contradictions of U.S. Policy* (New York: Seven Stories Press, 1999); and Tony Evans, *The Politics of Human Rights* (Chippenham, England: Pluto Press, 2001). But from the beginning, even U.S. residents criticized the U.S. notion of human rights, and other states rejected its claims to legitimate moral leadership.

116. Stettinius, quoted in Simpson, *Human Rights and the End of Empire,* 262.

117. The issue of recognizing the Chapultepec agreement caused a major internal rift in the U.S. delegation. Rockefeller, who served as the main liaison to the Latin American delegations, insisted on an approach of having the cake and eating it too—establishing the principle of universal security through the UN while carving out an exception for Latin America. A compromise was reached in which Article 51 of the UN Charter was

expanded to include "collective self-defense," an implicit recognition of regional security arrangements such as the one agreed between the United States and Latin American countries at Chapultepec. This seemingly innocuous addition later had major repercussions, opening the door for the possibility of war not approved by the Security Council, as in the case of Iraq and Korea.

118. The UK still proposed that the Economic and Social Council be empowered to establish all such commissions as it thought necessary without mentioning any specific commissions, whereas the United States favored an explicit reference to the Commission on Human Rights. Given strong support for this idea among Latin American countries and civil society groups, the U.S. position carried the day.

119. Simpson, *Human Rights and the End of Empire,* 262.

120. Ibid., 256–257.

121. Ibid., 256.

122. O. Franklin Nolde, a U.S. NGO representative, noted that at a luncheon meeting he attended, the Chinese expressed strong support for human rights; see Nurser, *For All Peoples and All Nations,* 114.

123. See Simpson, *Human Rights and the End of Empire,* 268–272.

124. Anderson, *Eyes Off the Prize,* 52–56. The Trusteeship Council did not have any indigenous representatives, and, under its policies, only the colonizers could determine if a colony was ready for independence.

125. See Russell and Muther, *A History of the United Nations Charter,* 808–848.

126. Quoted in Simpson, *Human Rights and the End of Empire,* 270.

127. Ibid., 272.

128. Ibid.

129. Tony Evans, *U.S. Hegemony and the Project of Universal Human Rights* (Basingstoke: Macmillan, 1996), 59.

130. Norman Lewis, "Human Rights, Law and Democracy in an Unfree World," in *Human Rights Fifty Years On: A Reappraisal,* ed. Tony Evans (Manchester, UK; Manchester University Press; New York: St. Martin's Press, 1998), 89.

131. Evans, *U.S. Hegemony and the Project of Universal Human Rights,* 64.

132. D. J. Llewelyn Davies, "Domestic Jurisdiction: A Limitation on International Law," *Transactions of the Grotius Society* 32 (1946): 60–67. Commentary, "The Domestic Jurisdiction Limitation in the United Nations Charter," *Columbia Law Review* 47, no. 2 (1946): 268–279; Hans Kelsen, "Limitations on the Functions of the United Nations," *Yale Law Journal* 55, no. 5 (1946): 997–1015; L. B. Shapiro, "Domestic Jurisdiction in the Covenant and the Charter," *Transactions of the Grotius Society* 33 (1946): 195–211.

133. Kelsen summarizes the Committee on Foreign Relations hearings, further noting that the committee's goals were in conflict with other objectives of the Charter. Senator Millikin was concerned that addressing economic and social problems in any country required investigation and intervention. Mr. Pasvolsky stated that the issue was the international nature of these problems, noting that "international problems may arise out of all sorts of circumstances"; Kelsen, "Limitations on the Functions of the United Nations," 1007 n10.

134. Simpson, *Human Rights and the End of Empire,* 265.

135. Ibid., 264–268.

136. Ibid., 266.

137. Dulles, quoted in Anderson, *Eyes Off the Prize,* 50 n159.

138. A. Glenn Mower, Jr., *The United States, the United Nations, and Human Rights: The Eleanor Roosevelt and Jimmy Carter Eras* (Westport, Conn.: Greenwood Press, 1979).

139. Quoted in Anderson, *Eyes Off the Prize,* 49. A British historian of human rights reached a similar conclusion: "Thus on a strict view of the founders' intention the Charter of the United Nations, settled after a war which had witnessed the most appalling violations of human rights, was drafted in a way which, had it been in force in the 1930s, would have seemed to exclude any action over the oppression of Jews in Nazi Germany"; Simpson, *Human Rights and the End of Empire,* 268.

140. For a general discussion, see James Fredrick Green, *The United Nations and Human Rights* (Washington, D.C.: Brookings Institution, 1956).

141. Archibald MacLeish, quoted in President Carter, "Continuing the CSCE Process," State Department Policy Paper 204, U.S. State Department, Washington, D.C., 29 July 1980.

142. Anderson, *Eyes Off the Prize.*

143. Lauren, *The Evolution of International Human Rights,* 201.

144. Ibid., 9.

145. Nurser, *For All Peoples and All Nations,* 119.

146. In San Francisco, the big issue was the veto power of the Big Five and whether it was open to revision (Article 109 of the UN Charter). Initially, there was no agreement in the subcommittee discussing the proposal, and therefore the recommendation was to place the question on the agenda of the tenth General Assembly meeting. The Soviets expressed concern about the temporary nature of the Charter. A compromise was reached (which the United States proposed) whereby the UN Charter would be reviewed by vote when two-thirds of the General Assembly and seven members of the Security Council agreed to do so. Any alterations to the Charter would require a two-thirds majority of the members.

147. Nurser, *For All Peoples and All Nations,* 119.

5. Laying the Human Rights Foundation

1. Humphrey is critical of ECOSOC, which was intended to be the liaison between the CHR and the General Assembly's Third Committee. Because of the number of items on human rights, ECOSOC had to set up a special human rights committee. "But like the Council," Humphrey notes, "this committee did very little of lasting value." There was a great deal of talk about procedure, and neither ECOSOC nor the Third Committee changed as much as a comma on any of the draft declarations or conventions that came to them. ECOSOC had no outstanding members and no well-defined role to play relative to the General Assembly's Third Committee and the CHR. John P. Humphrey, *Human Rights & the United Nations: A Great Adventure* (Dobbs Ferry, N.Y.: Transnational Publishers, 1984), 55.

2. The CHR's parent body is ECOSOC, which reports to the UN General Assembly;

in the case of human rights it reports to the Third Committee. Resolutions are passed between these three bodies. Philip Alston, "The Commission on Human Rights," in *The United Nations and Human Rights: A Critical Appraisal,* ed. Philip Alston (New York: Oxford University Press, 1992).

3. Norman Lewis, "Human Rights, Law and Democracy in an Unfree World," in *Human Rights Fifty Years On: A Reappraisal,* ed. Tony Evans (Manchester, UK: Manchester University Press, 1998).

4. Roger Baldwin, "International Agreements Can Protect Specific Rights," *Annals of the American Academy of Political and Social Science* 243, no. 1 (January 1946): 134–138; Taraknath Das, "Human Rights and the United Nations," *Annals of the American Academy of Political and Social Science* 252, no. 1 (1947): 53–62; Lyman C. White, "Peace by Pieces: The Role of Nongovernmental Organizations," *Annals of the American Academy of Political and Social Science* 264, no. 1 (1949): 87–97.

5. According to Robinson, all drafts came from the West, and all but two were in English; Nehemiah Robinson, *The Universal Declaration of Human Rights: Its Origin, Significance, Application, and Interpretation* (New York: Institute of Jewish Affairs, 1958), 20–22.

6. *Yearbook of the United Nations, 1948–49* (Lake Success, N.Y.: United Nations, 1949), 525.

7. Humphrey notes that the United Nations had received a great number of such communications from persons and organizations; Humphrey, *Human Rights & the United Nations,* 28.

8. Clark M. Eichelberger, *UN: The First Twenty Years* (New York: Harper & Row, 1965); Mary Ann Glendon, *A World Made New: Eleanor Roosevelt and the Universal Declaration of Human Rights* (New York: Random House, 2001).

9. See Commission on Human Rights, *Report of the First Session of the Commission to the Economic and Social Council,* ECOSOC document E/259, 1947, paragraphs 21–22. Humphrey remarks that at first the decision was to make communications from individuals available to members upon request, but the Philippines delegate feared state reprisals against the authors of such missives and moved that the matter be referred to a committee for further study. The committee took the view that it had no power to take any action on any complaint; Humphrey, *Human Rights & the United Nations,* 20.

10. Procedure 1503 was established in 1970 for confidential communications of gross and consistent human rights violations. The procedure is available after all domestic remedies have been exhausted; ECOSOC resolution 1235 (XLII), 6 June 1967; ECOSOC document E/4393, 17 June 1967; ECOSOC resolution 1503 (XLVIII), 27 May 1970; ECOSOC document E/4832/Add. 1. See in general R. B. Lillich, "The U.N. and Human Rights Complaints: U Thant as a Strict Constructionist," *American Journal of International Law* 64, no. 3 (1970): 610–614; M. E. Tardu, "United Nations Response to Gross Violations of Human Rights: The 1503 Procedure," *Santa Clara Law Review* 20 (1980): 559–601.

11. See *Report of the Drafting Committee to the Commission on Human Rights,* ECOSOC document E/CN.4/21, 1 July 1947.

12. U.S. Department of State, Office of Public Affairs, *Questions and Answers on the UN*

Charter, Genocide Convention, and Proposed Covenants on Human Rights (Washington, D.C.: Office of Public Affairs, 1952); John P. Humphrey, *The United Nations and Human Rights* (Toronto: Baxter Publishing Company, 1963).

13. The Panamanian draft was in the form of a declaration; Humphrey, *Human Rights & the United Nations,* 25. Similar arguments for a declaration had been made earlier by Dr. Héctor Reyes during the formative meetings of the UN in San Francisco.

14. Ibid., 14.

15. "Draft Declaration on Fundamental Human Rights and Freedom," General Assembly resolution 43 (1), 11 December 1946. In the preparatory meeting (August to October 1945), the fourteen-member Executive Committee of the United Nations had recommended that ECOSOC create six commissions, making the Commission on Human Rights its first priority. ECOSOC authorized the CHR to create three subcommissions composed of independent experts. The Sub-Commission on Freedom of Information and the Press met from 1947 to 1952 and then was dissolved. The Sub-Commission on the Prevention of Discrimination and the Sub-Commission on the Protection of Minorities were formed at the insistence of the Soviet Union. These two were folded into a single Sub-Commission on Prevention of Discrimination and Protection of Minorities, which became a permanent group. Humphrey, *Human Rights & the United Nations,* 18–19.

16. For a detailed analysis, see A. Loveday, "An Unfortunate Decision," *International Organization* 1, no. 2 (1947): 279–290. Loveday observes that of the eight advisory bodies constituted under ECOSOC, all but one suggested that members be experts serving as individuals rather than as government representatives.

17. The western contingent included Australia and Belgium and the three permanent members, France, United Kingdom, and the United States. Latin America was represented by Chile, Panama, and Uruguay. China, India, Iran, Lebanon, and the Philippines represented Asia. Egypt was the only African member. The eastern bloc was represented by Byelorussia, Ukraine and the Soviet Union, and Yugoslavia. The United States and its European, Asian, and Latin American allies had an insurmountable majority over the communists. All five permanent members of the Security Council were always represented in all UN bodies pertaining to human rights.

18. Humphrey, *Human Rights & the United Nations,* 18.

19. Loveday, "An Unfortunate Decision," 289. Loveday points out that there was no mechanism within the UN for discussion of the whole corpus of individual rights by other than government representatives. Even if private organizations took up the concerns of individual rights, they got a hearing only at the courtesy of the CHR.

20. Humphrey, *Human Rights & the United Nations,* 23.

21. John P. Humphrey, "Address to Opening Session of 3rd Plenary Session of World Jewish Council," UN document Pa 53/Spr/3, 4 August 1953, 7.

22. "Commission on Human Rights: Summary Record of Meetings," ECOSOC document E/CN.4/SR.1, 1–2, 28 January 1947.

23. John J. Mearsheimer, *The Tragedy of Great Power Politics* (New York: W.W. Norton and Co., 2002).

24. Eleanor Roosevelt, *The Autobiography of Eleanor Roosevelt* (Boston: G. K. Hall,

1961); David Emblidge, ed., *My Day: The Best of Eleanor Roosevelt's Acclaimed Newspaper Columns, 1936–1962* (New York: Da Capo Press, 2001); Allida M. Black, ed., *Courage in a Dangerous World* (New York: Columbia University Press, 1999).

25. Mrs. Roosevelt chaired the first six sessions of the commission (1947–1951). She was succeeded by Charles Malik for two sessions in 1951–1952 and by Dr. Mahmoud Azmi (Egypt) for two sessions in 1953–1954. This period was critical in preparing the international bill of rights. In 1953, with the change in U.S. presidency from Truman to Eisenhower, her term was not renewed, and she was replaced by Mrs. Mary Lord. Tolley, *The U.N. Commission on Human Rights*, 15.

26. Kirsten Sellars, *The Rise and Rise of Human Rights* (Thrupp, UK: Sutton Publishing, 2002), 18.

27. Lash, quoted in A. Glenn Mower, Jr., *The United States, the United Nations, and Human Rights: The Eleanor Roosevelt and Jimmy Carter Eras* (Westport, Conn.: Greenwood Press, 1979), 58.

28. Durward Sandifer had served as secretary-general and chief technical expert to the U.S. delegation to the UN conference in San Francisco in 1945 and acting director of the Office of United Nations Affairs. Mrs. Roosevelt noted the important influence of Sandifer: "[He] would climb into my automobile with the assurance that for the next forty minutes I would be his captive audience and that our discussion of the day's work would not be interrupted"; Roosevelt, *The Autobiography of Eleanor Roosevelt*, 316.

29. Sellars, *The Rise and Rise of Human Rights*, 18–19.

30. James Green (one of her advisors) noted that her views on human rights did not differ much from those of the State Department. See Mower, *The United States, the United Nations, and Human Rights*, 39.

31. Oral history interview with Durward V. Sandifer, 15 and 29 March 1973, Harry S. Truman Presidential Museum and Library, Independence, Missouri.

32. Sellars, *The Rise and Rise of Human Rights*, 17–19.

33. Mower, *The United States, the United Nations, and Human Rights*, 43.

34. A. W. Brian Simpson, *Human Rights and the End of Empire: Britain and the Genesis of the European Convention* (Oxford: Oxford University Press, 2004), 427.

35. Quoted in Paul Gordon Lauren, *The Evolution of International Human Rights: Visions Seen* (Philadelphia: University of Pennsylvania Press, 1998), 232.

36. Carol Anderson, *Eyes Off the Prize: The United Nations and the African American Struggle for Human Rights, 1944–1955* (Cambridge: Cambridge University Press, 2003).

37. E. J. Kahn, Jr., "The Years Alone—I," *New Yorker*, 6 December 1946, 33.

38. Humphrey felt that Mrs. Roosevelt had compromised her reputation as a symbol that stood above such political quarrels. John Hobbins, ed., *On the Edge of Greatness: The Diaries of John Humphrey, First Director of the United Nations Division of Human Rights*, vol. 1, *1948–1959* (Montreal: McGill University Libraries, 1994), 1:50.

39. Sellars, *The Rise and Rise of Human Rights*, 12.

40. Simpson, *Human Rights and the End of Empire*, 312–320.

41. Sellars, *The Rise and Rise of Human Rights*, 12–13.

42. Simpson, *Human Rights and the End of Empire*, 332.

43. For a full discussion, see ibid., 348–352.

44. Geoffrey Masterman Wilson was later knighted and served as the chairman of Oxfam (1977–1983).

45. By 1950, Lauterpacht was thoroughly disappointed with the work of the commission and even more so with the structure of the UN in terms of human rights and its lack of enforcement. See Humphrey's diary entry of 11 December 1948 in Hobbins, *On the Edge of Greatness*, 1:90.

46. Simpson, *Human Rights and the End of Empire*, 350. Lauterpacht had moved to London in 1923, and became a British citizen in 1933.

47. Peter Gowan, "US: UN," *New Left Review* 24 (November–December 2003): 17.

48. Karl Marx, "On the Jewish Question," (1843) available online at http://www.marxists.org/archive/marx/works/1844/jewish-question/.

49. J. Stalin, "Speech Delivered by J. V. Stalin at a Meeting of Voters of the Stalin Electoral District," Moscow, 9 February 1946, available online at http://www.marx2mao.com/Stalin/SS46.html. See also Fraser Harbutt, "American Challenge, Soviet Response: The Beginning of the Cold War, February–May 1946," *Political Science Quarterly* 96, no. 4 (1982–1982): 623–637.

50. Churchill's famous Iron Curtain speech of 5 March 1946 noted that a shadow had fallen on Eastern Europe and that it was now cut off from the free world; Glendon, *A World Made New*, 31.

51. These debates were most contentious in the Third Committee but also in the CHR. See Commission on Human Rights, *Report of the Drafting Committee to the Commission on Human Rights*, ECOSOC document E/600, 17 December 1947.

52. Humphrey notes Koretsky's legal acumen in comparison to that of other Soviet delegates; Humphrey, *Human Rights & the United Nations*, 38.

53. Sellars notes that at the end of the first commission session, a U.S. report indicated that U.S. positions were accepted on all important points. Sellars, *The Rise and Rise of Human Rights*, 23.

54. Ibid., 11.

55. Humphrey, *Human Rights and the United Nations*, 24–25. Humphrey felt that Ribnikar was one of the most interesting people on the commission.

56. "Commission on Human Rights: Summary Record of Meetings," ECOSOC document E/CN.4/SR.8, 30 January 1947, 4.

57. Humphrey, *Human Rights & the United Nations*, 23, 26. Humphrey describes Hodgson as "peppery" and notes that he also represented Australia on the Security Council. "Hodgson wanted a human rights convention with teeth in it," Humphrey noted.

58. Ibid., 24. "A determined woman," noted Humphrey. In his diary entry for 31 May 1949, Humphrey wrote that only René Cassin, Mrs. Mehta, and Col. Hodgson were really interested in implementation. Hobbins, ed., *On the Edge of Greatness*, 1:170.

59. For a study of Malik, see Glendon, *A World Made New*. Humphrey describes him as "a tall man with black hair and a nose like an eagle who would have made a good figure dressed as a sheikh galloping across the desert"; Humphrey, *Human Rights & the United Nations*, 23.

60. For a summary of his contribution, see Glendon, *A World Made New*.

61. Humphrey notes that Chang's gruff manner and uninhibited criticisms of the Sec-

retariat were offputting at first, but he soon learned to appreciate Chang's great human qualities and diplomatic skills. Humphrey, *Human Rights & the United Nations*, 23.

62. P. C. Chang is often labeled as a Confucian who represented a traditional eastern influence on the commission. However, Abdullahi An-Naʿim argues that while communitarian in thought, Chang was shaped by the western cultural tradition. The commission records indicate that it was Chang who proposed that duties be placed at the end (Article 29) rather than the beginning of the UDHR. His preference for civil and political over economic and social rights may have been a reflection of his connection to a Chinese government that was on the verge of falling to a communist revolution. Abdullahi Ahmed An-Naʿim, "Problems of Universal Cultural Legitimacy for Human Rights," in *Human Rights in Africa: Cross-Cultural Perspectives*, ed. Abdullahi Ahmed An-Naʿim and Francis M. Deng (Washington, D.C.: Brookings Institution, 1990).

63. Humphrey, *Human Rights & the United Nations*, 23–25.

64. Glendon, *A World Made New*, 33.

65. Ibid., 34.

66. Ibid.

67. Report submitted by the special rapporteur, Mr. Hernan Santa-Cruz, *Special Study of Racial Discrimination in the Political, Economic, Social and Cultural Spheres*, ECOSOC document E/CN.4/Sub.2/276, 24 July 1967.

68. "Chang and Malik were both seen as being broadly sympathetic to America's view"; Sellars, *The Rise and Rise of Human Rights*, 12.

69. Ibid., 16. Sellars notes that Malik and Mehta were favorites of the UK delegates. Interestingly, the delegates from both the UK and the United States were unenthusiastic about Cassin.

70. Sellars, *The Rise and Rise of Human Rights*, 16.

71. Karel Vasak and Jean Graven, *René Cassin: Amicorum discipulorumque liber* (Paris: Editions A. Pédone, 1969).

72. Sellars, *The Rise and Rise of Human Rights*, 16.

73. The British viewed Cassin as vain and verbose, noting: "His fondness for indefinable phrases like judicial personality and social security cause endless discussion"; ibid.

74. Johannes Morsink, *The Universal Declaration of Human Rights: Origins, Drafting, and Intent* (Philadelphia: University of Pennsylvania Press, 1999).

75. John Humphrey recorded his experience at the Secretariat in his diaries, which have become an invaluable source of information for individuals interested in events that took place in private. These fourteen diaries have been faithfully restored into four books edited by A. J. Hobbins: *On the Edge of Greatness: The Diaries of John Humphrey, First Director of the United Nations Division of Human Rights*, vol. 1, *1948–1949* (Montreal: McGill University Libraries, 1994); vol. 2, *1950–1951* (Montreal: McGill University Libraries, 1996); vol. 3, *1952–1957* (Montreal: McGill University Libraries, 1998); vol. 4, *1958–1966* (Montreal: McGill University Libraries, 2000).

76. He retired at sixty-one years of age and recalls leaving "without the formal thanks of the commission"; Humphrey, *Human Rights & the United Nations*, 388.

77. In the League of Nations system, largely based on the report of Tommaso Tit-

toni, onetime prime minister of Italy, the petitioner had no standing to raise the matter before the League and could only address the complaint as a communication. Once the League had received the information, its members could then choose to investigate or take action. Edwin Borchard, "Historical Background of International Protection of Human Rights," *Annals of the American Academy of Political and Social Science* 243, no. 1 (1946): 112–117; Hersch Lauterpacht, "The Law of Nations, the Law of Nature, and the Rights of Man," *Transactions of the Grotius Society* 29 (1943): 1–33; Mark Mazower, "The Strange Triumph of Human Rights, 1933–1950," *The Historical Journal* 47, no. 2 (2004): 379–398.

78. Mazower, "The Strange Triumph of Human Rights," 385.

79. It achieved inaction by avoiding the placement of such matters on the League's agenda.

80. See Patrick Thornberry, *International Law and the Rights of Minorities* (Oxford: Oxford University Press, 1991).

81. Quoted in Simon Segal, "Problems of Minorities Regarding an International Bill of Rights," *Journal of Educational Sociology* 18, no. 5 (1945): 305.

82. Baldwin, "International Agreements"; Segal, "Problems of Minorities"; Charles A. Baylis, "Towards an International Bill of Rights," *Public Opinion Quarterly* 8, no. 2 (1944): 244–253.

83. See generally the writings of Lauterpacht, including "The Law of Nations"; and *International Law and Human Rights* (New York: Frederick A. Praeger, 1950).

84. *Human Rights, the Charter of the United Nations, and the International Bill of the Rights of Man, Preliminary Report by Professor H. Lauterpacht*, ECOSOC document E/CN.4/89, 12 May 1948, 6.

85. Ibid., 14.

86. See ibid.; and Lauterpacht, *International Law and Human Rights*.

87. Herbert W. Briggs, "Implementation of the Proposed International Covenant on Human Rights," *American Journal of International Law* 42, no. 2 (1948): 389–397.

88. Quincy Wright, "Recent Trends in the Evolution of the United Nations," *International Organization* 2, no. 4 (1948): 617–631.

89. Ibid.

90. Quoted in Tolley, *The U.N. Commission on Human Rights*, 10.

91. Laugier also stated that he was inclined to doubt whether the right to appeal existed and that the CHR should submit proposals about the "setting up of machinery for hearing of such appeals"; "Commission on Human Rights: Summary Record of Meetings," ECOSOC document E/CN.4/SR.1, 27 January 1947, 2.

92. See generally "Commission on Human Rights: Summary Record of Meetings," ECOSOC documents E/CN.4/SR.2, 3, and 4, 28–29 January 1947.

93. Mrs. Mehta (India), "Commission on Human Rights: Summary Record of Meetings," ECOSOC document E/CN.4/SR.2, 28 January 1947, 3. The summary records of UN bodies were written in the past tense. We have changed the tense to present here, showing the change in brackets. In all subsequent quotations from summary records, we have made this change silently.

94. Simpson, *Human Rights and the End of Empire,* 353.

95. "Mrs. Roosevelt Is Elected Chairman of the U.N. Human Rights Commission," *New York Times,* 28 January 1947.

96. Quoted in Anderson, *Eyes Off the Prize,* 97. Also see Sellars, *The Rise and Rise of Human Rights,* 18–19.

97. Frank E. Holman, "An International Bill of Rights: Proposals Have Dangerous Implications for U.S.," *American Bar Association Journal* 34 (1948): 625–632. Holman also stated that U.S. participation was unconstitutional and that the human rights program embodied a threat to free enterprise.

98. Charles Duke (UK), "Commission on Human Rights: Summary Record of Meetings," ECOSOC document E/CN.4/SR.2, 28 January 1947, 5.

99. *Yearbook of the United Nations 1946–1947* (New York: Columbia University Press, 1947), 121.

100. "Commission on Human Rights: Summary Record of Meetings," ECOSOC documents E/CN.4/SR.9, 16 and 48, 28 January– 27 February 1947.

101. Mr. Tepliakov (USSR), "Commission on Human Rights: Summary Record of Meetings," ECOSOC document E/CN.4/SR.16, 1947.

102. Simpson, *Human Rights and the End of Empire,* 417.

103. *Report of the Drafting Committee to the Commission on Human Rights,* ECOSOC document E/600, Annex C, Suggestion B on the right of individuals to petition the United Nations to initiate the procedure for enforcing human rights. See also Howard Tolley, "The Concealed Crack in the Citadel: The United Nations Commission on Human Rights' Response to Confidential Communications," *Human Rights Quarterly* 6, no. 4 (1984): 420–462.

104. Eleanor Roosevelt, "The Promise of Human Rights," *Foreign Affairs* 26, no. 3 (1948): 470–477.

105. ECOSOC resolution 75 (V), 5 August 1947; ECOSOC document E/573, 2 September 1947. ECOSOC placed a similar restraint on the Commission on the Status of Women. This self-denying rule was reaffirmed in 1959; ECOSOC resolution 728 F (XXVIII), 30 July 1959.

106. For a full review, see Tolley, "The Concealed Crack in the Citadel."

107. Humphrey, *Human Rights & the United Nations,* 28. Humphrey notes that this façade ended in 1959 when the Soviet Union attacked the Secretariat for compiling a list that contained a large number of complaints from Poland.

108. See Anderson, *Eyes Off the Prize,* 79.

109. For a vivid description of the violence in the U.S. South, see ibid., 58–65.

110. Charles H. Wesley, "The Dilemma of the Rights of Man," *The Journal of Negro History* 38, no. 1 (January 1953): 10–26. Wesley wrote: "The truth about peoples, their rights and their duties, is basic to peace in our day. Just as a good life cannot be built on lies, the life and reputation of a nation cannot be built on falsehood and error" (26).

111. Anderson, *Eyes Off the Prize,* 105–106.

112. "U.N. Mass Protest on Housing Today," *New York Times,* 17 July 1947.

113. The 1946 report was prepared by historian Herbert Aptheker and included a wide range of statistical evidence, such as infant mortality rates among blacks that were double those of white southerners; see Anderson, *Eyes Off the Prize,* 80.

114. In 1938, the Carnegie Corporation commissioned Swedish economist Gunnar Myrdal to undertake a study on the conditions of African Americans. Myrdal employed forty-eight writers and researchers, including Ralph Bunche and Kenneth B. Clark. Clark, an educator and psychologist, was one of the originators (along with his wife) of the famous doll studies on the harmful effects of racism on black children, cited in the Supreme Court's landmark 1954 ruling in *Brown v. Board of Education.* See Gunnar Myrdal, *An American Dilemma: The Negro Problem and Modern Democracy* (New York: Harper and Row Publishers, 1944).

115. NAACP, *An Appeal to the World: A Statement on the Denial of Human Rights to Minorities in the Case of Citizens of Negro Descent in the United States of America and an Appeal to the United Nations for Redress* (New York: National Association for the Advancement of Colored People, 1947).

116. George Streator, "Negroes to Bring Cause before U.N.," *New York Times,* 12 October 1947.

117. Anderson, *Eyes Off the Prize,* 86–87.

118. *Yearbook of the United Nations 1946–1947,* 144–148. UN General Assembly resolution 44(1), Treatment of Indians in the Union of South Africa (8 December 1946).

119. Sellars, *The Rise and Rise of Human Rights,* 78.

120. Streator, "Negroes to Bring Cause before U.N."

121. Walter White, secretary of NAACP, regretted the limitation on the number of persons who could be admitted to the ceremony marking the official submission. In his official invitation letter to Mrs. Roosevelt, he wrote:

> We have invited approximately 125 distinguished white and Negro Americans to be present as well as the heads of all delegations to the United Nations. We estimate that between 100 and 150 persons will be present. In addition we have notified the newspapers, newsreel and radio companies.
>
> The fact that such attention is being paid to the petition seems to disturb some of the United Nations personnel and there has been indicated to us a desire to limit the number of persons to not more than five or six including newspaper men.

White to Eleanor Roosevelt, 20 October 1947, Eleanor Roosevelt Papers, available online at http://www.gwu.edu/~erpapers/documents/correspondence/doc007690.cfm.

122. Harley Notter, state department advisor on UN human rights issues, had earlier said that "no nation, including the United States, had yet been able to reach the first rung of the [human rights] ladder, namely elections which are free enough to provide the prerequisite basis for the honoring of even the most tangible of human rights, which are the legal ones. American human rights leadership should rest on the cornerstone of its First Amendment, namely freedom of speech." Quoted in Anderson, *Eyes off the Prize,* 73.

123. Mrs. Roosevelt (United States), *General Assembly Official Records,* Third Committee, Sixth Session, 371st meeting, 20 December 1951, 144.

124. "U.N. Group Rejects Negro Study in U.S.," *New York Times,* 4 December 1947.

125. Du Bois quoted in George Streator, "U.N. Gets Charges of Wide Bias in U.S.—3 Centuries of Discrimination against Negroes Cited in NAACP Pleas for Justice," *New York Times,* 24 October 1947.

126. Humphrey, *Human Rights & the United Nations,* 23–25.

127. In 1947, the members received a draft outline prepared by the Secretariat (E/CN.4/AC.1/3 and Add. 1), the text of a letter from the UK representative and a draft covenant and resolution for the General Assembly (E/CN.4/AC.1/4), and U.S. proposals for rewording the Secretariat's outline (E/CN.4/AC.1/8 and Rev. 1 and 2, 5 December 1947).

128. Glendon discusses this period in *A World Made New,* 53–71.

129. *Yearbook of the United Nations 1948–1949,* 525–526.

130. *Report of the Drafting Committee to the Commission on Human Rights,* ECOSOC document E/CN.4/21.

131. Mrs. Roosevelt noted that she had devised a plan to keep eighteen noses to the grindstone: "I immediately laid out a schedule of work that, with night sessions, I believed would enable us to adjourn by eleven o'clock on the evening of December 17"; quoted in Glendon, *A World Made New,* 83.

132. Humphrey, *Human Rights & the United Nations,* 48.

133. Lord Dukeston (UK), "Commission on Human Rights: Summary Record of Meetings," ECOSOC document E/CN.4/SR.25, 2 December 1947, 5–6.

134. Charles Dukes (UK), "Commission on Human Rights: Summary Record of Meetings," ECOSOC document E/CN.4/SR.11, February 1947, 11.

135. Simpson, *Human Rights and the End of Empire,* 394.

136. Vratislav Pechota, "The Development of the Covenant on Civil and Political Rights," in *The International Bill of Rights,* ed. Louis Henkin (New York: Columbia University Press, 1981), 34.

137. Dehousse (Belgium), "Commission on Human Rights: Summary Record of Meetings," ECOSOC document E/CN.4/SR.25, 2 December 1947, 7.

138. "Commission on Human Rights: Summary Record of Meetings," ECOSOC document E/CN.4/SR.25, 2 December 1947, 8.

139. Hodgson (Australia), "Commission on Human Rights: Summary Record of Meetings," ECOSOC document, E/CN.4/SR.28, 4 December 1947, 6.

140. Hodgson further noted, "This Court would be the Central Appeal Court to which States, groups of individuals or even single individuals could appeal when all domestic possibilities of appeal had been exhausted"; "Commission on Human Rights: Summary Record of Meetings," ECOSOC document, E/CN.4/SR.15, January–February 1947, 2–3.

141. Mrs. Mehta (India), "Commission on Human Rights: Summary Record of Meetings," ECOSOC document E/CN.4/SR.2, 28 January 1947, 3.

142. See generally Nehemiah Robinson, *The United Nations and the World Jewish Congress* (New York: Institute of Jewish Affairs, World Jewish Congress, 1955).

143. *Human Rights, the Charter of the United Nations, and the International Bill of the Rights of Man. Preliminary Report by Professor H. Lauterpacht,* ECOSOC document E/CN.4/89, 12 May 1948, paragraph 32.

144. The Soviets felt that any discussion of a convention was premature and that any interference in domestic affairs of states was unacceptable; see "Commission on Human Rights: Summary Record of Meetings," ECOSOC document E/CN/SR.25, 2 December 1947, 38.

145. Soviet Union position quoted in Humphrey, *Human Rights & the United Nations,* 54.

146. Roosevelt, "The Promise of Human Rights," 476.

147. Simpson, *Human Rights and the End of Empire,* 378.

148. "Commission on Human Rights: Summary Record of Meetings," ECOSOC document E/CN.4/SR.25, 2 December 1947, 10; quoted in Glendon, *World Made New,* 85. See also E/CN.4/SR.29, 8 December 1947, where Mrs. Roosevelt noted that "her Government did not consider it would be wise to draft the Convention until Member Governments had had an opportunity to comment on the draft Declaration" (5).

149. Simpson, *Human Rights and the End of Empire,* 416.

150. Sellars, *The Rise and Rise of Human Rights,* 11.

151. See in general Anderson, *Eyes Off the Prize,* 101–112.

152. Sellars, *The Rise and Rise of Human Rights,* 19.

153. Mrs. Roosevelt, clarifying the nomenclature for members of the commission, remarked that while "Paragraph (a) of the terms of reference spoke of an International Bill of Rights," it did not define the term. She maintained that whatever its meaning might be in the domestic field, the term had no accepted meaning in the international realm; there was no existing concept of "bills" in international law; Mrs. Roosevelt (United States), "Commission on Human Rights: Summary Record of Meetings," ECOSOC document E/CN.4/SR.29, 8 December 1947.

154. P. C. Chang (China), "Commission on Human Rights: Summary Record of Meetings," ECOSOC document E/CN.4/SR.30, 9 December 1947.

155. René Cassin, *La Pensée et l'Action* (Paris: Lalou, 1972), 105–106.

156. In the smaller working-group meeting, Mrs. Roosevelt stressed American support for a non–legally binding declaration that would be followed by a covenant. But, justifying the delay, she warned that the treaty would be undermined if adopted prematurely by states that did not intend to honor them: "Flagrant, prolonged and repeated violations of those Conventions could not fail to harm the United Nations"; "Commission on Human Rights: Summary Record of Meetings," ECOSOC document E/CN.4/SR.25, 2 December 1947, 10.

157. This view was also expressed in the drafting of the covenant; see Mower, *The United States, the United Nations, and Human Rights.*

158. Lord Dukeston (UK), "Commission on Human Rights: Summary Record of Meetings," ECOSOC document E/CN.4/SR.28, 7 December 1947, 7.

159. Simpson reported that the head of the British Foreign Office "treated the haste with which the UN had proceeded as little short of ludicrous"; Simpson, *Human Rights and the End of Empire,* 447.

160. *General Assembly Official Records,* Third Committee, Third Session, 30 September 1948, 32.

161. Ibid., 34.

162. Mower provides evidence of this attitude on the part of the U.S. government; Mower, *United States, United Nations and Human Rights,* 42.

163. *Human Rights, the Charter of the United Nations, and the International Bill of Rights. Preliminary Report by Professor H. Lauterpacht,* ECOSOC document E/CN.4/89.

164. "Commission on Human Rights: Summary Record of Meetings," ECOSOC document E/CN.4/SR.30, 9 December 1947.

165. Mr. Klekovkin (Ukraine), "Commission on Human Rights: Summary Record of Meetings," ECOSOC document E/CN.4/SR.38, 16 December 1947.

166. Commission on Human Rights, *Report of the Drafting Committee to the Commission on Human Rights,* ECOSOC document E/600, Annex C, paragraph 10.

167. Belgian Fernand Dehousse most strongly expressed this opinion in the working group; ibid., paragraph 11.

168. *Report of the Drafting Committee on an International Bill of Human Rights,* E/CN.4/21, Annex H, "Memorandum on Implementation Prepared by the Division of Human Rights of the Secretariat at the Request of the Drafting Committee," 68–74.

169. Rómulo (Philippines), "Commission on Human Rights: Summary Record of Meetings," ECOSOC documents E/CN.4/SR.2, 3, and 4, 28–29 January 1947.

170. *Report of the Drafting Committee to the Commission on Human Rights,* ECOSOC document E/CN.4/21, Annex C.

171. The original idea called for a public prosecutor who would receive petitions from individuals and organizations and act as an advocate in the Court of Human Rights. For the historical antecedents of the position of UN high commissioner for human rights, see Roger Stenson Clark, *A United Nations High Commissioner for Human Rights* (The Hague: Nijhoff, 1972).

172. These ideas were originally proposed in *Report of the Drafting Committee to the Commission on Human Rights,* ECOSOC document E/CN.4/21, 88. The right to petition was to be open to individuals, associations, and states and was to be included in the proposed convention on human rights.

173. Article 10 of the UN Charter states: "The General Assembly may discuss any questions or any matters within the scope of the present Charter or relating to the powers and functions of any organs provided for in the present Charter, and, except as provided in Article 12, may make recommendations to the Members of the United Nations or to the Security Council or to both on any such questions or matters. Article 12 limits the ability of the GA to intervene in the event of disputes, which are to remain the domain of the Security Council."

174. Article 62 of the UN Charter states:

(1) The Economic and Social Council may make or initiate studies and reports with respect to international economic, social, cultural, educational, health, and related matters and may make recommendations with respect to any such matters to the General Assembly to the Members of the United Nations, and to the specialized agencies concerned.

(2) It may make recommendations for the purpose of promoting respect for, and observance of, human rights and fundamental freedoms for all.

(3) It may prepare draft conventions for submission to the General Assembly, with respect to matters falling within its competence.

(4) It may call, in accordance with the rules prescribed by the United Nations, international conferences on matters falling within its competence. UN Charter, Chapter X, Article 62.

175. Discussed in "Summary Record of Working Group on Implementation," ECOSOC document E/CN.4/SUB.2/SR.27, July 1947.

176. The Sub-commission on Prevention of Discrimination and Protection of Minorities had just been formed under the CHR for the purposes of addressing discrimination and minority issues.

177. *Report of the Drafting Committee to the Commission on Human Rights,* ECOSOC document E/600, Annex H, comments of the U.S. representative in footnote 1.

178. Dr. Charles Malik, "Commission on Human Rights: Summary Record of Meetings," ECOSOC document E/CN.4/SR.39, December 1947, 7.

179. Ibid.

180. The Consultative Council of Jewish Organizations modified the functions and the title to a high commissioner for human rights, based on the adoption of the High Commissioner for Refugees; ECOSOC document E/CN.4/NGO/6, 1950. The NGO proposal was officially taken up by Uruguay in the 1950 session of the General Assembly calling for the creation of a high commissioner on human rights. "[This] special representative of the international community, of the highest standing and independence, would receive petitions from individuals and organizations relating to violations of the Covenant; . . . and would seek satisfactory settlements through negotiation with the States concerned"; "Bases of the Proposal to Establish a United Nations Attorney-General for Human Rights. Memorandum Submitted by Uruguay," General Assembly document A/C.3/564, 20 December 1951.

181. "High Commissioner for the Promotion and Protection of All Human Rights," General Assembly resolution A/RES/48/141, 20 December 1993; see also P. Alston, "Neither Fish nor Fowl: The Quest to Define the Role of the UN High Commissioner for Human Rights," *European Journal of International Law* 8, no. 2 (1997): 321–335; Andrew Clapham, "Creating the High Commissioner for Human Rights: The Outside Story," *European Journal of International Law* 5, no. 1 (1994): 556–568; B. G. Ramacharan, "Strategies for the International Protection of Human Rights in the 1990s," *Human Rights Quarterly* 13, no. 2 (1991): 155–169.

6. The Universal Declaration of Human Rights

1. For an excellent analysis of the UDHR, see Johannes Morsink, *The Universal Declaration of Human Rights: Origins, Drafting, and Intent* (Philadelphia: University of Pennsylvania Press, 1999). During the period between 1947 and June 1948, the declaration was still referred to as the International Declaration on Human Rights or the Manifesto in documents and discussions.

2. John P. Humphrey, *Human Rights & the United Nations: A Great Adventure* (Dobbs Ferry, N.Y.: Transnational Publishers, 1984), 29–30.

3. Morsink, *The Universal Declaration of Human Rights,* 7–9.

4. *Report of the Drafting Committee to the Commission on Human Rights,* ECOSOC document E/CN.4/21, Annex D, 1 July 1947.

5. *Report of the Drafting Committee to the Commission on Human Rights,* ECOSOC document E/CN.4/95, 21 May 1948.

6. Morsink, *The Universal Declaration of Human Rights*, 7–9. See *Yearbook of the United Nations 1948–1949* (Lake Success, N.Y.: United Nations, 1950), which observes that the Third Committee of the General Assembly discussed the draft in meetings 88 to 105, 107 to 116, 119 to 134, 137 to 167, and 174 to 179. It notes 85 meetings.

7. The proposal put forward by Malik (Lebanon) was adopted in General Assembly document A/C.3/380, 30 November 1948. However, translations created another problem that took several additional meetings (174 to 178) to work out.

8. "USSR Amendment to the Draft Declaration of Human Rights," General Assembly document A/C.3/407, 7 December 1948.

9. For a summary of views, see *Yearbook of the United Nations 1948–1949*, 525–542.

10. "Statement by Mrs. Roosevelt, Department of State, on 9th December to the General Assembly," State Department Bulletin, 19 December 1948, 751.

11. According to Humphrey, the UK draft defined civil and political rights with the great precision "appropriate to a text that was meant to become a treaty" and should have been used to draft the Covenant on Civil and Political Rights. In the UK draft, state parties would recognize that the rights defined in the covenant were founded on "the general principles of law recognized by civilized nations," a state-of-the-art term used to settle disputes in the World Court. This term would have imparted an enforceable character to the treaty, but the UK draft was not used. Humphrey, *Human Rights & the United Nations*, 38.

12. The Humphrey draft was not really an outline but a listing of provisions for a declaration. John Hobbins, ed., *On the Edge of Greatness: The Diaries of John Humphrey, First Director of the United Nations Division of Human Rights*, vol. 1, *1948–1949* (Montreal: McGill University Libraries, 1994), 21. Discussions of his submissions at the commission were noted in *Report of the Drafting Committee to the Commission on Human Rights*, ECOSOC document E/CN.4/21, 1 July 1947, and annexes A–E.

13. John Humphrey wrote: "The best of texts from which I worked was the one prepared by the American Law Institute, and I borrowed freely from it. This was the text that had been unsuccessfully sponsored by Panama at the San Francisco conference and later in the General Assembly. It had been drafted in the United States during the war by a distinguished group representing many cultures, one of whom was Alfredo Alfaro, the Panamanian foreign minister"; Humphrey, *Human Rights & the United Nations*, 32.

14. A. W. Brian Simpson, *Human Rights and the End of Empire: Britain and the Genesis of the European Convention* (Oxford: Oxford University Press, 2004), 412.

15. The American Law Institute draft included eighteen articles with a short preamble on freedom of the individual. Article 1 was on freedom of religion; Article 2 on freedom of opinion; Article 3 on freedom of speech; Article 4 on freedom of assembly; Article 5 on freedom of association (for political, economic, religious, social, cultural, or any other reason); Article 6 on freedom from wrongful interference; Article 7 on fair trial; Article 8 on freedom from arbitrary detention; Article 9 on retroactive law (prohibition of ex post facto); Article 10 on property rights; Article 11 on education; Article 12 on work; Article 13 on conditions of work; Article 14 on food and housing; Article 15 on social security; Article 16 on participation in government; Article 17 on equal protection;

Article 18 on limiting the exercise of rights. Committee appointed by the American Law Institute, "Statement of Essential Human Rights," *Annals of the American Academy* 243 (January 1946): 18–26.

16. "Secretariat Draft Outline of the Declaration of Human Rights," ECOSOC document E/CN.4/AC.1/8, 11 June 1947.

17. Mr. Koretsky (USSR), "Commission on Human Rights: Summary Record of Meetings," ECOSOC document E/CN.4/AC.1/SR.6, 16 June 1947.

18. Humphrey, *Human Rights & the United Nations,* 41.

19. Ibid., 42.

20. *Report of the Drafting Committee to the Commission of Human Rights,* ECOSOC document E/CN.4/21, 1 July 1947. For a comparison of Humphrey's draft with Cassin's, see UN Secretariat, "Draft Outline of the International Bill of Human Rights," ECOSOC document E/CN.4/AC.1/3, 2 June 1947, Annex A; and "International Bill of Rights, Revised Suggestions Submitted by the Representative of France for Articles of the International Declaration of Rights," ECOSOC document E/CN.4/AC.1/W.2/Rev. 2, 1 July 1947, Annex E.

21. Simpson, *Human Rights and the End of Empire,* 420–421.

22. ECOSOC document E/CN.4/21, Annex D, 1 July 1947, preamble. E/CN.4/21 is the Cassin draft.

23. The UK rejected the notion because it violated the rights of conscientious objectors, and Mrs. Roosevelt pointed out that military service was not a right or a freedom. See "International Bill of Rights, Revised Suggestions Submitted by the Representative of France for Articles of the International Declaration of Rights," Article 29.

24. "International Bill of Human Rights," General Assembly resolution A/RES/217 (III), 10 December 1948, Article 27(2).

25. Kirsten Sellars, *The Rise and Rise of Human Rights* (Thrupp, UK: Sutton Publishing, 2002), 23 nn89–91.

26. UNESCO, *Human Rights: Comments and Interpretations* (New York: Columbia University Press, 1949).

27. The meeting records show that although UNESCO sent the report to the CHR, it also chose to publish extracts in the *Weekly Bulletin* of the UN; see "Commission on Human Rights: Summary Record of Meetings," ECOSOC document E/CN.4/SR.26, December 1947, 11.

28. UNESCO, *Human Rights: Comments and Interpretations,* 263.

29. Ibid., 271.

30. Jacques Maritain, "Introduction," in ibid., 13.

31. Ibid., 255.

32. Ibid., 18.

33. Ibid., 94–95.

34. Ibid., 60.

35. Ibid., 189–190.

36. Ibid., Appendix II, 258–272.

37. Ibid., 268–271.

38. Ibid., 9.

39. "Commission on Human Rights: Summary Record of Meetings," ECOSOC document E/CN.4/SR.26, December 1947, 12.

40. Ibid., 17.

41. See in general "Commission on Human Rights: Summary Record of Meetings," ECOSOC document E/CN.4/SR.26, December 1947.

42. Since the CHR had decided that summary records of the two meetings (SR.25 and 26) would take the form of restricted documents, it was not necessary to make public the votes on the resolutions that were adopted. See ibid., 16.

43. See discussion in Morsink, *The Universal Declaration of Human Rights,* section 8.4. Morsink notes that the concept of rights was rooted in the writings of Thomas Paine and John Locke and that the concept of collective rights was derived from the rights of the individual.

44. State Department report, quoted in Sellars, *The Rise and Rise of Human Rights,* 15.

45. Preamble to the UDHR.

46. Humphrey draft (1947), quoted in Glendon, *A World Made New,* 271–274.

47. Bogomolov quoted in Morsink, *The Universal Declaration of Human Rights,* 284.

48. Ibid., 118.

49. Ibid., 116–129.

50. "Universal Declaration of Human Rights," General Assembly resolution 217A (III), 10 December 1948, Article 1.

51. Morsink, *The Universal Declaration of Human Right,* 269–280; and Simpson, *Human Rights and the End of Empire,* 441–442.

52. Humphrey, *Human Rights & the United Nations,* 69.

53. Sellars, *The Rise and Rise of Human Rights,* 22.

54. Morsink, *The Universal Declaration of Human Rights,* 99–209.

55. Ibid., quoted on page 205. Zakat is discussed on pages 204–207.

56. Frank E. Holman, "An International Bill of Rights: Proposals Have Dangerous Implications for U.S.," *American Bar Association Journal* 34 (1948): 625–632; Frank E. Holman, "International Proposals Affecting So-Called Human Rights," *Law and Contemporary Problems* 14, no. 3 (1949): 479–489. Holman opposed any mention of economic and social rights. For FDR's support for economic and social rights, see Cass R. Sunstein, *The Second Bill of Rights: FDR's Unfinished Revolution and Why We Need It More Than Ever* (New York: Basic Books, 2004).

57. The first of such remarks were made by Cassin at the plenary meeting of the General Assembly. His criticism was that the right to employment or social security required more material layout than traditional civil and political rights.

58. *General Assembly Official Records,* Third Committee, 88th–108th Meetings, 29 September to 18 October, 499.

59. "Commission on Human Rights: Summary Record of Meetings," ECOSOC document E/CN.4/SR.72, April 1948, 4.

60. On the typology of duties, see Asbjørn Eide, "Realization of Social and Economic Rights and the Minimum Threshold Approach," *Human Rights Law Journal* 10 (1989):

35; Henry Shue, *Basic Rights: Subsistence, Affluence, and U.S. Foreign Policy* (Princeton, N.J.: Princeton University Press, 1980).

61. "Commission on Human Rights: Summary Record of Meetings," ECOSOC document E/CN.4/SR.61, 11 June 1948, 17. The issue of placement of umbrella articles is more fully developed in Johannes Morsink, "The Philosophy of the Universal Declaration," *Human Rights Quarterly* 6, no. 3 (1984): 225–230, 331–332.

62. "Commission on Human Rights: Summary Record of Meetings," ECOSOC document E/CN.4/SR.67, 11 June 1948, 2. The word "good" was later deleted.

63. Mr. Pavlov (USSR), General Assembly document A/C.3/303/Rev. 1, 1948, 638.

64. Stephen Marks, "Emerging Human Rights: A New Generation for the 1980s?" *Rutgers Law Review* 435 (Winter 1981): 435–452; Philip Alston, *People's Rights* (New York: Oxford University Press, 2001).

65. Morsink, "The Philosophy of the Universal Declaration," 310.

66. Stephen P. Marks, "From the 'Single Confused Page' to the 'Decalogue for Six Billion Persons': The Roots of the Universal Declaration of Human Rights in the French Revolution," *Human Rights Quarterly* 20, no. 3 (1998): 459–514. Marks traces the similarities and differences in human rights ideas in the French Declaration and the UDHR. He comments that although the philosophical foundations of human rights in the UDHR mirror those of European liberalism, they contain other philosophical ideologies, such as the idea of racial and gender equality.

67. See Morsink, *The Universal Declaration of Human Rights,* 156–190, on economic and social rights.

68. Mr. Radovanovic (Yugoslavia), *General Assembly Official Records,* Third Committee, 183rd Plenary Meeting, 10 December 1948, 58–59.

69. The reasoning that human rights could not be conceived outside the state was repeated several times by representatives of all the communist states, who argued that the very concepts of rights and law were connected with the state.

70. This was stressed for the right to work and work-related rights in general. See Morsink, *The Universal Declaration of Human Rights,* 157–190.

71. Mrs. Roosevelt (United States) noted: "It [the U.S. government] did not believe that the economic, social and cultural rights listed in the latter part of the declaration implied the need for direct government action"; *General Assembly Official Records,* Third Committee, 89th meeting, 30 September 1948, discussing the *Report of the Third Session of the Commission on Human Rights,* ECOSOC document E/800, 28 June 1948, 33. The denial of any state obligation was a direct reply to the Russian delegate, Mr. Pavlov, who in discussions in the Third Committee had proposed that Article 22 include the statement that the state would undertake all necessary measures, including legislation, to ensure that its citizens would have these rights.

72. "American Declaration of the Rights and Duties of Man," Organization of American States resolution XXX, adopted by the Ninth International Conference of American States (1948), reprinted in *Basic Documents Pertaining to Human Rights in the Inter-American System* (Washington, D.C.: General Secretariat, Organization of American States, 1992), 17.

73. General Assembly document A/C.3/104, 16 October 1948, 164. The initial proposal was submitted by Cuba, Lebanon, and Uruguay. Mexico joined later. Article 3 in the UDHR says: "Everyone has the right to life, liberty and security of the person."

74. Mr. De Alba (Mexico), *Report of the Third Session of the Commission on Human Rights*, 143.

75. Sunstein, *The Second Bill of Rights*. Roosevelt had listed several rights: the right to a useful and remunerative job; the right to earn enough to provide food, clothing, and recreation; and the right to a decent living.

76. "General Assembly, Third Committee, Summary Records," General Assembly document A/C.3/SR.104, 16 October 1948, 164.

77. See "General Assembly, Third Committee, Summary Records," General Assembly document A/C.3/SR.103–104, 15 October 1948.

78. Some argue that the Convention on the Rights of the Child expresses a fully integrated view of human rights that does not recognize any distinction between sets of rights, but this convention did not come into force until more than forty years after the Universal Declaration on Human Rights.

79. Mr. Carrera Andrade (Ecuador), "General Assembly, Third Committee, Summary Records," General Assembly document A/C.3/SR.183, 10 December 1948, 918.

80. Mr. Louw, *General Assembly Official Records*, Third Committee, Third Session, 90th meeting, 10 October 1948, 39–40.

81. Baroody, quoted in Marnia Lazreg, "Human Rights, State and Ideology: An Historical Perspective," in *Human Rights: Cultural and Ideological Perspectives*, by Adamantia Pollis and Peter Schwab (Praeger: New York, 1979), 35.

82. Mr. Baroody (Saudi Arabia), "General Assembly, Third Committee, Summary Records," General Assembly document A/C.3/SR.90, 1948, 49. Mr. Baroody clarified that although the UDHR did not run counter to eastern values, it did not conform to them. At the time of adoption, he reemphasized that the drafters had only recognized western standards and that "it was not for the Committee to proclaim the superiority of one civilization over all the others or to establish uniform standards for all the countries in the world"; *General Assembly Official Records*, Third Committee, Third Session, 168th meeting, 1 December 1948, 370.

83. Statement of Mr. Vyshinsky, *General Assembly Official Records*, Third Committee, Third Session, 183rd plenary meeting, 10 December 1948, 926–928. Another Soviet delegate, Mr. Pavlov, declared the UDHR "absolutely unsatisfactory," arguing that it contained such "serious defects and omissions" that it should be rejected entirely and replaced with an instrument that would "effectively serve the cause of historical progress, democracy . . . [and] finally lead to an assertion of the principles of equality of nations, real respect for human rights and freedoms and the strengthening of international peace"; statement by the delegation of the Union of Soviet Socialist Republics, 18 June 1948, in *Report of the Third Session of the Commission on Human Rights*, ECOSOC document E/800, 28 June 1948, 37–39.

84. Mr. Pavlov (USSR), "General Assembly, Third Committee, Summary Records," General Assembly document A/C.3/SR.96, 7 October 1948, 110.

85. Humphrey, *Human Rights & the United Nations*, 32.

86. Asbjørn Eide, "The Historical Significance of the Universal Declaration," *International Social Science Journal* 50, no. 4 (1998): 494. Eide argues that by adopting the UDHR, member states of the UN attempted to make a break with traditional realpolitik that dictates normal intergovernmental relations. In his opinion, the UDHR is significant in the evolution of human rights ideas in the following respects: (1) restoring the process of normative development; (2) broadening the twin concepts of freedom and equality; (3) expanding the content of human rights by including economic, social, and cultural rights; (4) expanding rights to the whole world (widening the geographical scope); and (5) making human rights a legitimate concern of international law. See also Susan Waltz, "Reclaiming and Rebuilding the History of the Universal Declaration of Human Rights," *Third World Quarterly* 23, no. 3 (2002): 437–448.

87. Quoted in Carole Anderson, *Eyes Off the Prize: The United Nations and the African American Struggle for Human Rights, 1944–1955* (Cambridge: Cambridge University Press, 2003), 131.

88. Makau Mutua, "Is the Universal Declaration of Human Rights Truly Universal?" in *Harvard Human Rights Program 20th Anniversary Symposium* (Cambridge, Mass.: Harvard Law School, 2001).

89. Marc Agi, *René Cassin, Père de la Déclaration Universelle des Droits de l'Homme* (René Cassin, Father of the Universal Declaration of Human Rights) (Paris: Librairie Académique Perrin, 1998). See also Tony Evans, *U.S. Hegemony and the Project of Universal Human Rights* (New York: St. Martin's Press, 1996), 93.

90. Mary Ann Glendon, "The Forgotten Crucible: The Latin American Influence on the Universal Human Rights Idea," *Harvard Human Rights Journal* 16 (2003): 27–40; William Korey, *NGOs and the Universal Declaration of Human Rights* (New York: St. Martins Press, 1998).

91. Humphrey, *Human Rights & the United Nations*, 64–65.

7. The Human Rights Covenants

1. Summary available in Human Rights Commission, *Report of the Drafting Committee, First Session,* ECOSOC document E/CN.4/21, 1 July 1947. Annex B of this report identified the international bill of rights as a convention.

2. The nature of political negotiations between vastly unequal states resulted in outcomes that reflected the hierarchy of international power rather than a moral consensus or compromise based on principles of dignity and justice. Tony Evans, "Power, Hegemony, and the Universalization of Human Rights," in *Human Rights Fifty Years On: A Reappraisal,* ed. Tony Evans (Manchester, UK: Manchester University Press, 1998), 123.

3. The working group stopped meeting after 1950, although several of its proposals were later resurrected in different guises. For example, the individual right of petition was eventually recognized in the optional protocols to the covenants, and the office of attorney general for human rights was adopted in the form of the high commissioner for human rights in 1993.

4. Mr. Malik (Lebanon), "Commission on Human Rights: Summary Record of Meetings," ECOSOC document E/CN.4/SR.28, 1947, 10–11.

5. "International Covenant on Economic, Social and Cultural Rights, International Covenant on Civil and Political Rights and Optional Protocol to the International Covenant on Civil and Political Rights," General Assembly resolution A/RES/2200 (XXI), 16 December 1966. Despite its origin as a euphemism for imposing a hierarchy within the human rights corpus, the phrase "interdependence and indivisibility of all human rights" has become a boilerplate in recent UN discourse; a Google search of this term on 2 March 2007 turned up over 9,800 citations.

6. See Herbert W. Briggs, "Chinese Representation in the United Nations," *International Organization* 6, no. 2 (1952): 192–209.

7. See Gabriel Kolko, *Century of War: Politics, Conflicts, and Society since 1914* (New York: W. W. Norton, 1994), 395–411; Stanley Meisler, *United Nations: The First Fifty Years* (New York: Atlantic Monthly Press, 1995), 75–95; Martin Gilbert, *History of the Twentieth Century,* concise ed. (New York: William Morrow, 2001), 347–359. For a positive view of the General Assembly's "Uniting for Peace" resolution, see "The 'Uniting For Peace' Resolution of the United Nations," *American Journal of International Law* 45, no. 21 (1950): 129–137.

8. See Mark Mazower, *Dark Continent: Europe's Twentieth Century* (New York: Alfred Knopf, 1999), 263–277; Eric Hobsbawm, *The Age of Extremes: A History of the World, 1914–1991* (New York: Random House, 1994), 389–400.

9. See John P. Humphrey, *Human Rights & the United Nations: A Great Adventure* (Dobbs Ferry, N.Y.: Transnational Publishers, 1984), 134, 170–171; Meisler, *United Nations,* 81–84; Richard O. Davies, *Defender of the Old Guard: John Bricker and American Politics* (Columbus: Ohio State University Press, 1993), 153–184.

10. René Cassin, *La Pensée et l'Action* (Boulogne-sur-Seine: F. Lalou, 1972), 83.

11. See Hobsbawm, *Age of Extremes,* 344–371, 433–439; A. W. Brian Simpson, *Human Rights and the End of Empire: Britain and the Genesis of the European Convention* (Oxford: Oxford University Press, 2001), 1085–1086, 1099–1100.

12. *Report of the Drafting Committee to the Commission on Human Rights,* ECOSOC document E/600, 17 December 1947, Annex B.

13 Ibid., 27.

14. Cassin submitted a draft covenant that included these rights to the drafting committee; see ECOSOC document E/CN.4/82/Add. 8, May 1948.

15. *Report of the Working Group on the International Covenant,* E/CN.4/AC.3/1–9, June 1947.

16. *Report of the Drafting Committee to the Commission on Human Rights,* Part II, "Comments on the Draft International Covenant."

17. Ibid., Annex B, Part I contained general provisions on creating a framework. Part II, Articles 5–22, addressed civil and political rights, including the right to life, the prohibition of slavery, the right of personal liberty and due process, the right to leave one's own or another country, the prohibition of retrospective criminal laws, freedom of religion and belief, parental control over the religious education of minors, freedom of expression and association, and freedom of assembly. Articles 8 and 10 protected the rights of worker; the International Labour Organization was involved in drafting these articles. Articles

24 and 25 addressed issues of implementation and enforcement in federal states (federal clause) and for non-self governing-territories (the colonial clause).

18. "International Bill of Human Rights," General Assembly resolution 217 (III) E, 10 December 1948. The resolution was passed by 44 votes to 0, with 8 abstentions, and it requested that the Economic and Social Council give priority to preparing the draft covenant on human rights.

19. Humphrey, *Human Rights & the United Nations,* 83.

20. In the sixth session of the CHR, the USSR moved to expel P. C. Chang. In response, Mrs. Roosevelt read a statement prepared by the State Department ruling the motion out of order and rejecting further discussion. Humphrey commented that this was an unusual and authoritarian exercise of the chair's privilege. Humphrey, *Human Rights & the United Nations,* 105.

21. Quoted in Mary Ann Glendon, *A World Made New: Eleanor Roosevelt and the Universal Declaration of Human Rights* (New York: Random House, 2001), 211.

22. Humphrey, *Human Rights & the United Nations,* 85.

23. *Report of the Fifth Session of the Commission on Human Rights to the Economic and Social Council,* ECOSOC document E/1317, June 1949. Annex III included suggestions for adding articles on economic, social, and cultural rights that included the right to work for women and men, equal pay for women and men, and the right to rest and leisure, social security, and education.

24. William G. Cornelius, "The 'Latin-American Bloc' in the United Nations," *Journal of Inter-American Studies* 3, no. 3 (1961): 419–435. The Latin American view is also expressed in *Draft International Covenant on Human Rights and Measures of Implementation: Report of the Third Committee,* General Assembly document A/1559, 29 November 1950. In this report, the Uruguay representative proposed that a permanent agency of the UN be established to be known as the attorney-general's office or the high commission for human rights.

25. "General Assembly, Third Committee, Summary Records," General Assembly document A/C.3/SR.89, October 1948, 35.

26. Lord MacDonald (UK), "General Assembly, Third Committee, Summary Records," General Assembly document A/C.3/SR.288, 1950, 108. He went so far as to raise the specter of fascism to warn against granting international sanction to vague and meaningless human rights pronouncements: "When the Nazi and fascist governments before and during the war . . . consistently trampled on human rights, they did so by means of laws which were valid according to their national constitutions. If the final version of the covenant contains an article drafted in such terms, all that some future Hitler would require in order to avoid violating that article would be to pass a law making membership of a particular racial or religious group, for example, punishable by imprisonment" (ibid.).

27. Mr. Azkoul (Lebanon), "General Assembly, Third Committee, Summary Records," General Assembly document A/C.3/SR.289, 1950, 111.

28. Ibid.

29. *Draft International Covenant on Human Rights and Measures of Implementation: Report of the Third Committee,* 37–41.

30. Mr. Noriega (Mexico), "General Assembly, Third Committee, Summary Records," General Assembly document A/C.3/SR.306, November 1950, 225.

31. Mr. Pavlov (USSR), "General Assembly, Third Committee, Summary Records," General Assembly document A/C.3/SR.289, October 1950, 114–115.

32. Mr. Hoffmeister (Czechoslovakia), "General Assembly, Third Committee, Summary Records," General Assembly document A/C.3/SR.290, October 1950, 118.

33. Mr. Pleic (Yugoslavia), "General Assembly, Third Committee, Summary Records," General Assembly document A/C.3/SR.298, October 1950, 178.

34. "Draft International Covenant on Human Rights and Measures of Implementation: Future Work of the Commission on Human Rights," General Assembly resolution 421 (V), 4 December 1950. The resolution was based on *Draft International Covenant on Human Rights and Measures of Implementation: Report of the Third Committee.*

35. Mrs. Lionaes (Norway), "General Assembly, Third Committee, Summary Records," General Assembly document A/C.3/SR.307, November 1950, 228.

36. Sir Lionel Heald (United Kingdom), "General Assembly, Third Committee, Summary Records," General Assembly document A/C.3/SR.361, 1951, 88.

37. Mrs. Roosevelt (United States), "General Assembly, Third Committee, Summary Records," General Assembly document A/C.3/SR.364, 1951,105.

38. At the first meeting of ECOSOC in 1946, Mrs. Begtrup argued that the subcommission on women should not fall under the purview of the Human Rights Commission, declaring that women did not want to be "dependent on the pace of another commission." Humphrey opposed the idea and felt she had no mandate to speak on behalf of her colleagues. When the independent Commission on the Status of Women was formed, Mrs. Begtrup was elected as the first chair. She went on to serve as president of the Danish Council of Women. See Humphrey, *Human Rights & the United Nations,* 19, 30.

39. Mrs. Begtrup (Denmark), "General Assembly, Third Committee, Summary Records," General Assembly document A/C.3/SR.297, October 1950, 174.

40. Mr. Altman (Poland), ibid.

41. The vote for the draft resolution was put to vote at the 318th meeting of the Third Committee held on 17 November 1950. See "Draft International Covenant on Human Rights and Measures of Implementation: Future Work of the Commission on Human Rights," General Assembly resolution 421 E (V), 4 December 1950. Article 7 specified that a single covenant would include economic, social, and cultural rights.

42. *Report of the Seventh Session of the Commission on Human Rights to the Economic and Social Council,* ECOSOC document E/1992, July 1952. The CHR agreed that a human rights committee would be established to supervise implementation and that states would agree to work toward full realization of rights through the use of maximum available resources and submit periodic progress reports to ECOSOC. But members disagreed on whether economic, social, and cultural rights could be implemented in the same manner.

43. Humphrey, *Human Rights & the United Nations,* 144.

44. ECOSOC resolution 384 (XIII) C, 29 August 1951, summarizing previous ECOSOC resolutions E/L.233 and E/L.233/Add. 1, 1951, in *Yearbook of the United Nations 1951* (New York: Columbia University Press, 1951), 481. Belgium and Uruguay stated

that they did not disagree with the principle of including economic, social, and cultural rights but believed that separating them in different instruments would allow for more comprehensive and practical treatment. The resolution was adopted by 11 votes to 5, with 2 abstentions.

45. Views are summarized in *Yearbook of the United Nations 1951,* 479–481.

46. See Matthew Craven, *The International Covenant on Economic, Social and Cultural Rights: A Perspective on Its Development* (Oxford: Clarendon Press, 1995), 16–22.

47. "Draft Resolution to Include Economic, Social and Cultural Rights," General Assembly document A/C.3/L.182, 1951.

48. "Joint Draft Resolution to Draft Two Covenants on Human Rights," General Assembly document A/C.3/L.185/Rev. 1, 1951.

49. The General Assembly debate in the Third Committee is summarized in *Draft International Covenant on Human Rights and Measures of Implementation,* Section III, 8–12. Humphrey wrote in his diary on 18 November 1951 that Malik discussed with him the advisability of adopting two separate covenants instead of one, which could be submitted to governments simultaneously for signatures, adding "this of course is the American line." The next day he wrote that the Lebanese had consistently favored two instruments. A. J. Hobbins, ed., *On the Edge of Greatness: The Diaries of John Humphrey,* vol. 2, *1950–1951* (Montreal: McGill University Libraries, 1996), 285.

50. Chile submitted amendment at the 374th plenary meeting of the Third Committee of the General Assembly on 4 February 1952, the day before the final resolution was approved; *Yearbook of the United Nations 1951,* 484.

51. "Preparation of Two Drafts International Covenants on Human Rights," General Assembly resolution 543 (VI), 5 February 1952.

52. Ibid.

53. In its eighth session (April–June 1952), the CHR considered separate covenants for each set of rights and adopted an article on the right of peoples and nations to self-determination. For final text of substantive articles of the commission drafts, see *Report of the Commission on Human Rights (Ninth Session), Draft International Covenants on Human Rights,* ECOSOC document E/2447, 29 November 1954.

54. See Farrokh Jhabvala, "The Soviet-Bloc's View of the Implementation of Human Rights Accords," *Human Rights Quarterly* 17, no. 4 (1985): 461–491.

55. For a comprehensive review of the drafting history of the International Covenant on Economic, Social and Cultural Rights, see Craven, *The International Covenant on Economic, Social and Cultural Rights,* 106–152; and Philip Alston and Gerard Quinn, "The Nature and Scope of States Parties' Obligations under the International Covenant on Economic, Social and Cultural Rights," *Human Rights Quarterly* 9, no. 2 (1987): 156–229. For the drafting history of the International Covenant on Civil and Political Rights, see Manfred Nowak, *UN Covenant on Civil and Political Rights: CCPR Commentary,* 2nd ed. (Kehl, Germany: N. P. Engel, 2005); and Vratislav Pechota, "The Development of the Covenant on Civil and Political Rights," in *The International Bill of Rights,* ed. Louis Henkin (New York: Columbia University Press, 1981).

56. Compare "International Covenant on Economic, Social and Cultural Rights, International Covenant on Civil And Political Rights and Optional Protocol to the International

Covenant on Civil and Political Rights," General Assembly resolution A/RES/2200 (XXI), 16 December 1966, with "International Covenant on Economic, Social and Cultural Rights," General Assembly resolution A/RES/2200A (XXI), 16 December 1966.

57. International Covenant on Civil and Political Rights, Articles 6, 7, 9, and 14.

58. International Covenant on Economic, Social and Cultural Rights, Articles 6, 8, and 11.

59. International Covenant on Civil and Political Rights, Article 2(3).

60. International Covenant on Economic, Social and Cultural Rights, Article 2(1). The Committee on Economic, Social and Cultural Rights, established by ECOSOC in 1986 to monitor the covenant, has interpreted the "progressive realization clause" as a limitation on the ability of states to avoid meeting the demands of the covenant and a clear statement of their concrete obligations. See "General Comment 3 of the Committee on Economic, Social and Cultural Rights," ECOSOC document E/C.12/1990/12, 14 December 1990, paragraphs 8–11. Similarly, the UN special rapporteur on economic, social, and cultural rights has noted that under the covenant, "States are obliged, regardless of their level of economic development, to ensure respect for minimum subsistence rights for all." Danilo Turk, *Second Progress Report of the UN Special Rapporteur on Economic, Social and Cultural Rights,* ECOSOC document E/CN.4/Sub.2/1991/17, paragraph 10.

61. For a summary of discussion of amendments and the adoption of changes, see *Draft International Covenant on Human Rights; Annotation: Report of the Secretary-General,* General Assembly document A/2929, 1 July 1955.

62. Soviet opposition to any forms of implementation is described in James Simsarian, "Draft International Covenant on Human Rights Revised at Fifth Session of United Nations Commission on Human Rights," *American Journal of International Law* 43, no. 4 (1949): 779–786. See also Jhabvala, "The Soviet-Bloc's View of the Implementation of Human Rights Accords," 461–491.

63. The Committee on Economic, Social and Cultural Rights has over time expanded its limited grant of authority by developing innovative jurisprudence through specific observations on state reports and general comments elaborating broader points of law. Scott Leckie, "Another Step towards Indivisibility: Violations of Economic, Social and Cultural Rights," *Human Rights Quarterly* 20, no. 1 (1998): 81–124. Reflecting the perspective of progressive human rights scholars, Richard Falk has argued that any state that "maintains an economic situation in which a small proportion of the population gains most of the wealth while a large majority subsists at or below the poverty line is guilty of violating this category of human rights"; Richard A. Falk, *Human Rights and State Sovereignty* (New York: Holmes & Meier Publishers, 1981), 7.

64. International Covenant on Civil and Political Rights, Articles 28–45.

65. Cass R. Sunstein, *The Second Bill of Rights: FDR's Unfinished Revolution and Why We Need It More Than Ever* (New York: Basic Books, 2004).

66. Peter Gowan, "US: UN," *New Left Review* 24 (November–December 2003): 21.

67. See Tony Evans, *U.S. Hegemony and the Project of Universal Human Rights* (Basingstoke: Macmillan, 1996), 77; Durward Sandifer to Eleanor Roosevelt, 5 February 1947, quoted in A. Glenn Mower, Jr., *The United States, the United Nations, and Human*

Rights: The Eleanor Roosevelt and Jimmy Carter Eras (Westport, Conn.: Greenwood Press, 1979), 42.

68. In legal history, this broad transformation is called the move from status to contract, whereby legal relations formerly determined by birth status and feudal class were replaced by individual agreements memorialized by freely negotiated written contracts. Burns Weston, "Human Rights," *Human Rights Quarterly* 6, no. 3 (August 1984): 258–262; Lauren, *The Evolution of International Human Rights*, 14–36; Louis Henkin, Gerald L. Neumann, David W. Leebron, and Diane F. Orentlicher, eds., *Human Rights* (New York: Foundation Press, 1999), 30–41, 50–52.

69. Mr. Lesage (Canada), "General Assembly, Third Committee, Summary Records," General Assembly document A/C.3/SR.297, 1950, 174. His government considered that difference significant enough to prevent its support for including economic and social rights in the covenant.

70. Mr. Lesage cited Article 27 of the Universal Declaration of Human Rights, the right to participate in cultural life of the community, as an example of a basic freedom of the individual that could not be formulated in terms of a legal obligation or enforced through established judicial process; ibid.

71. Tony Evans highlights how this conception of economic, social, and cultural rights as "progressive" also found expression in the argument that the idea of human rights should be conceived of as a point of departure rather than one of arrival. See Evans, *U.S. Hegemony and the Project of Universal Human Rights*, 78.

72. Mr. D'Souza (India), "General Assembly, Third Committee, Summary Records," General Assembly document A/C.3/SR.361, 1951, 86. Mr. D'Souza commented: "India recognizes the need for unity, but has never confused unity with uniformity"; ibid.

73. Ibid.

74. Sir Heald (UK), ibid., 86–87.

75. Mr. Dehousse (Belgium), ibid., 83–84.

76. James Fredrick Green, *The United Nations and Human Rights* (Washington, D.C.: Brookings Institution, 1956), 41–42.

77. Mr. Hussain (Pakistan) noted that in the future the decision might be reversed by public opinion. Mr. Valenzuela (Chile) commented that there might be a movement towards a single covenant at the next General Assembly given the experience of the eighth session of the CHR. "General Assembly, Third Committee, Summary Records," General Assembly document A/C.3/SR.396, 1952, 2941.

78. Mrs. Afnan (Iraq), "General Assembly, Third Committee, Summary Records," General Assembly document A/C.3/SR.371, 1951, 142.

79. Mr. Najar (Israel) "General Assembly, Third Committee, Summary Records," General Assembly document A/C.3/SR.410, 1952.

80. Ibid.

81. Alston and Quinn, "The Nature and Scope of States Parties' Obligations under the International Covenant on Economic, Social and Cultural Rights," 177.

82. Craig Scott and Patrick Macklem, "Constitutional Ropes of Sand or Justiciable Guarantees? Social Rights in a New South African Constitution," *Pennsylvania Law Re-*

view 141, no. 1 (1992): 1–48. A global network of human rights groups called ESCR-Net has compiled a searchable database, in English and Spanish, of sixty-eight cases from jurisdictions worldwide in which economic and social rights have been adjudicated by competent tribunals. According to network's website, "The cases in this Database—and many others elsewhere—confirm that economic, social and cultural rights, like all other human rights, impose a series of obligations (both positive and negative) upon States and that courts and other adjudicative bodies may determine, on a case by case basis, whether the rights have been violated, either by state action, inaction or a combination of both." The database is available online at http://www.escr-net.org/caselaw/.

83. Asbjørn Eide, "Economic, Social and Cultural Rights as Human Rights," in *Economic, Social and Cultural Rights: A Textbook,* ed. Asbjørn Eide, Catharina Krause, and Allan Rosas (Netherlands: Kluwer Academic Publishers, 1995), 21–23; Henry Shue, "The Interdependence of Duties," in *The Right to Food,* ed. Philip Alston and K. Tomasevski (Dordrecht: Martinus Nijhoff, 1984), 81–93; A. Belden Fields and Wolf-Dieter Narr, "Human Rights as a Holistic Concept," *Human Rights Quarterly* 14, no. 1 (February 1992): 1–20; William Felice, *The Global New Deal: Economic and Social Human Rights in World Politics* (Lanham, Md.: Rowman & Littlefield, 2002).

84. Compare Theodore Meron, "On a Hierarchy of International Human Rights," *American Journal of International Law* 80, no. 1 (1986): 1–23; and Jack Donnelly, "Recent Trends in UN Human Rights Activity: Description and Polemic," *International Organization* 35, no. 4 (1981): 633–655.

85. For a review of how the trend toward increasing inequality has accelerated under a form of economic globalization detached from human rights considerations, see Michael Chossudovsky, *The Globalization of Poverty and the New World Order* (Shanty Bay, Canada: Global Outlook 2003); UNDP, *Millennium Development Goals: A Compact among Nations to End Human Poverty* (New York: Oxford University Press, 2003); Roger Normand, "Background Paper for HDR, Separate and Unequal: Trade and Human Rights Regimes," January 2000, available from the author.

86. In its general comment on the right to self-determination in 1984, the Human Rights Committee proclaimed that "self determination is a fundamental human right," yet it purposely avoided fleshing out the legal interpretation of self-determination on the political grounds that it is "one of the most awkward to define, since abuse of that right could jeopardize international peace and security in giving States the impression that their territorial integrity was threatened." *Report of the Human Rights Committee,* General Assembly document A/39/40, 1984, 142–43.

87. International Covenant on Civil and Political Rights and International Covenant on Economic, Social and Cultural Rights, Common Article 1.

88. Humphrey, *Human Rights & the United Nations,* 10.

89. Soon after the creation of the UN, major Asian nations, including India, Pakistan, Burma, Sri Lanka, Indonesia, and the Philippines, won independence. The pace of decolonization in Africa was slower; in 1955 there were only four independent states including South Africa, but the process accelerated, and in 1960 alone, seventeen African states declared independence. See Lauren, *The Evolution of International Human Rights,* 249–252.

90. As a measure of how unexpected this was, one scholar notes that delegates at the San Francisco conference believed that the UN could achieve disarmament in a decade but that decolonization might take a century. Antonio Cassese, *International Law* (Oxford: Oxford University Press, 2001), 285.

91. Hurst Hannum, "The Right of Self-Determination in the Twenty-First Century," *Washington & Lee Law Review* 55 (Summer 1998): 774.

92. See, for example, E. J. Hobsbawm, *Nations and Nationalism since 1780* (Cambridge: Cambridge University Press, 1990); Hans Kohn, *Nationalism: Its Meaning and History*, rev. ed. (Princeton, N.J.: D. Van Nostrand Company, 1967).

93. One historian notes that "As an agency of destruction the theory of nationalism proved one of the most potent that even modern society has known"; Alfred Cobban, *The Nation State and National Self-Determination*, rev. ed. (New York: Crowell, 1969), 36.

94. U.S. Secretary of State Robert Lansing, quoted in Cassese, *International Law,* 106.

95. David Chandler, "International Justice," *New Left Review* 6 (November–December 2000): 56.

96. Point 3, Atlantic Charter, in Roosevelt, *Public Papers and Addresses of Franklin D. Roosevelt,* 10:314.

97. UN Charter, Articles 1(2) and 55.

98. H. Quane, "The United Nations and the Evolving Right to Self-Determination," *The International and Comparative Law Quarterly* 47, no. 3 (July 1998): 537–572.

99. Clyde Eagleton, "Excesses of Self-Determination," *Foreign Affairs* 31 (1953): 592.

100. For a summary of arguments see *Draft International Covenant on Human Rights, Annotation: Report of the Secretary-General*; and opening remarks of Mr. Azmi in the Third Committee summarizing the commission debates, General Assembly document A/C.3/SR.443, November 1952, 149.

101. Mr. Kiselyov (BSSR), "General Assembly, Third Committee, Summary Records," General Assembly document A/C.3/SR.449,1952, 187–188; and "General Assembly, Third Committee, Summary Records," General Assembly document A/C.3/SR.451, 1952, 31. In another speech, he criticized the confiscation of Puerto Rican land for U.S sugar monopolies and drew attention to the colonial situation in British Kenya, where in 1949 the average annual income of a European was thirty-five times greater than that of an indigenous Kenyan. Mr. Kiselyov (BSSR), "General Assembly, Third Committee, Summary Records," General Assembly document A/C.3/SR.444, November 1952, 153–154.

102. Mrs. Lord (United States), "General Assembly, Third Committee, Summary Records," General Assembly document A/C.3/SR.827, 1957, 325.

103. "Draft International Covenant on Humans Rights and Measures of Implementation: Future Work of the Commission on Human Rights," General Assembly resolution 421D, 4 December 1950, 35.

104. "Inclusion in the International Covenant or Covenants on Human Rights of an Article Relating to the Right of Peoples to Self- Determination," General Assembly resolution 545, 5 February 1952, 36.

105. In Humphrey's opinion, self-determination was not an enforceable legal right and introducing it as such would further politicize the covenant by making it a weapon in the fight against colonialism. Humphrey, *Human Rights & the United Nations,* 129, 167.

106. David Emblidge, ed., *My Day: The Best of Eleanor Roosevelt's Acclaimed Newspaper Columns* (New York: Da Capo Press, 2001), 185.

107. Mr. Valenzuela (Chile), ECOSOC document E/CN.4/SR.256, 1952, 10.

108. *Report of the Eighth Session of the Commission on Human Rights,* ECOSOC document E/2256, 1952, 64.

109. The U.S. amendment was defeated by a vote of 28 to 22, with 5 abstentions; *United Nations Yearbook 1952* (New York: Columbia University Press, 1953), 444.

110. "The Right of Peoples to Self-Determination," General Assembly resolution 637 (VII), 20 December 1952.

111. Mr. Munro (New Zealand), "General Assembly, Third Committee, Summary Records," General Assembly document A/C.3/SR.450, November 1952, 196.

112. Mr. Demchenko (USSR), "General Assembly, Third Committee, Summary Records," General Assembly document A/C.3/SR.367, November 1951, 122.

113. Mrs. Menon (India), "General Assembly, Third Committee, Summary Records," General Assembly document A/C.3/SR.294, 1950, 151.

114. Mr. Beaufort (Netherlands), "General Assembly, Third Committee, Summary Records," General Assembly document A/C.3/SR.447, 1952, 171–172.

115. Mrs. Roosevelt (United States), "General Assembly, Third Committee, Summary Records," General Assembly document A/C.3/SR.447, 1952, 174–175.

116. Quoted in Henry J. Steiner and Philip Alston, *International Human Rights in Context: Law, Politics, Morals* (Oxford: Oxford University Press, 2000), 1251.

117. For a thorough treatment of this issue, see Hurst Hannum, "Rethinking Self-Determination," *Virginia Journal of International Law* 34 (Fall 1993): 1–69. The author notes, "Where independence is the goal, acceptance of one group's claim to self-determination necessarily implies denial of another group's competing claim of territorial integrity. When a self-determination claim comes from only a portion of the entire population of a state . . . denial of self-determination to the group can be seen as merely supporting the self-determination of the larger 'people'" (41).

118. Mr. Bey of Egypt quoted from Georges Scelle's book *Précis de droit des gens,* and later Mrs. Roosevelt, Mr. Cassin, and others mentioned it. See General Assembly document A/C.3/SR.443–452, 1952.

119. See, e.g., Hobsbawm, *Nations and Nationalism since 1780.*

120. Makau Mutua has criticized this decision as contributing to the structural weakness and instability of African states, leading to bloodshed in such countries as the Congo and Rwanda. See Makau Mutua, *Human Rights: A Political and Cultural Critique* (Philadelphia: University of Pennsylvania Press, 2002); Makau Mutua, "Redrawing the Map of Africa: A Legal and Moral Inquiry," *Michigan Journal of International Law* 16 (1995): 1113–1176; Makau Mutua, "Redrawing the Map along African Lines," *Boston Globe,* 22 September 1994.

121. Steiner and Alston, *International Human Rights in Context,* 1256.

122. Mr. Thierry (France), "General Assembly, Third Committee, Summary Records," General Assembly document A/C.3/SR.825, December 1957, 308.

123. Ibid.

124. Mr. Cheng Paonan (China), "Commission on Human Rights: Summary Record

of Meetings," ECOSOC document E/CN.4/SR.256, 1952, 3–4. The Pakistani delegate Mrs. Liaqat Ali Khan also noted that "the objections raised to the text of the article on self-determination arose mainly from a purely technical legal approach to the matter." Mrs. Liaqat Ali Khan (Pakistan), General Assembly document A/C.3/SR.448, November 1952, paragraphs 7–9.

125. "General Assembly, Third Committee, Summary Records," General Assembly documents A/C.3/SR.641–656, 1955, 667–677. The item was also discussed in the seventh (1952) and twelfth (1957) sessions. For the commission's discussion, see "Commission on Human Rights: Summary Record of Meetings," ECOSOC documents E/CN.4/SR.252–258, 1952. For a summary, see *Draft International Covenant on Human Rights, Annotation: Report of the Secretary-General,* 38–45; for comments from governments, see "Observations by Governments," General Assembly document A/2910/Add. 1–3, 1955.

126. See, "Observations by Governments," 1–4, 11, 14.

127. "General Assembly, Third Committee, Summary Records," General Assembly document A/C.3/SR.643, 1955, paragraph 10.

128. In 1955 the vote in favor of article 1 was 30 to 12, with 13 abstentions. "General Assembly, Third Committee, Summary Records," General Assembly document A/C.3/SR.676, 1955, paragraphs 21, 27.

129. For a summary of this debate, see "Draft International Covenant," General Assembly document A/3077, 8 December 1955, 11–31.

130. Mr. Abdel-Ghani (Egypt), "General Assembly, Third Committee, Summary Records," General Assembly document A/C.3/SR.651, 1955, 137.

131. The Third Committee rejected a U.S. draft along these lines; see *Yearbook of the United Nations 1950* (New York: Columbia University Press, 1951), 528.

132. Mrs. Roosevelt (United States), "General Assembly, Third Committee, Summary Records," General Assembly document A/C.3/SR.447, 18 November 1952, 174–175.

133. Mrs. De Figueres (Costa Rica), "General Assembly, Third Committee, Summary Records," General Assembly document A/C.3/SR.826, 1957, 315.

134. Mr. Mahmud (Ceylon), ibid., 314.

135. Ms. Addae (Ghana), "General Assembly, Third Committee, Summary Records," General Assembly document A/C.3/SR.827, December 1957, 319.

136. Mr. Nisot (Belgium), "Commission on Human Rights: Summary Record of Meetings," ECOSOC document E/CN.4/SR.252, 1952, 7–9.

137. Mrs. Mehta (India), "Commission on Human Rights: Summary Record of Meetings," ECOSOC document E/CN.4/SR.253, 1952, 13.

138. Mrs. Mehta (India), "Commission on Human Rights: Summary Record of Meetings," ECOSOC document E/CN.4/SR.256, 1952, 5.

139. "General Assembly, Third Committee, Summary Records," General Assembly document A/C.3/SR.570, 1954, paragraph 16. Hannum notes that "the distinction between minorities and peoples remains an article of faith for states and international bodies concerned with monitoring human rights"; Hurst Hannum, "The Right of Self-Determination in the Twenty-First Century," *Washington & Lee Law Review* 15 (Summer 1998): 774.

140. Ms. MacEntee (Ireland), "General Assembly, Third Committee, Summary Records," General Assembly document A/C.3/SR.825, 1962, 311.

141. "General Assembly, Third Committee, Summary Records," General Assembly document A/C.3/SR.649, 1955, paragraphs 9, 15.

142. See "General Assembly, Third Committee, Summary Records," General Assembly documents. A/C.3/SR.641–56, 667–77, 1955; *Draft International Covenant on Human Rights, Annotation: Report of the Secretary-General*; "Observations by Governments," 3. Hannum concludes that "a careful examination of the legislative history of the covenants leads to the conclusion that a restrictive interpretation of the right to self-determination comports with the views of the majority of the states that supported the right"; Hannum, "Rethinking Self-Determination," 23.

143. Humphrey, *Human Rights & the United Nations*, 129.

144. "Declaration on the Granting of Independence to Colonial Countries and Peoples," General Assembly resolution 1514 (XV), 14 December 1960. The unanimous vote was 89 to 0, with 9 abstentions, including the United States, the United Kingdom, France, and other former colonial powers.

145. Hannum, "Rethinking Self-Determination," 2.

146. Centre for Human Rights, *Human Rights: Status of International Instruments* (New York: United Nations, 1987), 9. The text of reservations by India and other countries is available online at http://www.unhchr.ch/html/menu3/b/treaty5_asp.htm.

147. Ibid., 18–19.

148. See Gerry J. Simpson, "The Diffusion of Sovereignty: Self-Determination in the Post-Colonial Age," in *The New World Order: Sovereignty, Human Rights and the Self-Determination of Peoples,* ed. Mortimer N. S. Sellers (Washington, D.C.: Berg, 1996), 35–65.

149. Mr. D'Souza (India), "General Assembly, Third Committee, Summary Records," General Assembly document A/C.3/SR.651, November 1955, 135.

150. Hannum, "Rethinking Self-Determination," 27.

151. Mr. Lopez (Philippines), "General Assembly, Third Committee, Summary Records," General Assembly document A/C.3/SR.825, 1957, 308–309.

152. Y. Liang, "Colonial and Federal Clauses in United Nations Multilateral Instruments, *American Journal of International Law* 45 (1951): 108.

153. *Report of the Drafting Committee to the Commission on Human Rights,* Annex B, Part I, Article 24 addressed the federal issue.

154. Paul Gore-Booth, quoted in Simpson, *Human Rights and the End of Empire,* 473.

155. Ibid., 467.

156. Mr. Hoffmeister (Czechoslovakia), "General Assembly, Third Committee, Summary Records," General Assembly document A/C.3/SR.293, 1950, 145.

157. Simpson, *Human Rights and the End of Empire*, 474.

158. "Commission on Human Rights: Summary Record of Meetings," ECOSOC document E/CN.4/SR.37, 1947. The proposal submitted during the first reading of the draft covenant can be found at A/C.3/L.421, 1947.

159. Mr. Moodie (Australia) "General Assembly, Third Committee, Summary Records," General Assembly document A/C.5/SR.292, 1950, 134. He argued that "for the central government to unilaterally accept and ratify the covenant would not only be provocative

to state feeling, but would be a breach of the whole spirit of federation." The Canadian representative, Mr. Lesage, pointed to the dichotomous nature of the problem: "While on the one hand the covenant creates an international obligation, on the other hand its aim is to determine the nature of laws which, with the country, should govern the juridical relations of individuals with one another and with the State"; "General Assembly, Third Committee, Summary Records," General Assembly document A/C.3/SR.292, 1950, 136.

160. For a review of whether the covenant limited U.S. constitutional jurisdiction, see Jacob D. Hyman, "Constitutional Aspects of the Covenant," *Law and Contemporary Problems* 14, no. 3 (1949): 451–478. He concluded that there was nothing in the Constitution to prevent the United States from ratifying or implementing the covenant; even the inclusion of economic and social rights would "create no special problem of federal-state relations. . . . Those rights are such as can be protected only by the kind of national action which has already been determined to lie within the competence of the Federal Government" (471).

161. Mrs. Menon (India), "General Assembly, Third Committee, Summary Records," General Assembly document A/C.3/SR.293, 1950, 144. She also asserted that the United States should take responsibility for its importance in international affairs and consider amending its Constitution to enable it to meet the growing demands of international participation. Within a few years, a constitutional amendment was considered, but one that would have prevented the U.S. president from signing international human rights treaties.

162. Mr. Dehousse (Belgium), "General Assembly, Third Committee, Summary Records," General Assembly document A/C.3/SR.292, 1950, 133–134.

163. Mr. Bokhari (Pakistan), "General Assembly, Third Committee, Summary Records," General Assembly document A/C.3/SR.292, 1950, 135.

164. Humphrey wrote that "Professor Bokhari of Pakistan made a brilliant speech opposing the inclusion of the clause, and it looked as if a majority would agree with him. This would create serious difficulties for countries like Canada and the United States"; Humphrey, *Human Rights & the United Nations,* 128.

165. Constitution of the International Labour Organization, Article 19(9). For discussion of this clause, see Manley O. Hudson, "Membership of the US in the International Labor Organization," *American Journal of International Law* 28 (1934): 673.

166. Mr. Moodie, the Australian representative, pointed out that "the idea of [a] federal clause is not new; it was applied by the International Labour Organization thirty years [ago]"; Mr. Moodie (Australia) "General Assembly, Third Committee, Summary Records," General Assembly document A/C.5/SR.292, 1950, 134.

167. Mr. Altman (Poland), "General Assembly, Third Committee, Summary Records," General Assembly document A/C.3/SR.293, 1950, 142, referring to the comment of the U.S. representative at the 292nd meeting of the Fifth Session.

168. Ibid., 141.

169. Mr. Danton Jobim (Brazil), "General Assembly, Third Committee, Summary Records," General Assembly document A/C.3/SR.293, 1950, 143.

170. Anderson, *Eyes Off the Prize,* 257–262.

171. Green, *The United Nations and Human Rights,* 5. James Green was Department

of State advisor to both Eleanor Roosevelt and Mary Lord and played an important role in the formation of U.S. policy regarding human rights.

172. Natalie Hevener Kaufman and David Whiteman, "Opposition to Human Rights Treaties in the United States Senate: The Legacy of the Bricker Amendment," *Human Rights Quarterly* 10, no. 3 (1988): 309–337. Whitton and Fowler note that some in the United States were concerned that the covenant might encourage more thinking in Congress about human rights, which might have led to a federal statute against lynching. John B. Whitton and Edward J. Fowler, "Bricker Amendment—Fallacies and Dangers," *American Journal of International Law* 48, no. 1 (1954): 23–56. Davies notes that scholars are divided about why Bricker chose to focus on human rights to restrict presidential powers in treatymaking, but in his view, Bricker's aim was to limit the role of the United Nations, which he viewed as a threat to American sovereignty. Bricker was vehemently opposed to including economic, social, and cultural rights and feared that these rights might be applied in the domestic setting. Davies, *Defender of the Old Guard*, 88–91.

173. Cassin, *La Pensée et l'Action*, 83.

174. Dulles, quoted in Evans, *U.S. Hegemony and the Project of Universal Human Rights*, 115.

175. Statement made by Mrs. Lord before the ninth session of the commission, Geneva, 8 April 1953, quoted in Sellars, *The Rise and Rise of Human Rights*, 83.

176. A. J. Hobbins, ed., *On the Edge of Greatness: The Diaries of John Humphrey, First Director General of the United Nations Division of Human Rights*, vol. 3, *1952–1957* (Montreal: McGill University Libraries, 1998), 3:58.

177. "Explanatory Paper on Measures of Implementation Prepared by the Secretary-General," General Assembly document A/5655, 1963, 25.

178. International Covenant on Civil and Political Rights, Article 50; International Covenant on Economic, Social and Cultural Rights, Article 28.

179. Even though it demanded the federal clause, Australia signed and ratified the Covenant on Civil and Political Rights in 1972 and 1980 and the Covenant on Economic, Social and Cultural Rights in 1972 and 1975. Canada ratified both covenants in 1976. The United States ratified the Covenant on Civil and Political Rights in 1992.

180. See *Report of the Drafting Committee to the Commission on Human Rights*, ECOSOC document E/600, Annex B and Article 25 (The Colonial Territories). The issue was raised by the General Assembly in resolutions 421 (V) and 422 (V), both 5 December 1950, calling on ECOSOC to request the CHR to study the issue.

181. *Draft International Covenant on Humans Rights and Measures of Implementation: Report of the Third Committee.*

182. "Territorial Application of the International Covenant on Human Rights," General Assembly resolution 422 (V), 4 December 1950.

183. Quoted in Simpson, *Human Rights and the End of Empire*, 489–490.

184. Ibid., 476–477 and 491–493.

185. Ibid., 491.

186. Ibid., 497.

187. Mr. Altman (Poland), "General Assembly, Third Committee, Summary Records," General Assembly document A/C.3/SR.295, 1950, 158.

188. See "General Assembly, Third Committee, Summary Records," General Assembly document A/C.3/SR.288–319, October 1950.

189. Lord MacDonald (UK), "General Assembly, Third Committee, Summary Records," General Assembly document A/C.3/SR.293, 1950, 150.

190. Mr. Chang (China), "General Assembly, Third Committee, Summary Records," General Assembly document A/C.3/SR.295, 1950, 159.

191. Mr. Mendez (Philippines), "General Assembly, Third Committee, Summary Records," General Assembly document A/C.3/SR.296, 1950, 169.

192. Mr. Valenzuela (Chile), ibid., 168.

193. Mr. Kayali (Syria), "General Assembly, Third Committee, Summary Records," General Assembly document A/C.3/SR.294, 1950, 153.

194. Simpson, *Human Rights and the End of Empire,* 490.

195. Ibid., 493.

196. John K. Gamble, Jr., "Reservations to Multilateral Treaties: A Macroscopic View of State Practice," *American Journal of International Law* 74, no. 2 (1980): 372–394.

197. See Jhabvala, "The Soviet-Bloc's View of the Implementation of Human Rights Accords," 461–491.

198. For a summary of different state views, see *Draft International Covenant on Human Rights, Annotation: Report of the Secretary-General,* 382–389.

199. Mrs. Roosevelt (United States), "Commission on Human Rights: Summary Record of Meetings," ECOSOC document E/CN.4/SR.42, 1947, 2.

200. Simpson, *Human Rights and the End of Empire,* 468.

201. UK representative Sir Geoffrey Wilson reported to London: "I was summoned to see Hendrick and Plaine [at the U.S. State Department] and they gave me the third degree on the general limitations clause idea. They say they have categorical instructions, and . . . it is clear they are going to turn up the heat and threaten to have nothing to do with the covenant unless their ideas are accepted. There are five of them here (plus Mrs. R) working night and day seeing people and producing masses of paper. . . . I'm not sure how many of the drafting committee will be able to stand up to the pressure." Quoted in ibid., 506.

202. Mr. Malik (Lebanon), "Commission on Human Rights: Summary Record of Meetings," ECOSOC document E/CN.4/SR.42, 1947, 3.

203. Sir Eric Beckett, quoted in Simpson, *Human Rights and the End of Empire,* 468. Simpson writes, "The clause proposed by the USA was regarded by the Foreign Office as 'a monstrosity.' . . . Earlier belief in hypocrisy was now confirmed; Eleanor Roosevelt simply wanted a convention which was sufficiently vacuous for the Senate to accept. The federal clause and the general limitations clause were both means to the same perfidious end" (475).

204. *Report of the Drafting Committee to the Commission on Human Rights,* ECOSOC document E/600, Annex B, Article 4.

205. See "General Assembly, Third Committee, Summary Records," General Assembly document A/C.3/SR.404, 1951. Byelorussia, Czechoslovakia, the Ukraine, and the Soviet Union all ratified the genocide convention with reservations.

206. International Court of Justice, "Advisory Opinion on Reservations to the Genocide

Convention," ICJ REP.15, 28 May 1951. The decision was conveyed at the same time that the general question of reservations to multilateral treaties was being discussed in the Third Committee. See Green, *The United Nations and Human Rights,* 57–59, 100–101.

207. Mr. Albornoz (Ecuador), "General Assembly, Third Committee, Summary Records," General Assembly document A/C.3/SR.405, 1952, 357.

208. Mr. Azkoul (Lebanon), "General Assembly, Third Committee, Summary Records," General Assembly document A/C.3/SR.404, 1952, 350. Mr. Alemayehou (Ethiopia), ibid., 352.

209. Mrs. Afnan, (Iraq), ibid. She had earlier noted the absurdity of accepting the principle of reservation before agreeing on the actual articles for the covenants; "General Assembly, Third Committee, Summary Records," General Assembly document A/C.3/SR.362, 1951, 91.

210. Mr. Valenzuela (Chile), "General Assembly, Third Committee, Summary Records," General Assembly document A/C.3/SR.404, 1952, 351.

211. Lauterpacht wrote a paper suggesting how states might address the issue of reservation in treaties by accepting a very limited set of circumstances, though he emphasized that being party to a treaty implied abandoning the strictly national view of law-making authority. Hersch Lauterpacht, "Some Possible Solutions of the Problem of Reservations to Treaties," *Transactions of the Grotius Society* 39 (1953): 97–118.

212. Mr. Mufti (Syria), "General Assembly, Third Committee, Summary Records," General Assembly document A/C.3/SR.404, 1952, 351. Mexico supported this view.

213. "Inclusion in the Draft International Covenants on Human Rights of Provisions Regarding Reservations," General Assembly resolution 546 (VI), 5 February 1952. Guatemala, which sponsored the resolution, hailed the decision to make the covenants "the first United Nations Conventions to contain such reservations"; Mr. Garcia Bauer, "General Assembly, Third Committee, Summary Records," A/C.3/SR.404, 1953, 349.

214. "Commission on Human Rights: Summary Records, Tenth Session," ECOSOC document E/CN.4/SR.477-448, April 1954.

215. *Draft International Covenant on Human Rights, Annotation: Report of the Secretary-General,* 382–383.

216. "Commission on Human Rights: Summary Records, Ninth Session," ECOSOC document E/CN.4/SR677, May 1953.

217. *Draft International Covenant on Human Rights, Annotation: Report of the Secretary-General,* 385.

218. Mr. Pavlov (USSR), "General Assembly, Third Committee, Summary Records," General Assembly document A/C.3/SR.405, December 1951, 356.

219. Mr. Hajek (Czechoslovakia), ibid., 357.

220. Article 5, Section II of the Vienna Convention on the Law of Treaties says that "a reservation is considered to have been accepted by a State if it shall have raised no objection to the reservation by the end of a period of twelve months after it was notified of the reservation or by the date on which it expressed its consent to be bound by the treaty, whichever is later." Available online at http://fletcher.tufts.edu/multi/texts/BH538.txt. The treaty was signed on 23 May 1969 and entered into force on 27 January 1980.

221. The figures for reservations and ratifications are available online at http://www

.ohchr.org/english/law/ccpr-ratify.htm (International Covenant on Civil and Political Rights) and http://www.ohchr.org/english/countries/ratification/3.htm (International Covenant on Economic, Social and Cultural Rights).

222. Reservations have had an even greater impact for subsequent treaties, such as the UN Convention on the Elimination of All Forms of Discrimination against Women; see Catherine Tinker, "Human Rights for Women: The UN Convention on the Elimination of All Forms of Discrimination against Women," *Human Rights Quarterly* 3, no. 2 (1981), 32–43.

223. *Yearbook of the United Nations 1946–1947* (New York: Columbia University Press, 1947), 556.

224. Summary records of debates at the CHR and Third Committee between 1947–1955 contain many such speeches; for example, see "General Assembly, Third Committee, Summary Records," General Assembly documents A/C.3/SR.562–564, 566, 573, and 575–576, 1955.

225. "Draft International Covenant on Human Rights and Measures of Implementation: future work of the Commission on Human Rights," General Assembly resolution 421 (V), 4 December 1950. The resolution was based on *Draft International Covenant on Human Rights and Measures of Implementation: Report of the Third Committee.*

226. Mr. Koretsky (USSR), quoted in Simpson, *Human Rights and the End of Empire,* 482. Mr. Ribnikar of Yugoslavia similarly decried this "new attempt to transform the U.N. into a kind of world government" (484).

227. M. de León (Panama), "General Assembly, Third Committee, Summary Records," General Assembly document A/C.3/SR.90, 1948, 43.

228. See letters from the American Bar Association to Eleanor Roosevelt, quoted in Evans, *U.S. Hegemony and the Project of Universal Human Rights,* 108.

229. James Hendrick to Mrs. Roosevelt, quoted in Simpson, *Human Rights and the End of Empire,* 378–379.

230. Mr. Lovett, memorandum for the president, 30 April 1948, approved by President Truman on 1 May 1948, quoted in ibid., 504.

231. Arthur Galsworthy, quoted in Simpson, *Human Rights and the End of Empire,* 497.

232. Sir Alexander Maxwell, quoted in ibid., 502.

233. Ibid., 496.

234. See *Draft International Covenant on Human Rights, Annotation: Report of the Secretary-General,* 28–31.

235. Mr. Soares (Brazil), "General Assembly, Third Committee, Summary Records," General Assembly document A/C.3/SR.300, 1 November 1950, 192.

236. *Draft International Covenant on Human Rights, Annotation: Report of the Secretary-General,* 31.

237. Mr. Sorenson (Denmark), "Commission on Human Rights: Summary Record of Meetings," ECOSOC document E/CN.4/SR.238, 1953, 7. Also see Philip Alston, "The United Nations' Specialized Agencies and the Implementation of the International Covenant on Economic, Social, and Cultural Rights," *Columbia Journal of Transnational Law* 18, no. 1 (1979): 79–118.

238. Michael J. Dennis and David P. Stewart revived some of the traditional arguments against economic, social, and cultural rights in "Justiciability of Economic, Social, and Cultural Rights: Should There Be an International Complaints Mechanism to Adjudicate the Right to Food, Water, Housing, and Health?" *American Journal of International Law* 98, no. 3 (2004): 462–515.

239. International Covenant on Civil and Political Rights, Articles 28–45. African states were skeptical of an expert monitoring body; many were disillusioned with expert bodies in the wake of the ruling of the International Court of Justice that South West Africa was to remain a mandate. "South West Africa Case," *International and Comparative Law Quarterly* 15, no. 4 (October 1966): 1219.

240. See Nowak, *UN Covenant on Civil and Political Rights: CCPR Commentary*; Pechota, "The Development of the Covenant on Civil and Political Rights," 25.

241. On the history and the workings of the committee, see Matthew C. Craven, *The International Covenant on Economic, Social, and Cultural Rights: A Perspective on Its Development* (New York: Oxford University Press, 1995), 35–105.

242. Philip Alston, "Out of the Abyss: The Challenges Confronting the New UN Committee on Economic, Social and Cultural Rights," *Human Rights Quarterly* 9, no. 3 (1987): 332–381. See also Philip Alston, "The Economic Rights Committee" and T. Opsahl, "The Human Rights Committee" both in *The United Nations and Human Rights: A Critical Appraisal*, ed. Philip Alston (Oxford: Clarendon Press, 1995).

243. General Comment No. 3, in *Report of the Fifth Session of the Committee on Economic, Social and Cultural Rights*, ECOSOC document E/1991/23, December 1990. In 1991, the committee proposed an optional protocol complaint procedure for individuals and groups, but it has yet to win General Assembly approval.

244. See Kitty Arambulo, *Strengthening the Supervision of the International Covenant on Economic, Social and Cultural Rights* (Antwerp: Intersentia-Hart, 1999).

8. The Human Rights of Special Groups

1. Mr. Radovanovic (Yugoslavia), *General Assembly Official Records*, 183rd Plenary Session, 10 December 1948, 913–914.

2. Article 2 of the UDHR states: "Everyone is entitled to all the rights and freedoms set forth in this Declaration, without distinction of any kind, such as race, colour, sex, language, religion, political or other opinion, national or social origin, property, birth or other status. Furthermore, no distinction shall be made on the basis of the political, jurisdictional or international status of the country or territory to which a person belongs, whether it be independent, trust, non-self-governing or under any other limitation of sovereignty." Article 7: "All are equal before the law and are entitled without any discrimination to equal protection of the law. All are entitled to equal protection against any discrimination in violation of this Declaration and against any incitement to such discrimination."

3. Douglas Sanders, "Collective Rights," *Human Rights Quarterly* 13, no. 3 (1991): 368–387. See also Mary Gardiner Jones, "National Minorities: A Case Study in International Protection," *Law and Contemporary Problems* 14, no. 4 (1949): 599–626. Jones

notes: "A minority exists if its members look upon themselves as possessing a distinct national consciousness accompanied by linguistic and/or cultural characteristics . . . [or] members of society may 'create' a minority in their midst through the practice of discrimination by reason of their religion, race, sex, color, social class and the like. . . . It is this dual nature of minorities as embracing both 'self-made' and externally 'created' groups which must be clearly perceived if effective and constructive solutions are to be found for the general problem of group frictions."

4. Self-determination was further associated with statehood by the General Assembly's adoption of the 1960 "Declaration on the Granting of Independence to Colonial Countries and Peoples," General Assembly resolution A/RES/1514 (XV), 14 December 1960, which stresses nonintervention and preserves territorial integrity. See Centre for Human Rights, *Human Rights: A Compilation of International Instruments* (Geneva: United Nations, 1994), vol. 1, part 1. Article 6 ruled out secession as a right for oppressed groups in the context of nation-states.

5. Mr. Lopez (Philippines), "General Assembly, Third Committee, Summary Records," General Assembly document A/C.3/SR.825, 1957, 308–309.

6. Joe Oloka-Onyango, "Heretical Reflections on the Right to Self-Determination: Prospects and Problems for a Democratic Global Future in the New Millennium," *American University International Law Review* 15 (1999): 1245–1273. Oloka-Onyango argues that "the doctrine of self-determination must be reconstituted so that it does not simply take 'the group' (or 'the state') as a given. Indeed, the exact content and application of the doctrine of self-determination must be revisited and reconceptualized as a whole" (1261).

7. Rupert Emerson, "Self-Determination," *American Journal of International Law* 65, no. 5 (1971): 459–475; K. J. Partsch, "Fundamental Principles of Human Rights: Self-Determination, Equality and Non-Discrimination," in *The International Dimensions of Human Rights,* ed. Karel Vasak and Philip Alston (Paris: UNESCO, 1982).

8. Hurst Hannum, "Minorities, Indigenous and Self-Determination," *Studies in Transnational Legal Policy* 26 (1994): 1–16.

9. There are other equally relevant areas such as migrant workers, refugees, and (to some degree) the rights of children that we do not discuss here.

10. Kunz observed in the 1950s that problems related to minority rights were still present in the South Tyrol between Austria and Italy; in Trieste between Italy and Yugoslavia; in the communist states of Czechoslovakia and Hungary; in Turkey; in the treatment of Indians in South Africa, Ceylon, and Pakistan (and conversely Muslims in India); and between the Arabs and Jews of Palestine and Israel. Josef L. Kunz, "The Present Status of the International Law for the Protection of Minorities," *American Journal of International Law* 48, no. 2 (1954): 282–287.

11. John Humphrey, "International Protection of Human Rights," *Annals of the American Academy of Political and Social Science* 255, no. 1 (1948): 15–21.

12. A brief history is included in United Nations, *Yearbook on Human Rights 1947–48* (New York: Columbia University Press, 1949), 425.

13. E/56/Rev. 1 and E/84, 21 June 1946, paragraph 4, in *Yearbook of the United Nations 1947–1948* (New York: Columbia University Press, 1948).

14. John Humphrey, "The United Nations Sub-Commission on the Prevention of Discrimination and the Protection of Minorities," *America Journal of International Law* 62, no. 2 (1968): 870.

15. The original members of the Sub-commission on Prevention of Discrimination and Protection of Minorities were William McNamara (Australia), Joseph Nisot (Belgium), C. F. Chang (China), A. M. Pallares (Ecuador), Samuel Spanien (France), Herard Roy (Haiti), M. R. Masani (India), Rezazada Shafaq (Iran), Elizabeth Monore (UK), J. Daniels (United States), and A. P. Borisov (USSR). Harvard Law School professor Inis L. Claude, commenting on the political nature of its composition, observed: "It is perhaps significant that the pattern of geographical distribution illustrated . . . coincides with the one which has become more or less standard in the political organs of the United Nations, even to the extent of including nationals of all the permanent members of the Security Council." Moreover, Claude notes, despite the fact that the subcommission was an expert body, its debates were filled with political innuendo and Cold War accusations. "The lay visitor at Lake Success would probably not be aware that he had discovered a special and distinctive sort of United Nations organ if he should inadvertently stumble into a meeting of the Subcommission, and hear its members assuring each other that minorities are treated well in their own countries, and engaging in polemics not very different from those which have become characteristic of most United Nations organs." In one particularly outrageous incident, the Polish expert attacked the Chinese member and then walked out in protest. Inis L. Claude, Jr., "The Nature and Status of the Subcommission on Prevention of Discrimination and Protection of Minorities," *International Organization* 5, no. 2 (1951): 312, 303.

16. The convention was adopted without any abstentions. See General Assembly document A/PV/179, 9 December 1948, 70. The meetings of the Ad Hoc Committee on Genocide that drafted the convention took place at Lake Success, the location where the Commission on Human Rights also met. There were most likely informal exchanges among delegates that served in these two bodies, but it is difficult to trace these discussions. For a history of the drafting of the genocide convention, see William A. Schabas, *Genocide in International Law* (New York: Cambridge University Press, 2000).

17. See Josef L. Kunz, "The Convention on Genocide," *American Journal of International Law* 43, no. 4 (1949): 738–746. Even though John Humphrey prepared the first draft, the CHR did not discuss the provisions of the treaty, and experts at the time considered the purpose of the convention to be the preservation of international peace. "Its purposes are objective, not subjective," Kunz noted (742). In this view, human rights were a subjective matter, and genocide was part of criminal law.

18. Johannes Morsink, *The Universal Declaration of Human Rights: Origins, Drafting, and Intent* (Philadelphia: University of Pennsylvania Press, 1999), 269–280.

19. Raphael Lemkin, "Genocide as a Crime under International Law," *American Journal of International Law* 41, no. 1 (1947): 145–151.

20. Lemkin's interest dated to the failed prosecution of those who were involved in Ottoman Turkey's massacre of Armenians in 1915. See Schabas, *Genocide in International Law*, 25n73; and Robert Melson, "Paradigms of Genocide: The Holocaust, the Armenian Genocide, and Contemporary Mass Genocide," *Annals of the American Academy of Political and Social Science* 548, no. 3 (1996): 156–168.

21. Raphael Lemkin, *Axis Rule in Occupied Europe: Laws of Occupation, Analysis of Government, Proposals for Redress* (Washington, D.C.: Carnegie Endowment for International Peace, 1944), 79. Quoted in Schabas, *Genocide in International Law,* 25n72.

22. A. J. Hobbins, *On the Edge of Greatness: The Diaries of John Humphrey, First Director of the United Nations Division of Human Rights,* vol. 1, *1948–1949* (Montreal: McGill Queens University Press, 1995), 30. Humphrey noted that Lemkin initiated the world movement against the outlawing of genocide. He also worked with the UN Secretariat in the drafting of the genocide convention and appeared to be opposed to any mention of international genocide in the international bill of rights. Humphrey commented on Lemkin's opposition to the right-to-life clause of the covenant: "Lost my temper yesterday with Lemkin who is conducting a campaign against the article on the right to life in the draft Covenant—because he sees in it a potential rival to the Genocide Convention" (2:21, entry for 25 March 1952).

23. See "General Assembly, Legal Committee, Summary Records," General Assembly document A/C.6/SR.22, 1946; for a history of the resolution, see ECOSOC document E/621.

24. "General Assembly, Legal Committee, Summary Records," General Assembly document A/C.6/SR.21–24, 1946, 83. "The Crime of Genocide," Resolution 96 (I), was adopted on 11 December 1946 unanimously and without debate. It eliminated any nexus between genocide and armed conflict and held individuals and officials responsible, excluding any notion of state responsibility. The resolution included the idea of culture: "[Genocide] results in great losses to humanity in the form of cultural and other contributions."

25. "Convention on the Prevention and Punishment of the Crime of Genocide—Secretariat Draft," ECOSOC document E/447, 9 December 1947. For detailed background on the preparation of the convention, see Matthew Lippman, "The Drafting of the 1948 Convention on the Prevention and Punishment of the Crime of Genocide," *Boston University International Law Journal* 3 (1985): 1–66. Also see Nehemiah Robinson, *The Genocide Convention: A Commentary* (New York: Institute of Jewish Affairs, World Jewish Congress, 1960); and Schabas, *Genocide in International Law,* 51–101.

26. Humphrey noted that although de Vabres was one of the three designated experts, he did not attend the meetings and was represented by a member of the French delegation. John P. Humphrey, *Human Rights & the United Nations: A Great Adventure* (Dobbs Ferry, N.Y.: Transnational Publishers, 1984), 54.

27. Schabas, *Genocide in International Law,* 25.

28. Ibid., 26.

29. See "Ad Hoc Committee Draft, Second Draft Genocide Convention," General Assembly documents E/AC.25/SR.1–SR.28, 5 April–10 May 1948; and *Report of the Ad Hoc Committee on Genocide, 5 April–10 May 1948,* ECOSOC document E/794, 1948, for the draft and accompanying commentary. This committee included representatives of all five permanent members of the Security Council. It emphasized separating the crime of genocide from other crimes against humanity and treating it as independent of the notions of crimes against peace and war crimes.

30. Vespasian V. Pella was an advocate for the International Criminal Court. He emphasized the setting up of an international criminal court, recognizing the complexities of the present world in which physical distances were being abolished but moral barriers

were becoming increasingly difficult to cross. Writing in 1950 of the political posturing of states in the General Assembly, he observed: "It is this circumstance which impels many jurists to adopt an attitude of 'cautious reserve' lest developments in international law should prejudice the freedom of action or reaction—of the state to which they belong. . . . This reserve . . . takes the form of legal dogmatism or infinite delay"; Vespasian V. Pella, "Towards an International Criminal Court," *American Journal of International Law* 44, no. 1 (1950): 43.

31. Mr. Maktos (United States), "Ad Hoc Committee Draft, Second Draft Genocide Convention, Session Reports," ECOSOC document E/AC.25/SR.10, 1948, 16; also emphasized in E/AC.25/SR.14, 1948, 10–11.

32. See "Convention on the Prevention and Punishment of the Crime of Genocide—Secretariat Draft," ECOSOC document E/447, 1947, 17, 27.

33. Egon Schwelb, "Crimes against Humanity," *British Year Book of International Law* 23 (1946): 178–226.

34. Article 2 of the genocide convention states: "In the present Convention, genocide means any of the following acts committed with intent to destroy, in whole or in part, a national, ethnical, racial or religious group, as such: (a) Killing members of the group; (b) Causing serious bodily or mental harm to members of the group; (c) Deliberately inflicting on the group conditions of life calculated to bring about its physical destruction in whole or in part; (d) Imposing measures intended to prevent births within the group; (e) Forcibly transferring children of the group to another group"; "Convention on the Prevention and Punishment of the Crime of Genocide," General Assembly resolution A/RES/260A (III), 9 December 1948.

The genocide convention was thus seen as an important instrument for clarifying the definition of crimes against humanity. But the drafters of the convention were nation-states, and they refused to include provisions regarding state action or policy, an important element of the definition of crimes against humanity. See Margaret McAuliffe de Guzman, "The Road from Rome: The Developing Law of Crimes against Humanity," *Human Rights Quarterly* 22, no. 1 (2000): 335–403.

35. This group had also supported the idea of including a minority rights article in the Universal Declaration of Human Rights. India, Liberia, Siam (Thailand), South Africa, Turkey, and most states from the Americas and Western Europe opposed this concept of protection of minorities. Four states (Afghanistan, Argentina, Cuba, and Venezuela) were sympathetic to the idea but did not feel that the convention was the right place for it. See Johannes Morsink, "Cultural Genocide, the Universal Declaration, and Minority Rights," *Human Rights Quarterly* 21, no. 4 (1999): 1009–1060.

36. In the first decade, the United Nations was predominantly a Euro-American club (Euro-American states constituted 73 percent of membership), and during this period it admitted only ten new countries.

37. "ESCOR Summary Record of Meetings," ECOSOC document E/3/SR.175–225, 1948, 6. The draft text of the article stated: "Destroying or preventing the use of libraries, museums, schools, historical monuments, places of worship or other cultural institutions and objects of the groups." France and the United States voted against its adoption

in the Ad Hoc Committee and joined China in abstaining in the second reading of the article. See "Genocide: A Commentary on the Convention," *Yale Law Journal* 58, no. 7 (June 1949): 1142–1160 for an analysis of the convention at the time it was adopted. The United States also objected to the reference to public propaganda that incited hateful and systemic destruction of a racial, ethnic, or religious group; it argued that this interfered with the free speech amendment of the U.S. Constitution. Thus, the text of the convention is limited by Article V—"the Contracting Parties undertake to enact, in accordance with their respective Constitutions, the necessary legislation to give effect to the provision of the present Convention"—the standard escape clause for sovereign states.

38. See Eric Markusen and David Kopf, *The Holocaust and Strategic Bombing: Genocide and Total War in the Twentieth Century* (Boulder, Colo.: Westview Press, 1995); and Morsink, "Cultural Genocide, the Universal Declaration, and Minority Rights." Morsink argues that the UDHR should be amended to include a separate article on the rights of members of religious, linguistic, and cultural minority groups.

39. Mr. Setalvad (India), "General Assembly, Legal Committee, Summary Records," General Assembly document A/C.6/SR.206, 1948, 206.

40. Morsink, "Cultural Genocide, the Universal Declaration, and Minority Rights." Morsink notes that European delegates felt that cultural genocide was a vague idea and fell within the sphere of human rights (also a vague concept). Mr. Federspiel, the Danish representative, commented that there was a big difference between "mass murderers" and "the closing of libraries" (1030).

41. Morsink notes that of all the drafts Humphrey had collected, only four contained some sort of provision on minority rights and that he drew inspiration from Hersch Lauterpacht's draft as he drafted Article 46. He presented this article with an explanation that nondiscrimination did not protect the rights of minority groups. Morsink, "Cultural Genocide."

42. Article 46 stated: "In States inhabited by a substantial number of persons of a race, language, or religion other than those of the majority of the population, persons belonging to such ethnic, linguistic or religious minorities shall have the right to establish and maintain, out of an equitable proportion of any public funds available for the purpose, their schools and cultural and religious institutions, and to use their own language before the courts and other authorities and organs of the State and in the Press and in public assembly"; "Report of the Drafting Committee to the Commission on Human Rights," E/CN.4/21, 1 July 1947, 23, Annex A.

43. Humphrey felt that Cassin weakened the text by omitting the issue of resources; see Humphrey, "The United Nations Sub-Commission on the Prevention of Discrimination and the Protection of Minorities," 872–873. Cassin also deleted the provision on the use of minority languages in the press and in public assemblies. See "International Bill of Rights, Revised Suggestions Submitted by the Representative of France for Articles of the International Declaration on Human Rights," ECOSOC document E/CN.4/AC.1/W.2/Rev. 2, 1947.

44. Section V discussed the scope of the terminology regarding prevention of discrimination and protection of minorities. The commission felt that it was not possible at that

time to frame definitions pertaining to the protection of minorities. Sub-Commission on Prevention and Protection of Minorities, *Report of the Drafting Committee to the Commission on Human Rights,* ECOSOC document E/CN.4/52, June 1947.

45. For a history of the formation of the Sub-Commission on Prevention of Discrimination and Protection of Minorities, see E/CN.4/Sub.2/2, September 1947.

46. Mr. Pallares (Ecuador), in Sub-Commission on Prevention and Protection of Minorities, *Report of the Drafting Committee to the Commission on Human Rights,* 14.

47. This reluctance was also based on the fear that immigrants, perceived by some as undesirable aliens who might foment internal conflict, would demand recognition or separate schools for their children. Prior to the San Francisco conference, the Latin American states hosted an Inter-American Conference on the Problem of War and Peace, where they discussed the issue of postwar immigration and concluded that any group that had the status of a minority was a direct threat to their sovereignty. Morsink, "Cultural Genocide."

48. The text of Cassin's article was as follows: "In states inhabited by a substantial number of person of a race, language, or religion other than those of the majority of the population, persons belonging to such ethnic, linguistic, or religious minorities shall have the right, as far as compatible with public order and security to establish and maintain schools and cultural or religious institutions and to use their own language in the Press, in public assembly and before the courts and other authorities of the State"; Sub-Commission on Prevention of Discrimination and Protection of Minorities, *Report of the Drafting Committee to the Commission on Human Rights,* 9.

49. Humphrey, "The United Nations Sub-Commission on the Prevention of Discrimination and the Protection of Minorities," 873.

50. The subcommission's debates are recorded in *Report of the Drafting Committee to the Commission on Human Rights* and "Commission on Human Rights: Summary Record of Meetings," ECOSOC document E/CN.4/SR.74, 1948. The commission debates are in "Commission on Human Rights: Summary Record of Meetings," E/CN.4/SR.31–32, 1947. The Third Committee debates are in "General Assembly, Third Committee, Summary Records," General Assembly document A/C.3/SR.161–162, 1948. The Third Committee proposed that groups that wanted differential treatment should have the right to it, and it acknowledged the rights of noncitizens despite strong protests from European delegates.

51. Mrs. Roosevelt (United States), "Working Group on the Declaration of Human Rights," ECOSOC document E/CN.4/AC.2/SR.9, 1947, 2–4.

52. Mrs. Mehta (India), ECOSOC document E/CN.4/AC.1/3/Add. 1, 1947, 380.

53. Commission on Human Rights, *Report of the Drafting Committee to the Commission on Human Rights,* ECOSOC document E/600, 17 December 1947, footnote 2 to paragraph 40.

54. The revised article with the article from the subcommission was forwarded to ECOSOC. The drafting committee's version of the draft text was as follows: "In States inhabited by well-defined ethnic, linguistic or other groups which are clearly distinguished from the rest of the population, and which want to be accorded differential treatment, persons belonging to such groups shall have the right, as far as is compatible with public

order and security, to establish and maintain their own school and cultural or religious institutions, and to use their own language and script in the Press, in public assembly and before the courts and other authorities of the State, if they so choose"; ibid., Annex A, Article 31.

55. The USSR resubmitted the original Humphrey draft article. Yugoslavia proposed three additional articles addressing minority rights that did not include the issue of protecting religious minorities from discrimination. *Report of the Drafting Committee to the Commission on Human Rights.*

56. By May 1948, Stalin and the Tito were no longer on friendly terms, and they submitted two separate articles. Morsink, "Cultural Genocide," 1057n167.

57. Mr. Radevanovic (Yugoslavia), "General Assembly, Third Committee, Summary Records," General Assembly document A/C.3/SR.161, 1948, 720.

58. A/C.3/307/Rev. 1/Add. 2, 1948, 724.

59. Morsink, "Cultural Genocide," 1045.

60. Mrs. Roosevelt (United States), "Commission on Human Rights: Summary Record of Meetings," ECOSOC document E/CN.4/SR.78, 1948. The allegations of the United States were supported by Brazil, Uruguay, Chile, and Canada.

61. Patrick Thornberry, "Is There a Phoenix in the Ashes? International Law and Minority Rights," *Texas International Law Journal* 15 (1980): 421.

62. The subcommission discussed the definition and protection of minorities from 1947 to 1952. There was no session in 1953, and in 1954 when the subcommission was reconstituted, it focused on discrimination. Kunz observes that there was a general reluctance to do something about the protection of minorities. Kunz, "The Present Status of the International Law for the Protection of Minorities."

63. James F. Green, *The United Nations and Human Rights* (Washington, D.C.: Brookings Institution, 1956); Humphrey, "The United Nations Sub-Commission on the Prevention of Discrimination and the Protection of Minorities," 875–876.

64. Humphrey, "The United Nations Sub-Commission on the Prevention of Discrimination and Protection of Minorities," 876.

65. Eide observes that while the memorandum may have been logical in theoretical terms, it was not helpful in practice because it allowed for racial discrimination under the pretext of differential treatment, as in the case of the "separate but equal" doctrine for African American residents of the United States or the policy of apartheid in South Africa. See Asbjørn Eide, "The Sub-Commission," in *The United Nations and Human Rights*, ed. Philip Alston (New York: Oxford University Press, 1992), 211–264.

66. The phrasing of Article 27 did not change from the language the subcommission proposed; see *Report of the Sub-Commission in 1950 to the Commission on Human Rights*, ECOSOC document E/CN.4/358, April 1950, paragraphs 39–41 and 42–47. Also see generally *Draft International Covenant on Human Rights; Annotation, Report of the Secretary-General*, General Assembly document A/2929, 1 July 1955, 181–184.

67. Mr. Panyushkin (USSR) suggested this idea during the discussions on the first draft covenant submitted by the United Kingdom. He noted: "States should also guarantee to their national minorities the right to use their own languages and to build their own schools, libraries and other cultural institutions"; "General Assembly, Third Committee,

Summary Records," General Assembly document A/C.3/SR.289, 1950, 11469. See the debates in "Commission on Human Rights: Summary Record of Meetings," ECOSOC documents E/CN.4/SR.303 and 368–370, March–May 1950.

68. *Draft International Covenants on Human Rights: Report of the Third Committee,* General Assembly document A/2808, 29 April 1954.

69. "International Covenant on Civil and Political Rights," General Assembly resolution 2200A (XXI), 16 December 1966. For an interpretation of negative and positive obligations imposed upon the state, see Ryszard Cholewinski, "State Duty Towards Ethnic Minorities: Positive or Negative?" *Human Rights Quarterly* 10, no. 3 (1988): 368.

70. Patrick Thornberry, "Self-Determination, Minorities, Human Rights: A Review of International Instruments," *International and Comparative Law Quarterly* 38, no. 4 (1989): 877.

71. Humphrey, disappointed at the failure of the CHR to initiate a study on minorities, summed up the situation in the subcommission by quoting the chair's statement that this was "the end of the beginning." In 1954, several members of the Secretariat, including Edward Lawson, were under investigation for communist activities. A. J. Hobbins, ed., *On the Edge of Greatness: The Diaries of John Humphrey, First Director of the United Nations Division of Human Rights,* vol. 3, *1952–1957* (Montreal: McGill-Queen's University Press, 2001), 54.

72. Francesco Capotorti served on the subcommission and as the Italian representative in the Third Committee during the drafting of the Convention on the Elimination of Racial Discrimination.

73. See Capotorti, *The Rights of Persons Belonging to Ethnic, Religious and Linguistic Minorities,* ECOSOC document E/CN.4/Sub.2/384, 1977. Capotorti submitted several other interim reports: E/CN.4/Sub.2/L.594, 1974; and E/CN.4/Sub.2/L.582, 1973.

74. Eide, "The Sub-Commission," 221.

75. Capotorti, *Study of the Rights of Persons Belonging to Ethnic, Religious, and Linguistic Minorities,* ECOSOC document E/CN.4/36, 1979, paragraph 217.

76. See *Report of the Working Group on the Rights of Persons Belonging to National or Ethnic, Religions, and Linguistic Minorities,* E/CN.4/1988/36, 8 March 1988, and *Report of the Working Group on the Rights of Persons Belonging to National or Ethnic, Religions, and Linguistic Minorities,* E/CN.4/1992/48, 16 December 1991.

77. "Declaration on the Rights of Persons Belonging to National or Ethnic, Religious and Linguistic Minorities," General Assembly resolution 47/135, 18 December 1992. Asbjørn Eide, chair of the Working Group, prepared a document summarizing the applicability of the declaration; see "Final Text of the Commentary to the Declaration on the Rights of Persons Belonging to National or Ethnic, Religious, and Linguistic Minorities," ECOSOC document E/CN.4/Sub.2/AC.5/2001/2, 2 April 2001.

78. For a study on the distribution of minorities, particularly those at high risk, see Ted Robert Gurr and James R. Scarritt, "Minorities at Risk," *Human Rights Quarterly* 11, no. 3 (1989): 375–405; Ted Robert Gurr and Barbara Harff, *Ethnic Conflict in World Politics,* 2nd ed. (Boulder, Colo.: Westview Press, 2004); and Rita Jalali and Seymour Martin Lipset, "Race and Ethnic Conflict," *Political Science Quarterly* 107, no. 4 (1992–1993): 585–606.

79. Philip N. S. Rumney, "Getting Away with Murder: Genocide and Western State

Power," *The Modern Law Review* 60, no. 4 (1997): 534–608; Samuel Totten and Paul R. Bartrop, "The United Nations and Genocide: Prevention, Intervention, and Prosecution," *Human Rights Review* 5, no. 4 (2004): 8–31.

80. *An Agenda for Peace: Preventive Diplomacy, Peacemaking and Peacekeeping: Report of the Secretary-General,* General Assembly document A/47/277-S/2411, 17 June 1992.

81. Michael Barnett, *Eyewitness to a Genocide: The United Nations and Rwanda* (Ithaca, N.Y.: Cornell University Press, 2002); Philip Gourevitch, *We Wish to Inform You that Tomorrow We Will Be Killed with Our Families* (New York: Picador, 1998); Linda Melvern, *The Rwandan Genocide and the International Community* (London: Verso, 2004); Linda Melvern, *The Ultimate Crime: Who Betrayed the UN and Why* (London: Allison & Busby, 1995). Melvern comments: "[Rwanda] then was the direst of all human situations—the systematic elimination of an entire people. Genocide is the first, last and most serious crime against humanity, and its prevention the single most important commitment of the countries who join together as the United Nations. But fifty years after the UN was founded, it cannot begin to delay genocide. Its member states know no better than to use the UN as a camouflage" (22).

82. Christian Jennings, *Across the Red River: Rwanda, Burundi and the Heart of Darkness* (London: Phoenix, 2000), quoted in Samuel Totten, "The United Nations and Genocide," *Society* 42, no. 4 (2005): 7. See also Barnett, *Eyewitness to a Genocide.* Barnett observes, "Humanitarian institutions can be run by decent and well-meaning individuals who become timid and fearful as a result both of the soul-breaking demands and of the knowledge that powerful benefactors want only a convenient façade of humanitarianism" (105).

83. David Carment and Patrick James, "The United Nations at 50: Managing Ethnic Crises, Past and Present," *Journal of Peace Research* 35, no. 1 (1998): 61–82. The authors note the paradox confronting the UN: "How does the institution maintain the integrity of the state system from which its political existence is derived and also promote and protect the interests of minorities from whom it was created?" (77). Also see Totten, "The United Nations and Genocide."

84. Samantha Power, *A Problem from Hell: America and the Age of Genocide* (New York: Basic Books, 2002).

85. Totten and Bartrop, "The United Nations and Genocide."

86. See generally *Law and Contemporary Problems* 59, no. 4 (1996). The issue is dedicated to accountability in the face of gross human rights violations and contains several excellent pieces. Also see C. M. Carroll, "An Assessment of the Role and Effectiveness of the International Criminal Tribunal for Rwanda and the Rwandan National Justice System in Dealing with the Mass Atrocities of 1994," *Boston University International Law Journal* 18, no. 1 (2000): 163–204; and Payam Akhavan, "Pushing War Crimes in the Former Yugoslavia: A Critical Juncture for the New World Order," *Human Rights Quarterly* 15, no. 2 (1993): 262–289.

87. Pella, "Towards an International Criminal Court." Also see Schabas, *Genocide in International Law*; and M. Cherif Bassiouni, "From Versailles to Rwanda in Seventy-Five Years: The Need to Establish a Permanent International Criminal Court," *Harvard Human Rights Journal* 10, no. 1 (1997): 11–62.

88. William A. Schabas, "United States Hostility to the International Criminal Court:

It's All About the Security Council," *European Journal of International Law* 15, no. 4 (2004): 701–720. The main objections of the United States are interference with its national sovereignty and a fear of politically motivated prosecutions.

89. *Report of the High Commissioner for Human Rights on the Rights of Persons Belonging to National or Ethnic, Religious and Linguistic Minorities,* ECOSOC document E/CN.4/2005/81, 1 March 2005.

90. In particular, the report noted that nongovernmental organizations supported the idea of a special representative but that they also wanted more effective measures of implementation in order to avert ethnic conflict.

91. "Rights of Persons belonging to National, Ethic, Religious, and Linguistic Minorities," ECOSOC document E/CN.4/2005/L.10/Add. 14, 21 April 2005.

92. Barbara Harff and Ted Robert Gurr, "Research Note: Toward Empirical Theory of Genocide and Politicides: Identification and Measurement of Cases since 1945," *International Studies Quarterly* 32 (1988): 359–371.

93. Mark Levene, "Why Is the Twentieth Century the Century of Genocide?" *Journal of World History* 11, no. 2 (2000): 305–336.

94. Vernon Van Dyke, "Collective Entities and Moral Rights: Problems in Liberal-Democratic Thought," *The Journal of Politics* 44, no. 1 (1982): 21.

95. The initial vote was 106 for and 0 against, with 1 abstention that was later changed to a positive vote. General Assembly, Third Committee vote on the International Convention on the Elimination of All Forms of Racial Discrimination, General Assembly resolution 2106, adopted 21 December 1965.

96. For the origin of and preparatory work for the convention, see Egon Schwelb, "The International Convention on the Elimination of All Forms of Racial Discrimination," *International and Comparative Law Quarterly* 15, no. 4 (1966): 996–1068.

97. Mr. Ketrzynski (Poland), "Sub-Commission on Prevention of Discrimination and Protection of Minorities, Session Records," ECOSOC document E/CN.4/Sub.2/SR.409, 1964, 6.

98. E/CN.4/Sub.2/L.214, 1961. The resolution that was drafted condemning the manifestation of anti-Semitism did not mention the actual country. Humphrey describes these anti-Semitic events in the Federal Republic of Germany as an epidemic; Humphrey, "The United Nations Sub-Commission on the Prevention of Discrimination and the Protection of Minorities," 882.

99. *Report of the Twelfth Session of the Sub-Commission on Prevention of Discrimination and Protection of Minorities,* E/CN.4/800, 1960. See generally the records of the twelfth session of the subcommission.

100. Howard Tolley, *The UN Commission on Human Rights* (Boulder, Colo.: Westview Press, 1987), 45–51. In 1959, nine African members were added, and by the end of the following decade another sixteen members had taken their seats. In San Francisco, only three African states were present: Egypt, Ethiopia, and Liberia. Michael Banton, *International Action against Racial Discrimination* (Oxford: Oxford University Press, 2005). Also see Arthur Lall, "The Asian Nations and the United Nations," *International Organization* 19, no. 3 (1965): 728–748.

101. One expert notes that the impact of Africa in the United Nations shifted the emphasis from East-West to North-South differences, with particular stress on moral-political issues and basic social and economic problems. Thomas Hovet, Jr., "The Role of Africa in the United Nations," *Annals of the American Academy of Political and Social Science* 354, no. 1 (1964): 122–134.

102. The resolution for a convention on the elimination of discrimination was submitted by a group of West African Francophone countries. For a history of the convention on racial discrimination, see Banton, *International Action against Racial Discrimination*, 51–60.

103. The General Assembly had asked the CHR to prepare a declaration and convention covering both racial discrimination and religious tolerance. The decision to separate "religious intolerance" from "racial discrimination" came from Arab delegates and reflected the Arab-Israeli conflict. Many delegates also felt that the issue of race was much more urgent than the issue of religion. "General Assembly, Third Committee, Summary Records," General Assembly documents A/C.3/SR.1165–1173, 1962; Bruce Dickson, "United Nations and Freedom of Religion," *International and Comparative Law Quarterly* 44, no. 2 (1995): 327–357. While it took two years to complete the convention on racial discrimination, it would take another nineteen years to agree on the Declaration against Religious Intolerance (1963–1981). Dickson assesses that the delay was not political but was due to a general sense of malaise in the commission.

104. When the General Assembly adopted the International Convention on the Elimination of Racial Discrimination, the Ghanaian representative commented: "This was its finest hour"; "General Assembly, Third Committee, Summary Records," General Assembly document A/C.3/SR.1345, 1965, 7.

105. Mr. Ketrzynski (Poland), "Sub-Commission on Prevention of Discrimination and Protection of Minorities, Session Records," ECOSOC document E/CN.4/Sub.2/SR.408, 1964, 5. Mr. Ketrzynski also commented that the Commission on Human Rights had received the subcommission's draft declaration "gingerly" but that the Third Committee "had taken a courageous and radical stand in the matter" (5).

106. Miss Malla (Nepal), General Assembly document A/C.3/SR.1220, 1963, paragraph 19.

107. The CHR had already adopted the Declaration on the Elimination of All Forms of Racial Discrimination (General Assembly resolution 1904 [XVIII], 20 November 1963). The declaration was prepared in record time during seventeen of the thirty-five of the CHR's meetings in 1963.

108. See "Sub-Commission on Prevention of Discrimination and Protection of Minorities, Session Records," ECOSOC document E/CN.4/Sub.2/SR.412, 15 January 1964, 6, for the adoption of a motion by Mr. Awad (United Arab Republic) to adopt the text by Mr. Abram (United States) as a basis for discussion. Mr. Abram's text of the Convention on the Elimination of Discrimination is in E/CN.4/Sub.2/L.308, 13 January 1964.

109. Article 21 states: "A State Party may denounce this Convention by written notification to the Secretary-General of the United Nations. Denunciation shall take effect one year after the date of receipt of notification by the Secretary-General."

110. Mr. Ivanov (USSR), "Sub-Commission on Prevention of Discrimination and Protection of Minorities, Session Records," ECOSOC document E/CN.4/Sub.2/SR.407, 14 January 1964, 10. The text in the preamble noted that "any doctrine of superiority based on racial discrimination is scientifically false"; Convention on the Elimination of Racial Discrimination, preamble paragraph 6.

111. Robert L. Carter, "The Warren Court and Desegregation," *Michigan Law Review* 67, no. 2 (1968): 238.

112. Mr. Abram (United States), "Sub-Commission on Prevention of Discrimination and Protection of Minorities, Session Records," ECOSOC document E/CN.4/Sub.2/SR.413, 5 February 1964, 5.

113. Mr. Ketrzynski (Poland), ibid.

114. Mr. Abram (United States), "Sub-Commission on Prevention of Discrimination and Protection of Minorities, Session Records," ECOSOC document E/CN.4/Sub.2/SR.410, 15 January 1964, 11.

115. ECOSOC document E/CN.4/Sub.2/L.345/Add. 4, Annex I, 30 January 1964, Article 1, paragraph 2.

116. Mr. Hakim (Lebanon), "Commission on Human Rights: Summary Record of Meetings," ECOSOC document E/CN.4/SR.787, 27 February 1964, 5.

117. Mrs. Berrah (Ivory Coast), "General Assembly, Third Committee, Summary Records," General Assembly document A/C.3/SR.1306, 15 October 1965, paragraph 23.

118. There was a debate over the initial term "underdeveloped." As Nigeria stated, "a large proportion of the world's population was underprivileged, while no group of human beings could justifiably be called under-developed"; Miss Aguta (Nigeria), "General Assembly, Third Committee, Summary Records," General Assembly document A/C.3/SR.1304, 14 October 1965, paragraph 25.

119. Mr. Benites (Ecuador), "Commission on Human Rights: Summary Record of Meetings," ECOSOC document E/CN.4/SR.784, 25 February 1964, 10.

120. Mr. Hakim (Lebanon), "Commission on Human Rights: Summary Record of Meetings," ECOSOC document E/CN.4/SR.785, 26 February 1964, 5.

121. Mr. Sperduti (Italy), ibid.

122. Mr. Caporoti (United Kingdom), "Sub-Commission on Prevention of Discrimination and Protection of Minorities, Session Records," ECOSOC document E/CN.4/Sub.2/SR.411, 16 January 1964, 6.

123. See Drew Mahalic and Joan Gambee Mahalic, "The Limitation Provisions of the International Convention on the Elimination of All Forms of Racial Discrimination," *Human Rights Quarterly* 9, no. 1 (1987): 74–101.

124. Mr. Abram, *Suggested Draft for the United Nations Convention on the Elimination of All Forms of Racial Discrimination,* ECOSOC document E/CN.4/Sub.2/L.308, 13 January 1964, Article I.

125. Ibid, Article II, paragraph 1.

126. Mr. Saario (Finland), "Sub-Commission on Prevention of Discrimination and Protection of Minorities, Session Records," ECOSOC document E/CN.4/Sub.2/SR.411, 16 January 1964, 12.

127. *Draft Convention on the Elimination of All Forms of Racial Discrimination adopted*

by the Sub-Commission, Report of the Sub-Commission, Annex, ECOSOC document E/CN.4/Sub.2/241, January 1964.

128. Mr. Brillantes (Philippines), "Commission on Human Rights: Summary Record of Meetings," ECOSOC document E/CN.4/SR.785, 26 February 1964, 5.

129. Mr. Hakim (Lebanon), "Commission on Human Rights: Summary Record of Meetings," ECOSOC document E/CN.4/SR.785, 26 February 1964, 6.

130. India, amendment to the draft International Convention on the Elimination of All Forms of Racial Discrimination adopted by the Commission on Human Rights General Assembly document A/C.3/L.1216, 11 October 1965. See Poland's comment on this in "General Assembly, Third Committee, Summary Records," A/C.3/SR.1304, 14 October 1965, paragraph 7.

131. United States and France, "Amendments to the Provisions of the Draft International Convention on Elimination of All Forms of Racial Discrimination," General Assembly document A/C.3/L.1212, 8 October 1965.

132. Mr. Combal (France), "General Assembly, Third Committee, Summary Records," General Assembly document A/C.3/SR.1299, 11 October 1965, paragraphs 37 and 36.

133. Miss Luma (Cameroon), General Assembly document A/C.3/SR.1305, 14 October 1965, paragraph 9.

134. Mrs. Mantzoulinos (Greece), General Assembly document A/C.3/SR.1305, 14 October 1965, paragraph 11.

135. See the compromise proposal: General Assembly document A/C.3/L.1238, 15 October 1965. Also see Schwelb, "The International Convention," 1001–1011.

136. "Revised Suggested Draft for United Nations Convention on the Elimination of All Forms of Racial Discrimination (Addendum) Article IX," ECOSOC document E/CN.4/Sub.2/L.308/Add. 1/Rev. 1, 14 January 1964. A revised amendment by the United States called for laws that punished any organization or individual that incited racial hatred or discrimination "resulting in or likely to cause acts of violence"; ibid., paragraph 1.

137. Mr. Calvocoressi (UK), "Sub-Commission on Prevention of Discrimination and Protection of Minorities, Session Records," ECOSOC document E/CN.4/Sub.2/SR.407, 14 January 1964, 5.

138. The USSR submitted a draft for consideration to the CHR: "Draft Convention on the Elimination of All Forms of Racial Discrimination," ECOSOC document E/CN.4/L.681, 18 February 1964.

139. Poland, "Amendment to the Provisions of the Draft International Convention on Elimination of All Forms of Racial Discrimination," ECOSOC document E/CN.4/L.699, 27 February 1964.

140. Mr. Ketrzynski (Poland), "Sub-Commission on Prevention of Discrimination and Protection of Minorities, Summary Records," ECOSOC document E/CN.4/Sub.2/SR.409, 15 January 1964, 7.

141. USSR, "Amendment to the Provisions of the Draft International Convention on Elimination of All Forms of Racial Discrimination," ECOSOC document E/CN.4/L.703, 4 March 1964.

142. Mrs. Tree (United States), "Commission on Human Rights: Summary Record of Meetings," ECOSOC document E/CN.4/SR.790, 28 February 1964, 8.

143. United States, "Amendment to the Provisions of the Draft International Convention on Elimination of All Forms of Racial Discrimination," ECOSOC document E/CN.4/L.688, 25 February 1964.

144. Mr. Morozov (USSR), "Commission on Human Rights: Summary Record of Meetings," ECOSOC document E/CN.4/SR.790, 28 February 1964, 8.

145. Commission on Human Rights, *Report on the Twentieth Session,* ECOSOC document E/37 Supp. 8, 1964).

146. Nigeria, "Amendment to Article IV of the Draft Convention on the Elimination of All Forms of Racial Discrimination," General Assembly document A/C.3/L.1250, 22 October 1965. Both sides welcomed Nigeria's suggestion, since the United States and the United Kingdom wanted a specific reference to freedom of speech while the Polish and Soviet delegations did not want any reference to this issue. Referring to the UDHR enabled both sides to claim victory, so the suggestion passed with flying colors with a vote of 76 to 1, with 14 abstentions. See "General Assembly, Third Committee, Summary Records," General Assembly document A/C.3/SR.1318, 25 October 1965.

147. ICERD's Article 4(b) stated that states parties "shall declare illegal and prohibit organization, and also organized and all other propaganda activities, which promote and incite racial discrimination, and shall recognize participation in such organization or activities as an offence punishable by law."

148. Mr. Ketrzynski (Poland), "Sub-Commission on Prevention of Discrimination and Protection of Minorities, Session Records," ECOSOC document E/CN.4/Sub.2/SR.409, 15 January 1964, 7.

149. Mr. Boquin (France), ibid., 13.

150. Mr. Calvocoressi (United Kingdom), "Sub-Commission on Prevention of Discrimination and Protection of Minorities, Session Records," ECOSOC document E/CN.4/Sub.2/SR.407, 14 January 1964, 4.

151. Mrs. Tree (United States), "Commission on Human Rights: Summary Record of Meetings," ECOSOC document E/CN.4/SR.789, 28 February 1964, 10.

152. Mr. Baroody (Saudi Arabia), "General Assembly, Third Committee, Summary Records," General Assembly document A/C.3/SR.1166, 1962, paragraph 3.

153. Poland, amendments to the provisions of the Draft Convention on the Elimination of All Forms of Racial Discrimination, General Assembly document A/C.3/L.1210, 8 October 1965.

154. United States and Brazil, amendments to the provisions of the Draft Convention on the Elimination of All Forms of Racial Discrimination, General Assembly document A/C.3/L.1211, 8 October 1965.

155. Mr. Baroody (Saudi Arabia), "General Assembly, Third Committee, Summary Records," General Assembly document A/C.3/SR.1300, 12 October 1965, paragraph 6. Colonialism was also another touchy topic, but in the end the convention condemned colonialism in its preamble, building on the Declaration on Granting of Independence to Colonial Countries and Peoples as an "elder sister, so to speak" of ICERD. Mr. Ivanov (USSR), "Sub-Commission on Prevention of Discrimination and Protection of Minorities, Session Records," ECOSOC document E/CN.4/Sub.2/SR.407, 14 January 1964, 8.

156. Mr. Olcay (Turkey), "General Assembly, Third Committee, Summary Records," General Assembly document A/C.3/SR.1313, 21 October 1965, paragraph 5.

157. The draft resolution from Greece and Hungary is in General Assembly document A/C.3/L.1244, 20 October 1965.

158. See "General Assembly, Third Committee, Summary Records," General Assembly document A/C.3/SR.1312, 20 October 1965. The preamble text says: "Alarmed by manifestations of racial discrimination still in evidence in some areas of the world and by governmental policies based on racial superiority or hatred, such as policies of *apartheid,* segregation, or separation."

159. For a thorough analysis of ICERD and its impact, see Theodor Meron, "The Meaning and Reach of the International Convention on the Elimination of All Forms of Racial Discrimination," *American Journal of International Law* 79 (1985): 283–318; and Banton, *International Action against Racial Discrimination.*

160. Mahalic and Mahalic, "The Limitation Provisions of the International Convention on the Elimination of All Forms of Racial Discrimination."

161. Anne Philips, *Which Equalities Matter?* (Oxford: Polity Press, 1999).

162. Mr. Ingles (Philippines), "Sub-Commission on Prevention of Discrimination and Protection of Minorities, Session Records," ECOSOC document E/CN.4/Sub.2/SR.427, 28 January 1964, 11–12.

163. Mr. Ingles (Philippines), "Sub-Commission on Prevention of Discrimination and Protection of Minorities, Session Records," ECOSOC document E/CN.4/Sub.2/SR.409, 15 January 1964, 5.

164. For the discussion, see ibid. For the draft articles, see Mr. Ingles, "Proposed Measures of Implementation," ECOSOC document E/CN.4/Sub.2/L.321, 17 January 1964.

165. Mr. Soltysiak (Poland), "Sub-Commission on Prevention of Discrimination and Protection of Minorities, Session Records," ECOSOC document E/CN.4/Sub.2/SR.427, 28 January 1964, 15.

166. Mr. Morozov (USSR), "Commission on Human Rights: Summary Record of Meetings," UN document E/CN.4/SR.810, 13 March 1964, 8. The USSR commented that the committee should be limited to nationals of state parties.

167. The draft articles were reissued in the Third Committee in General Assembly document A/C.3/L.1221, 11 October 1965.

168. Argentina, Chile, Colombia, Ecuador, Guatemala, Honduras, Mexico, Panama, Peru, Venezuela, "Amendments to the Articles Relating to Measures of Implementation Submitted by the Philippines," General Assembly document A/C.3/L.1268, 28 October 1965.

169. Netherlands, "Amendments to the Articles Relating to Measures of Implementation Submitted by the Philippines," General Assembly document A/C.3/L.1270, 29 October 1965.

170. United States, "Amendments to the Articles Relating to Measures of Implementation Submitted by the Philippines," General Assembly document A/C.3/L.1271, 29 October 1965.

171. Tunisia, "Amendments to the Articles Relating to Measures of Implementation

Submitted by the Philippines," General Assembly document A/C.3/L.1273, 3 November 1965.

172. Ghana, "Revised Amendments to the Articles Relating to Measures of Implementation Submitted by the Philippines," General Assembly document A/C.3/L.1274/Rev. 1, 12 November 1965.

173. Mr. Mommersteeg (Netherlands), "General Assembly, Third Committee, Summary Records," General Assembly document A/C.3/SR.1344, 16 November 1965, paragraph 71.

174. Lady Gaitskell (United Kingdom), "General Assembly, Third Committee, Summary Records," General Assembly document A/C.3/SR.1344, 16 November 1965, paragraphs 54–55.

175. Mr. Waldron-Ramsey (United Republic of Tanzania), "General Assembly, Third Committee, Summary Records," General Assembly document A/C.3/SR.1345, 17 November 1965, paragraph 40.

176. Mr. Waldron-Ramsey (United Republic of Tanzania), ibid., paragraph 39.

177. Mr. Cochaux (Belgium), "General Assembly, Third Committee, Summary Records," General Assembly document A/C.3/SR.1349, 19 November 1965, paragraph 5.

178. Saudi Arabia, "Amendments to the Articles Relating to Measures of Implementation Submitted by Ghana," General Assembly document A/C.3/L.1290, 18 November 1965.

179. Mr. Baroody (Saudi Arabia), "General Assembly, Third Committee, Summary Records," General Assembly document A/C.3/SR.1351, 23 November 1965, paragraph 57.

180. Mr. Lamptey (Ghana), "General Assembly, Third Committee, Summary Records," General Assembly document A/C.3/SR.1352, 23 November 1965, paragraph 18.

181. ICERD, Article 14.

182. ICERD, Article 11, paragraph 3.

183. See generally "General Assembly, Third Committee, Summary Records," General Assembly document A/C.3/SR.1344, 1965.

184. See Theodor Meron, *Human Rights Law-Making in the United Nations: A Critique of Instruments and Process* (Oxford: Clarendon Press: Oxford University Press, 1986).

185. In particular Article 5 obliges governments "to prohibit and eliminate racial discrimination in all its forms and to guarantee the right of everyone" to political participation and participation in public affairs and equal access to public services; civil rights, including freedom of movement, thought, conscience, religion, opinion, and expression, and peaceful assembly; the right to nationality, to own property, to inheritance, and to marriage and choice of spouse; economic, social, and cultural rights, in particular rights associated with work, housing, health, education, and participation in cultural activities; and the right of access to any public place or services. Also see William F. Felice, "The UN Committee on the Elimination of All Forms of Racial Discrimination: Race and Economic and Social Human Rights," *Human Rights Quarterly* 24 (2002): 205–236; Meron, "The Meaning and Reach."

186. Karl Josef Partsch, "The Committee on the Elimination of Racial Discrimination," in *The United Nations and Human Rights: A Critical Appraisal,* ed. Philip Alston (New York: Oxford University Press, 1992).

187. Michael Banton, "Decision-Taking in the CERD Committee," in *The Future of UN Human Rights Treaty Monitoring,* ed. Philip Alston and James Crawford (Cambridge: Cambridge University Press, 2000).

188. Humphrey, *Human Rights & the United Nations*, 23–28. Indians from Canada had served in World War II and had one of the highest voluntary enlistment rates of any group. They were extremely aware of their second-class citizenship in their own country. See Douglas Sanders, "Developing a Modern International Law on the Rights of Indigenous Peoples," note 11, research paper prepared for Canada's Royal Commission on Aboriginal People, 1994, available online without endnotes at http://www.anthrobase .com/Browse/home/hst/cache/Developing.doc.htm; available with endnotes from the authors. The involvement of indigenous peoples in their quest for recognition and justice through international institutions can be traced back to the League of Nations. Cayuga Chief Deskaheh traveled to Geneva in 1923 in the hope of addressing the issue of broken treaties, but he was treated with indifference and was not allowed to speak. The leader of the Maoris tried to approach the League in 1925, but he was also denied access. See Paul Gordon Lauren, *The Evolution of International Human Rights: Visions Seen* (Philadelphia: University of Pennsylvania Press, 1999), 105–138.

189. General Assembly document A/6101, 1948. The General Assembly passed the resolution to this effect in 1949 ("Study of the Social Problems of the Aboriginal Populations and Other Under-Developed Social Groups of the American Continents," General Assembly resolution 275 [III], 11 May 1949).

190. ECOSOC document E/CN.4/SR.397, 1951. The western majority, with the United States in the lead, decided that the subcommission should no longer continue and that its work could be handled by the Secretariat and the CHR. The General Assembly, with its majority of communist and Third World states, saved the subcommission. See also Humphrey, "The United Nations Sub-Commission on the Prevention of Discrimination and Protection of Minorities."

191. In 1957, the ILO formulated Convention 107 on the Protection and Integration of Indigenous and Other Tribal and Semi-Tribal Populations in Independent Countries. Indigenous peoples have rejected this convention because of its emphasis on assimilation. In June 1989, the ILO adopted a revised Convention 169 on Indigenous and Tribal Peoples, but it has not yet shelved Convention 107. The texts of these conventions are available online at http://www.ilo.org/ilolex/english/convdisp1.htm.

192. The report was based on a study conducted in 1967 by the Summer Institute of Linguistics, a Protestant organization. Joseph Novitski, "For Indians of Brazil's Interior the Choice Is the Past or the Future," *New York Times*, 28 July 1970. Soon after that, two groups on indigenous affairs were established. The International Work Group for Indigenous Affairs (1968), based in Copenhagen, and Survival International (1969), based in London, highlighted the massacres, land theft, and genocide that were taking place in the Brazilian Amazon in the name of progress and "economic growth." In addition, in response to the publicity surrounding indigenous survival in the modern world, the International Red Cross undertook a survey to assess the living conditions and health of thirty-six Indian tribes in the Amazon region. Victor Lusinchi, "Red Cross Says Aid Is Needed by Indians in Amazon Urgently," *New York Times*, 24 February 1971.

193. The "Declaration on the Granting of Independence to Colonial Countries and Peoples" (General Assembly resolution 1514 [XV], 14 December 1960) stresses nonintervention and preserving territorial integrity; Centre for Human Rights, *Human Rights: A Compilation of International Instruments*. The declaration's so-called blue-water or

salt-water principles limited decolonization to overseas territories but did not apply to internal collectivities. Article 6 ruled out secession as a right for oppressed groups in the domestic setting.

194. References were made to natives of trust or non-self-governing territories (euphemisms for colonized groups) or minorities residing within them, but these definitions did not include the tribes of the Americas, the Pacific, Africa, or Asia that had been displaced by arriving Europeans. Newly independent states were more concerned with issues of territorial integrity and economic development, and they subjected indigenous groups to new forms of oppression that ranged from genocide to variations on assimilation policies. The belief that only "civilized" members of society could improve the lot of indigenous groups, aborigines, and the like has resulted in their general invisibility in the developing human rights project of the United Nations. See James Anaya, *Indigenous Peoples in International Law* (Oxford: Oxford University Press, 1996).

195. See Sanders, *Developing a Modern International Law,* 6.

196. Ibid.

197. Ibid., 7.

198. Russel Lawrence Barsch, "Indigenous Peoples: An Emerging Object of International Law," *American Journal of International Law* 80, no. 2 (1986): 369–385.

199. Sami (or Lapps) are the largest indigenous groups in Europe, encompassing parts of northern Sweden, Norway, Finland, and the Kola Peninsula of Russia.

200. The final draft was released in 1987. *Study of the Problem of Discrimination against Indigenous Populations, Vol. 5, Conclusions, Proposals, and Recommendations,* ECOSOC document E/CN.4/Sub.2/1986/7/Add. 4, 1 March 1987.

201. Barsh, "Indigenous Peoples."

202. José R. Martínez Cobo, Special Rapporteur, *Study of the Problem of Discrimination Against Indigenous Populations,* ECOSOC document E/CN.4/Sub.2/1983/21, 30 September 1983, Add. 8, paragraphs 624–25, and 628.

203. Sanders credits the work of the Canadian-based World Council of Indigenous Peoples and the American-based International Indian Treaty Council. In addition, the government of Norway played a key role. Sanders, *Developing a Modern International Law.*

204. The subcommission proposed that a working group be created in September 1981; this suggestion was endorsed by the commission in its resolution 1982/19 of 10 March 1982. It was formally established by ECOSOC on 7 May 1982 in its resolution 1982/34. The study, largely written by Diaz, was completed in 1983 but it had little impact because it was "unmanageably long . . . outdated and incomplete." It was also not accessible in its entirety until 1987. Douglas Sanders, "The UN Working Group on Indigenous Populations," *Human Rights Quarterly* 11, no. 3 (1989): 412.

205. See the 1996 report of the working group on indigenous rights for a discussion of self-determination: "Sub-Commission on the Prevention of Discrimination and Protection of Minorities, Summary Record of the 21st Session," ECOSOC document E/CN.4/Sub.2/1996/SR.21, 26 August 1996. Also see Russel Lawrence Barsh, "Indigenous Peoples in the 1990s: From Object to Subject of International Law," *Harvard Human Rights Journal* 7 (1994): 33–86.

206. Eide was a member of the subcommission from 1981 to 1983 and 1988 to 1991. Since 1995 he has chaired the United Nations Working Group on the Rights of Minorities.

207. See Sanders, "The UN Working Group."

208. More precisely he had taken seriously and expressed concern about the alleged threats of reprisal by the Indian government toward Swami Agnivesh, the head of the bonded labor movement in India. When the Indian representative organized Third World votes against Eide's reelection, Eide's ouster was seen as a personal initiative and not as a policy of the Indian government. The government did seize the swami's passport upon his return to India, an action that supported Eide's initial concern; ibid., 408–409.

209. The fear among states is that the declaration will serve to censure their actions and promote the rights of indigenous people under the human rights rubric. For a summary of the discussion of the 1994 draft, see Barsh, "Indigenous Peoples."

210. For a summary of debates over the final text of the declaration on issues such as distinct nature of collective rights, territorial rights, the right to self-determination, and international legal protections, see Robert A. Williams, "Encounters on the Frontiers of International Human Rights Law: Redefining the Terms of Indigenous Peoples' Survival in the World," *Duke Law Journal* 1990, no. 4 (1990): 660–704.

211. Michael J. Dennis in a meeting with Native American tribes of the United States, quoted in James W. Zion, e-mail to the Native Law Centre, 22 November 2000; in authors' possession.

212. Countries of Asia, particularly India and China, argued that "autonomy" should be made subject to the existing political and legal system of the state. They also objected to a definition of indigenous peoples that included groups that had assimilated into the greater society.

213. Barsh, "Indigenous Peoples."

214. "Indigenous peoples have the right of self-determination. By virtue of that right they freely determine their political status and freely pursue their economic, social and cultural development"; Article 3 of draft declaration submitted by the CHR (ECOSOC document E/CN.4/Sub.2/1994/2/Add. 1, 1994).

The article in General Assembly resolution 1514 was worded as follows: "All peoples have the right to self-determination; by virtue of that right they freely determine their political status and freely pursue their economic, social and cultural development." "Declaration on the Granting of Independence to Colonial Countries and Peoples," General Assembly resolution 1514 (XV), 14 December 1960.

215. *Report of the Working Group on a Draft United Nations Declaration on the Rights of Indigenous People,* ECOSOC document E/CN.4/2005/89, February 2005, summarizes the tenth session of the working group, held from 13 to 24 September and 29 November to 3 December 2004.

216. The idea was proposed by Special Rapporteur Rodolfo Stavenhagen, and indigenous peoples endorsed it. See Stevenhagen's *Study of the Problem of Discrimination Against Indigenous Populations,* ECOSOC document E/CN.4/Sub.2/1986/7/Add/4, 1986. Other reports by the special rapporteur are available online at http://ap.ohchr.org/documents/sdpage_e.aspx?m=73&t=9.

217. Sanders notes that only sixteen or seventeen states would have supported an

amendment using the term "indigenous peoples"; Sanders, *Developing a Modern International Law.*

218. Indigenous peoples are listed under Section II—Persons belonging to national or ethnic, religious and linguistic minorities; "Vienna Declaration and the Programme of Action," General Assembly document A/CONF.157/23, 12 July 1993.

219. Quoted in Sanders, *Developing a Modern International Law.*

220. The removal of the "s" (from "Peoples" to "People") is linguistically significant; the word "peoples" was considered to imply the right to self-determination.

221. "Second International Decade of the World's Indigenous People," General Assembly draft resolution A/C.3/59/L.30, 22 October 2004.

222. Article 31 on self-determination is perceived by some indigenous groups as an elaboration of the right to self-determination and by other groups as a limitation of that right. Article 3 states: "All peoples have the right of self-determination in accordance with established principles of international law. This right applies to indigenous and non-indigenous peoples on the same basis and without discrimination." Article 31 states: "Indigenous peoples, as a specific form of exercising their right to self-determination, have the right to autonomy or self-government in matters relating to their internal and local affairs, including culture, religion, education, information, media, health, housing, employment, social welfare."

223. Their resistance is not surprising, given the dichotomous view that society has imposed upon them as either ignoble or noble savage. Tennat traces this development in the post-1945 literature: 1945–1958 as the backward, uncivilized populations leading lives of misery and 1971–1993 as the noble primitive whose culture is threatened by progress. In the first, the indigenous person needs assistance in order to assimilate into modern society. This reasoning was the basis for the Andean Indian Program (1954) sponsored by the International Labour Organization. In the second period, indigenous peoples were seen as connected to land with a wealth of ecological knowledge, and their extinction was linked with that of plants, animals, and ecosystems. Indigenous peoples have resisted both these classifications and instead have repeatedly demanded greater participation and asserted their right to self-determination in the international community and within the membership of the UN. Chris Tennant, "Indigenous Peoples, International Institutions, and the International Legal Literature from 1945–1993," *Human Rights Quarterly* 16, no. 1 (1994): 1–57.

224. See in general Hurst Hannum, "Minorities, Indigenous Peoples, and Self-Determination," *Studies of Transnational Legal Policy* 26, no. 1 (1994): 120–136.

225. Although indigenous people were present in great numbers at the Rio conference on the environment, there is little formal mention of them or human rights in the final declaration. However, the program of action, Agenda 21, includes a full chapter (chapter 26), that emphasizes indigenous participation in policymaking and land and resource management. See Economic and Social Affairs, *Agenda 21: Earth Summit—The United Nations Programme of Action from Rio* (New York: United Nations, 1993).

226. One writer suggests that the discourse on international human rights as defined by the United Nations has serious limitations for the indigenous in Mexico. See R. Overmyer-Valasquez, "The Self-Determination of Indigenous Peoples and the Limits of

United Nations Advocacy in Guerrero, Mexico (1998–2000)," *Global Studies in Culture and Power* 10, no. 1 (2003): 9–29.

227. The Permanent Forum was established in 2000 and is an advisory body to ECOSOC. Its mandate is to provide advice, raise awareness, promote integration, and prepare and disseminate information.

228. See Devaki Jain, *Women, Development, and the UN: A Sixty-Year Quest for Equality and Justice* (Bloomington: Indiana University Press, 2005).

229. UN Charter, Preamble.

230. Ibid., Article 8. The article, which is phrased in the negative, is not viewed as an obligation to include women.

231. Ruth B. Russell, *A History of the United Nations Charter: The Role of the United States 1940–45* (Washington, D.C.: Brookings Institution, 1958), 793–794n24. Cited in Hilary Charlesworth, Christine Chinkin, and Shelley Wright, "Feminist Approaches to International Law," *American Journal of International Law* 85, no. 4 (1991): 622. The authors note that in reality, women's appointments within the United Nations have not attained even the limited promise of Article 8.

232. Dame Margaret Bruce, personal conversation with the authors, June 2005.

233. Cited in Johannes Morsink, "Women's Rights in the Universal Declaration," *Human Rights Quarterly* 13, no. 2 (1991): 230. For a general history of the CSW, see Laura Reanda, "The Commission on the Status of Women," in *The United Nations and Human Rights: A Critical Appraisal*, ed. Philip Alston (New York: Oxford University Press, 1992).

234. *Yearbook of the United Nations 1946–1947* (New York: United Nations, 1947), 523.

235. "ECOSOC Resolution Establishing the Commission on the Status of Women," ECOSOC resolution E/RES/11 (II), 21 June 1946.

236. Humphrey, *Human Rights & the United Nations,* 19. Humphrey also notes that several women's groups came to him to protest this decision and that he also felt strongly that the status of women was a human rights issue.

237. Dorothy Kenyon, "Victories on the International Front," *Annals of the American Academy of Political and Social Science* 251 (1947): 17–23. Kenyon later represented the United States on the Commission on the Status of Women. Jain also notes that Eleanor Roosevelt was opposed to setting up a separate commission on women because it would marginalize women and their issues at the UN; Jain, *Women, Development, and the UN,* 17–19.

238. Kenyon, "Victories on the International Front," 20.

239. Ibid.

240. Mrs. Begtrup, quoted in Humphrey, *Human Rights & the United Nations,* 19.

241. "Commission on Human Rights: Summary Record of Meetings," ECOSOC document E/CN.4/SR.1, 1947, 6.

242. ECOSOC had passed a special resolution on participation inviting the officers of the CSW to be present and participate in the work of the CHR when the issue of women was being considered, but without voting rights; Morsink, "Women's Rights in the Universal Declaration," 231.

243. Ibid. Morsink notes many examples where Mrs. Begtrup suggested that a phrase

or word be modified to ensure that provisions keep in mind the issue of nondiscrimination against women.

244. Ibid., 236–241.

245. Article 3 in both covenants states that "the State Parties to the present Covenant undertake to ensure the equal right of men and women." Article 2 recognizes the principle of nondiscrimination with respect to sex.

246. International Covenant on Civil and Political Rights, Article 23.

247. The actual text stated its intent to raise the status of women irrespective of nationality, race, language, or religion to equality to men in all fields of human enterprise and to eliminate all discrimination against women in statutory law and legal maxims or rules or in interpretation of customary law. See Margaret E. Galey, "Promoting Nondiscrimination against Women: The UN Commission on the Status of Women," *International Studies Quarterly* 23, no. 2 (1979): 243–302. Galey reviews the work the CSW undertook in its early years. Also see Margaret K. Bruce, "An Account of United Nations Action to Advance the Status of Women," *Annals of the American Academy of Political and Social Science* 375, no. 1 (1968): 163–175.

248. "Convention on the Political Rights of Women," General Assembly resolution A/RES/640 (VII), 20 December 1952; "Convention on the Nationality of Married Women," General Assembly document A/RES/1040 (XI), 29 January 1957; "Convention on the Consent to Marriage, Minimum Age for Marriage and Registration of Marriages," General Assembly document A/Res/1763A (XVII), 7 November 1962.

249. The declaration was adopted in 1967 by the General Assembly. Details of the origins of women's rights are discussed in Arvonne S. Fraser, "Becoming Human: The Origins and Development of Women's Human Rights," *Human Rights Quarterly* 21, no. 4 (1999): 853–906.

250. The previous year, the World Conference on Population had been organized with a budget of $3 million for planning and execution. In contrast, the CSW had less than $350,000. Noted in Judith P. Zinsser, "From Mexico to Copenhagen to Nairobi: The United Nations Decade for Women, 1975–1985," *Journal of World History* 13, no. 1: 139–168.

251. Jain, *Women, Development, and the UN*, 65–71.

252. This tension is highlighted in the writings of international lawyer Hilary Charlesworth. She writes: "The fundamental problem women face worldwide is not discriminatory treatment compared with men, although this is a manifestation of the larger problem. Women are in an inferior position because they have no real power in either the public or private worlds, and international human rights law, like most economic, social, cultural, and legal constructs, reinforces this powerlessness"; Hilary Charlesworth, "What Are Women's International Human Rights?" in *Human Rights of Women: National and International Perspectives,* ed. Rebecca Cook (Philadelphia: University of Pennsylvania Press, 1994).

253. Fraser, "Becoming Human," 895–899.

254. Zinsser, "From Mexico to Copenhagen to Nairobi."

255. Kelly D. Askin and Dorean M. Koenig, eds., *Women and International Human Rights Law,* 3 vols. (New York: Transnational Publishers, 1999). Volume 2 examines the human rights instruments that affect women's rights.

256. "Convention on the Elimination of All Forms of Discrimination against Women," General Assembly resolution A/RES/34/180, 18 December 1979. The convention came into force in December 1980. For a summary of provisions and domestic applicability, see Catherine Tinker, "Human Rights for Women: The UN Convention on the Elimination of All Forms of Discrimination against Women," *Human Rights Quarterly* 3, no. 2 (1981): 32–43.

257. For a history of the early years of CEDAW, see Elizabeth Evatt, "Finding a Voice for Women's Rights: The Early Days of CEDAW," *George Washington International Law Review* 34, no. 3 (2002): 515–553. For a review on the Mid-Decade World Conference for Women, see Fran P. Hosken, "Toward a Definition of Women's Rights," *Human Rights Quarterly* 3, no. 2 (1981): 1–10.

258. Reanda notes that for other human rights instruments very few women are part of the supervisory mechanisms and comments on the absence of women's issues on their agendas. For example, in the Human Rights Committee, forced prostitution is considered slavery but has not been raised as such under the International Covenant on Civil and Political Rights. See Laura Reanda, "Human Rights and Women's Rights: The United Nations Approach," *Human Rights Quarterly* 3, no. 2 (1981): 11–31.

259. Hilary Charlesworth, "Feminist Methods in International Law," *American Journal of International Law* 93 (1999): 379–394. Charlesworth remarks that pigeonholing by theorists masks the obvious power differential that exists between men and women.

260. Radhika Coomaraswamy, "Reinventing International Law: Women's Rights as Human Rights in the International Community," *Bulletin of Concerned Asian Scholars* 28 (1996): 16.

261. Vern L. Bullough, Brenda Shelton, and Sarah Slavin, *The Subordinated Sex* (Atlanta: University of Georgia Press, 1988); Amartya Kumar Sen, "Gender Inequality and Theories of Justice," in *Women, Culture and Development: A Study of Human Capabilities,* ed. Martha Nussbaum and Jonathan Glover (Oxford: Clarendon Press, 1995). Sen writes that gender inequality is closely related to notions of legitimacy and correctness.

262. Andrew Byrnes, "Women, Feminism and International Human Rights Law—Methodological Myopia, Fundamental Flaw or Meaningful Marginalization," *Australian Yearbook of International Law* 12, no. 205 (1992); Charlotte Bunch, "Women's Rights as Human Rights: Towards a Re-Vision of Human Rights," *Human Rights Quarterly* 12 (1990): 486–498.

263. Bunch, "Women's Rights as Human Rights," 491.

264. For reservations to CEDAW by states, see "Declarations, Reservations, Objections and Notifications of Withdrawal of Reservations Relating to the Convention on the Elimination of All Forms of Discrimination Against Women," CEDAW/SP/2006/2, 23 June 2006.

265. Michele Brandt and Jeffrey A. Kaplan, "The Tension between Women's Rights and Religious Rights: Reservations to CEDAW by Egypt, Bangladesh and Tunisia," *Journal of Law and Religion* 12, no. 1 (1995–1996): 105–142.

266. Rebecca Cook, "Reservations to the Convention on the Elimination of All Forms of Discrimination against Women," *Virginia Journal of International Law* 643 (1990).

267. Bunch documents several examples: amniocentesis used for sex selection in India

and China, different care and weaning practices for female children, denial of reproductive rights, rape as an instrument of war, and others; Bunch, "Women's Rights as Human Rights."

268. Ibid.

269. "Convention on the Elimination of All Forms of Discrimination Against Women," General Assembly document A/44/38, 1989, General Recommendation 12. In 1992, CEDAW adopted General Recommendation 19 on violence against women.

270. Margaret E. Galey, "The Nairobi Conference: The Powerless Majority," *PS* 19, no. 2 (1986): 262. Galey comments that the very serious health consequences of female circumcision were initially discussed in the World Health Organization's Regional Seminar in Khartoum in 1979 and at a conference of Arab and African heads of state in 1984 with the goal of prohibiting its practice and making it illegal.

271. Paragraph 258 of the Nairobi Platform; quoted in *The Preliminary Report of the Special Rapporteur on Violence Against Women, Its Causes and Consequences*, ECOSOC document E/CN.4/1995/42, 22 November 1994, paragraph 22.

272. A draft was prepared and submitted to the UN in 1992. *Report of the Working Group on Violence against Women*, ECOSOC document E/CN.6/WG.2/1992/L.3, 1992. The "Declaration on the Elimination of Violence Against Women" was adopted by the General Assembly as resolution 48/104 on 20 December 1993.

273. Hilary Charlesworth, "Not Waving but Drowning: Gender Mainstreaming and Human Rights in the United Nations," *Harvard Human Rights Journal* 18 (2005): 1–18; Mary Robinson, "A Selective Declaration: Women's Human Rights in the New Millennium," *Harvard International Review* 21, no. 4 (1999): 60–63.

274. Anne Gallagher, "Ending the Marginalization: Strategies for Incorporating Women into the United Nations Human Rights System," *Human Rights Quarterly* 19, no. 2 (1997): 283–333; K. Tomasevski, "Rights of Women: From Prohibition to Elimination of Discrimination," *International Social Science Journal* 50, no. 158 (December 1998): 545–558.

275. "The Optional Protocol to the Convention on the Elimination of All Forms of Discrimination Against Women," General Assembly resolution A/54/4, 6 October 1999; entry into force 22 December 2000.

276. Charlesworth, Chinkin, and Wright, "Feminist Approaches to International Law," 622. The authors observe that states are patriarchal structures and that their foundations are reinforced by international legal principles of sovereign equality, political independence and territorial integrity. International organizations are functional extensions of states, and, not surprisingly, their structures replicate those of states, restricting women to insignificant and subordinate roles. In applying Article 8 of the UN Charter they note the inadequate representation of women in positions of power at the UN.

277. Oloka-Onyango, "Heretical Reflections."

278. A. Ording, "The United Nations and the World's Children," *Annals of the American Academy of Political and Social Science* 252 (July 1947). On 11 December 1946, resolution 57 (I) was passed in the General Assembly, establishing UNICEF.

279. M. Black, *Children First: The Story of UNICEF Past and Present* (New York: Oxford University Press, 1996). In particular, see Chapter 1.

280. "Declaration of the Rights of the Child," UN General Assembly resolution 1386, 20 November 1959. The ten principles associated with childrens' need for protection include the rights set forth in the declaration; special protection in the best interest of the child (this would later be an important concept for the Convention on the Rights of the Child); entitlement to name and nationality; social security and adequate nutrition, housing, recreation, and medical services; special protection for physically, mentally, or socially disabled children; public services to care for children without families and for families without adequate means of support; free compulsory education at the elementary stage; protection and relief under any circumstances, including economic exploitation, trafficking, and all forms of neglect and cruelty; protection from all forms of discrimination.

281. John Charnow and Sherwood G. Moe, eds., *Henry R. Labouisse, UNICEF Executive Director, 1965–1979*, UNICEF document CH/HST/MON/1988-011, June 1988, available online at http://www.cf-hst.net/UNICEF-TEMP/mon/cf-hst-mono-list-title-ext-ref.htm. The International Year of the Child successfully promoted the needs and rights of children and provided an unprecedented level of services and support for poor children. Michael Jupp, "The International Year of the Child: Ten Years Later," *Proceedings of the Academy of Political Science* 37, no. 2 (1989): 31–44.

282. "Convention on the Rights of the Child," General Assembly resolution 44/25, 20 November 1989.

283. For a complete discussion on the travaux préparatoires, see J. Le Blanc, *The Convention on the Rights of the Child* (Lincoln: University of Nebraska Press, 1995); Sharon Detrick, ed., *The United Nations Convention on the Rights of the Child: A Guide to the Travaux Préparatoires* (Boston: Martinus Nijhoff Publishers, 1992); and Maria Rita Saulle, ed., *The Rights of the Child: International Instruments* (New York: Transnational Publishers, 1995).

284. C. P. Cohen, "The Role of Nongovernmental Organizations in the Drafting of the Convention on the Rights of the Child," *Human Rights Quarterly* 12 (February 1990): 137–147. In 1983, an NGO ad hoc group on the drafting of the CRC was formed. At the close of negotiations in 1989, thirty-five NGOs had endorsed a joint statement. The core group of NGOs that represented the ad hoc group between 1983 and 1989 included Defense for Children International, the International Catholic Child Bureau, Radda Barnen, Human Rights Internet, and the International Commission of Jurists. The ad hoc group contributed significantly to raising awareness of the drafting process and of the convention through conferences, symposia, exhibits, regional workshops, and seminars.

285. Per Miljeteig-Olssen, "Advocacy of Children's Rights—The Convention as More than a Legal Document," *Human Rights Quarterly* 12 (February 1990): 148–155.

286. Le Blanc, *The Convention on the Rights of the Child*.

287. Article 45 of the Convention on the Rights of the Child states: "In order to foster the effective implementation of the Convention and to encourage international cooperation in the field covered by the Convention: The specialized agencies, the United Nations Children's Fund and other United Nations organs shall be entitled to be represented at the consideration of the implementation of such provisions of the present Convention as fall within the scope of their mandate. The Committee may invite the specialized agen-

cies, the United Nations Children's Fund and other competent bodies as it may consider appropriate to provide expert advice on the implementation of the Convention in areas falling within the scope of their respective mandates."

288. Convention on the Rights of the Child, Article 3.1. For a discussion of "best interests of the child," see *International Journal of Law, Policy, and the Family* 8 (1994). The full issue is dedicated to the topic and includes articles from Philip Alston, Stephen Parker, and Abdullahi An-Na⸱im, among others.

289. Thomas Hammarberg, "The UN Convention on the Rights of the Child—and How to Make It Work," *Human Rights Quarterly* 12, no. 1 (1990): 97–105.

290. *Question of a Convention on the Rights of the Child: Report of the 1989 Open-Ended Working Group on a Draft Convention on the Rights of the Child,* ECOSOC document E/CN.4/1989/48, 12 March 1989.

291. See Philip Alston, "The Unborn Child and Abortion under the Draft Convention on the Rights of the Child," *Human Rights Quarterly* 12, no. 1 (1990): 156–178.

292. Indeed, the Holy See became a signatory of the Convention on the Rights of the Child after expressing a reservation on this point.

293. Convention on the Rights of the Child, Article 37(a).

294. Hammarberg, "The UN Convention."

295. *Question of a Convention on the Rights of the Child: Report of the 1985 Working Group on a Draft Convention on the Rights of the Child,* ECOSOC document E/CN.4/1985/64, 3 April 1985.

296. "Setting International Standards in the Field of Human Rights," General Assembly resolution 41/120, 4 December 1986, stated that new standards should be consistent with the existing body of international law.

297. Jamie Sergio Cerda, "The Draft Convention on the Rights of the Child: New Rights," *Human Rights Quarterly* 12, no. 1 (1990): 115–119.

298. David A. Balton, "The Convention on the Rights of the Child: Prospects for International Enforcement," *Human Rights Quarterly* 12, no. 1 (1990): 120–129.

299. William A. Schabas, "Reservations to the Convention on the Rights of the Child," *Human Rights Quarterly* 18, no. 2 (1996): 472–491.

300. Ibid.

301. See S. Goonseskere and R. de Alwis, "Women and Children' Rights in a Human Rights Based Approach to Development," Gender Unit, Global Policy Section. UNICEF, May 2005; K. Mukelabai and A. Belembaogo, "How Does a Human Rights Approach Enhance Health Programmes for Children?" presentation at the conference "Lessons Learned from Rights-based Approaches to Health," Atlanta, 14–16 April 2005.

302. UNICEF, *The State of the World's Children 2005* (New York, Oxford University Press, 2005).

303. Carol Bellamy, "UN Reform: Working for Children," presentation to the Joint Meeting of the All Party Parliamentary Group on Overseas Development and the Overseas Development Institute, London, 9 March 2005, available online in audio format at http://www.odi.org.uk/speeches/MDGs_2005/meeting_9Mar/meeting_report.html.

304. This example is taken from Wolf Schafer, "The Uneven Globality of Children,"

Journal of Social History 38, no. 4 (2005): 1027–1039. See also UNICEF, *Birth Registration: Right from the Start* (March 2002), available online at www.unicef.at/fileadmin/medien/pdf/birthreg.pdf.

305. The conference identified a minimum list of activities for preventive health care: health education, sound nutrition, safe water and sanitation, maternal and child health care, immunizations, family planning, and the provision of essential drugs.

306. Philip Alston, "Ships Passing in the Night: The Current State of the Human Rights and Development Debate Seen through the Lens of the Millennium Development Goals," *Human Rights Quarterly* 27, no. 2 (2005): 755–829.

307. See UNICEF, *State of the World's Children 2006* (New York: Oxford University Press, 2006), which focuses on the Convention on the Rights of the Child and its relation to the Millennium Development Goals.

9. The Right to Development

1. Mbaye used the phrase "right to development" as the title of his opening address at a seminar at the International Institute of Human Rights at Strasbourg. Kéba Mbaye, "Le Droit du Développement comme un droit de l'Homme," *Revue des Droits de l'Homme* 5 (1972): 503–534, quoted in Russel Lawrence Barsh, "The Right to Development as a Human Right: Results of the Global Consultation," *Human Rights Quarterly* 13, no. 2 (1991): 322–338. Mbaye formally launched the idea in 1978 in a paper delivered at the UNESCO Meeting of Experts on Human Rights (Human Needs and the Establishment of a New International Economic Order), Paris, 19–23 June 1978; see "Emergence of the 'Right to Development' as a Human Right in the Context of the New International Economic Order," UNESCO document SS-78/CONF.630/8, 16 July 1979.

2. Articles 55 and 56 of the UN Charter focus on creating favorable economic and social conditions for international cooperation. Article 55 states: "With a view to the creation of conditions of stability and well-being which are necessary for peaceful and friendly relations among nations based on respect for the principle of equal rights and self-determination of peoples, the United Nations shall promote: a. higher standards of living, full employment, and conditions of economic and social progress and development; b. solutions of international economic, social, health, and related problems; and international cultural and educational cooperation; and c. universal respect for, and observance of, human rights and fundamental freedoms for all without distinction as to race, sex, language, or religion." Article 56 states: "All Members pledge themselves to take joint and separate action in co-operation with the Organization for the achievement of the purposes set forth in Article 55." In addition, Chapter IX of the UN Charter created the specialized agencies on international cooperation for achieving this purpose. Article 28 of the Universal Declaration states: "Everyone is entitled to a social and international order in which the rights and freedoms set forth in this Declaration can be fully realized." "Universal Declaration of Human Rights," General Assembly resolution 217 A (III), 10 December 1948.

3. For the view of a U.S. participant in these UN debates, see Clarence Clyde Ferguson,

Jr., "The Politics of the New International Economic Order," *Proceedings of the Academy of Political Science* 32, no. 4 (1977): 142–158. For the perspective of the Group of 77 on the NIEO, see Carol Geldart and Peter Lyon, "The Group of 77: A Perspective View," *International Affairs* 57, no. 1 (Winter 1980–1981): 79–101.

4. "Declaration on the Right to Development," General Assembly resolution 41/128, 4 December 1986.

5. Ibid., Article 1.1.

6. By the 1950s, Asian decolonization was complete, with the exception of Indochina. Ethiopia, Liberia, and Egypt were the only three African states represented at the San Francisco conference. South Africa was also present, but it was not considered an indigenous African nation because of its institutionalized policy of racial discrimination. See Thomas Hovet, Jr., "The Role of Africa in the United Nations," *Annals of the American Academy of Political and Social Science* 354 (July 1964): 122–131.

7. Since 1823, when the United States announced the Monroe Doctrine, it has dominated Latin America economically and politically. See David W. Dent, *The Legacy of the Monroe Doctrine* (Westport, Conn.: Greenwood Press, 1999).

8. See E. J. Hobsbawm, *The Age of Extremes: A History of the World, 1914–1991* (New York: Pantheon Books, 1994), 257–286.

9. Brian Urquhart remarked that "the avalanche started with the Indian subcontinent in 1947. And once that had happened, it was clear that this was going to be a rapid process." Brian Urquhart, quoted in Thomas G. Weiss, Tatiana Carayannis, Richard Jolly, and Louis Emmerij, *UN Voices: The Struggle for Development and Social Justice* (Bloomington: Indiana University Press, 2005), 171.

10. Abdullah El-Erian, "The Bandung Conference," in *Essays on International Law*, ed. Asian African Legal Consultative Committee (Jakarta, Indonesia: National Youth Committee, 1981), 159. El-Erian notes that their assertion of identity was not confined to the political field but also involved economic and cultural aspects. The Bandung conference, organized by Egypt, Indonesia, Burma, Ceylon (Sri Lanka), India, and Pakistan, was significant as the first major conference convened by poor nations whose fates had been largely determined by Europe. See Paul Gordon Lauren, *The Evolution of International Human Rights: Visions Seen* (Philadelphia: University of Pennsylvania Press, 1998), 250–253.

11. Final Communiqué, Asian-African Solidarity Conference, Bandung, Indonesia, April 1955, quoted in Karin Mickelson, "Rhetoric and Rage: Third World Voices in International Legal Discourse," *Wisconsin International Law Journal* 16 (1998): 357.

12. See Robert W. Cox, "Ideologies and the New International Economic Order: Reflections on Some Recent Literature," *International Organization* 33, no. 2 (1979): 257–302; Mahbub ul Haq, *The Poverty Curtain: Choices for the Third World* (New York: University Press, 1976).

13. Samir Amin, quoted in Weiss, Carayannis, Jolly, and Emmerij, *UN Voices,* 170.

14. "Declaration on the Granting of Independence to Colonial Countries and Peoples," General Assembly resolution 1514, 14 December 1960, paragraph 1. As with other resolutions concerning decolonization, the debates were affected by Cold War and North-South divisions. The Soviet delegate accused "the colonialists [of] trying in every way to postpone the granting of political independence and to guarantee for the future the position of

European minorities in those countries." David Ormsby-Gore of the UK responded: "The representative of the Soviet Union appears to wish to use the debate simply as another occasion for vilifying my country and for carrying the Cold War into Africa, in the hope that it can there be holed up to his advantage"; *Yearbook of the United Nations 1960* (New York: United Nations, 1961), 45.

15. Committee on Programme Appraisals, Economic and Social Council, *Five-Year Perspective, 1960–1964,* ECOSOC document E/3347/Rev. 1, 1960, 25.

16. Robert Wade, *Governing the Market: Economic Theory and the Role of Government in East Asian Industrialization* (Princeton, N.J.: Princeton University Press, 1990).

17. See Andre Gunder Frank, *Crisis in the World Economy* (London: Heinemann, 1980); Ankie Hoogvelt, *Globalization and the Postcolonial World: The New Political Economy of Development* (London: Palgrave, 2001).

18. "Declaration of the Establishment of a New International Economic Order," General Assembly resolution 3201, 1 May 1974.

19. Ibid., paragraph 1.

20. "Programme of Action on the Establishment of a New International Economic Order," General Assembly resolution 3202, 1 May 1974.

21. "Declaration of the Establishment of a New International Economic Order," General Assembly resolution 3201. The NIEO documents generally did not mention, or paid only lip service to, human rights. See *The International Dimension of the Right to Development as a Human Right in Relation with Other Human Rights Based on International Cooperation, including the Right to Peace, Taking into Account the Requirements of the New International Economic Order and the Fundamental Human Needs: Report of the Secretary-General,* ECOSOC document E/CN.4/1334, 2 January 1979, paragraph 4(f); and "Report of the Open-Ended Working Group of Governmental Experts on the Right to Development," ECOSOC document E/CN.4/1989/10, 13 February 1989.

22. "The Charter of Economic Rights and Duties of States," General Assembly resolution 3281, 12 December 1974. See also Burns H. Weston, "The Charter of Economic Rights and Duties of State and the Deprivation of Foreign-Owned Wealth," *American Journal of International Law* 75, no. 3 (1981): 437–475.

23. "The Charter of Economic Rights and Duties of States," Articles 1–4.

24. Quoted in Ferguson, "The Politics of the New International Economic Order," 142–143.

25. Philip Alston, "Revitalising United Nations Work on Human Rights and Development," in *International Human Rights In Context: Law, Politics, Morals,* ed. Henry J. Steiner and Philip Alston (New York: Oxford University Press, 1996), 1112–1113. For analysis of the debate on reparations for colonialism, see John Torpey, "Making Whole What Has Been Smashed: Reflections on Reparations," *Journal of Modern History* 73, no. 2 (2001): 333–358.

26. As one international lawyer observes, this contradiction rests on "the fiction of sovereign equality, meaning that these countries, while continuing to claim their political and economic independence, also assert [the] legal outcome of disadvantage"; Christine M. Chinkin, "The Challenge of Soft Law: Development and Change in International Law," *International and Comparative Law Quarterly* 38, no. 4 (1989): 855.

27. J. Frieden, "Third World Indebted Industrialization: International Finance and State Capitalism in Mexico, Brazil, Algeria, and South Korea," *International Organization* 35, no. 3 (1981): 407–431.

28. Quoted in *Yearbook of the United Nations 1977* (New York: United Nations, 1978), 393.

29. "Declaration of the United Nations Development Decade," General Assembly resolution 1710 (XVI), 19 December 1961.

30. The main impetus for the Kennedy administration's launching of the Alliance for Progress was the fear that Fidel Castro's Cuba would spread revolution throughout Latin America. See John Toye and Richard Toye, *The UN and Global Political Economy: Trade, Finance, and Development* (Bloomington: Indiana University Press, 2004), 175–179.

31. President John F. Kennedy, quoted in Richard Jolly, Louis Emmerij, Dharam Ghai, and Frédéric Lapeyre, *UN Contributions to Development Thinking and Practice* (Bloomington: Indiana University Press, 2004), 85.

32. The idea was that domestic and foreign capital investment would lead to economic growth, resulting in increased employment and income for the poor. See Betina Hürni, *The Lending Policy of the World Bank in the 1970s: Analysis and Evaluation* (Boulder, Colo.: Westview Press, 1980).

33. "Declaration of the United Nations Development Decade," paragraph 4(d).

34. Ibid. See also *United Nations Development Decade: Proposals for Action* (New York: United Nations, 1962), 12–13.

35. See *Yearbook of the United Nations 1967* (New York: United Nations, 1968), 228; Toye and Toye, *The UN and Global Political Economy*, 184–205.

36. "World Social Situation," General Assembly resolution 2436, 19 December 1968; "World Social Situation," General Assembly resolution 2771, 22 November 1971. Economists Sudhir Anand and Ravi Kanbur demonstrate that the 1960s strategy of economic growth and wealth accumulation did not alleviate poverty or reduce inequality; Sudhir Anand and Ravi Kanbur, "Inequality and Development: A Critique," *Journal of Development Economics* 41 (Spring 1993): 19–43.

37. *1970 Report on the World Social Situation* (New York: United Nations, 1971), 3; see Colin Legum, ed., *The First UN Development Decade and Its Lessons for the 1970s* (New York: Praeger, 1970).

38. "International Development Strategy for the Second United Nations Development Decade," General Assembly resolution 2626, 24 October 1970.

39. Ibid., paragraph 18.

40. Albert O. Hirschman, "The Political Economy of Latin American Development: Seven Exercises in Retrospection," *Latin American Research Review* 22, no. 3 (1987): 7–36.

41. See Charles Lipson, "The International Organization of Third World Debt," *International Organization* 34, no. 4 (1981): 603–631.

42. Jolly, Emmerij, Ghai, and Lapeyre, *UN Contributions to Development*, 138–168. The authors also highlight sharp regional differences. For example, in Latin America, the debt ratio rose from 20 percent in 1975 to nearly 40 percent in 1982; in Sub-Saharan Africa, it rose from less than 7 percent in 1975 to 19 percent in the 1990s. In Asia, the debt ratio

has remained remarkably stable at around 5–8 percent over the entire period, but in West Asia it has risen threefold from 3 percent to about 9–10 percent in 1990; ibid., 146.

43. It is estimated that by the 1980s, the non-oil-exporting countries of Latin America had transferred some $100 billion to banks in the North; Weiss, Carayannis, Jolly, and Emmerij, *UN Voices,* 262.

44. The International Commission on International Development Issues, named for its chair, former German chancellor Willy Brandt, took up some of the NIEO issues, linking poverty with trade, the arms race, and the structure of the international financial system. However, it did not recommend an obligatory redistribution, instead emphasizing the need for North-South dialogue and cooperation. See Jolly, Emmerij, Ghai, and Lapeyre, *UN Contributions to Development,* 124.

45. "Report and Recommendations of the Committee for Development," in *Yearbook of the United Nations 1973* (New York: United Nations, 1974), 273; ECOSOC resolution 1805, 8 August 1973.

46. Mr. Alvarez Vita (Peru), "Commission on Human Rights: Summary Record of Meetings," ECOSOC document E/CN.4/1982/SR.31, paragraph 91.

47. "International Development Strategy for the Third United Nations Development Decade," General Assembly resolution 35/56, 5 December 1980.

48. *The International Dimension of the Right to Development as a Human Right.* The basic-needs approach was also put forward by several UN agencies and was widely recognized at the World Employment Conference held in Geneva during the summer of 1976. By this time, the growing influence of civil society groups at such international conferences was being noted: "The constituency of concern within which these ideas and directions are being formulated extend beyond conventional governmental groups to include a new set of actors and participants in the development dialogue. These are loosely organized in a variety of 'people networks' at a national, regional, associational, and nongovernmental levels"; John McHale and Magda Cordell McHale, "Meeting Basic Human Needs," *Annals of the American Academy of Political and Social Science* 442 (March 1979): 14.

49. See Paul Streeten, *First Things First: Meeting Basic Needs in Developing Countries* (New York: Oxford University Press, 1981); Paul Streeten, "Basic Needs and Human Rights," *Development: Seeds of Change* 3 (1984): 10–12; Frances Stewart, "Basic Needs Strategies, Human Rights, and the Right to Development," *Human Rights Quarterly* 11, no. 3 (1989): 347–374; Jolly, Emmerij, Ghai, and Lapeyre, *UN Contributions to Development,* 112–122.

50. Robert McNamara, quoted in Cox, "Ideologies and the New International Economic Order," 10.

51. Toye and Toye, *The UN and Global Political Economy,* 184–205, 251–253.

52. See Howard J. Wiarda, "The Politics of Third World Debt," *Political Science and Politics* 23, no. 3 (1990): 411–418; Jahangir Amuzegar, "Dealing with Debt," *Foreign Policy* 68 (1987): 140–158; and Rudiger Dornbusch and Stanley Fischer, "Third World Debt," *Science* 234, no. 4778 (1986): 836–841.

53. Graham Bird, Tony Killick, Jennifer Sharpley, and Mary Sutton, *The Quest for*

Economic Stabilization: The IMF and the Third World (New York: St. Martin's Press, 1984), 2.

54. See ibid.; and Jolly, Emmerij, Ghai, and Lapeyre, *UN Contributions to Development*, 138–185.

55. Enrique Iglesias, president of the Inter-American Development Bank, coined the term "lost decade" to describe the impact of the 1980s debt crisis in Latin America and Africa; Weiss, Carayannis, Jolly, and Emmerij, *UN Voices*, 263.

56. See Giovanni Andrea Cornia, Richard Jolly, and Frances Stewart, eds., *Adjustment with a Human Face* (Oxford and New York: Oxford University Press, 1987). UNCTAD, the World Institute for Development and Economic Research, and the United Nations Research Institute for Social Development also prepared reports critical of structural adjustment as imposed by the Bretton Woods institutions.

57. See Howard Tolley, *The UN Commission on Human Rights* (Boulder, Colo.: Westview Press, 1987), 55–82.

58. "Balanced and Integrated Economic and Social Progress," General Assembly resolution 1161, 26 November 1957.

59. "Proclamation of the International Conference on Human Rights, Tehran," General Assembly document A/CONF.32/41, 13 March 1968, paragraphs 12–13.

60. "Declaration on Social Progress and Development," General Assembly resolution 2542, 11 December 1969, Articles 10, 25, and 27.

61. "Alternative Approaches and Ways and Means within the United Nations System for Improving the Effective Enjoyment of Human Rights and Fundamental Freedoms," General Assembly resolution 32/130, 16 December 1977.

62. The eight points were as follows: (1) All human rights and fundamental freedoms are indivisible and interdependent; (2) realization of civil and political rights without the enjoyment of economic, social, and cultural rights is impossible; (3) human rights and fundamental freedoms are inalienable; (4) human rights questions should be examined globally; (5) within the UN system, priority must be given to mass and flagrant violations resulting from apartheid, racial discrimination, colonialism, and threats against national sovereignty of both a political and economic nature; (6) realization of the NIEO is an essential element for human rights promotion; (7) member states must undertake specific obligations through accession and ratification of international instruments; and (8) the experience and contribution of both developed and developing countries must be taken into account by all UN human rights organs. Ibid.

63. See the summary of the report of the director general for development international co-operation of 2 January 1979 in *Yearbook of the United Nations 1980* (New York: United Nations, 1981), 487. This report assessed developments in international economic cooperation since the General Assembly adopted the NIEO resolutions in its 1974 session.

64. Stephen Marks, "Emerging Human Rights: A New Generation for the 1980s?" *Rutgers Law Review* 435 (1981): 435–452; Philip Alston, "Peace as a Human Right," *Bulletin of Peace Proposals Journal* 11, no. 4 (1980): 319–330. Karel Vasek, a Czech jurist who served as secretary-general of the International Institute of Human Rights in Strasbourg (1969–1980), introduced the concept of solidarity rights as the third generation of human rights. Johan Galtung assigned a color scheme to these rights: blue for civil and political

rights as belonging to the bourgeoisie, red for economic and social rights as belonging to the working class, and green for solidarity rights to development, environment, and peace as belonging to grassroots movements. See Hans-Otto Sano, "Development and Human Rights: The Necessary, but Partial Integration of Human Rights and Development," *Human Rights Quarterly* 22, no. 3 (2000): 734–752. Alston criticized Vasek's generational typology for establishing a hierarchy within human rights. See Philip Alston, "Third Generation of Solidarity Rights: Progressive Development or Obfuscation of International Human Rights Law," *Netherlands International Law Review* 29 (1982): 307–322.

65. M. Ganji, *The Realization of Economic, Social and Cultural Rights: Problems, Policies, Progress, Report of the Special Rapporteur of the Commission on Human Rights,* ECOSOC document E/CN.4/1131/Rev. 1, 1975. This report formed the basis for discussions at the CHR; "The Question of Realization of the Economic, Social and Cultural Rights Contained in the Universal Declaration of Human Rights and in the International Covenant on Economic, Social and Cultural Rights, and Special Problems Relating to the Human Rights in Developing Countries," ECOSOC document E/CN4/1334, 2 January 1979, item 7 of the provisional agenda.

66. Mr. Alvarez Vita (Peru), "Commission on Human Rights: Summary Record of Meetings," E/CN.4/1982/SR.31, paragraph 95.

67. Mbaye, "Le Droit du Développement comme un droit de l'Homme."

68. Mbaye, quoted in Simeon O. Ilesanmi, "Leave No Poor Behind: Globalization and the Importance of Socio-Economic and Development Rights from an African Perspective," *Journal of Religious Ethics* 32, no. 1 (2004): 84.

69. Ganji, *The Realization of Economic, Social and Cultural Rights.* The report sparked a protracted debate in the CHR on the indivisibility of human rights and whether priority should be given to civil and political rights or to economic, social, and cultural rights. See "Commission on Human Rights: Summary Record of Meetings," ECOSOC document E/CN.4/SR.1391, 1978.

70. Mr. Parashar (India), "General Assembly, Third Committee, Summary Records," General Assembly document A/C.3/41/SR.37, 1986, 5.

71. "Commission on Human Rights Resolution 4 (XXXIII)," ECOSOC document CHR/Res/4 (XXXIII), 21 February 1977. This was the first recognition of the right to development and signaled a series of activities.

72. *The International Dimension of the Right to Development as a Human Right,* paragraph 307.

73. Ibid., paragraphs 82–83.

74. *Regional and National Dimensions of the Right to Development: Study by the Secretary-General,* ECOSOC document E/CN.4/1421, 13 November 1980.

75. Mbaye and other experts, such as Professor Jean Rivero, focused on the legal aspect of the right to development. See "The Right to Development as a Human Right in the Context of the New International Economic Order," paper presented at the UNESCO Meeting of Experts on Human Rights, Human Needs and the Establishment of a New Economic Order, 19–23 June 1978, UN document SS-78/Conf.630/8.

76. See Hector Gross Espiell, "The Right of Development as a Human Right," *Texas International Law Journal* 16 (1991): 189–207.

77. "Establishment of the Working Group on the Right to Development," CHR resolution 37 (XXXVII), 11 March 1981.

78. Once the group decided that a declaration would be more appropriate than a convention, it could agree on little else. Tolley, *The UN Commission on Human Rights,* 152–153; Toye and Toye, *The UN and Global Political Economy,* 142.

79. See the reports of the Working Group of Governmental Experts on the Right to Development: ECOSOC document E/CN.4/1488, 31 December 1981; ECOSOC document E/CN.4/1489, 11 February 1982; ECOSOC document E/CN.4/1983/11, 9 December 1982; and ECOSOC document E/CN.4/1984/13, 14 November 1983. Mr. A. Sene (Senegal) chaired and Mr. G. Choaraqui (France) was the rapporteur. The working group presented a draft declaration in its 1984 report, ECOSOC document E/CN.4/1985/11, 24 January 1985.

80. *Report of the Working Group of Governmental Experts on the Right to Development,* ECOSOC document E/CN.4/1489, 11 February 1982, 10.

81. *Report of the Working Group of Governmental Experts on the Right to Development,* ECOSOC document E/CN.4/1983/11 and Annex IV, 9 December 1982.

82. Mr. Novak (United States), "Commission on Human Rights: Summary Record of Meetings," ECOSOC document E/CN.4/1982/SR.32, 23 February 1982, paragraph 60.

83. "Commission on Human Rights: Summary Record of Meetings," ECOSOC document E/CN.4/1982/SR.31, February 1982. The western states at times disagreed on the issue of collective rights. The UK member viewed the right to development as a synthesis of other rights and not as an independent right of states. The French member endorsed the right as having a collective element and felt that it could serve as the nexus for North-South cooperation. See "Commission on Human Rights, Summary Records," ECOSOC Document E/CN.4/1988/SR.23, 1988.

84. Mr. Novak (United States), ECOSOC document E/CN.4/1982/SR.32, 23 February 1982, paragraph 62.

85. The report of the working group summarized the difference in views. One group felt that various human rights instruments supported the idea of rights of states as a legal right in international law. The other group argued that a General Assembly resolution that presented norms to states was merely a recommendation and in that respect did not form a legal right under the present set of international rules. *Report of the Working Group of Governmental Experts on the Right to Development,* ECOSOC document E/CN.4/1489, 11 February 1982. Mr. Sene (Senegal) noted that "most experts regarded as more important, the principals of solidarity and interdependence uniting developed and developing countries"; "Commission on Human Rights: Summary Record of Meetings," ECOSOC document E/CN.4/1982/SR.31, 22 February 1982, 15. Mr. Colliard (France) noted: "At present, the right to development appears to be both a right of individual and a collective right; a right of a synthetic nature, as it were, could also be seen in it." "Commission on Human Rights: Summary Record of Meetings," ECOSOC document E/CN.4/1982/SR.32, 23 February 1982, 12.

86. *Report of the Working Group of Governmental Experts on the Right to Development,* ECOSOC document E/CN.4/1489, 11 February 1982.

87. *The Right to Development: Report of the Independent Expert on the Right to Development,* ECOSOC document E/CN.4/2000/WG.18/2, 2 January 2001, 10.

88. Ms. Byrne (United States), "General Assembly Third Committee, Summary Record," General Assembly document A/C.3/41/SR.36, 14 November 1986, 135. It is not surprising that the United States refused to accept even a weak declaration during the Reagan administration. The U.S. representative noted that references to the human rights of peoples were inconsistent with the proper concept of human rights as rights of the individual. "General Assembly Third Committee, Summary Record," General Assembly document A/C.3/41/SR.61, 1986, paragraph 190.

89. Morris B. Abram, "Human Rights and the United Nations: Past as Prologue," *Harvard Human Rights Journal* 4 (1991): 76.

90. Chile and Argentina, for example, had already been investigated by the CHR for human rights abuses. See Michael Stohl and George Lopez, eds., *The State as Terrorist: The Dynamics of Governmental Violence and Repression* (Westport, Conn.: Greenwood Press, 1984).

91. Pieter Kooijmans (Netherlands) remarked that "the ultimate goal is the integral development of the individual . . . according to which the weak and disadvantaged should be protected." "Commission on Human Rights: Summary Record of Meetings," ECOSOC document E/CN.4/1982/SR.30, 19 February 1982, 14.

92. Mr. Novak (United States) noted: "The individual in free association has the right to development that States have the obligation to respect. On the other hand, totalitarian states violate the right to developments of peoples and social groups. States can never be the subject of the right to development; only human persons, individuals, have that right." "Commission on Human Rights: Summary Record of Meetings," ECOSOC document E/CN.4/1982/SR.32, 23 February 1982, 14.

93. Ms. Clark (United States), "General Assembly, Third Committee, Summary Records," General Assembly document A/CN.3/41/SR 36, 30 October 1986, paragraph 23.

94. "General Assembly Third Committee, Plenary Verbatim," General Assembly document A/41/PV.97, November 1986, 7. These countries argued that labeling rights held by a collective as "human rights" could weaken the ability of the UN human rights system to respond to violations. The Swedish representative commented: "Human rights have their origin in concepts of natural law, and efforts to equate collective rights with human rights tend to create confusion between two separate concepts and to undermine the safeguards of the individual against oppression and abuse of power by authorities"; Mr. Ewerlof (Sweden), "Commission on Human Rights: Summary Record of Meetings," ECOSOC document E/CN.4/1982/SR.36, 26 February 1982, 16.

95. Murade Isaac Murargy (Mozambique), "Commission on Human Rights: Summary Record of Meetings," ECOSOC document E/CN.4/1983/SR.17, 15.

96. Mr. Alban-Holguin (Colombia), "General Assembly Third Committee, Plenary Verbatim," General Assembly document A/41/PV, 30 October 1986, 62.

97. *Study on the Right to Popular Participation in Its Various Forms as a Important Factor in the Full Realization of All Human Rights: Preliminary Report by the Secretary-General*, ECOSOC document E/CN.4/1984/12 and Add. 1, 24 January 1984.

98. Mr. Herdocia Ortega (Nicaragua), "Commission on Human Rights: Summary Record of Meetings," ECOSOC document E/CN.4/1983/SR.20, paragraph 21. A series of consultations with lawyers, development experts, and grassroots activists organized by the International Commission of Jurists emphasized the right of the poor to organize

themselves and meaningfully participate not only in formulating policies but also in applying and monitoring them.

99. International and local NGOs successfully established the linkage between development and human rights through their participation in the 1972 United Nations Conference on the Human Environment in Stockholm and their reporting on the adverse human and environmental costs of megaprojects financed by the World Bank and ruthlessly implemented by national governments.

100. Member states defined participation as the opportunity to shape one's own reality, including the right to education and many of the civil and political rights, such as the right to organize and participate in the political process. See C. J. Dias, "Realizing the Right to Development," in *Development, Human Rights, and the Rule of Law,* ed. J. Mestdagh (Oxford: Pergamon Press, 1980).

101. Mr. MacDermot (International Commission of Jurists), "Commission on Human Rights: Summary Record of Meetings," ECOSOC document E/CN.4/1983/SR.17, 17.

102. Mr. Roucounas (Greece), "Commission on Human Rights: Summary Record of Meetings," ECOSOC document E/CN.4/1982/SR.32, 23 February 1982, 12.

103. Mr. Sene (Senegal), "Commission on Human Rights: Summary Record of Meetings," ECOSOC document E/CN.4/1982/SR.31, 10.

104. See *Report of the Working Group of Governmental Experts on the Right to Development,* ECOSOC document E/CN.4/1984/13, 1984.

105. Mrs. Ito (Japan), "General Assembly, Third Committee, Summary Records," General Assembly document A/C.3/41/SR.61, 1986, paragraph 186.

106. Viscount Colville of Culross (UK), "Commission on Human Rights: Summary Record of Meetings," ECOSOC document E/CN.4/1982/SR.17, 11.

107. Ms. Clark (United States), "General Assembly, Third Committee, Summary Records," General Assembly document A/C.3/41/SR.36, 30 October 1986, paragraph 23.

108. Mr. Incisa di Camerana (Italy), "Commission on Human Rights: Summary Record of Meetings," ECOSOC document E/CN.4/1982/SR.30, 19 February 1982, 10. He stated that his delegation could not accept that "the right to development as a collective right is to be exercised solely or mainly by the developing countries. That opinion, in fact, denies the very nature of development, which is a continuous process of positive evolution of all societies, including those of the developed countries, and which certainly include, but are not limited to the growth of national income."

109. Mr. Akram (Pakistan) was one of the strongest advocates of the position that the North had a duty to provide aid for developing countries. See "Commission on Human Rights: Summary Record of Meetings," ECOSOC document E/CN.4/1982/SR.32, 23 February 1982, 7. The delegate from Mozambique stated that "the developed countries have an obligation to contribute to the development of the developing countries." Mr. Murargy (Mozambique), "Commission on Human Rights: Summary Record of Meetings," ECOSOC document E/CN.4/1983/SR.17, 5.

110. By the late 1970s and early 1980s, seventeen African nations had experienced severe drought and increased desertification and plagues of locusts, Sudan had experienced a devastating flood, and there was an ongoing civil war in Zaire and a refugee crisis on the continent.

111. *Report of the Working Group of Governmental Experts on the Right to Development,* ECOSOC document E/CN.4/1985/11, 10 December 1984, Annex VIII.

112. The Soviet delegate commented that the U.S. "since 1945 . . . has allocated $300 billion for official aid to other countries. It might perhaps be appropriate to recall some figures in order to understand why the United States is opposed to the concept of the right to development. In the period 1980–1984 alone, the United States has received from the third world countries directly $80 billion a year. . . . The drop in raw materials prices has resulted in the loss of an additional $100 billion for developing countries. According to data published in the annual report of the Inter-American Development Bank, the Latin American countries have lost since the early 1980s nearly a $100 billion in debt service, without taking account of unregistered capital transfers." Mr. Yakolev (USSR), "General Assembly, Third Committee, Summary Records," General Assembly document A/C.3/41/SR.38, 1986, 5.

113. Ibid., paragraph 24.

114. See Ms. Sinegiorgis (Ethiopia), "Commission on Human Rights: Summary Record of Meetings," ECOSOC document E/CN.4/1982/SR.30; Mr. Alvarez Vita of Peru also raised the need to regulate transnational corporations to prevent violations of human rights and dignity. "Commission on Human Rights: Summary Record of Meetings," ECOSOC document E/CN.4/1983/SR.18.

115. Mrs. Tawally (Egypt), "Commission on Human Rights: Summary Record of Meetings," ECOSOC document E/CN.4/SR.1391, 1977, paragraph 44.

116. Mr. Akram (Pakistan), "Commission on Human Rights: Summary Record of Meetings," ECOSOC document E/CN.4/1982/SR.32, 23 February 1982, 6.

117. For a history of disarmament and development initiatives, see "Establishment of an International Disarmament Fund for Development," UNIDIR publication 84/08, 1983. The link had been made at the founding conference of the UN but was set aside while the war continued. See Jolly, Emmerij, Ghai, and Lapeyre, *UN Contributions to Development,* 87–88.

118. Boilerplate language in the working group's summary reports always noted that the main obstacles developing countries faced were colonialism, racism, apartheid, and the arms race. See "Commission on Human Rights: Summary Record of Meetings," ECOSOC documents E/CN.4/1982/SR.31, and E/CN.4/1983/SR.17–20.

119. "Economic and Social Consequences of Disarmament," ECOSOC document E/3593, 28 February 1962.

120. *The Regional and National Dimensions of the Right to Development as a Human Right: Study by the Secretary-General,* ECOSOC document E/CN.4/1421, 13 November 1980.

121. "Study on All Aspects of Regional Disarmament," *Report of the Secretary-General,* General Assembly document A/35/416, 1981.

122. *International Conference on the Relationship between Disarmament and Development: Report of the Secretary-General of the Conference,* General Assembly document A/CONF.130/139, 13 April 1987, 15.

123. "President Reagan's Speech before the National Association of Evangelicals," Orlando, Florida, 8 March 1983, available online at http://www.presidentreagan.info/

speeches/empire.cfm. The "Star Wars" speech announcing the strategic defense initiative was delivered at the White House on 23 March 1983; available online at http://www .presidentreagan.info/speeches/sdi.cfm.

124. Mr. Zorin (USSR), "General Assembly, Third Committee, Summary Records," General Assembly document A/C.3/41/SR.38, 1986, paragraph 21. The Soviet representative accused the United States of hampering economic development with its military expenditures. "Commission on Human Rights: Summary Record of Meetings," E/CN.4/ SR.18, 1983, paragraph 58.

125. The Working Group produced a draft declaration in *Report of the Working Group of Governmental Experts on the Right to Development,* ECOSOC document E/CN.4/1985/11, 24 January 1985, its fourth report. Its second report included a compilation of proposals with bracketed provisions signifying disputed concepts and issues; see *Report of the Working Group of Governmental Experts on the Right to Development,* ECOSOC document E/CN.4/1983/11, 9 December 1982. The third report was a technical consolidated text that served as the basis of further work; see *Report of the Working Group of Governmental Experts on the Right to Development,* ECOSOC document E/CN.4/1984/13, 14 November 1983.

126. Philip Alston argues that the debates over the right to development are "little more than an exercise in shadowboxing" that drains the limited human and financial resources of the UN's human rights system. Philip Alston, "Making Space for New Human Rights: The Case of the Right to Development," *Harvard Human Rights Yearbook* 1 (1988): 21.

127. "Commission on Human Rights: Summary Record of Meetings," E/CN.4/1999/ SR.10, 6 September 1999, 6.

128. "Declaration on the Right to Development," General Assembly resolution 41/128.

129. Seeking to explain the gap between American rhetoric and practice concerning human rights, Mertus uses the analogy of a car dealer engaging in deceptive marketing. Julie A. Mertus, *Bait and Switch: Human Rights and U.S. Foreign Policy* (New York: Routledge, 2004), 209.

130. "Declaration on the Right to Development," General Assembly resolution 41/128, Articles 1 and 2.

131. Ibid., Article 3.

132. Ibid., Article 6.

133. Ibid., Article 7.

134. Ibid., Articles 8 and 10.

135. See N. J. Udombana, "The Third World and the Right to Development: Agenda for the Next Millennium," *Human Rights Quarterly* 22, no. 3 (2000): 753–787.

136. Mr. Bashir (Pakistan), "General Assembly, Third Committee, Summary Records," General Assembly document A/C.3/41/SR.37, 1986, paragraph 55.

137. In one of the first articles to dismiss the right to development, Donnelly argued that it is positively harmful because it allows governments to avoid responsibility for human rights violations they perpetrate on their own people. See Jack Donnelly, "In Search of the Unicorn: The Jurisprudence and Politics of the Right to Development," *California Western International Law Journal* 15 (1985): 473–510. Alston is more amenable to the

right to development in principle but cautions against accepting the idea of state rights. See Philip Alston, "Conjuring up New Human Rights: A Proposal for Quality Control," *American Journal of International Law* 78, no. 3 (1984): 607–621.

138. See Ian Brownlie, "The Human Right to Development," *Human Rights Unit Occasional Paper* 11 (1989); Stephen Marks, "The United Nations and Human Rights: The Promise of Multilateral Diplomacy," in *The Future of International Human Rights Law*, ed. Burns Weston and Stephen Marks (New York: Transnational Publishers Inc., 1999).

139. The Working Group produced three reports: *Report of the Working Group of Governmental Experts on the Right to Development*, ECOSOC document E/CN.4/1987/10, 29 January 1987; *Report of the Working Group of Governmental Experts on the Right to Development*, ECOSOC document E/CN.4/1988/10, 29 January 1988; *Report of the Open-Ended Working Group of Governmental Experts on the Right to Development*, ECOSOC document E/CN.4/1989/10, 13 February 1989. The United States withdrew from the working group in 1987, citing a variety of objections. Having cast the sole vote against the declaration, it noted that pursuing implementation efforts were pointless and did not constitute a responsible use of limited UN resources. In addition, it argued that the group was exceeding its mandate by focusing on economic policies, trade, and arms control.

140. ECOSOC resolution 1989/45, 24 May 1989. This was the principal recommendation of the working group in its last report, ECOSOC document E/CN.4/1989/10, and in "Right to Development," General Assembly resolution 44/62, 8 December 1989.

141. *Global Consultation on the Right to Development as a Human Right: Report by the Secretary-General Pursuant to Commission on Human Rights Resolution 1989/45*, ECOSOC document E/CN.4/1990/Rev. 1, 26 September 1990.

142. Ibid., paragraph 12.

143. The global consultation endorsed the recommendations of the United Nations Seminar on Indigenous Peoples of 1989 and proposed special measures to enable vulnerable groups such as indigenous peoples to participate: "Their direct participation and consent in decisions regarding their own territories are thus essential to protect their right to development." Ibid., paragraph 157. See Russel Lawrence Barsh, "United Nations Seminar on Indigenous Peoples and States," *American Journal of International Law* 83 (1989): 33–86.

144. *Global Consultation on the Right to Development as a Human Right*, paragraphs 112–125.

145. "Commission on Human Rights: Summary Record of Meetings," ECOSOC document E/CN.4/1990/SR.38.

146. Yugoslavia, which traditionally coordinated right-to-development issues for the nonaligned states, was convinced that strong U.S. opposition to any measures of implementation would derail the initiative and proposed a more gradual approach that used a committee or special rapporteur. See "Commission on Human Rights: Summary Record of Meetings," ECOSOC documents E/CN.4/1990/SR.18–21.

147. "Note by the Secretariat on the Provisional Work Program of the Independent Expert on the Right to Development," ECOSOC document E/CN.4/1999/118, 3 February 1999. Reports of the independent expert are available online through the UN High Commissioner's Office on Human Rights at http://www.unhchr.ch/.

148. *The Right to Development—Report of the Independent Expert on the Right to Development,* General Assembly document A/55/306, 17 August 2000; *The Right to Development—Report of the Independent Expert on the Right to Development,* ECOSOC document E/CN.4/2000/WG.18/CRP.1, 11 December 2000; *The Right to Development—Third Report of the Independent Expert,* ECOSOC document E/CN.4/2001/WG.18/2, 2 January 2001; *The Right to Development—Fourth Report of the Independent Expert on the Right to Development,* ECOSOC document E/CN.4/2002/WG.18/2/Add. 1, 5 March 2002. See also Arjun Sengupta, "On the Theory and Practice of the Right to Development," *Human Rights Quarterly* 24, no. 4 (2002): 837–889.

149. "Vienna Declaration and Program of Action," General Assembly document A/CONF/.157/23, 12 July 1993. See Mary Robinson, "Human Rights at the Dawn of the 21st Century," *Human Rights Quarterly* 15, no. 4 (1993): 629–639.

150. "Final Declaration of the Regional Meeting for Asia and the World Conference on Human Rights," adopted in Bangkok, 2 April 1993, pursuant to General Assembly resolution 46/116, 17 December 1991. During this conference, Asian countries questioned the focus of the dominant human rights paradigm on civil and political rights. They also asserted that countries as well as individuals are the holders of the right to development. See Rob Buitenweg, "The Right to Development as a Human Right?" *Peace and Change* 22, no. 4 (1997): 414–431.

151. "Final Declaration of the Regional Meeting for Asia and the World Conference on Human Rights," Articles 6, 12, and 17. See Joanne Bauer, "The Bangkok Declaration Three Years After: Reflections on the State of the Asia–West Dialogue on Human Rights," *Human Rights Dialogue,* 1, no. 4 (1993), available online at http://www.cceia .org/resources/publications/dialogue/1_04/articles/518.html.

152. "Final Declaration of the Regional Meeting for Asia and the World Conference on Human Rights," Article 18.

153. "Vienna Declaration and Program of Action," Article 10.

154. Ibid., Article 73,

155. Amartya Sen, *Development as Freedom* (New York: Knopf, 1999).

156. First advanced by academics, the concept of sustainable development arose from concerns about overexploiting the environment and natural resources. Those who advocated human development focused on human capabilities and the expansion of individual choice. Both approaches had an intergenerational dimension. See Sudhir Anand and Amartya Sen, *Sustainable Human Development: Concepts and Issues,* (New York: UNDP, 1997): 1–38; UNDP, *Integrating Human Rights with Sustainable Human Development: A UNDP Policy Document* (New York: UNDP, 1998), 2, available online at http://www .undp.org/governance/docs/HR_Pub_policy5.htm.

157. Pakistani economist Mahbub ul Haq put Sen's capabilities approach into practice, developing the Human Development Index (HDI), a composite of measures of life expectancy, literacy, and per capita income. The HDI, which was publicized through UNDP's Human Development Reports, altered the UN's perception of development by concretizing the move away from an economic growth model toward a human-centered model.

158. UNDP, *Human Development Report 2000: Human Rights and Human Development* (New York: Oxford University Press, 2000).

159. Ibid., 1–4.

160. Jacques Polak, a longtime IMF officer, has noted that "the Human Development Report is not put on the agenda of the Executive Board of the IMF. I doubt many people in this building have even looked at it. I don't think it is generally distributed even." Jacques Polak quoted in Jolly, Emmerij, Ghai, and Lapeyre, *UN Contributions to Development,* 180.

161. See Alston, "Making Space for New Human Rights," 3–40.

162. Ibid.

163. "United Nations Millennium Declaration," General Assembly resolution 55/2, 8 September 2000. The eight millennium development goals are accompanied by eighteen targets and forty-eight indicators. Available online at http://www.un.org/millenniumgoals.

164. A concept note was prepared by the Working Group on the Right to Development to address this gap. See "The Right to Development and Practical Strategies for the Implementation of the Millennium Development Goals, Particularly Goal 8—Preliminary Concept Note," ECOSOC document E/CN.4/2005/WG.18/TF/2, 20 September 2005.

165. See Philip Alston, "Ships Passing in the Night: The Current State of the Human Rights and Development Debate Seen through the Lens of the Millennium Development Goals," *Human Rights Quarterly* 27, no. 2 (2005): 755–829.

166. See "The Right to Development and Practical Strategies for the Implementation of the Millennium Development Goals."

167. See World Bank and International Monetary Fund Development Committee, *Global Monitoring Report 2004: Policies and Actions for Achieving the MDGs and Related Outcomes* (Washington, D.C.: World Bank, 2004).

168. See UNDP, *Human Development Report 2005: International Cooperation at a Crossroads—Aid, Trade, and Security in an Unequal World* (New York: Oxford University Press, 2005).

169. Alston, "Ships Passing in the Night," 755.

170. UNDP, *Human Development Report 1999* (New York: Oxford University Press, 1999), 38. See also World Bank, *World Development Report 2006: Equity and Development* (Washington, D.C.: World Bank, 2006); and *World Development Report 2001: Attacking Poverty* (Washington, D.C.: World Bank, 2001).

10. Human Rights after the Cold War

1. Francis Fukuyama, "The End of History?" *The National Interest* (Summer 1989): 3–18.

2. Boutros-Ghali quoted in George H. Fox and George Nolte, "Intolerant Democracies," *American Journal of International Law* 36, no. 1 (1995): 5.

3. UN Charter, Chapter IX, Article 55.

4. Preamble, Universal Declaration of Human Rights.

5. See Office of the President of the General Assembly of the United Nations, *Reference Document on the Participation of Civil Society in UN Conferences and Special Sessions of the General Assembly during the 1990s,* 18 May 2001, available online at http://www.globalpolicy.org/ngos/role/policymk/conf/2001/0518refdoc.htm.

6. Article 8 of the Vienna Declaration and Program of Action, A/CONF.157/23, 25 June, 1993.

7. "Renewing the United Nations: A Programme for Reform," General Assembly document A/51/950, 14 July 1997.

8. UNDP, *Integrating Human Rights with Sustainable Human Development* (Washington D.C.: CDI, 1998), 1.

9. FAO, *The Right to Food in Theory and Practice* (Rome: United Nations, 1998), 2.

10. UNICEF, "Guidelines for Human Rights-Based Programming Approach," CF/EXD/1998-04, 21 April 1998.

11. Office of the High Commissioner for Human Rights, *Human Rights in Development: What, How and Why* (Geneva: Office of the High Commissioner for Human Rights, 2000).

12. UNICEF, "Convention on the Rights of the Child: What Have We Achieved?" (2005), available online at http://www.unicef.org/crc/index_30223.html.

13. The major exception to this trend is the European regional human rights system.

14. James Baker, *The Politics of Diplomacy: Revolution, War and Peace, 1989–1992* (New York: George G. Putnam & Sons, 1995).

15. See Scott Peterson, "In War, Some Facts Less Factual," *Christian Science Monitor,* 6 September 2002, 1.

16. Philip Gourevitch, *We Wish to Inform You that Tomorrow We Will Be Killed with Our Families: Stories from Rwanda* (New York: Picador, 1998); Samantha Power, *A Problem from Hell: America and the Age of Genocide* (New York: HarperCollins, 2002).

17. Romeo Dallaire, *Shake Hands with the Devil: The Failure of Humanity in Rwanda* (New York: Avalon, 2003).

18. For contrasting views, see Bilahari Kausikan, "Asia's Different Standard," *Foreign Policy* (Fall 1993): 24–41; Aryeh Neier, "Asia's Unacceptable Standard," *Foreign Policy* (Fall 1993): 42–51.

19. See Joanne R. Bauer and Daniel A. Bell, eds., *The East Asian Challenge for Human Rights* (New York: Cambridge University Press, 1999); Peter Van Ness, ed., *Debating Human Rights: Critical Essays from the United States and Asia* (London: Routledge, 1999).

20. Abdullahi An-Na'im, ed., *Human Rights and Cross Cultural Perspectives: A Quest for Consensus* (Philadelphia: University of Pennsylvania Press, 1992); Makau Mutua, *Human Rights: A Political and Cultural Critique* (Philadelphia: University of Pennsylvania Press, 2002).

21. Samir Amin, the prominent development economist, has asserted: "I am not against globalization. I am against neoliberal globalization"; quoted in Thomas G. Weiss, Tatiana Carayannis, Louis Emmerij, and Richard Jolly, *UN Voices: The Struggle for Development and Social Justice* (Bloomington: Indiana University Press, 2005), 283.

22. See, for example, William Greider, *One World: Ready or Not* (New York: Simon and Schuster, 1997); Kenichi Ohmae, *The Borderless World: Power and Strategy in the Interlinked Economy* (New York: Harper Business, 1990).

23. Edward Goldsmith and Gerry Mander, *The Case against the Global Economy and a Turn toward the Local* (San Francisco, Calif.: Sierra Club Books, 1996).

24. J. Williamson, "What Washington Means by Policy Reform," in *Latin American Adjustment: How Much Has Happened?*, ed. J. Williamson (Washington, D.C.: Institute for International Economics, 1990).

25. Frank J. Garcia, "Symposium: The Universal Declaration of Human Rights at 50 and the Challenge of Global Markets: Trading Away the Human Rights Principle," *Brooklyn Journal of International Law* 25 (Winter 1999): 51–97.

26. Jagdish Bhagwati, *In Defense of Globalization* (Toronto: Oxford University Press, 2004). Also see John Williamson, "What Should the Bank Think about the Washington Consensus?" *The World Bank Research Observer* 15, no. 2 (August 2000): 251–264.

27. Chalmers Johnson, *MITI and the Japanese Miracle* (Stanford, Calif.: Stanford University Press, 1982): 3–35; A. H. Amsden, "The State and Taiwan's Economic Development," in *Bringing the State Back In*, ed. P. Evans, D. Rueschemeyer, and T. Skocpol (New York: Cambridge University Press, 1985), 78–106; T. Gold, *State and Society in the Taiwan Miracle* (Armonk, N.Y.: M. E. Sharpe, 1986); Robert Wade, *Governing the Market: Economic Theory and the Role of Government in East Asian Industrialization* (Princeton, N.J.: Princeton University Press, 1990); J. Schiffer, "State Policy and Economic Growth: A Note on the Hong Kong Model," *International Journal of Urban and Regional Research* 15 no. 2 (1990): 180–196.

28. Richard Appelbaum and Jeffrey Henderson, eds., *States and Development in the Asian Pacific Rim* (Newbury, Mass.: Sage, 1992).

29. Ibid., 21–22.

30. See, for example, Joseph Stiglitz, *Globalization and Its Discontents* (London: Allen Lane, 2000); Ha Joon Chang, *Kicking Away the Ladder: Development Strategy in Historical Perspective* (London: Anthem Press, 2004).

31. Walden Bello, *Deglobalisation: Ideas for a New World Economy* (London: Zed Books, 2002); Adrian Leftwich, "Governance, Democracy and Development in the Third World," *Third World Quarterly* 14, no. 3 (1993): 605–624.

32. Stiglitz, *Globalization and Its Discontents*, 6.

33. Chang, *Kicking Away the Ladder*; Dani Rodrik, "Governing the Global Economy: Does One Architectural Style Fit All?" in *Brookings Trade Forum: 1999*, ed. Susan M. Collins and Robert Z. Lawrence (Washington, D.C.: Brookings Institution Press, 1999), 105–126; Giles Mohan, Ed Brown, Bob Milward, and Alfred B. Zack-Williams, *Structural Adjustment: Theory, Practice, and Impacts* (London: Routledge, 2000); Dhahram Ghai, *The IMF and the South: The Social Impact of Crisis and Adjustment* (London: ZED books, 1991).

34. Stiglitz, *Globalization and Its Discontents*, 195–213.

35. Ghai, *The IMF and the South*; UNCTAD, *Trade and Development Report* (New York: United Nations, 1998).

36. See, for example, UNDP, *Human Development Report 2005: Globalisation and Inequality* (Oxford: Oxford University Press, 2005).

37. Ibid., 4.

38. Ankie Hoogvelt, *Globalization and the Postcolonial World: The New Political Economy of Development* (London: Palgrave, 2001).

39. Andre Gunder Frank, *Crisis in the World Economy* (London: Heinemann, 1980).

Many of the failings of the international economic order were predicted by the seminal dependency theorist Raúl Prebisch in works such as "The Latin American Periphery in the Global System of Capitalism," *CEPAL Review* 13 (April 1981): 143–150.

40. Weiss, Carayannis, Emmerij, and Jolly, *UN Voices,* 288.

41. See Chris Jochnick, "Challenging Impunity: Accountability for Non-State Actors," *Human Rights Quarterly* 21, no. 2 (1999): 56–79.

42. Ankie Hoogvelt, *Globalization and the Postcolonial World: The New Political Economy of Development* (London: Palgrave, 2001), 180–185.

43. Claudio Cocuzza and Andrea Forabosco, "Are States Relinquishing Their Sovereign Rights? The GATT Dispute Settlement Process in a Globalized Economy," *Tulane Journal of International and Comparative Law* 4, no. 2 (1996): 161–189; Kofi Oteng Kufuor, "From the GATT to the WTO: The Developing Countries and the Reform of the Procedures for the Settlement of International Trade Disputes," *Journal of World Trade* 31, no. 5 (1997): 118–145.

44. Garcia, "Symposium: The Universal Declaration of Human Rights at 50," 62.

45. Ibid., 71.

46. Ibid.

47. Robert Howse, "The World Trade Organization and the Protection of Workers' Rights," *Journal of Small and Emerging Business Law* 3, no. 1 (1999); Michael J. Trebilcock and Robert Howse, *The Regulation of International Trade,* 2nd. ed. (London: Routledge, 1999), 390–441.

48. Ibid.

49. Lori Wallach, "Transparency in WTO Dispute Resolution," *Law and Policy in International Business* 31, no. 3 (2000): 773–798.

50. These cases can be found online at www.worldtradelaw.net.

51. Gustavo Nogueira, "The First WTO Appellate Body Review: United States—Standards for Reformulated and Conventional Gasoline," *Journal of World Trade* 30, no. (1996): 5–29; Nancy E. Scott, "The WTO Appellate Body and the US-Venezuela Gasoline Dispute," *International Trade Law and Regulation* 2 (1996): 103–118.

52. Zsolt K. Bessko, "Going Bananas over EEC Preferences? A Look at the Banana Trade War and the WTO's Understanding on Rules and Procedures Governing the Settlement of Disputes," *Case Western Reserve Journal of International Law* 28, no. (1996): 265–290; Andrew S. Bishop, "The Second Legal Revolution in International Trade Law: Ecuador Goes Ape in Banana Trade War with European Union," *International Legal Perspective* 12, no. 1 (2001): 1–16.

53. Articles about an impending clash abound in mainstream publications. An example is Graham E. Fuller's, "The Future of Political Islam," *Foreign Affairs* (March/April 2002): 48–61.

54. The term "long war" was adopted after a speech Rumsfeld made on 2 February 2006 before the release of the Pentagon's quadrennial review. See "Rumsfeld Offers Strategies for Current War," *Washington Post,* 3 February 2006.

55. For support of the use of wide discretionary powers, see David Cole's review of John Yoo's book: "What Bush Wants to Hear," *New York Review of Books* 52, no. 18 (November 2005). One of the most famous examples of the Bush administration's contempt

for human rights is the memo by U.S. attorney general Alberto Gonzales dated 25 January 2002 that provided legal justification for torture and human rights abuses in the context of war. The full text of this memo and other Bush administration documents justifying human rights abuses is available at http://www.texscience.org/reform/torture.

56. Human Rights Watch, *World Report 2006* (New York: Human Rights Watch, 2005), 7–24.

57. On February 13, 2003 at a speech at Naval Station Mayport, Jacksonville, Florida, President George W. Bush spoke of the need to prevent the UN from fading into history as "an ineffective, irrelevant debating society."

58. Paul Hoffman, "Human Rights and Terrorism," *Human Rights Quarterly* 26 (2004): 932–933.

59. White House Press Release, "Statement by the President in His Address to the Nation," 11 September 2001, available online at www.whitehouse.gov/news/releases/2001/09/20010911-16.html.

60. Lisa Hajjar, "From Nuremberg to Guantánamo: International Law and American Power Politics," *Middle East Report* 229 (Winter 2003): 4–11.

61. Robert Scheer, "Is Al Qaeda Just a Bush Boogeyman?" *Los Angeles Times,* 11 January 2005.

62. President Bush quoted in Bob Woodward, *Bush at War* (London: Simon & Schuster, 2002).

63. Arundhati Roy, "The Algebra of Infinite Justice," *The Guardian,* 29 September 2001.

64. Human Rights Watch, *World Report 2006,* 7–24.

65. Charles Swift, "The American Way of Justice," *Esquire* (March 2007): 193–199.

66. See Hoffman, "Human Rights and Terrorism"; Human Rights Watch, *World Report 2005* (New York: Human Rights Watch, 2004); Anthea Roberts, "Righting Wrongs or Wronging Rights?" *European Journal of International Law* 15, no. 4 (2004): 721–749. For a country-by-country study of the abuse of traditional civil and political rights, see Human Rights Watch, *World Report 2006.*

67. A particularly telling example is described in Dick Marty's statement to the Council of Europe; see "Alleged Secret Detentions in Council of Europe Member States," January 2006, available online at http://assembly.coe.int/ASP/GNews/EMB_NewsView .asp?ID=1254.

68. Comment by Lord Johan Steyn, member of the Judicial Committee of the House of Lords, at the Twenty-Seventh F. A. Mann Lecture titled "Guantanamo Bay: The Legal Black Hole"; available online at http://www.statewatch.org/news/2003/nov/guantanamo.pdf.

69. See Lisa Hajjar, "From Nuremberg to Guantánamo," *Middle East Report* 229 (Winter 2003), 4–11; Hoffman, "Human Rights and Terrorism," 932–934; Roberts, "Righting Wrongs or Wronging Rights?" 721–749.

70. The idea of a U.S. global empire, popularized by influential think tanks, has been expressed in numerous journal and media resources in the past few years; see Michael Ignatieff, "Nation-Building Lite," *New York Times Magazine,* 28 July 2002; G. John Ikenberry, "America's Imperial Ambition," *Foreign Affairs* 81, no. 5 (September/October 2002): 44–60; and Sebastian Mallaby, "The Reluctant Imperialist: Terrorism, Failed States, and the Case for American Empire," *Foreign Affairs* 81, no. 2 (March/April 2002): 2–7.

71. See the summary of these ideas in Project of the New American Century, *Rebuilding America's Defenses: Strategy, Forces and Resources for a New Century*, September 2000, available online at http://www.newamericancentury.org/RebuildingAmericasDefenses .pdf. See also Robert Kaplan, *Warrior Politics: Why Leadership Demands a Pagan Ethos* (New York: Vintage Books, 2003); Henry Kissinger, *Does America Need a Foreign Policy? Toward a Diplomacy for the Twenty-First Century* (New York: Simon and Schuster, 2001).

72. Nafeez Mossadeq Ahmed, *The War on Truth: 9/11, Disinformation, and the Anatomy of Terrorism* (Northampton, Mass.: Interlink Publishing): 331–336.

73. The political imperatives of Israeli foreign policy tie in closely with those of the United States, as may be observed in the Institute for Advanced Strategic and Political Studies' "A Clean Break: A New Strategy for Securing the Realm," July 1996, available online at http://www.iasps.org/strat1.htm.

74. Zbigniew Brzezinski, *The Grand Chessboard: American Primacy and Its Geostrategic Imperatives* (New York: Basic Books, 1997); see also Joseph Nye, *The Paradox of American Power: Why the World's Only Superpower Can't Go It Alone* (New York: Oxford University Press, 2002).

75. Henry H. Shelton, *Joint Vision 2020* (Washington, D.C.: Government Printing Office, 2000).

76. Ibid., 6.

77. The UN Charter requires Security Council approval of the use of force (Article 42) and recognizes the right of individual and collective self-defense (Article 51).

78. Robert L. Jackson, August 12, 1945, quoted in *U.S. Department of State Bulletin* (Washington, D.C.: Government Printing Office, 1945).

79. John R. Bolton, "Is There Really Law in International Affairs?" *Transnational Law and Contemporary Problems* 10 (Spring 2000): 1–5.

80. See Phyllis Bennis, *Calling the Shots: How Washington Dominates Today's UN* (New York: Interlink Publishing Group, 2004); and Peter J. Spiro, "The New Sovereigntists: American Exceptionalism and Its Prophets," *Foreign Affairs* 79 (November/December 2000): 9–15.

81. Memorandum on "Humane Treatment of Al Qaeda and Taliban Detainees" to the vice president, the secretary of state, the secretary of defense, the attorney general, the chief of staff to the president, the director of the Central Intelligence Agency, the assistant to the president for National Security Affairs, the chairman of the Joint Chiefs of Staff, quoted in "Human Dignity Denied: Torture and Accountability in the War on Terror," Amnesty International Report AMR 51/145/2004, 27 October 2004, 3.

82. Memorandum to President Bush, quoted in "Human Dignity Denied: Torture and Accountability in the War on Terror."

83. Harold Brown, Tillie K. Fowler, Charles A. Homer, and James R. Schlesinger, *Final Report of the Independent Panel to Review DoD Detention Operations* (Washington, D.C.: U.S. State Department, August 2004).

84. ICRC reactions to the Schlesinger panel report, quoted in "Human Dignity Denied: Torture and Accountability in the War on Terror," Amnesty International Report AMR 51/145/2004, 27 October 2004.

85. See Human Rights Watch, *World Report 2007* (New York: Human Rights Watch Publications, 2007), available online at http://hrw.org/wr2k7/index.htm.

86. "Human Rights Council," General Assembly resolution 60/251, 15 March 2006.

87. UN, *A More Secure World: Our Shared Responsibility—Report of the Secretary-General's High-level Panel on Threats, Challenges and Change,* General Assembly document A/59/565, 2 December 2004.

88. Statement by Ambassador Richard S. Williamson, "Item 4: Report of the United Nations High Commission for Human Rights and Follow-Up to the World Conference on Human Rights," 19 March 2004, available online at http://geneva.usmission.gov/humanrights/2004/statements/0319Williamson.htm.

89. Reed Brody, "Will the New Human Rights Council Get Serious about Human Rights?" *Mail and Guardian,* 11 April 2006.

90. These quotes are from the commission session in 2005; cited in Philip Alston, "Reconceiving the United Nations Human Rights Regime to Fit the Needs of the Twentieth Century," paper for Columbia University Seminar on Human Rights, 27 October 2005, 3, in authors' possession.

91. Asian Center for Human Rights, "High Commissioner Louise Arbour: Reconsider Support for Universal Membership in the CHR," *Asia Center for Human Rights Review* 57 (26 February 2005).

92. Ken Roth, "The UN Reform Agenda and Human Rights," in *Irrelevant or Indispensable? The United Nations in the Twenty-First Century,* ed. Paul Heinbecker and Patricia Goff (New York: Wilfrid Laurier University Press, 2005).

93. Alston, "Reconceiving the United Nations Human Rights Regime," 7–12.

94. For a useful review of the council and analysis of the extent of its reforms, see Julie Mertus, "United Nations Human Rights Reform: Breakdown or Breakthrough?" discussion materials prepared for Columbia University seminar, 27 April 2006, in authors' possession.

95. Amnesty International, "New Website to Monitor Candidates' Human Rights Record," press release, 19 April 2006, available online at http://news.amnesty.org/index/ENGIOR400122006.

96. "Explanation of Vote by Ambassador John R. Bolton on the Human Rights Council Draft Resolution," USUN Press Release #51, 15 March 2006, available online at http://www.un.int/usa/06_051.htm.

97. Colum Lynch, "U.S. Will Not Seek Seat on UN Rights Panel," *The Washington Post,* 7 April 2006.

98. Mertus, "United Nations Human Rights Reform," 8.

99. See Warren Hoge, "New UN Rights Group Includes Six Nations with Poor Records," *New York Times,* 10 May 2006.

100. Thalif Deen, "UN Defies West in Vote for Human Rights Council," *Inter Press Service,* 9 May 2006.

101. See, for example, Anne Bayefsky, "A Mockery of Human Rights," *Washington Times,* 12 May 2006.

102. "Election to the UN Human Rights Council Important Victory," *Bahama Journal,* 12 May 2006.

103. Hersch Lauterpacht, "The Law of Nations, the Law of Nature, and the Rights of Man," *Transactions of the Grotius Society 29* (1943): 29.

104. C. Kondapi, assistant secretary of the Indian Council of World Affairs and an alternate representative for India on the commission on the Korean conflict (one of the few voices from the South) noted: "The basic causes of conflict have not been removed. Imperialism continues to reign supreme, thus bifurcating the powers into the have and the have-nots, and the peoples into half slaves and half free"; C. Kondapi, "Indian Opinion of the United Nations," *International Organization* 5, no. 4 (1951): 711.

Index

abortion, 285
Abram, Morris, 263
Acheson, Dean, 86
activism: and development rights, 305; and globalization, 328, 329; impact on human rights agenda, 24; and the North-South divide, 324; and the Paris Peace Conference, 54; and peace, 41, 126; and popular movements, 37; and protests and demonstrations, 54; and the San Francisco conference, 137; and trends in human rights, 316. *See also* civil society; nongovernmental organizations (NGOs)
advisory opinions, 233
advocacy, xxii, 319. *See also* civil society; nongovernmental organizations (NGOs)
Afghanistan, xxiii, xxv–xxviii, 333
Africa: and Cold War conflicts, 199; and decolonization, 24, 243, 400n89; and development rights, 246, 291, 298, 304–305, 306; and enforcement of human rights, 236; and globalization, 327; and the hierarchy of nations, 55; and indigenous peoples' rights, 275, 276; influence in the UN, 421n101; and minority rights, 249, 257, 258; and origins of World War II, 58; and the Paris Peace Conference, 43; poverty in, 446n110; and race issues, 163, 269; and self-determination issues,

218–219, 219–220; and World War I, 45
African Americans, 162–166, 254, 383n121
An Agenda for Peace, 258
AIDS, 287
Al Qaeda, xxv, 5, 332
Albright, Madeline, xxiv
Alfaro, Ricardo J., 97, 132, 146
Alliance for Progress, 295
Alston, Philip, 314
Alvarez, Alejandro, 74, 75, 144
Amazonian Indians, 273
American Bar Association, 116, 160, 229, 252
American Civil Liberties Union (ACLU), 168
American Declaration of the Rights and Duties of Man, 191
An American Dilemma (Myrdal), 163, 383n114
American Federation of Labor (AFL), 144
American Jewish Committee (AJC), 96, 116
American Jewish Conference, 128
American Law Institute, 74, 96–97, 102, 132, 180, 388n13, 388–389n15
American Peace Society, 38
American Society of International Law, 116
Amin, Samir, 292
Amnesty International, xxiv, 240, 344n8

About the Authors

Roger Normand is Associate Professor of Law at Lahore University, Pakistan, where he teaches human rights and humanitarian law. He holds graduate degrees from Harvard University Law School and Divinity School with specializations in international law and religion and the politics of the Middle East. He was the main organizer of the Harvard Study Team, which visited Iraq three weeks after the 1991 Gulf War to conduct the first assessment of the civilian impacts of the bombing campaign. In 1993 he co-founded the Center for Economic and Social Rights, a human rights group that addresses poverty and economic injustice from the perspective of international law, and has served as its executive director. Normand has lectured widely on topics related to international politics and human rights.

Sarah Zaidi is Associate Professor and Acting Head of the Social Sciences Department at the Lahore University of Management Sciences. She is also the coordinator of Relief Information Systems Earthquake-Pakistan (RISEPAK), a collaborative initiative that conducts field work and prepares policy analysis. Under her leadership, RISEPAK won the prestigious Stockholm Challenge Award for information and communications technology in 2005. She is co-founder and was previously research director of the Center for Economic and Social Rights. Zaidi has organized research missions to Iraq, Ecuador, Haiti, Afghanistan, and her native Pakistan and has written articles and advocacy reports based on the findings. She holds a doctorate in public health from Harvard University.

About the United Nations Intellectual History Project

Ideas and concepts are a main driving force in human progress, and they are arguably the most important contribution of the United Nations. Yet there has been little historical study of the origins and evolution of the history of economic and social ideas cultivated within the world organization and their impact on wider thinking and international action. The United Nations Intellectual History Project is filling this knowledge gap by tracing the origins and analyzing the evolution of key ideas and concepts about international economic and social development born or nurtured under UN auspices. The UNIHP began operations in mid-1999 when the secretariat, the hub of a worldwide network of specialists on the UN, was established at the Ralph Bunche Institute for International Studies of The CUNY Graduate Center.

The UNIHP has two main components, oral history interviews and a series of books on specific topics. The seventy-nine in-depth oral history interviews with leading contributors to crucial ideas and concepts within the UN system provide the raw material for this and other volumes. A CD-ROM containing complete and indexed transcripts is available from UNIHP; see http://www.unhistory.org.

The project has commissioned fifteen studies about the major economic and social ideas or concepts that are central to UN activity which are being published by Indiana University Press.

- *Ahead of the Curve? UN Ideas and Global Challenges,* by Louis Emmerij, Richard Jolly, and Thomas G. Weiss (2001)
- *Unity and Diversity in Development Ideas: Perspectives from the UN Regional Commissions,* edited by Yves Berthelot with contributions from Adebayo Adedeji, Yves Berthelot, Leelananda de Silva, Paul Rayment, Gert Rosenthal, and Blandine Destremeau (2003)
- *Quantifying the World: UN Contributions to Statistics,* by Michael Ward (2004)
- *UN Contributions to Development Thinking and Practice,* by Richard Jolly, Louis Emmerij, Dharam Ghai, and Frédéric Lapeyre (2004)

- *The UN and Global Political Economy: Trade, Finance, and Development,* by John Toye and Richard Toye (2004)
- *UN Voices: The Struggle for Development and Social Justice,* by Thomas G. Weiss, Tatiana Carayannis, Louis Emmerij, and Richard Jolly (2005)
- *Women, Development and the United Nations: A Sixty-Year Quest for Equality and Justice,* by Devaki Jain (2005)
- *Human Security and the UN: A Critical History,* by S. Neil MacFarlane and Yuen Foong Khong (2006)

Forthcoming Titles

- *Preventive Diplomacy at the UN,* by Bertrand G. Ramcharan
- *The UN and Transnational Corporations: From Code of Conduct to Global Compact,* by Tagi Sagafi-nejad in collaboration with John Dunning
- *The UN and Development Cooperation,* by Olav Stokke
- *The UN and the Global Commons: Development Without Destruction,* by Nico Schrijver
- *The UN and Global Governance: An Unfinished History,* by Ramesh H. Thakur and Thomas G. Weiss
- *The United Nations: A History of Ideas and Their Future,* by Richard Jolly, Louis Emmerij, and Thomas G. Weiss

The project also collaborated on *The Oxford Handbook on the UN,* edited by Thomas G. Weiss and Sam Daws, published by Oxford University Press in 2007.

For further information, the interested reader should contact:
UN Intellectual History Project
The CUNY Graduate Center
365 Fifth Avenue, Suite 5203
New York, New York 10016-4309
212-817-1920 Tel
212-817-1565 Fax
UNHistory@gc.cuny.edu
www.unhistory.org

CPSIA information can be obtained at www.ICGtesting.com
Printed in the USA
BVOW06s1424200116

433638BV00009B/221/P

9 780253 219343